P9-CKY-176

Waiting for
the Galactic Bus

Waiting for
the Galactic Bus

PARKE GODWIN

Doubleday
NEW YORK

All of the characters in this book
are fictitious, and any resemblance
to actual persons, living or dead,
is purely coincidental.

ISBN 0-385-24635-8

Copyright © 1988 by Parke Godwin

All Rights Reserved
Printed in the United States of America

To Marvin Kaye,
for more Incredible Umbrellas

Waiting for
the Galactic Bus

Charity, by way of prologue

Charity Mae Stovall spent her childhood in a county orphanage. Yearning for a mother or any kind of palpable parent, she sublimated in adolescence to a rigid Christianity. Charity was—and still is—a highly intelligent young woman, although for her first twenty years she never thought herself acute in this regard, nor was the quality noted by the school system that passed her through its portals and curricula without a second glance. Since she didn't read much and no one ever required her to think, Charity's potential remained a string unsounded in the decaying factory town of Plattsville.

She was very active in the house of her chosen faith, the Tabernacle of the Born Again Savior, where she accompanied congregational hymns on the hammer-worn piano, was wooed by an aggressive young man named Roy Stride and, to a more retiring extent, by Roy's self-effacing friend, Woody Barnes. Woody furnished trumpet obbligato for these musical effusions. He played well, Charity with more precision than talent. She was a Fundamentalist and earnest about it, distributing leaflets for the removal from libraries of harmful books like *The Wizard of Oz* and *The Diary of Anne Frank*. On a personal basis, Oz didn't do much for Charity one way or the other, though she did wonder why the Tabernacle was against *Anne Frank*. Outside of her being a Jew, the day-to-day life and thoughts of Anne were pretty much like her own at thirteen. Nevertheless, Reverend Simco thundered against it as an alien blot on a Christian land already imperiled. Dutifully, Charity demonstrated against an abortion clinic, opposed the teaching of evolution as a dastardly onslaught of secular intellect upon defenseless children and believed herself a direct descendant of Adam.

Not entirely without justification.

Barion found her earliest direct ancestor by a Pliocene water hole, a creature with no likeness to Adam other than health, appetite and uncertainty. Unlike Adam, the ape was quite savage. Anything outside its immediate family group was a dangerous enemy. The crucial difference in this primate, for Barion's purposes, was a brain verging on but not quite ready to be called a mind. In this regard, the creature had much in common with its descendant, Charity Mae Stovall.

1

SORT OF GENESIS

1

This was a real nice clambake . . .

Without question the grandest party of a brilliant season. Racketing across the universe through the myriad clusters of stars, across the dark void between galaxies, like a gleaming silver tear glistening on black velvet, the end-of-term celebration became an unbridled riot of the senses for the self-conscious students. On young worlds they bathed in the scarlet splendor of volcanoes, rhymed solemnly to each other and made love in the cold light of moons drawn close to dying mother worlds, dove headlong through the chromospheres of small suns to prolong their high on rarefied gases. They basked and swam in plasma-soupy primordial seas gravid with life to come; roared drunk in a perverse course counter to a slow-wheeling galaxy to reach the outer whorl simply because it was there and looked lovely; came to rest finally on a green savanna in an atmosphere so oxygen-rich that it shot their high even higher and they changed form again to complement it. No one expected a school's-out party to make much sense, not in this generation at least.

A magnificent time—yet Sorlij was bored.

They were the purest and most sublime of sentient life forms:

energy to matter to energy at will. Where their kind passed, less advanced creatures called them gods. This generated wise laws among the mature and in jokes among snotty adolescents like Barion and Coyul.

They were neither gods nor the only advanced mutable form, as the recent war had proven. Certain developments might have been predicted by far less advanced cultures, particularly the war's effect on the young. After the inconclusive hostilities, the anthropoid form became a dissident movement among students. Thinking themselves the first to be disillusioned and sold down the cosmos by craven elders, they brazenly adopted any lifestyle and form disapproved by the retiring generation. They transported blithely in their glittering, half-ethereal ships to any planet that pleased them and cavorted on two legs or three as the fancy took them.

Why not? Bodies were fun. They opened a whole new spectrum of sensory highs. Sexual possibilities were narrow and local but with interesting side effects. They found it a real kick to chew certain green leaves with actual teeth and feel the profound effect on a finite being, and if you overdosed, you could always dissolve to energy state to detoxify. Some substances were very dangerous; you had to identify the onset of physical death before coma set in. You could actually die, and some loved to see how close they could come before winking safely back to energy. Fun, danger, uncertainty, courage. Works of art perpetrated in this perilous state were considered ultimate truth. A few extremists formed death pacts, left bad verse in farewell and went all the way.

Older academics considered the anthropoid form an unprofitable dead end for study. The new generation loved being decadent and lost, reveled in irony and romantic self-pity, created sad or savage music like that of Coyul, Barion's bratty little brother. In the bizarre four-limbed form they leaned together, murmured solemn verities, felt doomed and dramatic or glittered defiantly in radical chic.

Though all this could pale. Sorlij, the class leader, was terribly bored. The party was coming down from its high, scattered about the moist grass, too exhausted now even for the queer, comic form of lovemaking peculiar to the bipedal body. They should

start home. A long way, Sorlij remembered fuzzily, five galaxies
away . . . or was it six?

"Which way did we come?" he asked about. No one remembered.

Meanwhile the party languished. Sorlij's pet hates, Barion and
Coyul, were not fun drunks. The brothers were not even of the
graduating class, sophomores in every sense of the word, but well
connected and precocious. A few of the seniors had thrilled for a
moment to Barion's poetry—

"It sings! It soars!"

—and someone else twittered over Coyul's music and flip cynicism. The brothers were invited along over Sorlij's objections. He
could always pass on Barion's poetry and interests which centered unhealthily on the possibilities of the anthropoid form. The
main thrust of all their studies was life-seeding on new worlds,
but Barion seemed obsessed with the one creature far beyond
the limits of fashion or fad. Anyone else would be laughed at or
disciplined. Barion, the spoiled darling of prominent family,
would probably win the coveted first prize in genetic science
that should go to Sorlij for his work in marine life forms. To most
observers, Barion's faults were drowned in his alleged charm,
and Sorlij politely detested him.

As for Coyul, Sorlij considered him a mere added irritant. His
ennui and affected decadence could wear on you, especially if
those poses had only recently been renounced in one's self. Nothing galled so much as yesterday's follies worn today by someone
else.

"The green shoot plays the autumn leaf," Sorlij quipped, not
above an epigram himself.

He gazed about at his friends lounging about the grassy slope
and found his favorite, Maj, whose radical concepts in the anthropoid form had prompted her to assume something dramatic for
the occasion: a scarlet mer-seductress with a broad tail that
changed colors with Maj's every whim.

"Stroke my fin?" she invited Sorlij.

"Maj, I think it's time to go home."

"Oh, not yet. The party's a huge success."

"Before it becomes tedious."

Maj covered a delicate yawn with cerise fingers. "There's that,

yes. Time to go, everyone. Don't have to be sober, just mobile."
Her mer-tail flirted suggestively at Sorlij and became a remarkable pair of female legs. "Shall we?"

One by one the party let go of physical shape and became daubs of silver light against the green and amber of late afternoon, flowing toward their ship. All but Barion and Coyul, prostrate on the grass. Sorlij lingered in substance to prod them with a custodial toe.

"Up, you two. We're going home."

Coyul hiccupped, rumbled somewhere in an unaccustomed digestive tract and passed out again.

"Barion! Gather up your unspeakable brother and bring him to the ship. Time to leave."

The young man turned over, labored up on one elbow. "Leave?" he said thickly. "Ridiculous."

Sorlij booted him again. "Party's over. Come on."

Barion pronounced with drunken care, "It has just begun." He gouged double handfuls of grass from the moist earth and flung them high. "Rich with promise and oxygen, new-made creatures pattering, thundering toward destiny. Primates . . . what's the literal meaning of 'primate' in our tongue? 'Those who look up.' Utter par-*hic*-adise."

Sorlij hauled him to his feet, on which Barion swayed like a tree about to fall. His chosen physical form was advanced primate. Millions of years later on this same world the image would be described as Byronic.

"I would take this birthing world into my hands"—Barion tried to focus on them—"and through my fingers run the saltwaters of oceans, the grains of earth, a cosmos of thought . . ."

"Meanwhile, let's go home."

". . . teach my creations to see the atom and through it to the larger worlds, galaxies within: one vast, concerted, soaring purpose . . ." Barion trailed off, wilting down onto the grass like a garment fallen from a hanger. "Soon's I get a nap."

"Serve you both right to be left here," Sorlij muttered. He nudged Coyul again. One bleary eye opened and found him. "We're going. Come on. You'll have to carry Barion to the ship."

"Abs'lutely. Common sense to the rescue." Coyul rolled over beside his unmoving brother, studied him and then Sorlij. "The lovely thing about being drunk: I don't have t'listen to him or look at you. My dear brother," Coyul mumbled on the verge of maudlin tears. "He believes all that cosmic-poetical nonsense, y'know."

Coyul squinted up at Sorlij with drunken malice and apparently came to a decision. Lurching erect somehow, he balled the novelty of his right hand into a clumsy fist. "I know you don't like him, but he's never been hurt. Which, as of this moment, is more than I can say for you."

Coyul launched a roundhouse right at Sorlij. Unused to real muscles, he aimed the blow where Sorlij's mouth was supposed to be. His target merely dissolved. Coyul passed through thin air, went down on his face and stayed there.

"All *right,*" Sorlij huffed, a little shaken by the sudden violence that recalled too sharply everything he disliked about the irresponsible siblings. "So be it. For once you two can get your precious selves out of trouble. Just stay here a while and cool off. I'm sick of you both."

"Where are the boys?" he was asked at the ship.

"They don't feel like coming." Sorlij bit off the words. "Frankly, I don't care. I don't want to be bothered with them now."

Maj tittered at the prospect. "That's amusing. Imagine them waking up with nothing to do until we come for them."

The notion caught on immediately. "Doomed!"

"Alone."

"No one to impress but monkeys."

The whole thing was a lark. After all, someone would return sooner or later. They were all still too partied out to care. Anyway, what harm could come to the brothers on a world where the highest form of life was an undersized primate? Crossing the orbit of the system's frozen outermost planet, more immediate problems beset them.

"I've been in some unfashionable neighborhoods," their navigator observed, "but this is really obscure, not even on our charts. Anyone remember where we came out of jump?"

No one did. They hadn't cared much about directions coming out, though in a curved, finite universe, they couldn't stay lost forever. On the other hand, the volunteer navigator was less than expert.

They landed many times on the way home, mostly for a change of scene, knowing certain systems to be in varying stages of civilization. After some bad experiences, they became discreet about asking directions. On worlds where they were not understood, the higher life forms proclaimed them deities, wrote sacred works, promulgated dogma on what they were supposed to have said, and flattered them with the sacrifice of surplus population. Where they were understood, the natives tried to sell them trinkets, real estate and surplus daughters.

"Thank you, no," they declined, "we're just passing through . . ."

"Unless perhaps you have a son with four arms," suggested Maj, who was quite jaded.

As their near-immortal kind went, they were not appreciably older when they found a familiar sun for reference, but the universe was. By then, no one even faintly remembered or cared much where they'd left Barion and Coyul.

Shortly after their return, a conservative administration came to power. Trends altered, youth no longer flamed. The few post-adolescent gatherings in the now unfashionable human form looked merely anachronistic. Primate studies languished. The family and friends of Barion and Coyul found themselves less well connected than before, though it was understood that Sorlij would have to return for the boys since he knew the way. More or less. Sooner or later.

Meanwhile Sorlij's discipline became high-priority for a newly discovered batch of sea worlds, his academic star in the ascent.

"Of course you'll go back for them one of these days, no question. But now, dear boy—how do you like advanced studies?"

■ 2 ■

Killing time: genius ad lib

Barion stood on the brow of a low hill, seven feet tall, idealized in every fine-chiseled feature, a time bomb of idealism. Eons later in the Age of Romance, this likeness would inspire a plethora of sonnets by repressed ladies who played the spinet and reproduced parthenogenically by thinking of England. A little later, Whitman would write much the way Barion presently conceived existence. By then Barion would be more restrained in taste and method, but the errors of early enthusiasm would be irreversible.

He felt buoyant this primal morning, breathing deeply of the oxygen-rich air and the heady impurities exhaled by this fecund planet. On the flatland below, a mild breeze stirred the tall savanna grass—no, not breeze but movement. A small group of the fascinating primates noted yesterday: two males, three females, shambling through the high grass in search of food, physical differences barely discernible under the silky black hair that covered most of their body.

Their stereoscopic vision and acute color perception would register Barion as alien. Yes; they saw him and halted. Barion faded to energy phase, moving closer. With nothing to see or smell, the primates went on foraging. Barion concentrated on one of the males turning over a stone in search of grubs. It had no forehead at all, merely a thick supraorbital ridge of bone. The brain was almost entirely instinct.

Almost, Barion knew, excitement rising. There were possibilities.

The ape's blunt head swiveled toward a flicker of light, screeching at the others. On the hilltop something like sunlight began to take definite shape. Barion flowed away toward his brother.

Physical but motionless, the brothers watched the wary primates move away from them. "As anthros go," Barion judged, "these are interesting."

"Try this for laughs," Coyul glowered in frustration. "They've left us here. Sorlij, Maj, the whole considerate pack of them. We're stuck."

Absorbed, Barion said, "Nothing to worry about. Probably a side trip. They'll be back."

"I lack your faith in Sorlij."

There were large differences of temperament between Barion and Coyul, quite obvious in human form. As stated, Barion's fancy ran to the Byronic. Smaller Coyul looked like an overdressed Dylan Thomas. Where Barion's costume was thrift shop casual, the fretful Coyul stumped up and down in a gold lamé dressing gown that startled his brother as much as it had the retreating apes.

"Left!" Coyul berated the heavens. "Lost, abandoned, ma-rooned!"

"Relax; they'll be back. You know Sorlij."

"I do," said Coyul, not at all reassured. "I have work at home: a whole new cycle of études. Notes for a major orchestral piece."

Which demonstrated another basic difference in the brothers. Both were trained to the primary work of their kind, genetic seeding. Barion considered himself a scientist with artistic leanings. Coyul was at heart an artist and something of a dilettante, happy only at his music, competent but halfhearted at the discipline into which fate arbitrarily dumped him.

"I've got a bad feeling about this," he brooded. "Remember the way we came?"

"Not really. Toward the outer edge of the galaxy . . . sort of."

"Ah—which galaxy?"

"Oh, I don't know," Barion confessed without much concern.

"How many are there?"

"Your complacency boggles the mind. I hope someone knows. Without a ship we are in trouble."

Relative trouble: in energy form they could streak across short distances, perhaps half the diameter of the present galaxy. Beyond that presented serious dangers of energy dissipation, radiation effects, pollution from star scintillation, all possibly mortal to their electron-cycle life.

"Barion, what can we do?"

"Come on, little brother." Barion grinned. "Where's your creativity, your initiative?"

"I've got plenty of initiative," Coyul blazed. "Just wait'll I use it on you sometime."

"How about now?"

"This is your kind of place," Coyul retreated. "What can we do?"

"Oh, well." Barion looked off after the primates receding across the grassland. "All sorts of things."

Lost on this mud-ball world while more time passed. Whenever Barion disappeared for long periods, Coyul could always find him indulging his obsession with primates, observing the nearest family group in physical form, allowing them to get used to him. On this unknown, uncharted planet, Coyul feared that Barion would find the lure of experiment irresistible, and therein lay the problem. Penalties for premature seeding were stiff enough; for unauthorized experiment they were virtual death: exile for eons on the Rock, some utterly or near-lifeless planet, until the solitary prisoner gave up and bled his energy out into space and oblivion.

Coyul found it ironic that he should be considered the irresponsible one, but a large part of this general opinion was his own doing. Competent enough at carbon-cycle life studies, he had no interest in science at all. Part of his youthful dilettante pose was an affectation of boredom toward any discipline save art, deriving a perverse pleasure from letting elders and peers alike think him an utter waste of time. He reasoned that by the time he was independent they'd just leave him alone to dabble and compose.

On this unpromising day, he found Barion observing a single primate under a tree. Coyul's sudden appearance made it start and gibber.

"Soften your colors," Barion suggested. "The bright confuses it."

Coyul's toga-like creation faded from scarlet and silver to buff-green. "What's it doing that's worth watching?"

"Found some nuts. Tried to gnaw through one and broke a tooth. Doesn't feel at all good about that. Now it'll try that stone."

The ape raised the stone and hurled it at the nuts, missing them altogether. Coyul stirred restlessly. "I hope this improves— *ow!*"

He sprang up, rump stinging, as the offending snake coiled to strike again. "You little—"

The Ur-cobra was evolving a neurotoxin to paralyze its dinner, but the concept was still on the drawing board. Coyul glared murderously, then flowed as energy into the reptile brain, raging, bloating it to grotesque activity. For tortured seconds the snake suffered from conscience, questioned existence, then thrashed away through the undergrowth. Shortly afterward, with suicidal relief, the snake allowed itself to be eaten by a wild dog with fewer scruples.

"Charming place: one huge digestive tract," Coyul muttered, corporating again. He glanced at the bewildered ape pawing at his gritty nutshells. "Any news from the cutting edge of science?"

Suffering with the broken tooth, the ape scooped up the stone with a scream of frustration and smashed it on a larger one. The missile split evenly along a seam.

"Cutting edge," Barion mused. "I wonder . . ."

"Leave the animals alone," Coyul warned. "Don't tinker."

"Obviously on its way to becoming human."

"With all the implied instabilities. Even if he creates beauty at breakfast—and he's not exactly expert at simple feeding yet—you can never be sure he won't murder before sundown."

But Barion heard the siren song of possibility. "At least I can help him with the nuts. Before that other specimen grabs them away."

A smaller male, foraging himself, had wandered close. The first male chattered a warning. When the newcomer made a snatch at the nuts, he scooped up the broken stone—

—the difference was subtle but apparent to Coyul: a little more control in the grip, better aim as the cutting edge slammed down on the marauder's skull. With a shrill scream the smaller male rolled in the grass, clutching its furry head. Reclaiming the prize, the victor laid the nuts on the rock that had shattered and shaped his own missile and pounded at them with the cutting stone.

"Barion, quit messing *around!*"

"I didn't," Barion whispered, jubilant. "Well, not much."

Just a nudge here, a hint there in the small proto-brain, turning it precocious just a little ahead of evolutionary schedule. "Show-off. At least give the loser the same break."

"What, him?" Barion started away toward the hilltop. "Controlled experiment; always a loser. Smart eats, stupid starves. I have some thinking to do."

Coyul sat alone, brooding on the grave and very possible consequences of Barion's impulse, staring morosely at the relative genius picking edible morsels from the mashed shells.

"Congratulations. Try not to get eaten yourself before the day's out. Now get out of here. Move!"

The sudden thunder of Coyul's voice sent the ape fleeing away across the savanna. Safe for the moment, the smaller male brandished a stick after him, achieving moral victory at low cost and healthy distance, then rummaged among the nutshells for bits of meat.

Coyul watched him, thinking on balances of power, his brother's arrogance, the wounded monkey. Blood from its lacerated scalp spattered over the stone missile. The creature hefted the stone in one hand, picked up its stick in the other, looking off after the departed enemy.

"Just this once," Coyul decided. "Only fair."

He made no major intrusion in the small brain, just enough to push one fact toward another to make a working combination. Still intent on his distant assailant, the ape's bright eyes gleamed with new tactical purpose. It remembered dimly making a few tentative swipes at soft wood with harder stone . . . something stone could do to wood.

The nimble fingers with their unique opposable thumbs began to work—clumsily at first, then more surely through a hundred tries until the ape learned how to strike most effectively with the tool. Until there was a formidable point.

With a scream of triumph, the little creature plunged its weapon again and again into yielding earth, brandished vengeance high overhead, then darted away on a direct course after the enemy who hurt it.

Coyul lingered a moment to wonder which would survive, then put his figurative money on the spear maker. The other ape might be bigger, but this one was vindictive and *mean.*

■ 3 ■

The serpent's gift

The spear maker became head of his family group by the logical expedient of skewering his larger rival. Barion was peeved at his brother's interference—

"Keep your hands *off*, Coyul."

—but on reflection found aspects of the victor too tempting to pass up. Perfect serendipity: this backwater world would never matter to anyone. Sorlij or someone would pick them up soon enough; meanwhile he could experiment toward results that would surely win him a science prize for seeding in one of the more important galaxies. Barion was young. The urgent rightness of his theories spurred him like a pebble in his shoe.

Suppose . . .

Ninety-five percent of hominid species never went anywhere. Another three percent did somewhat better but coasted eventually down evolutionary dead ends. The viable two percent were no end of trouble, but only—Barion theorized—because no one was allowed to work them to Cultural Threshold until they'd attained 1050 cc of cranial capacity. At that tardy point, the primal tendencies were too deep-rooted a part of them, the memory of the dark in which their nocturnal ancestors foraged while the great reptiles slept.

"No one has ever tried CT at the level of these subjects."

"An unencouraging and totally illegal 900 cc," Coyul reminded him.

But the prospect caught fire in Barion's imagination. "An expendable world not even on the charts at home. An expendable species that won't . . . Look, you know this kind of planet always tends to radical polar tilt sooner or later. They won't make it through the ice. We'll be gone by then, but at least I'll know I'm right."

Coyul shook his head, resigned to sad truth. "You won't breed the darkness out of them no matter when you start. It's part of them."

"Isn't."

"It is when you're a mind capable of conceiving eternity trapped inside a body that dies. I didn't sleep through *all* the lectures, you know."

"Yes, yes." Barion waved the objections aside with his usual know-it-all gesture. "Religion, dualism. Predictable stages."

"Not stages, you idiot! Propensities!"

"Hush, be still. My subject's coming."

The ape moved cautiously to the water hole to drink, wary of the two still figures a little distance away, hissing a challenge out of a mouth and throat still limited in the sounds they could produce. Were she of an empirical bent, Charity Stovall might have been edified to know her direct ancestor was the smartest ape on its metaphorical block. Relative to body mass, the brain was already huge. Other survival traits would have sent Charity gibbering back to Genesis for reassurance.

Above all, the ape was marvelously adaptable. Omnivorous as a rodent, thriving on any food available. Three and a half feet tall: the most acquisitive, curious, aggressive, inventively vicious hominid Barion had ever found, and quite the hardiest on this violent world next to the cockroach and the rat. Long after this day's work the ape would produce Christ, Beethoven, Auschwitz, thumbscrews and philosophy, Magna Carta and White Supremacy, poetry, poison gas, nuclear fission and romantic love. For the moment it crouched by the water hole, munching a succulent grub discovered under a stone, warning off the large creatures that somehow would not be frightened away. They were unclassifiable, therefore a threat. The ape made the brave noises of its kind.

"Good morning," Barion said softly. "Welcome to evolution."

The ape jumped at the sound, afraid but curious.

"I may be wrong about you. You and I have a great deal to learn."

The ape made a clicking sound of puzzlement.

"You won't understand any of this. Even when your mind is clear enough to send your little cutting stone to the moon and beyond, you'll still wonder about this moment but never quite forget the truth of it. Wrap it in religion, a hundred flattering myths, in music, painting and exaltation of pure spirit—"

"Why all the lyrics?" Coyul wondered sourly. "You're only giving it a boot in the evolutionary butt."

"Can't you see it? The implications, the greatest of all dramas, when life stands erect to contemplate itself—"

"My brother, the scientific lemming, headlong over the edge of folly. Don't do it."

"Shut up. This is *his* triumph: this one moment of knowing, when the atom contemplates an electron navel and finds worlds within worlds, will stay in that small brain forever. Your nature will always be to believe," he prophesied to his quivering subject, "but your destiny always to question. I can't make that any easier for you."

Barion began to dissolve, flowing toward the creature. Coyul pleaded one last time. "Barion, don't! It's—"

Too late. His brother became a brief sparkle in sunlight before pouring into the little ape's brain.

"—madness."

Under the beetling brow, it—*he*—blinked. A great light had flashed somewhere behind his eyes. Blood pounded in his ears. He was alone by the muddy water hole and still thirsty, but now, as he bent to drink, there was a difference. Always before, he'd seen the other creature come up to meet him out of the water, then vanish somehow in the small ripples caused by his drinking. The image had always frightened him; now he knew it was his own. He snarled at it, knowing he existed and would end, rejecting that horrible truth for all time with a howl of terror and rage and a primal loss he would labor through countless eons and creeds to rationalize and define. With all the terrible weight of consciousness, *knowing* he was. The beginnings of expression in the eyes, a dawn-sense of the tragedy Barion had taxed him with. As for the lost thing never to be found again, even his far-distant daughter Charity would call it the Fall.

Stunned by sentience, the miserable human did what came naturally—growled as Barion reappeared beside Coyul.

"Now you've done it," Coyul reproached him with a full measure of disgust. "I don't care if you are my brother. You're a rotten kid."

"We'll see." Barion inspected his handiwork like a critical painter gauging perspective on a canvas. Abruptly he swung away, covering the ground in great strides.

"Where are you off to now? Haven't you done enough damage?"

"Got to do the same for his group," Barion flung back. "Can't have him maundering around thinking all alone."

"Fine . . . just fine." Coyul dissolved to energy out of compassion for the miserable creature that Barion had just kicked upstairs. Whimpering with a new fear all the sharper for having no clear shape, the creature bowed his besieged head in hairy paws and felt vastly sorry for himself.

"All right," Coyul sighed. "You're a self. Suddenly apart where you used to be part of. I'd have left well enough alone."

The same sympathy kept him from leaving the human, who was weeping now, already trying to make sounds for unguessed meanings.

"It's not all bad. There'll be insights now and then. I suppose there's a chance."

The pathetic human went on sniffling. He didn't seem to know where he was anymore.

"Look, it's not my fault, not up to me to help you at all. He shouldn't have done it. So many other life forms more suited to sentience than you'll ever be. Oh, stop whining, will you?"

The weeping human raised his blunt head at the sound of a distinct reluctant sigh.

"All right—here: it's the least I can do."

Weeping made him feel thirsty again. As he bent to drink once more, knowing the reflected image for himself, fear transmuted to something lighter, the ugly sound of his sadness to an even more alien emotion. He couldn't help it. The effort strained his throat that barely had the muscles for laughter.

So much for motivations. Barion wanted to win a science prize, Coyul only to go home and write music, but the thing was done. A great deal of bloodshed, art and religion would be perpetrated in both their names, and neither would be understood at all. As they had done to him, the human modified them to a lesser but more flattering truth he could live with.

Dazed, intermittently sobbing and laughing like a squeaky hinge, the creature deserted the water hole and scampered away toward history and other mixed blessings.

4

Topside/Below Stairs

The relief ship didn't come. And *didn't* come.

A great deal of time went by. The Pole tilted, the ice came and went. Barion's creature moved across the land and oceans, the skies, touched the moon and groped beyond. Barion began with a passionate belief, encouraged to vindication with every advance. Coyul took his own conclusions from the dismal weight of evidence.

Humans *were* dualistic. Consciously forgotten, the primitive eons still lurked in the subsconscious, a huge dark forest against the small bright leaf of civilization. With new language they put new names to the gods of light and dark, put them at a distance but could not escape. Called the dark evil but found it always there inside them, a kind of spiritual schizophrenia. Persisted in seeing existence in terms of this struggle between "good" and "evil," producing a great deal of belief, violence and, now and then, actual thought.

"The darkness will wear away," Barion was certain.

"Sure," said the dubious Coyul. "Any millennium now."

And then a new problem cropped up in which dualism was only an aggravating part. Matter could be neither created nor destroyed. The human brain was matter that generated energy.

At a certain point in its evolution, a residue of personally defined energy began to stockpile, wanting somewhere to continue after physical death and, above all, something to do. Even Coyul had no flippant answer for the quandary. The small body of work their kind had done with the ill-regarded species never included sufficient follow-up on side effects. A few inspection reports on this post-existent energy pool (couched in *very* cautiously conservative terms) filtered in, were misinterpreted, buried and forgotten in the academic catacombs for irrelevant information and the pressure of more immediate problems at home. Barion never realized—

"They don't die, Coyul. They just go *on*. And they keep asking about one god or another."

"Me, too. I tell them I'm just waiting to go home. Then I tell them where home is and nobody believes me. For all their violence, they have a remarkable capacity for supine adoration. Throw 'em a grand party; that always works."

Worked for some and for a while. Egypt and Sumer passed. Most of them forgot about gods and creeds after a time and got on out of habit with the kind of life they'd known on Earth. Babylonians came, greased and gauded, brought wine and cheese and loved the party. Britons sang, Irish drank and mourned, Chinese discussed aesthetics, Indians chased phantom buffalo, Jews argued. Their combined energy was incredible, but Barion managed after a fashion, directing by indirection.

Then the Christians started to arrive, simple folk for the most part who didn't want much. Nevertheless, the Apostles had definite and aggressive views, the martyrs felt they were owed the Presence of God and grew sharp with Barion, who was, to them, merely a ubiquitous handyman and certainly dressed like one. Unlike Coyul, Barion dressed for function, inventing denim ages before America popularized it.

Very few had the perception to discern Barion's real power. One who did was a young Nazarene named Yeshua who had problems of his own in what people thought he was and expected of him.

"Sometimes," he admitted to Barion, "I wish I'd minded my own business."

"*You* wish? Have you met Augustine yet?"

"I've avoided him," said the candid Yeshua. "He doesn't like Jews."

"Well, he's after me all the time about seeing God. And you: where and when does he come into the Presence?"

Yeshua gazed out over the grassy riverbank he and Barion had imagined for a few moments of relaxation. There was a directness to his glance and a stillness that the unsure found disturbing, the pompous insolent. "Just tell him you're . . . You, I guess. Something."

"You were an extraordinarily wise man in your time," Barion said, "and even you had to use parables. You think Augustine, that doggedly passionate saint, would accept what I really am: a student from a galaxy on the other side of the universe and likely to be in a lot of trouble when I'm found? He's growing insistent on seeing you, too. What he thinks you are."

"He'd just be disappointed. They all are. A pity, too. I like being with people." Yeshua rested his chin on drawn-up knees. "There's one friend I'd give anything to see . . . talk to. He hasn't come here."

"Judas?" Barion guessed. "He's with Coyul."

"Judas could have understood the truth, but he ran from it."

"You two!" The stentorian voice startled them.

Barion winced. "Speak of saints . . ."

"I would speak with you." The short, bull-shouldered man in late Roman dress strode along the bank and halted before them, peremptory as a drill sergeant. His wide-set eyes gleamed with strength and the steely light of the Believer reborn from self-defined sin.

Nothing for it; Barion greeted him pleasantly. "Hello, Augustine."

The Bishop of Hippo brushed the courtesy aside. "Give me no more excuses or subterfuge. Tell me where I may find what I have in life suffered, fought, endured enmity and slander for. Where—is—He?"

"Haven't seen him."

"Oh, not again!"

"I've never seen him." Barion shrugged, choosing his words carefully. Augustine was skilled in debate and played dirty. "But in time you'll understand more than you did."

Augustine bridled: a strong, courageous but narrow man. "I need no nondescript porter in outlandish garb to give me understanding. Where, then, is my Lord, Jesus Christ?"

"Visiting a troubled friend," Yeshua volunteered truthfully.

Augustine, that most embattled of the early saints, subjected Yeshua to disdainful scrutiny from the sensitive face to the provincial garb of Galilee. "And here another riddle. I do not understand, among other mysteries sufficient to drive the Faithful to drink or women, why *you* people are suffered to remain here. You destroy, you question everything and accept nothing. When Christ offered you salvation, you spit on it and nailed Him to a cross."

"That was a bad day," Yeshua agreed with authority. "I was against it myself."

So it went. Time continued to pass. More people arrived, prejudiced as Augustine. Barion was forced to subdivide his nebulous domain into different realities. Pagans were no problem so long as they had sunlight and greenery, nor the Jews so long as they could suffer and argue and Hasidim didn't have to deal with the new Zionists. If you needed to feel Chosen or Elect, there were miles of exclusive high rises set aside for the purpose, and never a wait for vacancies. Only the most radical few made permanent residence there. A lifetime of extremity was one thing, eternity quite another.

With the Protestant Reformation and its spread to America, Barion's problems became truly complex. In their passion for exclusivism and damning others, they gave his establishment so many names that Barion simply affixed a nonsectarian title that stuck.

Newcomers were greeted: "Welcome to Topside."

Coyul could look to no more respite than his brother. Postexistent energy began collecting in his vicinity as early as in Topside. Like Barion, he was forced to maintain an office for some kind of organization. Barion's taste in decor never got beyond functional government surplus, but Coyul's office was more of a salon, reflecting the march of style through the ages—grand during the Egyptian Middle Kingdom, a fine Athenian period. He went a little gaudy with Imperial Rome, overtapestried during the Renaissance. The seventeenth century grew a bit lacy, the nineteenth very busy and Pre-Raphaelite, the twentieth by turns Art Deco, Scandinavian, chrome-and-Lucite. The grand piano obligingly modified its finish to match changing styles.

Those lusty ancients who came to Coyul just wanted to relax and enjoy themselves. Romans were marvelous in this respect, especially Petronius and Martial, but eventually Coyul had to subdivide to accommodate the variety of human experience, prejudice and folly. Seeding Cultural Threshold so early had lasting repercussions; by the time of the late-medieval Christians, human notions of an afterlife were as violent as the one they'd suffered Earthside. Since Coyul's neighborhood was clearly not heaven, they considered themselves damned and expected to suffer. Coyul found that they ultimately defined themselves by pain and were used to it. After a time he gave up trying to dissuade them and provided a space large enough but of no specific character—until he read Dante and comprehended their geometric and grisly expectations.

"These people are sick. Well . . . all right."

Drama they wanted, drama they got with full staging, lights and stereophonic sound. Their subdivision hell was very German Expressionist—dark, windswept and romantically bleak. Coyul provided only scenery and props, leaving pain to humans with more talent for it. As with Topside's high rise for unreformed ecstatics and the insufferably blessed, the reality of eternal penance quickly palled. The sector had well-lighted exits, and their use was encouraged.

Occupied with their own problems, the brothers saw less and less of each other as the ages passed. When Barion did visit he was appalled.

"What do you call this—whatever it is going on here? Looks like a cross between a procession of flagellants and a Polish wedding."

"Hadn't thought to name it," Coyul said, stroking idle chords from the piano. "Topside is catchy; what should I be? Downstairs? The Cellar? No, it doesn't ring."

"I heard you visited Luther Earthside."

"For all the good it did. I presume you got him."

"Didn't I just. Don't meddle, Coyul."

"Oh—the original pot blackening the kettle. Did you straighten him out?"

"I don't try anymore," Barion said unhappily. He no longer looked Byronic, just hassled. "Left off that with the Druids. They all think I'm sort of a janitor."

Coyul surveyed his brother's worn denim jeans and work shirt. "Can't think why. Now, drama works very well here—below stairs, as it were."

"But do they believe you?"

"No." Coyul played a few minor chords. "Most don't believe me, the rest don't give a damn. I hope they find us soon—fun as this place can be sometimes."

"Just keep your hands off Earthside. We're in enough trouble—" Barion broke off abruptly, listening intensely. "There—you hear it?"

"Hear what?"

"That sound. Voices. Been hearing them on and off for several years. Americans," Barion concluded vaguely. "Don't like it at all."

"Wait. Where are you going?" Coyul asked hastily as Barion began to dissolve.

"Out . . ."

His curiosity tweaked, Coyul turned his ear Earthside, sifting the voices and spirits that echoed as energy from that violent little ball in space. He heard them soon enough: American voices that somehow didn't *sound* American, like a sudden change of pitch in a smooth-running engine. Coyul sought out Barion's energy, found him sweeping over American mountains and flatlands, a solitary hound on a scent. Blending with that energy, Coyul knew what his brother did, read the names though they meant nothing to him.

Charity Stovall. Roy Stride.

To Barion came the masses of simple folk, lost, neglected and ground down through history, bearing nothing but their bewilderment, injustice and the brutalized monotony of their lives. The passionate but inarticulate needers of a flaming God to redeem their humble faith or at least help them get even.

Coyul fared better for personalities. There were problems, to

be sure: malcontents, injury collectors, bureaucrats (dull but useful for keeping records), fascists, reformers, assorted chauvinists
and bigots. Coyul grew adept at fitting the right ambience to the
individual spirit. As time went on, this rather than any schism
became the difference between Topside and Below Stairs. Both
were more or less efficient without much organization, but Coyul
maintained the more colorful establishment. Along with the
thorns of the professional sufferers came the occasional blossoms:
the musicians, the stimulating thinkers from the Vienna coffee-
houses. The artists, the newsmen with cynical eyes and large
thirsts, rowdy poets and agnostic scholars. The actors like Edmund Kean, whose visceral *Othello* could thrill new generations
of deceased . . . and the dashing, incendiary, utterly mad John
Wilkes Booth, who came bathed in his own perpetual spotlight,
ready as ever to be a star.

Early on, there came one man who wanted absolutely nothing
except to be left alone. He lived in solitude on an isolated moor
on the fringe of suffering, received no guests, troubled Coyul not
at all. Now and then he drove a cab or did other odd jobs for the
mislabeled Prince of Darkness, who knew him immediately but,
out of courtesy, did not trouble him for a name.

"Jacob will do," the newcomer said—a brooding, sardonic man
with troubled eyes and a manner designed to keep folk at a
distance. In later times, tooling his cab through the byways of
Below Stairs, he simply offered, "Call me Jake."

■ 5 ■

Management problems among the mad

"No! I will not! Never, ever again!"

Wilmer P. Grubb was not an aggressive man, but driven by last-ditch frustration, he barged into Coyul's salon, slamming a pale hand on the piano top to punctuate his passion. A slight, sallow academic who never looked quite kempt, his happiest expression that of a child forced to drink something good for him.

"I will not!" he bleated. "Excuse me for not knocking, Prince."

"No one ever does," said the inured Coyul, "but you might start a trend. What is it, Mr. Grubb?"

"Booth."

"Again?"

"As ever, the bane of my existence."

In life Wilmer Grubb had been a professor who wanted nothing more than to teach Shakespeare as a poet, not a playwright. The immortal lines, he felt, were fragile and unsafe in the braying mouths of players. Not choice but biology sent Grubb to a galley oar in theater. He had an ardent love for his comely wife, Elvira, and stated it redundantly with eight children, forcing him to earn extra money as a drama critic during Lincoln's administration. In his jaundiced scholarly view, actors were déclassé, plays the opiate of a benighted public—but the mad John Wilkes Booth, younger brother to Edwin, was Grubb's bête noire. When Booth opened, Grubb quite often wrote his review before trudging to the theater as to execution, sometimes without bothering to go at all. He died of acute gastritis brought on by questionable oysters and Booth's *Hamlet*, never once blaming the seafood. Wafting Topside to the requested strains of Handel, Grubb was told that his wife had preferred Coyul's establishment. Before departing south, the scholar indulged the dream of a lifetime and asked to meet his icon, Shakespeare.

The meeting was unfortunate. The balding, bibulous son of a Stratford glove maker possessed a lyrical vulgarity that might tickle his tavern cronies but revolted the prim Grubb, especially when well-oiled Will did his uncensored Mercutio. Grubb fled the Mermaid and the neighborhood, arriving Below Stairs in profound cultural shock. He was greeted by an affable Coyul in a lilac chesterfield.

"Do come *in*, Mr. Grubb. Your charming wife is already with us, presently doing—uh—social work in the downtown area. We have lacked you, sir. Our actors, particularly Booth, need your critical rein."

Grubb blanched and shuddered.

"House rules are quite lenient, though we discourage children and pets."

After eight children, so did the Grubbs. They renewed their connubial passion unfettered by issue. Paris being worth a Mass, Grubb continued to review and flay the impossible Wilksey Booth—but enough was enough.

"Prince, I am, in most respects, a happy man. If I must review, I am allowed infinite space—"

"Infinitely employed."

"But far too often"—Grubb's tone went pallid—"I have to review that . . ."

"Booth. Yes." Coyul struck an idle chord on the piano. "And you are driven now to Draconian measures? Miltonian depths? Want to review books?"

"Anything!" Grubb seized on the notion as on a life preserver in a maelstrom. "Even the new works of Hitler."

"He's Topside with Eva." Coyul rippled an arpeggio. "Never sees anyone but Wagner, reviews his own books."

"Possibly romance novels," Grubb offered with waning hope—then, in broken tones, the final indignity: "Even epic fantasy."

"Grubb, remember your pride. All those unicorns . . . I'm in a bind where Wilksey's concerned," Coyul confessed. "Groundlings dote on him, uncritical virgins swoon, older women pursue him with Merovingian intent. No one reviews that painful ham with any detachment except you, Mr. Grubb. My last, best critical hope. You can endure actors."

"I don't like actors," Grubb complained in a voice like a damp sock. "I don't like writers. They're never as nice as their books. All they do is get drunk and arrogant and sick all over the furniture."

Well, Coyul suggested, he might relocate Topside. "There's Woolf and T. S. Eliot: they're frightfully sane."

"HA! *There*, villain!" They were transfixed. "There you are!"

"Booth!" Grubb paled at the sight of the vengeful figure in the entrance. "Protect me, Prince. He's violent."

"Nay, stand! Your next move is your last." The hissed command became the *whish* of a rapier unsheathed, the lethal point on a line with Grubb's pigeon chest in the grip of a black-clad, lithe young man. Still in his Hamlet costume, John Wilkes Booth crouched before them, malevolent and handsome, bathed in his ubiquitous spotlight. He advanced like a demented but purposeful cat. "Grubb, you ratcatcher, I have found thee."

"Provincial raver!" Grubb retreated behind the piano. "Confederate assassin!"

"Prince, I entreat you." Booth suited word to action, down on one knee. "Have you heard what this baneful scribbler wrote about my current Hamlet? List then: 'a hyperthyroid mannequin,' says he, 'overstuffed with conceit as his codpiece with batting.'"

Coyul frowned at the cringing critic. "Now, that was mean."

"Puissant Prince, hear the most loyal among thy liege men. Is't not enough I had to live in Edwin's shadow? Nor that I died for the Confederacy? Now in death must I suffer and create only to endure the calumnies of this unfeeling fungus on the fundament of art? The sword's too noble for such as he." Booth dropped the rapier, drawing a wicked dagger. "A bodkin's work, by heaven!"

He launched himself at the miserable Grubb, spotlight following the fine body as it hurtled to vengeance. A scant inch from Grubb's breast, the dagger became a limp daisy. Not that Booth could have done any damage, but Coyul hated even the idea of violence.

"Wilksey, you silly ass, knock it OFF! Mr. Grubb, if you please." Coyul ushered the trembling teacher to the door. "The matter is in my hands. Meanwhile, you need no longer review."

"Thank you, Prince. Thank you," Grubb effused. "It means so much. So far behind in my professional reading."

"Not at all, I completely understand. Once a scholar . . . good day."

With Grubb no longer part of the problem, Coyul addressed himself reluctantly to the ongoing burden of idiotic Booth, who brooded now in the center of his amber spot. "Wilkes, we're closing *Hamlet.* The women love it, yes, but even those loyal ranks are thinning."

Booth raised his head with its fine raven curls. "My finest role."

"With the imagination of the ages at beck, why always Hamlet?"

"Because he suffers," Booth intoned. "Torn by what he must do and cannot until too late—as I was torn between art and my country. As I suffered."

"Edwin suffered." Coyul turned critical. "Edwin *was* Hamlet. You were too busy drinking, wenching and having a darkly dramatic good time plotting against Lincoln to suffer for a moment. Please turn off that ridiculous light. Jake is the only man Below Stairs who broods with any depth. You look merely petulant or constipated."

"Though you wrong me, that is true." Booth dimmed his aura. "Jake broods like a definition of sorrow itself. But close *Hamlet?* For what, pray?"

"*Romeo.* There, Wilksey, was triumph unalloyed."

"Play again that puling Veronese adolescent?"

"By Thespis, not as *you* played him," Coyul reminisced. "Well do I remember."

So did the women among Booth's audiences, who still grew

faint with the violence of his passion; so did his leading ladies, who usually sustained a bruise or two, and the hapless Tybalts, who had to fight in earnest to remain unmauled. Even Shakespeare, down for a weekend, was impressed: "There, sirrahs, is a Romeo with a scrotum."

"In your reading of 'she doth teach the stars to shine,' one could hear the undiluted hormones of a mating call." Coyul did not flatter in this. Edwin's brother was mad as a hatter but not without talent. But for his deplorable eleventh-hour politics, the world might have loved him as well.

"Close *Hamlet,*" the Prince bargained, "and I myself will find a part worthy of you—or a vehicle, playing all the roles if you like. Sparing no expense for lighting, scenery, costumes or music."

Booth was skeptical but interested. "With love scenes and swordplay? Can I die?"

"In color and often. Strong men will weep and ladies faint."

"Don't they always?" Booth preened. "What is this role?"

Coyul had nothing in mind beyond getting back to his music— and perhaps wondering what Barion heard from America to trouble him. He tried to keep his people happy or at least short of revolt, slanderously called King of Liars because no one really wanted truth, Wilksey least of all.

"Do Romeo first," he hedged. "Make Edwin green. He was never your equal in the role. Then we will follow it with . . ."

"Nay, speak," Booth urged, hooked solidly now. "With what?"

"Well may you ask." Coyul favored the demented actor with a smile of pure anticipation, then dissolved in flattering, soft blue light. "The ages will remember you for it."

Booth stretched out a staying hand as to a ghostly father. "Stay and speak—"

"Remember thee for it . . ."

You had to stage everything for Booth. Like most actors, that was the only way it sank in.

Meanwhile the voices from America grew louder, uglier.

6

Slouching toward Plattsville

Barion rode the wind over desert and flatland, listening to the sound of American voices. Hovered over the steel-and-glass cities, drifted in autumn haze over gas station and 7-Eleven store crossroads, back and forth along the freeways of a country sliding down the long decline toward second-class nationhood while still the most powerful in a turbulent world. The voices he searched out would not be in the cities but out somewhere beyond them across a widening gap, among the have-nots, the small, the disenfranchised and vengeful. The common people toward whom Lincoln had presumptuously ascribed a large affection on Barion's part. As he turned east again, hunting with the concentration of a hawk, he heard the sought voices more clearly. He was coming closer.

Government? Sell us downriver like always. Give the country away to niggers and queers. Don't give a shit about folks like us.

Never had much school, but I know what's right. Liberry full of dirty books, Commoniss books. Klan got the right idea: kill 'em all.

Well, I don't hold with that, but you can't make a living. Man can take a lot if there's enough to live on. Closed the plant . . . ain't worked since. Bad as '29.

Barion veered north now, closing on one place, one town where the voices resolved to dangerous coherence and—somehow known in the eons of his experience—a pivot point in American time. He knew that cry made up of many cries, remembered how it muttered through the sixteenth century, became an ugly but catalytic insanity in the eighteenth, an obscenity in the Germany of the 1930s. The place changed or the language, but not the voice. Coming from America now, from the great vindictive mass, always vocal but never heeded—ignored through the '50s, lampooned in the liberal '60s, polarized in the apathy of the '70s, returning now with ax-grinding leaders. True believers coming to the fore with the same old theme—*don't you make out you're better than us*—defining a narrow God by what they themselves hated and feared.

Contrary to American myth, Barion was no fonder of that nation than he was of Ghana or Finland; just that America bothered him more and more as the twentieth century grew old.

"Cash-register heart and a fairy-tale mentality," he fumed to Coyul in the early '70s. "Savage, sentimental and moralistic."

"Well, that's the thing about the Charmed Princess mystique," Coyul observed. "As often as they lose their virginity, it always grows back."

Barion's pulsing energy followed the great, rounded wrinkles of the Appalachians north. *We the people*, he remembered, recalling the look of the mountains when transplanted Englishmen wrote those words and few but Indians cut trail over the smoky ridges.

We the people, the ones who came first, turned out of England, Ireland, the Highlands for the sake of sheep; out of Newgate and debtors' prison scabrous and dying, but living long enough to sow an American seed. Someone wrote a paper calling us free and equal, but no one made it stick.

Hard men and women, from Barion's firsthand recollection: not always thinking of God but seeing Him hard as themselves when they did. Their descendants much the same, not as hard but needing that peculiarly American form of religious ecstasy blended of poverty, ignorance, degenerated mysticism, collected injuries and the need for vengeance. Helped to some extent by social advances, unions and insurance, but somehow always at the bottom and the last in line.

The plant closed, relief checks run out. No more credit at the store. Sweet Jesus, Sweet White Jesus who wasn't never a Jew, give us—

A target! "That's Roy Stride." Barion dipped sharply, shot down through darkness to the dim lines of light clustered along a highway. "Charity, are you there, too?"

Sweet Jesus, tell us who to blame, that's all. Give us a government with balls that ain't ascared of Russia or niggers, queers and Jew liberals. Give us the true faith of Jesus Christ.

All of which might have sickened Yeshua were he not grown used to it through the Inquisition, the Protestant Reformation and other outbursts of sanctity perpetrated by the true believers.

"What is this White Jesus nonsense?" he implored of Barion once. "They've spent two thousand years turning me into something out of Oxford or a Tennessee Bible college. *Both* my parents were Hebrews, I look like an Arab, spent all my life in the desert, and if they let me into one of their nice 'white' restaurants at all, I'd get the table by the kitchen door. What do these people *want?*"

"You know the lyrics," Barion reminded him. " 'Gimme that old-time revulsion.' "

Roy Stride knows folks that been buying guns, says a day's coming when they send 'em all back to Africa or Jew-rusalem and sink the boats halfway.

The muttered threats, the idle talk, but the anger very real under it and the message clear even though no one listened. No one had ever listened.

Listen, you fuckin fat rich bastards: you cry over Indians and send money to Africa, but when you see our homes and farms going up for taxes, three, four generations of blood gone down under the gavel, that's just five minutes on the late news to you. Heart of your country gone, it's nothing to you but a few more cents at the supermarket.

Hey, listen good: we may be rednecks but some of us are rich rednecks now. You watch on TV what we say and do. Watch the

*folks in the TV tabernacle, plain folks come to hear the Word
with their own kind of understanding—*

Barion had seen them, the tears washing down the faces
scarred with work and want, broken promises and broken
dreams, pustulant with anger—

*We got the TV now and a media voice. Think we'll go down
without someone's to blame? Roy's got the right idea. Roy
says . . .*

The Plattsville town square with its ancient obelisk could manage no charm even in soft autumn dusk. A greenish plaque admitted the town's founder and age to an uncaring present. The
World War I cannon's mouth was a trash-lined haven for transient
birds.

"Depressed," said Barion. "In every sense of the word." His
energy drifted like purposeful mist toward what remained of
Plattsville's commercial area, past the closed and padlocked defense plant, the one movie house, letters awry on the worn run-
ners of the marquee. Past the dark bar, sullen with slow-drinking
men whose anger slammed at Barion out of the entrance along
with the loud country-and-western music. Through the ship's
graveyard of the failing used-car dealership, no car that Barion
saw less than five years old.

Prosperity was a brief, bright strip along Main Street. Very
quickly the street ran to boarded-up stores. Like a garish gold
molar in a row of bad teeth, McDonald's was still open for business.

Still early in the evening; McDonald's had a dinner crowd of
families, work-tired husbands, house-tired mothers trying to get
fast food into squirming, bickering children. Young people—
brusque, callow young men munching hamburgers and wondering what, if any, excitement the evening might bring. More cautious girls with essentially the same question. Young couples . . .

Barion moved, invisible, through the loud babble and paused
at one wall table. Roy and Charity. Their physical attitude at the
table, close as possible though straining together from separate
seats, told the story. They were in love—as they defined that
agony—and physically possessive of each other.

Young as he was, Roy's face brought the word "ravaged" to

Barion's mind: gaunt cheeks, thin black hair already receding swiftly, complexion scarred from acne. A mustache, carefully nurtured but of no specific character. Poor nutrition and worse circumstance, a face festered with violence that Barion knew from every riot or protest meeting since Imperial Rome. What character or statement there was resided in Roy's self-conscious costume: camouflage fatigues, jump boots and field jacket, a black beret bearing some insignia in pewter shoved through one shoulder strap.

Charity Stovall was even more poignantly familiar to Barion, who had glimpsed that face through Europe since the fall of Rome or even earlier, seen it suffer and starve under successive waves of Huns and Vandals.

I know this girl.

Charity Stovall died, raped and burned, under the westward sweep of the Visigoths; burned in her thatched hut along the Humber or drowned in it at the hands of Viking raiders. She searched the field at Hastings and after a hundred other battles to find her own dead. Died in the Black Plague or survived pox-scarred; burned for her Protestant faith in France, raped for her Catholicism in Germany. Her face glared out of the surge of doomed peasant revolts with a growing genetic rage that carved its God and faith from bloodstained granite. Rembrandt painted it and found a deep spirituality. Delacroix romanticized her, but Goya and Breughel knew her better.

Her genes were worn out as Roy's, not much color left to Charity Stovall, the blush gone from her DNA. Below average height because her meagerly nourished bones never lengthened to their full potential. Mouse-brown hair and pale blue eyes, a cast of features the superficial might call plain except for a blunt stubbornness and a set to her eyes that Dürer caught in one or two canvases of German peasant women. Delacroix was a damned fool, Barion reflected. He glorified that face into a singing symbol of liberation. Not so. Mere survival. She hadn't had much of a chance to do anything else for two thousand years.

Just now Charity Stovall's mind was muddled with glandular longings, definitely ambivalent. Barion paused to note the symptoms before digging deeper into her psyche. Gazing fondly at Roy Stride, fingers intertwined with his, Charity was torn be-

tween standards and inclination, a moral skirmish that her subconscious had just ordered her to lose as soon as possible.

Working swiftly through the convolutions of Charity's mind,
Barion found more disparities. Mentally, Roy Stride was average
to the point of mediocrity. He would never be more than he was,
though his fantasies were totally unfettered by reality. But Charity . . . here, in this twenty-year-old woman, rusted from little
or no use, was an actual mind, capable but anchored like the
town-square cannon in the cement block of convention and
habit. The capabilities of that mind, its potential for many states,
good and bad, went far beyond anything Barion would have
suspected or Miss Stovall would ever need in Plattsville. Sooner
or later, tied to Roy, that mind would ferment to bitterness. All
this in predictable futures; right now the major decision of her
life was: should she give in and go to bed with Roy?

He followed them out of McDonald's, table by table as they
greeted young friends. They were the center of the energy that
caught his attention in the first place, the names he heard and
had to seek out. Now they paused on the sidewalk to embrace
and grope at each other in a manner (it seemed to Barion) more
urgent than pleasurable. Charity rested her chin over Roy's
shoulder.

"Yes," she whispered, but her eyes were not that happily decided.

Futures and possibilities radiated from these two in this moment as surely as from Bethlehem.

Roy and Charity turned, still clinging to each other, and
walked slowly up the sidewalk past the boarded-up stores to the
lighted establishment known in better times as La Mode Dress
Shoppe—now reborn as the TABERNACLE OF THE BORN AGAIN
SAVIOR. Roy kissed Charity once more, almost conspiratorially,
then they went into the storefront church.

Barion had known them as types through the ages. He needed
to know their specific probabilities as individuals, all the more
since he'd caught the message from Roy's mind just before the
door closed behind them. The message that had disturbed Barion
in the first place, the essence of Roy and so many like him whose
combined frustration rose from them like the smell from a garbage dump in a long, hot summer.

We know the kind of leader we need. Give us a hero, Sweet White Lord. Someone to look up to who'll waste those rich wimps and Commoniss niggers and Jews without even thinking twice. And give us someone to look down on, too, the way so many look down on us. Give us a victim, Lord, someone to hang from a tree and pay us back. Before we find one for ourselves like we always have to. Amen.

Barion floated just outside the tabernacle entrance, flashing a message to Topside:

BARION TO FELIM: RECORDS RETRIEVAL, PLEASE.

A brief pause only, then the answer burst on his mind in a fervent rush:

ALLAH IS THE ONE TRUE GOD. ALL PRAISE TO—

BY ALL MEANS, BUT FOR NOW JUST GET ME PERSONAL AND FAMILY HISTORY ON ROY STRIDE AND CHARITY STOVALL, THIS LOCATION.

A professional terrorist during his short life, Felim had also been a hacker whiz who nearly accessed Israeli intelligence computers before the Sabras punched his ticket for good. He spent a great deal of time Topside chanting and praying in his own custom-conceived mosque, but his eidetic memory was invaluable in retrieving information on the spot.

FELIM TO BARION: SUBJECTS: R. STRIDE/C. M. STOVALL. SPIRITUAL STATUS INFIDEL, MORE TO FOLLOW . . .

Barion quickly digested the information Felim transmitted from Topside. When the flow ceased, he absently materialized against a streetlight, tasting the cool night air as he pondered the problem. He'd always disapproved of Coyul's random interference in human affairs, much of it from worry and guilt about his own youthful mistakes. Leave bad enough alone, he always said after that. Coyul had been right about propensities, but bad enough could no longer be left to get worse.

"Well, why not?" he rationalized darkly. Governments and corporations used plumbers and played dirty pool every day. Without working up a sweat, his little brother was the master plumber of them all, and never a greater need.

COYUL, CAN YOU HEAR ME?

The instant answer: WHAT'S THE MATTER? YOU FEEL WORRIED.

HOME IN AND JOIN ME.

Moments later, Coyul appeared in blazer and foulard, a camel-hair coat thrown over his shoulders to dashing effect. He inspected Barion's watch cap, pea coat and jeans gone ragged at one knee. "Don't you ever dress?"

"Only for ex-popes and defunct Episcopalians," Barion retorted brusquely. "Listen, kid—we're in trouble."

7

A conspiracy of princes

"Let's be unobtrusive," said Barion, dissolving.

Coyul followed suit. "By all means. I'd certainly not want to be seen here."

They passed like radiation through the tabernacle door. Inside the crowded store-cum-tabernacle, Coyul read the charged ferment of frustration like heat from an oven. Rows of people on metal or rickety wooden folding chairs, intent on the preacher on the small raised platform at the front. Taking Gomorrah as his text, Purdy Simco strode dramatically up and down, open Bible held aloft like a waiter serving dinner.

"Those are the Lord's words, my friends. That is what He said: that if He found twenty good men, He would not destroy Gomorrah for their sakes."

From a point just below the preacher's outthrust jaw, Coyul studied him. "Gomorrah's old hat. Why doesn't he pick on something timely?"

"Mr. Simco is a true believer, but no fool," Barion said. "He knows what he can play to his audience. You won't hear a word about war or an inflated defense budget. Their factory used to turn out missile components, and they'd like it back, thank you.

They want to be saved but they also want to eat. Deviant sex is a safer bet and a hotter ticket."

Purdy Simco challenged his flock: "Did He find twenty?"

A ragged but fervent spattering of *no* from the faithful.

"And you wouldn't either in the Gomorrahs we have now, my friends. New York and Los Angeleez, places like that, places just down the road from us, right? Isn't it a Gomorrah that allows so-called gay rights? And lesbeen rights?"

Coyul looked to his brother for enlightenment. "For this I gave up an evening with Noel and Gertie? You said trouble."

"So I did."

"From what? The Classic Comics theology of Mr. Simco?"

"Smell the anger around you," Barion bade him. "The yearning, the frustration."

"I did. The whole place could do with a spritz of emotional air freshener."

"Pure explosive," said Barion. "I want you to meet the sparks."

Building to the climax of his excoriation of Gomorrahs past and present, Purdy Simco screwed his doughy face in mincing mimicry of his version of a city academic, his voice a nasal mew.

"He said to me, this college professor, when I spoke to him of the homa-sexuals and lesbeens I saw prancing down Fifth Avenue in their own licensed parade in that so-called great city of New York, he said to me: 'You have to regard this in its legal and social context.'"

Purdy Simco impaled his audience with a glare of righteous disgust. "Social context. I said to him: Sir"—straight face now, the soft, manly voice of Revealed Truth—"I am looking at it in the context of the most important text in the world. I don't care what it is in your social context, it's an abomination in the sight of the Lord!"

The open Bible on high, Simco served dinner again, striding the platform, going for his cadenzas as the applause spattered about him like rain. "SHALL I HIDE FROM ABRAHAM THAT THING WHICH I DO FOR HIM? . . . WE WILL DESTROY THIS PLACE, BECAUSE THE CRY OF THEM IS WAXEN GREAT BEFORE THE FACE OF THE LORD!"

The applause mounted to fervor. In the front row, Roy Stride leaped to his feet, pounding his hands together. "With sword and fire!"

"There's our boy, Coyul. Roy Stride."

"Oh-h, yes," Coyul remembered. "That's one of the names I heard."

"Compulsive joiner. Used to be a Satanist."

Since the seventeenth century, Coyul had little patience with Satanists of any stripe. Beyond burning black candles and desecrating graveyards, most of them would be just as happy in the local drama club. "Rather inconsistent."

"Not at all. Read him."

Blending with the churning essence of Roy Stride, Coyul knew the extremes of Satanism and narrowly defined Christianity were not inconsistent at all in this case. Roy was looking for power and identity. He'd plug into anything that promised deliverance from helplessness and nonentity. All of it tangled now with a strong biological urge toward Charity Stovall—*there she is, that must be her.* Because young Mr. Stride's simpler motivations were overlaid with sentiment and a panting Protestant need for respectability, he imagined himself seriously in love with Miss Stovall.

"I tried to warn Luther about this: throwing morality back on the frail human conscience," Coyul reflected. "He threw his inkpot at me. They still show the splat to tourists."

"Roy has been trying to get it on, as they say, with Miss Stovall for some time. Charity has rationalized it as love herself."

Coyul turned his attention to the young woman at Roy's side. "Meaning, I suppose, that she's found a way to reconcile what she ought to do with what she wants."

"Precisely. And tonight's the night."

Coyul was a study in indifference. "So?"

"They're the wrong people at the wrong time."

"So why do you need me? I'm just waiting for a bus, remember?"

"I sampled some background on them. Not the happiest. Please read Miss Stovall."

Coyul gave Charity another cursory glance—then a closer look. The flicker of interest was not lost on Barion.

"Shall I put time out of joint?" he offered delicately.

"Yes. Just for a moment."

Tableau in time frozen between one nanosecond and the next: Roy on his feet, Charity yearning up at him with the dazed aspect of someone who has found Ultimate Truth, too dazzled to examine it critically.

Coyul slipped into and blended with her mind. Where Roy was concerned, her mental and physical promptings were hopelessly muddled. Below that level, as Coyul had found with Roy, the years of deprivation, envy and inarticulate rage. Like Barion, he'd already detected the long, brutal history of Europe in her face. Nevertheless, even deeper . . .

She was like a person with a large house, living in only a few of the ground-floor rooms, the rest gone to dust and waste, although some oddments of emotional bric-a-brac here and there interested Coyul. Charity "guessed" she was in love with Roy because her painful Christianity would not allow physical gratification without the lapidary settings of true love and morality. In one room just off her mental parlor, not often used but not entirely abandoned, Charity had strong feelings for a young man named Woody Barnes, evidently the one seated on her left, a polished trumpet in his lap. Everything about Woody Barnes looked average—hair the color of sand, slightly wiry, freckled hands, blue eyes mild but observant, focused now in frozen time on Charity's face.

Sifting through the female psyche, Coyul paused at the Woody Room before passing on. Charity did not spend much time there. TV and romance novels had left their simplistic message. Woody was very close, but love was supposed to be an earthquake. Not a very intelligent attitude for the cortex he discovered, fine but unused.

"Not a bad sort," he judged, popping free of her. "A little cluttered, thinking with her glands. All the objectivity of a mating moose. Not terribly stable."

As he gazed down at Charity just then, Barion's expression was not unlike her blossom-bordered concept of him as Him. "I get millions like her. People with nothing to hang on to but a gnarled belief in cosmic cops and robbers, a hero and a heavy. Life as drama with themselves as star. Divine purpose as salvation, guilt for conflict. I thought dualism was only a stage."

"I told you so," Coyul singsonged.

"Yes, I know. I was wrong, but I won't compound the error. Coyul, we're going to work on this one together."

"Am I hearing right?" Coyul wondered. "Here on this cultural slag pile, listening to God Almighty suggest putting in the fix? The mind boggles."

"While you've *never* interfered," Barion shot back testily.

"Only in cases of exceptional talent."

"You read her: the girl's ten times smarter than she or anyone thinks, and a wellspring of possibilities, not all of them salutary. The miasma comes from imagining herself in love with Roy Stride. If she had a stronger sense of self, she'd just take this malignancy to bed and get him out of her system."

"Or just laugh him off." But Coyul knew her upbringing didn't program Charity that way. "Just a moment."

He immersed himself in the essence of Roy Stride—measuring, analyzing—and emerged very quickly with the energic equivalent of nausea.

"See what I mean?" Barion divined his distaste. "If there was ever a need for a stacked deck . . ."

"Yes," Coyul agreed, still a little queasy. "Not quite like Hitler, but . . ."

"But very like some of his satellites in the early days, remember? Röhm and his SA troopers, some of those charmers in the Gestapo. I have background on Roy and Charity," Barion said. "What they came out of, what they are, what they might be. Blend with me . . . Coyul?"

Barion's brother seemed preoccupied and uncharacteristically serious. Odder still that his mind was masked now. "Go ahead."

Filtered through Barion's mind, the data on Roy Stride were only a little less sickening. Age twenty-six, the ground-down descendant of ground-down ancestors, unremarkable for anything but his smoldering rage and its classic symptoms. His own history was one of failure and frustration, a bomb looking for a place to explode. A compulsive joiner, evidenced in his belief-shopping from Satanism to Born Again Christianity without losing a beat, and his boasted affiliation with the White Paladins, the paramilitary group reflected in his costume. Roy had an armchair lust for Armageddon, for bloody and dramatic goals. With these went an overwrought, distorted set of values and more hang-ups than a coat closet, including an agonized sense of purity where Charity was concerned.

There was more intelligence in Charity's background but, as Coyul noted earlier, not much stability. Her grandparents had worked with religious tent revivals. The anonymous couple who bred Charity and left her with the county stayed together for a while, alternating fits of Fundamentalism with others soaked in alcohol until they drifted apart. The father died in a distant hospital, bloated with cirrhosis, scribbling an ecstatic but incoherent history of human creation, convinced his pen was spirit-guided by John the Baptist. Charity's mother drifted to San Francisco and the last psychedelic love-and-flowers gasp of the Haight-Ashbury scene, where, in a microcosm not known for mental equilibrium, she earned the sobriquet of Franny the Flake. She OD'd on heroin in 1971 and was buried by the city when they could locate no relatives. Their daughter hadn't known much love in her twenty years; the mere possibility of it, of a chance to identify with *anything* beyond her loneliness, would fever Charity's blood like a virus.

She stood poised at the convergence of several paths; what happened tonight could send her down the wrong one. She'd go to bed with Roy because she was lonely. She would marry him because she was a "nice" girl by stringent Plattsville standards—and for the more banal reason there was nothing better in town or in her life already dead-ending to nowhere.

Barion's comment broke into the flow of information: *factor, Coyul. Both these families breed more boys than girls. Charity would have a number of sons. Statistically one would grow up with the worst of both of them in him.*

A son maturing in the damp fog of poverty, feeling hopeless and abandoned as his parents, raging at the world; who grew up with a paranoid warrior-manqúe father, racist and soured, a child literally weaned on hate. A mother frustrated without clearly knowing why, whose bitter, fermented energies would turn more and more toward this tabernacle or one like it. A child growing up with the rage and rotted dreams of both parents beating in his ears, making him quiver, making others see this malignant vibrance as charisma where it was truly a predatory instinct for the vulnerability of those around him.

The sort of man who gets noticed by people who bankroll Christian Identity groups, Barion's energy whispered to his brother. *There are avowed racists running for office now. This statistically probable kid would be a natural.*

Wholly possible, Coyul agreed, materializing to his brother again, lounging atop the battered piano. "You said there were millions of them. The same son could be born to a million sets of parents. Why these two in particular?"

"What I heard," Barion said in a troubled voice, "what led me to these people I've heard all through history when something was about to change. I was too inexperienced, too busy or whatever to take notice, but I always *heard* it. The sound of catalysts, Coyul. Cassius, Moses, John Brown . . . Hitler. I'm not sure. I'm never exactly sure anymore, but I've never heard it so clearly. Roy or his son. You read them. The odds are bad."

Leaning against the lip of the stage in his old pea coat, Barion awarded a loveless glance to Roy Stride, something of pity to Charity Stovall. "And there's this: you know they'll be coming for us someday. Sorlij or someone else."

Coyul nodded slowly. "I know," he said with unwonted gravity.

"And I'll get hell at home for the mess I've made here," Barion stated, and accepted the inevitable in a breath. "But I'm going to do something about this now. Whatever it costs. Help me, Coyul. Stack the deck, deal from the bottom, but *something.* Because if we don't, there's not going to be an America or a world worthy of the name."

"Well, it's always been a second-rate sideshow." Coyul tried to sound flip; for the first time in his very long life, he failed utterly. "Aren't you overstating?"

"You think so? This country has gone to the right before but always with a balance to straighten them out. The balance simply isn't there anymore. The middle class isn't that secure, the same as Weimar Germany in 1932. Look around, Coyul. These are the people who'll call the shots if this country swings to the extreme right. Look at these faces. You think they're *kidding?* Look at me," Barion concluded in dry disgust. "I wanted to win a prize.

You told me not to tinker. You were right. Nothing but a mess, five million years of mess—but *this* one I'm going to clean up before it spills."

"Don't wallow in self-condemnation," Coyul admonished with surprising gentleness. "You've had some fine moments."

For one instant, before his brother's mind curtained itself behind the habitual cynicism, Barion caught an unusual emotion from Coyul. Something like guilt.

"Well." Coyul fluffed out his foulard. "What do you require of our hard-breathing heroine?"

"To marry someone else."

"Anyone in mind?"

"Anyone would do." That was secondary to Barion. Perhaps Woody Barnes, whose most incendiary ambition was to work as a jazz sideman at Jimmy Ryan's or the Blue Note in New York. Woody had more talent than drive, but a musician, even a poor one, was preferable to a fanatic. He could only assault the ear.

Coyul studied the three, ruminating, one knuckle to his lips. "If you're in trouble, so am I. Two rowers in a sinking lifeboat telling each other 'I told you so' doesn't keep either from drowning. I don't know . . . there *is* an element of creativity in all this."

"Carte blanche," Barion promised. "No questions asked."

"Perhaps that's best," Coyul considered honestly. "It *just* so happens that certain friends of mine need something to keep them out of trouble and my hair. I'll need complete Topside cooperation."

"Got it," Barion responded staunchly, already seeing daylight at the end of a long, dark tunnel. "As for Woody Barnes, I have a few ideas for him. He's a friend of a friend. So, deal?"

"Deal. And I'll probably live to regret it."

Barion's hand arced in a peculiar gesture—

—and Purdy Simco's hand descended with the Bible, the congregation stirred, Roy's hands went on applauding his idea of magnificence.

"While Roy takes up our offering," Purdy Simco crooned to the faithful, "let us sing together. Sweet Jesus, hear our lifted voices and the need in our hearts."

Charity climbed the precarious steps to the platform stage, Woody close behind with his trumpet. Charity seated herself on the old-fashioned round piano stool and struck the first chords of "Amazing Grace." The instrument was badly out of tune. Coyul winced in actual pain.

"My God, they mean it." He retreated far as possible from the offending sound while Purdy Simco and his congregation assaulted the hymn like amphibious marines.

"A-*maz*-ing Guh-*race*—" In support of their attack, Charity played determinedly, which is not the same as well. Woody's horn had more encouraging overtones for Coyul. There was a quality to his style, hard to pin down but interesting. Too good to waste here.

"When Luther broke with Rome, the Church kept all the good music. This does nothing for theology or the muse. Shall we wait outside?"

"No, wait." Barion stayed him. "Stride: I want to catch this."

While Charity and Woody reprised the hymn, Roy took a small basket from the platform and flourished it before the congregation.

"Offering time!" he called in an abrasive but compelling voice. "You all know what the tabernacle needs. We all know how hard it is, don't tell me that. Don't show me silver, show me green! The tabernacle's important as meat on the table, because we are the people, yes we are. Ain't nobody gonna save us but us. We been down, but we're going UP!"

Roy moved from row to row with the basket. To a balding, florid-faced donor: "Mr. Beasley, you just put fifty cents in this basket. Ain't you ashamed? I *know* you got a dollar, 'cause I seen you break a five in McDonald's. There you go"—as the extorted and sheepish Beasley produced a limp single—"never mind the fifty cents, it won't get lonely."

Roy's challenging finger swept over the congregation. "Do you trust the government? Hell no! You feel sold? Betrayed? Do you hear the true word of Jesus Christ in your heart? Lemme see the green, then. New day coming, hallelujah! New day coming when the people rise up. Don't trust Washin'ton. They sold out the farmers, closed the factories, sold mosta New York to the Ay-rabs. I read that in a book, you can look it up. But the people will rise— thank you, sister—the people will rise in a triumph for Jesus, a triumph of the will!"

"See what I mean?" said Barion darkly. "A catalyst looking for a disaster. We can go now. We'll meet them at McDonald's. They'll probably stop there when this is done."

"Already our plot shows its darker side." Coyul steeled himself. "McDonald's, then. If we must."

■ 8 ■

The hero is the one who just wants to finish his drink and go home

The garish orange and Formica decor of McDonald's appalled Coyul, as did the notion of fast food or the amounts of it humans could ingest without mishap.

"Do you see what they call a well-done hamburger? Looks like it was dragged too late from a burning house."

"Very popular place," Barion remarked. "Some of my people want a franchise Topside."

"Shoot them."

"Business at hand, remember? Shall we proceed?"

Reluctantly Coyul turned his invisible attention to the three young people at the table: Roy and Charity against the wall, Woody sprawled back on the outside seat, fitting the mute to his trumpet. With his leg rubbing against his woman's (the possessive notion excited him), Roy told Woody, "Get us some more napkins, okay?"

Charity held hers up. "We got napkins."

"Yeah, but they're all wet. And Charity needs a new straw."

Woody went obligingly for the setups. Under the table, Roy added bourbon to his Coke. "You want a taste, honey?"

"Gee, I don't know. Does it go with diet cola?"

"Goes with anything your heart desires. Come on, ain't polite to let me drink alone."

"Well . . . just it's cold outside," Charity accepted with a prim giggle. "But you tell me if I start to get bad."

She slipped her plastic glass below the tabletop and Roy hardened it a little. "Sort of a wedding toast," he said, smiling at her. "Tonight's our night, honey."

—while Coyul sighed with the burden of the duty-bound. "I regret this already. The dialogue's as bad as the drinks."

"Be a little kind," Barion admonished. "This is going to be Charity's first time and very important to her. Actually, she's readier than he is. Why don't you read Roy; he's sending signals pertinent to our case."

Charity's all mine—Roy glowed with a flush of macho. Nicest girl in town and she's all mine. Thought once it might be Woody. I like Woody, like the way he does what I tell him, long as I make out like I'm asking, but that just shows you the difference. I'm a leader natural born, Woody just ain't aggressive at all. Even in the Marines he barely qualified with a rifle, he told me. Wouldn't touch the piece I got under the back seat. Just looked shit scared when I showed him the ammo and grenades for the Paladins. Threw him one: he caught it all right but just gave it back and looked sick. Ought to come out and join the Paladins. We need good boys been in combat, even the little bit Woody saw. Couldn't be much, he don't never talk about it, just mostly about some Jew bastard he knew in the Corps. He don't think right. He's pure White American like me and we need all we can get, being a minority ourselves now.

For sure it's tonight for me and Charity. Man, about time something worked out right in this shit-ass life. All three of us out of work, and we deserve just as much as the Commoniss niggers riding in Cadillacs in Washington, which, hell, it's all black now anyways. I read that in a book. President steps off the White House lawn, must feel like he's in Africa.

We Paladins gonna take this country back someday, and I'll be there, breaking bad and spitting lead, a natural leader. Gonna be

blood spilled, the only way, gonna take America back for God
and the Aryans.

But tonight I'm gonna take a little for myself—except, shit, I
hope I don't have the usual trouble. No problem at all with some
old whore, but somebody nice like Charity . . . you can't fuck
goodness and look her in the eye at the same time. I mean, that's
a problem. She's the girl I'm going to marry, and I wouldn't be
spiking her drink except I'm nervous. Only time it was ever
super good was in that whorehouse in that hunky town near
Pittsburgh. Big Polack whore didn't give a damn what you
wanted done, she served it right up. Just you can't go on paying
for it to get what you need, that ain't the way for a man to do.
Maybe another shot in this lousy Coke, just enough so I won't
worry . . .

Coyul snorted: "If this tumor had a brain, he'd be neurotic."

"Think what his son will be with the same problems and more
intelligence," Barion urged. "Does it suggest an approach?"

For a moment, Coyul's expression came close to his popular
image. "There could be some good dirty fun in all this. Being a
son of a bitch in a worthy cause."

"That's my little brother."

"Woody." Roy nudged him under the table. "How about getting me another Big Mac?"

"I just went," Woody protested mildly. "Whyn't you go yourself?"

"Because I'm all tucked up with my woman and I ast you nice."

"Okay, okay. In a minute."

While Roy rubbed up against Charity, Woody tried to be cool
about the whole thing and not notice. He took a deep breath and
let it out through the muted horn in a long, sleepy, drawling
phrase like Winton Marsalis on "Melancholia," or the other
jazzmen whose records he could seldom afford. They made a
whole new language with the horn, not playing the melody but
knowing all about it anyway in that special tongue.

"What you doing with that thing?" Roy wondered.

"Marsalis. Blows a good horn."

"Yeah, I read about him." Roy was always talking about what

he read, although Woody never saw any books in his house except *Soldier of Fortune* or *Guns and Ammo*. "Smart nigger, thinks he got all the answers. Whyn't you play like a white man?"

Woody put down the trumpet. "Char, you want anything?"

"No, I'm just fine." She wiped her lips too daintily. "I like the way Woody plays."

"Nigger music. Listen, Woody: you come to the next Paladin drill with me. They'll straighten you out. Old marine like you, we need guys with combat time."

"No way."

"You always say that. I'm serious, man. Why not?"

"I'm a pacifist," said Woody Barnes.

"That's what the Commonists like," Roy asserted with the air of an insider. "That's what they want when they come marching down Main Street. Where'd you get to be a pacifist?"

"In Beirut." Woody drained his Coke and slapped the paper cup on the table, rattling the ice. "What you say you wanted?"

"Big Mac again. Extra French dressing 'n' pickle." Roy splayed a couple of dollars on the table, mostly change. "Hey, you see how I took up the collection tonight? I know how to squeeze it out of 'em."

"They know five percent of what you squoze gets back to the Paladins for guns and ammo?"

"Hey, not so loud." Roy glared at Woody, then glanced at Charity to assure himself the effect wasn't lost on her, then around at the nearby customers with overdone caution. In a tense whisper: "We got enemies."

"Just a passing thought," said Woody.

"Well, you just go on and let it pass."

"Positively wallows in the role of conspirator," Coyul remarked.

"To the hilt: the drama, the air of danger. The Paladins can't afford much ammunition," Barion recalled from Felim's briefing. "They have to be very good shots, although so far they've only destroyed a few paper targets and someone's window. But they feel terribly clandestine." To Coyul's appreciative smile, he amended: "I'm sorry. I shouldn't joke about him."

"Difficult not to."

"Just so. The Nazis were a joke to Germans in 1925, remember? The upper classes found them a never-ending source of amusement." Barion looked toward Woody at the counter. "Let's read Mr. Barnes in his heart of hearts. It may be of service."

All right, Woody thought, that's the way it is. Roy's gonna score with Charity at the White Rose. He shouldn't take her there, that's the best-known make-out spot in ten miles. And talking about it all week; some spy he'd make. We've been friends since eighth grade; when I went into the Marines, he enlisted in the Air Force. Gonna be a top-gun jet pilot. Except his eyes weren't good enough or his teeth or his education or anything else. This town doesn't grow a lot of college graduates. We used to have more to talk about, but now listening to Roy gets real old. It's all one thing, race and politics. Last couple of years, he's got a hard-on for niggers and Jews, all he can talk about, and he can't understand why I ˙ eep remembering Milt Kahane so much. More like I can't ever forget. Milt and that old black man.

I was in New York with Milt before we shipped for Beirut, three straight nights checking out the jazz joints. The last night we found that place where drinks were mucho expensive but the combo—oh, man, they were worth it. That old black man with a lifetime in his horn. The way he talked to me between sets: not polite at all, just an old-timer giving it straight to a kid. Shit, he didn't *think* he was good as me, he knew he was better where that horn came in, and damn if he wasn't right. Thought a lot about that old man in the hospital; about him and Milt Kahane. Still thinking about them, but everything gets mixed up together, like will I ever make it back to New York where it's all at or just sit around here forever, wondering if I want Char enough to do something about it? Or if I'll ever be good enough to even play backup for that old man who knows it all.

Milt was that good. That's how we got together, rapping music at Parris Island. Too damned good to go out fragged and bagged in Beirut. He talked about the Israelis like they were a separate people he didn't agree with, like the way they sent in Lebanese Christians as hit men at Beirut. That bothered him, but when he got it squared away, he said to me, Barnes, I have planted my last fucking tree in Israel, and I'd like the last one back.

I said, Hell, ain't you sticking up for your own people? What people? he asks. I'm a financial analyst from Long Island, or I will be if I ever finish at NYU. Just don't want to hear any more Zionist bullshit.

I remember: that was at chow the day he got zapped and damn near me, too. We sat down in the shade of a half-track, eating corned beef and carrots and fruit cocktail. Milt bummed a cigarette from me, angry not because he couldn't figure it out but because he had. Barnes, he said, countries are just like women. Sooner or later everyone loses their cherry and gets to be just another broad on the block. I don't know if I'm a Jew anymore.

What do you mean? I said. You were born Jewish.

You were born dumb, Barnes. That mean you gotta stay that way?

We pulled detail after chow, humping ammo to the M-60. Not expecting trouble; didn't even see that grenade come out of a window until it fucked us up good. Milt got most of it, but there was enough left over for a nice road map across my stomach. So Milt Kahane went home on the same hospital ship with me. I got a bed, he got a box in the hold.

When Roy mouths off about Jews, I see Milt eating those goddamned peaches and smoking my cigarette, asking questions and not liking the answers he got. Me and Milt and that old black man with his trumpet, I guess we're pacifists. Once you're nearly blown away, you get real picky what you'll die for. Roy really got off on the scars where my belly button used to be. I said they were religious medals, not that he'd understand. Roy never wasted anyone but he'd sure as shit like to. Going to declare war all over Char tonight.

Wish I knew what the hell bothers me so much about that. Maybe—hell, no maybe about it. Char deserves better than what Roy's turned into, but I'm not fool enough to say so. Already did my gig in somebody else's war.

"Not a bad sort." Coyul watched Woody carry the fresh tray back to the table. "Eloquent in his way. The ones who've done the bleeding always have a great respect for peace. Attila, for example. Very keen on animal husbandry now. Goats, that sort of thing."

"They'll be off to the White Rose soon," Barion said. "Will you be ready to take it from there?"

"Of course. I'll make an appearance."

"Let the blandishment fit the time," Barion advised. "Don't think about them, think *like* them."

A crucial aspect, as Coyul knew. In a careless moment a few years back, he'd appeared in slacks and an Izod shirt to a cult of California Satanists. They threw wine bottles at him. Charity Stovall would be no less hag-ridden with stereotype. You couldn't hurl new ideas head-on at old notions. It never paid.

■ 9 ■

H hour minus one

Charity liked riding in Roy's car the way the three of them always did: holding hands with Roy in the front seat, old Woody in the back talking softly to himself through the muted trumpet. The old car was like a house and they were the family, the realest she ever knew. Roy in his old field jacket and that black T-shirt with the skull and KILL 'EM ALL. LET GOD SORT 'EM OUT on the front —which she really didn't believe in that, it was just Roy's sense of humor. Beer cans rattling around on the floor and over the tire iron. Big sponge-rubber dice hanging inside the windshield and the two tiny baby dolls banging suggestively against each other.

So tonight they'd do it. That troubled her more than a little, but yes, she did love Roy. Especially tonight in the tabernacle, the way he made those folks dig down a little deeper for Jesus.

I wonder if Jesus will call tonight a sin. I couldn't do it unless I loved Roy and was going to marry him, which we'll do it as soon as we can afford to, and live our lives in Jesus anyway, so maybe He won't mind if we are a little ahead of time.

"Night, Woody," she said when they let him off at his house. She liked the way he leaned in through the window to kiss her on the cheek like family.

"Take care of yourself, Char. Don't do anything I wouldn't."

Wouldn't you, Woody? What did you mean by that? I know you like me, but you don't know about tonight because Roy certainly wouldn't talk about it. Good night, dear Woody. When you see me tomorrow I'll be a whole different person—

"Quite," promised Coyul from the back seat.

—married in the sight of God, kind of, but I'll always think of you as family.

"Of course, the tasteful Mr. Stride has been bending Woody's ear about it all week." Coyul remarked.

"He's on the intelligence team for the Paladins," Barion noted, "usually disseminating more than he gathers, but then you have to realize, as the current phrase has it, where Mr. Stride is coming from. Drama is essential. He and Charity are true lovers silhouetted against the fiery backdrop of strife-torn Plattsville and the Cause. Like the motorcycle he couldn't afford: one way to put some kind of power between his legs."

After Woody's door closed, Roy pulled Charity closer to his side for a long kiss. Charity felt the warmth and roughness of his cheek against hers and the slight thrill of knowing Roy was always a little dangerous. You never could tell what he'd do.

I said yes and I guess I meant it, she thought. *Face it, I'm twenty and it has to be sometime, so might's well be with somebody I love. Just I wish I knew if it is the right thing to do. I'm glad Roy didn't let me put Jesus on the dash when I wanted to. He'd be looking at me now, maybe making me change my mind, maybe damning me to hell.*

Just that I hate going to the tacky old White Rose, which everybody knows about it, but we can't go to his house or mine, and the car's okay for fooling around but too damn uncomfortable and cold for anything else . . . boy, when I set out to be bad, I am really a New York Saturday night.

Roy drove without haste, not wanting to seem like he was rushing her. Charity wished he'd hurry before she changed her mind.

"Until later," Barion excused himself to Coyul. "I must see to Woody."

"You always get the nice jobs."

"Woody's on my end. Never in the world or even in the fe-

vered indulgences of Wilksey Booth has there been such a need
for careful casting. Have a nice evening."

"I just might," Coyul predicted. "For Charity, an education.
For Roy, enough rope."

Charity stayed in the car while Roy got the room. Coyul drifted
in after them like the night chill before they closed the door.

"Well, hey," Roy bluffed to cover his awkwardness. "We finally
got here. Let's get comfortable."

With elaborate casualness, he took off his jacket and hung it on
the rack near the door, then took Charity's coat. Charity made an
instinctive female assessment of the room and sat tentatively on
the bed, an acknowledgment of their purpose, though still tensed
to fly.

There followed a strained interlude while Roy tried to hide his
nervousness. Charity opted for demure silence to cover moral
panic, spending much time in the bathroom and in finding the
right music on the small FM radio. Finally Roy sat down on the
war-worn bed beside her.

"Well," he said by way of prelude, "I guess."

Coyul tactfully removed to the unlit bathroom. Behind him,
the lights went out. Murmurings, the rustle of sheets and blan-
kets. Neither of them noticed the soft closing of the bathroom
door.

Coyul knew to its core the essence of Charity Stovall, who had
lived her twenty years in the lower echelons of Christian belief, a
lurid topography with no middle ground. Her theology was banal
but rendered in full color, a Caucasian *Green Pastures* at one end,
smoke, fire, pain—the whole Faustian, *Exorcist* claptrap at the
other.

Coyul conjured a soft, indirect light over the bathroom mirror,
admiring his makeup and costume—impressive mustachios and
spade beard, cruel, chiseled features. He added a fastidious pat of
Givenchy to the gaunt cheeks and gave serious thought to his
scenario, flashing an urgent message—

PRIORITY, WILKES: DROP EVERYTHING.

The classic figure of Booth took shape at Coyul's side, cloak
gathered and draped over one arm. "I love the beard, Prince.
You are Lucifer, point-device! What's to do?"

"I promised you a great part. I have one: a zinger, possibly the keystone in the vaulting arch of your career."

Booth bowed with panache. "Your servant, sir."

"A role with range and depth," Coyul embellished. "Exquisite suffering, color, your own choice of music."

"Steiner," Booth opted eagerly. "No one scores drama like Max —if we can ask him of Topside."

"It can be arranged." Coyul admired his finished Luciferian effect in the mirror. It would scare them to death. It scared the hell out of *him*.

"Our drama?"

"Damnation."

Wilksey Booth's eyes flashed like black diamonds. "Jesuit or Joycean? Something medieval?"

"Beyond that," Coyul urged. "Beyond Doré, beyond De Mille. They're Born Again. You may indulge."

"Ah! A moment, if I may." The handsome actor assessed his image in the bathroom mirror. "God, I am magnificent! Perhaps in the future a surprise appearance on *Dynasty?*"

"Wilksey, we are gentlemen. The shlock is for the customers."

"A passing thought, no more. Watch!"

"Oh, Wilksey—that's good." Coyul observed with admiration as Booth's fine head became something foul, green and misshapen, medieval in its darkest concepts but with an obvious debt to George Lucas. Charity Stovall would—oh, it was to quiver!

"Remember me, Prince," the green thing rasped, "when thy sublime brothers find thee. Also that my name appears over the title and in larger type."

Woody had a cup of coffee in the kitchen with his uncle before going up to bed. Still not terribly late, but there was nothing to do in the morning except wait at the unemployment office for a job that wouldn't be there, wait for his union relief check and maybe clean up the yard.

Climbing the squeaky stairs, he thought on Charity, Roy and himself with some sadness. Since the Corps, he had more of his shit together, enough to get sour knowing he'd never make it back to that uptown club in New York unless he had the price of a bus and a drink; that Roy would never make it anywhere, just go on boring the shit out of everyone about the coming racial wars. And Charity? Hell, she'd never see anything until she woke up twenty years from now, still in Plattsville, making dinner for the same Roy but with a beer belly and four kids mean as their daddy.

He shouldn't take Char to the goddamned White Rose. Everybody driving by knows who's inside just from the cars. Am I feeling sorry for her or just wishing it was me instead of Roy? Me that don't even know where I'm going myself.

"A long way, Barnes."

He couldn't tell if he'd heard an actual voice or his own thoughts, but it sounded like Milt Kahane. Woody opened the door to his room, threw the down vest where his old easy chair would be, snapped on the lights and felt his heart stop.

Milt Kahane lounged on his bed—beefy, vital and sardonic, crisp black curly hair, wearing the same wild Hawaiian shirt he had on the night they made it to the jazz club. "Hey, Woody."

When Woody's heart jump-started up, he backed against the undeniable reality of the door. "Milt?"

"Uncle Milty, live and in person. More or less." Milt grinned expectantly. "Dummy, you can't say hello?"

"Uh . . . hi, Milt."

"Semper fi, Barnes."

The groan of his unoiled clock was conspicuous by its absence, the second hand petrified just short of 2. "Milt, is this really happening? Aren't you . . . you know?" Then, in panic: "God, am I? All I had was a burger and—"

"Relax, it's not the big one." Milt laughed, swinging his legs off the bed. "Got us a gig, that's all. See your vest?"

The garment was an impossible still life where Woody had thrown it, one edge caught mid-crumple, the rest still defying gravity over the chair.

"That's—interesting."

"Boss calls that trick time out of joint. Lets me prove my point without a lot of *Topper* dialogue."

Woody swallowed hard. "Yeah, well, I definitely believe it."

"Just like the Corps, Woodrow: the Boss is looking for a couple of good men on brass who can also bullshit a little in a good cause." Milt raised his horn and spurted a clean run up to high C.

"Haven't lost your lip, Milt."

"Never." As usual, Milt Kahane looked like he was thinking something funny and sad at the same time. "Why do you hang out with that putz Stride?"

"Roy? I dunno," Woody hedged, hands in his pockets. "We grew up together. He's kind of crazy, but—"

"But he loves his mother, yeah, I know. Personally I'd like to give him a briss from the neck down, but the Boss works in mysterious ways."

"What you got against Roy? You don't even know him."

"I've known that shmuck for two thousand years," Milt said. "And you just follow him around. A natural follower, Barnes. You were following me the day that Shiite mother fragged us. Our fire team got him a few minutes later. Man, was he surprised to see me! Don't ask." Milt Kahane chuckled. "Tell you about him sometime. Roy Stride in a polka-dot headdress."

Milt rose, tucking the trumpet under one arm. "Time to ship out, Barnes. Travel and adventure! The Boss wants to brief us."

"The Boss?" Woody hesitated, still trying to get a handle on all this. "You mean—"

"Numero Uno," Milt corroborated with a bright smile. "But most of the clowns Topside don't know it. He keeps a very low profile. I said *relax*, Barnes. This is no shit detail. He's a cool guy, very laid-back. Doesn't come on or anything like that."

The walls of Woody's room began to blur, fade, darkening to the midnight blue of infinity.

"First time I saw him," Milt remembered, "I thought he was some shlub from California."

■ 10 ■

The woman taken in adultery, and other set pieces

Roy was very still beside her. Charity thought he might be asleep. They had to go home soon. Late she could explain; all night was pretty obvious.

When Charity sorted out her feelings as a retired virgin, they resolved to disappointment. Nothing specific; she couldn't make any kind of comparison because she wasn't that kind of girl. All the same, this was what all the shouting was about? Her expectations had come mostly from a little petting in Roy's car, mostly from the movies and TV. Reverend Falwell was right: certain things just shouldn't be brought right into your living room where you might have company or children. Movies went even further, soft lights and softer music with the man and woman photographed from the shoulders up, and you knew what they were doing and that they enjoyed it. Transports of joy—that was the phrase she heard somewhere, except she wasn't transported at all, just stayed there.

Roy seemed to have some kind of trouble, she couldn't tell what, but he acted embarrassed even after the lights were out. The whole thing was over in a hurry, just when she was beginning to relax and enjoy it. Afterward he asked if it was special for her. She said yes.

Charity stared up into the darkness with emotional second thoughts. They had sinned—well, not much since they were practically married, but still a sin. Come down to it, she wasn't sure bad girls got punished all that much. What they got were children.

Which it's just about the same thing in this town. I love Roy, I guess, so it'll be all right when we're married.

How? How would anything be all right or even different? She had married friends; when did anything change for them?

The though was so clear and frightening that Charity blotted it out, shifting closer to the warmth of Roy beside her. There were a lot of thoughts like that in the last year that she kept from Roy and Woody, notions she barely had words for. Like Reverend Simco saying most of the world was unsaved. That meant a lot of people. All those people and the way they lived, were they *all* wrong? Like, when you were poor, you couldn't afford to waste anything. Saving got to be a part of you, so God must hate waste as much as she did.

So would he waste all those million-billion people just because they're not exactly like us? Gol-lee, that's like chopping down a whole forest just to get one toothpick. If I got better sense than that, God sure has.

Roy lay on his side facing her. In the dim light she could just see the dark smudge on his shoulder that would be his White Paladin tattoo with the skull. He got more excitement out of belonging to the Paladins than anything else. All those secret communications with groups in Alabama and maneuvers in the woods, when all Charity could see was a bunch of out-of-work hunks who liked to play with guns, drink beer and talk about the "coming Armageddon."

They ought to get up soon and go home . . .

She must have dozed. Charity was suddenly aware of Roy turning over. The air in the room smelled horrible. Roy sniffed distastefully. "What's that?"

"Like sulphur." Charity tested the air. "Ten times worse." Besides the intolerable odor, something else. "Roy," she quavered. "L-look."

"What?"

"There," said Charity, terror rising like a tide. "There!"

"Where? There ain't any—"

"Look!"

The darkness around them had taken on the hue of blood. As Charity stared, numb with fright, the blood resolved to a smoky, infernal scarlet. With a deafening *whoosh* the room seemed to implode. The light went garish fire engine red as the far wall sprang up in a solid barrier of flame.

Charity screamed. Roy tried to.

Against the wall of fire, amid the choking stink, two nightmare images were silhouetted. One of them Charity knew in every detail from God-fearing childhood: the horns jutting from the narrow, saturnine head, the pointed beard, eyes like hot coals. The lashing tail and hooves. Her deepest fears incarnate.

"Heel, Damocles!"

The huge figure of Satan jerked at the chain wound on his wrist. Straining at its check, something scaly with large bat wings gurgled uncleanly and slavered at Charity. As she and Roy cringed on the bed, Satan stroked his beard with the back of one claw and smirked at his leashed minion.

"I call him Damocles because, like the mythical sword, he hangs over wretches like you." An exquisite sneer. "Just waiting to fall. And you yourselves have cut the thread."

Charity felt for the silver cross around her neck. It felt hot. "Please . . . God in heaven, please . . ."

"Too late for that," Satan told her in tones that would have thrilled Bellini or Gounod. "You're both dead."

"Dead?" Roy found his voice somewhere. "We're too young to die."

"Coronary, you clods. Both of you. Unusual in humans so young, the more so during a fornication not rigorous enough to tire a terminal emphysemic. Nevertheless, dead in the act."

"With no relish of salvation," the scaly demon paraphrased in a voice that made the *Exorcist* demon sound like Linda Ronstadt. Damocles' leathery wings flexed with impatience. He ravaged the rug with his foreclaws.

Charity and Roy were jolted upward from the bed like shells ejected from a rifle breech to hang suspended and nude in midair. Satan gestured negligently at the bed, where two forms gave a convincing impression of very dead.

"Dead and damned."

"We can't be," Roy attempted pathetically. "We're members of the Tabernacle of the Born Again Savior. Good Christians."

Damocles chuckled, a sound like scratching on a coffin lid. "Our favorite kind."

"No." Roy groped for the nearest part of Charity to hang on to. "My White Christian God—"

"Oh, shut up. Where do you think my authority comes from?"

Roy found a vestige of his courage. "You ain't no Christian, never were. You look like a lousy Jew."

"A touch of the Levantine." Satan bowed. "Beelzebub and all that. A touch of the Egyptian as Set, various Etruscan and Roman . . . this is really a set piece. Benét did it so much better. In the main, Mr. Stride, a Wasp like yourself. Hit it, Damocles."

Damocles pointed a foreclaw at the two shuddering wraiths. "You have the right to remain silent—"

"Never mind the Miranda," Satan prompted. "Skip to the appeal."

"All right," Damocles sulked. "You get a phone call."

Floating helplessly, hanging on to Roy, Charity stammered, "Wh-who can we call?"

"Why not God?" Satan suggested. "You've been bending His ear for the last few minutes. Give Him a buzz."

Charity did. "God! Please help us!"

The air tore visually, like something out of a Cocteau film. An imposing patriarchal figure blossomed out of nothing, brilliant white against the crimson nightmare, very much like Charlton Heston in *The Ten Commandments.* He inspected Charity and Roy like smudges on glassware.

"Forget it," God said, and disappeared. Damocles' wings flared in triumph.

"Ha! Ours!"

"Appeal granted, heard, denied. Damocles, the lady was thinking of transports. Give her one."

Foaming from an obscene mouth, Damocles plucked the two gibbering forms out of the air and tucked each under an unpleasant arm. Charity had just enough mind left to see Roy, eyes bulging and mouth working in a silent prayer, before the dark came down on her with a last sensation of falling . . .

"Don't slaver so, Wilksey," Coyul remarked as they descended. "They've got the gist."

"Oh, but, Prince, how often do we have the chance for such good trashy fun?"

"Don't get carried away. You have a makeup and costume change. Mr. Steiner, Mr. Shostakovich—cue music, please. The damnation bit."

11

THE EDUCATION OF
CHARITY STOVALL

■ 11 ■

One man's media . . .

Dead and damned. Alone. Roy, the world, life gone. Dead and damned.

Stunned.

Charity couldn't make a sound beyond a pitiful squeak forced out between chattering teeth. No sense of time. She couldn't tell how long she'd huddled naked in the limbo of oily fog. Any attempt to think trailed off in whimpering terror.

Gradually she became aware of her surroundings. Limbo resolved as the fog sank to a thick, writhing carpet. No color, only barren black rocks jutting here and there. No hellfire as she'd learned from childhood and bad dreams, only damp cold and the fog coiling about her bare legs. Here and there, plumes of dark, stinking smoke rose out of the fog into a gray sky. Naked and shivering in a hell not cold enough to kill the sickening stench from the oily pools surrounding her.

And the sounds. She wasn't alone. Even gratitude for that had to be fumbled at before she could be sure of it. Thin, piping agony floated eerily on the fetid air. At last Charity dared to stumble toward the nearest sounds that might at least mean companionship.

Incredibly, there was music, deep, booming and grim, of a

piece with the total absence of color. Charity hugged herself tight against the chill. As she groped forward, she heard a shift in the music, a definite beat to it now, stroked on deep bass strings.

She moved timidly, expecting demons behind every dark-rearing boulder. "Oh!"

She started; a naked arm thrust upward out of the mist just in front of her. She felt herself beginning to sink in clammy ooze. The bog's obscene odor clogged her nostrils. Charity scrabbled backward to firmer ground. The arm became a shoulder and then the head and torso of a man covered with numbers in red dye.

"Help me," he moaned. "Mercy! A good pilot, anything. I lived by the media and died by the rating."

The pitiful wretch went down again before Charity could summon the courage to help him. There were reaching arms all about her now, dyed with numbers, faces rising a little way out of the mist to implore her aid before falling back.

Charity wondered aloud, "Is this the hell for fornicators?"

"No, not quite."

"EEEE!" Charity jumped as if she'd been goosed with a cattle prod. To her left, seated on a mountainous stack of *TV Guides*, a monstrous thing with television screens for eyes and a speaker mouth hulked over two tiny men cavorting between his cable cord legs. One gesticulated continuously. His head was no more than a huge mouth that worked furiously without sound but produced a constant shower of popcorn. The other puppet-thing giggled and gibbered, rocked back and forth with the edged inanity of an idiot brushed for one terrible moment by the truth of the world.

"This section is for the abusers of media," said the electronic nightmare. "Actually designed for romance writers, but our place isn't ready yet. What are you?" The blank eyes peered at her. "A televangelist?"

"No, I—" Charity shivered with the damp cold. "I'm just me. Charity Stovall."

"Mm-hm. Don't look smarmy enough, in any case. Now *this* one." One jack-plug finger tapped the popcorn purveyor between its spindly power-cable legs. "He was a Fundamentalist politician who proclaimed himself God's candidate." The jack finger flicked at the laughing fool. "This one believed him."

Dumb as the popcorn man, Charity backed away from the horror, remembering how she'd rung doorbells for the same cause in Plattsville.

"This, as you've noticed, is a rather Brontëan neighborhood," the monster said. "It's for gothic writers. How can you be gothic without bad weather? Ah-hah! Hear that? Please stand by." The ugly head swiveled on its circuitry neck. "They're coming for you."

"Me?"

"Listen." The voice trailed off in speaker hiss. "Lis-sen . . ."

Under the sobbing wind, the strange deep music resolved to a descending motif of three notes in the strings. Long, short, long under a haunting human voice.

Charity. Char-i-tee . . .

"This also is reality," the speaker voice informed her.

"It's not real!" Charity wailed. "I'm supposed to be in hell, punished. This is crazy."

"I didn't say whose reality. The popcorn always suited you. You never asked for anything better."

"Who's following me? Tell me that much, will you?"

"In this place," said the TV creature, "most likely the last person you'd want to meet. Unless you care to remain for my editorial—public service, carefully laundered of damaging inference, station not responsible for content—you'd better run like hell."

Amid swirling fog, ominous music and the inane cackling of the true believer, Charity Stovall fled away.

■ 12 ■

Prometheus in Dolby

The pursuing voice faded, but she heard another just ahead. A man's voice like a clear trumpet, like Richard Burton in *The Robe*. One fearful glance over her shoulder, then Charity found the courage to call out.

"Hey! You out there, where are you?"

"Here!" the voice summoned. "Here, come to me, whoever you are. Now, you nighted ranks, you host of villainous shades, do I yet defy you! Time and again, though you pursue and yet I strive, and to your darkness give the lie—it is not the winning but the quest that raises me anew from your defeats."

She didn't know what he was saying, but the quality of that voice galvanized Charity in a place untouched before: powerful and heroic, yet vulnerable, racked with anguish of spirit.

The mist shifted slightly and she saw him, spread-eagled against a huge boulder by chains spiked into the rock. Not embarrassingly bare like herself, but his black tights and sheepskin vest set off a body heroic as the voice: slender, tight-muscled, smooth chest heaving under an open linen shirt, the finely shaped head crowned with unruly black curls.

"Come, child. Free me."

With her hands a poor makeshift for modesty, Charity approached the pinioned hero. Black eyes pierced her through out of the pain-drawn face. Under that gaze Charity knew, dead or not, she was still female.

"Uh . . . hi."

"Take the hammer, girl. Free me."

"Hammer?"

"Even there by your foot." He laughed bitterly. "That with which they pinned me to this rock thinking none would have the heart to help."

Groping under the carpet of fog, Charity found the heavy sledgehammer. "Batter at the spikes," he directed. "If my arms are free I can loose myself from the manacles. Haste you."

As Charity lifted the heavy hammer, the ground trembled and shifted beneath her feet with an ominous rumble.

"Quickly," he urged. "This ground is perilous."

She could barely lift the sledge at first, but spurred by fear and the quaking underfoot, Charity drove it faster and faster at the prisoning spikes. The first of them came loose with a hollow clang. The earth shifted sickeningly. Not far away a great gout of flame shot up through the mist, showering them with fiery needles of pain.

"Hurry, girl!"

His voice drove her to pound maniacally at the remaining pinion until it fell away. The young man brought his lacerated hands together with a concentrated energy fierce enough for Charity to feel. The entire charisma of tension and conflict in him focused in the hands as he grasped one manacle and writhed his wrist through it. The skin tore and bled; his lips drew back in a grimace from the effort.

"Careful, you're cutting yourself."

"The blood will—ease—the—passage." One lacerated hand sprang free as the ground beneath them palpably sank and heaved again. "Hold the chain, girl, it's coming . . . there!"

He stood a moment, flexing the torn hands, then allowed her a fleeting, distracted smile. Considering their plight, Charity could still find it devastating.

"Dane." He bowed his head briefly. "Once heir to a crown, now but a poor, tormented shade like yourself. Though not so

poor that I lack thanks, nor so dull"—his smile turned warmer—
"as to overlook your dire need of costume. Allow me."

Dane shed the sheepskin vest and draped it about Charity's
shoulders. With considerable gratitude, she found it large
enough to cover the conventions.

"Th-thank you." The ground surged again, throwing her
against him. "My name is Charity Mae Stovall from Plattsville, 'n'
can we please get out of here?"

"The wish is the act." He grasped her hand. "Come."

They set off at a jolting trot across the dreary landscape, Charity clinging for dear life to Dane. The rumble of the treacherous
ground grew to a roar. To their left and right the earth ripped
apart, belching flame and ash into the sooty air, pushing back the
mist in hissing retreat from blackened heath. Charity caught a
glimpse of some hapless creature disappearing into the flaming
maw.

Still Dane hurried her on, dragging her over rocks, guiding her
surely toward some distant goal she could only guess at, and
always the music under the roar of laboring nature. In a lull
between quakes they stopped to rest. Charity wilted to her
knees, panting. Dane knelt beside her; even through the sheepskin his hands were a comforting human warmth in the middle of
chill horror.

"Just a jot further, Charity." He pronounced her name in a way
that made it sound noble, full of meaning.

"Someone's following me, Dane."

"And me," he said. "There's always someone. And he will find
me. Come, the ground's not safe."

"Not yet," she protested. "I can't even get up. Where are we
going?"

"Where I must." Dane paced forward alone. Blinking through
her fear and exhaustion, Charity saw something about him that
escaped her before. Dane moved in a definite light that defined
him from his drearier surroundings. It must be his goodness, she
thought. Just like a spotlight on Bruce Springsteen. *Gol-lee, he
must be important.*

"We go to all that should have been precious to me." His
sadness was audible. "All I should have clung to, honored, but
never did." He swung about to Charity. The mist swirled be-

tween them, and the poignant music. "And you? What condemned you to this place, child?"

"I wish you wouldn't call me child. You're not all that much older than me."

"Hurrying the pleasures of wedlock?"

Charity found she could still blush. "That's kind of personal."

"Be not amazed that I can so divine; your namesake virtue's written in your eyes. No sins I find but they were writ by love."

A little hard to understand, but he certainly said it real nice. "Well, I guess modesty don't cut much here. That was it. Just . . . I wish I could've enjoyed it more. I mean, long as I had to get a heart attack. Boy, who could've figured on that? Is that your sin, too?"

"No." Dane's sorrow emanated from a great distance with an underlying rage that drew it taut. "Far worse, Charity. In the terms of the world, you only crossed a boundary without the passport of Grace. I . . . ran from all meaning. So now I must ever run toward it, fight and lose. In the matter of *hell*"—the magnificent voice hurled the word like a missile at a dull gray sky. "Demons, you lack imagination!"

The organ tones thundered away, mocked with echoes and the growing roar of the earth itself. Charity was flung backwards as the heath writhed up under her and opened in a great rift between her and Dane, belching fire and black smoke to dirty the mist.

Dane held out his arms. "Jump, girl. I'll catch you."

"I can't, it's too far."

"Try."

She scrambled to her feet, moved back from the yawing chasm already widening as she crouched for a running start.

"Now, ere it's too far."

With a quick prayer—not certain to whom under the circumstances—Charity churned toward the rift. She leaped, felt empty, scorching air on her bare legs—then nothing, no solid ground to meet her descent, hands scrabbling in panic at the lip of the rift, the rest of her dangling over searing void. Her fingers lost their grip, clawed, slipped, then Dane caught her and drew her up onto solid ground.

"The whole moor's sinking," he shouted over the thunder of chaos. "Tearing itself to pieces. Come on."

He dragged Charity after him toward a barren promontory rising high over the mist. "Take heart: even surviving is an action. To choose and act, even in hell, we are alive."

"How can we be alive?" Charity ran a dirty hand through her hair stringy with damp and singed ends. "We're as dead as you can get."

"Life's not state but quality. Here, this will help." Dane drew the lace from the front of his shirt and tied back Charity's hair. "In the far kingdom of Plattsville, would you ever know a day like this?"

No, Charity reflected honestly. I'd be working in the kitchen or just riding around with Roy or watching dumb old TV. Scary as this place is, and for all his weird talk, Dane is the beautifulest man I ever saw.

"Now you get down to it," she allowed, "things could be a lot worse."

"So they could." Dane swept her clear off her feet and kissed her. Charity's heart definitely missed a few beats. She felt his kiss down to her dangling toes.

"Just a little further now."

At the summit only a vast blanket of white fog lay before them, dirtied with smoke and reddish ash. The rock beneath them trembled. When Charity looked back, she saw the earth convulse once more in a scream of sundered stone. The last spasm subsided in echoes that stumbled away across leaden skies like fading timpani. "Is the weather always this bad here?"

"No. Quite oft it turns truly foul." Dane touched her cheek. "You're a brave lass, Charity Stovall. And very lovely."

Charity gulped. He said it easily enough, as if a little surprised at the discovery. No one had ever called her lovely. Now, suddenly, she felt that way. But Dane was pointing, a gesture weighted with more doom than hope.

"There. My father's keep."

■ 13 ■

Yonder lies the castle
of my father

From somewhere, dry strings swept up to be capped by a single piano note from which a chilly figure shuddered away in woodwinds. The mist eddied and parted to reveal a brooding castle of black stone rising from the heath. Over the single tower a banner turned in the wind.

"There's a flag, Dane. Someone's home."

"No one is there. But one will come."

The ubiquitous music turned rhythmic as they jolted down the last slope and on toward the drawbridge. They crossed it, passed under the portcullis across a cobbled courtyard and up a spiraling set of damp steps, Dane's boots ringing on the stone. They moved down a long, gloomy corridor toward a widening flicker of light.

"Told you someone's here."

"There's always a light," Dane answered. "And someone always comes."

"Your folks?"

"No."

The vast hall stretched away before Charity, an ocean of dark with one small island of light from a wall sconce. Dane took the torch and set it to logs and kindling laid in the huge fireplace. With more light came welcoming warmth. Giant shadow snakes danced up the high walls. Charity could see the size of the hall now, big as the Plattsville High School gym. Over the mantel a single lion's head glared at her in bas-relief. Just under it, Charity caught the transient gleam of light on cold metal. All of it gloomy and depressing; yet that odd, steady light followed Dane. Like the music, it must be awfully annoying, but Dane seemed to accept it as part of himself like Roy's camouflage fatigues.

"We sort of never get hungry here, do we?"

"No. Not for food." Dane left her by the fire and vanished into the gloom. He emerged again carrying something, which he held out to Charity: the most gorgeous pearl-gray velvet gown she'd ever drooled over in a movie or on the cover of a paperback romance. She thrilled to the sensual crush of the material. The neckline alone was illegal. "It's beeyootiful! Where'd you find it?"

"My mother's."

"Oh, Dane, I couldn't."

"Of course you can. It's yours."

"All right. Turn your back and I'll give you back your vest." Charity let the luxurious weight of the velvet fall about and caress her body. What could be so bad for people who can dress like this? she wondered with a shade of mean envy. At least they had fancy problems. "Oh, it's really *neat*, Dane. Thank you very much."

"Stay by the fire. Stay in the light." Dane prowled the shadows beyond their fire, the musical voice coming out of gloom. "This was my father's house, seat and symbol of that honor to which he hoped I might aspire. Remember me in your prayers, Charity. Say that when I might have mattered, I would not. That even now I need to act and choose when action mocks me with futility."

All that was pretty, but she did wish he could talk a little plainer so she wouldn't feel like a fool trying to answer what she could barely understand.

"Do you know poetry, girl?"

"Just what we had to read in school. Woody Barnes gave me a book of poems for my birthday once." By Rod somebody, she recalled imperfectly, though one of them was enough. It was about a man in love with a man, which she didn't approve of that at all and didn't bother with the rest. Anyway, why was Dane going on like this, so far away from her? "Come sit by the fire, it's real toasty now."

Dane knelt by Charity. Even kneeling he conveyed the effect of a taut athletic effort, like Gene Kelly. But now Charity could see the firelight dancing in his eyes and understood very well the feelings they stirred.

"There was a poet of Italy," Dane said, "who wrote of hell for those who changed allegiance or had none. Ever must they pursue, this way and that through a mist, one banner that ever eluded them. In this place I should have honored am I damned ever to find it empty, ever to lose and know too late what winning might have been." The fine head bowed over his knee. "Pray for me."

His voice was like an open wound. Charity's heart opened and reached for his pain, closed tight around it. "Dane, I'm sorry."

He flung himself on his back, searching the darkness above for a hope that would not be there.

"You're crying. I never saw Roy cry." He would have let himself be run over first, though tears took nothing from Dane's manhood. "He was my boyfriend."

"The boy who loved you?"

"Yes. Well, just that once."

"Oh, there's the sin." Dane wound his fingers in her hair. "That such a woman was loved only once."

When he drew her down to him, Charity knew the meager statistic was about to rise and loved the whole notion. She slid her arms around Dane's neck while the violins overhead haunted them with melody. "I don't want you to hurt, Dane."

"Or I you. We'll help each other." His body moved against hers, sending a different heat through every part of her. This was a fringe benefit she hadn't counted on.

"Can we? Even dead and all?"

"Why not feast on the lamb?" Dane chuckled with the dry ghost of humor. "We've already been hanged for the sheep."

"Sure enough," she whispered against his lips. "Way I figure, they owe us."

■ 14 ■

Enter Nemesis, pursuing

Something woke her.

The fire had burned low. She lay with her head on Dane's arm in a soft glow from the embers. Then Dane gently slid his arm away. She felt his movement. When she turned over, he was dressing rapidly.

"Did you hear it?" he muttered.

"Something woke me up."

"Yes." Dane threw on the sheepskin and thrust his feet into boots. "They have found me. They will not do't in the dark." He threw another log on the fire in a shower of sparks, then came back to Charity. "Stay in the shadows. Do not speak or cry out at what you see. All was foreordained." He handed her the gown with a remembrance of their earlier tenderness. "I should have known you in life. But it is enough."

"There wasn't anybody like you in Plattsville," she blurted—an admission of wonder and regret not unmixed with a certain relief. Dane was pure electricity, ten times what Roy would ever be or even Woody, but a woman could get very tired loving a raw wire. Roy and Woody she understood; besides, he might not even be Protestant.

"Well, then, come on," Dane challenged the dark. "Come and

make an end." His hand swept over the mantel and came away with a magnificent rapier that flashed in an arc of light. *"Listen!"*

Hurrying into her gown under a muted cadence from plucked bass strings, Charity heard the hollow echo of a male tread over the courtyard stones—up the stairs, striding toward the hall. Illumined in his own light, Dane bounded across the vast chamber onto a low dais, whirling, rapier held high.

"Nemesis, come! And you unfeeling stars, I hurl defiance for reply, and cast into the balance for the world to see, my soul 'gainst thy insensate cruelty."

As Dane's ringing challenge died away, Charity started at the answer, a blast of horns descending in a minor mode. Another spotlight revealed a figure leaning, negligent but coiled, against the entrance arch. Even in apparent relaxation the black-clad stranger had about him the same dangerous energy as Dane. His sardonic laughter echoed off the stones.

"Bravo, Dane. Pentametric to the end." He lifted his rapier. "But I have found you."

A stifled scream of tension tore from high-pitched strings. Muffled timpani measured the intruder's cat tread across the hall as Dane stepped down to meet him.

Charity swallowed hard. *Oh, man, it's Darth Vader.*

"So you have," said Dane. "But think no more to follow me. Here upon my father's hearth, with all he left me, this sword, I speed you home to the deeper hell that spawned you." The sword cut a hissing swath through the air. "Come, sir."

Moving in his own light, the stranger's blade crossed Dane's with a chilly *ting* and slithered along its middle third. The two slender threads of steel were no more than moving light, flashing about each other. The two men circled like lethal dancers, the nasty *ting-tack!* of the blades a deadly dialogue. The steel threads wove about each other, crossed, disengaged, beat with resonant echoes over the inexorable trombones that measured them.

Then in a blur too swift to follow, the dark little man thrust and lunged like a striking snake. As quick, Dane parried overhand with a twist of his wrist; the blade streaking for his heart swerved far aside, tore from the attacker's grasp and clattered on the stone floor. He stepped back.

"Your father taught you well, Dane."

"Had he schooled me so in honor, or were I pupil apt, I should be with him now. But as to sword—" Dane speared the fallen rapier guard on his own point and launched it toward his enemy's grasp. "Well enough. Come again."

"You should not lend me mercy I may not repay." The stranger leaped at Dane again in a slashing attack, closed and tripped him. Dane lost his balance and fell. The dark man's blade whirled in a circle of light, came down just as Dane rolled aside and sprang to his feet. They closed again, beat, disengaged; then the smaller man slipped under a slight miscalculation in Dane's guard and lunged.

Dane faltered; the sword dropped from his fingers. Charity cried out as he sank to his knees with a strangling cough and fell on his side. His enemy regarded him with remote pity as the music melted to poignant strings.

"Victory," he pronounced with no joy in it. "Rest, most noble among the damned."

Dane lay in his light, a stain spreading over his shirt. With a sob, Charity ran to cushion his head in her lap.

"Dane. Dane!"

His eyelids fluttered open. "Aye, Charity. Well enough."

The grave, tender music brooded over them, a repeated figure in muted brass. Dane listened with a wan smile of satisfaction. "For the time . . . you made me very happy."

"Oh, Dane. Honest, for all the trouble, I was never so happy in my whole life." A rage welled up in Charity, a fury with a virulence to frighten her. Even her voice was different when she turned on Dane's killer. "You son of a bitch."

He stepped back, offended. "Madame, please."

"Pardon my language, but damn if I don't wish I was a man for two minutes. I'd take his sword and shove it where the sun don't shine for what you done."

"For what you *did*," Dane corrected weakly. "So please you . . . a little of your namesake for our mother tongue."

She hugged him close, desperate. "I don't want you to die."

"I must." Dane's hand faltered up to touch her lips and hair. "My father's waiting. My . . . spirit fails. But I did love you. That . . . makes fair end."

"Please don't die. It ain't fair!"

"Don't blame this churl; he's but transport. He sends me home. Oh, Father, I stained your life. For earnest, take . . . my death."

The somber music faded to silence. Dane lay still in Charity's arms.

"Oh, Dane." With infinite tenderness, Charity eased his head down onto the stones and bent to kiss the stilled lips. "I should have gone with you. You were a man to die with."

"You are worthy, child." The stranger sheathed his sword. "The sentiment becomes you."

Charity was a little impressed herself. She'd never felt that depth or voiced anything like it in her life.

"You must go now."

"Go where?" she asked listlessly over Dane's body.

"Where you will, but with dispatch. Hark!"

The wind had risen outside, a pitiful moaning sound, bleak as her own sorrow, and a voice rode on it.

Char-i-tee . . .

"I came for him," the dark man said. "They come for you. His ghosts o'ertook him; yours will come betimes. Quickly begone."

With a last adoring look at Dane, Charity hurried away from the hall, down the worn steps and across the gray courtyard while the wind cried with its terrible summons.

Charity?

She fled across the drawbridge into the fog.

In the gloomy hall, the victor gazed down at the body graceful even in death—and signed plaintively. "Wilksey, your pauses are interminable."

One baleful eye opened and impaled him with accusation. "That is the way to play it, Mr. Kean."

"Indeed." Edmund Kean snorted with dry disgust. "Is there no o'erdone reading, no tattered cliché, no cheap effect to which you will not plummet?"

"You amateur!" Wilksey Booth shot to his feet like a jack-in-the-box released. "You charge me with overplaying?"

"Amateur? I was playing the Bard before you were born."

"Precisely, Ned. One wouldn't mind your Shakespeare lit by flashes of lightning—"

"Just so." Kean's intensity softened with satisfaction. One's better reviews were delights evergreen. "Coleridge did say that."

"Were it not for all the darkness in between."

"Take care." Kean's sword flashed again from the scabbard. "I might school you in earnest."

"You?" Booth derided. "The bawdy-house school of fencing?"

"Oh, did I tax you beyond competence?"

"Beyond patience, Kean. You know the disengage one-two-three always comes before the parry-quatre-thrust-lunge and you *always* forget. Not to mention that you lunged when I was out of my light."

"Allowance must be made for colonials. Let us rehearse once more," Kean said. "And whilst we do, remember who was called in his day the very Sun's Bright Child—and who merely assassin."

"Oh, base prompter's boy!" Booth recoiled, wounded. "Come you over me still with that? I shot *one* Republican. Have at you, villain."

Ned Kean crouched *en garde*—then lowered his point. "Stay, it's no fun without an audience. She sorrowed with heart, that girl, and raged with natural fire. But that accent . . . ?"

"Allegheny," Booth agreed. "Eerie, isn't it?"

"Nor did I recognize your death music."

"Oh, that? Walton: the passacaglia from the film *Henry V.* Falstaff's death."

"The death of a clown; how apt," Kean sniped. "Now my choice was Shostakovich."

Booth sniffed. "Bit much on the kettles and brass."

"It likes me well. The ghost and duel music from *Hamlet.* Ah, those minor thirds in the horns—ominous, fated. I say, Dimitri?" Ned Kean petitioned the dark overhead. "Could I hear my entrance again, old boy? Rather fancied it. And, Wilksey, do shorten those pauses when you die. One tends to nap."

Together in their universe, the circle of light, the actors listened to the reprise of music and were stirred.

■ 15 ■

Aryans in the fast lane

No pain, nothing clear except terror.

When Roy could think straight, he found himself in a small chamber inviting as a dentist's waiting room. Table, lamp, modern chair, a copy of *Soldier of Fortune,* a worn book with no dust jacket—and to Roy's huge relief a cotton bathrobe hanging on the coat rack. He put it on immediately; he found it hard to feel secure fully clothed, but naked was unbearable.

Time, if there was such a thing for him now, passed and kept on passing. Nothing. No sound. No one came. His tension began to ebb to the point where he could relate to his surroundings. Dr. Corbett once had a waiting room just like this, and the magazines were just as out-of-date. The copy of *Soldier of Fortune* was six months old. Roy paged through the book's first leaves. *Mein Kampf* by Adolf Hitler, who was one of his gods along with George Lincoln Rockwell and Rambo.

"Never knew he wrote a book."

He tried a few pages and gave up. Hitler was an unappreciated hero of the race struggle, but whoever wrote it in English made it boring as hell. Suffice to say, Roy never spent an evening trapped with the inexhaustible Austrian.

More waiting. Roy thought of Charity: where did they take her? More to the point right now: what would they do to him?

The very silence was oppressive. "If this is it for eternity," he judged aloud to shatter it, "I think I can handle it."

When the door opened behind him, he jumped clear out of the chair, clutching the bathrobe around him.

"Roy Stride? I'm Drumm."

"I didn't do anyth—"

Roy caught himself, not knowing whether to be scared or plain laugh. A squat, unimposing little man, Drumm was decked—stuffed, rather, into the dress finery of the White Paladins: tailored camouflage fatigues, white silk scarf and red beret, web belt under a double strain to contain his girth and support the heavy Magnum revolver in its tooled holster. With all the authority these might have lent, Drumm didn't make it. His paunch betrayed the military intentions of his blouse. His glasses were thick enough to make his eyes look like small, distant clams within concentric rings. The vague mustache added no character, merely coexisted with his upper lip. Drumm removed his beret with the care of a cardinal divesting after Mass to reveal a toupee neither subtly matched nor firmly allied with his sparse indigenous hair. He greeted Roy with the fervor of adoration.

"At last the day. We've been waiting, sir."

Roy backed away, trying to keep the bathrobe closed. "Hey, look, I just got here."

"On a trumped-up charge."

"I'm innocent . . . who are you?"

"My cause is yours," Drumm said with dramatic urgency.

"You with the Paladins?"

"We're everywhere." Drumm patted the toupee for evidence of wanderlust since last contact. The two clams fixed on Roy. "We know you; we intercept the dossiers. And Charity? Was she pure?"

"We're gonna get married," Roy maintained, but the tense was obviously wrong. "Were gonna get married."

"I mean was she Aryan?"

"One hunnert percent pure White American Aryan like me. The purest."

"And like so many capable men, you are here through the

judgment of inferiors." Drumm rubbed his pudgy hands together. "As myself. I was with Rockwell in Arlington."

Roy regarded Drumm with new respect. "The American Nazi Party." The last of his fear vanished. Drumm was no threat but an ally with major-league credentials.

"With me to guide him, George Rockwell formed and headed the ANP. He saw the merit and the truth in the plays I wrote that no one would produce; that no one *here* will do anything but throw back at me, thanks to Jason Blythe, our pristine prime minister. The truth of the world was in my work, Roy Stride. And that truth is the God-ordained and inevitable supremacy of the White Race."

Roy even found the composure to grin. "Right on."

"Your hand, sir."

"Gimme five."

"There are those who guide, those who lead, many who follow. I am a prophet; you may be much more than that. Wait." Drumm peered suspiciously about the chamber with an air of habitual caution, bent to inspect the inside of the lampshade and under the table, ample rump presented to Roy, who quelled a profitless urge to boot it.

Satisfied, Drumm beckoned him close. "I don't think we're bugged, but Blythe's spies are everywhere. All of us are marked. We must move soon. You may be the leader we have waited for. Rockwell was shot, cut down in his prime. His followers wait even here to carry on his cause, needing only the day and the man. Are you fit for it? A leader seizes the moment. Will you?"

Will I? Roy felt ambition surge in him like a shot of whiskey. *Damned, no chance at all, call that a trial we had? All of you just watch. Just one chance, all I ask, and he's handing it to me. Get set up, find Charity, and won't be any son of a bitch on two legs big enough to fuck me over anymore.*

"Okay. Your people ready?"

"And waiting. A coup," Drumm said. "A purge. One lightning strike."

This wasn't hell but heaven. "Weapons?"

"All we need, the latest. AR rifles, ammo, C-4 plastic, LAW rockets, men in the right place ready to move. The government has a rotted will; the danger is in fanatics and interference from Topside. But the time and stars are right, Roy Stride!"

"Lead me to it." Roy felt marvelous—until second thoughts nudged him. "No, wait. I gotta get some decent clothes." Not even Hitler could conquer in a bathrobe.

"Before all else." Drumm clicked his heels and flung open the door. "The Whip & Jackboot will furnish all you need. Run by a nigger and a Jew, but we can't purge them all."

"Yet," Roy corrected with the first overtones of authority.

"Well put, sir." Drumm motioned Roy first through the door. "I was not mistaken in you. You show genius."

The Whip & Jackboot: the glories of the display window alone convinced Roy that Drumm knew his taste to a T, his brightest fantasies. Within the window there were many metal-studded styles and a great deal of leather.

"I'll leave you here." Drumm searched the mall both ways with his perpetual air of secrecy. "Remember, you're being watched. I'll get word to the others and to you when it's safe to meet."

"Yeah, cool." Roy wanted to get off the sidewalk. The bathrobe didn't do anything for a man of destiny.

"The code word for the takeover is Case White. Leader, the pistol is cocked." The metaphor pleased Drumm. "You will pull the trigger. *Auf Wiedersehen.*"

"Stay cool. No, wait a minute." Roy found he was thinking clearer and more confidently with each passing minute. Never mind the people on the sidewalk; they didn't seem to think a man in a bathrobe was ridiculous or even interesting. Looked like a bunch of stuck-up yuppies, didn't know their ass from a hole in the ground. "You said you know everybody that comes here."

"Everyone," Drumm confirmed. "We make it our business to know. Not hard, a few favors here and there. Now and then for the right person an agreeable girl in the right motel. I mean— that is to say . . ." Drumm looked away, awkwardly conscious of a gaffe. "Excuse me, Leader, I—"

"That's okay, just watch it. Pass an order to the troops."

Click! "Immediately, Leader."

"Find Charity Stovall for me. I don't give a shit who you put in what bed with his own mother even. Charity's my woman and I want her, understand? That's General Order *numero uno*, got it?"

"Sir." Click! "Until then, may I suggest A Son Goût, just down the mall? Adrian the sommelier personally extends his invitation."

"Adrian the what?"

"In charge of the girls." Click! "Until later, my Führ—my Leader." Drumm bustled away. He had very little military bearing and digging in his nose destroyed that.

Roy entered the Whip & Jackboot. Before him stretched rows of gleaming, studded jackets and matched uniforms, shelves of precisely arranged peaked caps like a squad on parade, racks of leather whips, whole tack sections of leather strapping. Midway down one row, a balding black man with bulging eyes and enormous white teeth fussed over an item on a rack. Seeing Roy, he shuffled forward with a servility that warmed the customer's heart.

"Mistuh Roy Stride, suh! Lan', it *good* to see you in a gent'man's shop where y'all belong."

Roy felt better already. He straightened up. The demeaning rag of a bathrobe took on regality. He liked a nigger who knew his place; didn't have anything against that kind at all. Tell them a Mandy and Rastus joke, they'd laugh hard as you did.

"Well, now, first we gone take you back to this li'l old booth, get you some trousers and shirt while Jacob measures you. Come 'long, Mistuh Roy."

The black man shuffled classically, using a great deal of graceful effort to cover very little distance. Hell, they all had rhythm.

"What's your name, boy?"

"Washington Moonlight Jones, suh." He revealed again the vast expanse of gossamer teeth. "Mama call me Moonlight 'cause that when Daddy done his bes' work among de neighborin' stills."

Roy swelled with pleasure and ventured a Rhett Butler grin of roguish but patrician understanding. "Moonlight, you black rascal, give me the best you got."

"Don' fret. We gone get you lookin' fine."

In a few moments Roy was in and out of the booth, the silly

robe traded for shirt and trousers. There were several small holes in the shirtfront and faded stains around them, but he wouldn't have them on for that long.

Moonlight gestured like a majordomo. "Now, y'all come 'long with me in the back. We got Jacob. He trash but he do know what a mil'tary gent'man need for wear. Ja-cob? Gent'man need some outfittin' right now." Moonlight lowered his voice in confidence. "He try to Jew you on price, old Moonlight set him straight. Been took care of. Jacob?"

Moonlight thrust aside a curtain. "G'wan in, Mistuh Roy."

The dingy back room was rack-lined with uniforms in various stages of completion. At the end of a long table, tape measure draped about his oddly twisted neck, a bearded Jew of indeterminate age hunched over a thick book. Bespectacled and ringleted, the fringes of a prayer shawl splayed from beneath the hem of his shabby vest.

Roy sneered: a real one, all right. "Work hours, Ikey. You praying to Moses on company time?"

The tailor gave Roy an unhurried inspection before closing his book. Somehow, under that gaze, Roy recalled the factory worker he bad-mouthed in a bar once, a man who stood much bigger than he sat. Roy had the same second-thought prudence then as now. Jacob exuded an undefinable force that belied the humble appearance. In a dark alley, he might be dangerous. Though his head canted at an unnatural angle, his gaze was pitilessly direct.

"Not prayer, no. Thinking on the nature of belief. Like the Talmud, a preoccupation of mine." Jacob clapped his hands briskly and rubbed them together; the image of quiet strength vanished. "But business is business. It's good you come by my shop. Something in a uniform, yes?"

Jacob undraped his measure and subjected Roy to professional scrutiny, tugging at one ringlet. "It wouldn't need to be made special. From looking alone, I can suit you from stock."

He puttered about Roy, measuring fore and aft, up and down, noting the results on a greasy slip of paper. When he stooped to gauge an outseam, Roy saw the livid rope scar that ringed his neck.

"The *shwartzer* says I must always measure. Feh! Who has

been a tailor so long? Go give advice but leave to me clothes. So: didn't I say? A perfect size forty all around. Wait, I will bring it all for approval." Jacob vanished into another dark recess and shortly reappeared with an armload of boxes. "You will try them on and say I know my business?"

Dressed before the full-length mirror, Roy palpitated: what approval was needed for sheer magnificence? Black the uniform, stern black and cut in SS style with silver buttons, even a death's-head ornament on the peaked cap. Flared riding breeches fitted perfectly into high, polished boots perfect for striding over a conquered city. *Too much, oh, Jesus, too much.* In the mirror the magic uniform converted his whole image to strength and dominance. With a sense of ritual, he centered the cap on his head, tried a rakish angle, straightened it again and patted the heavy Lüger at his hip.

"Gotta hand it to you, Jacob."

"Only wait." A protesting hand. "Something is missing, I think."

"Hey, what?" How could perfection lack?

"Maybe a swagger stick like the Englishers? No, they are not a generous people. How long before they gave back Jerusalem? Who needs the English? We will keep it good and German. Moonlight! Bring to me, *bitte,* the Gauleiter Special."

From the remote front of the shop: "Comin' fas' I can." Followed by a considerable hiatus.

"Which means, we can hope, sometime before evening prayers." Jacob lifted his eyes to Jehovah. "Meanwhile we will settle on the price."

"Don' you fret Mistuh Roy with no bill, you trash." Moonlight hovered, stern, between the parted curtains. "All took care of by the Paladins. Here you is, suh: just what y'all need."

Now, truly, perfection was improved. The black whip coiled in Roy's hand with the lead-weighted feel of authority. He cracked it once; the sound was music. *All right, you motherfuckers, come on.*

Jacob beamed approval. "You should wield it in good health. Maybe on the Arabs."

With what he meant to be a superior smile, Roy nodded curtly and stalked out of the shop, cracking the whip. When the front door slammed, Moonlight and Jacob went through profound metamorphosis. Moonlight stood much more erect, chuckling as the whole cast of his features shifted.

"It's impossible to insult them or overplay, Jake. New York, Harvard or the boonies: a nerd is a nerd, world without end, amen."

"Yours to shuffle, mine to cringe and fawn." Jake divested himself of the grizzled wig and spectacles to reveal youthful black hair. The gabardine, vest and prayer shawl added to his discards. He slithered quickly into a work shirt and corduroy trousers. "Honor thy stereotypes, the authors of thy thinking, for without them, thou wouldst have to see."

"You dig El Shmucko with that whip?"

"He's a fish," Jake said with cold contempt. "And he's going to get everything he always wanted."

"What's his bag?" Moonlight wondered.

"Power. The Prince is going to give him all he ever longed for."

"He must be pretty rotten."

"No more than most; just hungrier. The world shut him out. Never turn your back on a small man," Jake said with conviction. "We're a dangerous breed. Catch you later. Got a call on my cab."

16

Problems of the whore/
madonna syndrome (Aryans at
half-mast)

Mirrored dramatically in A Son Goût's polished window, Roy let his own image ravish him. From cap to boots and whip, he had never felt so tuned to his inner essence. He felt secure and strong, a man with an identity and a destiny at last, seduced as Narcissus.

When something else could intrude on his rapt self-admiration, the displayed pictures and X-rated toys in the window told him this was a place for kicks of a very special kind. A small rubric lettered low on the glass—CATERING TO YOUR REFINED NEEDS—confirmed the impression. Drumm had steered him right.

Entering, Roy found himself in an opulent anteroom done in red velvet plush. Two young men in White Paladin uniforms, on their way out, snapped to rigid attention, puzzling Roy until he realized he was the recipient of the courtesy. Good enough. He touched the whip to his cap bill.

"As you were. I was enlisted once myself. Carry on."

"Good *day,* sir!" A distinguished older man in tux brushed through beaded curtains at the rear, menu tucked under one arm, manner silken. "We hoped you might honor us with a visit. Welcome to A Son Goût, Mr. Stride." A slight but impeccable bow. "Adrian at your service."

"Heard you had a real nice place here. Take care of, uh, special needs?"

"Absolutely," Adrian assured him quickly. "A Son Goût has earned its reputation: purveyors of the best and the unusual, an oasis to the male libido athirst."

"Huh?"

"My own little joke." Adrian waved it away. "This way, sir."

Roy followed him through the beaded curtains to another room in the same plush with more gold trimming and tables covered with crisp white damask. Adrian seated him with a flourish and opened the menu with a practiced twist—frowned and closed it again. Kind of a queer, Roy guessed, but he had to admire the flashing choreography of the white hands. Strictly class. Adrian reminded him of that guy who used to advertise expensive booze in magazines.

Adrian snapped his fingers. "Esmeralda?" A rear door opened and a thin girl of about eighteen skittered into the chamber. She looked passably slutty to Roy; he could make it with her in a pinch: thin hips, way too skinny, in ratty black tights and a leather miniskirt. The pouting face with its carmine mouth, green eye shadow and frowzy, peroxided hair over dark roots might interest him on an odd night—but not special. Too punk rock.

"Esmeralda, this is yesterday's menu. Today's please." The girl changed them quickly and slipped out after a sultry glance at Roy.

"Esmeralda is one of today's specials." Adrian pursed his lips over the current bill of choices. "We are expecting a party from SoHo." He beamed at Roy, hands laced. "Do we have an appetite today, sir? Truly lustful? A full repast or just something to pick at?"

"The full treatment." Roy settled back. "Best you got."

"Good, sir."

Roy twitched his whip. "No spades or losers, you got it? That special don't look so hot. And no Jews."

Adrian stiffened. "But of course not, sir. We prepare to order.

Esmeralda was prepared for the disco trade. We offer as well an *haute monde* selection, very popular with the New York set. And for the palate beyond astonishment, an anorexic double amputee. Then there is the consideration of vintage. For example, the '67: an excellent year but still a trifle young."

Roy whetted to the prospect. "I like 'em young."

"And the '70," Adrian ventured. "Naïve but a fun libation." The delicate turn of a pale hand. "Though for a true Sauvignon complexity, may one suggest the '54, which should be superb now. And absolutely Wasp, sir."

Roy nodded. "Now you got the idea."

"Untainted with, shall we say, Mediterranean influences."

"Pure blood is very important."

The white hands described a precise sine qua non. "To the discriminate, quite everything."

"That's what I want. But, you know . . . kinky."

"Kinks, sir?" Adrian managed to correct and reassure in one breath. "Proclivities, rather. By a miracle of serendipity, we have a selection of two today, each a masterpiece." The sommelier's gift for description grew to rhapsody. "Ms. Eleanor Padgett-Clive, vintage '60. Niece to an earl. Down from Cambridge, firsts and blues. An enormous, one might say legendary, appetite for men, curbed only by her breeding and the restraints of civil law."

"Hey, a real nymphermaniac?"

"With frequent relapses," Adrian blandished, "which allow us to feature her as a selection of rare value. And—if it is not redundant to observe—dying to meet you, Mr. Stride. Are we tempted, sir?"

"Right on!" Roy bumped back the chair. "Lead me to it."

Adrian wheeled with the precision of a sergeant major on parade. "This way, please."

The bedroom was something out of old movies, done mostly in merciless scarlet and electric blue. To any taste but the most diseased, the colors alone might have precluded sleep or even relaxation; for Roy they were Uptown.

"Bon appétit, sir." Adrian withdrew.

If this was hell, it was definitely the high-rent district, and why not? Damned for making it just once with Charity, and that once not all that good. Face it, she didn't know much, and he had his usual troubles like with any respectable girl. Why shouldn't he land in clover just once: power, girls, every dream about to come true? He could really get comfortable here, make it every time with the right kind of woman.

"That's our wish," the low, musical contralto voice read his thought, "and our purpose, Roy."

Eleanor Padgett-Clive poised in the doorway like an exquisite painting, marvelously sexual without working at it in the least, in a diaphanous dressing gown that left just enough to erotic imagination. She glided to Roy and slipped her arms about his neck. "Sorry to be late. I was reading and the time just stole away. Hello, darling."

Roy felt bleak. To most men this side of terminal impotence, Eleanor would be a love call in herself. She resembled several English film stars of the '60s and '70s: full, luscious mouth, her face sculpted over exquisite bones. Her voice alone, low and musical, could remind a man of biological imperatives.

Could but did not; for Roy, everything about Eleanor was wrong. Wrong voice, wrong face, too damned high-class. Classy women made him feel angry and inferior, but he allowed her to lead him to the bed. Eleanor began to undress him. Her hands moved faster and faster, her breathing rapid and shallow with desire, until she was tearing the clothes from him.

"Hey, careful of the shirt, it's new."

In a very short time, Roy was naked as a peeled egg. Eleanor let her gown slide from creamy shoulders and pulled him eagerly down onto the bed, her heavy sensual mouth crushed to his. "Take me, darling. Use me. Ravage me."

He wished he could.

"Darling, what's the matter?" Eleanor searched Roy's face for some answering spark and found none. "Is something wrong?"

"No," he evaded. "Just . . ."

"Please, I'm so ready for you." Eleanor writhed against him.

"Hey, take it easy, okay? Shit." The same old trouble, no different here than back home. He could never make it with a nice girl like Charity that you wanted to marry. Even if Eleanor was just a whore, she *looked* nice. And there were other things needed that he usually had to pay for.

"A challenge," Eleanor whispered. "Shall we not rise to it?"

She was more than beautiful, she was admirably deft and proved it in the next few minutes. The range of her erotic skill was phenomenal, employing the full gamut of her own marvelous equipment and parts of Roy even the Air Force doctors had missed. He only became more depressed and angry, thinking of all the guys who would've died happily by this time, how good it could be without that lousy hang-up, but . . . nothing.

At length, Eleanor desisted. "Love's labors are definitely lost. Your sort are so predictably alike."

That did it. She wasn't his type but no woman talked to him like that. "What you mean all alike?"

Eleanor glanced down at his defeat. "A midsummer's night dream turns to a winter's tale or a comedy of errors."

He didn't know what the hell she was talking about but it sounded like she was making fun of him. A stud like him who could go all night with the right kind of woman. "Hey, listen, bitch. With a man sometimes the woman don't turn him on, you know? Not my fault if you don't do nothing for me."

"The point is moot." Eleanor slid from the bed and into her gown. "But then you're not my sort either, you inadequate little man."

"You shut your fuckin mouth, bitch!"

"Certainly." Eleanor knew how to make a graceful exit with ruin in her wake. "This place isn't your hell, darling. Nowhere you go will ever be. You carry it with you. For you, nice girls don't, isn't that so? You can never quite reconcile sexuality with virtue. Actually nice girls have more talent for sex. Less guilt, more imagination and a great deal more fun."

"I said shut *up.*" Roy swung off the bed, ugly and dangerous. "You don't talk to a man like that."

"A man?" Eleanor's laughter cut like shards of crystal. "And you're what busy little Drumm dredged up for the people's choice? White Paladin to the unwashed. *Bon chance*, darling. Hail and farewell from the gratefully obsolete."

"Listen, you—" Roy took a vicious swing at her. She hardly moved, but whatever she did Bruce Lee would have paid to learn. Roy went tail over teakettle against the wall and landed head down, blinking at an upside-down Eleanor.

"Filet's not for you, Mr. Stride. Adrian will fetch you something more in the line of grits." The door closed behind Ms. Padgett-Clive.

Cold, shaking, Roy sat down on the bed, staring at the door. They knew. Everything. Got right down to the problem, even laughed at him. He cursed with feeble rage at Eleanor and Adrian and the whole goddamned lousy system that made things and people the way they were.

I didn't make the rules about what's nice and what ain't. Just I'm a White Christian and that's the way things are.

"Precisely, sir." Adrian poised in the doorway, an étude in apology.

"Hey, man, do you people know what I'm thinking even?"

"Not exactly, but we have done business for ever so long. One hopes you will pardon my deplorable lapse of judgment. Eleanor of *course* was completely wrong for your specifications. Actually she specializes in the younger novelists. I insist on making amends. Our remaining selection is Florence Bird."

Roy was in no mood to be gracious. "She better be the right stuff. Won't be long 'fore I got some pull around here. The business will go where I go, you got it? Who is she?"

Once more Adrian was the compleat sommelier. "Florence Bird: vintage '54. Robust, assertive as Pinot Noir. And absolutely Wasp."

"For real?"

"On the house's reputation: the last honest-to-Goebbels bottling Below Stairs.

"Well, run her in here before I go somewhere else. Can't be only one whorehouse around here."

"There is Club Banal for the pedestrian trade," Adrian informed him with a definite chill. "Whatever *they* can make ordinary, A Son Goût can render sublime. Miss Bird, sir."

Once more Adrian bowed and withdrew. Only a short wait, then the door flew open and Florence Bird gusted in. Roy's heart leaped.

" 'Allo, luv!"

Florence was large, frizzy-haired and utterly bare under the open nylon wrapper trimmed in rabbit fur that fluttered in her bold wake like the train of a raffish empress. Florence was nothing if not forthright.

"Had to spend a linnet up the apples for an 'it and miss from all the pig's ear and mother's ruin down the rub-a-dub. Like me Bristols?"

Roy licked his lips in tumescent excitement. Florence was stout and coarse with a merry lasciviousness, though her very direct handshake was definitely not what he was used to from businesswomen. She sounded like some foreigner, very difficult to understand. "Hiya, honey. Where you from?"

"Lunnon," Florence pealed like Bow Bells. "Carnt yer tell?"

More bullshit. He didn't want to talk at all. She worked for him, all right, the kind that always did: loud, cheap, lay it on the line. Right on. There'd be no problems with Florence beyond translation. She was late, she explained, having been down at her pub having a few gins and beer chasers and had to stop at the bathroom for that and to rouge her nipples, knowing a man of his hearty tastes would appreciate the effect.

Right stuff, right on, Roy thrilled. *Oh jeez, if she can only do the rest of it.*

Subtle as a bayonet charge, Florence cupped Roy's genitals and wiggled her hips. "Right bit o' wick'n awls." She winked, undulating her belly against his. "Like me Khyber?"

Whatever her Khyber was, Roy was all for it. "Yeah. Come on."

"A course, for you, might have to down a few more pints to give yer what yer need, but we'll give it a bash. Down on the floor, luv. Might be a bit left for yer."

"Oh yeah. Yeah, that's it, you got it." Roy got ready, tingling with anticipation and need. "Give it to me, you lousy slut. The whip, too."

Florence was cheerfully accommodating. Roy closed his eyes in bliss and pain under the benediction and the whip. Love had found Andy Hardy.

17

Faith, hope and Charity
Stovall

Charity didn't dare stop for long. Of all the terrors hell might hold, she most feared that unknown voice pursuing her, though she could no longer hear it following on the wind. No real time in this place, no real distance she could measure with any certainty. The gray velvet gown was a Hollywood dream but not much for traveling, sodden and heavy with mist.

She stopped suddenly. Just ahead through the swirling fog hulked a large house surrounded by a high iron fence. No lights showed but smoke curled from one chimney. The gloomy presence of the house contrasted with a gleaming, fresh-waxed taxi near the front steps. The driver's door bore the device:

BELOW STAIRS CAB
"ANYWHERE TO HELL AND BACK"
CALL 666-JAKE

Charity pushed at the wide gate. At the groan of rusty hinges, a huge hound raised his head from a nap on the crumbling stone steps with an inquisitive *woof.*

"Got no time for games," Charity told the dog. "Hope you don't bite."

"Not at all." The hound yawned to his ears. "But beware the owner. He thinks."

Charity was only moderately surprised. After a monster made out of television, an earthquake and a thrill-packed but exhausting interlude with Dane, a talking dog was not all that new, except he sounded kind of snooty. City people were always putting you down, trying to sell you something or draft your friends. "You got a funny accent. Where you from, doggie?"

"Boston, girlie," said the hound with audible disdain. "I will not comment on your accent. Similes founder, metaphors fail."

"I speak good American."

"And I only English, alas. Yale, '52. Summa cum maxima, Skull and Bones."

"Plattsville High School, class of '85." Charity would not be outdone. "You don't have to be so stuck-up about it. Everybody goes to school." *Will you listen to me?* she caught herself. *I'm arguing with a watchdog.* "Anyway, is your owner home?"

"He's not my owner." The hound indulged in a thorough fore-and-aft scratch. "But he's in. What do you want?"

"I guess a cab to town. Somewhere. Maybe get warm first."

"The cab you can get; the warmth comes harder. His name is Jake. With a J."

"I know, I know." Charity grasped the heavy bronze knocker and banged it twice.

"Oh, go on in, it's never locked," the dog told her. "Jake had only a few things he valued and lost them ages ago. Some ideals and a friend." He licked his chops and settled down again into his nap.

Charity had to ask. "How does a hound dog go to college?"

One eye opened. "I'm only a dog on duty. Good hours, great for catching up on sleep, which was very difficult for a successful embezzler. Worries, occasional conscience. This is like keeping a lighthouse, not much traffic. So if you don't mind, sayonara." The eye closed.

Charity pushed the door in and found herself in a dark hall, musty with the long absence of light. The only illumination flickered feebly on a wall from a room far down the passage. Charity moved unsurely along the hall to pause in the entrance to a large living room lit only by a fireplace.

There was a man in front of the fire. He didn't look up. "Prince?"

He slumped in his armchair, absorbed in a chess game on a small table on his near side. Charity saw at first only a brooding profile. Too young to read men with any accuracy, Charity still felt the profound sorrow of that presence. He barely acknowledged her, first moving a piece on the board.

"Yes?"

"The door was open," Charity attempted, a little embarrassed. "The dog said just come in."

"Of course." Jake rose with a distant courtesy and came to meet her. His head canted at a weird angle as if the neck had been broken and badly set. A small leather bag hung around his throat and chinked dully with his movement: seemed an odd place for a cabdriver to carry change.

"Come in. Warm yourself if you can."

"I saw your cab out front. Thought maybe you could drive me out of here."

"There is no out." Jake looked right through her, clearly disinterested. "Where would you like to go?"

"Somewhere," she guessed with her small knowledge of Below Stairs. "Just I don't have any money. I'll have to owe you."

"Don't worry about that. Come by the fire."

She spread her hands to the pale flame that she could barely feel. "What are you burning?"

"Old vanities, dry regrets," Jake told her. "They don't throw much heat. *Shalom*, Miss Stovall. Have a chair."

"Do we know each other?"

"New arrivals: the news gets around. We don't recruit as many as you'd think. It's still a small town. You came with Roy Stride. He was my last fare."

"Roy?" She twisted to him in her deep chair. "How is he? Where is he?"

"Doing quite well," Jake reported. "Stiffed me for the tip."

"Take me to Roy, please. Can you?"

Jake nodded. "Anywhere you want. I'd imagine there's a great deal you want, Charity." He ranged about the large room, turning up lamps here and there. "You haven't changed for hundreds of years, and your sins, such as they are, have not grown in complexity. A moment of yes in a lifetime of thou shalt not. Certain punishment out of a steaming Protestant imagination." He laughed as at an old, familiar joke. "Not that Catholics lack melodrama. In the thirteenth century, they imagined me hanging feet downward from Satan's mouth. Next to Brutus."

"Who?"

"A man with similar questions, similarly resolved."

Nobody in this whole damn place can talk straight, Charity thought restlessly. She couldn't understand a word of Jake although he had his own fascination, quieter—thank goodness— than Dane, who had been exciting as could be, but he could wear you out. Now, Jake was . . . definitely good-looking, even a hunk by back-home standards; not so much the looks but the manner and voice. He reminded Charity of James Mason on the Late Show. Hell might be a strain, she concluded, but you couldn't beat it for the new and different or the interesting men. Not that Jake put himself out to be polite. She wondered if folks were this hard to talk to in heaven.

"Sure is quiet here."

"You object to that?"

"No, no, it's a nice change."

"One can think," Jake mused over the chessboard. "If thought is desirable. For me it was a curse, an obsession, like chess. Always the intellectual yearning to be the man of action. To be, like Brutus, a fulcrum of history. That was denied me until one day when I—acted. I'll never know whether I was right at the wrong time for my own sake or wrong at the right time for the sake of history."

Well, how does a person answer something like that? "Gee, I got good marks in history, but . . ."

"I wouldn't expect you to understand."

His quiet bitterness shriveled Charity. He could be a nice man if he let himself; what would that cost him? This was no way for a man to live, all alone in the dark, even visitors kept at a distance. Dane made her feel woman enough to be a fire hazard, but this Jake, it was like she was wallpaper or something. Not natural. The worst thing in the world, even in hell, was being alone. He didn't notice her. He irritated the living Jesus out of her.

"You don't have to be so mean about it."

Jake waved it away. "Nothing personal. History's full of sink-holes. Today's moral bedrock is tomorrow's quicksand."

He *really* ticked her off, partly for what she couldn't understand, mostly for what she could. Real men like Roy or Clint Eastwood didn't talk so wimpy. "When it comes to morals, right is right and wrong—"

"Is debatable. Don't argue morality or guilt with a Jew. We invented them."

"You don't look Jewish."

"My God, she said it!" Jake's laughter was a dry, wondering bark that had no warmth in it. "She actually said it. You must have been an evangelical."

"Tabernacle of the Born Again Savior," Charity owned with wistful pride. "Not that it helped a whole lot."

"Indeed." Jake sank again in his chair. "Tabernacle of the . . . the more shriveled the existence, the more elaborate the credentials. Virtue measured by what you wouldn't do, at least under scrutiny, and others judged for what they would and got caught at. You don't want Grace, Miss Stovall. You want to get even."

She didn't get that at all. "Get even with what?"

"I'll show you." Jake touched a button on the arm of his chair. Across the room a four-foot screen jumped to life in ravishing color subtly enhanced by soft music.

"This is the ultimate," a deep male voice oozed from the screen. "This is Ultimate Rise. What you've worked for and deserve, and it's waiting for you."

The camera moved over stunning vistas of sunken living rooms in luxurious cream leather, each casual furniture piece worth a fortune. Bedrooms of imperial opulence, kitchens that inspired domesticity and did all the work, cozy dens, conversation pits cunningly designed around fieldstone fireplaces, bathrooms of unbridled hedonism with heart-shaped tubs and frothing Jacuzzis. Charity ogled.

"Where's that? They don't have that in Pittsburgh even."

"I'd say not," Jake remarked with a sideways glance. "I'll bet you never missed *Dynasty* or *Knots Landing*."

"Course not. I even wrote a letter to Alexis telling her what a slut she is."

"But such a rich slut, eh? All that scheming and immorality in the middle of all that wealth. The painful fascination of pressing your cold little nose against the windowpane and deciding that rich is nasty, virtue is just plain folks and the American Way. The envy of the have-nots: Alexis will get what's coming to her, evil will be punished. And you sure as hell want yours. Religion is what you sing on Sunday, Miss Stovall. Your true faith is what you want all week."

"Hey, you make me sick, you know that?" Charity flared, surging out of the chair. "What do you know how hard it is to get anything nice? There was a factory in Plattsville, now there's nothing. Just a mis'rable piddly little town full of people that have to stand outside—that's true, that much, what you said—stand outside looking in at folks no better than us taking the best while we get the leavings.

"What do you know about living on welfare checks or credit run out at the store? Huh? I grew up with not enough; with stepparents because my own was . . . were a couple of God knows what from God knows where. You try that, Jake: nothing to call your own and nowhere to go but down or dead. You watch all the pretty, silky commercials like this one about all the nice things you can buy with the money you'll never have. You try that—"

"Admirable," Jake acknowledged. "At least you've learned to state the problem."

"Don't you laugh at me," Charity seethed. "Don't you laugh at us. All we got in Plattsville, all the rest of you goddamnit *left* us is the kind of God and Jesus Christ we can understand. Look at me! Forget this bullshit movie dress that'd take me six months to buy if I didn't eat or pay rent. Do I look fat? Like I never missed a meal or a trip to the dentist? Last one we had moved out three years ago, couldn't make a living. You get a toothache now, you gotta drive twenty miles. If the car will make it.

"Your kinda people laugh at us for crying in church when we feel like crying all the time. Why shouldn't we want a Jesus with sword and fire? If He's got no sword and fire when He comes, by God, we'll give Him ours. We got lots of that."

"And anger. Envy. Getting even."

He seemed to be goading her. With nothing at hand to throw at him, Charity threw the truth. "Damn right we want to get even. *Everyone else does.*"

Until she heard it, Charity never guessed such a rage lived in her, that rush of deep emotion always prayed and sung out of her in the Tabernacle, cleansed and released until the need built up again. She always thought it was the Holy Spirit. More frightening than that, but damn right she wanted hers. Why not?

Jake moved another piece on the chessboard, considered the consequences, then rose and took his cabby hat from the mantel.

"You sound ready to get some of yours."

"I sure am." Charity clawed at her hair gone frizzy and hopeless from damp. "Between Dane and his poetry and you, gimme a break. I want to find Roy."

Jake escorted her down the hall to the entrance. "No fear, he's doing very well. The Paladins pounced on him the minute he arrived. No different here than on earth. Messiahs are a weekly special."

"Oh. Where can I find him?"

Jake gave her a searching glance. "Why not let him find you? Ultimate Rise just happens to have a vacancy, and I'd say you're entitled to the good life for a change."

Charity remembered that sinful bathtub and the acre-wide living room and was tempted. "Maybe for a little. Just to rest."

"You'll love it," Jake promised. "Fully automatic, live-in butlers, magnificent view. On a clear day you can see Robin Leach. I wouldn't be surprised if they didn't expect you. What's the matter, woman? I'm tempting you to a freebie paradise and you look positively ill."

She did feel sick, cold with a winter thought. "Gol-lee. Jake. All that stuff I said . . ."

"All quite true."

Was that what all my praying was about? "Lord Amighty, no wonder I'm damned."

"No, Miss Stovall. Love and hell are alike in that respect; they are what you bring to them. The script is yours; only the props are furnished." Another keen scrutiny. "And growing always hurts."

Damn, Charity yearned as Jake's cab whisked her away. *Doesn't anybody around here talk straight?*

Drained, quivering with the release of emotion. Not even Roy would guess there was so much mean in her. Or maybe he did.

Was that what got us together, each wanting to get even any way we can and seeing the same thing in the other?

"The weather's better in the high-rise district," Jake tossed over his shoulder as they drove through clammy fog.

"That's nice." Charity sat back with her own thoughts. Strange thoughts with a disturbing familiarity, like ugly cousins met for the first time who resembled her too closely for comfort.

■ 18 ■

This can't be hell, the plumbing works

From the taxi window, Charity goggled up at the splendor of Ultimate Rise. "Now, that is class!"

"As advertised." Jake handed his card over the seat. "Anytime you need a cab."

"I sure will, thanks. You're nice when you don't talk so weird." When Jake came around to open her door, Charity noted the pallor of his face and neck. "You ought to get out more, Jake. Be with folks."

"I've been there."

"It's kind of embarrassing. I can't pay you. Not even a tip."

"On the house. Your new condo, Miss Stovall. Corrupt yourself in good health." Jake slid into the front seat, meshed gears and drove away.

A uniformed doorman spun the revolving doors at just the right speed to receive her smoothly. Across an opulent lobby large as a parking lot, a tailored, obsequious desk clerk held out her keys. "Your duplex, Miss Stovall. Elevators to your right. Welcome to Ultimate Rise."

The elevator whispered open, wafting light, breezy music to

her ears from an old Audrey Hepburn movie. A cool voice inquired: "Floor, please?"

"Uh. Floor." Charity always flustered when singled out for a decision. "I don't know. Do I press a button or something?"

The elevator voice had the sepulchral hush of an undertaker's receptionist. "Floor, please?"

"I don't know," Charity implored the upholstered walls. "What do I do with an elevator that talks?"

"What do I do with a human who can't?" The retort held a nuance of electronic bitchery. "I'm just a machine. Now, at least. I used to be a high-fashion model. Died of drugs, but I did have lovely cheekbones. Name, please?"

"Charity Mae Stovall. From Plattsville."

"Finally. Penthouse duplex," the elevator confirmed. "Going up."

The music breezed and sparkled as the doors swept open on paradise. Charity gasped.

Definitely nothing like it even in Pittsburgh. A white apartment, everything perfect. The parquet foyer led down three steps to a sunken living room wall-to-walled in white carpet. Gleaming chrome-and-glass coffee table topped with oversized art books left at just the right angle. Cream the walls, ivory the grand piano, gossamer the powered silk drapes that slid noiselessly aside to reveal a spacious balcony and, beyond, a breathtaking panorama of fashionable Below Stairs.

"I'm rich." She said it again as the truth sank home. "I'm RICH. Just like in the movies. WOWIE!"

Charity skipped from one vast room to another, wonder treading on wonder's heel. Downstairs alone was big as two houses together. Living room, guest rooms, extra baths, kitchen, pantry, a whole freezer room, more rooms just for the hell of it.

"GOOOINNG UP!" Hiking the velvet skirt, Charity took the spiral designer stairs two at a time to the master bedroom with its emperor-sized water bed covered with an eiderdown and CMS-monogrammed silk sheets in powder blue. The master bath was done in pink.

Charity wallowed and rolled on the water bed like a contented puppy. The quilt hissed gorgeously as it slid against her skin. She paraded in front of the huge mirror and decided that gray velvet looked kind of tacky here, and then yipped with new delight to discover a full dressing room with three full racks of dreamy clothes, all in her size. Charity stepped out of the movie dress into nylon underwear and a soft linen caftan. Mirrored results were edifying. Feeling audacious, she wondered if she could get away without a bra—but no, that was for the liberated city women she disapproved of on principle.

"On second thought, why the hell not?"

Charity hiked up the caftan, popped the bra and let it drop on the carpet. She wasn't a feminist, but the Devil had already liberated the hell out of her at the White Rose Motel, and this was her house, so she could be comfortable without feeling, you know, trashy or common. Besides, she wasn't big enough to be all that floppy without a bra.

Descending the stairs, she felt exotic in caftan and bare feet. The cream leather sofa invited her; she melted into it before a four-foot television wall screen. The remote control was near her hand; one touch blossomed the screen to life, panning slowly across a snowy and familiar interior. Charity's eyes widened.

"That's this place. Mine, right here."

"That's right, Char."

Even the voice was familiar, a nasal London yelp out of the speakers just as she remembered from *Lifestyles of the Rich and Famous.* "This gowerjus condo in the carefully secluded and mowst expensive paht of Below Stairs is the hideaway of glamorous Char Stovall."

She giggled. "You better believe it."

"Char has been the constant companion of Roy Stride, rising young political leaduh."

Gol-lee, where was Roy now? Well, she thought, he won't be hard to find. If he's no worse off than me, he sure ain't hurting.

The screen blushed pink as the picture segued to the lush bathroom with its foaming Jacuzzi. "And it's here," the voice-over brayed enthusiastically, "that Char lives with her new love interest, Randy Colorad."

"Hey. Who?"

"—her every wish fulfilled by her houseman, Simnel."

Charity hugged her knees, wide-eyed. All too much, but *fun.* The camera cut to a beige kitchen where a mild, pudgy little man in livery busied himself twirling a bottle down into an ice bucket. "Wonder what heaven's like."

"Miss Stovall?"

Simnel hovered just behind her, holding a tray with champagne and several small but interesting plates of the stuff called "ordooves." Charity flicked off the TV as he set the tray on the coffee table. "Mr. Colorad called earlier, mum. He should be here directly."

There was a curious blob of something dark on one plate. "What's this?"

"Caviar, mum."

"Oh. Sure. Come to think of it, I ain't had a bite since I got here. Dane said we don't get hungry."

"No, mum," Simnel said pleasantly. "It's one of the advantages. However, you may indulge if you care to. I also took the liberty of chilling an excellent year." He poured the champagne into a tall, shallow glass. "Moët, '76. Shall I prepare the Jacuzzi?"

The champagne tingled delightfully in mouth and nose. *So that's what it tastes like.* And Simnel looked like every butler she ever saw in old Fred Astaire movies. "Yes, indeedy. You may do that thing." Charity flicked the television on again, unable to get enough of it. "Gol-lee."

Simnel watched her with discreet amusement. "Jacob was right."

Another gulp of Moët. "Say what?"

"This is your real religion."

"I don't want to go into that again."

"Excuse me, mum. Merely by way of orientation. Your real religion is what you really want. I'll ready your bath, mum."

He sounded like a stuck-up Englishman or something. She ought to get rid of him and find a good nigger maid that knew how to keep her place.

The champagne made her tingle with well-being. She ordered Simnel to bring the ice bucket and caviar to the bathroom, then trailed upstairs to watch the Jacuzzi churn in readiness for her. Charity slithered out of the caftan and lowered herself bit by luxurious bit into the foaming bath.

"Oh, God, if I wasn't already dead, I could DIE."

The bathroom had its own thirty-inch screen with remote control. Charity swallowed more champagne to wash down the caviar—which she didn't like all that much but it came with the place—and pressed the TV on switch.

There she was, herself, in salmon-pink lounge pajamas, sexy enough to ruin someone's life, right there on TV.

"Oh, man, I look like red-hot Saturday night."

She gulped more Moët and thrilled to her own image on the tube: half reclining on the white leather sofa, one knee drawn up, winsome with a blue teddy bear hugged to her breast.

"The trooly mahvelous thing about Char Stovall," the narrator yelped, "is how she's never forgotten her roots or the people that raised her."

"But I'd sure love to," Charity talked back. "Who the hell wants to remember Plattsville?"

She felt defiant, daring and just a little drunk.

"Here in this fabulous but secret five-million-dollah condo, Char Stovall works constantly to better the lot of the humble folk she comes from. A simple, poignant story, an American rags-to-riches tale of an orphan gel active in the little church in her hometown."

Gorgeous color faded to grainy home-movie black and white with sepia hints of aging: Charity at ten with her adoptive parents, all waving at the camera and looking uncomfortable. Then a shot of Roy sitting with studied nonchalance on the hood of his car, rifle in hand. Woody playing with another local musician—

I really liked you, Woody Barnes, know that? You didn't ask me to be anything but me and I could always sort of take my shoes off with you. One mistake, Woody. One. Am I still a nice girl?

She took larger gulps of champagne, guzzling it like her usual diet cola. Combined with the hot Jacuzzi, the effect relaxed her, made her quickly drunk and not a little maudlin. She wept incoherently over Woody, Roy, herself and the pathetic sight of ten-year-old Charity in a greasy potato-sack shift.

Then realized: "I never wore anything like that."

"Yes, yew did, Char," the narrator prompted. "It goes with the American Dream."

Cut back to silken Char on her divan, cuddling her teddy bear, a close-up that caught all the honesty and wistfulness of her thoroughly American face. "Until I was ten," the screen Char spoke to someone off camera, "I never had any clothes that weren't hand-me-downs. So now I want to write my story as an inspiration for other people and to show that the American Dream is real. Somehow, any way I can, dead or not, I want to go back and help my people."

"You kiss my ass," Charity blurted, dropping her glass in the bath. "I ain't never going back there, never! Damn dead town where there wasn't anything to do but work and pray and pay and get kids."

"Char is a *deeply* religious gel," the voice-over nasaled. "She led the prowtest against the Planned Parenthood clinic ten miles from Plattsville."

"Sure I did." Charity found her glass, rinsed and refilled it. "And I wish I didn't. My best friend got pregnant first time with a boy. What kind of lies you telling?"

"Why, Char," the narrative voice protested, "the truths you've always lived by."

"That ain't the way it was, no way."

Not even close to truth. Bea got pregnant and scared, and the first thing her father did was beat hell out of her because Bea's mother made him. Liars! Charity raged. You goddamn phonies, you weren't thinking of Bea, just how it would look with the neighbors. So Bea married Roland, and when I saw her after, it was like more than the baby got taken out of her. She shouldn't've had that baby, but there wasn't any more clinic even if she could've gone. After all that protest and screaming we did, Roy and the Paladins bombed it in the name of White American motherhood or something. I think Roy did it to impress me.

"Char Stovall, this is your faith. Brought to you by Slick Shave, the blade that starts your day—"

"And can damn well end it any ol' time you get sick of the stupid game." Charity switched off the set in disgust and reached for the white Princess phone.

"Simnel, that you? Listen, how do I get outside? I want to call a friend."

"Sorry, mum. The entire phone system is out for the whole building. We have intercom but nothing outside."

"Oh, fine."

"And Mr. Colorad just arrived. He'll be up in a minute."

Was up already, smiling at her from the bathroom door. "Hi-i, gorgeous."

Charity gazed with bleary appreciation at the muscular young man who stood before her stripping down to a pair of immaculate white briefs. "Hi," she breathed. "I bet your underwear don't even get dirty."

"Not the kind I wear." Randy Colorad winked from the mirror, lathering himself.

"Y'know, Jake's right," Charity mumbled, sinking to her chin in the whirlpool. " 'S my religion. I want. Wanted all my life. That's a main occupation back home. Right, right, right. First offender: think I'd get off with probation, but no-o-o. To hell with *you*, Stovall! And there's Dane with all that fog and poetry and then Jake who jus' sits around feeling sorry for hisself. What the hell's he got to be sorry about?" She smiled foggily at Randy, her mood shifting softly. Talk about ruining somebody's life; he looked like he might enjoy it. "You're a real hunk, y'know that?"

"It's easy with my Slick Shave." Randy flashed thirty-two blinding teeth at her. "I'm smooth all the time."

"C'mon in here and prove it. What the hell, I'm just what the man said. A simple down-home girl living the American Dream."

"Love to." Randy slipped out of his briefs and into the whirlpool. Charity snuggled up to him.

"Already been damned," she murmured woozily, "and I got change coming."

■ 19 ■

Money can't buy happiness, but why not be miserable in comfort?

Charity opened her eyes to sunlight and strange sounds. Feeling delicious, she yawned and squirmed contentedly between the blue silk sheets. Hell could be a lot worse.

A series of grunts issued from an angle of the bedroom beyond her vision. She turned over to see Randy Colorad laboring with a Nautilus weight machine like a guillotine, muscles rippling, glistening with sweat.

"Twenty-three—*huh*. Twenty-four—*agh*. Twenty-*fi-i-ve*—URKK!"

"For God's sake, you'll rupture something!"

"When the going gets tough . . ." A last herculean effort. Randy lowered the weights and sat up, favoring Charity with a charming smile, no tooth uncapped. He sprang up, beautiful above the neck and all a girl could wish below. "Now for that morning shower that gives all-day protection."

Charity draped herself on one elbow, feeling sultry. "Hurry back."

Randy came out of the shower carrying a spray deodorant.

"Here." He slipped under the sheets. "It's strong enough for me but made for you."

"So are you." Charity attacked him joyfully.

The ensuing two hours demonstrated that she really ought to work out more herself. In the bookstore back home, voyeuristic peeks into *The Joy of Sex* (when nobody was looking) dazzled her with possibilities that seemed languorous only in theory. In practice they required a certain facility and a great deal of limberness. Silk sheets were great to dream about but always slidey when you needed four-wheel traction, and the damn water mattress made her almost seasick, zigging when it should zag. Nevertheless, her climaxes were symphonic. She never thought she was that kind of girl; now she knew there wasn't any other.

In the brief respites between onslaughts, by way of critique Charity could wish now and then for the poetry that turned Dane's passion tender (God, he could suffer!) and even once, in an athletic moment, for the pungent honesty of Jake. She closed her eyes over Randy's shoulder and thought of him. That helped her get there, but it was Woody's face she saw at the end. That was strange; she felt treacherous and terribly fallen. Anyway, Randy never said anything she hadn't heard on TV before.

When she was gasping with surfeit and yearning seriously for a little rest, Randy bounced out of bed with the same energy that propelled him into it.

"Hey, kid." The white smile flashed like a bathroom light at 4 A.M. "Gotta go to work. Got a shoot later."

Charity picked up on that much from TV. "You in a movie?"

"No." Randy flexed his shoulders and trotted into the bathroom. "Gotta shoot someone. But first—that all-day protection again with a man's kind of soap."

"You just took a shower."

"Yeah, but then we screwed for a while."

"Don't talk dirty. All that washing's not good for your skin."

From the depths of the thundering shower: "I'm Beautiful People!"

"Yeah, but are you gonna itch." Charity yawned. "Idiot."

With the detachment of a definitely slaked thirst, she watched with decreasing interest as Randy trotted out of the bathroom in pale blue one-piece underwear, slipped into slacks and a Members Only jacket and placed his Foster Grants with the care of a coronation. Again the measured, roguish grin. "See you later."

"Sure. It was real nice."

"That's what friends are for." Another devilish grin and Randy was gone. Charity drowsed a while before plumping the pillows to sit up against. She touched the call button, only to find Simnel in the doorway.

"You rang, mum?"

"Breakfast would be nice. Not that I'm hungry but, you know, a change. Oh, how about the phone?"

"Still out, I'm afraid. They are working on it."

"Honest to Pete, you'd think once a girl dies she wouldn't have to hassle stuff like this."

"No, mum. The upwardly mobile concept is a Christian notion. We have our problems." The mild little butler withdrew.

"Even dead the phone company gets you." Charity turned on the wall TV, quickly adjusting the volume as the fifty-inch screen roared to furious life across the bedroom.

"—can feel that these are indeed the last days of a dying regime. Here in the teeming downtown streets, a drama is being enacted, one that may be fraught with significance for Below Stairs tomorrow—indeed, may be that tomorrow."

Music up with telegraphic urgency as the news continued with voice-over. A street, soldiers in White Paladin fatigues and swastika armbands straining to hold back the screaming crowds.

"We're here in the main thoroughfare, which you can see is packed with the largest crowd since the arrival of Lord Byron. In a moment—yes, here they come!—in a moment we'll see the massed demonstration and its dynamic new leader, Roy Stride. This demonstration follows by less than twenty-four hours the threat of a raid on black and Jewish homes by Paladin squads. The government's failure to make any effective answer to this threat may be seen as a death rattle. There's our camera truck."

The open truck came into shot and passed beyond; as it did, the view on Charity's set cut to a dolly from the truck itself. She sat bolt upright. "Hey-y."

There was Roy striding along in precise step with the ranks of Paladins behind him, head high, confident and flushed, the star of his own drama at last.

"Roy!" Charity bounced up and down with delight. "Roy!"
ROY! STRIDE! ROY! STRIDE! ROY! STRIDE!

". . . and here he comes. Roy Stride, the youngest political
contender in the long history of Below Stairs. An American from
the Heartland, the first candidate to be endorsed by the Prince
and Topside alike. Even as we speak, the messengers from Topside are said to be on their way with formal ratification."

"Gol-lee, Roy." Charity melted back on her pillow. "Even angels. Oh, wow!"

"We're trying to reach Judas Iscariot for comment," the telereporter informed her. "The most reclusive of all Below Stairs
citizens, Judas has always been distrusted by the popular vote,
particularly the Christian Identity groups and the Paladins, who
consider him a dangerous adversary. Certainly he has never allied himself with any party."

"Well, he shouldn't." Charity put the TV on hold as Simnel
entered with a bed tray bearing champagne, coffee, strawberries
and whipped cream, setting it across her with a flourish.

"Strawberry Decadence, mum. One of my specialties."

"Super." Charity dipped a plump berry in the mound of
whipped cream and munched it. "Mmm . . . Do you know Judas?"

"Quite well," Simnel said.

"No, I mean the man who—"

"I'm familiar with the case." Simnel poured her coffee. "Very
good company, Judas. Sharp mind. Mean chess player."

Charity frowned over her coffee. "You could like a person like
that?"

"One man's meat, you know. There are celebrities I avoid out
of self-preservation. Beethoven, for example. The personality of
a chain saw. Yes, I like Judas for an evening's chat now and then.
When he condescends. Not very gregarious."

Charity turned on the TV again. The same reporter had just
poked his microphone in the face of a clearly disinterested man
leaning against a car door, cigarette dangling from lips curled
with an ancient, bitter joke. As the camera went to close-up,
Charity choked on a swallow of champagne.

"That's Jake," she wheezed after a coughing spasm. "I know
that guy. Honest, he drove me here in his cab."

"Best service in town," said the imperturbable Simnel. "More coffee, mum?"

"We're here with Judas Iscariot on the fringe of the delirious demonstration for Roy Stride. Judas, can you comment on the meteoric rise of Stride and the White Paladins?"

Judas reached through the cab window and fetched his cap. "I'd say the hopeless shmucks have found the kind of government they deserve. Always do."

The reporter pressed for more. "And his rapid rise?"

"So *nu?*" Judas shrugged. "He's taking their own fear, frustration and anger and selling it back to them with a new ribbon around it. Easy answers, easy targets: out with the Jews and blacks, down with the intellectuals, which means anyone who's better off or disagrees with them. Slogans, marching bands and the promise of blood. How can he miss?" Judas flicked away his cigarette and opened the cab door. "Buzz off, I've got a call."

Still the reporter persisted. "Could your views be construed as a class-oriented remark?"

"Look, these clowns need a messiah because the truth of the world always goes down easier with a few miracles and a lot of blood. It's a very old game, the rules don't change. I'd say Stride is a flaming, fourteen-karat folk hero. Look at this crowd; you're not talking about contented, mature people. You ever see a happy man who needed to conquer the world?"

Judas/Jake got into the cab and drove out of shot.

"So that's the evilest man in the whole world ever." Charity pondered the screen. She dunked a strawberry in champagne. "Talks mean about folks."

"With considerable authority," Simnel said. "A true believer at one time who would do anything to make need into truth. Now he watches the rest of them doing the same thing over and over again one way or another."

"He talked like he was real angry, only just at himself, you know? Funny"—Charity considered it—"I couldn't hate Jake."

Charity missed Simnel's approving glance. "No, mum. He does that for himself."

"Well, I'm real happy for Roy. I guess. This is a neat breakfast. Can you make eggs like McDonald's?"

"There is no such franchise here yet," Simnel informed her coolly. "Though I'm sure Mr. Stride will insist on one. As Judas remarked, a ray of hope to the benighted. Good morning, mum."

The late, late show

Charity woke in the dark. Randy wasn't beside her in the bed; that didn't bother her at all. Outside of sex, he wasn't much company. Everything he said sounded like a commercial.

Just . . . she felt creepy and more alone than she ever had since dying. She rang Simnel and heard only the quiet intermittent buzz. Randy gone, Simnel out. She was alone and couldn't sleep. She tried the outside phone: nothing, still out of order. From habit, she reached for the TV remote and turned on the wall set.

The screen sprayed garish color and flickering shadows over the dark bedroom, resolving to a night scene with a telereporter's voice-over—

"—just an hour ago the peace of these black and Jewish homes in a quiet neighborhood of Below Stairs was shattered by devastating White Paladin raids led personally by Roy Stride, new head of the Paladin party."

Cut to Roy himself standing in an open car, leather-coated, whip in hand, black peaked cap perched at a cocky angle, and—

Cut to a black family being dragged from their front door by huge Paladin guards. Husband, wife, three children being hustled ungently toward a waiting van. When the father broke away and resisted, one guard simply shot him. The action was brutally graphic: two guards slammed the man up against the van and a third opened fire with a submachine gun. The gunfire went on and on, his body disintegrating in sharp detail and color.

"No . . ." Charity recoiled from the scene, tried to change channels. They were all the same but someone was playing tricks with the camera. The black man fell and fell with his head coming apart—and then Roy again, standing in the open car. He turned to Charity as the camera came in close, and looked directly at her, found her, his mouth twisted in a smirk of macho triumph and pride.

"Hey, Charity, that you? Where are you? Look: I told you how it would be."

And once more the scene cut to another home, smoke and flame spurting from a shattered window, Paladins sprinting out of the front door. A man and woman lay crumpled on the front steps. The camera zoomed in on them. It looked to Charity as if someone had cut every artery in their bodies. *You wouldn't think there was that much blood in just two bodies.*

"The general feeling in the political air," the telereporter's voice-over went on dispassionately, "is that these raids have the tacit assent of the White Christian populace."

"Who said?" Charity blurted. *"I didn't."*

"—certainly no government troops or police have made any move to intervene, as though quietly allowing political force of gravity to take its course. This act is seen by some as a definite referendum. It is increasingly clear that the confidence of Below Stairs at large is with Roy Stride's party rather than the Wembley administration."

Only half listening, Charity couldn't take her eyes from the bodies. *Dummies,* she thought. *They look like doll-dummies sprayed with red paint.*

"Charity!"

Roy again in huge close-up with that twisted grin. "Where are you? I told you how it would be."

"NO!"

She jabbed desperately at the remote control but each channel was the same, not even a lag in the film.

"Simnel-l!"

"—how it would be."

Charity screamed silently at the vicious grin on the screen. *No, I didn't believe you. I didn't believe it would be like this—*

—as the camera caught a little girl darting around the corner of the house, shrieking in terror. She turned to see the Paladin guard trotting after her, not even hurrying. The child ran blindly to the natural place, the bleeding sack of offal that had been her mother, screaming for help.

"My God," Charity writhed. "Don't hurt her. She's just a baby. Don't."

The Paladin guard loomed over the tiny child as the camera came in tight on them—

"These Jewish homes were the first target," the voice-over stated with no emotional color. "The black homes were hit a few minutes later in an apparently coordinated attack."

Something was happening to the film. Somehow it went to slow motion as it focused tight on the face of the blond, blue-eyed child. Hypnotized with horror, Charity let the irrelevant thought skitter through her mind—*I didn't think Jews could be blond.* But they could; she'd seen plenty that weren't anywhere near the picture conjured up when somebody said Jew. She'd just never connected images, never thought beyond the stock picture. This little girl was very fair and—

Very familiar. More than familiar.

"Jesus, that's—"

The child was *her* at age ten. She remembered the picture her new parents took when they adopted her, before her hair darkened to brown. But undeniably her in the picture, screaming for help from her dead mother.

And then not screaming at all.

The child looked up at the guard, mute. The only sound came from Charity herself, a wordless whine of empathic terror as the Paladin pointed his pistol at the tiny face. Her own child face but changed forever. More than horror in those wide eyes, a terrible knowledge that there was no help anywhere, no pity or escape. For those few slow-motion seconds, the child was not mad but her eyes knew madness, swallowed it whole and recognized it as the truth of existence. Knew it as her head disintegrated and spattered blood and brains over the twisted flesh bag of her mother, and—

Charity wanted to be sick and couldn't. You couldn't be sick after death, but the nausea rolled through her stomach, all the more exquisite torture since she couldn't even retch with it. She fled the bedroom to splash her face with cold water, but the bathroom screen was on as well—the same film repeating and repeating—Roy standing in the car, the camera zooming in on that dirty, mean grin of his that she hated—*always hated it. Why didn't I ever realize then?*

"—are you? Look! I told you how it would be."

For the first time in her life, Charity Stovall snarled. "You get away from me. YOU GET AWAY FROM ME, YOU . . . SIM-NEL-L-L—"

She ran out of the bathroom and stumbled downstairs. As she hit the bottom step, all the screens went on—kitchen, living room, guest rooms; a repeating loop, the child running to the butchered sack of her mother, screaming in slow motion, then not screaming but looking up with Charity's own eyes at the pistol barrel with that obscene knowledge in her eyes.

"—told you how it would be."

"Stop. *Stop,* you son of a bitch."

"—how it would be."

Her instinct was to bury herself deep in the pillows of the sofa, blot out the sight and sound, but as the loop repeated, shorter and shorter now—Roy's leer, the words, her own eyes staring not at death but a sudden understanding of life—something else began to counterbalance the horror in Charity Stovall. The fruitless nausea passed, replaced by a wholly alien emotion more powerful than she'd ever felt. Detached, from a long distance, she turned her gaze back to the screen, to Roy's gloating face and swaggering words, and the nightmare of her own violent child death.

That's me could be me is me . . .

"—told you how it would be."

Yes, you did, she thought, watching the screen from the depths of an icy calm. You sure as hell did, and I heard it and didn't think about it.

Faster and faster the loop ran: Charity at ten, screaming, then no voice left to scream, only her own eyes lifting to the gun, knowing what a child shouldn't have to know but so many did and had and would.

"—told you how it would be."

Scream. Silence. Look up. Knowing.

Until at last the film froze on the eyes and their final recognition of horror. The child, with one second, one century or an infinity to exist, would never again look on anything or anyone unshadowed by that terrible knowledge.

Obscene . . . I never used that word, always thought it meant dirty movies. But this is obscene. I could scream from now until the end of time, every dirty word I ever knew, they wouldn't be as obscene or dirty as this. Not that you kill a child, but that you could put such a knowledge into her.

Now she knew the passion churning in her: rage—not from any wound to her but simply that humans could do that to children, take the brief innocence and stain it forever with the knowledge that there was no safe place anywhere ever. Forever or for a few seconds, children shouldn't know that much about the world.

The gun didn't kill her. She was dead when she looked up at him. Like some old people in Plattsville who came from Europe after we beat Germany. You could see that shadow of a gun barrel all their lives.

No music, love or joy would leach that shadow from the little girl's eyes.

"—told you how it would be."

"Damn straight you told me," Charity lashed back. "You murdering piece of shit, I should've seen you coming. But I'm glad, Roy. Glad I'm dead; that's cleaner than being alive with you. You better hope you never meet up with Jesus. He's sure as hell not gonna like the way you use His name. I'm afraid of you, Roy. And I think you like that."

Trembling, near-traumatized by the force of her own rage, Charity didn't notice Simnel switching off the set or the silence that followed.

"Can't sleep, mum?"

"Where were you?" Charity mumbled in a voice with no life in it. "I called and called but you weren't here."

"Sometimes I go for a walk in the wee hours."

"Do you know what I just saw?"

"The purges? Yes, I was there. You can see the fires burning from the balcony."

"No, Simnel. I don't want to."

"The government conveniently did nothing to stop them. No one did."

"No one?" Charity whispered, still trembling. "Not one person? Did you see what they were doing?"

"Yes, of course," said mild little Simnel. "I expect things will change at Congress Hall. The government won't last. Not to worry; none of this will touch us in Ultimate Rise. Shall I fix some hot cocoa, mum?"

"It's already touched me," Charity muttered. "I feel dirty just watching that."

"The postmoderns would call you sentimental," Simnel observed. "Trying to encompass inhuman behavior with human sensibility."

"Dirty . . . They ain't fixed the phones yet?"

"No, mum."

That was good, that gave her time to think. "Simnel, I don't live here. Just like before, you never heard of me."

"Charity who?"

"Right. Good night, Simnel."

"Good morning, mum."

Charity tried to climb the stairs. All of sudden there were too many of them. "Oh, Simmy—Jesus!" She slumped down on the steps. "Even . . . even dead, how can they do this to people? To children?"

She felt a hundred years old, too utterly spent to climb the rest of the stairs. Like a child herself, she allowed Simnel to guide her upward, his wise, gentle voice close to her ear though she didn't understand any of what he was telling her. Something about a tiny animal who developed in the dark while bigger animals ruled the day. A funny little thing with big eyes and fur and fear, born looking over its shoulder for danger, and out of this twitching bundle of need and terror came humans never to be wholly free of the dark or their own nightmares.

When Simnel tucked her in like a tender parent, Charity saw a wisdom in his eyes older than mountains, and a pity beyond tears.

■ 21 ■

Doing the Reichstag rag

The Case White takeover had been accomplished without a shot fired. Roy might have relished at least a little shooting after his bold blood-purge raids, but the Wembley wimps gave in to the will of the people. That will was a steady roar as Roy's armored Cadillac inched through the Paladin-lined streets toward Government Square and drew up before the marble steps of Congress Hall. The armored car carrying his personal guard slowed in his wake.

"We're the fuckin Congress now," Roy smirked to Drumm beside him. "Gonna be some changes."

"Don't lean out too far," Drumm cautioned. "There's a possibility of snipers."

"Hey, yeah." Roy ducked back inside. They waited until the police and hulking Paladin security guards shouldered and heaved the screaming crowd back from the cars to clear a path up the steps.

"Okay, let's go." Roy stepped out of the car and stood a moment as the crowd caught sight of him and loosed a roar of delirious excitement.

Roy! Stride! Roy! Stride!

He basked in the sound like sunlight after long winter. It

warmed and sufficed him. All they had to do was follow his word
and Below Stairs would be their kind of paradise. A new order,
rough on some, but you couldn't fry eggs without breaking shells,
he thought in a flush of originality. Impulsively, Roy flung up his
right hand with the whip. The screaming cut like edited tape.
The crowd hovered, quivering, for his words.

"We been down! Going UP!"

The mob roared like maddened animals. GOING UP!

"Damn right," Roy muttered to Drumm as they mounted the
steps inside a cordon of armed Paladins. "They waiting for us?"

"Shaking in their boots," Drumm assured him. "Ready to agree
to anything."

Looked that way: the guards at the door stood to nervous
attention when Roy passed. They were pointedly unarmed and
looked anxious to leave. Roy's entourage commandeered two
elevators to the executive floor, alighted and formed again, the
guards flanking Roy and Drumm. Roy took a moment to
straighten his tunic and hat, tug at the holstered Lüger. "Let's go.
Short and sweet."

Their jackboots rang in unison down the marble hall.

"Here." Drumm halted before open double doors. Roy felt
disappointed; he'd hoped the guards could kick them in. The first
four guards swept into the chamber, weapons at the ready. One
of them nodded to Drumm, who stood aside for Roy. "After you,
my Leader."

Roy stalked into the executive chamber. The guards' precau-
tion was hardly necessary. A small elderly man huddled behind a
large, ornate desk, head in his hands. Next to him stood another
man, somewhat younger and much more vital, quiet defiance
flashing in his eyes. This was the one who might be trouble, Roy
decided. Looked like a smart-ass college boy lieutenant always
used to hard-ass him in the Air Force, always thought he was
better than anybody.

Drumm strutted to the desk, a parody of protocol. "Leader
Stride, may I present the former president, Ronald Wembley.
And"—a studiedly contemptuous glance at the distinguished
man at the president's side—"the former prime minister, Jason
Blythe."

"The papers are executed," Wembley began in a haggard

voice. "The transfer of power is complete. For the people's sake, I ask—"

"You're in my chair," Roy cut him short. "Move it, Wimpley." A nod to the guards: two of them hauled Wembley out of the leather chair and pushed him to one side.

"What the fuck would you know about the people, Wimp?"

"The president's name is Wembley," Blythe snapped.

Drumm spun on him, vibrant with malice. "You shut your mouth. You had your say a long time, Blythe. From here on, it's ours."

"And what price the Leader's loyal right hand?" Blythe posed the acid question. "His own theater? Perhaps a decent toupee?"

"Hey." Roy pointed at Blythe. "You got something personal against my minister?"

"No more than against the spread of roaches," Blythe retorted. "Mr. Drumm is a former clerk from this office with a habit of opening private mail."

"The right mail at the right time," Drumm admitted with malicious satisfaction. "That's how I learned of your personal vendetta against my plays."

Blythe seemed to find that amusing. "Plays? Ah, yes—*More Stories from the Toilet Zone.* The smaller the man, the larger his power fantasies. Mr. Stride, I would prefer to be liquidated now, if you please."

Roy had to grin at the guy's balls. "What, you crazy?"

"No. Just tasteful."

"Mr. Stride, if I may." Wembley approached tentatively; the guards moved to intervene but Roy waved them away. "I wanted to say for the people that you must be sensitive to their greater needs."

"Cut the shit, Wimp. What do you think I'm doing? Hear them out there? I *am* the people."

"Yes." Beyond the weariness and defeat, Wembley's tone was faintly ironic. "I should like to retire now."

Roy laughed at him. The poor old bastard looked pathetic. "Sure, go ahead."

Drumm drew himself up as far as five foot four could manage and ran the back of one gloved hand across his mouth. "Guard, let the old gentleman go home."

"But not him." Roy jerked a thumb at Blythe. "I don't like his fuckin mouth. Take him to solitary."

Blythe was marched out after Wembley. Drumm held the executive chair for Roy. "Sir?"

Roy went to the chair as a king to coronation, settled in it, spreading his hands over the polished desk top. "That Blythe is a smart-ass. Sit on him."

The small dead oysters behind Drumm's thick glasses registered their closest to pleasure, momentarily less cold. "Done, Leader."

"I'll count on that." Roy couldn't like Drumm, no one really could, but he was loyal to the point of adoration and very efficient. "So you wrote horny plays, huh?"

"I wrote truth. Only leftist liberal hypocrites called them pornographic."

"Yeah, well now you're in the top ten, maybe you can have your own the-ayter."

"Thank you, sir." Drumm clicked his heels. He did it so well that Roy glared around at the guards, who looked too damned casual. "Nobody gave you at ease! Hit it!"

They jerked to rigid attention.

"That's better." Roy lifted his booted feet onto the desk. "I used to be enlisted myself. Discipline's the backbone of any outfit. When I say jump, you jump. When I say shit, you squat and strain, got it? Okay. At ease. Drumm!"

Click! "Leader?"

"Something missing in here. Yeah. Take down Wimp's picture. I want one of me, like an oil painting, you got it? And bigger."

Ever resourceful, Drumm knew just the artist to execute the commission, one who'd done covers for barbarian fantasy novels.

"Ri-i-ght." Roy glowed, hands behind his head. "Somebody who can draw guys with balls and women that look like women. Which reminds me. How about—" Roy broke off and glared at the guards. "Hit it!"

Clack!

"Dismissed. But wait outside."

Alone with Drumm, Roy became confidential, almost friendly. "You know how it is with a real man. Got certain needs, but he knows what's right. That's what bugs me about that Blythe.

Smart-ass fuckers like him think we're dirt, don't know shit about good manners or what's the right thing to do. I know what the people expect from me that way. The hell I ain't a gennelman. I'm gonna get married to Charity Stovall soon's you find her, and you do that real quick, you got it? Gonna do the right thing by her. Where's Florence?"

Drumm didn't smile at the revealing non sequitur. "Watched over, sir."

"Give Florence her own house, all the beer she wants. But out of the way, you know what I mean?"

Drumm knew. "A discreet location."

Roy chucked the little man under one of his chins with the whip. "Discreet and close."

"May I suggest Blythe's former accommodations? Lovely house, very secluded."

"Right on. I like that." Roy snickered, swinging his boots off the desk. He swaggered about the chamber, hands on his hips. Perfect, sure enough. He peered out from the curtained double windows at the crowd seething beyond the balcony. The sight was more than beautiful; he felt like crying. He couldn't tell what his feelings were, but there was the purest joy he'd ever felt and still an unslaked rage at people like Blythe who looked down on him. He needed respectability. He *was* respectable, otherwise he wouldn't trouble to marry Charity, who was the right kind of girl. What else he needed on the side, like Florence—well, that was private, no need to flaunt it. And those people out there waiting for him, he needed them too.

Trouble is, you don't know who your enemies are. You gotta watch everyone.

But while they screamed for him, Roy knew what to do. What he'd dreamed of.

Going to show you people the truth of the world. What you always want. Like the raids which they did exactly what you didn't have the balls for, and you are going to love me for it, because I am the goddamned people. Love me!

"Get the guards back in here," he ordered, not taking his eyes from the milling thousands beyond the window. "Time to let them see me."

■ 22 ■

The rewards of faith and
their avoidance

Streaking through limbo with Milt Kahane, Woody Barnes marveled at the black, bright, star-winking universe around him. "Man, you really get a different picture from up here."

"Very impressive," Milt agreed. "No view like it, although the Hudson Valley comes close. The whole thing is a helluva show, Barnes. Being alive, being at all. That's what this gig is all about. Remember your trumpet voluntaries from practice?"

They shot through gaseous clouds, played tag with asteroid belts, hitched a short ride on *Voyager 1* snail-pacing past the orbit of Pluto. The frail little contraption looked lonely but familiar to Woody. Milt hurried him on.

"It'll get shmutz all over the costume. Come on, we're late." With the whoop of a raucous diver, Milt kicked off from *Voyager* and whizzed on, Woody close behind. "Everyone wants a reward, especially shmucks like Roy. What do you want?"

"Never thought much about it," Woody reflected. "At least, not until they zapped Charity. Enough gigs to pay the rent, I guess. Chance to play with some good sidemen. Get married."

"Like Charity?"

"No, she's all hung up on Roy. I never said anything to her anyway."

"Wouldn't've done any good," Milt was sure. "Love is a matter of when."

A sudden, nearby nova turned the universe blinding white.

"Wheeee! Feel the breeze! You know the worst thing in the world, Woody? Getting what you thought you wanted. Never looks as good on you as in the store. Take that mother who fragged us in Beirut. He got zapped the same day and came Topside looking for Mohammed and Allah, the whole shmeer. The Boss really has trouble with Moslems, and this dipstick was a Shiite, sort of an Islamic Fundamentalist. They don't even like other Moslems."

But there were great fringe benefits. As Milt explained it, radical Moslems had an ancient but precise idea of heavenly reward for defenders of the faith.

"Houris: sort of super Arab hookers. These guys believe they get an eternal shtup with orgasms that last a thousand years. Sexual Valhalla."

Woody considered the prospect. "Not only couldn't I stand it—hell, I'd get bored."

"That's the point, but (a) you're not dumb and (b) you're not a fanatic. If these clowns had any smarts, they'd be raising poppies or selling rugs."

Milt did a graceful loop and figure eight, waving his trumpet at eternity. "The Boss gives Dipstick his houri just to get rid of him. Not a real houri: actually she'd been a waitress in Newark who belly-danced on weekends. But sexy? You could get seasick watching her navel. So she goes in, she told me, and this turkey gets it on after a lot of bullshit about the infidels he scored, meaning you and me, and he cranks up on paradise."

As Milt had it from the part-time houri, when paradise arrived as advertised, with no sign of cessation, the Shiite felt it was really worth dying for. Gibbering with faith and gratitude, he labored to redeem his spiritual green stamps. Ten minutes into his thousand years, he wondered if the Koran mentioned anything about a break now and then. After twenty minutes he was ready for Sundays off.

"What the hell, the Thousand-Year Reich only made the first

twelve," Milt observed. "So—half an hour and he throws in the towel. Totaled, sick at heart. In tears, yet. The dangers of literal belief: what's eternal reward when there's nothing left to want, right? So the Boss sits him down—believe me, he had to sit down —to find out what he really wanted to do. Which was all uphill, because I met this clown and he had the IQ of a Venetian blind; even Arabs had trouble getting through to him. That's why they put him in that window alone and told him carefully who to waste and who not, hoping Dipstick would remember some of it.

"Anyway, the Boss finally gets out of him that he was a baker, a whiz on baklava. He gives him the last known address on Mohammed, and off goes the Lion of Islam to find the place—which turns out to be in Greenwich Village. So now he's the patron spirit of a falafel hut on Macdougal Street, inspiring the best Middle Eastern desserts in town, happy as a clam. There we go! Hang a right, Barnes."

Woody dove after Milt toward a tiny point of light from whence came a growing roar of human frenzy. "Must be Roy's crowd whooping it up."

Milt listened as they drew closer. "That's them. Can't use your mute this gig. Subtle is not in. These turkeys are all Venetian blinds."

"Roy wasn't too dumb, I guess. He was always reading."

"Yeah?" When Milt turned to glance at Woody, he looked rather like Jake. "Who do you think I've been talking about? Arabs?"

They swooped toward the distant point of light that became a city, a street, a screaming crowd. A high balcony . . .

■ 23 ■

The clear vistas of paranoia

Drumm at his shoulder, Roy ogled the crowd below like an orphan given a birthday party.

"Microphones ready, sir."

"Listen, what about Topside?" The memory was all too recent for Roy. "I seen God close up and He ain't no wimp. He could really fuck us up."

"Hardly." Drumm seemed unconcerned. "Topside is not all God, just as Britain was not all Churchill. Topside has always observed strict neutrality where Below Stairs is concerned; not to mention the vast numbers of them in open or secret sympathy with the Cause. The rest don't want trouble, which is fine until we're ready to enlarge our ambitions. Their emissaries will put in an appearance today as promised. Listen to your people, Leader: *there* is reality. You are eternal. Be Brutus. Seize the time. Below Stairs is ours today." Drumm let the seductive implication hover at Roy's ear. "Tomorrow . . . ?"

Tomorrow Topside. Roy thrilled to the first frisson of invincibility. Heaven and hell all his for all time, bought and paid for with a heart attack. *Jesus, too fuckin much. Like he says, seize the time.* "Okay. Guards out first. Let's go."

At Drumm's order, the guards, vigilant mastiffs, filed in and through the balcony doors. As Roy Stride stepped onto the balcony, the roar burst from the crowd like a single crazed animal. He raised his arms, asking for silence but content to let the storm of frenzied triumph roll over him forever. Drumm waited at the other microphone until he could be heard.

"The Wembley government has stepped down." Another wave of delirium, which Drumm stayed with an upraised hand. "A worn-out garment discarded by a healthy body."

Pandemonium. Roy felt close to tears.

"A new day! Topside itself has agreed to a non-aggression pact following the Leader's assurance that, with this assumption of power, he has no larger political demands. We ARE the future!"

Again the energy exploded from thousands of upturned throats. ROY! STRIDE! ROY! STRIDE! ROY! STRIDE!

"We expect momentarily the emissaries of Topside to ratify our assumption of rule," Drumm told them. "Of our destiny!"

STRIDE! STRIDE! STRIDE!

Arms lifted, Roy beamed down upon his destiny. *You motherfuckers are gonna kiss my ass and love me for it.*

"Liberated Aryans of Below Stairs"—Drumm drew out the vowels in a stentorian voice—"greet the morning of your own new day!"

Hysteria again as Drumm stepped away from his microphone and saluted Roy Stride. Roy waited full minutes until the screaming went ragged from collective exhaustion and subsided to the tense, murmurous anticipation of a single beast straining to be unleashed.

"WE BEEN DOWN!" Roy boomed over the expectant acres of them. "GOING UP!"

The roar from them was music to his ear as he raised his fist in what was to be a new salute—knuckles not forward as with the radicals of the '60s and '70s, but turned in naturally, fist ready to fall like an avenging hammer. He found he didn't have to think of the words, they simply came to him. "They always laughed at us, right? We were the trash, the rednecks, the clowns at the back door of their yuppie paradise. And every four years they promised us whatever we wanted just so's we'd vote. Sure they did—while the farms got sold and the factories closed down. They did everything but listen, right? Well, they'll listen *now.*"

STRIDE! STRIDE! STRIDE!

He found his rhythm, learned from Purdy Simco. "Hallelujah, a new day come! They don't write the word of truth, we do. From now on, they don't speak for the White Christian American Way, *we* do. That's for us. By God and all that's holy—"

In nearby limbo, Milt Kahane nudged Woody. "That's our cue. Let's give him the shtick."

Trumpet ready, wig straight and lines learned, Woody Barnes still marveled at the monumental travesty of what he saw. "If this was on TV, I'd turn it off."

"You might." Milt worked the spit valve on his polished instrument. "They won't. Look at those clowns: are they laughing? Myth is in, kid. And . . . go!"

Strauss or Berlioz would have wept for sheer musical ecstasy. The effect was staggering. Over pedal tones deep as from the organ at the heart of the world, a great celestial chord of massed brass blared in a symphonic hosanna as two columns of dazzling light appeared above the balcony and resolved to white-gowned, Aryan-blond angels who lifted their trumpets in an electrifying fiat to the stunned crowd.

"Topside and the ranks of heaven, the halls of ultimate truth and justice, proclaim and ratify the sovereignty of Roy Stride Below Stairs."

"Second in sway only to the Prince himself," the second angel declared in a marked New York accent.

Another riff from the first angel, curled about the edges by a subtle drawling style. The trumpet came down smoothly to rest on his hip. "For unto the chosen people is come a chosen Leader. All hail to the people of Below Stairs and the Leader they have so long deserved." He nodded to his gossamer-robed companion, sotto voce: "Hit it, Milt."

Blazing in the light, the two trumpets lifted in a stirring voluntary. One broke off while the other slid up into a high-flirting riff—

—that bolted Charity straight up in bed. The face she'd recognized for one moment under that silly blond wig was unmistakable. The music was like *Star Wars*, but only one guy in the whole world blew a horn that way.

Cut to a close-up on the angel.

"WOODY!"

He peered out of the screen, surprised and delighted. "Char! Hey, this is a real kick, ain't it?"

"I didn't know you were dead, Woody."

"Came as a complete shock to me, too."

"What's the wig for?" Charity wondered. "Not like you at all."

"These people dig blonds. They're Aryans or something."

"Woody, we're Aryans."

"No fooling?" Woody considered it. "Didn't get us much, did it?"

"Not much." Charity chilled with the memory of Roy's blood raids that brought him to that balcony. "Don't let on you see me, okay?"

"Okay." Woody peered into the bedroom. "Great place you got there."

Charity hiked the sheet higher around her cleavage, grateful that Randy Colorad was out. He wanted to make love all the time. That was okay at first, but lately she'd taken to watching television over his shoulder because even the commercials were more interesting. Him and his exercise machine and his twenty-four-hour freshness soap. Nothing was fresh about Randy; even his sweat was boring. She'd always thought someone glamorous like that—

No. She *never* thought, that was the problem. In her whole dumb-ass life she never thought for one minute. About anything, goddamnit, pardon her lang—no, the hell with that. Don't pardon anything. Dumb-ass. Had to *see* what Roy was before she caught on. Had to die to realize what she'd missed in Woody Barnes.

"I'm sorry you're dead, but it's nice to have friends around. I mean—oh, damn, Woody, I miss you."

"I miss you too," he confessed. "Only hung around the Tabernacle because you were there. Too late now, I guess."

"I wish it wasn't," she yearned.

"I never had anything to give you. And you were always for Roy."

"That's over." The finality of the sound surprised Charity.

"Well, look at him now," Woody glanced out of shot. "He's got it all now."

Yeah, Roy and me, we got it all. Our real religion, like Jake said. I guess he should know. "One thing you can do real good here is learn, Woody. When you get Topside again, you tell them I've seen the pits, and they were smart to make you an angel. You're a good person. I mean the best." Charity's eyes smarted with sudden tears. "I just wish to hell—"

"Hey!" Woody's bewigged head jerked aside at something off-screen. Behind him, the crowd noise had changed to something shocked and then dangerous, a huge gasp, then a roar for blood. "Char, they shot him. Somebody shot Roy."

As Charity gaped at the screen, the live event cut to a news anchorwoman with the blankest expression since Mount Rushmore.

"Good afternoon, I'm Nancy Noncommit—here's what's happening. An as yet unidentified gunman has wounded Leader Roy Stride in the middle of his apotheosis. No details yet, we'll have that story live—after this."

CUT TO FEMININE-HYGIENE COMMERCIAL. (Music: poignant violins. The honey-haired young woman with the heart-shaped face presses a letter to her breast.)

SOFT, INTIMATE FEMININE VOICE-OVER: "There are days when nothing should interfere with feeling like a woman—"

"STICK IT, BEAVER!" Charity shot from the bed, grabbing for the channel switch. All the channels were the same commercial.

Cut back to the balcony. Roy's face, dull with shock, looking straight at her in huge close-up.

"Charity," he croaked. "They shot me."

—and pull back to reveal him holding his bloody sleeve. "Don't worry, it's just a flesh wound." Roy winced and staggered—kind of actorish, Charity felt. "I'll take care of it myself. We're gonna get married. You and me, just like I promised. Listen to these people. Did you see? I'm the Leader! And you're . . . you're going to be . . ."

She didn't know what to say, just wanted to hide. "Mrs. Leader?"

"Where are you?" Roy strained. "You're gonna share all this with me. Where the hell are you?"

Charity panicked and blanked. "I don't know the address." With a sick rush of fear, she saw again her child self aged with that horrible knowledge in the split second before her head splattered open like a broken egg. *And I don't want you to know it. Talk about a good time for a commercial—*

—and cut with blessed serendipity to a well-groomed, smiling young Japanese spokesman: "Three-point-nine financing, five hundred cash back on the new Wasabe XL with underpaid Japanese engineering. You only *thought* you won World War II."

Charity dove for the remote switch and turned the set off. "What's the use of being dead? It's just like being alive, only worse."

"Mum?" Simnel waited, polite and impassive, in the bedroom entrance. "A Mr. Veigle called. An agent, apparently lives here in the building. Naturally I told him he had a wrong number. I'm not sure he believed me."

Charity was in no mood for this. "Make him believe you. Who's this Vague anyway?"

"Veigle, mum. A very powerful agent. They say he gets ten percent of the Prince. I'm sure that's a bit strong."

Charity turned away, wrapping the sheet around her. She felt cold. "I don't want to see anyone, Simmy. Anyone! Understand?"

■ 24 ■

Romanticism as theology: Is there hope for the spiritual drunk?

Gorgeous; the million-dollar wound that looked spectacular and didn't hurt much. Roy surveyed the dramatic stain spreading over his shirt sleeve between shoulder and elbow. The whole thing was a beautiful movie, better than Bronson or Eastwood, and Charity saw it.

"Drumm, will it show on color TV?"

"If it doesn't, we can touch it up."

They were momentarily alone just inside the balcony doors, guards three deep in the hall, the crowd screaming outside as the assassin was torn like an unclean thing from their seething mass by Paladin guards and dragged up the marble steps to his doom.

"You bring that sumbitch here," Roy seethed. "I want him to see me to my face."

Click! "Instantly, Leader."

He felt like the next thing to—no, he *was* God now, at least here. The Devil didn't seem interested—Roy couldn't figure that at all—but the rest sure loved him all right. They'd follow him.

He'd find Charity, tuck Florence away for rainy days . . . he had the whole thing knocked. Even Topside got out of his way. Damn if one of those angels didn't look like . . . No. No way. Woody was alive. A live nothing back in Plattsville.

Roy gazed at Wembley's picture in the space where his would hang in nobler majesty. Secretly he wished the portrait could be bare-chested, but that wouldn't be dignified. Respectability warred with inclination and won. But still . . . maybe a sword and lots of fur like Conan.

Drumm entered, followed by three guards and a shabbily dressed prisoner, whom they sent sprawling at Roy's feet.

"Get up, motherfucker. I want to get a good look at you."

Roy realized he should have kept the man on the floor. Middle-aged and schoolteacherish, he wasn't tall but seemed so because of a determined dignity.

"What are you?" Roy wondered. "Besides a lousy shot. You look like some kind of college perfessor."

"I was a teacher, yes," the prisoner admitted. "May I have my glasses back?"

Drumm laughed unpleasantly. "Old man, you won't be around long enough to need them. Name?"

"Ernst Stahler." There was a trace of High German in the accent.

"I remember him, Leader Stride," Drumm explained. "Stahler: fled Germany when Hitler came to power. Under suspicion as a Communist in the U.S. during the fifties. An enemy."

"I was a political writer." Stahler tried to focus his deficient sight on Roy, one eye already closing from a well-aimed blow. There was another bruise on his chin. His clothes were badly torn.

"You got guts, old man," Roy said with thin admiration. "Just stupid. You're gonna apologize. Say you're sorry for shooting at me."

"I am sorry," Stahler admitted easily. "Sorrier than you think. More than that, I was totally wrong."

"How about that?" Roy smirked to Drumm. "Even the losers are with us."

Stahler managed to stand like a granite statue even bleeding and handcuffed. "You misunderstand. The bullet only dignified you."

"Hey look, scumbag, I got things to do and people to see. Roaches like you I just spray, you got it?"

"The image is apt," Stahler said with his quiet academic precision. "In the fifties I wrote that fascism was a propensity of the schizoid German mind. Not so. It is universal as influenza and as tenacious. When healthy resistance wears down, you will appear. For a time, Mr. Stride. Because it is not only the power you need but the cosmic drama. Ask your resident dramatist, Drumm. That truly was the romantic German part of it. But even the Germans realized, if only subconsciously, that their own mythology ends in defeat and loss. *Götterdämmerung.*"

A snap of Roy's fingers and his Lüger was fetched from the desk by an obedient guard. Roy leveled the weapon at Stahler. "You gonna tell me in straight talk, old man."

Stahler didn't flinch. "You will come to it in time, as I did. As Hitler did. Until then, every wise decision will be nullified by two of sheer stupidity and indulgence. It must be so, and you know why it must be so."

"You—" The son of a bitch made him so mad, Roy began to shake. He yanked back the pistol slide and pointed the weapon again. "You got five seconds to live. Talk *straight.*"

It was unnerving; Stahler didn't even blink. "You even have the wrong symbol, Mr. Stride. Your sign is not the fist of power, it is Florence Bird."

Aiming the pistol between those steady, knowing eyes that stripped him naked, Roy had a red-sick moment of recognition. *This* was his real enemy, not the Jews or blacks or any of the easily visible targets the Paladins held up to the mob outside. This one here. The ones who knew and had the power to describe him; who made him a white nigger, only one step up from the black ones and no different at all when it came to money or getting fired first. The ones who got to be officers, got the best jobs and the best cars and women; who never had to work for power but always got it somehow. Not only the inferiors would go but these motherfuckers, too. Before anyone else. Now. Because of the answer in his hand. *You don't look down on me.*

But they did.

Roy fired. Stahler's head snapped back, spraying blood and flesh. The rest of him went down like a pile of rags. Drumm stepped over the mess, unconcerned.

"Get rid of that," he ordered.

When the guards were gone with the remnant of Stahler, Drumm adjusted his toupee and reassured Roy. "Don't worry, my Leader. The rug is washable."

"How'd he know about Florence?"

"I don't know, sir, but—"

"If he knows, who else does, huh? She's my private business." Roy turned on Drumm, shaking with rage and the exhilaration of a new kind of power. Blooded and blood drawn. He'd never felt anything like it, not even in good sex.

"And now possibly the business of others," Drumm reflected prudently. "Especially after you marry Miss Stovall."

Roy dropped the Lüger on his desk. "You got Florence hid good?"

"Trust me, Leader. But we must be prepared. If respectability is the daughter of morality, her jealous sister is blackmail."

Roy understood. More than respectability's sister, blackmail was her shadow, especially now. He really needed Florence tonight, but that would be asking for it. Where the hell was Charity? The high-rise district wasn't all that big they couldn't find her. House to house if they had to.

"We must be prepared," Drumm cautioned. "A scenario, orchestrated circumstances. We must make the disclosure work for us. That will be my personal operation. Trust me."

"Yeah. I got to, don't I?"

"Everything must work for us now." Drumm pointed a pudgy finger at Roy's bloody sleeve. "Even that."

Lovingly, Roy fingered the stained sleeve with its bullet holes as credential. "He was right, that old man, he did me a favor. Listen to them out there." He drank in the thunder, the music. "That fucker made me God."

With grand panache, Drumm threw open the balcony doors. The roar invaded the chamber like floodwaters from a burst dam. "Show them their God, Leader! Oh, and the blood. Cheat your left arm down—that is, be sure the wound is slightly turned toward them. After you, sir."

Roy stepped out onto the balcony, bathing in the sweet balm of total power.

STRIDE! STRIDE! STRIDE! STRIDE!

▪ 25 ▪

Meanwhile, back at reality . . .

Woody and Milt sped Topside across the void. The first trip had been a bit unsettling for Woody, though not all that different from good science fiction movies. Once used to it, he found the whole experience a hoot, and how many nights like this could you expect in Plattsville?

"We might make another appearance sometime," Milt supposed, "depending on how the script goes."

"I'm worried about Char."

"Writhing in the torment of a luxury duplex? What's to worry?"

"It's all phony," Woody complained. "And Char's a real person."

"That ought to clue you, Barnes. She's smarter than Roy, but still no hundred-watt bulb yet. She's gotta learn for herself. Meanwhile you can't complain about the scenery."

That you couldn't, Woody marveled: worlds and space and more worlds, colors he'd never imagined possible let alone seen, flickering through million-mile clouds of dust and gas alive with more worlds to come. Compared to this, Roy's triumph was bush league; just that Woody knew the guy too well.

"Roy's a dumb prick, but a dangerous one."

"Hey—take advice," Milt counseled as they soared through the black and silver of endless space. "My family were experts on the fascist mind. Roy's a fuck-up like Hitler. What's the opposite of fail-safe? Success-safe. These turkeys have got to lose because most of their thinking is off the wall to begin with. Think about it: there's Adolf rearranging Europe like a hyperactive housewife, shrewd as they come, and still getting his horoscope done every goddamned day, which is like seriously figuring Santa Claus into the national budget. These people are not coming from common sense; they simply can't think big. Give Stride a steady job and his own mediocrity would keep him in his place." Milt Kahane laughed suddenly, twisting around to grin at Woody. "Now there's a thought. If Hitler could've made it as an artist, we might've skipped a whole war—hey!"

Milt looked quickly over his shoulder as a series of flashing lights bathed them in hard brilliance, then rolled over in a steep dive. "INCOMING!"

Woody banked in a tight turn after him as the swift ship slid past them, glittering in and out of visibility before it vanished in the distance. The damn thing barely missed them. It could have . . . Woody felt at himself to see if the whole inventory was there and not hanging off the damn hit-and-run ship. "Ho-*ly*, Milt. What the hell was that?"

"You got me." Milt swerved back on course, fuming. "Dumb son of a bitch almost ran right up our tails. Just like the Long Island Expressway: long as their horn works, who needs brakes?" He bellowed his scorn after the alien ship.

"Tourist!"

Their ship had been in matter phase for the few instants Maj needed for control calibration. The two human-energy readings came up on them so quickly that she flustered for a moment. Beside her, Sorlij scanned the readouts.

"Whatever that was," he said, "I don't believe it."

"Conventionalized human-energy forms."

"Can't be. Scanner malfunction." Sorlij punched in a system

check, then called up various star charts on the screen. "We're getting close, I'm positive. I think it was the fourth planet in this system."

Maj disagreed: the fourth planet could barely sustain microbe life when they visited last. "The third."

"You're sure?"

"How could I forget?" Maj was in a particularly seductive form now, favored by the more successful women of her kind. She shimmered like bright metal immersed in clear water, and the gently reminiscent emotions turned her to a rainbow shower. "We made love in human form there. You remember how fashionable it was then."

Sorlij didn't remember all that well but was diplomatic enough to share her smile of pleasurable recollection. "Who cared then where we were? But I'm sure it's this system."

"There it is." Part of Maj's rainbow elongated to a pointer as the definitely familiar clouded blue ball loomed on her viewscreen.

"So it is. I wish I hadn't been so drunk when we landed."

"Darling, I'm glad you were. You tended to be terribly serious." Maj's colors dulled slightly as her mood turned analytical. "Reading the third planet now."

Absorbed with the world growing on the screen, Sorlij didn't notice Maj's chromatic change from faded rainbow to the dull brown of shock. "Sorlij, listen!"

More than just listening, they *felt*—a torrent of human energy, a cacophony of languages, mechanical and even nuclear activity.

"No malfunction," Sorlij stated grimly. "Those were human-energy forms."

Which raised questions troublesome as they were intriguing. "Sorlij . . . could it be?"

Sorlij didn't want to believe what the readouts told him: relatively advanced human life infecting not only the planet but polarized in two distinct post-physical energy pools. "Maj, enter a problem. Precise time point of our last visit."

She formed a delicate hand with seven agile digits that danced over the computer keyboard. "Entered."

"Primate parameters as observed then, approximate brain development in cc."

"Entered."

"From elapsed time, extrapolate anthropoid development to present. Query: nuclear technology possible?"

Maj's slender temporary fingers tap-danced over glittering inductance squares. "Computed."

They read the dismal results expressed in formulae. Maj summarized them on a sinking note. "From our givens, some extraordinarily gifted specimen might just about have discovered the bow and arrow. However . . ." She broke off to scan a parenthetical insert to the results. Sorlij read it with her.

"However," he echoed hollowly.

Based on the developmentary arc of twenty other primate species over two galaxies, the ape should have been too stupid to meet nine out of ten predictable early challenges. The few prodigies that developed beyond the point of their last visit would not have survived the probable polar tilt and the first long winter. Not to mention their penchant for intramural slaughter.

"Forced development," was Sorlij's inevitable conclusion.

"Oh yes."

Nor was that the worst of it. Intellectual growth could be augmented or accelerated. Emotional growth, too random a process, could not, though its relation to the former could be stated as a fairly predictable arithmetical lag behind the logarithmic progress of intellect.

Maj ran a swift line check to verify their results. No error. If she was a hedonist in her youth, Maj was now very practical. "The disparity is monstrous. I'd say they're technically brilliant, emotionally primitive and not a few of them quite mad."

Even superior beings had limits to their comprehension. Sorlij was close to his. "This is not supposed to happen. It's not my field. How do I deal with this?"

Instantly Maj was all comfort, entwining her essence with his. "There, dear. Whatever it takes, you'll manage."

"But how could it *happen?*"

"Don't be dense, dear. Our little lost lambs."

Sorlij changed color dramatically as he realized the unthinkable. "Oh no. No . . ." He materialized a specialized rump and collapsed on it. "Barion. That disgusting, egotistical, irresponsible—"

"And as of now, criminal fool." Maj's reflections were weighted with delicious malice. "And his musical brother. The matched banes of existence."

"Excuse me, Maj. I'm going to go human for a moment." Sorlij did just that. "I want to feel sorry for myself. I was so happy, Maj. So successful with marine organisms."

"Darling, it's hardly your fault."

"I left them there, both of them too drunk to move. A degree of culpability, that's what they'll say at home. Why, Maj? My mollusks were showpieces. I was working toward a decorative form of kelp. A really fine lungfish. Why me?"

Maj turned human to complement him, managing a lustrous cross between a sitcom wife and a centerfold. "Because you're the best for the job and everyone knows it."

"Yes," he admitted with manly resignation. "That's true."

Maj guessed from experience: now he would say *it's a dirty job but someone has to do it.*

"It's a dirty job—"

"Yes, darling."

Sorlij glared at the energy readouts emanating from the third planet and its vicinity. They were spectacularly mad. "Those two little *brats*. There's not even a word to do them justice."

"Excuse me, dear." With the flick of one delicate finger, Maj brought the ship out of jump to sublight. "The word for them is 'finished.'"

26

A rescue! A rescue!

From her Jacuzzi or watching over the shoulder of the inexhaustible Randy Colorad, Charity followed the mounting TV drama of Roy's fevered quest for her. BSTV made the most of it—

"This is Nancy Noncommit, BSTV news anchor. Top story this hour: the Paladin search continues for Char the mystery star."

Quick cut to Drumm close-up, smoothing his little mustache. "Below Stairs is simply not large enough to hide a woman of such importance. The Black-Jewish-Catholic-Communist dissidents responsible will pay severely when apprehended. I would also like to say for the record—"

Cut back to Nancy Noncommit: ". . . idiot will talk all night." (Sees her camera light on. The blank smile flashes automatically.) "Meanwhile White Paladin guards are combing the streets and residential neighborhoods for any lead to the missing fiancée of Leader Roy Stride. BSTV news is on the spot with one interrogation team."

Outdoor shot of a sleepy-eyed Paladin by a bullet-pocked wall, fondling his rifle. Several bodies lay at the foot of the wall.

TELEREPORTER: "We understand that these people resisted interrogation."

PALADIN: "That is correct. I asked them if they knew where

Char was, and they said they was Catholics and didn't give a big rat's (bleep), and I shot them as per the orders that I was given."

TELEREPORTER: "Do you usually have this difficulty with interrogation subjects?"

PALADIN (stroking his rifle absently): "Sometimes, yes, sir. Like this morning someone said he knew where Char was gone to but we was already shooting him."

TELEREPORTER: "Did your superiors consider this hasty?"

PALADIN (frowns in thought, takes a slip of paper from pocket and reads it): "We cannot be blamed for patriotism, but we are working to upgrade interrogation procedures."

And back to Nancy Noncommit: "One thing is certain, Char is difficult to find, especially when you can't get good help. Paladin search parties, ranging across Below Stairs, usually find themselves back at the Leader's Palace. This is seen by Minister Drumm as the work of dissidents. Others suggest the use of a compass."

So it went. Charity lounged in her tub, nibbled lox and admitted a select few neighbors from the building, like the past-life therapist from Venice, California, who volunteered to help her work through historical personalities allegedly seething in Charity's subconscious.

"She says I could've once been Cleopatra," she confided to Simnel over a hand of gin rummy, "but she says that's a very hard life to work through."

"Usually means there's a waiting list." Simnel laid down a deuce on the playing board across the white plateau of bubbles that encased Charity to the shoulders. "Cleo is very popular; never gets a moment's rest. Why not try for Calpurnia?"

"Who?"

"Caesar's wife. As advertised, above reproach."

Charity picked up the deuce. "I don't know. Liz Taylor was so great in the movie. Gin."

"GIN?" Caught with a ruinous handful of points, Simnel forgot himself. "You larcenous wench, you *can't* have gin this soon unless you're cheating. And you shuffled."

"Sure. Gin."

"You're not playing the game, mum."

"It ain't playing the game. It's winning. Gin."

"If I may say so, Miss Stovall, you never learned that Below Stairs."

"No. I learned that being poor in Plattsville."

The intercom phone buzzed softly. Charity yawned. "Get it downstairs, Simmy."

Simnel withdrew to do his office; shortly thereafter the bathroom phone beeped again. "It's Mr. Veigle again. About business, he says. Wants to come up. He lives here in the building, mum."

"Oh . . . why not," Charity decided, thoroughly bored. "It beats wrestling with Colorad, which I want you to tell him when he comes in that I have a headache."

"Mr. Colorad won't be back until this evening."

"It's a bad headache, it'll last."

When Simnel ushered in Eddie Veigle and added more bubble bath, Charity's head in its red shower cap looked like a maraschino on whipped cream. Veigle struck her as somehow sinister; even in the hot bath he made her feel clammy cold. She greeted him with a noncommittal "Hi."

"No." The bulky visitor shook his brilliantined head. "Absolutely not. We build the image from the first. You're a nice girl from Pottsville."

"Plattsville."

"Never mind. We're creating a product. The word is 'How do you do, Mr. Veigle?' Your parents were poor but they taught you good manners."

"They never taught me anything," she contradicted truthfully. "They didn't even care if I did my homework or not. Look, I'm doing you a favor just letting you in. How'd you find me, anyway?"

"I'm a businessman," Veigle said flatly. "We always know more than the government. And I live here in the building. Word gets around."

Eddie Veigle was moon-faced, bespectacled and deceptively benign, a fat man in a tasteful, perfectly tailored double-breasted gray suit. Next to Veigle, Ronald Reagan looked seedy. His nails were manicured, not one glossy black hair strayed out of place, not even the short gray ones around his ears. He smiled a great deal—just that, Charity discovered quickly, the smile could go bleak and cold as the moor around Dane's castle even as he beamed at her.

"Not even the Paladins know where I am."

"Bet your buns they didn't; not till I got the scenario worked out." Veigle drew a satin-upholstered stool close to the bath and rested his ample buttocks on it. "But they do now."

"Huh?" Charity sat up so fast she had to scoop in extra bubbles for modesty. "SIM-MY!"

"Because now is the right time for you to be found." Veigle inspected the shine on his nails. "Don't worry, you'll make a mint. Wait'll you hear what I've worked out."

Charity felt suddenly very afraid.

"What's the matter, kid? You look like you just lost your last option." Veigle leaned closer, solicitous but still oddly menacing. "The scenario's a winner. First the book, then the movie. That's why we ran the lifestyle segment on you."

"That wasn't me." She needed to escape from him. The vague threat of him filled the whole bathroom. "That was mostly bullshit."

"Look, baby, we're not amateurs. We used the best actress we could find. We had to to get that boondock accent of yours. The dream is what they'll buy."

Charity felt herself trembling in the warm, sudsy water. If he called the Paladins, they'd be here any minute, the same ones that killed the little girl. "I can't write any book. I wasn't good in English."

"Honey, it's a package," Veigle told her as if tutoring a backward child. "I got ten ghostwriters screaming for this assignment. Title alone can't miss. *American Dream.*"

They had the rags to riches, he explained; that was a natural, he loved it, but . . . getting a little, you know, tired. The package needed something else. Market studies showed greater impact when a spiritual element was included.

"That's it. A spiritual rags to riches." Veigle's oil and honey tones enriched with revelation. "Look at Colson after Watergate: found God in prison. How many sales? TV movie. Larry Flynt of *Hustler* magazine: up to his kishkas in a lawsuit, saw the light on a plane trip. I FOUND GOD AT 35,000 FEET. The drunks and druggies who fell from the big time and fought their way back, always with a book and a movie coming out of it. Goodness is admirable," that deep, insinuating voice told Charity, "but the fall-down is prime time. Jim and Tammy Bakker struggling to be brave on camera. Even the highbrows watched. They made jokes about it, but they watched. Drama, Char!"

Of the names he rattled off, Charity remembered only Reverend and Mrs. Bakker. She'd liked the PTL ministry on TV. He seemed like a nice man, but someone ought to teach his wife how to put on her makeup.

"Now do you get the picture?" Veigle urged. "This is high concept. Every one of those stories was a hit book or a boffo flick. Virtue is nice and sweet, but pain—the fall and redemption are the drama, the money in the bank. And you, doll face, are a mint. I want you to sign with me now."

"Pardon, mum," Simnel barely edged through the open door with a polite knock. "Mr. Colorad is home early after all."

"Great. I really need that. Mr. Vague here—"

"Veigle, baby."

"He says my story is the American dream."

"American dreaming has a high sugar content," Simnel observed, fussing with a shelf of towels. "Spiritual junk food."

"Simnel, I love ya!" Veigle boomed. "Always good for a zinger." The grin petrified as he turned back to Charity. "Now listen, kid—"

"I'm home, lover." Randy Colorad bounded into the bathroom in candy-striped bikini briefs. "Hey, Eddie, what's going down?" He stripped quickly and slithered into the tub. As always, the lighting went commercial bright to accommodate him.

Veigle groaned. "Christ, it's Tennis Anyone. Don't splash on the suit, okay?"

"Miss me?" Randy leered at Charity.

"No. I have a headache. Stay on your own side of the tub. I'm busy. Simnel"—a meaningful glance she hoped Veigle missed—"I'd like the kosher special for lunch and put a rush on it."

"Kosher special. Very good, mum." Simnel modestly eclipsed himself.

"Quit futzing around," Veigle snapped. "I'm talking megabucks. Got the contract in my pocket."

"I'm not sure about my future plans," Charity hedged. "I may have to move real quick."

"Char, when you sign with me and this deal goes down, you'll have a pad like this for every day of the week. Listen to this story," Veigle persuaded. "Nice American girl from a small town in the American heartland dies in the middle of her first boff, right? Damned with her lover, Roy Stride, a nobody from nowhere who rises to become a leader of his people Below Stairs." Veigle's organ tones began to sound like a coming attraction in Dolby. "Alone, terrified, she flees across the bleak landscape of damnation—lotsa special effects—one breathtaking escape after another. In color, score by Korngold."

"Oh, shit," breathed the mesmerized Randy. "That is wonderful."

"Just wonderful? It's fucking dynamite. And all the while . . . Are you getting this, Char?"

She smiled demurely. "I'm starting to."

Veigle's voice softened with pathos. "All the while, Roy searches for his high school sweetheart. Pain nothing, wounds nothing, triumph dust and ashes without her. Without . . ."

"Without the world in his arms," Randy offered, totally caught up in the magic.

Veigle grudged Randy something like admiration. "That's good. You ought to write jacket copy. The world in his arms." He savored the words, rising, uplifted by the pure helium of his vision. "A best-seller book, a miniseries. A forty share on BSTV."

"I don't *wanta* get rescued or anything!" Charity wailed.

"Say what?" Veigle blinked, brought back to a world not in anyone's arms. "You're kidding."

"I don't wanta get saved or shot on film or any other way, which it's very easy to do around here even dead. As for Roy and the one time—*once* in the tacky old White Rose Motel—I had more fun playing gin with Simmy. Now will you please get out of here so's I can get dressed?"

"You're not thinking positively." Veigle took a folded contract out of an inner pocket.

"I am thinking of getting out of here and I am not signing any stupid contract."

"Yes, you are." Veigle speared her attention on one pudgy

forefinger. It was very white, white as the rest of his skin, blood-less pale. Everyone was dead here, but under his manicure and hair comb, Veigle *looked* it. "Listen, you are nobody until I make you somebody, you understand? You don't do a thing without me. Nobody'll look at you twice without packaging. You're his sweet-heart, his true love—"

"The hell I am!"

"Listen to him, Char." Randy wriggled closer under the water. "He knows the business."

"I'm sick of the business and everybody trying to give it to me," Charity raged in a spray of water and bubbles. She found Randy's rump by Braille and applied a foot to it. "Get out of here, you horny seal!"

"But I want to hear the end of the story," Randy pleaded. "It's gripping."

Veigle's voice dropped to a husky whisper. "I was just coming to it. The two of you, success hollow without true love, Lazarus at the feast, and then finding each other at last. I see the shot already: both of you on an empty, lonely street late at night. You turn and see him a block away. He turns. Slowly you recognize each other. You move toward each other, faster and faster. Close on him, close on you as the music rises up in the kind of triumph only Korngold can write—the soundtrack alone will go platinum. Two American kids who went all the way down and up again. Underdogs who stumbled, but even after death came from be-hind to win."

"Oh, shit, Eddie, that's—" Words threatened to fail Randy Colorad. "That's more than good. It's *profound.*"

"And about as real as you are," Charity seethed, near violence herself. "Lordy, would I love a little real. Even a roach in the kitchen."

"No, you wouldn't." Veigle shook his head, sure of himself. "You never did. The world is made up of losers like you who just go on losing. How much did you ever pay for a look at one more? You wanted the prime-time glitz like the rest of the grunions. You begged for it with your snotty little nose pressed up against the screen. Don't kid yourself: without me, without the buildup, you're not even a thirty-second spot on late night."

"I don't *want*—"

"Who cares what you want, you little twat? *We're going to make money out of you!* It's inevitable, so relax and enjoy it."

At this tense juncture, Drumm shouldered through the bathroom door followed by an armed Paladin big enough to have been manufactured by the GM truck division, Simnel hovering in their wake. Charity's heart sank. Her goose was cooked. Furthermore, she was running out of bubbles.

"At last, Miss Stovall!" Drumm flourished. "My respects and my regrets for your trouble. If these people have harmed you—"

"Sorry, mum," Simnel apologized. "They forced their way in."

"Can we talk without the gun?" Charity appealed. "How'd you get past security?"

"We persuaded 'em, ma'am." The lumbering guard ogled the receding froth over Charity's bosom. "My name's Roy, too. Roy Earl Holub from Yazoo City, Mississippi, and I'm pleased to make your acquaintance. I'd do anything for the Leader."

"If you'll dress, Miss Stovall, we'll escort you to—"

"Hold it, Drumm," Veigle butted in, waving his contract. "She signs with me first. Favor for favor."

"Roy Earl." Drumm motioned to the guard. "Some persuasion for Mr. Veigle."

The rifle trained on Eddie Veigle. He went, if possible, even paler, wilting down onto the stool. "Now, that's not fair. Who tipped you she was here?"

"Fair is what right-thinking Americans say it is," Drumm snapped. "Miss Stovall will have no need of your services."

"Char, this would be a great time for those new stress vitamins," said ever-helpful Randy.

Drumm motioned impatiently. "Miss Stovall, if you please."

"Simmy, how about my kosher special?"

"On the way, mum." Simnel took a giant towel from the rack— only to have it plucked from his grasp by the kosher special, who opened it invitingly for Charity. Her heart leaped: God and the Mounties had arrived in time.

"Jake! I've been living right after all."

"Charity—" Surveying the astonished and suddenly respectful faces around him, Jake couldn't supress a giggle. "Let me take you away from all this."

"Jake, I never saw anyone so beautiful in all my life or so in time," she vowed passionately, booting at Randy with the vigor and precision of a halfback. "Outa the pool, Flipper! Towel, Jake. I mean please, Mr. Iscariot."

He spread the towel expertly between Charity and the other men as she rose to wrap herself in it. "The rest of you freeze. You, the brain trust with the gun: you're tired of carrying it, so put it down."

Dazed but obedient, Roy Earl leaned the rifle against the tub. Charity skittered out of the bathroom, grabbing for the first clothes to hand. "Thanks, Jake. I'm always getting rescued without a stitch."

"Won't hurt sales," Veigle offered. "Don't worry, we'll find you. You're money in the bank."

Jake turned on him lethally. "I said freeze. All of you."

Something in the voice. Dressing hurriedly, Charity herself froze at the sound of it. Everything about Jake now was scary, even his back. She wriggled into jeans and a T-shirt, jammed her feet into tennis shoes.

"You won't get away with this, Iscariot," Drumm blustered. "Friend of the Prince or whatever, you're not big enough to cross the Leader."

"Oh? Anyone want to get paid off now?"

Charity couldn't see the exact movement of his right hand, but Drumm, Veigle and the guard shrank as far from him as possible. With a yelp of pure terror, Randy jumped clear out of the tub like a hyperactive salmon and sprinted out of the bathroom, trailing wet bubbles down the stairs.

"Ready, Charity?"

"Got my running shoes on. Think I'm gonna need 'em."

Judas/Jake scooped up the rifle and tossed it to Simnel. "Entertain the callers until we're gone."

Hurrying downstairs to the open elevator, Charity remembered her fled roommate. "Randy?"

Hidden but plaintive: "He's not going to pay anybody off, is he?"

"No, but there's some Seconal in the bathroom. Take the whole bottle." She jogged into the elevator after Jake and punched for down. Nothing happened. "Hey, elevator, move!"

"Please enter correct instructions," the elevator balked. "I used to be a—"

"I *know,*" Charity screeched. "You had great cheekbones. GO, stupid!"

"I most certainly will not." The elevator didn't.

"How'd you like to start life over as a stamp pad?" Jake offered with the calm of a poised cobra. "Basement, please."

The doors closed. They wafted downward to the piped music of Lawrence Welk. With a moment to breathe at last, Charity gazed adoringly up at her savior, the Archvillain of the Christian World. He looked beautiful. "Jake, did I ever tell you you remind me of James Mason?"

"Thank you. I always liked his work."

"Would you mind just this once if I kissed you?"

"Delighted, Miss Stovall. It's been a long time since the last. Ruth Snyder," Jake recalled tenderly. "Incompetent murderess but a very nice woman. Be my guest."

He didn't kiss well at all. His lips were slightly cold. Charity was faintly disappointed. She felt the hard knot of the leather bag against her throat and went cold herself. Under the ricky-tick elevator music, she heard again the voice almost forgotten—very familiar and much closer now.

Char-i-tee . . .

III

BANALITIES

27

Judas with strings

Jake ran red lights with such reckless abandon, Charity kept looking back to see if they'd picked up any traffic cops.

"Don't worry about that." Jake took a corner with squealing tires. "The heat leaves me alone."

"Where are we going so fast, anyway?"

"A place you're ready for."

"Someplace real that makes sense," Charity yearned.

"With rules, order, regulations."

"Where people live like folks—*look out that car!*"

Jake swerved with the reflexes of a fighter pilot, throwing Charity against her door. "Lordy, where'd you learn to drive?"

"Never did, actually. Just sort of picked it up. No accidents yet."

"We're not there yet." Charity crossed her fingers and prayed silently. "Wherever there is."

"As requested, reality." Jake kept his eyes on the street ahead. "And Alice said, 'Who cares for you, anyway? You're nothing but a pack of cards.' And as the pack rose up and came pelting down on her, Alice woke up to reality. Getting dark."

Jake switched on his high beams. A startled pedestrian leaped back out of their lethal trajectory. Jake geared down and curved smoothly into a side street. Downtown Below Stairs slid by Charity's open window, garish with neon.

"Where are we going? 'Suming we get there in one piece."

"The Club Banal."

"Club what?"

"Banal," he defined: "the classically ordinary, predictable, unremarkable, unchanging. Not the worst, a long way from the best. Boring."

"That's a dumb name for a club. I already got bored out of my gourd by Randy Colorad."

"The Banal is much more than that," Jake explained. "The working heart of Below Stairs. Leaders come and Drumms go, but the bureaucracy remains. And there's the brothel."

Charity hoped she hadn't heard him right. "The what?"

Jake shrugged. "I believe the American term is cathouse."

"Now, look," Charity argued, offended. "All right, I made some mistakes, and maybe I'm not a real nice girl anymore, and maybe that ain't much of a loss, but I don't deserve to be sent to a . . . a white slave house."

"White slave?" Jake laughed with honest amusement. "Melodramatic wench, the Banal has a variety of jobs, and you'll like Elvira Grubb, the manager. Everyone says what they mean. What they've got to say, that is, and as far as it goes. But as ordered, reality. Reason and order, ponderous sanity, regulations. The very cosmos invalid until reviewed, countersigned and filed in triplicate. Very safe and no surprises. And . . . here we are. Feel at home."

The cab slid to the curb before a neon-fronted building with a crowded bar from which brassy music blared out over the whole sleazy block. A little daunted, Charity didn't want to leave the safety of Jake just yet.

"Thanks again. Every time I need saving, there's you."

"Scared, Charity? It's just like the world, the same confusion. Don't be impressed."

Charity's glance dropped to the age-blackened leather pouch around his scarred neck. "There's something I—don't be mad, but I just gotta ask."

"I know." He tapped the pouch. "They all do."

"You can tell me to mind my own business."

"Perhaps you're not ready for it yet."

She met his gaze levelly. "Hey, Jake, I'm getting readier by the minute, or ain't you noticed? I mean about what I used to think was good and bad."

"Ah—a sea change."

She slid over to touch his cheek, caring about him. "Why, Jake?"

"The same old question. Why did I do it?" He looked past her in that distant, detached way of his. "You know, all those films you saw never got it right. Yeshua was my friend."

"Who's he?"

"Jesus: that's what the Greeks made out of his name. He was my friend, he loved me. Actually Yeshua was one of the two best minds in Judea. I was the other. Freely admitted; my modesty fell with the rest of me. But in those days I was something of a Fundamentalist myself and not at all forgiving. I never forgave him for not being what I wanted him to be . . . a god, a messiah. We needed to believe in miracles then, too; nor were we any more critical than you."

Charity found it difficult to stay on the subject with him that close. "I was taught you were the lowest thing on earth or in hell."

Jake laughed again. "That's leaning on it, don't you think? What I am in fact is the oldest but most effective plot device of the trite world. People need a villain, Charity. Without me, Yeshua would have been a ripple in Roman history. One dissident rabbi leading one splinter group out of dozens, a footnote for Hebrew scholars. People have short memories for also-rans. The way things turned out, I don't imagine he's any happier than I am. I have to go." Jake leaned over and brushed her lips with his. They weren't warm, but Charity felt the sincerity. "The ride's on the house, Miss Stovall."

"Don't you ever get lonely, Jake?"

He took a moment to consider the question. "No, not the way you mean it. Besides, who'd live in that house of mine?" Jake slipped the gear into neutral. "Rotten weather, a snotty embezzler for a watchdog, and I'm not much company."

"Don't put yourself down." Charity opened her door and got out.

"Don't go sticky," Jake snorted. "You'll spoil my theological image."

"Don't worry about that. You'll always be a son of a bitch." Charity slammed the car door and leaned in through the window. "Just kind of a nice one."

"Queen of the Treacle Harvest." Jake gunned the motor. "If you'd been with us, you'd have fallen in love with Yeshua just as Mary did. Women have a weakness for celebrity. Go on, I've got a call."

BARION TO COYUL:	SINCE STOVALL NO LONGER INTERESTED IN STRIDE, OBJECTIVE SEEMS ACCOMPLISHED. SHOULD EXPEDITE. STRONG REASONS TO TERMINATE.
COYUL TO BARION:	WHAT'S ACCOMPLISHED? SHE IS MERELY AFRAID OF HIM. WILL TERMINATE WHEN SHE'S SICK OF HIM. YOU SAID NO QUESTIONS. DON'T BUG ME.
BARION TO COYUL:	I SAY QUIT NOW. WHY MAKE A FEDERAL CASE?
COYUL TO BARION:	YOUR KNOWLEDGE OF WOMEN STILL NEOLITHIC. SUBJECT LOOSENED UP BUT NOT YET RESTRUCTURED. PRESENTLY AS LIABLE TO FALL IN LOVE WITH JUDAS AS WOODY BARNES OR ANYONE ELSE. BESIDES, I'M BEGINNING TO LIKE THE LASS.
BARION TO COYUL:	PSYCHOBABBLING SENTIMENTALIST.
COYUL TO BARION:	NEXT TO VIOLENCE I REALLY HATE DIRTY LANGUAGE.

28

Everyone comes to the Banal

A week without Paladins assured Charity that her trail was cold. She relaxed into the humdrum of the Club Banal, which combined all the functions Jake listed. There was the bar, built in the Tijuana-Juárez style of the late '40s, with rickety tables and a brass ensemble that played interminably. Just off the bar down an atmospherically dim passage were the brothel rooms. Behind this vigorously active function lay BSA (Below Stairs Accounting, office of), a huge open space like five airplane hangars end to end. From the entrance, BSA receded into a dim infinity of desks, workers, the *chitter-clatter-ting!* of office machines and the asthmatic buzz of government phones obsolete in 1960.

"What do they do here?" Charity asked Elvira Grubb, who conducted her introductory tour.

"I'm not sure, lamb. No one is."

If the function of BSA remained obscure, the people were more than familiar to Charity, like the VA and post office workers at home. They filed into the bar on their breaks to hunch over the tables in disconsolate huddles, bawling at each other over the deafening music. None of them could tell Charity Stovall what BSA ultimately produced, being employed strictly on a need-to-know basis. They needed to know very little and were not at all curious about the end product. They processed mountains of paperwork, all requiring triplication and interoffice memos, listless, disinterested and permanently dissatisfied. Since time meant nothing, the smallest mistake in the endless lists of numbers and names jarred the Leviathan process off its treadmill track. Back came whole Himalayas of completed lists for checking, recopying, rechecking, review and countersigning once again. Conversations in the bar centered obsessively on who made the most mistakes, who was getting kicked upstairs or who was next in line for promotion. They endured a grinding, lowgrade misery but no one ever left except to visit the girls.

"They could leave anytime," Elvira told her, "but no one ever does."

The whole thing seemed pointless to Charity. "Gol-lee, why would the Devil make up such a wimpy kind of punishment?"

"Bless you, child, the Prince doesn't punish anyone any more than *I* do. They brought all this with them." Elvira Grubb had a comfortable, sensual laugh and the relaxed plumpness of a woman come to middle years by an enjoyable road. Her life, she felt, had been marvelous and death was even better. "I take care of things and water the drinks and—if I do say so—give the establishment what decorum it possesses. My husband is an eminent critic and friend to the Prince. Did I tell you that Mrs. Lincoln was a confidante of mine?" Elvira had, more than once. "She didn't deserve her bad reputation in Washington society. Let me tell you, that husband of hers was not an easy man to live with. You watch out for these humanitarians. Someone close wants a little affection, they're always off loving Mankind. Now, Wilmer is a perfect husband. A real bear cat."

And off she'd go, telling once more of her romantic marriage while Charity tried to enjoy her diet cola and found she could no longer stomach anything so insipid.

"Give me a bourbon straight up, please?" said the suddenly needful Charity. "This stuff tastes like these people look."

True, gray and unhappy as they were, no one left the club or the accounting office. They hung over the tables or the bar, complaining about the petty but endless injustices of civil service or what hell should really be, but no one really tried to change anything.

"Why should they when it's all so nice and steady and safe?" Elvira philosophized from her high desk between the bar and the annexed house of qualified joy. "Babies always rattle their cribs, but they wouldn't be comfy anywhere else, I say. The girls are fantasy . . . Good evening, Mr. Pugh! Nice to see our regulars, go right up. Domination on the second floor, same as always . . . Where was I?"

"The girls are sad as the office." Charity swirled the swizzle stick in her bourbon. "And those old ladies up in Accounting. Work, work, work, and once a week, big deal, they put on an awful hat with fake flowers, and go across the street where there's girl waitresses and fancy cocktail napkins and get blind. They sweep 'em out in shifts."

This was also true. The retrieval of genteel and very blitzed old ladies from the lounge across the street was a cottage industry in itself.

"Never mind." Elvira stuck to her point. "Whatever they dreamed, this is all they ever really wanted and the office is all they ever got. Used to it. Be scared to death of anything else."

You get what you pay for, Charity knew, *which means what you can afford, and you get used to that. Even me, my big night, the first night of my really being a woman, and what do I look back to? The White Rose Motel, which it was probably built by the same people thought up this place.*

One worker, mired in the quicksand of Accounting, was still defiant. Leon Pebbles was thin, red-eyed and always looked slightly feverish. Leon went an extra mile to do his job well and to search out ways to improve efficiency. Naturally his co-workers hated his guts.

"They don't want efficiency," he grieved to Charity. "They're afraid of it."

For his integrity, Leon lived on the Cross. Much table kvetch centered on his wild-hair schemes to cut down paperwork, which would mean less employment. His memos were few, brief and lucid, heretical to calcified supervisors who saw ruin in their comprehensibility.

"He don't read the Style Manual. You don't *begin*, you *imple-ment*. You don't *rush*, you *expedite*. Pebbles is a square peg in a round hole."

"But what are we *doing?*" Leon lamented to Charity over his mineral water and ulcer tablets. He didn't need the pills since his death, but they were habit, like his compulsive efficiency. "Nothing, that's what. Pounding sand down a rat hole, and the less they do, the longer the job description."

Heads turned at the bar: Pebbles had spoken a taboo word. In this area Leon was Judas himself to other workers. Lengthy memos were always coming down from somewhere to be read, initialed and passed on. Never less than ten single-spaced pages, they boiled down to the need for efficiency and cutting paperwork. To keep one's job from going under the ax, one's function must be represented as vital, complex and sufficiently incomprehensible to dazzle the job analysts. Trash burners alone, Leon's department, became End Product Evaluation Engineers with job descriptions couched in syntax that defied translation—

—conceive, establish and maintain an effective system of end product evaluation and final action implementation of same . . . (see para. 27a above).

Not so the traitor Pebbles, who, throwing caution and the Manual to the winds, was brash enough to write: *All material comes to me in large bundles, which I bag and burn. There are twenty-five of us to do this where ten would be enough.*

A marked and friendless man. Bloody but unbowed, Leon prophesied to Charity with Old Testament wrath: "Someday, the Lord's anger and just plain COMMON SENSE, by God, is going to reach down and rewrite every by God job description in this dead-ass place. BOOM! You wait."

Leon plodded back to his job, threading his way through the tables, glowering at the sludge in the wheels of progress. "Just wait . . . boom."

The band played on, workers muttered into their watered drinks. Barion sent more agitated messages to his brother—

BARION TO COYUL: ADVISE. READY YET?

COYUL TO BARION: NOT. WILL NOT OPEN UNREHEARSED.

BARION TO COYUL: HURRY REPEAT HURRY. IF
SUSPICIONS CORRECT, OUR TYPE
ENERGY FORMS WITHIN SOLAR
SYSTEM, GROWING STRONGER.

COYUL TO BARION: YOU MEAN WE CAN GO HOME?

BARION TO COYUL: YOU UNBELIEVABLE ASS, I AM
TALKING ABOUT JUDGMENT DAY.
OURS. VERY LITERAL AND VERY
NEAR. HURRY.

■ 29 ■

The treadmills of your mind

The Club Banal and her own place in it were faintly absurd to Charity. The description occurred to her out of the blue like so many others lately. Absurd. Pathetic. She'd always recognized the words in reading but not often enough to work them into her own vocabulary.

"Ab-surd." She tasted the word. "Ridiculous. Re-dundant. That's me, all right."

The threefold business of the club churned onward through eternity. The bad brass ensemble slammed its musical assault against the harsh-lit tiles of the bar walls, the men of Accounting brooded and complained, Leon Pebbles seethed and muttered, "Boom . . ." The line of glum men shuffled forward to see the girls, browsed the Green Room and from there passed on to see what fantasy might beckon from the rooms.

With Charity's outbreak of new vocabulary came an increased desire to read, although the Green Room held little nourishment, mostly Harlequin romances read and reread by the girls until they had to be held together with rubber bands. Charity once devoured them like potato chips; now they seemed insipid. The heroines were all vanilla versions of herself in better clothes, the heroes all Woody Barnes with better chances. For the waiting male customers, there was a shelf of "Bor" novels or something like that, not very interesting to Charity although she hewed her way through one or two from desperation. The men in these stories were all grim studs and all the women started out getting raped and ended up loving it. These books were kept on a shelf labeled "comedy" by the Puerto Rican girl, Esperanza, who had been raped at the age of thirteen and hadn't cared for it at all.

"Guy who wrote this oughta do three to five in a horny cell block, see how he likes it," Esperanza suggested darkly. "Hey, who took my Harlequin? I ain't done yet."

There were also some fat paperbacks called sword-and-sorcery, usually in three or more unreadable volumes each. Charity couldn't relate to fairies beyond Walt Disney. As for destiny-haunted princes—always getting hidden with poor folks at birth and then going on dangerous quests to find out who they really were—well, she'd been there with Dane and came close to a second heart attack and didn't need a replay. But fat Shirley (a.k.a. Lady Ellivare) read them over and over, sometimes starting with volume five and working backward.

"I can't help it," she confessed to Charity over her book and a box of chocolates. "I relate to all the destinies within me. How could I not, being Dion Fortune in my last life?"

There were other neo-pagans like Shirley among the Club ladies. They practiced a religion of emancipation and joy and were terribly serious about it, chanting their prayers to the Goddess in the fruity overtones of Eastern Star chapter ladies attempting *Medea*. They reminded Charity of Purdy Simco on a fired-up night in the tabernacle. The Catholic girls burned candles to the Virgin in their rooms, and gossiped back and forth through the thin walls between tricks and often during them. Protestant and Jewish girls just got bored and did their nails, talked about leaving and finding a steady man and never did either.

Essie Mendel loved to talk about her boyfriend in Accounting, upon whom her eye was fixed with iron patience but dimming hope. This swain, like his father, had died of overwork, prostate cancer and his mother.

"But he still spends every weekend with her in Ultimate Rise. Even with her around, I'm going to live there one day," Essie vowed. "Oh, Char, those hu-*mong*ous living rooms where all your friends can come and see and owe you. The icebox with all that *food*. It's to die."

"You never get hungry," Charity reasoned, already jaded with Ultimate Rise. "Bor-ing."

Essie Mendel was a born consumer. "How can anything so rich be boring?"

Monotony was usual, but now and then diversion reared its head when a holy war broke out among the girls. The neo-pagans were always swiping novena candles from the Catholics to use in their circles. The most recent skirmish pitted wiry little Esperanza against Shirley, goddamning and screw-you-ing each other to a standoff, Elvira wedged between them laboring for peace.

"Shirley, give Esperanza back her candles right *now*. I gave you a nice new Bic lighter just last week."

"I will *not* use a plastic lighter to purify my circle! The candles were mine to begin with. And my name, goddamnit, is EL-LIVARE!"

Esperanza strained to get at her. "It's mud you don't gimme my candles, *puta*. All that goddess 'n' nature shit and running around in a fancy bathrobe and stealing *my* candles ain't got *nada* to do with God."

"Of course not!" Shirley screeched, stung in the center of religious principle. "You sellout female eunuch!"

"Elvira, what the fuck she talking about? Some witch," Esperanza jeered. "Couldn't even charm the fat off her own ass."

"Oh, give her the damn candles." Shirley-Ellivare retired with the tatters of her dignity. "How can she understand the Goddess? Never even finished high school."

Charity could never see any sense in the physical inspection for the customers beforehand or the forms they filled out or the pro station stop afterward. "I mean, they're dead, aren't they? What can they catch? Jake said this place was real." Charity wailed her frustration and perplexity. "*None* of it is real!"

"Well, of course it's not." Elvira went on checking her bar invoice. "And then again it is. Look at those men in the line. What else was ever more real to any of them? They never knew much about women or sex or anything outside of their silly jobs. What else would they bring along?"

They'd tried dropping the pro station and the forms, Elvira pointed out. The customers missed the gap in normalcy. They enjoyed waiting in line, telling the same old jokes to the same friends, visiting the same women, creatures of habit even beyond death. They needed to touch something. Charity's working room was situated between the pro stop and the bar. The men came and talked to her for a few minutes before returning to work or another drink.

She'd never understood men very much, she realized now, or her own role in relation to them beyond a gut-level knowledge that life was not all that easy before marriage and tough as hell after, and you put up with each other.

A few passed up her open door; most came in, sat down on the off-yellow futon and talked to her. Talked at her, rather, falsely hearty, ultimately shy and wary of women on a one-to-one basis beyond the sexual mechanics. The rules, the forms and pro station helped them keep at a distance an experience and a being they knew very little about and feared a great deal. In time Charity came to feel her ten minutes the most essential in the whole production line. More than sex, it was the communication they starved for, part of them knowing what the rest denied, that they needed to touch, make contact with something beyond themselves.

Virgil Bassett was with her now. Virgil died of weight and worry as a surrogate for identity, reciting his life in tones leaden with resignation. Always there had been his gray job on a diaper service delivery route, and his discontented wife, whose chief ambition had been to head the Myrtle Beach Daughters of the Confederacy but who never flowered beyond the entertainment committee, thwarted throughout her days. Joy for Virgil Bassett translated to the few hours in his basement shop for meditation and the delicate art of kite making.

"Most relaxing thing I can think of, 'less it's flying 'em," he rambled pleasurably. "Certain summer days on the beach you get them updrafts, thermals, and that old kite'll stay up there breakfast to sundown. No strain, just a gentle pull on your line, but you know you got a friend up there. It's beautiful . . ."

He never knew the score any more than I did. Charity felt the compassion well up from deep inside for all of them and not a little for herself. *Hell, there's no mystery between men and women, except why some poor damn fool like me ain't figured that out yet. He's just like me, spent a lot of time just wishing someone would really look at him and listen to him like he was a human being and mattered. We lived with bullshit rules back there and more down here. Least we can do is make up our own.*

With the subversive insight came an irrepressible urge. "Hey, Virg." She winked at him. "Knock knock."

Interrupted in his dearest soliloquy, thermal updrafts and the nagging tyrannies of his wife, Virgil could only stare at her.

"Come on, knock knock. Say who's there?"

"Who's there?"

"Sonya."

Virgil snickered. "Oh, yeah, I remember this. Sonya who?"

"Sonya shanty in o-old shantytown. Knock knock."

"Who's there?"

"Slagle."

"Slagle who?"

Charity crooned: "Slagles ri-i-ing, are ya listenin'? . . . Now I got a hard one for you. What is two hundred feet long, green, with warts all over, and sleeps at the bottom of the ocean?"

Not ready for any of this, Virgil Bassett pulled nervously at an earlobe. "Warts and what?"

"Give up?" she brimmed.

"Hell yes."

"Moby Pickle! Got another," Charity threatened, definitely on a roll. "What's purple, wears a Scout hat and stamps out forest fires?"

Virgil foundered and went down. "Nothing is—"

"That's what you think." Charity zoomed off the futon, pirouetted and broadcast the answer to a cosmos agog. "SMOKEY THE GRAPE!"

Virgil gaped, trying to understand and failing. "That's dumb."

"Got a big fat headline for ya, Virg: so are we."

Dizzy all of a sudden, sight blurred, Charity wove on her feet. *What . . . what's happening to me?*

"Char-i-tee?"

In the process of pulling at his ear, Virgil Bassett became a still life. All sound ceased. Charity stood like a last survivor, able to hear and move in a vacuum. "What's—?"

"Charity?"

The voice was just down the hall, coming toward her room. She knew who it was now.

Charity Stovall appeared in the doorway, waving casually to Charity Stovall. "Girl, you have been hell to catch up with."

Herself to every feature—clothes, hair, probably the fillings in her back teeth, yet with a subtle difference. Identical lines but each one more relaxed from head to toe and more clearly defined, the facial expression quite changed. Charity II *saw* everything she looked at but didn't put labels on it.

"Hi." She plopped down on the futon. "Surprised it's me?"

"Not a whole lot," Charity supposed after honest reflection. "Way things happen around here. Well, I look pretty good."

"Thanks." Charity II inspected the petrified Bassett. "Customer?"

"Mr. Bassett. Champion kite maker of Myrtle Beach, but he never got much time for it."

"Let me guess," Charity II divined. "When he flew the kite, he worried about keeping his job. On the job he dreamed about kites."

"That's about it."

"Never met himself coming or going. But we have. Let's work together, Char. We're better as a team."

"Weren't we always?"

"Gol-lee no." Charity II stretched her legs and crossed her arms, a disconcerting double image making herself at home. "Not in Plattsville, for sure not with Roy Stride. Not until just this moment, girl. We're not exactly each other. You're what I used to be. I'm what you could be. No big deal, just playing with a full deck, and didn't you run me ragged catching up."

"You know?" Charity said thoughtfully. "Like Leon says, you are by God right. I was just thinking—"

"I know, hon. That's why I'm finally here."

"Just listening to Virgil go on about his job and his miseries when he can do whatever he likes anytime he wants. And then . . . hell, I said, so can I. Elvira told me and told me."

"Doesn't count until you tell you," said her vibrant counterpart. "Lordy, but you were a case back in Plattsville. The resident Nice Girl on which the factory seal ain't been broke. Some virgin, Char: you screwed yourself for years, right up to five minutes ago." Charity II stood up, opening her arms for an embrace. "Gimme a hug, I've missed you."

Charity hesitated, a little wary. "You're not one of those actors, are you? There's a lot of them around."

"Guaranteed pure Stovall. C'mere."

Alone again. Or joined. Whatever, something very strange was happening to her mind. Pieces of it reaching to other pieces, straining to connect, one and one somehow making three. Charity squeezed her eyes shut and open again to clear the sudden blur. She remembered something without sense or reason. Water . . . leaning over a pool of water, her own flat, ugly face coming up in reflection to meet her—at first frightening but then so damn silly she *had* to laugh, though the effort hurt her throat.

She must have dreamed it before to recall the image in such detail. Someone was standing on the other side of the water, telling her about . . . a gift? And for the gift, something paid or lost.

Charity's sight cleared. The ancient, fragile dream faded, leaving an afterimage, a bright flash still glowing behind her eyelids when she closed them, then . . . gone.

Charity looked down at the sleeping Virgil Bassett. She smiled at him. "We're in an absurd place doing ridiculous things." She bent close to the lost kite maker of Myrtle Beach, lulling him in the manner of a movie hypnotist. "You're deep asleep, Virg Bassett, but you can still hear me. When I say the magic word, you will leave this room and this whole dumb place, bag and baggage. Do you hear me, Virg?"

"Yes," he sighed in sleep. "I want to, but . . ."

"But nothing. The magic word is *fly.* When I say fly, you will go Topside. Go directly Topside. Do not pass Go, do not collect any more bullshit. That includes your wife, who won't care anyway. You got better things to do."

Virgil drowsed; his lips relaxed into an unaccustomed grin. "Cer'nly do."

"Wake up, Virg."

He woke feeling utterly marvelous, as if a light had gone on inside him. Charity was very close and—Je-sus!—ten times more beautiful than when he dozed off. And while Virgil rubbed his eyes and tried to put it all together, Charity bestowed on him the most thoroughly feminine and satisfying kiss of his bereft existence.

"Virgil Bassett," she whispered tenderly, "go fly a kite."

◼ 30 ◼

Barion explains; it doesn't help

"Post-life energy. We're in the thick of it." Maj removed the tiny earplug that emitted a cacophony of human speech. "All my readings are unreliable. What *is* that madness out there?"

"Go to matter phase," Sorlij ordered.

The corporeal ship drifted in space like a sea vessel becalmed. In matter phase, the viewscreens showed nothing but the monotony of space. They decided to leave the ship in matter and return to energy phase themselves for compatibility. At least they could read brain waves.

Once away from the ship they needed some time to adjust to a kaleidoscope of visuals and the deluge of raw emotion bombarding them: changing landscapes of pastoral serenity, city buildings, meadows, a pulpit or two, dwelling places of austere simplicity or garishness, all under a continual verbal roar. Sifting through the storm of voices and energy, Sorlij's worst fears plummeted to new depths. "Oh, Barion . . ."

"It's the Rock for them," Maj knew. "Shall we ask directions?"

"Got to start somewhere."

They found themselves on desert sand under a blistering sun. Not far away, an oddly garbed human crouched on his knees, face to the earth in an attitude of fervent prayer.

"Excuse me," Sorlij began. "We're strangers here. Could you tell us—?"

The worshipper glared around, sprang up and charged at them with a wicked curved sword. "ALLAH IS THE ONE TRUE GOD!" *Swoosh!*

The blow merely passed through Sorlij, who dissolved and materialized further away, a little put out. "Now, see here, who-ever you are—"

Maj made a stab at it. "We're looking for someone—"

The mad alien turned on her, swinging the sword. "PIGS!"

Maj discorporated and reappeared next to Sorlij. "Look, you might show a little court—"

"*Allah el Allah-h-h. The one, the all-merciful,*" the Moslem yodeled, winding up for another try at them—

But they were long gone before the sword completed its futile arc, passing over landscape that changed with disconcerting frequency along with a colorful cast of characters. They had bewildering adventures. A large, scented female with plastic flowers on her powdered bosom exhorted them to join something called the Brotherhood of the Holiest Elect. Someone named Scotty invited them for the weekend at Pola Negri's. A group of intense women, ignoring Sorlij, made a breathy, hands-on fuss over Maj and invited her to a sisterhood party "without the sexist." Twice more they were attacked, once with something saw-toothed and nasty, once with a tube that went rat-tat-tat. They managed to escape through montaging scenery to a quiet, empty street with small dwellings in white plaster and ocher tile. Maj wilted down on the lip of a quaint stone well, confused and discouraged.

"Somewhere in this madness I can read Barion," Sorlij maintained.

"If someone would just give us clear directions before they turned religious, erotic or homicidal. Sit down, dear, you look done in."

"I am." Sorlij drew a deep breath, enjoying the tranquillity of silence. "At least it's quiet here."

"You two!"

Maj sighed. "At least it was."

"Get ready to move. I'm tired of being polite."

Their interceptor bore down on them, a short, powerfully built man in late Roman dress.

"Greetings," Sorlij attempted. "We're a bit new around here—"

"No." Bishop Augustine inspected Sorlij up and down. "You are not Him."

"No, I suppose not," said Sorlij, staying carefully in neutral.

"I have sought Him for sixteen hundred years. I will find Him if it takes that long again."

"Our wish to the smallest syllable," said the diplomatic Maj. "We're looking for him, too."

Augustine surveyed Maj with unconcealed disapproval. "Cover yourself!" After observing the better local female forms, Maj had refined the concept to a dazzling image with a charmingly minimal regard to costume. "You are a woman."

"As you build them, more or less."

"The beauty of woman is a snare."

"I did hope I was in good taste. The one we're seeking is unusual to your sort. Very handsome." Maj had always thought Barion attractive when he wasn't suffering from poetry or cosmic purpose. "Blondish, tends to be tedious. We call him Barion."

"Oh, *that* one." The contempt was audible. "He is always underfoot somewhere. I think he is a little dim."

Sorlij agreed. "Quite possibly."

"I purpose to see that one myself—scant joy or profit as it holds. Come along."

Once more the scenery dissolved with unsettling rapidity. The street became a plain hallway spaced with office doors. They followed the bull figure of Augustine until he halted at one, knocked explosively and entered without invitation.

"Here is where he works. If the verb applies," Augustine qualified. "Sort of a general fetch-and-carry. Barion, are you here?"

"Augustine? Just a moment, Your Grace." A drawer slammed shut somewhere behind a row of ancient green filing cabinets. Barion emerged, hands full of papers. "Sorlij and Maj! I knew someone was in the neighborhood."

"Of course it's us," Sorlij acknowledged brusquely. "What's the meaning of this dissonant lunacy?"

"Tact, dear," Maj intervened delicately. "I'm sure Barion has an interesting explanation."

"Well, Maj: after all these eons." Barion made a valiant try at gallantry. "You've matured splendidly."

"And yourself, although you look a little drawn."

"I can't tell you how happy I am to see you," Barion confessed with more honesty than was apparent. "Overjoyed is not the word. Sit down."

Sorlij and Maj settled into wooden office chairs that creaked in protest at every move. Augustine remained standing, a rock of long-thwarted purpose. "Attend me, Barion. I have been trying for sixteen centuries to extract from you a plain answer as to—"

"EEEE!" Maj shrieked and turned dark blue with horror. A nightmare loomed suddenly in the open doorway, most of its body burned to char, the rest caked with blood.

"Which way to the martyrs, please?" the apparition inquired.

"Martyrs." Barion riffled through a Rolodex. "Martyrs . . . yes: William James, just down the hall."

"Thanks awfully." The horror bobbed out of sight.

"Have to be a little patient with martyrs," Barion explained genially. "They tend to feel *arrivée*. Mr. James helps them put it all in perspective. Well." Barion sat down at his desk. "I suppose you're here to collect us—a-and I imagine you have a great many questions."

Masking his mind from them, Barion fired an urgent message at Coyul across the void—

SORLIJ AND MAJ: READY OR NOT, HERE THEY ARE. GO WITH WHAT YOU'VE GOT.

The reply came instantaneously, hurried and harried:

YOU THINK YOU'VE GOT PROBLEMS? FORGET IT.

No help there.

Sorlij and Maj demanded to see Coyul as well. They assumed he was in the other messy pool of post-life energy.

"Coyul calls it Below Stairs. Very much like this place," Barion explained. "Just less organized."

Sorlij tried to imagine a place less organized than this. The concept was a challenge. "Well, we'll be taking you both back. And if you or Coyul have perpetrated what every indication leads us to believe, it's the Rock."

"Premature seeding with no authority." Maj shook her head in dire accusation. "You've always been spoiled, self-satisfied, self-indulgent and undisciplined, and now it's all caught up with you."

Augustine had lost any sense of direction or meaning in the discussion. "What means all this?"

"What it means, dismally, is a specimen like you," Sorlij snapped at him. "Please don't interrupt. What did you start with, Barion? Must have been far below standard CT."

"About nine hundred cc."

Maj blanched with utter shock. "Nine—"

"But that was part of the experiment," Barion amended quickly. "Combining augmented intelligence with the raw animal. You must consider success along with failure. I've produced some admirable specimens."

Augustine's brows shot up. "*You* have produced?"

"Yes. You may not be the most tolerant of men, but you did change the shape of European history and thought."

"Nine hundred *what?*" Augustine didn't understand any of this; there was a sensation in his stomach akin to indigestion that hinted he didn't really want to, but he must. "What is a CT?"

"There's another truth I want in your report," Barion went on, ignoring Augustine, who was suddenly seeing the fetch-and-carry bane of his existence in a new and horrible light. "Coyul wanted no part of this experiment. He was against it from the start."

"Anything that took him away from his silly music," Maj noted with honeyed malice. "We'll be questioning him, too."

"Well, Below Stairs is a bit chaotic, but my brother does what he can to keep things tidy."

"Your brother?" Augustine began to make even more unpleasant connections. "*Your* brother?"

"Coyul," Barion admitted with fraying patience. "Your Grace has given him less flattering titles. Please don't interrupt." He turned back to Sorlij and Maj, urgent. "Coyul is helping me now with a vital corrective measure. There's a girl Below Stairs. She's very important. You must let us complete it."

"This is enough to make a man mad," Augustine despaired. "No one knows where God is. All manner of undesirables wander in from anywhere"—a pointed glare at Sorlij. "One has to put up with heretics like Pelagius and that barbarian Luther—"

"Who is very much like you." Barion cut him off with even more fragile patience. "Utterly sure he's right and the rest of the world will realize it one day. Your Grace will recognize the tendency."

"Barion." Augustine drew himself up in last-ditch desperation. "What do you mean *you* produced—you and your brother—are you saying that *you* created the world?"

"Of course not. You were already here . . . sort of. I just improved you."

"THEN WHERE IS GOD?"

"A fine rhetorical. Where indeed?" Sorlij acknowledged. "But don't confuse the creature, Barion. He can't understand any of this."

—as the new message tinged with panic whispered into Barion's mind:

CHARITY READY BUT EMERGENCY REPEAT EMERGENCY AT CLUB BANAL.

What could happen at the Club Banal? Barion wondered. The place was a definition of fail-safe mediocrity. Nothing ever happened there.

All this in a nanosecond plus a fraction more to remember the tyrannies of Murphy's Law and that this was definitely not his day.

For a strong man Augustine seemed suddenly juiceless and brittle, though he was never a frail spirit. The implication was nakedly evident. "Barion—are you . . . ?"

"This primitive is not important." Sorlij rode over him with brusque purpose. "There's a great deal we have to know."

"If you are," Augustine struggled, a tragic figure, "then where is the City of God? Where the majesty of the spirit, where the mystery, the fall or the redemption?"

"Augustine, not today," Barion warned at the end of his tether. "Not today."

"Yes! Today! If *you* are—"

"All right! I *am.*"

"Then—what remains but madness?" Augustine drew on his last resources of intellect, courage and dignity, all formidable.

"Madness or low comedy. Shall we not then run wanton in the street? Why not? What remains?"

"A great deal remains, you relentless man," Barion said. "That I *did* build into that splendid mind I gave you. Though it's very like building a magnificent car for someone who obstinately refuses to learn to drive."

"You have riven meaning from existence. If you and these misbegotten sprites are gods—"

"You said it; I didn't," Barion countered. "You and your agonized ilk made it into heaven and hell, *I* didn't. The question was never fall and redemption but simply where and how high you can reach. There was a time when thunder and lightning were gods to your kind. The Egyptians improved on that. Moses built on them. Someone will build on you. That is the process."

"Barion, will you get back to relevance and stop wasting time on this creature." Sorlij jabbed a finger at the stricken Augustine in utter disbelief. "You think he understands any of this? You're talking to an *ape.*"

"Well, that's the heart of it. I think he can. As long as I'm going to jail, one of the best minds up here along with Yeshua and Tom More ought to know what's happening." Barion regarded Augustine with a deep respect for that strong man's convictions and his own. "You *can* understand; I built you for it. You see, a long time ago, not far from where you were born, there was this monkey . . ."

31

Roy Stride and the First Amendment

At the bar, Charity had one for the road with Elvira to say good-bye. She was very pleased with herself. "See old Virgil finally walk out? Guess I did the Lord's work today."

"Topside's very nice when you're ready for it, dear. Hel-*lo*, Mr. Pebbles. Mineral water as usual?"

"Yes, thank you, Mrs. Grubb." Leon set a tight-wrapped package by his stool. Charity tapped it with her toe.

"What's that? More health food?"

"Absolutely," said Leon, even more febrile than usual. "Makes the system efficient." He scooped up his drink and package and headed for an empty table near the bandstand.

"Don't know what I'm ready for, Elvira," Charity reasoned, "but I sure know what I'm finished with, so I guess it's time to go."

"Good luck, dear. By the way, someone's been asking for you over on the bandstand."

Out of self-preservation, Charity always ignored the Club band, but today they sounded good enough for most of the tables to quiet down and listen; two soft trumpets in a relaxed, meditative rendition of "Body and Soul."

"That's an old one," Charity murmured into her drink. "Used to be one of Woody's fav—" When the thought connected, she did the largest double take in the annals of American romance. "WOODY!" And shot across the room, dodging tables and customers in a broken-field run to hurl herself into the arms of the most beautiful man she ever found too late.

"Woody." Charity crushed herself to the marvelous reality of him. "Oh, Woody, am I glad to see you. I was just leaving for Topside 'n' thinking I'd never see you again, and—"

"Hey, doll," the other musician broke in, wry and gentle, "We're doing a gig."

"Forget it." Woody introduced them warmly. "Char, this is Milt Kahane, my buddy from the Corps. This is Char Stovall, and she's with me."

"Don't you know it," Charity breathed.

"Time for a break, anyway, Milt."

"So it is." Milt took up the mike and addressed the tables. "Gonna take a break, timeservers. End of the set, but don't you fret. We'll be back on our stools with some oldie jewels."

"Hey." A drunk wobbled erect at a near table. "Can you play 'Unchained Melody'?"

Milt frowned at him. "Not with a clear conscience. Don't applaud, just grovel and throw large bills. Hey-y." His dark eye brightened with incentive as a thin woman undulated past the bandstand. "Who is *that?*"

"Essie Mendel," Charity filled him in. "Sort of engaged to a Jewish guy in Accounting. She's very Orthodox."

"I knew it; I can spot a *shayna maidel* at a hundred yards. They're always ripe for a little reform." Milt took a deep, zestful breath and clapped his hands together, a man about to party. "Take ten, Barnes." He sauntered away in Essie's wake.

"Woody." Charity still couldn't believe he was here next to her. "What are you—I thought you were Topside."

"Oh, things were kind of slow, and we heard the burritos were good here, and—honest to God, Char, ain't this a trip?"

"Yeah," she agreed with some irony, "how they gonna keep us

down in Plattsville after we've seen Below Stairs? I didn't know you like Mexican food."

But then, come down to it, how much did she ever really know or see about Woody Barnes? Except he'd been her friend forever. She could recall him at any given moment, but never, she realized now, in clear detail: how the wiry hair over his forehead sort of shone with red hints under the bandstand light, or how good-humored his blue eyes were. Or how, while no taller than Roy, Woody's frame was lankier and more relaxed. She never looked or noticed any more than she really saw the rest of the world around her. Like the thin pale scar between thumb and forefinger that streaked two inches across the back of his left hand. She'd never noticed that. Charity wondered fleetingly if left-handed people ever looked much at other people's right.

"Where'd you get that scar?"

"This?" He turned the hand over, taking a second to recall. "Beirut; the day Milt and I got fragged. Corpsmen loading me on a stretcher, my damn hand fell over the side right onto broken glass. Couldn't win for losing that day." He stretched out the hand to touch her cheek. "Really missed you, Char."

"Same here," she said fervently. "A lot."

"Guess I was a damn fool just standing around letting Roy have you."

"That's done."

"But that's the way it was." Woody fussed with his horn. "You couldn't see anyone else."

That plus the old Plattsville brainwash bullshit, Charity remembered honestly. Save yourself for marriage and marry as soon as you can, before you know anything at all, let alone how to love. By the time you do, it's worn out as the car and the furniture. "Jeezooee, I was dumb, Woody. Anything worth doing takes practice, doesn't it? Like playing the trumpet."

"Sure. If you've never been bad, how do you know when you're good?"

"Or being a doctor or even roller skating. But they expect us to be good at love right off."

That one true love stuff never did much but sell houses and diapers and keep dummies like me off welfare as unwed mothers.

There's no more one true love than one true song to sing or dress to wear. Totally ridiculous, but so was I for buying it.

But—here she was being intelligent for a change, even if she had to die to achieve it, and Woody Barnes was laughing at her, grinning like a stupid kid. "What the hell's so funny?"

"No . . . no. Just you look kind of different."

"I feel beautiful, Woody. Just when I thought I lost you for good, I find you when I'm going Topside myself. Now we can go together." She snuggled close to Woody, reveling in the security of his arms around her.

"I always loved you, Char. Took me a while to know it, too." A beautiful thing to say—too beautiful for the fresh convulsion of giggles that followed. "Listen, you have to trust a little, okay?"

"Maybe I will if you'll stop laughing like a fool."

"I can't go with you, Char."

She looked up at him in surprise. "You're not gonna stay here, are you?"

"Well, no." Woody seemed to be choosing his words with excessive care. "There's a lot I can't tell you."

Charity felt a chill grow over her happiness. "Why not?"

Woody Barnes was not supple at evasion. "Well, I'm not dead."

She didn't understand that at all. "But—your friend Milt, you said he died in Beirut, and here you are with him. There's not a lot of rules around here, Woody, but that's one of them. What do you mean, you're not dead?"

"Just sort of drafted. For the duration."

"Duration of what?"

"Well, that's what I can't tell you. Just my part's done, so I'm going home."

Too damned much. Staring at Woody, she felt the second loss of him like a physical ache. Lost once out of ignorance and now again for no reason she could understand, and here he was telling her to trust . . . men.

"Always telling me what to do!" she flared suddenly. "First Roy, now you. Goddamnit, Woody Barnes, you are not in charge of the world—"

Only one answer. Woody Barnes finally made the right one. He kissed her. Thoroughly. In the lovely middle of it, Charity knew even more poignantly what she'd missed and would be missing for forever yet to come, but now at least she had some experience to judge from. Woody didn't have Dane's electricity or the bitter-tangy fascination of Jake, but . . . oh, yes. The kind of kiss you could live with a long time like a good, comfortable bed, and it tore her heart out with so much wisdom come too late.

"Damn, Woody," she said weepily against his cheek. "You're going home and you'll be married to someone else—"

"No way, Char."

"Come on, be real. You'll find someone else 'n' have kids and a whole life to live. And when I see you again, if I ever do, there'll be so much you lived that you can't share with me, and it's so damn, rotten un*fair*—and here I am putting my heart out for you to walk on and what the hell are you *laughing* at?"

All through her bittersweet lament, Woody's grin had grown even broader. "I can't tell you, but will you trust a little?"

"Like a stupid hyena: yuk yuk yuk."

"Girl." Woody kissed her again. No mistake, he was very good at it. *Talk about can't win for losing,* she lamented through his embrace. "I promise you, Char Stovall, you won't miss a thing. Whatever comes to me, I'll share with you."

She punched his arm in frustration. "How about sharing the joke?"

He still shook his head with that stupid-pleased grin. "No joke."

"Not to the late Miss Stovall it ain't."

"But it's big, Char. I don't know if anything like this ever happened before in the whole world."

"That's a safe bet." Charity glowered.

"I told you to listen, okay?" Woody shook her gently by the shoulders. "We'll see each other again. Trust me, okay?" He brushed the hair from her forehead delicately as if just discovering it. "Don't be sad, honey."

"Easy for you to say." With feminine practicality, Charity thought of Jake. She could go anywhere and, face it, a girl could do her waiting with a good deal worse. "I'll try not."

"Fall in, Barnes!" Milt reappeared, balancing a platter of burritos in one hand, Essie Mendel latched on to the other. "They didn't lie about the nosh, it's great. My treat, enjoy. This is Essie, also a winner."

Her own feelings very sensitive just now, Charity could read them in Essie like a neon sign. She clung to Woody's good-looking friend close as after-shave, and her introduction was clearly proprietary. "Char, this is Milton Kahane. He's Reform from Long Island."

"Reform?"

"The next thing to Unitarian," Milt translated. "Let's grab a table and assimilate."

They were moving to join Leon Pebbles at his eager invitation when the front doors exploded inward like a broken dike, loosing a tide of armed Paladin guards. The shock squad fanned out from the entrance, leveling submachine guns and bad dialogue at the startled customers.

"Freeze, mothers!"

"Nobody move!"

"Hold it, turkey—don't even think about it."

"Me?" Woody eased between Charity and the weapon trained on them. "Mind not pointing that thing at me?"

"Shut up, pussy." The gun muzzle swung on a slight movement from Milt. "Don't try it, dogshit. I'll mess you all over the wall."

"Please, not again."

"Everybody over toward the bar. Move."

Charity had a bad feeling that she understood more of this than she wanted to. The next moment proved her dismal theory. Fat little Drumm strutted through the door, flicked his clams-under-glass over her, then the room at large, and motioned to someone outside. Roy Stride stalked into Club Banal in SS black, whip in hand. He took the moment, giving them all, including Charity, the full effect of his absolute power.

"Hi, honey. Said I'd find you. C'mere. Okay, Drumm, everything's cool."

"This is not a general raid," Drumm announced. "We want only Miss Stovall. No one but her abductors will be arrested."

"Come on, Charity." Roy gestured with his coiled whip. "You're rescued."

Charity was sick at the sight of him but more afraid for Woody than herself. These people could hurt him. She started falteringly to obey. Woody's grip tightened on her arm.

"No way," he said.

"Hey, Woody." Roy strode to him, offering his hand. "Didn't know you were here. When you get it?"

Woody ignored the hand. "I got you way back, Roy, just wouldn't face it. Char's going Topside."

"You think so?" Roy smirked confidently. "Where've you been lately? I got those wimps in my pocket, boy. And the Prince. Shit, I ain't seen that sucker since I got here. Nobody fucks with me, Woody." He threw the fact to the room at large. "Nobody! You seen it on TV. Even Topside's playing ball with me."

Chewing on his burrito, Milt Kahane commented: "Hardball."

Roy turned on him, dangerous. "You got something to say?"

"You heard me," Milt said calmly. "And when you fan on your last strike, they're gonna ram the bat up your ass."

Roy looked Milt up and down with a grudging admiration: a badmouth but with guts and . . . somehow familiar. Maybe it was just the superior smile he'd writhed under all his life. In the lethal silence Leon muttered about Judgment and efficiency.

"Who are you?" Roy demanded. "You got a Jew look, boy."

"Me? I'm practically Swedish."

"I don't think so." Roy snapped his fingers. "This one to the camps."

"You always were a fuck-up." Woody stepped out in front of his friends. "Couldn't get out of boot camp without doing bad time. I was Topside when they cut orders on you, Roy, and you are in deep shit already. So take a little advice from the heart. Back off. I mean it."

Woody's still determination stopped Roy for a second before he remembered who had the guns and the power. "That you talking? Old go-along-with-the-program Barnes? Forget it. Charity, let's go."

She shrank back from him, remembering her own horror-filled eyes looking up at a gun barrel. "I can't."

"Charity, I don't wanta get personal in front of all these people, but you're already my wife, if you know what I mean."

Along with the fear, she felt disgust. "That's not personal, just tacky."

"Uh—excuse me, Leader Stride?" A small man with hunched shoulders and a potbelly edged forward from a huddle of his co-workers, hands still up. "If you don't propose to facilitate any arrests, I've really extended my break and have to return back forthwith to my duty station."

"What *is* this?" Roy's frustration blew up in a vicious crack! of his whip. "You want trouble? You scumbags want arrests?" He whirled on Charity and Woody. "You think I'm shitting you? Okay. Drumm!"

Click! "Sir."

"Every third one to the camps. I don't care—man, woman or queer." Crack! "I'll show you suckers trouble—"

"Ow, *there* y'are luv!"

Her strident cheer barely diminished by a long troublesome search, Florence Bird shouldered and flounced her way through Paladin guards toward Roy—who went sallower than usual against his SS black at the sight of her. Florence by contrast was an animated Cézanne in a painfully bright flower-print dress with bits and ends that bobbled with the jiggling of her Junoesque proportions, topped off with precisely the wrong hat skewed at a precarious angle. She bore down on the speechless Leader with a bear hug and lipsticky kiss.

"Crikey, dear, been 'avin a butcher's all over Below Stairs for you. Try to get you on the phone, this little pouv"—a contemptuous thumb jerked at Drumm—"says you carn't be disturbed. Not 'arf short wiv me. Y'orta talk t'im about it."

Roy's mouth worked. His eyes tried to deny what they saw even as he realized that dictators like anyone else could be caught with their image down. His colorless complexion went even paler; to Essie Mendel, the whole picture was a contradiction in obscenities.

"You've got to have good coloring to wear black," she whispered to Milt. "He looks like mayonnaise on my cocktail dress."

Roy managed to escape from Florence's possessive grip but found only part of his voice—a sort of squeak. "What the hell—are you crazy coming here?"

"Well may y'arsk, dearie. Got tired of sitting on me Khyber in front of the goggle box all day, nuffin to do but watch me gentleman friend prance all over town."

"Christ, will you cool it?" Roy hissed between clenched teeth. "This is Charity!"

"Not with *me*, luv," Florence vowed with gale-force lung power.

"Christ, you dumb—it's my fiancée. Charity Stovall."

"Ow, lumme! A *course!* Where's me 'ead?" Forthright and unabashed, Florence strode to Charity, offering her hand. "Sorry, dear. Needn't take on: just business with me and Roy. Cash and carry, hands across the sea and that. Florence Bird. Very pleased to make your acquaintance, I'm sure."

"Oh, that's all right." Charity didn't know what to say, nor did she trust herself to try. "I was just leaving."

"There's nice." Florence beamed. "Lor, what's on in the high street outside? Pushed this way 'n' that by bleedin hordes of telly men, and look at this hat what I bought just yesterday, all bashed in. Lot of right brutes, got no respect for a lady."

"Telly?" Her meaning galvanized Roy Stride. "You mean television?"

"Don't I just?" Ruffled, Florence inspected the damaged hat. "Weren't for that nice Mr. Veigle, wouldn't've got in here 'tall."

Drumm made a sound like a man dying under a curse. "Veigle . . ."

Roy cast about wildly. "Drumm, do something!"

Too late. Whatever blitzkrieg strategy sprang to Drumm's mind, Eddie Veigle was already sweeping through the doors, the double-breasted, brusquely confident point for a flying squad of BSTV technicians, some shouldering cameras, others paying out cable for a makeshift monitor control, grips and makeup people in their wake, Nancy Noncommit bringing up the rear.

"Well, well, well," Veigle purred. "Everybody's here. Who's minding the revolution? Char, the mystery star *and* Florence Bird." Veigle couldn't resist a chuckle of pleasure. "Perfecto. A fifty share. Even Topside won't be watching anything else."

"HOLD IT!" Drumm tried in vain to stem the stampede of technicians around him. The guards weren't much help. Hoping for some more television exposure, they started straightening uniforms and hats. "You can't do this, Veigle. This is an official government rescue."

"My Polish grandmother had such a rescue," Essie muttered. "One kiss from the magic mamzers, she turned into soap."

"Oh, this is a class act," Milt sighed. "History as drama: what do we get? Reruns."

A camera focused on Drumm; a light meter flirted near his mustache. He was becoming spastic. "THE LEADER FORBIDS THIS!"

"How?" Veigle chortled from his monitor. "This is news, lovey. Ratings. I told you Char couldn't move without me. You don't want to work with Veigle? Okay, Veigle works without you. Cue Nancy."

Freshly primped by her hovering makeup woman, Nancy Noncommit spiked herself beside Florence and turned to the camera with blank-eyed authority. "This is Nancy Noncommit at the Club Banal. The suspected other-woman scandal shadowing Roy Stride broke here a few minutes ago when, acting on an anonymous tip—"

With malicious emphasis, Veigle mouthed it to Drumm: *Me, Drumm-bum.*

"—BSTV news broke the story in a deluge of disclosures. We found the Leader, his fiancée, Char Stovall, and the other woman, Florence Burns—"

"That's Bird, y'little git." Florence moved firmly into frame, nudging the smaller anchorwoman aside, flashing a toothy smile at the camera. "Florence Bird from Lambeth, and lor yes, we been together *ever* so long."

In the backwash of the storm, Woody and Char stuck close together. "Char, who is this Veigle guy, anyway?"

Charity's expression was not easily decipherable. "Whatever he is, he just hit the fan."

32

Blossoms and thorns of
the media culture

Despite the media cyclone whirling about them, Roy and Drumm fought a brief, sibilant battle.

"Leader, you have to make a statement. The whole thing is out."

"Not if we shut them up good and quick."

"We can't arrest everybody. It's bad press."

"We're getting that now or maybe you din't notice."

"The scenario."

"What?"

"The scenario. I wrote it out. We talked about it as a contingency plan."

Roy found it difficult to think fast at bay. "Oh. Yeah, I remember."

"And you must weep, my Leader. For the camera."

"No." Roy was adamant. "I can't do that."

"Why not?"

Roy fidgeted; Drumm pried at the bedrock of deep beliefs where his icons were enshrined. "Ain't what a man would do."

Drumm's little eyes blinked behind their thick lenses. "Why do you think all this is news in the first place? Because you have transgressed? Rather that they recognize it. Not a real man Below Stairs who won't identify with you. Not a woman who won't sympathize: he's human, he's like us. They will know you for a man of large appetites as powerful men always are."

Still not convinced: "But why do I have to cry?"

"Because, my Leader, with the macho comes the marshmallow. The emotional response of people conditioned to believe anything they see on television as truth. The camera giveth and the camera taketh away. They will believe your repentance: the good man strayed but anguished for the pain he's caused. A man gone wrong, but a man throughout."

Roy began to like the image. "Yeah . . ."

"Leader, you'll be more popular than ever, Topside as well as here. Not a dry eye in the cosmos. You heard the Jew Veigle: no one will be watching anything else. We can deal with him anytime; meanwhile we must turn this to our advantage."

"But I can't *cry.*"

"It's simple. Pull the short hair in your nose, right . . . there. If that doesn't work, we have glycerin."

Roy surrendered to the imperatives of destiny. "Ah, shit. Let's do it."

Nancy Noncommit turned to the monitor. "That's it on the Bird."

"Okay, where's Char?" Veigle took center stage, an impresario committed to producing a miracle whatever the cost. "Hey, Stovall! You're on."

"No, she's not. Leave her alone," Woody fended him off. "Get away from her. She doesn't want to talk to anybody."

True: Charity struggled with every appearance of distress. "I— I can't talk now, honest." She collapsed in a chair at Leon's table. "Now, now . . ."

"Okay, cue the Leader." Veigle spun around, pointing at Roy. Drumm nudged the reluctant subject forward.

"From the left side only," Drumm ordered the cameramen. "Cameras three-quarter angle from the left *only.* Your best angle, sir."

Thrust into the glaring lights, nose hair tortured into yeoman service, a tearful Roy Stride went on camera—incoherent with shame for a watching cosmos, struggling with the demands of honor. Nancy Noncommit pushed the hand mike close to his face. Hushed, expectant silence.

"I can't—I don't know how to say this," Roy choked. Suddenly he turned away, hands to his face. At the monitor, Veigle talked into his headset.

"Close-up. Get the sweat and tears. I want his *pores.*"

One more furtive yank at the nose hair filled the monitor with Roy's moral agony. "What I did—I can't undo. I just wish—" He stopped, swallowed hard, then went on. "I can only ask the forgiveness of the good people who—who believe in me."

Once into his role, Roy was surprisingly good. Even Essie was stirred. "It's sad, Milt. Look at that big English *bummerkeh* and tell me who's really to blame."

"Essie, you make me wish I were alive again. I could be sick all over you."

"What are you talking? Look at Char."

Under Woody's soothing hands, Charity's shoulders heaved tragically; from the hollow of her cradling arms came the strangled sound of deep emotion.

"But I—I won't hide anything from my people," Roy went on valiantly. "I only wish to God I could undo what I've done." He faltered on the verge of fresh tears, then got it out in a ragged rush. "And that I can earn the forgiveness of the fine, good woman I asked to be my wife."

Roy's face filled the monitor—agonized, streaked with tears. "My office is new. I was—under a lot, a great deal of strain. Charity—honest to God, Charity—"

"Is that tomorrow's headline or is it not?" Veigle crooned into his headset. "Camera two on Char . . . beautiful. Now split one and two."

Roy and Charity now, split screen. Charity raised her head to Roy, equally racked, fighting to hold her feelings in check.

"Never top this," Veigle knew. "Never."

"Roy. Oh, Roy—" Charity struggled and lost. The words splintered, sputtered, roared into a raucous gut-hoot of hysterical laughter.

"Never . . . in all my li-life," she gasped. Out of control, clutching at her ribs, Charity collapsed on the floor by Leon's

feet. Spastic, beyond control, she grabbed for something, anything to keep her this side of lunacy. She hung on to Leon, came
away with his package squeezed to her own heaving chest. For a
fifty share of Below Stairs and Topside, Charity Stovall imprinted
her judgment on the cosmos.

"Y-you gotta be the b-biggest asshole that ever died."

Charity surrendered to a fresh onslaught of coughing and hic-
cups. Sadly, Veigle drew the finger of doom across his throat.
"Cut, for Christ's sake." He glared balefully at the monitor,
prompted to murder before his practical side came to the fore
with an angle. "Save her tape," he growled into the headset. "We
can sell it to the opposition."

Meanwhile, back at madness, Charity held out Leon's package
to Roy, still sputtering. "Listen: even the groceries are laughing
at you."

Roy charged at her. "What're you, crazy? This is going out
live—"

"Hear it, Roy?" She jittered on the edge of fresh hysterics.
"Even the bag is laughing."

Roy tore the bag out of her grip and threw it aside, raging. "You
don't laugh at me. You ain't so much, you goddamn whore. *You
don't laugh at me—*"

—while Nancy Noncommit talked into a headset in a steely
whisper: "Veigle, we're still rolling."

"I know." His voice oozed confidence again, buttered with
delight. "We'll hide at least one tape. Did I say fifty share? Sixty!
This belongs to eternity."

"Nobody laughs at me!" Roy raised his fist to batter the laughing truth from Charity's mouth. Before the blow could launch, he
was caught by the collar and flung violently backwards on his
butt, gaping up at Woody Barnes. Not a protracted gape. Into
that classic study in astonishment, Woody hurled a juicy burrito
with unerring accuracy and a *splat!* that would have thrilled
Mack Sennett.

Incoherent with fury, Roy clawed at his holster and brought up
the huge Lüger. "Shoot 'em all, Drumm! Every mother—" Point-
blank at Woody's face, he squeezed the trigger.

There was a sharp report but not much else. A baby-pink flag
unfurled from the pistol barrel, bearing the rubric: BANG!

Those few guards who had presence of mind to obey his final-solution order rather sheepishly discovered similar flags fluttering from their weapons, advertising MCDONALD'S—BILLIONS SERVED. Milt Kahane raised his hands in praise of celestial genius.

"Boss, Prince, I love you. The universe is sane, after all."

Then—acute hearing and traumatic memory wiped the joy from Milt's face. His eye shot to Leon's package, now busily ticking. He groaned with horrible prophecy. "Barnes . . . listen."

"YES! LISTEN!" His hour come round at last, Leon Pebbles, man of destiny, did not slouch toward Bethlehem but sprang to it atop the table, package held high with maniacal triumph. "I told you bastards the day would come. The day of total efficiency. Minimum paperwork and everyone sees the end product of his labors. FIVE SECONDS—BOOM!"

A frenetic five seconds, most revealing of character. Accounting personnel, used to doing nothing without directives, did just that. Elvira ducked behind the bar, mourning her freshly laundered tablecloths. Woody dove for Charity, upending a table for cover. Bug-eyed, Roy swerved for a second to Drumm for advice he'd never have time to heed, then hurled himself at Florence to protect the last, best pure Wasp piece of tail in the universe. Milt grabbed Essie and launched them both toward the deck—

"INCOMING!"

COYUL TO BARION: PLEASED TO REPORT CHARITY VERY READY, VERY BEAUTIFUL.

BARION TO COYUL: THEN PULL THE PLUG.

COYUL TO BARION: LOVE TO. ALL BEST, XXXX

33

All this significance—what does it mean?

Reeking of smoke and burrito, Roy Stride booted open the door to Coyul's salon and invaded with Drumm behind him. He'd left his Lüger behind, not trusting any weapon that read BANG instead of doing it. Right now his fury was a more formidable threat.

"Where is he?" Roy fumed. "Where's the Devil?"

"Ah, Mr. Stride. Just a moment." Coyul paused to feed a notation to his computer with two fingers, orchestrating with the remaining three. "We were expecting you. Good of you to be prompt."

Roy dismissed the ineffectual little man with one contemptuous glance. "I got no time for you, pussy. Wanta see the Honcho, you got it? The Devil."

"The term is considered gauche, old boy," said Drumm, whose flat American accent waxed suddenly British.

"True," said Coyul. "I prefer simply Prince."

Seething with his recent humiliation, Roy didn't connect at first. Not this nerdy little wimp in a business suit. "Don't shit me, man."

"Wouldn't think of it. Sit down."

"Fuck I will!"

"Over there." With no effort of his own, Roy floated swiftly toward and into a designer chair, unable to leave it. "All right, Barion."

Two men entered the salon—one dark, about Roy's size, who looked like he didn't have a single spot in his body without steel springs, the other big as a Redskin lineman in jeans. One of those blond college jokers he always saw in soft-drink commercials, making out with prime tail. Fucking big fag with muscles. He sat down across from Roy.

"Listen carefully, Mr. Stride," Barion began without prelude. "Your future depends on it. To begin with, you're not dead."

"Not . . . Drumm, what the hell is this?"

But even that stalwart's manner had changed. "It's the plot resolution, laddie. Do you gentlemen mind if I get out of costume? Awfully tired of it."

"By all means, Ned." Coyul's manicured hands fluttered in gracious assent. "And well done."

The sardonic Booth clapped slowly. "Applause, applause."

While Roy gaped, Drumm's image blurred, sloughing pounds, mustache and toupee, resolving to the fine-trained figure of Edmund Kean. He bowed to Roy. Coyul applauded lightly, presenting a second player.

"And a call for the ubiquitous Wilkes Booth."

With negligent ease, the lithe figure of Booth went squat and leathery green, quite vivid in Roy's memory.

"As Damocles." Coyul applauded. "Marvelous invention, Wilksey."

"You honor me, Prince. I was also outstanding as Dane." Another quick dissolve to the romantically tragic form of Charity's doomed lover.

"We don't need the entire dramatis personae," Kean reminded him sourly.

"The laborer is worthy of his hire," Booth countered with dignity, "and the player of his calls." The larger-than-life tragedy of Dane became something mundane out of daytime TV in tailored slacks, designer haircut and a Members Only casual jacket. "As Randy Colorad."

Kean sniffed. "Juveniles were always your forte."

But Booth was not finished. While Roy stared, a horrible realization dawning, the vacuous good looks of Randy Colorad aged, lined, set into the sensitive and thoughtful image of Ernst Stahler.

"No! I blew you away," Roy denied. "I saw your fuckin head go six ways from Sunday."

And again Booth stood before him. "Stahler was my finest work. Deep, thoughtful. I may consider character work henceforth. Nevertheless—John Wilkes Booth at your service."

Roy had never been that good in school, but some names stayed in the pantheon of memory. "I remember you. You shot Abraham Lincoln."

"As a soldier of the Confederacy, sir."

"Stahler was utterly fine," Coyul appreciated sincerely. "I saw new depths and colors, Wilksey. Restrained, sincere . . . impressive. One was reminded of Schofield."

"Thanks, my liege. I believed in what I was saying," Booth recalled soberly. "Futile, even laughable I might have been in life, but at least in my time life meant something. Your world is a sewer, Mr. Stride. One can almost absolve you for being one of its diseases."

"Time, Coyul," Barion put in. "Sorlij and Maj, remember?"

"Right." Coyul struck his hands together. "Wilksey, I made you a promise."

"Please, Prince: not *Romeo*."

"Not a whit. We'll leave that to Leslie Howard. You may remount *Hamlet*."

Booth went down on one knee in gratitude. "Oh, my liege. My Prince—"

"Now, now. Don't gush, there's a catch. You'll alternate Hamlet and Laertes with Ned."

"You give me leave to kill, sir." Kean bowed with relish. "After that fruity Dane, I'll eat this buffoon for breakfast."

"Will you?" Booth rose to the challenge. "Look to your own ratty laurels, you laboring-class lout."

"Gentlemen, allow me to finish." Coyul's machinations were subtler than they knew. "Ned, you'll keep Wilkes within the bounds of good taste. And he in turn will teach you to fence like a gentleman."

"And somewhat less like a dancing bear," Booth sniped.

"With less mayhem to the scenery," Coyul hoped, escorting them to the door. "Now off with you both. Don't call me; I'll call you."

"You first, Ned." Booth stood aside. "You're considerably my elder."

"Ah, well—wisdom before folly." Kean swept out, but Booth lingered expectantly, raising his eyes in supplication. "Max? It's my *exit.*"

The musical leitmotif of genial bonhomie sparkled in the salon. Booth's amber spotlight washed over him. Satisfied, with a heave of the shoulders, he followed Kean.

"You said I ain't dead," Roy blurted. "I don't get it. What's all this about?"

"Shut up. You'll get it. Believe me, you're going to get it." Barion's tone chilled Roy to the bone. His skin began to crawl under that merciless scrutiny. The son of a bitch looked like . . . eternity.

"You bug me, mister," Barion said.

"So who the fuck are you?" Roy bluffed. "Look, I'm covered, okay? I got treaties, Topside's word. No interference. I came here to see the Prince and it's this little wimp. So no bullshit, okay? Lemme go to the top."

Barion leaned back in his chair. "You're there."

Roy took a moment to digest and discard the absurdity. God did not wear Levi's. "Not you, man."

"In your parlance, you got it. As close as you'll ever get."

"Hey, listen, I *saw* God close up at the White Rose Motel. He sentenced me—"

"My friend Walter Hampden," Barion admitted. "Doesn't act much now but still does an occasional God, Moses or prophet. You're not dead. Charity's not dead, nor Woody. You can go home now if you want."

"Which we would prefer," Coyul remarked with a tinge of distaste. "The twentieth century is the foulest on record; makes the fourteenth immaculate by comparison. And it has produced, in a country like America, far too many like you."

"I wasn't ready for Hitler in 1933," Barion confessed. "I really didn't know how to deal with the danger of your kind or your sick needs. We've learned since then. Stahler put it nicely, you're a disease. The worst of what I could never breed out of humans."

"Though we certainly don't want to breed it into more," Coyul extended his brother's point. "If you married Charity—grisly prospect, but she was ignorant enough to go through with it—we shuddered to think what you'd have done to each other."

"Or your children to the world," Barion finished. "Charity is a great deal more intelligent than you. A son of hers could be quite gifted in beneficial ways. On the other hand, growing up under your benevolent influence, these gifts . . ." The beleaguered Lord of Creation let the obvious point dangle. "For Charity to put you aside as a reasoned act of will or even simple good taste was too risky in a place like Plattsville, where people pair at disastrous random for lack of wider choice."

"What are you trying to lay on me?" Roy sputtered. "You ain't neither one of you what you say. Look, I ain't dumb. You saw me on TV. You saw how they loved me. They fuckin *loved* me. I raised my hand and changed everything."

Coyul wandered to the piano, running a scale. "We do crowd scenes well."

"No." Barion shook his head. "He doesn't believe it. He can't. Like higher math to that monkey at the water hole. His whole cosmos is drama, magic, fable. A vision of Christ and Salvation awash with melodrama, God as a white man, himself as hero. Minorities for villains. But he's going to believe it."

Barion rose deliberately and stood over Roy. "You're going to. Charity saw the truth when she was ready for it. But you, little man, you're going on cold. Coyul?"

Coyul ran an arpeggio into a Gershwin phrase. "I did this with a snake once. Ready or not, Mr. Stride—it's magic time."

His tormentors shimmered, dissolved to pure white light, became one glow as they flowed toward, into and through Roy. The last thing he clearly remembered was an instant of euphoria as that light became limitless understanding and infinite vision.

He was pure mind, pulsing in space, no division between sight and comprehension. He saw the solar system, then the galaxy dreaming through its eon-slow revolution. His view pulled back and back to encompass the unimaginably vast, wheeling universe, video-split with the movement of atoms within a molecule. Clear, painful intellect himself, he saw everything Coyul or Barion had ever seen—worlds men would not contact for thousands of years, if ever. Civilizations, concepts of God undreamable by humans. He knew horrors beyond simple brutality or destruction, complex beauties, a peace in being one with the universe, and the loneliness of being inexpressibly small, apart and insignificant.

Roy heard and understood languages whose simplest concept strained his mind to tortured sentience, heard music of a sublime, limpid simplicity. He observed the rise, flourishing and decline of noble and brutish races, watched them voyage out into space with the same greedy wonder as savages pushing log canoes toward the plunder of a neighboring island. Time spooled out, an endless film strip of still frames to which his hurtling consciousness gave the illusion of movement. Light-years, light-millenniums, light-eons. More galaxies and more beyond them, to worlds still forming, cooling, thunderous with the struggles of small-brained monsters that knew only hunger and rage.

Time and again the nascent worlds; time and again, given the narrow conditions of climate and distance from a sun, inevitably there rose one creature, manlike or utterly alien, racked for one moment/millennium with the terror and beauty of self-knowledge, drawn onward ever after, unable to retreat. And worlds beyond these, but nowhere an end. Nothing that glorified Roy Stride, nowhere a destiny in his size begun in the writings of a people he despised, attaining dramatic close in a crucifixion, endlessly vindicated in the violence of men like himself—none at least without a pathetic ending. Myriads like him came to power, shadows on film as his mind sped across time, rose, conquered, added their madness to the rubble spinning between the worlds, then died reviled or forgotten. Or worse, lampooned, made a sad or faintly ridiculous footnote in the dry histories of aberration.

Roy's cry of horror filled the universe, more horrible for the indifferent silence that swallowed it up. He wept with double pity, for himself and a knowledge of tragedy too huge for expression; whimpered in his smallness and fear, shrieked through the soundless void—

—put his hands to his face, shattered in the chair while the Devil played Gershwin and God spoke quietly to him.

"So much for the universal. Not much from your point of view. No MGM cosmos to answer the subjective hungers of your life. No denouement where God's lost will is found in the chimney naming you the Pure White Chosen One. Only worlds beyond worlds and a chance to understand in a place where death comes to all, even Coyul and I." The brothers exchanged a look of profound weariness. "After several hundred million years, that's not horror but relief."

"One tires of repetition," said Coyul at the piano.

"But what's it *mean*," Roy cried, agonized. "What is it for?"

"Not for anything. It exists."

Roy glared from one to the other. "I wanta go home. You said I could go home."

"You can." Barion nodded. "But there's a catch."

"Neat but nasty." Coyul struck an ominous minor chord.

"You'll remember everything, Roy. You'll see everything you were or wanted for its pointlessness, understand every motive for its cowardice and frailty. You'll know."

"Everything I just seen?" Roy faltered. "I gotta live with that?"

"You got it: everything. You won't know a day, an hour, a minute without that burden. You're not any more intelligent than you were, just more informed and defenseless against honesty. You'll spin out your life in an ordinary job with an ordinary wife dim enough to think you a blessing, until your kidneys or your heart fail or your cells begin to ad-lib with cirrhosis or cancer. You'll always know the meaning of what you've seen but never be able to express or accept it."

"It's—" Roy broke off, wincing as something happened in his head, like parts of his brain stretching to touch others. "It's insane."

"Oh, not as bad as all that." Coyul polished off " 'Swonderful" with a flourish and bounced up, shooting his cuffs meticulously. "There's the good side. Allow me, Barion?"

"Please do. I wouldn't want our hero to think us inhumane."

"You can always come back Below Stairs—permanently this time—with no unpleasant memories at all," the Prince of Darkness offered. "No strings, even a Drumm to support you, armies of illusions to hail you, inexhaustible minorities to massacre, mountains of architecture to express your magnificence. Even Florence Bird to defile you cheerfully on demand, since you seem to need that. They won't be real but you won't know that—except now and then, perhaps, in dreams you'll never quite remember."

"Or quite forget," Barion finished reminiscently. "You're the underside of my errors. Char Stovall is what I meant by human."

"Which reminds me. Will you excuse me?" Coyul appealed to his brother. "I've grown very fond of the lass. Like to take her home myself."

"By all means, but don't dawdle. There's Sorlij and Maj."

"Dear Sorlij. Lovely Maj." Coyul's smile was small and cryptic. "We'll have to deal with them, won't we? *Auf Wiedersehen,* Mr. Stride." Coyul glowed, sparkled and was gone. Barion turned back to business, unpleasant as it was. "Well, Roy?"

"It ain't fair."

"No, it ain't. But that's the deal."

Still numbed by the horror of the indifferent universe, Roy felt himself lifted out of the chair and set on his feet before the huge man who was close as he'd ever get to God. *Why you gotta be so big? Why do you always get to look down on me? Son of a bitch, you done that all my life.*

"Size is irrelevant," Barion noted casually, shrinking and modifying to a new appearance—shorter than Roy, dark as Moonlight Jones. "You dig it better this way, white boy?"

The rage dimmed Roy's mind, blotting out even the fear. Even though he knew why the red sickness boiled up in him and that the black man was only a cartoon of his own fear, his fists balled around the hate. Roy sprang at the figure.

"You black mother—

34

The catsup factor

—over and over again, Leon screaming about judgment and efficiency, Roy grabbing for fat Florence. Woody pushed her down behind a table and landed between her and the bomb just as it went off. God, the blast hit Woody all over and leaked through like a sieve *Woody, Woody, don't die for real.* And then, with his mouth close to hers, he simply kissed it to shut her up.

"Who's dead? It's catsup."

"Catsup." Her ears still rang from the explosion, too numbed to be sure she heard him right.

"And fake blood. It's all bullshit, Char. Just a little messy."

"Catsup . . ."

Charity sighed, close to waking. If Roy was the biggest asshole ever born, Woody was the biggest clown, with a nice kind of crazy in him. If she saw all this on the Late Show—

"Wouldn't believe it . . ." Charity's head lolled the other way on the seat, jolted by movement. She opened her eyes. Dark outside, shadows and fog blurring past the cab windows. She recognized the back of Jake's head, cap perched at a familiar angle. "Jake?"

Someone was holding her hand. "Well, Char?"

She blinked hard, rubbed the last sleep-fuzz from her eyes. "Simmy?"

"Even he. How goes it?"

"Don't know." Her stomach felt definitely odd. Misty limbo streamed by the car windows at great speed. "Where are we?"

"Almost to Plattsville," Jake tossed over his shoulder.

She tried to grasp the fact but failed, though one question formed itself loud and clear. "Simnel, where's Woody? What happened to him?"

"Waiting for you in McDonald's. I suppose I should clarify," Simnel offered in his kindly/careful manner. "The good news is, you're not dead."

"Not . . ." No, that couldn't be. "But I saw. I saw in the motel—"

Simnel looked slightly embarrassed. "Shameless special effects."

"I had a heart attack—"

"Real as the blood on your dress."

Dear old Simmy—laying a bolt of lightning on her in the same meticulous way he served champagne and strawberries. Charity was a very practical girl; she reacted in character. "*That's* why my stomach feels weird: I'm hungry." The backlash was swift and predictable. "Simmy, what the hell is going on?"

From the driver's seat, Jake reproved gently: "That's no way to speak to the Prince."

That took a moment to sink in before Charity rejected it. No way. She remembered the horned nightmare who got her number at the White Rose. "You are the—"

"Prince will do," Simnel/Coyul suggested. "We keep it nondenominational. "As for Simnel: from Lambert Simnel, another pretender. I wanted to look after you personally; you were very important to me."

"Thank you," said Charity, a little abashed. "You were a nice butler."

"We try to make it fun." Coyul nodded to the compliment. "Now and again things turn serious. Roy was serious. That's the bad news. He's not dead, either."

Charity struggled to comprehend, battling the last tatters of deep-rooted superstition. "But the—" She made vague pantomimic allusion to claws, horns and the unspeakable Damocles. They were exactly what she would have expected to see dying in sin. But that seemed a very long time ago. She could far more readily believe in plump little Simmy in his pinstripe suit, even liked the muted paisley tie.

"The night we abducted you," Coyul explained, "you were about to make a ruinous pact with your own scruples and marry Roy."

"No, I wouldn't" she denied vehemently. "I don't even hate him anymore. I don't feel anything for Roy but sad."

"You would have married him," Coyul was gently certain. "This is Plattsville."

"Just passed the city limits," Jake put in. Charity began to recognize houses and streets through the thinning mist.

"And here in Plattsville, there weren't that many options open to you."

No, she refused stubbornly. *I would have seen through him. I would've picked Woody.*

"In time, perhaps," Coyul answered her thought casually. "After the white dress, the wedding, the years and the children. One of whom would have been bright as you but tending to his father's failings. What Roy did with shadows Below Stairs, his son—the seething product of his ignorance and your inevitable frustration—could very well perpetrate here in a country susceptible to charismatic charlatans as a dog to fleas."

Charity needed no great mental leap to know that for truth. When she'd thought of God before, she always saw Purdy Simco, and maybe Jeffrey Hunter as Jesus, but always Roy as John the Baptist. As the cab turned into Main Street, Charity wasn't all that sure whether she was glad to be in Plattsville again, except Woody would be there.

And yet . . . something else, something once a part of her but gone forever now. "I feel like I lost something, Simmy."

"Not to worry; quite natural." He patted her hand. "One of your ancestors felt the same way. But you'll manage. Never fails, Char: every so often at the beginnings of your kind"—Coyul kissed his fingertip and transferred the blessing to the tip of her nose—"comes one smart little monkey. There."

Once again, as at Club Banal, Charity experienced an almost

subliminal frame of memory—a pool of water, a dim image reflected . . . then nothing.

"But I do apologize for the theatrics at the White Rose."

"I think you should, Simmy. I might have had a real heart attack."

"Look at it this way," said the Prince of Darkness as the cab slid to the curb before McDonald's. "If I'd knocked on the door in a pinstripe, what could I sell you? Goodbye, Miss Stovall."

"Ms." Charity corrected him. "I just got liberated, remember?"

Jake alighted to open her door, but Charity lingered long enough to give Coyul an impulsive kiss and a squeeze. "Listen: if you have to pull this on anyone else, don't use the horns, okay?"

"I give you my word, that was an absolute first. If it's any consolation, tomorrow I may be out of a job altogether."

She cocked her head quizzically. "Would God let that happen?"

"He's in trouble, too. It's all very involved. Go on, now. Have talented children. At least one musician."

"Bye, Simmy."

Jake lounged against the front fender, hands in his pockets. "I suppose I'll miss you, Char."

"Don't say that," she said with no exaggeration. "I'll be wishing I was dead for real."

"Not you; not with all that living to do."

"Tell the truth, Jake, I almost—"

"No." He stopped her, pulling Charity close to him. "Never mistake compassion for something else. You could end up making a career out of it like Mary Magdalene," he recalled. "Always getting had and left. But she was that sort, an injury collector."

Charity understood him with canny female instinct. "You want to be alone always? I don't think so, Mr. Iscariot."

"It suits me."

Her affection just then was not at all myopic. "You haven't burned all your old vanities, Jake. There's a few left."

"Well." Jake opened the cab door brusquely.

"Don't tell me." Charity held on to him. "You've got a call."

He seemed anxious to be gone, glancing both ways along the street. "Maybe. Hate to deadhead all the way back."

"Wait, will you?" Charity pulled his head down to hers and kissed him. No, he wasn't good at it as Woody, but still almost worth being dead for. "I don't care if Simmy is the Prince and all that. Take him at gin rummy. He's a pushover."

"So are you." The sudden, urgent pressure of his embrace surprised Charity; dead or alive, still a definite hunk. "An abyss of sentiment."

"Go to hell," she murmured against his cheek.

"On my way."

Charity watched him slide across the front seat and drive away, turning at the next corner, cruising, ready to stop for a fare.

My God, I'm alive. I remember the water hole and being lost and afraid. I remember someone making me somehow human, and the other one who took my fear of the face in the water and made me laugh at it. If that's the truth under all the Sunday-school trappings, I guess I can live with it. Have to.

A little giddy; she'd never had thoughts like that or so easily expressed. *They've kicked me upstairs, just like they did at the water hole. Please, Simmy, help us to keep laughing.*

When Charity turned to go into McDonald's, the first human being she saw through the windows was Woody Barnes, looking alive as she felt.

35

The higher education of Roy Stride

—fucker!"

The blow launched at Barion found nothing to land on, threw Roy off balance. He sprawled on oily, stinking gravel. Roy blinked, shook his head, stared groggily at the man-made hills of the Plattsville garbage dump and up at the universe.

"I'm not dead. He said I'm not dead."

He lurched up, brushing garbage from the SS uniform; they'd left him that. They left him a lot more. His head hurt. His mind felt like a push-button FM tuner punching back and forth between two stations, two voices, his own and the scary one.

And the nightmare visions: pure mind again, watching from a great distance as the planets, from blistering Mercury to the dark ice ball of Pluto, wheeled about the roaring sun.

. . . **worlds beyond worlds, nothing finite or contained but opening out forever in an infinite process of becoming. Intelligence subjective, flawed, needing ever to renew itself, cleanse vision, reform with no truth ultimate.**

No!

Roy squeezed palms to his ears to shut out that serene, cruel voice. *NO!* he defied the broken refrigerators, plastic food containers, greasy tinfoil and rusted, skeletal Chevies. "It ain't like that. You can look it up in the Bible—"

Consider "Aryanism" first as a careless misinterpretation of a blanket term for a prehistoric people, later as an apology for white supremacy. This compounded error served as dogma for the diseased pseudophilosophy of Adolf Hitler, itself based on his severe paranoia.

"I don't know these words," Roy bellowed to the sprung-out sofas, broken kitchen chairs, pyramids of Hefty-bagged garbage and the incurious rats. "I'm alive. What you doing to my head?"

The visions would not leave him alone any more than the voice. Longer view now, beyond the solar system to the cold, bright stars, other systems whirling indifferently about the driving furnace of their suns.

Paranoia, the common cold of neurosis. The paranoiac, perceiving all external stimuli as threat, needs to see his enemies, not merely sense their external presence. Being imaginary, these threats must be fleshed out to visible targets, the more clearly defined the better. Thus the emotionally defeated German worker was given the Jew. His disadvantaged, disenfranchised American counterpart is offered not only the Jew but the Negro and Catholic—together with any group, way of life or system of belief not harmonious with his own, stamped with the label ENEMY in large red letters.

"You stop!" Roy sobbed to the microcosmos of broken Styrofoam, spent toothpaste tubes, Tampax, condoms, Kleenex and the small, night-foraging animals surviving now as his own kind once did. "Holy Jesus, get out of my head . . . STOP."

With his whole shriveled soul, he begged the voice to leave him alone. Against that gigantic clarity, he struggled to regain a small, neat box for a cosmos to believe in, with strong walls to contain all the truths he lived by, but the walls caved in under the pressure of what he knew and could never again deny.

He saw other systems now, the whole galaxy revolving with its own motives, rank with hatreds, vibrant with love, brilliant with alien striving in which he had no place or dramatic destiny, all wheeling ponderously through impersonal space and time.

Subconsciously aware of the fragility of his artificial reality, the

paranoiac must ever reinforce its defenses with more and more elaborate rationale. His virtues must be defined, his enemies painted in primary colors. The basic motive of fear is raised to mystic proportion: a cause, a uniform, a symbol. He proclaims his purposes one with God's.

"NO—"

The central infection inflames and eventually mortifies the entire psyche until any healthy stimulus becomes alien.

Roy stumbled through the reeking, rusted mountains of garbage toward the lights from Plattsville.

The fundamental problem of identity—

"I got no fuckin problems, man. None!"

—reaches to the core of being until even sexuality may be stunted. In males the basic relationship to women becomes dysfunctional. Commonly the subject may not be able to separate pleasure from guilt, and therefore pays with pain, quid pro quo. When this compensation becomes an intrinsic part of the natural pleasure principle, there can be no gratification without pain or defilement.

"This is . . . insane."

No, just reality. Being finite and wholly fallible myself, I have my own prejudices. What you call hang-ups.

"Why do you hate me?"

Because I'm subjective enough to be disgusted with a flaw in my own work. Because I'm in trouble, too, but you I can deal with. Live with it, Roy.

"That's right, live!" Roy hurled to the uninterested stars. "I'm alive. Nothing's changed. I win, you fuck."

Infantile, needing to be the center and reason for creation, the less educated or advantaged subject needs a distorted miraculous theology to support a perilous existence, externally and constantly threatened as it is by "them."

Howl.

Tightening, darkening, narrowing in ever-smaller circles—

Howl.

—until as your human joke puts it, the paranoiac eventually flies up his own metaphorical ass and disappears.

Roy reached the limits of Main where it became a feeder road to the Interstate. He hooked his arm around a lamppost, tottering, while the brutal light in his brain grew brighter and brighter. *Can you cut it?* the cruel voice challenged, *or just give up?*

36

Perks for the upwardly mobile

Woody it was, solid, warm and alive in her arms, with all the customers in McDonald's gaping at them, some of the vocal opinion that young people had no manners, and if they wanted to make out they should go home or to a drive-in.

Charity came up for air somewhere around the fifth kiss. "Woody, we're alive."

"Promised you, didn't I?" he murmured into her hair. "Nothing will happen for me that you won't share."

She still hung on to him for dear life. "You did. You promised. Gol-lee, I must be alive for sure or I wouldn't be so hungry."

They dropped into two empty seats at a vacant table. "Oh, Woody—where we've been and what we've seen. Can we live with it?"

Woody laced his fingers with hers, still delighted with the reality of her next to him. "It wasn't your usual vacation. But what's so bad, Char? I've seen heaven and you've seen hell, and they're just what? Common sense, funny and horrible with a lot of bullshit thrown in, just like the six o'clock news."

When the adrenaline rush of excitement passed, both of them slumped with exhaustion, still holding on to each other. "Tell you what I can't do," Charity allowed on sober reflection. "Can't go back to the tabernacle."

"Not hardly."

That kind of faith was simply outworn. The revival-tent gyrations of Purdy Simco would rouse no more fervor in either of them than a storm-window commercial.

"Maybe we can be Unitarians."

Charity knew little of the breed. "What do they believe in?"

"Can't say for sure," Woody admitted, "but I don't think they want to kill anyone."

"I'm for that." Charity inhaled the ambrosial aroma of broiling burgers. "We got any money? I'm star—" She broke off mid-syllable at sight of the two familiar figures at the serving counter; this she had not figured on. "Woody, is that who it looks like?"

"Sure," he confirmed, quite used to miracles now. "Just came along to say goodbye."

Well, she had a new concept of normal now herself. Charity welcomed the sight of Milt Kahane, bouncing with more life than most live people she knew, charging down at their table laden with shakes and burgers, Essie Mendel in tow. "Hey, Char! Quite a show, huh?"

Charity blinked at him. "Can I ask a dumb question?"

Milt struck a chairman-of-the-board attitude. "I suppose you're wondering why we're here."

"Just stopped off on our way Topside," Essie twittered, opening her cheeseburger with the curiosity of an Egyptologist. "May my family never hear of this."

"I'm giving trafe lessons." Milt attacked his Big Mac with gusto. "You believe this woman has never been in McDonald's or Burger King? Life in the fast-food lane, lover. Try the shake."

Essie took an experimental bite and then sipped judicially at the vanilla shake. "The shake is nice. The burger kind of sticks in my throat. Maybe it's guilt. Finish it, Char."

Charity dove gratefully at the food. "What about your boyfriend in Accounting?"

"I wouldn't cry," Essie said primly. "Didn't I wait long enough for him? In a hundred years he'll still be going home to his mother. Which reminds me, Milton. I want to keep kosher when my parents come to visit, they'll expect. And furniture, leave the selection to me. I saw a really bee*yoo*tiful cream leather in an Ultimate Rise ad, really classy, and Topside we wouldn't have trouble keeping it clean, am I right? Speaking of clean, trust me, you wouldn't go wrong letting me pick out a few nice clothes for you, Milton. God maybe can get away with ratty jeans, he's eccentric, but you are still on the way up, and they don't do anything for your character or your position as an angel."

"What?" Charity choked on a mouthful. "Milt, you're a what?"

"An *arch*angel," Essie announced with a death lock on Milt's arm. "My fiancé, the Right Hand of God."

"Oh, hell." Milt just looked embarrassed. "They commissioned me after Beirut. Ninety-day wonder. Big deal."

"Anyway, people respect what they see." Essie was not to be deterred. "And an archangel in skuzzy clothes, what will they think? I don't keep a decent house? If you ask *me*, Milton, assimilation is one thing and plain sloppy is another. I wouldn't say a word if you want to look like a nebbish day laborer, but—"

Through all of which, Milt's tolerant smile grew slightly strained. "The next time I see something cute, please let it be a car."

"Hey, Milt." Charity noticed that both he and Essie were paling, losing natural tone like turning down the color on a TV set. "What's happening to you?"

"Oh." Essie jumped as if she'd spilled something on herself. "Milton, I think we have to go."

"I guess. Semper fi, Barnes. See you both not too soon." He rippled his trumpet valves. "Essie, let's make a memorable exit for the underpriviledged Wasps of Plattsville."

McDonald's customers, never used to the extraordinary in any sense, were rocked to their roots by Milt's piercing cavalry charge played triple forte as Essie bowed gracefully to the house.

"I want to thank all the little people," she effused, blowing kisses. "The technicians, the grips, my aunts in Hadassah—"

"And for your sterling support of the Jewish Defense League." Milt took his bow. "Which helped us this year to blow up more Lebanese and Palestinians than ever before. *Shalom havarim,* and for our final impression of the evening, something in your own ballpark: a televangelist's bank account."

With a final wave to Woody and Char, they simply vanished.

One woman ran gibbering for the door, but that was extreme. Another customer said aloud it was probably just a publicity stunt for the new shopping mall on the Interstate. It was all done with mirrors, and they'd seen David Copperfield vanish the Statue of Liberty on TV. Just they didn't know Woody and Charity hung out with Jews, you know? They went back to eating.

"Know what I'll miss?" Charity mumbled through a mouthful. "I'll bet there's not one place in this whole damn town where you can get good Brie or smoked salmon, something you can really taste . . . Woody? What's wrong? You look—"

He was staring through the front window, the happiness washed out of his eyes. Charity turned to see what it was and went cold. The wraith framed in the restaurant window stared back at them, then passed out of sight.

Woody got up, tight and quiet. "Come on, Char."

She was suddenly afraid for both of them. "No. I don't want to see him. He's *sick*, Woody."

"He saw us." Woody picked up his trumpet case. "I don't want him hanging over our heads."

Like Damocles, Charity thought numbly, following Woody.

The night air was chill with the mist seeping along Main. Charity shivered. Woody took off his jacket and slipped it around her shoulders. They saw Roy a few doors down, leaning against the tabernacle window.

"Woody, I don't—"

He led her firmly on toward the desolate figure in the torn, fouled uniform, now a sardonic comment on the tragedy of Roy. From his attitude, face in his hands, Charity thought he was weeping, but no. When he raised his head, there was light enough from the streetlamp to know that those eyes would never weep again. They were the dry-scorched exhaustion after the last weeping of the world.

"I won," Roy told them. "They couldn't hold me. I can stay here if I want or go back if I want. The first sumbitch in the history of the *world* can go anywhere I want. I got it all." The swaggering tone softened with a note of pleading. "Come back with me, Charity."

Revolted, she didn't want to touch him, as much pity as she felt. "I can't, Roy."

"Shit you can't." Roy's eyes, dangerous and a little mad, slid to Woody. To Charity, they were the most frightening thing about him. "You got lucky. You caught me off guard in the club. Things'll be different when I go back."

"We can't go back," Woody told him quietly. "Char can't. She's alive."

Roy's crafty grin went colder. "I can take her."

"Why?" Charity blurted. "You don't want me. I *saw* what you want. I was there, I saw it on TV, again and again. You telling me how it would be, while a little girl got her head blown off."

"There's always blood at the beginning of a new order, got to be. Cleaning house."

"That baby was me, Roy."

He didn't understand. "You crazy? I was there; just a little Jew kid—"

"*She was me.*" The passion propelled her closer to Roy, and the clarity of the next thought surprised her. "Because if it wasn't, it wasn't anyone."

Roy pushed himself away from the window; the act seemed difficult for him. He wobbled as if both legs had gone to sleep. "Look, I ain't got much time." Even his voice sounded dry, coming from a long distance. "Have you seen it? Have you seen it all? The *nothing.*" Roy stared beyond the fog. "Just space and balls of rock, out and out and on and on forever and nobody, nothing out there to make us mean anything . . . Stop. Please, stop."

They edged back from him. He was a dead man come back for something after his own funeral.

"Come on, Charity." Roy reached for her. "I don't belong here no more."

She knew he was right. Nowhere in life, nowhere real.

"All those voices," Roy whispered. "All those lousy fuckin books, they're in my *head* and they won't shut up. They make me know things—STOP!"

Charity yearned from her heart, "I wish to God I could help you, Roy. But I can't."

"Don't shit me with that God stuff!" The words came out half snarl, half despair. "I seen God and the Devil. Couple of wise-ass wimps, that's all. But they never showed me Jesus Christ. They knew they couldn't sell me a phony Jesus Christ."

"I saw him," Woody said. He felt a pity, too, but even that was running out. "You wouldn't buy him either. He looks like an Arab. Come on, Char."

Roy lurched toward them. If his coordination was poor, nothing diminished the danger of him. "You ain't taking Charity. I got it made back there, anything I want. What she gonna do with a dumb shit horn player can't make a dime?"

"She's going to live," Woody said. "That's more than you can cut."

"You gonna stop me?" Roy drew the small ceremonial dagger from his belt. Light glinted from the honed edge. His laughter was a fading echo. "What you gonna do, Barnes, kill me?"

Woody moved between Roy and Charity. Roy slashed suddenly with the knife. Woody grabbed for his wrist but the movement was too quick. Woody felt the hot sting of the blade across his upthrust palm. He blinked at it; the blade should have cut deep but there was no more than a scratch.

"Woody—" Charity saw what was happening before he did. Roy was fading, piece by piece like bits taken at random from a jigsaw puzzle, not so much disappearing as becoming less defined from the night around him. "Look at him . . ."

Woody saw now. Poised with the knife ready to come up, Roy was only half in the real world, his very image being washed away like sand from a shoreline.

"*Kill* you—" The knife swept up, but for all the fury behind it, the thrust was insubstantial as double-exposed film. Instinctively, Woody tensed for the shock but the knife and Roy's hand only passed through him, a faint shadow across his body. He felt nothing except revulsion, a *wrongness*. When he pushed at Roy he could barely feel the contact.

Woody swallowed hard, feeling sick. He backed away, holding Charity. "He's going. Walk away and don't look back."

Roy was fading to something like grainy old black-and-white film, screaming at them with a voice weirdly distant. "Charity, we can have it all. They *promised* me."

Pulled along by Woody, she started to cry. "Dear God, Woody, I feel so sorry for him."

Woody didn't slow. "Don't," he muttered. "He doesn't feel a thing."

"What you gonna do with him?" Roy wailed after them. "Live in shit like we always did. Nothing, that's what you got. That's what you are! You saw on TV. The people . . . all the people, the crowds. *They fuckin loved me . . .*"

They weren't that far but they could barely hear him now.

"Woody, I can't just—"

"Yes, you can. Keep going."

"Come back, Charity—"

"No." Charity pulled away from Woody's grip. "I know what's in his head. I *know*. It's beautiful and horrible and—"

"I've seen it, too," Woody said. "And we can get up in the morning and live with it all day for the rest of our lives. He can't. That's the difference, Char. That was always the difference. Forget it."

No, she couldn't just walk on, walk away, but twisted around to see Roy because he hurt so. She prayed for him, the only kind of prayer she could believe in now: *Simmy, take care of him. The light's too bright and the truth is too cruel.*

Charity searched the sidewalk up and down the street on both sides. She thought she saw something move, but it was only a shadow in the thin fog wisping between her and the streetlight.

Roy felt marvelous, renewed power surging through him. Drunk with his own charisma, he didn't notice he wasn't breathing at all, didn't need to. His uniform was crisp and new as the day he swaggered out of the Whip & Jackboot. No voices but his own echoed in his head, and the adoration of the crowds. No other truth had ever disturbed that perfect balance. He remembered only the balcony, the reaching arms and hoarse voices raised to him—needing, loving, validating him. Making him God.

He was the Man now, Topside no problem, the Devil a fat little faggot. One day that little shit would get dumped on his ass, and when he looked around to see what hit him, there'd be Roy Stride in his chair.

His boots rang on the deserted sidewalk in cadence with the cleansing, conquering thought. He didn't hear the car round the corner behind him and purr silently to the curb.

"Leader Stride?" The cabby snaked out of the driver's seat and came around to open the passenger door. "Cab?"

"You got it." Sure of his destiny, Roy touched the whip to his cap. An image flickered in his memory wiped clean of everything else. The driver's face was familiar. He reminded Roy of some actor. "Don't I know you?"

"Sure you do." Judas lifted the money bag from his own breast and dropped it around Roy's neck. "We're practically blood brothers."

The small bag of silver coins was surprisingly heavy and would not come off.

37

Doom at the top

If Sorlij and Maj were appalled at Topside, Below Stairs was sheer trauma. A rapid but thorough survey of Earthside records only darkened their findings. With each new aspect, the problem grew more complex. They weighed observations, consulted law precedents in their library banks and finally summoned the errant brothers to a meeting in the matter-phased ship poised to streak home across the universe.

Sorlij broached the inevitable. "I don't quite know how to begin."

Maj knew very well how. "A crime has been committed: of error or gross assumption, call it what you will. The only question is: which of you is guilty of what?"

Coyul pondered the deck under his feet and wished he was Below Stairs drinking with Dylan Thomas.

"The magnitude of your presumption," Sorlij accused Barion. "The rampant disregard for law or ethics. That emotional rain forest you call Topside—"

"That chaos you call Below Stairs," Maj added. "And Earth itself."

"And Earth," Sorlij echoed. "That garden of lethal delights, churning out art, morals and murder. Never . . . never in all my experience." Sorlij paced the deck, lower lip jutted out in deliberation. "The greatest crimes. The gravest charges."

"Sorlij," Coyul interjected casually, "did I ever tell you that you render pomposity into art?"

"I have no love for either of you, never did," Sorlij snapped. "What Maj and I had to work for, the little darlings of the gods had handed to them. I'm not blameless, I left you here. This will reflect on my career."

"And mine," said Maj. "We had attained some prominence."

"What a shame." Barion shrugged. "A bad day for the Kelp King."

"And his wife, the cosmic yuppie. Can you believe this, Barion? We're getting class struggle. *A bas les aristos.*"

"Go ahead, laugh," Sorlij warned. "There'll be charges and conviction. I need not enlarge the consequences."

"And there are further complications," Maj took up the indictment. "If your post-life playpens are beyond description, Earth is not. In the midst of all that mess, there appears to be a great deal of healthy good. Admirable aspects. Some grasp, however inept, of real significance."

Sorlij agreed wearily. "An anomalous mutant."

"Transient is a better term, dear: halfway between what it was and whatever Barion wanted it to become. Quite unique."

"As anthropoids go," Sorlij qualified. "What you have is a weird neurotic balance. On the bottom end, this primitive dualism; on the high end, something I can only call sublime. If only they could *grow up!*"

"And that is our point." Maj's exquisite brows furrowed in a deep frown. "As one of their major languages puts it, you've painted yourself into a coroner."

"I think you mean corner," Coyul assisted delicately. "That's English, very metaphorical tongue. Yes, hoist by our own petard."

"Out on a limb with a power saw," said Barion, already seeing the barren vistas of the Rock.

A no-need-to-prolong-it glance passed between Sorlij and Maj. "The point is," Sorlij plunged into the thick, "these anthros are too good to waste but far too unstable to be left unattended. However traumatic, they must be reeducated very quickly. Barion, I'm sorry"—Sorlij even managed to look it—"Coyul will be allowed some time at home before sentencing. You'll have to be left here. I doubt if anyone will be returning for you."

Barion expected to do time, but—"Never?"

"I doubt it," Sorlij judged. "The balance here is too delicate. They're not just a lab culture but humans with obvious and unexpected potential. We can't just leave them."

"No, we can't," Barion admitted, glancing at Coyul. He already missed his brother.

"You must finish what you started. Though honestly"—Sorlij gestured vaguely—"I would have thought it not only illegal but impossible. I don't know how you managed it."

"He didn't." Coyul rose, adjusting his tie. "I did. We needn't go on with this. I confess. Oh, Barion was tempted, but . . ."

Sorlij and Maj were not minded to parse degrees of guilt; Coyul was in enough trouble already and Barion, they reminded him, had already confessed.

"Of course he would." Coyul grew more supercilious by the moment. "That mountainous ego won't share guilt any more than glory. Regarding humans, Barion was always more romantic than competent. He simply didn't realize the errors in our own technology."

"Didn't real—" Barion shot to his feet, stung and confused. "Look, I cleared you. I confessed."

"An egotist to the end. I did it, Sorlij. I had to do *something* until you paragons of responsibility came back for us."

Barion began to heat up. "He's lying through his teeth. Why are you doing this, Coyul?" He appealed to the inquisitors. "You remember him in school. Carbon-cycle life classes were his nap time. He couldn't augment a respectable paramecium without a crib sheet."

"Ha! Couldn't I?"

"The point is valid, Coyul. We have serious doubts, easily resolved." Sorlij activated a keyboard, fingers dancing over inductance pads that sprayed formulae over a large screen behind him. "The simple chemistry of primitive apse-to-synapse combination, with one minute error. Barion, find the error and restate."

Barion scanned the formulae, obvious as a child's cartoon,

found the error in the amino-protein elements. He corrected and restated. "First-year stuff."

Sorlij wiped the screen. "Quite correct. Now—"

Coyul contradicted him. "Quite wrong."

"Coyul, don't be an ass," Barion beseeched. "Not now."

"You were wrong because the whole theory is wrong."

"Really?" Sorlij smiled at Coyul like a spider about to lunch. "We'll find a different set of errors for you. Something simpler."

"Don't bother. These will do." Coyul flexed his fingers like a pianist warming up. On each hand the five fingers divided in two. Twenty slender digits stabbed at the keyboard in a swift toccata of statement, foresting the screen with symbols. "Stated. And here—"

The screen wiped to one subformula in the amino-protein group from which Coyul generated a whole family tree of results.

"You've only restated the error," Maj said.

"No. Science is only exact when experimentation proves it so. We should begin by assuming we're wrong. Unfortunately, we have certain failings in common with humans."

Prominent among which, Coyul noted, was not liking to be wrong even in regard to a remote study like carbon-cycle life in which none of their own electron-cycle kind had much prolonged empirical experience. Formal academics had generated plausible theory which worked in enough cases to be complacently accepted as law.

"What you call error is the actual propensity of protein enzyme acting as catalyst in evolving the anthropoid cortex—as you can see at a far greater rate than theory conceived. What theory fails to take into account is protein variation in a creature whose survival lies in its intelligence and ability to adapt. Barion was as hidebound as the rest of you in this."

"That's an assumption, not a factor," Sorlij challenged. "Show me the numbers."

"The precise variable," Maj specified. "What accelerated the protein?"

"Excuse me, I did forget." Rapidly, Coyul stated the oxygen components in the accepted theory. Underneath, the actual, richer oxygen content of Earth's Pliocene atmosphere and its more rapid effect on protein enzyme action, neatly stated in percentage. "There we are, children: how Daddy did the guilty work of the Sixth Day. Accept no substitutes."

A silent but sufficing bombshell. Staring at the formulae, Barion tried to find some point for refutation and saw none. Out of their own field, Sorlij and Maj could still see the obvious on the screen. These figures made Cultural Threshold at 900 cc not only possible but predictable.

Maj spoke first. "Would it be tedious to ask *why*, Coyul?"

"There was nothing else to pass the time." His silly titter nailed the lid on Coyul. "It amused me."

"But he *didn't*," Barion sputtered. "His figures are right, I admit, but *I* did it. I can re-create my process step by step."

Sorlij just shook his head. "Barion, please. We admire your loyalty, but . . ."

Shielded from them, Barion's mind leaped at Coyul's—

YOU IDIOT, WHAT ARE YOU DOING? YOU KNOW I DID IT.

NO, Coyul thought back with a ripple of humor, WE DID IT. HARDLY WORTH MENTIONING AT THE TIME, LIKE ONE BUTTON LEFT UNDONE. I JUST DID YOU UP. WE WERE YOUNG THEN. LIKE THE YOUNG ANYWHERE, YOU ADORED DABBLING WITH THE RADICAL, BUT INEVITABLY WENT HOME TO DINNER WITH THE ORTHODOX. CHECK MY FIGURES. Q.E.D.

Barion raged: MARGINAL VARIATIONS. THEY WOULDN'T MAKE THAT MUCH DIFFERENCE.

BUT THEY DID. AND WHEN IT COMES TO ANTHROS, THESE TURKEYS DON'T KNOW ENOUGH BEYOND BASICS TO ARGUE THE POINT.

Apparently they did not. "Coyul, you'll have to leave the ship now. Maj, prepare for energy phase."

"It's still a good question," Barion pressed, no longer caring if the others heard him. "Why?"

"You'll do time as an accessory, of course, but wherever they put you, brother, you'll go on doing what you do."

"And what about you?" Barion urged, concerned. "You can't run Topside like a demented B movie. What will you do?"

"What Sorlij ordered," Coyul said simply. "Make them grow up. Always wanted to. Now I've got to, haven't I?"

In truth, Coyul's motives were not entirely fraternal. Five million years had left a considerable human residue in his personality. He thought in human languages, spent more time than not in their form, understood them better by now than his own arid kind. He found it difficult, even deprivation to imagine existence without a Jake, a Wilksey, or an Elvira Grubb. Not to mention half a dozen musical compositions in various stages of completion that would find no audience on the Rock.

"I have a knack and I've really grown to like them," Coyul summed it up. "Go goose an amoeba." The rest of the sentiment was for Barion's mind alone—

DROP BACK WHEN THEY LET YOU OUT. I'LL SHOW YOU WHAT A PIANO PLAYER CAN DO.

Coyul blew a kiss to his brother, presented an expressive middle finger to Sorlij—which blossomed on afterthought into an American Beauty rose for Maj. "Here: stick it"—blazed into pure energy and was gone.

■ 38 ■

The new, the terrible and the maybes

The intense young man with the James Mason looks lounged in one of Coyul's salon chairs, listening as his abdicating Prince cleaned up last business. Jake admired Coyul's ability to communicate on any level, even the gaseous hype of Eddie Veigle. Coyul reclined in a contour chair, loafer-shod feet crossed on the Danish Modern desk, phone propped against one ear.

"Eddie, sweetheart: listen. The *putz* is back and you've got him. Yeah, he picked up his option. But let's not make things too easy for him. Did you save the tape? Dynamite. Tear your heart out until Char blew it with the yuks, right?"

Coyul listened to Veigle's woes, the dramatic possibilities gone down the tube with that uncontrollable explosion. The phone emitted a rancorous drone of disgust which Coyul gleefully turned out for Jake's benefit.

"I know, Eddie. Tears are prime time, laughs are late night. So anyway, Stride's all yours. Keep him happy, give him what he wants. All the extras and day players you need. Just don't frighten the horses or pedestrians in the better neighborhoods . . .

Okay, so *build* permanent sets. When did you ever go broke on overstatement?

Listening to the super-agent, Coyul winced at the smallest possibility of misunderstanding. "Eddie, are you trying to hurt my feelings? *Moi* who gave you exclusives on Bormann and Oswald? Of *course* you've got all rights: TV novelization, film, the whole enchilada . . . no problem, bubby. I always like doing business with people I love. Think big on this one; think Riefenstahl. *Triumph of the Will.* I'm bringing in a load of Topside talent. You can have C.B. Of *course* I mean De Mille. You're expecting Charlie Brown? What?" Coyul rolled his eyes at Jake in strained tolerance. "Eddie, what can I tell you? You want Griffith, you got him. What the hell, he needs a hit. Right. Terrific. Keep in touch. We'll have lunch. *Ciao,* kid."

The Prince of Darkness (or Light, depending on your translation) dropped the phone on its cradle. "Mr. Veigle is not an intellectual, Jake, but he is a predator. I made it worth his time to keep Roy Stride happy and off your back. That's how it goes; you'll have to talk to people in their own language, hold a few hands now and then, listen to problems. Develop outside interests, Jake; that helps on the bad days. Get out more, see people. You're getting a bit gloomy—but I think you'll manage smashingly."

Jake wasn't all that sure. "In your place? I'm just afraid . . ."

"Of what? You said it yourself, one of the two best minds in Judea, far from the worst Below Stairs."

"I certainly know Roy Stride, at any rate," Jake observed dryly. "I was once the kind of person who needed miracle workers. Messiahs. Now I wouldn't have one in the house."

"I understand Yeshua feels the same way now." Coyul swung his feet off the desk, checking his watch. He moved to a gilt-framed mirror. "Stroke them, Jake. Tell them what they want to hear, that's all they want."

"I'm not a leader, Prince."

"And I am?" Coyul countered out of the mirror. "I'm just a piano player, and precious little time I'll have for that now. Besides, you won't have to do it alone. I relied a great deal on your common sense for two thousand years, so I'm sending you real talent for Number Two. The other best mind in Judea."

"Yeshua?" Jake looked even more uncertain. "No, please. Not him."

"Bears no grudges. And he is the best."

"It's not that, Prince. You never had to live with that . . . He's impossible! He's always right."

Coyul smiled reminiscently, recalling Barion in his first few million years. "He's mellowed, Jake. And he misses you. Hasn't had a decent game of chess in ages. Well, it's your office now. Redecorate if you want, but avoid your habitual RKO Gothic; tends to depress visitors."

"Don't you understand?" Jake implored, desperate. "I'm *scared*."

"What can they do? Sue? Vote you out?" One more critical inspection in the mirror. No, Coyul decided: definitely the wrong look for Topside. The rich maroon tie became tasteful white on white. The off-white shirt went pastel blue in complement. As his costume modified, so did the Prince himself—taller, less corpulent, shoulders broader and straighter. The emotional mouth with its hint of petulance firmed to strength. "That will do it."

The figure who turned to Jake bore a resemblance to Lincoln or perhaps Gregory Peck. There were nuances of Clarence Darrow's bulldog tenacity and Truman's down-home integrity. The gravity of a wise king, the wry wit of a prairie philosopher quite at home in a barn or a summit meeting. The world-class wisdom and quiet authority in that image could sell oil to Arabs, Amex cards in the Kremlin.

"Yes, that will do it. Jake, you're an absolute power because over the ages you've learned absolute compassion and restraint and the knowledge that none of it is new and most of it is violence, treacle or pure hogwash. But . . . you're scared. So am I, Reb Judas. Talk about opening nights. As of now, I'm overdue Topside to meet a very confused delegation including Luther and Augustine—that eminently reasonable duo—Paul of Tarsus, Thomas Aquinas, a gaggle of the better popes, Joseph Smith, Jesuits, Taoists, Buddhists, disputing rabbis, Irish saints and God knows *how* many Fundamentalists still waiting like Oliver Twist with his bowl for their own kind of rhinestone salvation—and try to make them understand that all of them are the result of an

experiment neither well conceived nor even finished. Hah!"
Coyul snorted. "And *you're* scared?"

Coyul gave his tie a final tug. "Well, I asked for it, I guess. We
ultimately do what we want, though I don't have the foggiest
how to go about it. The therapists will have a field day and we'll
probably lose hordes to schizophrenia. But cry all they want,
stomp around, kick furniture, the human race will get rid of their
fairy-tale notions of good, evil and the cosmos, and by God—by
Me, I guess—they will grow the hell up."

Coyul subsided with a rueful chuckle. "You've got problems?
Forget it, I'll call you." With no further farewell, he vanished,
heading for a tight schedule—to reappear immediately with a
last afterthought.

"By the way: see that Wilksey gets a couple of good reviews for
the new *Hamlet.* Means so much to him. God bless, Jake."

God II went to work.

Alone, Judas Iscariot didn't move at first; when he did, his
actions were cautious, even timorous. He sat down tentatively at
Coyul's desk, lifted the phone, then put it down. He didn't want
to deal with anyone yet. His hypercritical eye gauged Coyul's
taste in decor, ending with the white piano. At a mental suggestion, the instrument blushed to dark mahogany and began a
pianissimo passage from the *Goldberg Variations.* Jake listened
for some moments, then materialized his chess set on the desk
before him.

Start small, he decided. Leave the glitz to Veigle. Do the big
stuff when you're ready.

He was definitely not ready for the young man who simply
appeared across the desk from him.

They could have said a great many things to each other, and no
doubt would have two thousand years earlier, but both were
much wiser now. Judas no longer needed a messiah at any price.
Yeshua no longer expected the world to buy spiritual common
sense even in parables. Both would do what they could with the
cosmos as it was. Perhaps this tacit understanding passed between them before Judas moved a white piece on the board.

Pawn to king four.

Yeshua responded: pawn to queen three.

"There you go," Judas growled, "being devious again."

"Shut up and move," Yeshua muttered, absorbed in the myriad possibilities of the opening.

■ 39 ■

Back to the drawing board . . .

The planet had no name. As it was so far out on the edge of the known universe, Barion's meticulous kind had noted it with a number on survey charts. Development of such worlds was not usual, their use rare and only for penal purposes. With very little water, the highest form of life was protozoan.

This was Barion's Rock. In a few million of its solar years, he might make parole, but the arch-instigator Coyul would never see home again.

Moving as restless energy over the near-barren face of the small planet, Barion couldn't deny a feeling of personal contentment and admiration for Coyul's wisdom, a quality heretofore not fully appreciated. Coyul remained where he wanted to be and was most suited: concierge to a maddening, murderous, occasionally gifted mutant. Barion had theories to restructure, new concepts to distill—only slightly chagrined that Coyul had shown up his errors, more that his own thinking, which he considered in youth to be chic and radical, was ultimately rooted in comformity.

Rethink. Start again.

The surface slid under him as he searched for moisture. Mere sight was not enough. The flashing animus of Barion melted into the equatorial soil, flowing like a subterranean river, divining, shaping new ideas. *What if? Suppose.*

All carbon life begins with a need for sustenance, therefore a challenge which must be met. The organism must develop a means to propel itself toward nourishment or draw it inward. Suppose . . .

He found the small patch that smelled encouragingly of water. No more than a trace, no thriving colony of protozoa rummaging through its elements for food.

But there was one.

The single organism Barion found had very little talent even for an amoeba, having just coalesced with the sluggish chemical agreement of proteins. The rank beginner had to nourish itself before it could divide, with no idea how to go about it.

But just suppose . . .

Like a human infant, the amoeba lay there knowing only hunger. The fact that bacteria existed close by was, in amoebic terms, of prime interest but little help. Vacuoles to envelop and ingest nourishment were barely functional.

Suppose we accelerate the whole protein process. Since specialization begins at this level anyway, suppose the learning/retention aspect is speeded up, so that selected unicellular life can specialize and evolve exponentially faster than before; faster than anyone thought possible.

"Come on," Barion urged as the tiniest part of him flowed into and endowed the single cell with relative genius. "We call this a pseudopod. You use it to reach for that snack over there. Tha-at's right."

The amoeba extruded a peninsula containing a vacuole. New at the business, the pseudopod merely pushed at the bacterium.

"No, now you open up. I'll show you. There you go, you're in business."

Refreshed, with an atom of learned behavior snugly tucked away, the amoeba thrust out another pseudopod, faster this time.

Barion felt the old thrill of creation, but the monkey had schooled him. "Don't get smug. That was my mistake. Lesson two is fission. No hurry. We'll be out here until you get it right."

You walk before you run before you fly. Concentrate the aminos more rapidly, accelerate specialization. The pseudopod gradually phases from temporary to permanent. Undifferentiated plasma divides to functions, learns. Get the food, reinforce the outer cell wall, which, in turn, senses food more quickly. More specialized functions: digestion, faster locomotion, eventually a central complex to coordinate the whole organism, evolving at a supercharged rate, already tougher and smarter than previously thought possible.

Always possible; just that no one ever did it.

There would never be a warm primordial sea for this creature, but maybe—just maybe—the speeded conditioning would produce a relative intelligence to adapt and cope on its way upward.

"Worlds within worlds," Barion murmured with a vast fascination. "Unconquerable."

His creation was already fighting outside its weight, as it were, laboring but game. Barion hovered, following each step. "Come on, turkey. I know I'm right."

And then something remarkable happened . . .

About the Author

PARKE GODWIN graduated third in his class from the Yerkes Institute. Enjoined by concerned friends and family to take writing seriously, he made an honest effort, producing the work of his Serious Period—*Beloved Exile, The Last Rainbow,* and *A Truce with Time.* This stage ended abruptly when, inexplicably, the Author began to giggle.

Godwin's brief career ended in tragedy at a fantasy convention banquet when he accidentally consumed the entrée. He is remembered mainly through the scattered recollections of other writers. *The Curse of Testosterone,* the autobiography of the radical feminist Roberta Drear, recalls Godwin with no affection at all, making rather much of his relationship with a Bulgarian succubus, an episode now considered apocryphal.

WALDEN REVISITED

WALDEN
REVISITED

A Centennial Tribute to Henry David Thoreau
By GEORGE F. WHICHER

PACKARD AND COMPANY
CHICAGO

PS 3053
W5
T39lw

COPYRIGHT, 1945, BY PACKARD AND COMPANY

All rights reserved. No part of this book may be reproduced in any form, by mimeograph or any other means, without written permission from the publisher.

45 - 6603

DESIGNED BY BERT KEMPSHALL, CHICAGO, AND PRINTED IN THE UNITED STATES OF AMERICA BY KENAGA PRESS, CHICAGO, ILLINOIS

52096

WALDEN REVISITED

STRAHORN LIBRARY
THE COLLEGE OF IDAHO
Caldwell, Idaho

PREFACE

Walden Pond, in spite of the twentieth century mania for calling every body of fresh water a lake, still keeps its old-fashioned name. Beside the heap of stones that marks the site of Thoreau's cabin the young pines are springing up. Standing there in the hush of an early morning in summer, one may look across the unruffled surface to wooded shores and recapture momentarily the sense of a landscape attuned to leisurely living and the delights of meditation.

But the drive and grind of modernity are not far distant. A glance at the ground where bottle caps and torn papers mingle with the dry pine needles or a whiff, not of a chance traveler's pipe, but of a passing motor-car's exhaust brings back the insistent realities of an era of speed and waste. Though Walden Pond is preserved as a State Reservation, it is no longer a refuge of the spirit. Free enterprise has exploited its bathing beach as a location for hot-dog stands and amusement booths. Official tests of the water at the beaches of popular resorts within the reach of Greater Boston show that Walden sometimes ranks among the most favored in urine-content.

Of more concern than the state of Walden's water or the beauty of its shores is the moral heritage of human freedom and loyalty to principle that descends from Thoreau. Nothing could be more opposite to the totalitarian doctrines of our times than the transcendentalist's belief in the dignity of man and the supremacy of individual conscience over a debased collective authority. The hope that these ideas may still be cherished and made valid is the mainspring of this essay.

G.F.W.

Amherst, Massachusetts
February, 1945

ACKNOWLEDGMENT

Passages from the *Journal of Henry David Thoreau,* edited by Bradford Torrey (Vols. VII to XX of the Manuscript and Walden editions of Thoreau's *Writings*) 1906, and passages from the *Journals of Ralph Waldo Emerson,* edited by Edward Waldo Emerson and Waldo Emerson Forbes, 1904-1914, are quoted by permission of Houghton Mifflin Company.

Passages from *The Journals of Bronson Alcott,* edited by Odell Shepard, 1938, are quoted by permission of Little, Brown and Company.

CONTENTS

1

WALDEN REVISITED

No doubt the townsmen of Concord, Massachusetts, celebrated the anniversary of national independence on July 4, 1845, with the customary effusion of gingerbread, spruce beer, and popular oratory. The cradle of liberty may even have been rocked more violently than usual that year, since it was a time of mounting tension. War was gathering on the southern borders. United States troops under General Zachary Taylor were massed at the Sabine River ready for an advance to the Rio Grande. On that very July 4, though Concord would not hear of it until two weeks later, a convention assembled in the Republic of Texas had voted all but unanimously in favor of annexation to the United States. By May, 1846, President Polk had committed the country to a vigorous expression of the bad neighbor policy, otherwise known as manifest destiny. The famous States, as Ralph Waldo Emerson wrote, were soon to be

"Harrying Mexico
With rifle and with knife!"

Concord, whose westernmost section commonly went by the name of "Texas," could hardly have failed to feel that the air was electric with great events.

Or if the town, like New England in general, disapproved of territorial expansion engineered for the benefit of the slave states, it might still be stirred by the unresolved Oregon boundary dispute with Great Britain. A generation before, the British had seized John Jacob Astor's fur-trading post at the mouth of the Columbia River. Now "Fifty-four forty or fight!" was the popular slogan. Two wars threatening to burst into flame were surely enough to make the patriotic kettle simmer.

11

Yet the most memorable event of that Independence Day passed uncelebrated and almost unnoted. Henry David Thoreau, a young man just short of twenty-eight, moved from his parents' home in the village to a cabin he had built with his own hands on the shore of Walden Pond, a mile and a half away. There was no special significance attached to his selection of a day for his going; the Fourth of July, viewed in the light of eternity, would serve as well as any day. Young Mr. Thoreau was a friend of Ralph Waldo Emerson's, and had often met in the study of that advanced thinker the little group of serious souls whom the neighbors referred to with a smile as the Transcendental Club. A witty lady supplied a definition of transcendental: it meant, she said, "a little beyond." You could think it a little beyond common sense if you liked. Thoreau had recently contributed poems and articles to the short-lived and esoteric *Dial*. But he was also in his own peculiar way a shrewd and practical man who could tell where blueberries grew thickest and was likely to bring home a good string of fish when he chose to go fishing. He seemed to know instinctively how to find the crops that he was best able to gather.

When young men have something to do, they not uncommonly hunt for a place where they may work without distraction. An attic room or a lonely hut in the woods seems at such times the first necessity of their being. Soon after 1840 Thoreau's journal bears witness to the consuming desire for self-realization that possessed him. "It is a great relief when for a few moments in the day we can retire to our chamber and be completely true to ourselves," he wrote in March, 1841. And by December comes this revealing entry: "I want to go soon and live away by the pond, where I shall hear only the wind whispering among the reeds. It will be success if I shall have left myself behind. But my friends ask what I will do when I get there. Will it not be employment enough to watch the progress of the seasons?"

12

Thoreau was probably thinking at this time of the reedy island in the middle of Flint's or Sandy Pond in the township of Lincoln, where his friend Stearns Wheeler had built a shack to study in. He had lived with Wheeler for possibly as much as six weeks. This taste of unimpeded existence only whetted his appetite for more. He was drawn to solitude by what was deepest in his nature. He could no more tell what it was than a lover can set down in words the reasons for his devotion. There was nothing any more original in Thoreau's going to the woods than there is in a young man's falling in love, but in both cases the participant feels that no one has ever had such an experience before.

At various times Thoreau attempted to explain why he elected to live for two years alone in his cabin by Walden. It was the fulfillment, he said, of a dream of his childhood that he should make the spot a nursery of his spirit. Again he declared that he could not account for his action: "To speak sincerely, I went there because I had got ready to go; I left it for the same reason." Even when writing *Walden* he could not decide what his true motives had been. "My purpose in going to Walden Pond was not to live cheaply nor to live dearly there, but to transact some private business with the fewest obstacles." We know that he had a book to put together and wanted long uninterrupted hours for the task. This would have been a sufficient reason if he had left it at that. But there was more to come:

"I went to the woods because I wished to live deliberately, to front only the essential facts of life, and see if I could not learn what it had to teach, and not, when I came to die, discover that I had not lived. I did not wish to live what was not life, living is so dear; nor did I wish to practice resignation, unless it was quite necessary. I wanted to live deep and suck out all the marrow of life, to live so sturdily and Spartan-like as to put to rout all that was not life, to cut a broad swath and shave close, to drive life into a corner, and

13

reduce it to its lowest terms, and, if it proved to be mean, why then to get the whole and genuine meanness of it, and publish its meanness to the world; or if it were sublime, to know it by experience, and be able to give a true account of it in my next excursion."

This ringing statement is no afterthought composed for purposes of publication. It is an expansion of a passage beginning, "I wish to meet the facts of life," written down in Thoreau's journal two days after he had moved into his cabin.

None of these various explanations need be discarded, for all are in some measure true. Yet their variety is significant. Thoreau was usually very conscious of his motives and ready to render an account. But in building a house where he could feel to the uttermost the beauty of solitude he was simply obeying an impulse akin to that which draws the sap upward in spring.

Since he was not aware of a definite motive, some interpretations that have been placed on his retreat to Walden may be ruled out at once. It was not an act of discouragement, nor was there anything sullen in his withdrawal. Thoreau was certainly innocent of any intention to break relations with his family or fellow-townsmen when he left the village. He was not in any serious sense a hermit. The house that he had helped his father to build on the Texas road was still his home, and few days passed that he did not visit it. He saw the friends that he cared to see. Except in his refusal to pay a poll tax to a government whose acts he could not condone, he was not conscious of any falling out between society and himself.

Furthermore, Thoreau was not setting up at Walden a model community of one, with the thought that others might go and do likewise. He did have a message for the discontented and the maladjusted, but it was couched in general terms: "Simplify your life." What form the simplification should take was for each to decide. For Thoreau himself

Walden was conceived in other terms than the Utopian experiments at Brook Farm or Fruitlands. He was not a philanthropic social theorist like George Ripley nor an idealistic reformer like Bronson Alcott. His supreme intention was to mind his own business.

At Walden Pond Thoreau kept house for two years and two months. Then on September 6, 1847, he returned to the village as casually as he had left it, to take care of Emerson's house and family while his friend made a voyage to Europe. The fruits of his stay in the woods were two book manuscripts, one which was practically complete, built around his notes on a boating trip that he had taken several years before, and the other, then only beginning to round into shape, based on the journals that he had kept while living in his cabin. These two products of the years 1845 to 1848 were eventually published as *A Week on the Concord and Merrimack Rivers* in 1849, and *Walden; or, Life in the Woods* in 1854. Out of twenty volumes that now constitute the definitive edition of Thoreau's writings only these two were issued in book form before his death.

His second book, *Walden,* is by common consent the finest expression of New England idealism and one of the greatest books of the nineteenth century. It has been called an American *Robinson Crusoe,* because it tells how a man by his own efforts managed to feed, warm, and shelter himself. But this is to belittle it. Thoreau's book is more many-sided than Defoe's. What he chiefly accomplished was to convey better than any other writer the sense of a special American experience. He knew the meaning of contact with unspoiled wildness, and how it seemed to confirm the hope of a world that was all to be begun anew. Thoreau embodied in the symbol of an independent forest-dweller the American dream of an open frontier and of unlimited expansion. *Walden* like Whitman's *Leaves of Grass* brings to imaginative fulfillment the

New World promise of dignity to the individual man. It marks a culmination of the faith implicit in the Declaration of Independence.

A war and a book, both products of American expansiveness, were in the making on the day when Texas voted to join the Union and Henry Thoreau went to live among the pines. Before reading the book it is worth while to consider what kind of man made it, for though Thoreau believed that he had put the best of himself into his books, he committed to life much that he never had opportunity to commit to paper.

2

BIOGRAPHY

Thoreau's life is full of apparent contradictions. It is paradoxical, to begin with, that he, a quintessential New Englander and the only writer native to Concord among those who came to be associated with the town, should be the grandson of a French-speaking immigrant from the Isle of Jersey and should himself have retained slight traces of a French accent. Moreover his father's mother and his mother's father were both of Scottish ancestry. Only through his maternal grandmother, a daughter of the Tory Colonel Elisha Jones of Weston, could Thoreau claim descent from a family long established in Massachusetts. It was in the house of this grandmother on the Virginia Road east of the village that he was born on July 12, 1817.

The following year the Thoreaus moved away from Concord, first to near by Chelmsford, then to Boston. Consequently Henry did not grow up to take his native town for granted, but discovered it with the eager curiosity of a six-year-old when his parents reestablished a home there. John Thoreau, the father, a not quite successful storekeeper, was a reasonably ingenious mechanic and made a comfortable living by the manufacture of lead-pencils, a home industry in which all the family helped. His lively and voluble wife, born Cynthia Dunbar, was not unwilling to take boarders to increase the family income. There were four children, Helen, John, David Henry (as he was christened), and Sophia. Mrs. Thoreau with her younger daughter lived to make a home for Henry until the time of his death.

Northward from Concord lay a great tract of little settled country, full of ponds and streams, where wild creatures were still abundant. The beaver had been hunted out, but muskrat and mink were often seen. Old trappers still recalled anec-

17

dotes of wolves and bears. Henry Thoreau and his brother John lived a free outdoor existence, ranging the woods and clearings for nuts and berries and becoming expert with rod and gun. Later in life Henry never hunted bird or beast, and seldom fished, but he was always ready to entertain children with endless stories of his boyish sallies into the wilds. "We seem but to linger in manhood to tell the dreams of our childhood, and they vanish out of memory ere we learn the language," he confided to his journal. Memories of his early days remained vivid to Thoreau all his life.

His parents were respecters of education and ready to deny themselves in order that their children might have it. With some difficulty they managed to acquire a piano for the two girls, who proved to have some musical talent. Henry turned out to be a studious boy, fond of reading, and so when he had finished Concord Academy the family scrimped and saved to send him to Harvard College, where he held a scholarship and contributed what he could earn occasionally by teaching school. In college he spent much time in the library, especially in the alcove where English authors were kept. Though he became reasonably conversant with Latin and Greek classics and remarkably well read in English poetry, his standing in his class was no more than moderately high. Already he was showing a strong preference for going his own way rather than following in the path marked out for him. During his college years Thoreau read Wordsworth, Coleridge, and Carlyle with enthusiastic approval, and he bought and presumably read the little book called *Nature,* Emerson's first publication, which was a kind of manifesto of transcendentalism. But not until he returned to Concord to live was Thoreau really drawn into the current of new thought that was flowing so strongly there.

He graduated from Harvard with the class of 1837. As yet he had discovered no affinity for any particular profession. The great resource for the uncommitted, then as now, was

schoolteaching, but an experience of a few days in the common school at Concord convinced Thoreau that he could not succeed as a teacher if he were obliged to use the rod as convention then demanded. Accordingly he joined with his brother John in opening a private school, where discipline was enforced without whipping and where teachers and pupils often took long walks together to study the plant and animal life of the countryside. The routine pursuits of an academy were not neglected. Henry, as the more learned brother, taught Greek, Latin, French, and higher mathematics when it was called for, while John acted as principal, business manager, and teacher of elementary mathematics and English studies. The school, notwithstanding its unusual methods, was a decided success. It flourished for the short time until John's uncertain health obliged the brothers to discontinue it.

Meanwhile Henry had begun to keep a journal and was secretly writing verses. He took a great interest in the village lyceum and regularly lectured before it. His vocation as a writer was declaring itself. One literary man Concord already possessed in Emerson, a tall clergyman-scholar in his middle thirties, who in the year Thoreau graduated from college had electrified Harvard by his address to the Phi Beta Kappa society. As yet Emerson had published little, but he was clearly marked as an intellectual leader. Orthodox people were even beginning to suspect that he might prove a dangerous heretic. Some sentences that Thoreau had written came to the attention of Emerson's sister-in-law, who was boarding at the Thoreaus', and soon the two men were taking walks together and exchanging thoughts. Both secretly longed for perfect companionship; in practice neither could pass the barrier of an ingrained reserve.

Yet even their unconsummated friendship was immensely stimulating. It was Emerson more than anyone else who confirmed and brought to the surface Thoreau's innate powers.

19

Through Emerson the younger man became a "transcendental brother." He had previously known as his college tutor in Greek the eccentric poet and essayist Jones Very, and during one of his vacation intervals of teaching country school he had met the dynamic Orestes W. Brownson, with whom he had read a little Goethe in the original. But these were uncertain guides. Emerson more than any thinker of the moment was becoming the prophet of New England idealism and self-sufficiency. Under his encouragement Thoreau read oriental scriptures and found himself as an author. His first outpouring of poems occurred while he was living as an inmate of Emerson's house. But something else happened too. A young man in daily contact with a forceful personality must either turn into a disciple or fight hard to preserve his independent identity. Thoreau fought. To the end he never let his sympathy with 'Emerson's ideas deflect him from the convictions he had decided on for himself.

One freedom that he jealously guarded, no matter what occupation he was nominally pursuing, was an ample leisure for doing what he wanted to do. A broad margin of time was his only luxury. He did not believe in postponing the best of life to some other occasion. He wanted to catch the full savor of experience at once. So he seized the hours that he needed for reading and writing, and saw to it that there was room in the day for rambles afoot or excursions on the placid Musketaquid or Concord River. Now and then he was able to go farther afield. With his brother he had even planned to set up a school in Kentucky, and when this project fell through he made his first visit to Maine in an unsuccessful search for a position as schoolteacher there. It was partly an accident that he remained so closely bound to his native village. He enjoyed the trips he was able to make to distant mountains and waters, and his journal records of such excursions often served him as material for essays or as frames upon which he constructed his books.

Early in 1842 Thoreau suffered the sudden and agonizing loss of his brother John, who died of lockjaw. He and Henry had been inseparable companions. They were both attracted by a sensible, merry-hearted girl of seventeen named Ellen Sewall, whose brother Edmund had been a favorite pupil in the Thoreaus' school; and each without knowing what the other was doing proposed marriage to her. Though she liked Henry very much, she refused both offers because of her father's opposition. Later she married happily an undistinguished clergyman. Years afterward Thoreau told Ellen's aunt that he was thinking of Edmund Sewall, his brother John, and Ellen when he wrote of "a hound, a bay horse, and a turtle dove" that he had lost and was forever seeking.

Thoreau never married. His emotional need of a home was satisfied by his attachment to his parents and sisters. It is doubtful if he ever cared for anyone with as deep a devotion as he felt for his brother. For years he could not speak of John's death without tears. Within a few weeks of his own bereavement he was again afflicted when Emerson's entrancing child Waldo died at the age of six. Companionship in grief drew the two friends together more closely than at any other time in their lives.

At Emerson's insistence a quarterly review named by Bronson Alcott the *Dial* was launched late in the year 1840, in the hope that the thinking and writing of the transcendentalists might reach a larger public. The effort was greeted with some amusement. It is doubtful if the *Dial* ever had more than a few hundred readers, but even this limited audience called out the best talents among Emerson's friends. Thoreau, who was living in Emerson's house and attending to Emerson's garden and woodpile, contributed a poem and an essay on the Roman poet Aulus Persius Flaccus to the first number of the new publication. While the *Dial* lasted he continued to offer poems from his now considerable stock and to prepare prose papers on a variety of subjects from

notes on the ethical books of the Orient to the "Natural History of Massachusetts." Though Margaret Fuller, who remained the magazine's somewhat captious editor for two years, did not always accept the material Thoreau submitted, she never declined his work without giving ample reasons for her refusal and stimulating suggestions for improvement. Under discipline Thoreau's work did improve. Along with translations and much hack writing that he did for the *Dial* appeared one of his best country essays, "A Winter Walk."

Except for contributing to the *Dial* and to a very few other publications Thoreau was showing little interest in the ordinary occupations of men. At home he helped his father grind graphite for superior crayons, at Emerson's he acted as general handy man, and for the community at large he occasionally accepted a job as a surveyor. On his small earnings he was contented to lead a life of Spartan simplicity, provided he might be unhindered in his favorite pursuits. Like Longfellow, Lowell, and others he was trying to find out how an author could make a living in a country where there was no recognized way of following a literary career. His ultimate solution was highly original in that it involved no compromise of his ideals. But before he came to that he tried teaching once more, spending most of 1843 at Staten Island as a tutor to the children of William Emerson, Ralph Waldo's uninspiring elder brother. There he first saw the ocean, which he was later to know better from Cape Cod. In New York he made the acquaintance of Horace Greeley, founder of the *Tribune,* who had a partiality for radicals and who remained Thoreau's loyal and serviceable friend.

With Greeley's expert help Thoreau was able to place two or three articles in such periodicals as the *Democratic Review* and *Graham's Magazine,* and even to wring payment for his work from reluctant editors. But when the *Dial* ceased publication at the end of its fourth year, he was deprived of the principal medium that brought his writings before the

public. Perhaps it was just as well that his energies were not dissipated in minor enterprises. Thrown back upon himself, he did not try to earn his living by his pen—an almost hopeless endeavor, as Edgar Poe was currently proving—but settled the problem of his livelihood by removing to Walden Pond, where he could live on almost nothing and write such books as pleased his fancy. The best years of authorship for him were those that followed.

After a second residence in Emerson's house Thoreau lived for the last thirteen years of his life with his family in a sprawling yellow house not far from the center of Concord. The year that he came home, 1849, was that of the stampede to California. In "Life without Principle" he was later to make his protest against the insensate scramble for wealth. The year was marked for him by the death of his elder sister Helen, by the unsuccessful publication of his first book, by the printing of his powerful essay on "Civil Disobedience" under the title "Resistance to Civil Government" in a kind of aftermath to the *Dial* called *Aesthetic Papers* edited by Elizabeth Peabody, and by his first visit to Cape Cod. He was now well into his thirties, and the exquisite freshness of youth, which Thoreau like Wordsworth felt with exceptional keenness, was passing from him. After the Mexican War and the Gold Rush the high hopes that the transcendentalists had cherished of human nature being born again were likewise fading. Only one decade elapsed between Brook Farm and the Fugitive Slave Law!

Through the 1850's Thoreau occasionally interrupted his quiet routine of reading and writing in the mornings and exploring the neighboring countryside in the afternoons to make excursions to Maine or the White Mountains, or in another mood to New York, where he met Walt Whitman and Henry Ward Beecher. These journeys and their relation to his work will be considered later. After *Walden* appeared in 1854 he became known to a wider public, though he com-

pletely avoided the perplexities incident to popularity. Nevertheless, young men were moved to seek him out, and with a few of his admirers he formed warm and lasting connections. The most striking change in his way of life during this period, however, was due to his increasing concern over the question of slavery. Stirred by the humiliating seizure of alleged fugitive slaves in Boston, he delivered a strong address on "Slavery in Massachusetts" before an Anti-Slavery convention at Framingham in 1854. Twice John Brown of Kansas fame came to Concord, and Thoreau was captivated from the start by his simple, uncompromising fervor. After the raid on Harper's Ferry Thoreau was sickened by the pusillanimous tone of the northern press and immediately came out with a flaming defense of Brown's character. Anyone who may be inclined to take seriously Stevenson's too hasty charge that Thoreau was a "skulker" from the normal obligations of society should recall that he was probably the first man in the United States to speak an unhesitating word in favor of a conscientious assailant of the national crime of slavery.

His outburst over John Brown was the last important concentration of Thoreau's powers. Through 1860 and 1861 he was slowly dying of tuberculosis. The Civil War saddened and depressed him. He resented the fact that he was obliged to hear about it. Too late he realized that he would not be able to use a tithe of the enormous accumulation of material gathered in his journal and in his notebooks devoted to Indian lore. As long as he could hold a pen he labored grimly to prepare for the press the five papers that were printed in the *Atlantic Monthly* shortly after his death. In his final revision he cut away every hint of levity such as had once delighted him. With stoical fortitude he bore his wasting illness, trusting in the universal frame of things, and died peacefully on May 6, 1862. His friend Ellery Channing, leaning over to catch his last mutterings, thought he distinguished the words "moose" and "Indian."

In a deeply felt eulogy of his dead friend Emerson said: "His soul was made for the noblest society; he had in a short life exhausted the capabilities of the world; wherever there is knowledge, wherever there is virtue, wherever there is beauty, he will find a home." The truth at the core of this tribute has been proved by the steady growth of Thoreau's reputation.

3

JOURNEYS

Few writers have ever studied the countryside about them with more devoted interest than Thoreau lavished on the woods, meadows, and streams around Concord. During most of his mature life he made it his business to spend some part of every day in a tour of observation by field or river in order that he might note the progress of the seasons in the minutest detail. Often he was abroad at all hours of the night. The many volumes of his journal are an assiduous record of the work of sun, rain, wind, frost, and flowing water, the state of vegetation, the habits of muskrats, frogs, toads, turtles, and fishes, the migration, songs, and nesting of birds. Thoreau was not systematically classifying these things as a scientist might do; he was engaged in deeply absorbing them for the sake of the pleasure that such intimacy with the ways of nature brought him. Bronson Alcott declared that Thoreau was destined to write the perfect "Atlas of Concord." There can be no doubt that he assembled voluminous materials.

Yet for a person so firmly attached to a single spot Thoreau managed to make a fairly large number of excursions to distant points. Two circumstances, moreover, are notable about these travels. He seldom made them because he had business to transact, but purely for the sake of recreation; and though he was a confirmed lover of solitude, he almost always took one companion with him.

Exception to the first of these rules must be made for his journey to New York with his father in 1836 for the purpose of promoting the sale of lead-pencils; for his visit to Maine two years later in search of a school to teach; for his long sojourn on Staten Island while he acted as tutor in the family of William Emerson; for his hurried trip to Fire Island in July, 1850, in the hope of finding relics of Margaret Fuller

after her death by shipwreck; and for his third journey to New York and its environs in 1856 when he had the excuse of surveying Marcus Spring's estate at Perth Amboy. Thoreau seldom went to cities unless he had an errand that obliged him to go there, and he commonly left the crowded streets as soon as possible. "I am afraid to travel much or to famous places," he wrote, "lest it might completely dissipate the mind." The only time when he deliberately went sight-seeing was when he and Ellery Channing took a brief excursion by train to Montreal and Quebec in the early autumn of 1850.

But wild places he visited for the joy of the experience. There was no danger that nature would exhaust him. No precise record of all his travels can be recovered from his letters and journals, but by 1852 he could say that he had camped out all night on the tops of four mountains,—Wachusett, Saddleback [Greylock], Katahdin, and Monadnock,—and had rambled over the summits at midnight by moonlight. To the first and last mountains he frequently returned, sometimes merely to climb them in the course of a day's outing, sometimes to camp out for several nights with such companions as Ellery Channing, Harrison Blake, or Edward Hoar. With Channing he made a pedestrian tour in 1844 over the Hoosacs and the Catskills. He first visited the White Mountains and climbed Mount Washington, which he preferred to call by its Indian name of Agiocochook, with his brother John in 1839 as an extension of their boating trip on the Concord and the Merrimack, and he ascended Mount Washington a second time in 1858 with Edward Hoar and others, spending several days perforce at the foot of Tuckerman's Ravine as a consequence of spraining his ankle. His last camping out trip was taken with Channing in 1860, when the two friends passed five nights in a brush shelter on the shoulder of Monadnock.

Thoreau visited Cape Cod four times in all, in 1849, 1850, 1855, and 1857, twice with Channing for company. From the beaches of Staten Island he had gained some first impres-

sions of the ocean, or at least of the lower bay of New York, but on Cape Cod he came as close as he was ever to come to feeling a sense of how the ocean might dominate the lives of those who lived beside it and who looked to it for a living. His was the view of an outsider. He was always emphatically a landsman, more at home on inland rivers than at sea.

The most extensive and on many accounts the most rewarding of his excursions were undertaken partly to observe the methods of river travel in the wilderness of Maine. At the end of his second summer at Walden Pond, on the last day of August, 1846, he journeyed to Bangor and accompanied by a Thatcher cousin who had some connection with the lumber business he penetrated the forest to Mount Katahdin. Only half a dozen ascents of this mountain had then been recorded. Thoreau on this occasion had his first experiences of the untouched wilds. In 1853 he returned to follow the inland waterways of Maine in a birch canoe and see how the moose was hunted. He was again accompanied by his cousin, this time with an Indian hunter as guide. Thoreau's third trip, in July, 1857, took him into the still wilder region of the Allegash and the East Branch of the Penobscot, and brought him into contact with a remarkable personality, the Indian Joe Polis, from whom he learned much of the elemental wisdom of a people long adapted to life in the forest. This taste of the wilderness was the last that deeply affected him. He was to see something of Plains Indians during his journey to Minnesota in 1861, but by that time Thoreau had no energy to absorb what he was seeing. His intention to write a book on the Indians was never carried beyond the preliminary stage of amassing a quantity of notes from the narratives of explorers and fur-traders.

Out of the more than two million words that Thoreau wrote in his journal between 1837 and 1861, the most readily detachable sections were those that had to do with his travels, and it is out of these that all the books that he had

time to prepare for the press were made, with the single exception of *Walden*. And even that may be considered in some sense a travel book if one takes literally Thoreau's remark that he had traveled much in Concord. All of his works were the unforced emanations of episodes that he had lived through before he wrote them down.

Yet the best of Thoreau does not lie in mere descriptions of scenery and incidents of travel. His journeys in fact supplied only the framework on which he wove poetic tapestries of reflection and allusion. It is worth while to study briefly the ways in which he secured the kind of heightened effect that distinguishes the work of a master artist in prose from the uncomplicated style of plain communication, which is his basic medium. "In writing," Thoreau said, "conversation should be folded many times thick." The folding in some of his books was quite literal, so that it is possible to distinguish several of the layers.

Probably the thinnest of the narratives of travel is *A Yankee in Canada,* the record of a tour which touched little that deeply concerned Thoreau. He was not at home in French Canada. Neither the grace of its Old World Catholic tradition, as felt in Willa Cather's *Shadows on the Rock,* nor memories of the great historical drama once enacted at Quebec, memories so lively to Francis Parkman, moved him. He gazed at the Plains of Abraham with lack-lustre eye, and passed somewhat carping remarks about the primitive shiftlessness of sawing logs by hand when water-power from the Falls of Montmorenci might be made available. The only overtones awakened by what he observed were overtones of prejudice. Thus at the sight of redcoats in the citadel of Quebec all his dislike of regimentation comes to the surface, and he applies caustic reflections to the scene he is describing, as for example: "It is impossible to give the soldier a good education without making him a deserter." This may be a profound observation in its way, but making it just at this point

29

is like propounding a critical comment on the textile industry at the moment when the flag is being raised.

When Thoreau is truly at ease and happy in his material, the incongruous superposition of thought upon fact yields at once to more subtle implications. The tensions of emotional involvement multiply the interfoldings of awareness. So in the following sentence from "A Walk to Wachusett" the primary factual perception of the degree of light within the tent is overlaid first by a sense of the immensities of space in the night outside, then by a whimsical feeling of fellowship with the heavenly bodies, and finally by a realization of their infiniteness and mystery: "It was at no time darker than twilight within the tent, and we could easily see the moon through its transparent roof as we lay; for there was the moon still above us, with Jupiter and Saturn on either hand, looking down on Wachusett, and it was a satisfaction to know that they were our fellow-travelers still, as high and out of reach as our own destiny."

Or consider, overleaf in the same essay, a description of sunrise where the actual scene is sublimated by imperceptible stages into a poetic comparison: "At length we saw the sun rise up out of the sea, and shine on Massachusetts; and from this moment the atmosphere grew more and more transparent till the time of our departure, and we began to realize the extent of our view, and how the earth, in some degree, answered to the heavens in breadth, the white villages to the constellations in the sky."

These passages are good examples of Thoreau's almost magical power to convey in words the effect of space and cold pure air and the light of dawn. He found the perfect word for his style when he spoke of it as "hypaethral," borrowing a word that is applied to a type of Egyptian temple open to the sun and air.

He can also be of the earth earthy and write with undiminished gusto. In the three papers that make up his book on

The Maine Woods he was recording impressions of the wild, half brutal world of the backwoods, where the savage up-thrust of the forest was only varied by the reckless slashings of lumbermen and the wanton killings of moose and deer by hide-hunters. Plenty of rawness and ugliness is in the book, the squalor of the roving natives, the putrifying carcasses of moose lying in the shallows where they have been slaughtered and skinned. But in the midst of his faithful and often prosaic recording of these things there are moments when the spirit of the wilderness is marvelously rendered. The following passage has been often quoted: "Once, when Joe had called again, and we were listening for moose, we heard, come faintly echoing, or creeping from far through the moss-clad aisles, a dull, dry rushing sound with a solid core to it, yet as if half smothered under the grasp of the luxuriant and fungus-like forest, like the shutting of a door in some distant entry of the damp and shaggy wilderness. If we had not been there, no mortal had heard it. When we asked Joe in a whisper what it was, he answered, 'Tree fall'."

The fact that Thoreau returned at intervals to the Maine woods gives his account of these excursions a cumulative force which is missing from the slender narrative of his Canadian tour. Each time he comes back he seems to be penetrating further into the mystery of the forest, and to go on from where he left off before. The "Ktaadn" chapter gives a general first impression of the forest itself as a phenomenon, the "Chesuncook" excursion is concerned mainly with how lumbermen and hunters live and travel on the lakes and rivers of the interior, and finally in the paper on "The Allegash and East Branch" Thoreau is exploring not so much the country as the mind of the Indian. The superposing of each successive chapter upon the insights that have gone before gives the book as a whole a power of density and depth that is impressive.

Cape Cod like the Maine woods was strange country to a

resident of an inland town. In writing of it Thoreau again had the advantage of several sets of observations or field notes made at different times. When he composed a book out of his journal entries, he adopted a device more elaborate and more successful than that of printing in succession the narratives of his various trips. Taking his first pedestrian tour as a basis, he imposed upon it materials subsequently gathered, thus fusing all that he had to say into one unified and enriched narrative. A happy consequence of this method, which Thoreau was to use again when he compressed the story of his two years at Walden within the compass of a single year, was the multiplication of encounters with people of the region and other incidents of travel. In any one trip such meetings would be infrequent and hence vividly remembered. In combination none of the vividness is lost, while the intervals of sheer factual description are shortened. By such interfolding the whole book is enlivened. It is no accident that readers have found *Cape Cod* the most human of Thoreau's travel books.

In none of these works, however, does Thoreau's writing reach the level of sustained power that marks his *Week* and *Walden*. Something more went into the making of these two projections of a soul in matter than mere honesty of recording, or deftness in expression, or skill in the combining of factual impressions. Still the basis on which Thoreau worked was invariably a solid foundation of fact drawn from his journals.

4

TRANSCENDENTAL MISCELLANY

Thoreau would hardly have said of any of his books, "God wrote it," as Mrs. Stowe in her old age was accustomed to say of *Uncle Tom's Cabin*, yet he with other transcendentalists was suspicious of books produced by conscious intention. More than the surface of the mind should be involved, they thought, in the creation of a work of enduring worth. It should rise from the depths of a man's being as though dictated by a more than human power. It should be an irresistible outpouring like the flow of lava from a crater. It should have organic growth like a tree. "God lets alone," as Thoreau put it, "the work we choose should be our own."

This theory of literary creation is expressed with perfect clearness in Thoreau's poem entitled "Inspiration." What is written out of a man's "poor love of anything" is sure to prove "weak and shallow as its source," no matter how cleverly it may be contrived.

> "But if with bended neck I grope,
>   Listening behind me for my wit,
> With faith superior to hope,
>   More anxious to keep back than forward it,

> "Making my soul accomplice there
>   Unto the flame my heart hath lit,
> Then will the verse forever wear,—
>   Time cannot bend the line which God hath writ."

By some such process of spontaneous upwelling may indeed be produced a striking phrase or a memorable single line. It may even suffice for the making of an epigram or a brief lyric cry. But sheer inspiration seldom provides the principle of construction on which long and complicated

works can be based. Emerson found it next to impossible to weld his sparkling single sentences into coherent wholes, and other transcendentalists when they wrote books were driven to adopt sundry mechanical devices to secure an appearance of unity in a composition which not infrequently failed to sustain the hopeful notion that whatever is sincerely spoken by a simple separate person will be found to have a sufficient inner consistency. In theory the ideal book should unfold into form as naturally as leaves in the spring. In practice what the transcendental writer produced was often a miscellany on which a semblance of form was imposed as by afterthought.

One way of obtaining an artificial beginning and end was to build the book around the record of a journey or excursion, even though the "middle" which Aristotle also held to be necessary should turn out to be little else than a mere undifferentiated continuum. This device, as has already been noted, Thoreau frequently employed. Another kind of mechanical form might be secured by limiting the work to a single unit of time, such as a day, a week, a season, or a year. In this respect Thoreau was anticipated by Margaret Fuller, whose first piece of original writing was the narrative of a journey to the unsettled frontier country of Illinois and Wisconsin under the title *Summer on the Lakes*. Since the author's death this work has always been reprinted in an edited version which reduces it to three-fifths of its former length and makes it a simple description of travel. As Margaret Fuller composed it, however, the book was a characteristic transcendental miscellany which deserves examination for its possible influence on Thoreau's practice.

Miss Fuller had no idea of limiting her material to external observations of the country she was to pass through. Her opening sentence invites the reader to share "such foot-notes as may be made on the pages of my life during this summer's wanderings." The book, in other words, was to be a record

34

of random thoughts as well as sights, and anything that occupied the author's mind might be considered germane to her subject. So among verbal pictures of Niagara, Mackinaw, and the prairies, and pertinent remarks on the Indians and the life of the white settlers, are mingled poems composed during the trip, a tale of Mariana which is not improbably a bit of disguised autobiography, reflections on books read, a long digression on a German girl who possessed visionary powers, and other extraneous material. Miss Fuller even manages to insert a glowing appreciation of Titian's painting of Venus and Adonis "with no excuse, except that it came to memory at the time." The saying that all is grist that comes to the mill has seldom been given more uninhibited application.

Written by a member of Thoreau's intimate circle and published a year before he went to Walden and five years before his own first book, *Summer on the Lakes* must have been a kind of model for him to excel when he meditated on the writing of the *Week*. Both books are ostensibly records of travel, but records enriched by occasional verses, philosophical and moral reflections, essays, and digressions of all kinds. Each takes as its ultimate object the entertainment of the reader by a great variety of substance, which will also prove instructive and will in a way not too clearly defined indicate the scope of man's powers and the interactions of man and nature.

In 1839 John and Henry Thoreau, young schoolteachers in their early twenties, launched on the placid Concord River a boat that they had built themselves and named the Musketaquid. It was large enough so that both could row at once and was rigged with two small masts and sails. In this craft they loaded provisions, buffalo robes, and a home-made tent, and on the last day of August pushed off for a thirteen-day adventure, partly afloat and partly ashore, from Concord to the summit of Mount Washington. The expanded journal

of the fluvial portion of this excursion, the first of Henry's longer camping trips, made up approximately one half of the book that he put together during the first year that he lived at Walden.

The first step in preparing the manuscript for publication was the decision to omit entirely the half of the diary that had to do with land travel and mountain climbing. This aspect of the trip is summarized in a few pages. There remained the cycle of one week, Saturday to Friday, and Thoreau took his luck as he found it and wrote one chapter around each day with a slight prologue to introduce the whole. It was part of his theory not to disturb the setting of his thoughts any more than he could help. Better print them in journal form as they actually occurred than try to detach and rearrange them in coherent essays. If his thoughts had been golden, he would have wanted to present to his readers not the refined metal, nor even chance nuggets, but the whole mine.

Next, as a beginning of the process of elaboration or enrichment, Thoreau did what Herman Melville and other travel writers have commonly done: he read widely in town histories, colonial chronicles, and such descriptive books as were available and collected a mass of anecdotes, adventures, statistics, and picturesque factual material that might be worked into his record from point to point. Thus in connection with the scenes he was reviewing he was led naturally to recall the old frontier ballad of "Lovewell's Fight" and to retell the story of Hannah Dustin's exploit in escaping from the Indians that had taken her captive. A great deal of such local detail, culled from various records, is given incidentally as he goes along.

But besides supplementing the journal of his travels from local history, Thoreau like Margaret Fuller inserted in the book pieces of verse and prose that were little or not at all connected with the rowers' progress on the rivers, except that like the essay chapters in Melville's *Moby Dick* these digres-

sions serve to give the reader a sense of the passage of time and of distance covered without the necessity of watching every operation that carries the vessel onward. In thus alternating selections from his commonplace book with pages from his diary Thoreau was not merely inventing a device to secure variety, as Mark Twain, for example, did when he interjected "Jim Baker's Blue-Jay Yarn" in the midst of a description of student life at the University of Heidelberg. He was attempting to create a new species of travel book, one that would parallel the physical journey of a young man on the waters with the procession of a soul on the stream of time. Hence he drew largely on work that he had already published as well as on new pages from his notebooks. Readers should have him in the lump. From the *Dial* came essays on Aulus Persius Flaccus and on Anacreon, and a number of the more than fifty poems or scraps of poems that he scattered through the text. Besides a discussion of fishes which rose naturally from a consideration of the watery road on which the voyagers were proceeding and from the sight of a fisherman on the bank, Thoreau took advantage of the coming of Sunday to air his views on mythology and religion, Greek, Hindoo, and Christian. But with no shadow of excuse he introduced in his Sunday chapter also an essay on Books and Reading, and in the course of Wednesday the famous essay on Friendship, while his discussion of Poetry is intermittent and ranges over Homer, Ossian, Chaucer, and Goethe, in addition to the two classical writers previously mentioned. Lowell, who seldom did justice to Thoreau, missed the point when in reviewing the *Week* he spoke of these digressions as "snags" and considered them "out of proportion and out of place." They are essential to the kind of work that Thoreau planned. Without them it would have been impossible for him to achieve that effect of "happy fortuity" as of thoughts bubbling up from a living spring which Lowell rightly praises.

The "hypaethral" quality of Thoreau's writing is very pure in some of the fluvial passages of the *Week* and in descriptions of rambles in the Hoosacs and on Greylock. Only Hazlitt can so describe the lift of spirits that comes of going a journey. But there are many good outdoor books, full of sun and air, that do not impress the reader as so vitally a part of the writer's being as this one. Probably Henry Seidel Canby in his ample biography of Thoreau has come as near as a critic can to explaining the elusive and dynamic power of these pages. "I believe," he writes, "that his deep love for John, the tension which rose between them over Ellen, which must have colored the memory of those intimate days on the rivers, and John's sudden and terrible death, gave to his many tentative records of the voyage a significance and a worth which no casual tramping over the Catskills or on Cape Cod with Ellery could equal." It is possible also to suppose that the freedom of his life at Walden had something to do with the buoyancy and exuberance of his writing and with the extraordinary release of his energies between 1845 and 1848 when both the books that appeared during his lifetime were in effect composed. The *Week* may be in some conventional respects an ungainly book, but it indubitably comes alive as few books of travel ever do.

By the time he left Walden Thoreau had the manuscripts of his two books in hand and was ready to look for a publisher for the first. As the author of a few pieces of prose and verse in the transcendental *Dial* he could hardly have expected that a commercial firm would see much profit in his volume, and in fact none did. After four different publishers had declined to undertake the work at their own risk, Thoreau commissioned the house of James Monroe of Boston and Cambridge, the publishers of Emerson's *Essays* and *Poems,* to bring out the book at his expense. Many hours of surveying and many gross of lead-pencils went to the paying for it. When *A Week on the Concord and Merrimack Riv-*

ers appeared in the summer of 1849, it was reviewed not unkindly by friends such as Lowell and George Ripley, but roused little general interest in that feverish year of the California Gold Rush. In the autumn of 1853 the publishers ("falsely so called," muttered Thoreau) insisted on returning to the author 706 unsold copies out of an edition of one thousand. After stacking up the bundles like cordwood along the wall of his attic bedroom Thoreau entered in his journal the immortal comment: "I have now a library of nearly nine hundred volumes, over seven hundred of which I wrote myself."

No external appreciation was needed to confirm Thoreau's conviction of the soundness of his work, yet it is pleasant to recall that a just appraisal of the book which the public would not buy was put on record even before the manuscript was completed. After hearing some passages from the work in progress read in Thoreau's cabin, Bronson Alcott entered in his journal for March 16, 1847, a verdict which may still stand as definitive:

"The book is purely American, fragrant with the lives of New England woods and streams, and could have been written nowhere else. It preserves to us whatever of the wild and mystic remains to us along our brooksides and rivers, and is written in a style as picturesque and flowing as the streams he sails on . . .

"It has the merit, moreover, that somehow, despite all presumptions to the contrary, the sod and sap and fibre and flavour of New England have found at last a clear relation to the literature of other and classic lands . . . Egypt, India, Greece, England, flow from the poet's hand as he scoops the waters for us from the rivers . . .

"Especially am I touched by this soundness, this aboriginal vigour, as if a man had once more come into Nature . . .

"I came home at midnight through the woody snow-paths and slept with the pleasing dream that presently the press

39

would place on my shelves a second beside my first volume, also written by my townsman, and give me two books to be proud of: Emerson's *Poems* and Thoreau's *Week*."

5

READING

Alcott's testimony to Thoreau's familiarity with the literatures of other lands is not to be dismissed as a mere rhetorical flourish. His knowledge was genuinely acquired by hard reading. Books to him were not, as Emerson intimated they should be, "for the scholar's idle times," but for hours of strenuous application. "To read well," wrote Thoreau, "that is, to read true books in a true spirit, is a noble exercise, and one that will task the reader more than any exercise which the customs of the day esteem. It requires a training such as the athletes underwent, the steady intention almost of the whole life to this object." His specifications for satisfactory reading matter are surely such as only a reader of athletic mind would make. "Books, not which afford us a cowering enjoyment, but in which each thought is of unusual daring; such as an idle man cannot read, and a timid one would not be entertained by, which even make us dangerous to existing institutions,—such call I good books." On subjects that concerned him Thoreau read widely, but his preference was for a few inexhaustible books to which he could return again and again.

Before he entered Harvard, if we may believe tradition, he had performed a feat of reading that required no little steady intention: he had read straight through the twenty-one volumes of Alexander Chalmers' *Works of the English Poets, from Chaucer to Cowper* (London, 1810). He is said to have repeated the same exploit at a later date. These comprehensive assaults on the whole realm of English poetry made him familiar with several early writers that are seldom opened, such as Gower and Lydgate as well as Chaucer. They also determined his taste for the late Elizabethan and early Jacobean authors, such men as Daniel, Drayton, Ra-

41

leigh, and Donne among Shakespeare's contemporaries, and from the later group the religious poets Herbert, Vaughan, and Crashaw. A special favorite, Quarles, was a later discovery. Thoreau preferred Milton as a poet to Shakespeare. It is noteworthy that his taste was not for poets that the nineteenth century delighted to honor. With the possible exception of Herbert none of the lesser men that he speaks of were greatly admired at the time. In reading as in life Thoreau liked to find his own way about.

He was reasonably acquainted also with the prose writers of the seventeenth century, as may be evident to one who listens for echoes of the English Bible or the rhythms of Sir Thomas Browne in the cadences of Thoreau's sentences. An obviously imitative passage, with a geographical borrowing from *Paradise Lost* to boot, is the last paragraph of the chapter on "The Pond in Winter" in *Walden*.

Next to English writers he early felt the influence of the Greek and Latin classics, in which he was thoroughly drilled both in school and in college. Thoreau was in fact the best linguist of the Concord group. According to his friend and biographer Frank Sanborn, he could read Latin and French as easily as English, was conversant with Greek, and possessed some knowledge of German, Spanish, and Italian. He was not fond of the modern languages, however, and he seems to have read few masterpieces in the original, except in the ancient tongues. His enthusiasm for Greek gradually waned. While he was spending six hours a day, in his early twenties, in the drudgery of schoolteaching, he was as willing to read a few extra pages of Homer as to go for a walk. He made English translations of two Aeschylean plays and of a few poems by Pindar and the pseudo-Anacreon. The *Iliad* was one of the few books that he took to his Walden cabin, but he confessed that he seldom found time to look at it. Thereafter there are few records of his reading further in Greek. Unlike Emerson he was not attracted by Plato.

In Latin, on the other hand, he continued to explore with zest, soon turning away from the generally read masters of prose and verse to less known satirists such as Persius and to writers of utilitarian prose like Columella and Varro. He was as ready as ever to justify his idiosyncrasies. "If the writers of the bronze age are most suggestive to thee, confine thyself to them, and leave those of the Augustan age to dust and to the book worms." Though Thoreau's sense of style was no doubt shaped in some degree by his early immersion in the classics, he was not one to follow tamely the ancient models. Before long he was asserting his own taste in the selection of writers who handled plain factual matters connected with plowland and vineyard, and leaving his Virgil and Horace to teach elegance to those who might value it.

In Thoreau's opinion no poetry, either English or classical, adequately expressed the freshness and vigor that he felt in wild nature. All the literature he knew seemed tame and artificial. Only in momentary flashes in works of the highest genius, in *Hamlet* or the *Iliad,* could he discover passages whose inevitable perfection suggested the expanding of buds at the approach of spring. He was demanding what no civilized culture could achieve, an unconscious flowering of man's being into art. Mythology, the age-old accumulations of folk-wisdom, came nearer than any premeditated poetry to satisfying his yearning for unspoiled primitive naturalness, "wild lands where no settler has squatted." Nothing was more characteristic of him than his quaint way of fusing scraps of Greek myth and legend with the New England countryside, as when in *Walden* he sees the weeds in his beanfield as "Trojans who had sun and rain and dews on their side," or as when he revives the obscure tradition that Hebe, the cupbearer of Jove and the personfication of immortal youth, was the "daughter of Juno and wild lettuce." One can hear the Yankee twang as he adds: "She was probably the only thoroughly sound-conditioned, healthy, and

robust young lady that ever walked the globe, and wherever she came it was spring."

It was typical of a mind early stored with classical images that the hum of telegraph wires should seem to speak of Greece and the Muses. Let us grant that in Thoreau's youthful writing the frequent resort to classical allusion seems often far-fetched and pedantic. It is difficult to believe that Achilles and Hector have left footprints on the Concord meadows. Yet the same miracle of imaginative acclimatization that made the Athenian Theseus a duke and citizen of Shakespeare's London can at moments almost persuade us that Homer's trumpets still sound along the Musketaquid. Consider the poetic fusion of the disparate elements in the following passage: "Morning brings back the heroic ages. I was as much affected by the faint hum of a mosquito making its invisible and unimaginable tour through my apartment at earliest dawn, when I was sitting with door and windows open, as I could be by any trumpet that ever sang of fame. It was Homer's requiem; itself an Iliad and Odyssey in the air, singing its own wrath and wanderings." What two words can more fittingly convey the thin, angry whine of the mosquito's air-borne assault than the two key-words of Homer's epics, Achilles' *wrath*, Odysseus' *wanderings?* Only a fancy akin to Donne's, however, could detect and successfully exploit such remote analogies, and only a master of tonal effects could so concentrate nasal consonants as to make the words faintly vibrant with an echo of the mosquito's hum.

A desire to deepen his mystical love of nature was probably what led Thoreau to explore the scriptures of India, China, and Persia, the third great reservoir from which he drew inspiration for his work. Emerson likewise was a devotee of oriental writings, and it was in Emerson's study that Thoreau first soaked himself in the books of the East. This was in the year 1841, when at the age of twenty-four Thor-

eau seems first to have made up his mind to devote himself to a literary career. Previous to this he must have known the paraphrases of oriental poems by Sir William Jones and the comprehensive essay "On the Poetry of the Eastern Nations" contained in Chalmers' *Poets*. He was not entirely a novice in respect to the great books of Asia when he set himself to examine them more closely and to make excerpts for several articles that appeared in the *Dial* in 1843 and 1844. Vigorous entries in his journal attest his first ardent enthusiasm for Manu, Confucius, Zoroaster, and the like, and reveal the deeper insight into these writings that came to him after he had spent years in their company. When in 1855 a British visitor named Thomas Cholmondeley wished to give Thoreau what would please him most, he sent from London a "nest of Indian books" consisting of forty-four volumes of Hindoo scriptures, some in English, French, or Latin translation, others in the original Sanskrit. By that time the oriental classics were familiar friends to Emerson, Alcott, and Thoreau. From them they drew telling sayings in support of the ideas that were already theirs. It should not be supposed that any of the transcendentalists penetrated to the actual meaning and spirit of the wisdom of the East.

The effect of Thoreau's reading of oriental philosophy is superficially evident in the quotations scattered through his works and in the occasional parables modeled on the oriental pattern that occur in *Walden*. How far he accepted some of the religious practices and underlying ideas of Hindoo ascetic philosophy it is not possible to say precisely. During his sojourn at the pond he seems to have experimented with austerities of diet and other ascetic practices, and what he records on one occasion about sitting in his sunny doorway from sunrise till noon, rapt in revery, would lead one to suppose that he was attempting to induce a state of mystical contemplation akin to that sacramentally practiced by oriental devotees of the *yoga*. With the rules of this system of ascetic discipline

45

Thoreau was certainly acquainted, since he wrote to his friend Harrison Blake in 1849: "To some extent, and at rare intervals, even I am a yogi." Such exercises, even amateurishly and unsystematically followed, may have served to deepen Thoreau's sense of the spirituality of life and to carry him above the petty routine of a small New England village.

From Concord Thoreau liked to send his imagination ranging to distant lands and strange seas. He was an avid reader of travel books, including narratives of Elizabethan exploration such as *Purchas His Pilgrimes*. He kept up with recent voyages of discovery also, often noting in his journal some curious bit of information relating to Africa or the Arctic or Australia and the South Seas. Bits of this flotsam and jetsam are strewn through his works. He was not neglectful of American travels either, but showed an acquaintance ranging from Timothy Dwight's account of his trips through New England to Benjamin G. Ferris's *Utah and the Mormons*. Perfect books for Thoreau were Charles Darwin's *Voyage of the Beagle,* which combined descriptions and anecdotes of South America with much scientific lore, and William Bartram's *Travels,* with its accounts of the virgin forests and Indian tribes of the southern United States.

To supplement his own observations of the flora and fauna around Concord Thoreau had browsed through all the natural histories and herbals he could find. He knew Topsell's quaint *History of Four-Footed Beasts,* Gerard's *Herbal,* Evelyn's *Sylva,* and other authorities of the Renaissance and seventeenth century. He refers to John Josselyn's description of *New England's Rarities* and to Gilbert White's *Natural History of Selborne.* More modern scientific books and government reports on animals, birds, reptiles, fishes, insects, and plants were his constant study.

Whenever he visited a place like Cape Cod or Plymouth, he was sure to look up the histories of its discovery and settlement. As connected with the former he had read the voy-

ages of Gilbert, Gosnold, Archer, Brereton, Pring, and Captain John Smith. Of the colonial chronicles of Plymouth he was familiar with Bradford, Winslow, and Mourt's *Relation,* and he had read the journal of Boston's Governor Winthrop. He also consulted such later histories as Edward Johnson's *Wonder-Working Providence* and Cotton Mather's *Magnalia Christi Americana.*

The literature of the early Indian wars and captivities had from the first attracted his attention. Partly from still surviving local traditions and partly from books he had derived the story of Hannah Dustin's famous escape. He knew the vivid narratives of Mrs. Mary Rowlandson and of Joseph Bartlett. Samuel Penhallow was his authority for the Indian wars of Maine, and he enjoyed repeating the stirring ballad of "Lovewell's Fight" which commemorated a bloody episode of the struggle down east.

Much of his detailed information about the New England past was gained from such books as J. W. Barber's *Historical Collections,* or from state and town histories. He mentions at one time or another reading histories of New Hampshire (Jeremy Belknap), Virginia (Robert Beverly), Vermont (Zachary Thompson), and Connecticut (Samuel Peters).

He had scanned extensively the records of the American frontier, beginning with such French sources as Champlain's *Voyages* and the Jesuit *Relations* and continuing with Charlevoix and other historians of New France. Jonathan Carver's *Travels Through the Interior Parts of North America* and Alexander Henry's *Travels and Adventures in Canada* were favorite classics of the fur-trade with many anecdotes of Indians in the western regions. In the later years of his life Thoreau read everything he could find on the American aborigines, as well as studying the red men wherever he could meet them from Maine to Minnesota. His voluminous notes are now in the Pierrepont Morgan Library in New

York. The book that he dreamed of making on the Indian was never written.

In these factual books and records of travel and exploration Thoreau encountered the kind of gritty, unaffected prose that pleased him. Here was the antidote to the effeminacy of his contemporaries. "The sentences written by such rude hands are nervous and tough, like hardened thongs, the sinews of the deer, or the roots of the pine." Here were "sentences which . . . lie like boulders on the page, up and down or across." They supplied him with ballast while his contact with the mystical writings of the orient served as a great wind to fill his sails and to drive him forward in a quest for perfection. It should be remarked that Thoreau, like Herman Melville, felt no opposition between lofty spiritual contemplation and an abundant sensuous delight in the earth. The perfection that he wanted was not to be gained by a denial of what was dear to him in this world. And so his choice of reading reflects his attachment to both realms of being.

6

FRIENDSHIPS

Friends, Thoreau found, are not easily subordinated to a program of perfection. Books, nature, the day's tasks, may all be manipulated to suit the soul's needs, but friends constitute an unpredictable element. It is too much to hope that a friend's arrival will never be untimely, nor his departure welcome. Perhaps a perfectionist can only exist in solitude. In the give and take of human intercourse the illusion of spiritual advancement is difficult to maintain. Consequently in so far as Thoreau became the Yankee counterpart of a *yogi* he was unfitted for friendship. It is significant that his most successful human relations, outside his own family, were established with children, or with farmers, woodchoppers, and village reprobates. In the presence of respectable folks he generally maintained a polite but impenetrable reserve. "I love Henry," said the intellectual Elizabeth Hoar, "but I cannot like him; and as for taking his arm, I should as soon think of taking the arm of an elm-tree." Emerson endorsed, if he did not originate, this remark.

Nevertheless Thoreau gave a great deal of attention to elaborating a theory of friendship and to testing it in practice. His experiments were not as devoid of success as one might suppose from reading the passages in his journal where he bemoans the fact that friends in actuality never come up to expectations. If he was never able to find the ideal friend of his imagination, he was not unwilling to acknowledge the solid satisfactions he derived even from the partial fulfillment of his dream.

Both Emerson and Thoreau published essays on Friendship during the 1840's, Emerson in the first series of his *Essays* (1841) and Thoreau in the *Week* (1849). To place them side by side is to illuminate some important differences

49

between the two men. Each, as might be expected, had no use for the merely utilitarian aspects of friendship, yet Emerson in the midst of his etherealizing of the friendly relationship never lost sight of the principle of self-development. "We must be our own before we can be another's." Friends supply one of the conditions that enable a man to realize his personality. "The soul environs itself with friends that it may enter into a grander self-acquaintance or solitude; and it goes alone for a season that it may exalt its conversation or society." Society and solitude are the systole and diastole of life. But Emerson recoiled from any thought of combining friendship with "politics and chat and neighborly conveniences." These can be had cheaply. "Should not the society of my friend be to me poetic, pure, universal and great as nature itself?" The ideal of friendship "may be said to require natures so rare . . . that its satisfaction can very seldom be assured." "Friends such as we desire are dreams and fables." So difficult is perfect intercourse on the high ground that Emerson takes, that before he has finished he has in effect abolished the conception of friendship and set up instead a solipsistic ideal of benevolent friendliness that never asks to be requited. When indeed did Emerson ever know an intimacy such as he describes? His essay gives the impression of comment by an outsider.

In the case of Thoreau, however, the actuality of the experience is written in his pulse-beats. "The only danger in Friendship is that it will end." He like Emerson is aware of the possibility of disappointment when friends fail to meet on an ideal level. He knows that friendship is evanescent and cannot be long sustained at its best, that its joys must be mainly of expectation and retrospect. But what for Emerson is essentially a form of education is for Thoreau a means of rapture. "There are passages of affection in our intercourse with mortal men and women, such as no prophecy had taught us to expect, which transcend our earthly life, and

50

anticipate Heaven for us." Defects in intimacy he can take in his stride. "Ignorance and bungling with love are better than wisdom and skill without." And though he also realizes that intercourse with friends is improved by intervals of solitude, he conceives of these intervals not as occasions for consolidating one's gains in a grander self-acquaintance but for preparing oneself for a loftier intimacy. His tone is poetic. "Silence is the ambrosial night in the intercourse of Friends, in which their sincerity is recruited and takes deeper root."

There can be little doubt that Thoreau's essay on Friendship is a tribute to his brother John, his only close comrade until the elder brother's sudden and painful death. And mingled with recollections of that dear companionship were ecstatic memories of an idealized relationship with Ellen Sewall, a friend whom he cherished all the more because she remained aloof. Embedded in the essay is a poem that he had written to express his affectionate regard for the boy Edmund Sewall, her brother, on whose potential but unripened friendship Thoreau set a romantically high value. Other poems that spoke of Ellen herself appeared on an earlier page. Indeed he could hardly think of boating on the Concord without recalling the brief and happy visit that she had paid to his family when he and John had taken her rowing. The reference is explicit:

"On this same stream a maiden once sailed in my boat, thus unattended but by invisible guardians, and as she sat in the prow there was nothing but herself between the steersman and the sky. I could then say with the poet,

> "Sweet falls the summer air
> Over her frame who sails with me;
> Her way like that is beautifully free,
>   Her nature far more rare
> And is her constant heart of virgin purity"—

51

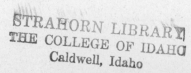
STRAHORN LIBRARY
THE COLLEGE OF IDAHO
Caldwell, Idaho

"At evening, still the very stars seem but this maiden's emissaries and reporters of her progress.

> "Low in the eastern sky
> Is set thy glancing eye" . . . .

Thoreau's most noted friend was Emerson himself. Their relationship was at first extremely cordial. The younger man, just out of college, responded to a personal stimulation that was proving extremely attractive to young men everywhere. In Emerson he saw "more of the divine realized" than in any other person. "In his world every man would be a poet, Love would reign, Beauty would take place, Man and Nature would harmonize." Emerson in turn enjoyed the singular experience of discovering a living embodiment of his American Scholar, moulded by nature, books, and action, right in his home town. It should be noted that Emerson's Phi Beta Kappa address was written before he knew Thoreau, and equally that Thoreau had shaped his character independently of Emerson. There could be no question of imitation or discipleship.

But it is not certain that Emerson was able to avoid a few proprietary airs. "My good Henry Thoreau," he wrote in 1838, "made this else solitary afternoon sunny with his simplicity and clear perception." And again in 1841: "I told Henry Thoreau that his freedom is in the form, but he does not disclose new matter. I am very familiar with all his thoughts,—they are my own quite originally drest." Thoreau may have had his own ideas about his originality. If he became aware of the local jests that pictured him as trying to imitate Emerson in gait and gesture, he could hardly have avoided being sensitive on the subject. After James Russell Lowell in *A Fable for Critics* (1848) had associated him with one who was accustomed to

"Tread in Emerson's tracks, with legs painfully short,"

52

Thoreau cannot have failed to know that he was being ridiculed. The natural effect would have been to make him emphasize in every possible way his divergencies from the man who was popularly regarded as his master.

By 1853 each man was confiding to his journal how difficult he found it to converse with the other. On a day late in May Thoreau wrote: "Talked, or tried to talk, with R.W.E. Lost my time—nay, almost my identity. He, assuming a false opposition where there was no difference of opinion, talked to the wind—told me what I knew—and I lost my time trying to imagine myself somebody else to oppose him."

In the course of the following month Emerson noted that Thoreau was "military" and "rarely sweet." "One would say that, as Webster could never speak without an antagonist, so Henry does not feel himself except in opposition. He wants a fallacy to expose, a blunder to pillory, requires a little sense of victory, a roll of the drums, to call his powers into full exercise."

Thoreau was fully conscious that he was parting company with the most sympathetic friend he ever had. Each was pursuing his proper path. The nature of the divergence was perhaps not as clear then as it has since become. The early years of their acquaintance had coincided with the peak of the transcendental excitement, when Emerson was sounding the call for a new relation of man to the universe and pleading with Americans to discover the divine nature inherent in their being. But, as Thoreau wrote in one of his letters, the whole enterprise of the nation was "not an upward, but a westward one, toward Oregon, California, Japan, etc." The message of the transcendental prophet was unheeded, and he remained an increasingly lonely figure on his mount of vision. Thoreau and Emerson differed profoundly in the way each proceeded from that point. Emerson tended to recede more and more into a mild and mystical meliorism which held that nature would inevitably right what was wrong and

bring all back to an even keel. Thoreau, on the contrary, though seemingly in retreat from men to muskrats, moved in the direction of civil disobedience. If the state was dull and evil, it was for men of conscience to do something about it. At the time of the John Brown incident Thoreau could not have been mistaken as a follower of Emerson.

Bronson Alcott, as early as 1852, became aware of the difference in the quality of his two friends. We find him writing in his journal for January 6: "Emerson said fine things last night about 'Wealth,' but there are finer things far to be said in praise of Poverty, which it takes a person superior to Emerson even to say worthily. Thoreau is the better man, perhaps, to celebrate that estate, about which he knows much, and which he wears as an ornament about himself. . . . Eloquent, wise, and witty as were the orator's praises of Gold, and just to this transition period of civilization, the merchant's day as none ever before—still the moral laws were too faintly implied, and so left not without detriment in the auditor's mind." Alcott was correct in discerning a Cromwellian fiber in the younger man.

With the high-minded and intransigent Alcott himself Thoreau remained in close accord. Though the Connecticut idealist was three years older than Emerson, he seemed to Thoreau at thirty "the youngest man of his age we have seen, —just on the threshold of life." He went about his business of being a spiritual philosopher with a directness and sincerity that won respect. Thoreau found his attitude "one of greater faith and expectation than that of any man I know." Alcott was the first resident of Concord to be put in jail for conscientious refusal to pay a tax in support of a government he considered unjust; and Sam Staples, the local constable, who was later to lock up Thoreau on a similar charge, declared, "I vum, I believe it was nothing but principle, for I never heerd a man talk honester." Where principle was concerned Alcott demonstrated on several occasions that he did

not know the name of fear. Nor was he afraid to earn his living on occasion by menial labor. Thoreau found his ideas indefinite and undisciplined, yet was unwilling to cavil at his impracticality. "The feelers of his thought diverge,—such is the breadth of their grasp,—not converge; and in his society almost alone I can express at my leisure, with more or less success, my vaguest but most cherished fancy or thought. There are never any obstacles in the way of our meeting. He has no creed. He is not pledged to any institution. The sanest man I ever knew; the fewest crotchets, after all, has he." At the end of the chapter on "Winter Visitors" in *Walden* may be found Thoreau's considered tribute to the least worldly of philosophers.

Alcott's crotchets did not escape the amused notice of his irreverent friend, who found it incongruous that the genealogy of the Alcock family should absorb so much of the sage's interest,—"he whom only the genealogy of humanity, the descent of man from God should concern!" The rustic summerhouse that Alcott constructed in Emerson's garden also awakened Thoreau's mind to derision. But the two men shared too many loyalties to have any serious falling out.

Alcott on his part early acknowledged the spiritual kinship of the younger man, but in terms that derogated nothing from his independence. "Emerson, Miss Fuller, Thoreau, and myself," he wrote in 1846," are the only persons who treat things in the new spirit, each working distinct veins in the same mine of Being." He perceived at once the poetic quality of Thoreau's mind, but considered his a "walking" (he did not say pedestrian) Muse. "But this fits him all the better for his special task of delineating these yet unspoiled American things, and of inspiring us with a sense of their homelier beauties—opening to us the riches of a nation scarcely yet discovered by her own population." Admiring and perceptive comments on Thoreau's writing and conversation are thickly scattered through the pages of Alcott's jour-

nal. Perhaps the most condensed appraisal is this, written in 1859:

"He is less thinker than observer; a naturalist in tendency but of a mystic habit, and a genius for detecting the essence in the form and giving forth the soul of things seen. He knows more of Nature's secrets than any man I have known, and of Man as related to Nature. He thinks and sees for himself in ways eminently original, and is formidably individual and persistent."

Alcott was often accused of having his head in the clouds, but he saw things on earth with extremely clear vision. Practically all the things that are important to say about Thoreau are contained in his journal.

With other Concord writers Thoreau was acquainted, though his shyness kept him from reaching anything like intimacy, except with one or two. He and Margaret Fuller learned much from each other. Hawthorne, who bought Thoreau's boat and rechristened it the "Pond-Lily," was a more distant friend, accustomed to move in a different social sphere. The man who came nearest to becoming a companion of Thoreau's later years was the poet William Ellery Channing, the namesake of the well-known Unitarian clergyman and the husband of Margaret Fuller's sister. But Channing, though an admirable partner on what he called their *riparial* excursions along the river, was intellectually of flimsy stuff. He never managed to make even one passably good poem, though he could sometimes produce an arresting phrase. Thoreau called his way of writing the "sublimo-slipshod style," and thought it would be good discipline for him to write in Latin, "for then he would be compelled to say something always, and frequently have recourse to his grammar and dictionary." Edgar Allan Poe mercilessly dissected his failings in a review full of animus against the New England "school" of writers.

Other men, too, many of them younger, came to know

Thoreau through his books and articles and to occupy a station between that of friends and disciples. Among them were Harrison Blake and Theodore Brown of Worcester, Daniel Ricketson of New Bedford, Edward Hoar of Concord, Thomas Cholmondeley the English visitor, and Horace Mann, Jr., who accompanied Thoreau on his last long journey to Minnesota. There were many who delighted to share his walks on occasion and to join him in serious reflection, for though Thoreau has written vehemently of the joys of solitude and self-sufficiency he was not indifferent to the pleasures of companionship with his peers. But let the companions come one at a time, so that there might be a true exchange of thoughts, not a mere bandying of compliments.

Alcott, who so often spoke the definitive word about Thoreau, may appropriately offer a final definition of the kind of response he aroused in those who best knew him: "I should say he inspired love, if indeed the sentiment he awakens did not seem to partake of something yet purer, if that were possible, and as yet nameless from its rarity and excellency."

7

LIFE IN THE VILLAGE

Airplane pilots have commonly remarked that merely by flying high among the clouds they acquire an extraordinary detachment from the concerns of men on the ground. They have an intoxicating feeling of superabundant power, of room to expand in all directions. They are released from the pressure of the crowd, and forthwith they are no longer afflicted by the worries and apprehensions of life at the customary level.

Thoreau attained somewhat the same detached point of view in regard to human affairs, not by soaring above the earth, but by identifying himself with the earth and its various natural phenomena more closely than the average man is likely to do. The earth was his airplane swung in space. The planets were his neighbors. His mind was so occupied with moon and stars, clouds and winds, swamps and woods and their inhabitants that he had little time to bother about what his human neighbors were doing. Toward them and their affairs in fact he adopted a slightly quizzical attitude which can hardly have increased his popularity with the majority of Concord citizens. His opinion of their importance was obviously low, and he had an irritating forthrightness in saying so. They seemed to him to swarm like ants by his woodpile or tadpoles at the pond's edge. As he put it in *Walden*: "In one direction from my house there was a colony of muskrats in the river meadows; under the grove of elms and buttonwoods in the other horizon was a village of busy men, as curious to me as if they had been prairie-dogs, each sitting at the mouth of its burrow, or running over to a neighbor's to gossip. I went there frequently to observe their habits."

The relations between Thoreau and the villagers were

often little better than an armed truce. His way of life was a criticism of theirs. His negations challenged their scheme of values. Emerson summed it up in a striking if slightly exaggerated sentence: "He was bred to no profession; he never married; he lived alone; he never went to church; he never voted; he refusd to pay a tax to the State; he ate no flesh, he drank no wine, he never knew the use of tobacco; and, though a naturalist, he used neither trap nor gun." Considering what human sensibilities are, it speaks well for Concord that Thoreau was even tolerated. Many resented and ridiculed him, many regarded his supposed shiftlessness as a scandal. When on one occasion a campfire got away from him and burned over a tract of woodland, it was only the lucky circumstance that the son of Judge Hoar was with him and equally guilty that saved Thoreau from vigorous reprisals. For years afterward he was not allowed to forget that he was the man who set the woods afire.

Yet once Thoreau's wide divergence from conventional attitudes of mind is realized, it is necessary to add immediately that he expressed his radicalism far more in words than in action. It is only in comparison with Emerson that he seems a doer rather than a thinker. He was not anti-social, though he favored a stringent revision of social values. And above all, his opinions were not those of a misfit or a failure. When he chose to do so he could adapt himself to ordinary standards. It was several times within his power to be what his neighbors would have considered successful. His early venture at keeping a private school was prospering until his brother's failing health put an end to it. The pencils that the family manufactured were of superior quality, and the plumbago, ground by a secret float-process invented by Thoreau and his father, was the finest that lithographers could obtain. If he had cared to devote his time and energy to the pencil business, he could almost certainly have developed a thriving trade. He was also a competent surveyor, and found

as much to do in that way as he wished to undertake. And finally in the unremunerative profession of authorship, where few Americans of his generation were able to make a living without resorting to other callings, Thoreau worked out as successful a *modus vivendi* as anyone and before he died in middle age had published a book that was distinctly a success by commercial standards. It is impossible, therefore, to dismiss Thoreau as an embittered failure.

In *Walden*, when he announces that he is addressing primarily those of his countrymen who are dissatisfied with their lot and don't know what to do about it, Thoreau is careful to dissociate himself from the discontented and to reckon himself among "those who find their encouragement and inspiration in precisely the present condition of things, and cherish it with the fondness and enthusiasm of lovers"— at least this is where he thinks he belongs "to some extent." It would not be easy to cast doubt on Thoreau's sincere attachment to the place of his birth. In spite of the faults he saw in Concord, he was willing to present himself with the freedom of the village.

Nevertheless this indigenous New Englander was a persistent critic of what the universal Yankee nation most prided itself upon and worshipped, its increasing material prosperity and its progress in mechanical invention. By 1845 the industrial revolution was in full swing in the northeastern section of the United States. Steamboats were running, railroads were being built, textile mills were in full operation, the electric telegraph was being extended, and the successful laying of a cable between France and England forecast the Atlantic cable to come a decade later. Except for the regression caused by the financial panic of 1837, wealth was increasing and the standard of living was steadily advancing. Who could look upon these multiplied wonders as anything but unalloyed benefits? Only a few perfectionists and cranks such as Emerson, who declared that

"Things are in the saddle
And ride mankind,"

and, of course, Thoreau, who persisted in describing all modern inventions as improved means to unimproved ends.

Thoreau's transcendental economics was not concerned with wealth as understood on the stock exchange. As he figured it, the fundamental questions were: What kind of life is a man enabled to lead? How much of his time is consumed by distasteful drudgery incident to earning a living merely? What margin has he left for doing the things that he really wants to do? Thoreau did not feel (and here many plain people who enjoy the occupations whereby they earn their livings may disagree with him) that time spent in providing the necessaries of life could possibly be as well invested as free time. Consequently, if all his waking hours were to be used up in earning his living, he would consider his life a blank. His problem was to secure as large a portion of time as possible for voluntary occupations. The richest man by his scheme of values would be the one who could devote the greatest amount of time to his own affairs. Thoreau is assuming, of course, that his economic man is high-minded and will not choose to waste his spangle of existence in riot and indulgence.

The test of value that he applied to any item that might be included in the apparatus of living was, therefore, determined by the question: How much life is required to be exchanged for it, either immediately or in the long run? In Thoreau's opinion the comforts, conveniences, and luxuries of civilized living had so multiplied that many men virtually made slaves of themselves in the effort to secure them, or to keep up the properties that they supposedly owned, but which in reality possessed them. His first suggestion to those who were discouraged in the struggle was to simplify their lives by seeing how much they could manage to do without.

This was a solution that he found eminently satisfactory in his own practice, and in *Walden* he describes with an elaborate parody of economic statistics his not too serious demonstration that the problem of earning a living need occupy only a small fraction of the time, if a man is young, unburdened with a family, in good health, and not eager to encumber himself with many possessions. This "experiment" in the art of simple living is partly a burlesque, put forward with tongue in cheek. Thoreau did not even adopt it for himself as a permanent way of living. But the advice to center one's aims in something other than material possessions is earnestly meant.

Thoreau perceived at once that an economic system based on sheer acquisitiveness could not lead to the beneficent effects that current theory claimed would flow from it. The inhuman conditions that workers had to face in British mines and mills before working conditions became subject to government regulation were notorious in the United States, and it was hoped that such brutality might be avoided here. The managers of the textile mills at Lowell, for example, took pains to provide proper housing for the girls they employed and to see that the operatives were not driven to the limit of their endurance, even though they spent a twelve-and-a-half-hour day at the looms. They encouraged the formation of "improvement circles," and were proud of the literary magazine called the *Lowell Offering* which the young women conducted without outside assistance. To Whittier, who wrote a series of journalistic articles collected in 1845 as *The Stranger in Lowell,* it seemed that the American industrial experiment was avoiding the worst mistakes of the British and was a marvel of efficient economic organization.

In Thoreau's opinion, however, production for profit was vitiated at the start by the low motives that inspired it. "I cannot believe," he wrote, "that our factory system is the best mode by which men may get clothing. The condition of the

operatives is becoming every day more like that of the English; and it cannot be wondered at, since, as far as I have heard or observed, the principal object is, not that mankind may be well and honestly clad, but, unquestionably, that the corporations may be enriched. In the long run men hit only what they aim at. Therefore, though they should fail immediately, they had better aim at something high."

For similar reasons Thoreau looked upon railroads with suspicion, and amused himself by making somewhat specious calculations to show that a man who traveled afoot could cover as much ground as one who must first earn his carfare by working as a common laborer at a dollar a day. It was not so much that he resented the intrusion of the locomotive into his solitude at Walden Pond; that he found companionable. But he distrusted mechanical improvements as irrelevant to the main issue, which was the improvement of the quality of human living. He could not overlook the exploitation of the miserable Irish immigrants by whose toil the railroad was built. And to what end was all this toiling and wretchedness? Few readers of *Walden* will fail to recall Thoreau's gibe at the project of "tunneling under the Atlantic" in order that America may know instantly that the Princess Adelaide has the whooping-cough. There was nothing in Thoreau's disposition to match that elation which Whitman so clearly felt in contemplating the triumphs of mechanical ingenuity:

"The seas inlaid with eloquent gentle wires!"

Whitman was the more modern in accepting uncritically such watchwords of the nineteenth century as science and progress. Thoreau insisted with old-fashioned caution on examining at once their bearing on man's welfare.

To him the problem of improving society was a matter of self-improvement many times multiplied. Let every man live up to his highest possibilities and there would be no need to worry about the state of the nation. Anything other than

individual improvement was beside the point. Hence Thoreau's sturdy independence was revolted by humanitarian projects for doing good to one's fellow-men, and to the subject of philanthropy he devoted some of his most astringent comments. He understood completely the degradation of being pawed over by a would-be benefactor. Let the charitable keep their hands off. The best service that he could render to mankind lay, he thought, in developing his specific talents to the height of his capacity. Even in preaching and practicing simplicity he did not aim at starting a movement. "To what end do I lead a simple life at all, pray? That I may teach others to simplify their lives?—and so all our lives be *simplified* merely, like an algebraic formula? Or not, rather, that I may make use of the ground I have cleared, to live more worthily and profitably?"

From what has been said it can easily be seen that Thoreau's ideas of how social conditions might be ameliorated were directly opposite to the techniques of social service as practiced at the present time. The basis of his thinking was religious, rooted in the Puritan conception of man's responsibility to God for the disposal of his talents. Man became his brother's keeper most effectually when by means of his own self-fulfillment he set a high standard for others to live up to. What we should labor to do unto others is to impart the courage of our example. The essence of Thoreau's social philosophy may be summed up in the following two quotations from his personal letters:

"Happy the man who observes the heavenly and the terrestrial law in just proportion; whose every faculty, from the soles of his feet to the crown of his head, obeys the law of its level; who neither stoops nor goes on tiptoe, but lives a balanced life, acceptable to nature and to God."

"Do not be too moral. You may cheat yourself out of much life so. Aim above morality. Be not simply good; be good for something."

8

CIVIL DISOBEDIENCE

Thoreau's conception of the proper relations between the individual and his government was at the farthest remove from the totalitarian policy of subordinating the rights of the subject to the demands of a Moloch-state. Like all the transcendentalists he exalted the "simple separate person" whom Whitman so amply celebrated. But Thoreau, unlike Whitman, never uttered the word *en masse*. A man was primarily an integer of soul. As a corollary he should be a distinct and independent economic and political unit. Instead of the necessities of statecraft exercising an ultimate compulsion upon each and every citizen, he would make the conscience of the private man the highest law of the state. It can readily be supposed that in holding these opinions Thoreau was making it impossible for himself to live easily under any form of organized control. In his view government could only be justified as "an expedient by which men would fain succeed in letting one another alone." It could be tolerated, in other words, only in so far as it protected the private man from the anarchy that might still more restrict his freedom if government did not exist.

Milton's social ideal of a people bred up in "strenuous liberty," Locke's assumption that the governed should choose the directors of their destiny by means of republican institutions, Jefferson's dream of a nation of independent yeoman-farmers, and the instinctive democracy of the American frontier, all were elements in Thoreau's political attitude. It would be difficult to carry the implications of liberalism further than he was willing to carry them. Not for nothing did he tread the ground "where once the embattled farmers stood." "This man," said Alcott, "is the independent of independents—is, indeed, the sole signer of the Declaration,

65

and a Revolution in himself—a more than '76—having got beyond the signing to the doing it out fully." Ideally Thoreau was prepared to go beyond the saying that that government is best which governs least and to state flatly that that government is best which governs not at all. But if man's present imperfections demanded some form of regulation, concession should extend only to the establishment of a kind of invisible civil service.

The essays called "Civil Disobedience" and "Life without Principle," in which Thoreau's views are asserted without qualification, are landmarks of an unfashionable and perhaps impossible radicalism. They are not reconcilable with Socialism, Communism, or any modern program for the conversion of society to a classless basis through the domination of a class. They do not contemplate the fusion of individuals into masses, nor the hammering of masses into pressure-groups and parties. Nevertheless they have not been without effect, even in a world which seems to be discarding as rapidly as possible Thoreau's basic philosophy. "Civil Disobedience," read by an able political agitator among the Hindoo workers of South Africa, bore strange fruit in Gandhi's powerful weapon of passive resistance. The chapter called "Economy" in *Walden* became a minor gospel of the British Labor Party because of its uncompromising emphasis, not on reform, but on proceeding at once to realize the ultimate values of life and on living only for them. "I came into this world, not chiefly to make this a good place to live in, but to live in it, be it good or bad," wrote Thoreau. He belived in having his share of immortality now. One man thoroughly imbued with such convictions is a force to be reckoned with. Several such men might constitute a silent revolution.

It is conceivable that a resurgence of religious conviction might unite men's wills in a passionate determination to make justice prevail in human affairs. The enormous force of inflexible and fanatical resolution which is now commonly

66

manipulated for the gaining of political or economic advantage might thus be turned to helpful social uses. If this should happen, Thoreau would at once be recognized as a prophet who prepared the way. The final defeat of demogogue and dictator occurs when no one can be found to think them important.

The creaky operation of government and politics in Massachusetts seemed to Thoreau less worthy of interest than the perfect functioning of muskrat society on the Concord meadows and the timeless mysteries of the seasons. But if the administration of human affairs interfered with the cosmic duties of citizens, or if the degradation of the state humiliated them by outraging their sense of justice, then the state had to be attended to. Otherwise it did not deserve to occupy a man's thought.

The issue of negro slavery was a case in point. Thoreau did not wish to have any truck with the foul institution, but it would not leave him alone. He was forced to consider it, and having considered it to condemn it, and having condemned it to take action. The Thoreau house was a well-recognized station on the underground railroad, and on at least one occasion Henry himself convoyed a fugitive slave on his way to Canada.

Emerson, it will be recalled, was unwilling to enlist as an anti-slavery agitator, partly because he had to guard his none too robust health, but partly also because he regarded slavery as only one monstrous symptom of the corruption at the heart of society which he was trying to combat by intellectual and spiritual means. Yet when the Fugitive Slave Law was passed, early in 1850, Emerson's reserve was broken and he entered in his journal a white-hot resolve, the most furious words that ever came from his pen: "This filthy enactment was made in the nineteenth century, by people who could read and write. I will not obey it, by God."

Thoreau, like Alcott, had reached a similar stage of in-

transigence at a considerably earlier date, and his response to an offense against his sense of right and wrong was uncompromising. He had discovered the pattern of dissent that he was to follow later, when in 1838 he "signed off" from the village church and refused to pay his tax for the support of the minister. There remained still a long list of institutions from which he would prefer to sign off. The war with Mexico, even if it were not inspired as most northern idealists believed it was by a desire to extend slave territory, was in his eyes an unrighteous war. "When . . . a whole country is unjustly overrun and conquered by a foreign army, and subjected to military law, I think that it is not too soon for honest men to rebel and revolutionize," he wrote, and added by way of pay-off: "What makes this duty the more urgent is the fact that the country so overrun is not our own, but ours is the invading army." His method of rebelling was more drastic than the making of any number of pacifist speeches would have been. Thoreau as a sovereign political entity seceded from the state of Massachusetts by ostentatiously neglecting to pay his poll-tax. As a consequence, he spent one night in jail. A friend intervened by paying the tax, and in the morning he was released.

The famous story that Emerson accompanied the jailer to the door of the cell and that gazing reprovingly on the delinquent he remarked, "Henry, why are you here?" only to have Thoreau reply with blazing indignation, "Waldo, why are you *not* here?" is probably apocryphal. It seems to be true, however, that Emerson at first deplored Thoreau's action as "in bad taste," but before the month was out he was comparing Webster's truckling to the politicians with Thoreau's uncompromising firmness. "My friend Mr. Thoreau has gone to jail rather than pay his tax. On him they could not calculate."

It was characteristic of the two men that, if we may judge by what they confided to their journals, Emerson was more

disturbed by the passage of the Fugitive Slave Law and Thoreau by the concrete application of it in the forcible return to slavery of certain colored residents of Boston, notably by the seizure of Anthony Burns. Thoreau could not say enough to express his contempt for the compliant officials of the State who permitted an injustice to be enacted under the sanction of a national statute. "Every man in New England," he wrote, "capable of the sentiment of patriotism must have lived the last three weeks with the sense of having suffered a vast, indefinite loss . . . I feel that, to some extent, the State has fatally interfered with my just and proper business. It has not merely interrupted me in my passage through Court Street on errands of trade, but it has, to some extent, interrupted me and every man on his onward and upward path, on which he had trusted soon to leave Court Street far behind." And his counsel was again that of a confirmed come-outer: "My advice to the State is simply this: to dissolve her union with the slaveholder instantly. She can find no respectable law or precedent which sanctions its continuance. And to each inhabitant of Massachusetts, to dissolve his union with the State, as long as she hesitates to do her duty."

All that Thoreau had ever said in contempt of a government that paltered with moral issues pales before the words that he uttered when the one man who dared to assault the very stronghold of a great wrong lay wounded and awaiting death on the gallows. Old John Brown of Kansas had visited Concord in March, 1857, and had taken meals at Thoreau's house. His homely rustic manners and simple directness had strongly appealed to Thoreau, who could recognize a man when he saw one. Early in October, 1859, Brown was again in Concord to secure funds that his supporters had been collecting for him. From there he proceeded directly to conduct his raid on Harper's Ferry. The news of his immortal failure shocked the nation, and the first response even of northern abolitionists was to disown Brown's act. He was attacked in

the press and from the pulpit as a misguided and insane fanatic, who had succeeded only in making mischief.

Less than two weeks after the raid, and while the country was still seething with indignation, Thoreau announced to his neighbors that he intended to speak in behalf of John Brown the next Sunday evening in the Town Hall of Concord. To some who sought to dissaude him he replied sharply that he had not asked for their advice but for their presence to hear what he had to say. Before a large audience he delivered his "Plea for Captain John Brown," the most forthright of his utterances. It was not, as its title might suggest, an appeal for clemency for the old fighter. It was the vindication of the character of a hero by a man who shared the same qualities of straightforwardness and independence. Two days later Thoreau read the same speech in Boston, and the day following in Worcester.

Seldom has a magnanimous deed been more nobly interpreted. Thoreau perceived at once the moral force of Brown's example. Here was the antidote to the long course of shuffling evasion that politicians had been pursuing. "For once we are lifted out of the trivialness and dust of politics into the region of truth and manhood." He reviewed Brown's character and personal history, contrasting his courage and the generosity of his aims with the apathy and caution that editors, clergy, and other public men had everywhere exhibited. The Day of Judgment for Massachusetts was at hand. "No man in America has ever stood up so persistently and effectively for the dignity of human nature, knowing himself for a man, and the equal of any and all governments."

Thoreau took part, with Emerson, Alcott, and others, in the services held at Concord on December 2, the day of John Brown's execution, and a little later he recorded in his journal a passage which contains the gist of his final tribute to the completest man he had ever known, a warrior-saint whose heroic stature matched Cromwell's in his imagination: "On

the day of his translation, I heard, to be sure, that he was hung, but I did not know what that meant,—and I felt no sorrow on his account; but not for a day or two did I even *hear* that he was dead, and not after any number of days shall I believe it. Of all the men who are said to be my contemporaries, it seems to me that John Brown is the only one who *has not* died. I meet him at every turn. He is more alive than ever he was. He is not confined to North Elba [where he was buried] nor to Kansas. He is no longer working in secret only. John Brown has earned immortality."

The American tradition is rich in the memorable sayings of our statesmen which have lived in popular esteem long after the occasions that gave rise to them. "Give me liberty or give me death!" . . . "All men are created free and equal" . . . "government of the people, by the people, for the people." But nothing Jefferson or Lincoln ever said is more inherently American or deserves to be more deeply engraved on the minds of a free people than a sentence wrung from Thoreau in the agony of his sympathetic comprehension of what John Brown had died for:

"The only government that I recognize—and it matters not how few are at the head of it, or how small its army—is that power that establishes justice in the land, never that which establishes injustice."

9

UNDERSTANDING NATURE

Defiance of American orthodoxy and respectability was endemic among finer spirits of the nineteenth century, particularly among men of letters. Emerson, Poe, Hawthorne, Melville, and Whitman were all at odds with the world as they found it. Emerson in early resigning from his pulpit, Hawthorne in joining the social reformers at Brook Farm, Melville in shipping on a whaler, each in his separate way was testifying to a sense of alienation from a society more and more standardized and dominated by material concerns.

No protest was more dramatic than Thoreau's. In the opinion of a recent student of Melville, the late William Ellery Sedgwick: "It is as if the long process of revolt which originated in England in the seventeenth century and was carried forward by successive generations of Puritans and pioneers, which dissented from the Church of England and broke away from the British government, came to a climax when Thoreau turned his back on civilization and went to live alone at Walden Pond." If it seems fantastic to suppose that a process of such proportions should culminate in an event of such small consequence, we may recall, following the way of analogy dear to the transcendentalists, that the significance of a mountain's peak is not due to its area as compared with the size of its base. The logic of Calvinism and Democracy alike pointed to the symbolic figure of a plain man with his feet on earth and his head among the stars.

In setting up a communion of saints in the American wilderness the Puritan founders of New England accepted an ideal very different from that involved in establishing a government for all sorts and conditions of men. A government theoretically intended to include everybody must be adjusted to a catholic conception of human nature, while a com-

munion of saints implies drastic exclusions. Though Puritan clergy and magistrates liked to argue that they had not left the Church of England but had only separated themselves from its errors, the distinction seemed immaterial to Anglicans who found themselves banished from Massachusetts Bay. Somehow a line had been drawn and men were required to toe the mark. In spite of occasional politic relentings such as the adoption of the "half-way covenant" to permit unconverted but substantial Christians to become members of the Puritan church, the policy of Calvinism was inherently exclusive. It magnified the small group of the elect, the Gideon's band who could show evidence that they were indeed chosen of God.

Democracy likewise, and paradoxically enough, was not available for all men. Born of the Protestant revolt against the traditional order, it commended itself to vigorous radicals as a method of discarding institutions which had become encumbrances. Democracy was justified in view of the dilapidations committed in its name. In one of his most cryptic sentences Melville remarked that, "Democracy lops, lops." The process of stripping government of its outworn trappings, however, could be carried out only as long as the citizenry remained alert and militant. Only the strenuous could keep Democracy from degeneration.

The winnowing implied in both Calvinism and Democracy might lead ultimately to profound spiritual isolation. The communion of saints, refined by successive purges, could in the end resolve itself into a community of one. Or in the political sphere the standard of fitness in the body politic might be raised until the majority of those fit to rule consisted of no more than Luther's "one with God." Sensitive men in nineteenth century America were becoming increasingly aware of the tendencies making for individual isolation. The thought of aloofness was dreadful to Hawthorne and he constantly recurred to it in his stories. Both Melville and

Thoreau were obliged to cope with the same specter. Captain Ahab in *Moby Dick,* like the Puritan spirit constantly discarding appliances and rejecting human sympathies in his fanatical desire to pursue and grapple with the white whale of universal mystery, is an incarnation of loneliness. Melville, however, after following his thought to a dead end of disillusionment, recoiled and gradually recovered. Thoreau, who experienced no powerful revulsion of feeling, dallied with solitude until his death.

Two quotations from the journal for the summer of 1852 show that Thoreau was beginning to feel that his closeness to nature was cutting him off from human associations. The first entry is admonitory: "Nature must be viewed humanly to be viewed at all; that is, her scenes must be associated with humane affections, such as are associated with one's native place, for instance. She is most significant to a lover. A lover of Nature is preeminently a lover of man. If I have no friend, what is Nature to me? She ceases to be morally significant." Only a month or two later seclusion is announced as an accepted fact. "By my intimacy with nature I find myself withdrawn from man. My interest in the sun and the moon, in the morning and the evening, compels me to solitude." Thoreau's resignation to loneliness might be called stoical if he had not been so vocal about it.

His chapter on "Solitude" in *Walden* is a masterpiece of extravagance compounded of paradox and romantic fallacies. "Why should I feel lonely? is not our planet in the Milky Way?" "I find it wholesome to be alone the greater part of the time . . . I never found the companion that was so companionable as solitude. We are for the most part more lonely when we go among men than when we stay in our chambers." "Society is commonly too cheap . . . We meet at meals three times a day, and give each other a new taste of that old musty cheese that we are." "I am no more lonely than the loon on the pond that laughs so loud, or than Wal-

den Pond itself . . . I am no more lonely than a single mullein or dandelion in a pasture, or a bean leaf, or sorrel, or a horse-fly, or a humblebee. I am no more lonely than the Mill Brook, or a weathercock, or the north star, or the south wind, or an April shower, or a January thaw, or the first spider in a new house." A truce to similitudes! Is this the Thoreau who as a young man burst into tears at the mere thought of leaving his home and family?

A note of false sentimentality very infrequent in Thoreau's writing occurs at the end of this same chapter where he personifies external nature as "an elderly dame . . . invisible to most persons, in whose odorous herb garden I love to stroll sometimes, gathering simples and listening to her fables." The enjoyment of solitude depended in a measure on the fancied sympathy of the out-of-door world. For a time the companionship of nature seemed a happy substitute for the more exacting association with men and women, and so Thoreau's isolation was at once deepened and made to seem tolerable. If we may trust certain entries in his journal that become more numerous toward the end, Thoreau was increasingly aware of a growing impoverishment and emptiness in his life. It is doubtful if he ever realized explicitly that worship of nature is only a thinly disguised form of self-worship, leading to sterility. Walking and boating trips had always been a part of his life before he exalted them into a chief concern. By the time he perceived that the path he was following did not lead where he wanted to go, it was too late to change. His quest for a free, abundant life ended in his being committed to comradeship with rocks and stones and trees. There is a trace of defiance in his later comments on his situation, as for example the following: "My work is writing, and I do not hesitate, though I know that no subject is too trivial for me, tried by ordinary standards; for, ye fools, the theme is nothing, the life is everything. All that interests the reader is the depth and intensity of the life excited . . .

That is, man is all in all, Nature nothing, but as she draws him out and reflects him."

There were two levels in Thoreau's attitude toward nature, and his shifting from one to the other leads to frequent inconsistencies. As a country-bred boy he had ranged the woods with his brother, deeply absorbing the healthy animal joys of fishing and hunting and camping out. Later in life memories of these rambles were associated with the closest human intimacy that he had ever known. His excursions also supplied him with the raw material for the making of essays, and after all he was primarily a writer. Hence Thoreau insisted on saving a generous portion of every day for trips afield. His delight in these jaunts was exquisite and wholesome, if still somewhat boyish.

But his preference for nature also rested on transcendental theorizing. His intense enjoyment of outdoor life led him to accept without hesitation the rhapsodic and reckless glorification of nature and of nature's beneficent influence on man, of which Emerson, outdoing Wordsworth, had made himself a major prophet. Emerson had missed the *caveat* which Coleridge, disillusioned after his early raptures, addressed to his brother poet:

> "O William! We receive but what we give,
> And in our life alone does Nature live."

Possessed by his mystical confidence in the immanence of the universal spirit in nature as well as in man, Emerson could see God in the meanest of inanimate objects. "What is there of the divine in a load of bricks? What is there of the divine in a barber's shop? . . . Much. All." The enthusiast found no difficulty in perceiving in the pleasanter aspects of nature a power to confirm the soul's health and to discipline the moral sense. The laws of spirit seemed to merge into one system with the laws of matter, and the ancient precept, Know Thyself, became identical with the modern slogan, Study nature.

As a poet Emerson, like Wordsworth, was capable of imposing serenely ethical interpretations on natural phenomena, sometimes with tonic effect, but as a thinker he was essentially uncritical of ideas that commended themselves to his blandly optimistic temper. Speaking of Emerson's philosophy of nature Professor Joseph Warren Beach observes: "Must we not admit that it is, for the most part, a loose and popular rendering of Coleridge, who gives a loose and popular rendering of (mainly) Schelling, who—for all his magnificent show of dialectic—is no better than a Kant run wild."

Thoreau, whose element was excess, carried the transcendental personalizing of nature even further than Emerson. What the Puritans had regarded as the garment darkly veiling God's majesty, and what Emerson had celebrated as a flowing revelation of the Over-Soul, he wholeheartedly took to his bosom as "friend" and "bride." Nature could give him the perfect response, the complete toleration that he could not expect from men and women. Nature demanded nothing in return. "If I am too cold for human friendship," he wrote in 1852, "I trust I shall not soon be too cold for natural influences. It appears to be a law that you cannot have a deep sympathy with both man and nature. Those qualities which bring you near to the one estrange you from the other." Association with human beings, in other words, checks a tendency to unimpeded expansion of the ego, but nature leaves one gloriously free: free but unchallenged, unprovoked to supreme effort, not subject to criticism.

Thoreau, even while passionately identifying himself with nature, seems to have felt that something was amiss: "I seem to be more constantly merged in nature; my intellectual life is more obedient to nature than formerly, but perchance less obedient to spirit. I have less memorable seasons. I exact less of myself." But he did not stay to analyze his difficulties. "The meaning of Nature," as Emerson noted, "was never attempted to be defined by him." A greater assimilation

77

either of Christian doctrine or of the spirit of the Greek and Roman classics might have preserved him from the bacchic excesses of transcendentalism; but Christianity was obscured for him by his dislike for its institutions and the ineptitude of its ministers, and with the passing years his reading of the classics grew less frequent. Though he cherished independence of mind, he was not independent enough to scrutinize with appropriate skepticism the romantic doctrines of the benefits of solitude and the kindliness of nature.

It is significant, pathetically so, that Thoreau made much of a remarkable echo that he encountered while surveying the Hunt farm. After days of unimportant drudgery with stupid companions, he says, here was "somebody I could talk with." When it is said that in devoting himself to nature Thoreau was "pursuing perfection in a vacuum," it should be added that the vacuum was not altogether of his own making.

There was one important difference between Emerson's attitude toward nature and Thoreau's, a difference that suggests one of the channels by which the too placid accumulations of transcendental speculation might ultimately be drained off. Emerson, who went to nature chiefly for mental refreshment, held the world of woods and streams generally at arm's length. He was satisfied to theorize about nature in general terms. Thoreau, on the other hand, could never saturate his senses enough with the concrete and specific items from nature's store. His journal for the last ten years of his life reads like a vast inventory, often tediously detailed, often repetitious. But there is this to say for it, that it points away from the conception of nature as a projection of universal mind in matter. It testifies to an implicit conviction of the separateness of the inner and outer worlds, to a respect for the unspoiled integrity of the latter, to a suspicion that even the transcendental temperament might profit by "the discipline of looking always at what is to be seen."

Thoreau was not a scientist, and his persistent measuring of the girth of trees, the height of floods, the thickness of ice, and so on would be dismaying in their clumsiness if regarded as attempts to collect scientific data. But probably they were not that. They were the awkward caresses that Thoreau lavished on the one consuming love of his life. He simply could not know enough of the world around him. If he was at rare intervals a visionary, he lived most commonly in the almost savage delicacy of his senses. He guarded them carefully from blunting by overstimulation. Fair Nature, which demanded no hard service, smiled upon him and he responded by recording in innumerable pages every least shade of expression on her countenance. He found his true vocation in being the enamored prose-poet of the countryside.

10

LITERARY ARTISTRY

Thoreau was inclined to simplify the business of writing as well as the business of living. Toward the close of the year 1841, when he was still thinking of himself as a poet rather than a prose writer, he adopted in extreme form the idea of the poet's community with other men. "Good poetry," he declared, "seems so simple and natural a thing that when we meet it we wonder that all men are not always poets. Poetry is nothing but healthy speech." Prose, he was later to discover, was also nothing but healthy speech with the weight of a man's full conviction behind it. In 1859, when he was deeply stirred by the John Brown affair, he reasserted a conception essentially Miltonic that good writing "demands earnestness and manhood chiefly" and is a matter of plain integrity. All else is mere flummery. "Literary gentlemen, editors, and critics think that they know how to write because they have studied grammar and rhetoric; but they are egregiously mistaken. The *art* of composition is as simple as the discharge of a bullet from a rifle, and its masterpieces imply an infinitely greater force behind them . . . It suggests that the one great rule of composition—and if I were a professor of rhetoric I should insist on this—is to *speak the truth.* This first, this second, this third; pebbles in your mouth or not."

The tone of depreciation that he employed in speaking of mere literary craftsmanship is occasionally repeated. When Thoreau noticed in turning over the biographical sketches in *Homes of American Authors* that many of the New England group had at one time or another contributed to the *North American Review,* he asserted at once, "It is one of my qualifications that I have not written an article for the *North American Review.*" As Emerson explained when he first mentioned Thoreau to Carlyle: "There is a universal timidity,

conformity, and rage; and on the other hand the most resolute realism in the young." Thoreau typified youth in revolt. Like Emily Dickinson he found it impossible to speak the truth within the decorous literary conventions of late romanticism and the genteel tradition. He was groping his way toward a technique of sincerity beyond anything that his literary contemporaries had yet grasped.

As an experimental poet he met a defeat attributable to two causes. The first was his own uncertainty, not of aims, but of means; the second was the failure of even the most friendly readers to perceive the basis on which he was working. Even Emerson, who shared in theory many of Thoreau's principles, did not see how close the young poet was coming to realizing them in practice. People were obsessed by literary tradition. Ultimately it took the robust self-confidence of a Walt Whitman to burst through the net of convention. Thoreau's confidence wavered. His poems, when some specimens were published in the *Dial,* were too radical for the public taste and were ridiculed by the uncomprehending for their "ragged and halting lines." Later he gave a number of his pieces, or fragments chipped from them, a setting in the pages of the *Week,* but there too they remained unappreciated. On the advice of Emerson he burned the bulk of his early poems. At the end of his life he looked back on this action with regret. Perhaps, he surmised, the poems were not as bad as they had thought them twenty years before.

His final opinion was indeed prescient. Though his contemporaries considered that his poems "lacked lyrical fire and melodious utterance," it has at long last been perceived that they possess other and more interesting qualities. After noting that Thoreau's search for a satisfactory poetic style led him to range over an unusual variety of models—the Greek anthology, Horace, the medieval mystery plays, Skelton, Ben Jonson, Herbert, Thomson and Cowper, Blake and Wordsworth—Professor Henry W. Wells, who has made the only

81

competent critical study of the complete poems, comes to the conclusion that the largest number of his most memorable pieces have no specific connection with the past but in a remarkable way anticipate the poetry of the present moment. "Thoreau, like Emily Dickinson or Baudelaire, anticipates the bold symbolism, airy impressionism, stringent realism, and restless inconsistencies of twentieth-century poetry." And again: "Thoreau's breadth of vision is precisely what our own age, tragically seeking a new consolidation of mankind, most of all requires." The one thing his poetry seldom does is to lapse into the facile sentimentalism and smooth nullity characteristic of the nineteenth-century imitators of such fashionable models as Byron and Tennyson.

It is possible to regret the loss of Thoreau's youthful poems without deploring his early change to prose writing. He did not feel with Matthew Arnold that any lowering of intention was involved. "Great prose of equal elevation," he thought, "commands our respect more than great verse, since it implies a more permanent and level height, a life more pervaded with the grandeur of thought. The poet only makes an irruption, like a Parthian, and is off again, shooting while he retreats; but the prose writer has conquered, like a Roman, and settled colonies." The instrument of prose was well suited to his genius, and within its broader scope he could employ the powerful concision and quick responsiveness that distinguished his poetry.

What Thoreau aimed at from first to last in all his writing was the expression of ultimate truth or reality. "You may rely on it that you have the best of me in my books," he wrote to a young inquirer during his last illness, "and that I am not worth seeing personally . . . what am I to the truth I feebly utter?" One of the most vigorous passages in *Walden* states his determination to penetrate through all shams and illusions to the very heart of actuality. "Let us settle ourselves, and work and wedge our feet downward through the mud

and slush of opinion, and prejudice, and tradition, and delusion and appearance, that alluvion which covers the globe, . . . through church and state, through poetry and philosophy and religion, till we come to a hard bottom and rocks in place, which we can call *reality,* and say, This is, and no mistake; and then begin, having a *point d'appui,* below freshet and frost and fire . . . Be it life or death, we crave only reality." Eloquent as these words are, they do not tell us how and by what tests Thoreau proposed to distinguish what was real from what was appearance or delusion. Perhaps like jesting Pilate on a famous occasion he was more interested in asking, What is truth? than in staying for an answer.

He seems to have recognized in practice, however, two sorts of reality, one of which he called "poetry" and the other "fact." The first consisted of an inward and overwhelming vitality of conviction, the second of a minute faithfulness to the external world. Theoretically the two seemed entirely distinct, yet he found that they tended to overlap. "I have a commonplace-book for facts and another for poetry, but I find it difficult always to preserve the vague distinction which I had in my mind, for the most interesting and beautiful facts are so much the more poetry and that is their success . . . I see that if my facts were sufficiently vital and significant,— perhaps transmuted more into the substance of the human mind,—I should need but one book of poetry to contain them all." And as late as 1854 he makes the characteristic transcendental affirmation that "there is no such thing as pure *objective* observation." He continues: "The sum of what the writer of whatever class has to report is simply some human experience, whether he be poet or philosopher or man of science. The man of most science is the man most alive, whose life is the greatest event. Senses that take cognizance of outward things merely are of no avail . . . All that a man has to say or do that can possibly concern mankind, is in some shape or other to tell the story of his love,—to sing; and if he

is fortunate and keeps alive, he will be forever in love." In passages like these our Bachelor of Nature is verging strongly toward a rhapsodic humanism.

As one surveys Thoreau's total deposit of words on paper, from his early journals and the *Week* through *Walden* to his posthumous travel books and the ten years of bookkeeping for all outdoors that constitutes the later journal, one cannot help being struck by an almost imperceptible shift of emphasis in practice from the poetic to the factual. It is as though Thoreau were passing within the compass of his own brief lifetime from a seventeenth-century view of a unified world of experience to a partial anticipation of the multiple universe characteristic of our own times. His earliest concern was for the depth and intensity of the life excited by his writing. He would attain to truth by the power of his pulses. "We cannot write well or truly but what we write with gusto. The body, the senses, must conspire with the mind. Expression is the act of the whole man, that our speech may be vascular . . . It is always essential that we love to do what we are doing, do it with a heart." Thoreau possessed by the vital urgency of his youth is not indifferent to the solidity and impact of his pages, but he is stimulated by the sheer ebullience of his energy into sportive pirouettings, puns, conceits, paradoxes, and verbal ingenuities. He is too effervescent to care greatly for the form of his writing. Any kind of framework will serve.

But as he becomes more sedate and factual the effervescence disappears, leaving only a negative scorn for the formal elements of composition. "It is surprising how much, from the habit of regarding writing as an accomplishment, is wasted on form. A very little information or wit is mixed up with a great deal of conventionalism in the style of expressing it, as with a sort of preponderating paste or vehicle. Some life is not simply expressed, but a long-winded speech is made, with an occasional attempt to put a little life in it." Instead

of settling down to a "certain dryness" that he considered not incongruous with maturity of mind, Thoreau tried the dubious expedient of accumulating larger and larger stores of fresh factual impressions. Insensibly facts came to bulk larger than the use he could make of them. The sparkle of his earlier manner dimmed to sobriety.

The increase of information at the expense of wit was a natural consequence of the reaction from the artificial or mechanical sublimity of much early nineteenth-century romantic writing. With Emerson, Thoreau sought to poetize the commonplace, "the meal in the firkin, the milk in the pan." Homeliness stood high in his list of literary virtues. "There is a sort of homely truth and naturalness in some books," he wrote in 1841, "which is very rare to find, and yet looks quite cheap . . . The scholar rarely writes as well as the farmer talks. Homeliness is a great merit in a book; it is next to beauty and high art . . . I like better the surliness with which the woodchopper speaks of his woods, handling them as indifferently as his axe, than the mealy-mouthed enthusiasm of the lover of nature." It is possible to trace through the journals a gradual deterioration from homeliness to barrenness. At first Thoreau is captured by the challenge of making something out of a common theme. "I omit the unusual—the hurricanes and earthquakes—and describe the common. This has the greatest charm and is the true theme of poetry. You may have the extraordinary for your province if you will let me have the ordinary." Several years later the solid substance of out-of-door experiences is needed "as a ballast to thought and sentiment." Finally in 1858, still shying away from lofty subjects, Thoreau remarks: "It is a great art in the writer to improve from day to day just that soil and fertility which he has, to harvest that crop which his life yields, whatever it may be, not to be straining as if to reach apples or oranges when he yields only ground-nuts. He should be digging, not soaring." Thoreau had never been

inclined to let his feet leave the ground. In the later years he became reconciled to digging.

The special luck of *Walden* among Thoreau's writings was to come neither too early nor too late, but at the happy moment when poetry and fact were in exquisite equilibrium. Some shadow of what was to come rests upon his recital of sundry measurements of the depth of the pond, the thickness of the ice, and the like, but on the whole it rests lightly. Meanwhile the "flame in the mind" illuminates with playful wit Thoreau's discussion of the economy of his sylvan retreat, and a passionate enjoyment of the freshness of life breathes from every page. The sentences are nervous and sensitive, stripped of all excess and flabbiness. Alcott paid his friend a deserved tribute in declaring: "Of Americans, Thoreau speaks and writes the strongest English . . . Nothing can be spared from his sentence; there is nothing superfluous or irrelevant, but all is compact, solid, and concrete, as Nature is."

11

HIGHER LAWS

The keynote of literary aspiration for the period between 1830 and the Civil War was sounded by the elder William Ellery Channing, the Unitarian divine, when he replied to Charles J. Ingersoll's *Discourse Concerning the Influence of America on the Mind.* Speaking in Philadelphia before the American Philosophical Society in 1823, Ingersoll had argued that the mind of the new nation was practical and utilitarian, and that in consequence a true national literature should be expressed in works of utility rather than in *belles lettres.* Channing in his reply, published in 1830, was willing to agree that literature should not be divorced from life, but he could not tolerate the idea that either literature or life should be dominated by material interests. Instead he rèaffirmed the conviction previously voiced by Crèvecoeur that "the American is a new man, who acts upon new principles; he must therefore entertain new ideas, and form new opinions." But the novelty must attain the heights of a moral and spiritual revival. Here on an unpreempted continent mankind might be privileged to make a fresh beginning, sloughing off the old errors and inherited injustices of past centuries. Our literature should be founded on our hopes for the future, not on dark recollections of old-world defeats nor on a dull and sordid present.

"We want a reformation," exclaimed Channing. "We want a literature, in which genius will pay supreme, if not undivided homage, to truth and virtue . . . We should have no heart to encourage native literature, did we not hope that it would become instinct with a new spirit. We cannot admit the thought, that this country is to be only a repetition of the old world. We delight to believe that God, in the fulness of time, has brought a new continent to light, in order that

87

the human mind should move here with a new freedom, should frame new social institutions, should explore new paths, and reap new harvests. We are accustomed to estimate nations by their creative energies, and we shall blush for our country, if, in circumstances so peculiar, original, and creative, it shall satisfy itself with a passive reception and mechanical reiteration of the thoughts of strangers."

This appeal for literary independence prepared the way for Emerson, who was but following out Channing's thought when he asked in *Nature* the fundamental question: "Why should not we also enjoy an original relation to the universe?" and proceeded in the *Essays* to develop his teaching of reliance on the godlike powers implicit in man's being. In an age of intellectual ferment newness and virtue often seemed synonymous, yet in actuality the two ideals that Channing hoped to realize in a national literature were not in all respects compatible. It is one thing for a writer to illustrate a lofty morality, and quite another for him to be informed by a new spirit. The principles of ethics are not a discovery of yesterday, but matter of venerable antiquity. Somewhere in the background of Channing's thought there seems to be lurking the characteristic American preconception that Europe holds a monopoly on sin. Our native genius would pay instinctive homage to truth and virtue if not contaminated from abroad. But Socrates and Saint Paul were not born in Boston.

The bifurcation, if not contradiction, inherent in Channing's argument did not lessen its attractiveness to American men of letters who immediately followed him. The notion of a fresh beginning which should involve at the same time a release from the baser side of human nature ran its course in the books of the three decades after 1830. The identification of newness and naturalness with truth and virtue is frequent in Thoreau, and traces of the same attitude may even be found in Henry James. Hawthorne was possibly the first

to detect a potential opposition, as of Siamese twins, between the ideals of moral excellence and originality, while Melville may be said to have performed the fatal operation in his *Pierre* of cutting the two apart.

In the chapter of *Walden* called "Higher Laws" Thoreau is paying his homage to truth and virtue. The particular quality under discussion is purity of heart, which Thoreau associates with virginal freshness of the senses. "If the day and the night are such that you greet them with joy, and life emits a fragrance like flowers and sweet-scented herbs, is more elastic, more starry, more immortal,—that is your success." But the process by which Thoreau would attain this crowning bliss turns out to be the time-worn process of ascetic negation. He "would fain keep sober always; and there are infinite degrees of drunkenness . . . Of all ebriosity, who does not prefer to be intoxicated by the air he breathes?" Such a one may revel at a proper remove with Emily Dickinson, that "debauchee of dew," but he will be unprepared to sit down with Falstaff.

To a seeker after new ideas Thoreau's reflections on the satisfactions of a life of high moral purity must prove very disappointing. They would not be out of place in the mouth of a medieval anchorite, but they hardly advance the credit of a transcendental thinker. They are an almost perfect example of what Channing called the "mechanical reiteration of the thoughts of strangers," or of what are properly called ethical truisms. "Our whole life is startlingly moral. There is never an instant's truce between virtue and vice. Goodness is the only investment that never fails . . . We are conscious of an animal in us, which awakens in proportion as our higher nature slumbers . . . Chastity is the flowering of man; and what are called Genius, Heroism, Holiness, and the like, are but various fruits which succeed it . . . Nature is hard to be overcome, but she must be overcome." Some of these apothegms might worthily adorn *Poor Richard's Almanac.*

In the pages of *Walden* they represent a lapse into moral commonplace. Why go to the woods for such thoughts as these?

It may as well be conceded that Thoreau is somewhat deficient on the side of heartiness. This does not mean that he was gloomy. He could even be gay in society on rare occasions. There is a record of his singing his favorite song, "Here a sheer hulk lies poor Tom Bowling," with immense gusto and dancing a faun-like impromptu dance to the music of the piano in Daniel Ricketson's parlor, taking pains to tread now and then on the guileless Alcott's toes. But this outburst of high spirits appears almost unique. Either an acquired Puritanism or an ascetic strain derived from his oriental studies made Thoreau exaggerate the benefits of austerity and forget that to cultivate one's higher powers solely is not to improve but to mutilate human nature. It was an excessive prudery that made Thoreau reject Rabelais as coarse, and an excessive solemnity that induced him to qualify his admiration for Chaucer's *Prologue* by the remark that "it is esentially humorous as the loftiest genius never is," a remark which if taken literally would immediately relegate most of Thoreau's writing to the status of the second-rate. There was a vein of adamant in Thoreau's nature, and in some of his judgments he was inflexibly conventional.

But it is fair to say that he sometimes felt the burden of his derivative ethics and dropped them with relief. The chapter on "Higher Laws" opens significantly with Thoreau's confession that he would like to pursue a woodchuck and devour him raw. The flavor of wildness seemed to him a premonition of a sort of virtue that would never stale. A tangle of swamp where no man before him had penetrated was his substitute for Eden. "I love Nature partly *because* she is not man, but a retreat from him. None of his institutions control or pervade her. There a different kind of right prevails. In her midst I can be glad with an entire gladness. If this world

were all man, I could not stretch myself, I should lose all hope. He is constraint, she is freedom to me. He makes me wish for another world. She makes me content with this." In preferring the "kind of right" that nature offers, Thoreau was becoming an American writer instinct with a new spirit.

It was not nature merely as the exterior world nor as the open air that he delighted in, but nature in its untouched and unsubdued wildness. He liked to keep out of sight of houses. In this respect he parted company with Wordsworth, who never wandered far from cottage and sheepfold. To Thoreau in his youth wildness was a thrilling and romantic experience, valued on the ground of its opposition to civilization. He hinted at its attractions in a famous passage in the *Week*:

"There is in my nature, methinks, a singular yearning toward all wildness . . . Gardening is civil and social, but it wants the vigor and freedom of the forest and the outlaw. There may be an excess of cultivation as well as of anything else, until civilization becomes pathetic . . . The young pines springing up in the corn-fields from year to year are to me a refreshing fact. We talk of civilizing the Indian, but that is not the name for his improvement. By the wary independence and aloofness of his dim forest life he preserves his intercourse with his native gods, and is admitted from time to time to a rare and peculiar society with Nature. He has glances of starry recognition to which our saloons are strangers. The steady illumination of his genius, dim only because distant, is like the faint but satisfying light of the stars compared with the dazzling but ineffectual and short-lived blaze of candles. The Society Islanders had their day-born gods, but they were not supposed to be 'of equal antiquity with the *atua fauau po,* or night-born gods!'"

From nature Thoreau next abstracted the quality of wildness and hypostatized it as an entity that might exist in the mind of man, in books, in actions. It was the matchless source of life and vigor, a reservoir of inexhaustible energy.

"In literature it is only the wild that attracts us." It is synonymous with genius. And finally, "in Wildness is the preservation of the World," the nourishment and tonic of mankind, as the still unsettled West was proving to be the salvation of the populated states. In the end nature was not sufficient to contain the degree of what might be called aboriginality that Thoreau desired. He was homesick for a wildness that could only be realized in imagination.

"We soon get through with Nature. She excites an expectation which she cannot satisfy. The merest child which has rambled into a copsewood dreams of a wilderness so wild and strange and inexhaustible as Nature can never show him."

"I long for wildness, a nature which I cannot put my foot through, woods where the wood thrush forever sings, where the hours are early morning ones, and there is dew on the grass, and the day is forever unproved, where I might have a fertile unknown for a soil about me. I would go after the cows, I would watch the flocks of Admetus there forever, only for my board and clothes. A New Hampshire everlasting and unfallen."

The dream of wildness thus came to stand to Thoreau as a symbol of the individuality, tang, and freshness of underivative things, and as such he held it precious. The exquisite unfolding of the leaves to fill out the pattern implicit in the seed, the unstudied grace of the bird balancing on the bough, the sureness of instinct in wild animals, these things were to him akin to the fulfillment of man's intellectual and spiritual powers. "We wish man on the higher plane to exhibit also the wildness or nature of that higher plane," wrote Emerson, and Thoreau entirely concurred. Beauty and integrity, magnanimity and a luminous mind should not be conscious contrivances, but organic flowerings of the primitive stock of human nature.

Toward the end of his life Thoreau ceased to look to nature as a means of romantic escape. He had come to see that wildness begins at home. "It is in vain to dream of a wildness distant from ourselves. There is none such . . . I shall never find in the wilds of Labrador any greater wildness than in some recess in Concord, *i.e.* than I import into it. A little more manhood or virtue will make the surface of the globe anywhere thrillingly novel and wild." So in his last phase Thoreau set to work to run down and corner the wildness that he could create in Concord. The enterprise was a part of his passionate pursuit of reality, which refused to stay put in either the inward or the outward world. Hundreds of pages of journal entries keeping minute record of the countryside in all its aspects, a million words of excerpts dealing with Indians, remained among his papers to testify to his unflagging zeal in the quest.

Francis Parkman is the only American writer comparable to Thoreau in his eagerness to capture in literature the most unique feature of American experience, the contact of civilized man with unbroken wilderness. His "History of the Forest," as he called his volumes on the struggle for the North American continent, is a magnificent achievement that by glimpses and flashes of indirection brings home to its readers a sense of how Europeans responding to a new environment were subtly changed into Americans, new men with new ideas. Thoreau attempted in a more personal way to portray the inwardness of this experience. For the last time in the world's history the freshness of an unviolated country, the wildness of the primitive forest, as American colonists had felt these things and as Thoreau could still in a measure recover them in Concord, were available to a writer who received them with deep reverence and attempted with vehement sincerity to transfer their inmost reality to his pages. Alcott has truly declared, "Of New England men, Thoreau came nearest to being indigenous."

GEORGE F. WHICHER has been since 1915 a

professor of English at Amhe

ALBERTSON COLLEGE OF IDAHO

3 5556 0012 7782 1

WITHDRAWN

APR 22 '71

P9-CKY-174

F

PS3053
W5

52096

TERTELING LIBRARY
THE COLLEGE OF IDAHO
CALDWELL, IDAHO

To Dione Lucas, a beautiful being, and to those who aim at combining exquisiteness and health in their eating habits. In short: to the ultimate gourmet.

Purpose

We believe that the art of eating should embrace both the *sensuous* and *nutritious* aspects of food. In this book we take a first step by incorporating natural, healthy ingredients into classic French cookery—replacing those refined, chemically processed, and artificial commodities we now know to be damaging our bodies. Our aim is to enhance the taste and the nutritive value of the foods we eat through reoriented menu planning and cooking methods.

This book is devoted to the dual objectives of gourmandise: To the sensuous: "it is an impassioned, rational and habitual preference for all objects which flatter the sense of taste." To the organic: "it is the result and the proof of the wholesome and perfect state of the organs destined to nutrition." (Brillat-Savarin, *The Physiology of Taste,* 1825)

Preface

For the last 30 years or so, Americans have become increasingly eager gourmets and have created a whole new market for sophisticated food products, equipment and utensils, books, food services, etc., that continues to grow and grow. We are even on our way to becoming a wine-drinking and wine-producing nation, an event thought inconceivable as little as ten years ago.

In the vanguard of this acculturation of a nation was Dione Lucas, my mentor, coauthor, and dearest friend. Craig Claiborne, the respected food writer of *The New York Times,* declared in 1970: "Dione Lucas pioneered French cooking in this country about 25 years ago, when the average American couldn't distinguish a crêpe Suzette from a flapjack or a scrambled egg from an omelet. As the high priestess of high cookery, she taught many of the people who now earn a living running cooking schools their basic techniques." Propelled by her popularity on the first and longest-running television cooking show (launched on WCBS-TV in the late 40's), she accelerated the passion for gourmet cooking. Gourmet cooking has become big business, and today conditions all American cooking and eating.

Mrs. Lucas's and my final work together just prior to her death in December, 1972, *The Dione Lucas Book of French Cooking* (Little, Brown, 1973), is a recipe compendium of her life's work in *traditional* classic cookery. During Dione's last years, however, through her interest and instigation, we began to experiment with *natural* ingredients and cooking methods that would improve the vital food value of dishes within the classic repertoire. During that period when Dione visited my home she would bear gifts of organic eggs, goat's milk, organic fruits and vegetables from her trips to Bennington, Vermont, where her younger son and sister lived. (The omelet queen had been raised as a vegetarian and was much taken with organic eggs.)

Dione always had an abiding love for natural richness and purity. She insisted on the "fresh" and "pure" in her recipes, avoided canned or frozen ingredients, advocated minimum cooking times, saved cooking water for stock, etc. On one occasion, when she was visiting her sister Orrea Pernel in Vermont, she expressed her interest in writing to Adelle Davis with the idea of having the two of them collaborate on a cookbook whose recipes would be truly healthy and at the same time delectable. Clearly, Dione herself anticipated the eventual need for the blending of the two great traditions: *haute cuisine* and natural foods.

Since that time, the new health-food* market has grown to the point where, in 1975, J. D. Power & Associates of Los Angeles estimated it to be a one-billion-dollar industry, with over 13 million U.S. homemakers as health-food consumers to some extent. This market is receiving boosts daily from the meticulous research of dietetics (the science of nutrition) which conclusively links aspects of our modern diets to the ghastly diseases that are also uniquely "modern," including the No. 1 killers—heart disease and cancer.

A few years ago Felipe de Alba, a nutrition expert who has devoted a lifetime to the study and practice of modern nutrition, asked me: "Why can't you prepare the dishes of *haute cuisine* with health (natural) foods?" Felipe's query caused me to realize that despite all of my gourmet interests I had been a one-track gourmet—concerned with appeals to the eye and the palate and assuming that the most expensive ingredients were the healthiest of all. I also realized that our daily food, including the gourmet repast, is dangerously overchemicalized and that this trend toward unhealthy food must be reversed before it is too late. At least we should be offered a choice to improve the meals we prepare and the foods we eat.

Thus Felipe and I began the joint project of converting the classic recipes of Dione Lucas into dishes with the maximum use of natural ingredients. (In addition to my own files from my years of association with Dione, I was given all of her unpublished files with the sole right to use them. Many of the recipes in this book are published for the first time.) Also, in a broader sense, we took a critical nutritional look at the classic menu concept and at traditional cooking methods.

The aims of our project were: (1) to maintain the sensuous plea-

* "Health food" is a broad term encompassing foods and supplements which claim to be free of chemical additives and to be of natural origin with a greater content of vital substances than foods which have been commercially mass-produced, processed, or refined. Included as "health foods" are "natural" and "organic" foods. The meanings are similar. (See "Natural" and "Organic" in the Encyclopedia, pp. 19 and 20–21.)

sures of gourmandise for which the great dishes of classic cookery are distinguished; (2) to reduce as much as possible the use of ingredients with harmful or questionable chemicals (which can enter a foodstuff at various stages of its production—breeding or planting, growing or manufacturing, distribution or storage) ; (3) to use ingredients which contain the maximum amount of natural life substances (vitamins and minerals, etc.) ; (4) to adapt cooking techniques which would preserve rather than destroy those life substances; (5) to develop a menu code which incorporates the principles of good nutrition into gourmet-quality meals. It seemed to us that *cuisine santé*, meaning healthy French cooking, was the best name to describe our new approach.

Felipe and I have lived this project every day since it began and attest to its merits: The conversions of classic dishes to natural ingredients and methods provide dishes that are substantially healthier; they are discernibly tastier; and they are easier, cleaner, faster, and more economical to prepare.

A note for the cook

We would like to suggest some attitudes to be taken toward this book. First, we emphasize that our effort is a beginning step; we sincerely hope other cooking authorities will also offer the American cook more recipes expressed in health-food or natural ingredients and methods.

To the cook we would like to point out that while *cuisine santé* is not a "diet" per se, its philosophy can be successfully applied to attain either the loss or gain of weight. *Cuisine santé* is different from *cuisine minceur* and *la nouvelle cuisine*. *Cuisine minceur* (meaning "food for slimming") is oriented toward people who are consciously trying to reduce their calorie and cholesterol intake, and some exponents of this method endorse the use of an artificial sweetener. *La nouvelle cuisine* is the general movement toward more emphasis on natural or primary ingredients and less complex sauces and flavorings, but to date its recipes do not identify the best natural form of the ingredients used. *Cuisine santé* encompasses both these ideas and goes beyond. But should you choose your menus unwisely, be they of natural food or traditional orientation, you could develop a weight problem. We defer to Dr. Roger J. Williams' term "body wisdom" for appetite control which should be cultivated and exercised at all times.

May we also alert you to our rather unorthodox organization for a cookbook. Because as of this writing we know of no other book which interprets the ways and means of French cooking in natural foods, we felt that an orientation was necessary. To avoid redundant and cumbersome explanations in the recipes with so many recurring ingredients and procedures, we have provided a small encyclopedia of explanations up front. If you want to know "why no chocolate," just look up "chocolate" in the encyclopedia; or "why cold-pressed safflower oil," refer to "cooking fats." The encyclopedia provides explanations that apply wherever an ingredient may or may not be used. Also, our Orientation section contains a substantial chapter on the menu. Actually, the recipe chapters are organized in terms of menu consideration—first course, main course, and desserts. This function is explained in detail in the Introduction.

Dear reader, Felipe de Alba and I hope this work will in a small way be useful to you in your pursuit of the fuller meaning of "gourmandise," and will enhance your joy of eating through the timeless talent of Dione Lucas, now expressed in *natural* goodness.
    Santé.

MARION GORMAN

New York City
April, 1977

Contents

PART I
Orientation

Introduction

TO THE "ULTIMATE GOURMET"

A person who enjoys delectable foods and who brings eating to the level of an art is a gourmet; for many centuries, one of man's most earnest and pleasurable pursuits has been the collection of outstanding formulas of sophisticated eating.

Eating gracefully has always been associated with living gracefully. Perhaps nowhere else is this as true as with classic French cooking. The very mention of *haute cuisine* specialties, such as *filets de soles Dugléré, tournedos Béarnaise,* and *mousse au chocolat,* evokes a feeling of anticipation toward food that is hard to equal.

What then can be held against the gourmets who champion such exceptional eating? Just this: the so-called gourmet of today has failed to use foods that include the most valuable natural nutrients, and has instead used ingredients which not only lack nutritional value, but are actively harmful to our health. He has allowed his specialties to be prepared with devitalized white flour, white sugar, synthetic eggs, saturated-fat-laden butter, chemically processed ingredients containing poisonous coloring and preservatives, and poultry or meat from chemically injected animals—some of which have now been officially linked with producing forms of cancer, heart disease, and other disorders. He has permitted depleted, overrefined, and at times openly harmful and/or poisonous foods to replace the original, natural, healthy ones. Thus he has seriously jeopardized his health.

Published books and investigative reports have made us painfully aware of our dangerous eating habits—from the clarion prophecy of Adelle Davis in 1954, *Let's Eat Right To Keep Fit,* to the warnings we see and hear daily in the press and on radio and television. These warnings link nitrates and nitrites to cancer; nutritional factors—including a diet high in animal fat, excessive alcohol intake, deficiencies in vitamins A and C, certain food additives, and natural as well as man-made contaminants of food—to cancer of the colon, stomach, esophagus, breast, liver, and uterus, and to heart disease; and synthetic flavors and colors to hyperactivity and learning disorders in children. These health-degenerative, disease-risk additives and natural imbalances in so many of our modern foods have created time bombs in our bodies. The factors are so complex that modern research cannot yet determine the point when individual nutritional imbalances will succumb to one of various diseases now known to be caused by vitally deficient and unnatural foods.

Ironically, the gourmets, who pledge themselves to discriminating eating, have been as guilty as anyone of abusing their health with the foods they eat. In the *Journal of the International Wine & Food Society* (London, November, 1975), devoted to one of the most prestigious gourmet organizations in the world, Barbara Cartland declares: "You Are What You Eat . . . 5,000 chemicals are added to our daily food. They fatten, they thin, they emulsify, they flavour, they colour, they preserve, but none of them has any nutrient value! What all these chemicals do is destroy the vitamins by which we live. You don't have to be a mathematician to realize that if you destroy more vitamins than you are able to replenish through eating, then you will not only feel ill, but become run down and easily prone to diseases."

Now, people who concern themselves with quality eating have been asking the question: Is it possible to enhance the nutritional values in recipes from classic French cuisine without impairing taste and delectability?

Our aim in this book is to suggest the sources for a valid and needed change in our diets, sources found in the new science—nutrition. Already a group of valiant dissidents has been making health discoveries related to this science. They are the young, unorthodox, "organic" cognoscenti whose numbers have been increasing fast and steadily and who have given impetus to the entire field of organic (health) food production.

We have browsed in natural-food shops with great fascination and joy, and we have been struck by the array of cookbooks based on nutrition. But, for us, there was one thing missing. Nowhere did we find a book containing recipes for the classics of French cuisine and telling us how to prepare these favorites with *healthful ingredients*. Why not? Is it not possible to harmonize the creative concepts of the classic cuisine with the better nutritional ingredients which are available to us?

Can *quenelles de brochet* still be a dining sensation if made with stone-ground whole-wheat flour instead of white flour? Or hollandaise sauce as exquisite if prepared with fresh lemon juice instead of vinegar, and with cold-pressed safflower oil (richest in unsaturated fatty acids) instead of saturated-fat-laden butter? Or stock-based sauces, soups, and ragouts if prepared with vegetable and soy stocks instead of animal-based stocks? Or mousse if made with carob instead of chocolate, and with organic eggs instead of the usual nutritionally impoverished commercial eggs?

This book is born out of our belief that gourmandise must address itself to nutrition *as well as* to sensuous eating, represented on the one hand by the health-food cognoscenti and on the other by the traditional gourmets. It is time for such a union to be attempted. The best of both worlds should be brought together to achieve the ultimate blend of the sensuous and the organic. The traditional gourmet—by incorporating into his meals an array of rich and healthy ingredients—will not only improve his health but will find to his gratifying surprise that the taste of his recipes has been enhanced. The young health-food cognoscenti will be introduced to the delights of *haute cuisine*.

Now we will truly be "ultimate gourmets."

THE PROJECT: CUISINE SANTÉ

When you think about it, *cuisine santé,* cooking classic French dishes with natural (health) foods, is not revolutionary at all. In fact, using natural ingredients is really a return to the origin of many of the present classic dishes. Many were created in the provincial kitchen, in the farm country, and were the product of unadulterated and unstripped natural resources of the region. If we were given the opportunity to compare side by side the preparation of a classic dish by a fine restaurant in Paris or New York with the same dish cooked in the region of its origin with the local ingredients (in European farm areas much is still organic), we might find the city version to be fancier in presentation, but it would probably be considerably lower in food values and higher in harmful additives. In an honest taste evaluation, we would likely concede the city version to be lackluster (sometimes called "subtle" in sophisticated company), compared to a fresh, stimulating, and more flavorful regional organic version.

But even though *cuisine santé* has its roots in tradition, the conversion to natural-food ingredients and cooking methods is a major departure for the home chef. Therefore, in writing this book, our first resolution was that the translation should be as simple and uncomplicated as possible. For example, a set of primary ingredients used frequently in cooking have been altered as follows:

FROM	TO
Butter	Vegetable oils (Our preference is cold-pressed safflower oil because it has the lowest saturated-fat content and highest unsaturated-fat content which represents the essential fatty acids needed by the organism.)
Pasteurized dairy products	Certified raw milk, raw sweet cream, raw sour cream, natural cheeses
Commercial eggs (nonorganic, infertile)	Organic eggs
White "enriched" wheat flour and other grains	Stone-ground whole-grain flours (whole wheat generally); natural brown rice, buckwheat groats, and other whole cereals (which have not been hot-rolled)
White sugar, all forms	Raw sugar or organic honey
Animal products (poultry, meat, and derivatives such as stock)	Organic poultry and meats when available; increased frequency of no-meat main-course dishes, and stock made with soy sauce and/or vegetable cooking water.
Seasonings and spices	Sea salt for salt; avoidance of pepper; more use of herbs, including herb salt; reduced use of spices with irritant quality; substitution of fresh lemon juice for vinegar.
Commercial produce	Fresh organic produce whenever available. More natural-food stores and greengrocers are stocking organic fruits and vegetables. In the summer, if possible, grow your own; also investigate farmer resources—enlist them in the movement back to natural health through more organic agriculture.

A small encyclopedia has been prepared (pp. 10–27) which provides basic explanations concerning the natural or health-food ingredients and terms used in the recipes in this book, including fuller discussions about those mentioned above.

In working with Mrs. Lucas's files, it was interesting to see that early recipes from her student days at l'Ecole du Cordon Bleu were in certain ways more oriented toward better nutrition than later versions. "Fat or oil" was often the ingredient given, instead of "butter" which was specified in the later years (the 50's and 60's) when butter, eggs, and cream were part of the mode of gastronomic affluence. In the early years lower cooking temperatures (300°) were more often specified. There was the frequent note to save vegetable cooking waters for soups and sauces. We also discovered some "new old" recipes for more substantial vegetable dishes which correspond to the current interest in no-meat main-course menus. Also we have included different omelet recipes which Mrs. Lucas contended were meals in themselves.

Some colorful and tasty differences

"Naturalized" cooking is immediately apparent in its color. If the chef has used stone-ground whole-wheat flour in the velouté sauce, for instance, or in the pastry cream along with raw sugar, the golden hue which results sets it off from its refined, devitalized counterpart. This golden complexion is the badge of good health, just as a white pallor is a sign of ill health. Also, the natural-appreciative eye senses and withdraws from brightly colored foods; artificial dyes are usually present. Nature's food basket is a blend of harmonious colors—rich, deep, and warm.

Any significant changes in cooking methods are discussed within the respective recipe chapters. In general, browning of meats and vegetables should be very light. The brown residue left on the bottom of the pan as a result of hot searing is actually burned food particles and can be toxic. This is the reason for our change to Marmite (brewers' yeast extract) in place of meat glaze. Vegetables should be barely cooked; they should still have crunch when served, unless they are puréed. This treatment of cooking vegetables has always been a principle of good cookery.

A new look at menu planning

We also offer some thoughts concerning menu planning for better nutrition. Nutritionists generally advise that some raw vegetable or fruit should be eaten at the start of every meal because it increases the flow of gastric juices. It is suggested that fresh fruit be the first course for breakfast and that lunch and dinner commence with a raw vegetable salad, usually with a raw green represented. While we recommend a salad with every meal, for some of us any attempt to diversify the salad repertoire is difficult. Therefore, we have provided a substantial chapter of salad ideas, which are taken from our own actual menu experiences. To consolidate the place of raw vegetables in the gourmet meal, we call *the salad "the first course,"* and continuing in our unorthodoxy, we position the salad chapter as the first chapter of recipes.

There is a modern tendency to simplify menus—which is nutritionally wise—and today even elaborate gourmet functions are being scaled down in courses and portions. Rarely does anyone require or desire a 5-, 6-, or 7-course meal. In principle a fine formula for a gourmet repast consists of salad, main course, and dessert. If a soup is offered, the salad precedes it. Good eating form has always preferred the salad as a separate course rather than as accompanying the main course.

Another important aspect of contemporary diet and menu planning is that we should eat less meat (and commercial poultry), if only to reduce the risk of cancer and heart disease. To assist in planning more no-meat menus, we have reframed the concept of "the main course." The recipe chapter entitled "Main-Course Dishes" has been divided into sections representing different food categories which offer substantial dishes for main-course service. The sections are: Vegetable; Fish and Shellfish; Poultry and Meat; Eggs; and Grain, Pasta, and Savory Pastry. We hope it presents a broader scope of thinking about main-course dishes. More eating of fish is highly recommended by nutritionists, and here the gourmet is blessed with a preponderance of delicious fish and shellfish dishes, which are superior when prepared with natural ingredients. On pages 28 to 34 we offer some examples of no-meat menus (meaning in this case no fish, poultry, or red meat) as well as with-meat menus.

The recipe section of this book is designed to reflect these menu-planning precepts and to make your planning for new first-course and main-course ideas more convenient. We group the recipes by their menu purpose rather than by technical food categories:

The First Course:	Salads
Soups	
The Main Course:	Vegetable
	Fish and Shellfish
	Poultry and Meat
	Eggs
	Grain, Pasta, and Savory Pastry
Vegetable Garnishes	
and Accompaniments	
Desserts	
Staples, Stocks, and Sauces	

Above all, menu planning should incorporate your particular nutritional needs. Would that there were such an institution as the "family nutritionist" to keep us in good health and prevent sickness, just as we have the "family physician" to help us when we do become ill. Generally, to learn how to build and maintain health, we must seek out the rare consulting nutritionist or learn about vitamins and minerals from books. The Scientific Council of the International Society for Research on Nutrition and Vital Substances (the world's most objective, qualified nutritional authority, composed of over 400 scientists from 75 countries, including many Nobel Prize winners) recommends the following diet for maximum health and nutrition: natural foods, free from harmful additives; an adequate supply of vital substances (vitamins, minerals, enzymes, proteins, fatty acids, trace elements, etc.); a moderate supply of calories and energy-producing foods such as refined carbohydrates; a lacto-vegetarian diet of fresh foods (whole grains, vegetables, fruits, seeds, nuts, and milk and milk products).

For a handy reference when you wish to know the specific nutritional values in given foods, we urge you to consult Handbook No. 8, published by the United States Department of Agriculture (available by writing to the Superintendent of Documents, U.S. Government Printing Office, Washington, D.C. 20402). We feel that this handbook is the most complete, authoritative guide to the nutritive values of foods now available. It lists over 2,400 foods and with easy-to-read tables provides a breakdown of:

1) *the composition of foods*—indicating, per edible portion, the amount of water, calories, protein, fat, carbohydrates, ash, calcium, phosphorus, iron, sodium, potassium, vitamin A, thiamine (vitamin B_1), riboflavin (vitamin B_2), niacin (vitamin B_3), and ascorbic acid (vitamin C);
2) *the fatty acid, cholesterol, and magnesium content of foods*

as well as other vital information. We believe you will agree it is one of the best efforts our government has made in the battle to maintain healthy nutritional standards and good eating habits.

Most of the natural or health-food ingredients specified in these recipes are available in natural-food stores or natural-food sections in other stores nationally. Organic produce, poultry and meat products, and dairy products are slowly making more frequent appearances. Should you not be able to obtain them, the recipes can, of course, be prepared with the standard commercial counterparts. And, should you not be able to find the natural dry products and staples in your area, some mail-order sources are listed on pages 281–282 in the Appendixes.

A Small Encyclopedia
for
Natural French Cooking

The following brief encyclopedia explains our position toward some of the basic ingredients and food preparation methods now used in classic cooking and those suggested in the conversion to *cuisine santé*.

ALCOHOL: The recipes and menus in this book include the use of wine and fortified wines (containing under 20 percent alcohol), and their nutritional value and use is explained in the general discussion about "Wine" on page 26. The use of high-proof alcoholic spirits is avoided. To flame a dish for flavor enhancement, we find dry sherry a very good agent.

ASPIC: Aspics offer an excellent way of eating nutritious stocks plus protein-rich gelatin. Good aspic can be made with vegetable, soy, or chicken stock. For a general discussion on basic stocks and aspic, please refer to pages 261–264.

BAKING POWDER: Check the contents; some brands contain aluminum compounds. Baking powders which do not contain aluminum are recommended and are available in natural-food stores.

BARLEY: Barley has been a staple food in European countries and the Middle East since ancient times. Hippocrates used barley water as a curative. It is rich in natural nutrients, and should be used increasingly in modern menus, as a gnocchi, for example.

BREAD (INCLUDING BREAD CRUMBS, CROUTONS, TOASTS): The only breads recommended in the menus and recipes of this book are *stone-ground whole-grain breads*. Because the wheat germ in whole-grain breads can become rancid, and because chemical preservatives are avoided, these breads must be refrigerated. Any whole-wheat bread that is sold on an open rack likely contains chemical preservatives.

In these conversion menus and recipes we depart from the use of traditional white French and Italian bread. For cooking and table use, we prefer a whole-grain bread called "Seven Grain Bread" which is made and nationally distributed by Shiloh Farms and contains sprouted whole grains of wheat, oats, rye, barley, corn, rice, and millet, as well as water, unbleached flour, gluten flour, honey, yeast, molasses, salt, and malt. (For eating, it is absolutely addictive.) Bread crumbs, croutons, toasts, and canapés are also made with whole-grain breads. Their preparation is described on pages 258–259. The conversion of these "incidental" garnishes to whole-grain bread results in a richer quality that is readily apparent.

BUCKWHEAT: Buckwheat is a type of grass indigenous to Central European cuisines which has now become popular in North America. Buckwheat groats are hulled crushed buckwheat. This nutritious, delicious grain is available in whole or crushed kernels or flour. See "Kasha" (which is cooked buckwheat), page 17.

BUTTER: Please refer to "Cooking Fats: Butter and Vegetable Oils," page 12.

CAROB: Carob is also called St.-John's-bread. The bean-shaped pod is the fruit of the *Ceratonia siliqua* tree, found around the Mediterranean and North African area. When carob is ground and cooked, it has a chocolatelike flavor. If you are concerned about your intake of calories and high acidity, as many Americans are, you will be glad to know that you can forswear chocolate and still enjoy delicious chocolate-flavored desserts made instead with carob. In one edible portion (100 grams), carob has 180 calories and 1.3 grams of fat; semisweet chocolate has 507 calories and 35.7 grams of fat.

Carob is available in powder, nugget, and solid bar forms. Mrs. Lucas generally preferred solid chocolate in cooking, and her recipes convert successfully with solid carob.

CHEESE: Cheese is an important ingredient for both fine cooking and good nutrition. This is especially true of "natural cheeses." Natural cheeses are those which are unpasteurized and unprocessed; they contain the whole untampered content of the natural nutrients but no coloring additives, preservatives, or commercial salt. An increasing variety of natural cheeses including Swiss-type, cottage, Monterey Jack, Cheddar, mozzarella, ricotta, goat's-milk, and cream are now available in natural-food stores; in our experience they are quite good.

Unfortunately in the U.S. we cannot get the great soft cheeses such as Brie and Camembert in their natural state (as one can enjoy them in Europe) because their best maturation process uses unpasteurized milk which the U.S. Department of Agriculture forbids entry, if aged under 60 days. Therefore, these imports are made especially for the American market with pasteurized milk.

Solid cheeses are less advisable than the sweeter soft cheeses (unless they are totally natural cheeses) because the solid (semihard and hard) cheeses usually contain more salt which is not likely to be pure or sea salt. Unless one knows that the salt content is sea salt, these cheeses are not recommended. These recipes do use commercial imported Parmesan cheese which is aged over 60 days and must be made with raw milk in order to mature as Parmesan. The specification of "natural Swiss-type cheese" in the recipes in this book refers to domestic natural cheeses identified as Swiss-type. It is not possible for totally natural Swiss cheeses such as Emmenthaler and Gruyère to be imported into the U.S. because they would contain non-pasteurized (raw) milk.

CHOCOLATE: Chocolate is a difficult food for many people to assimilate properly. It has a high caloric and saturated-fat content and its high acid excess puts it often on dermatologists' lists of foods that contribute to complexion problems. All chocolate dishes in this book have been converted to the use of carob with gratifying success. See also "Carob," page 11.

COFFEE: According to Adelle Davis in *Let's Eat Right To Keep Fit,* coffee stimulates "the production of adrenal hormones which cause the blood sugar to be increased, thereby producing the needed 'lift,' but insulin is quickly secreted, causing the sugar level to fall again." Also, coffee produces multiple B vitamin deficiencies—as does a large amount of any liquid—by washing these vitamins out of the body.

From this we deduce that coffee with or without caffeine (according to one's insomnia quotient) should be taken in moderation, if at all. When coffee flavoring is desired in cooking, we use an instant decaffeinated coffee (ask at your natural-food store or food specialty shop about suitable brands).

COOKING FATS: BUTTER AND VEGETABLE OILS: Our position on the use of fat and what type of fat to use in the conversion to health foods, is succinctly stated by Adelle Davis in *Let's Eat Right To Keep Fit:*
"Avoid hydrogenated fats such as hydrogenated peanut butter, processed cheeses, and solid cooking fats and the French-fried foods cooked in these solid fats; limit the solid, or saturated, animal fats obtained mostly from beef and lamb and increase your intake of fish and fowl having less saturated fat; eat no food containing coconut or palm oils, both saturated vegetable fats used in imitation cream, filled milk, and even infant formulas; have at least one to three teaspoons of vegetable oil daily. Use unrefined, or cold-pressed, oils and keep them refrigerated after they have been opened. If a fat is treated so that it cannot become rancid, do not buy it; if any fat does become rancid, throw it away."

In the converted recipes we have been able to *avoid* the use of butter almost completely. Only where the solid factor of butter is required to achieve a consistency does butter appear as an ingredient in this book. We are not total iconoclasts, however; we do put butter (natural sweet, unsalted) on the table for those who wish it. But we believe that most classic dishes can be reproduced in good quality with the use of certain vegetable oils instead of butter.

For an all-purpose fat, instead of butter, we propose the use of vegetable oil in general, avoiding coconut and palm oils. Our preference is cold-pressed safflower oil. (We do use olive oil in dishes that originated in Italy or Provence, for example, where it seems appropriate.) Safflower oil has the lowest ratio of saturated fats and the highest ratio of essential fatty acids (those which cannot be made within the body itself and are necessary for the support and growth of health, namely, linoleic acid, linolenic acid, and arachidonic acid). In addition to its nutritional superiority, safflower oil has, in our judgment, a lighter taste quality, which does not impose its flavor upon the true natural flavors of the primary cooking ingredients. Most commercial oils are hot-pressed; however, the high heat kills most of their natural nutrients. The cold-press process retains them. Natural-food stores carry a variety of cold-pressed oils. *Unrefined oils,* which retain the precious lecithin lost through refining or hydrogenation, are more difficult to obtain.

In the conversion to cooking with oil instead of butter, less fat is required because oil does not burn away as does butter. Therefore, each recipe has been tested and adjusted for the oil ingredient replacing butter. For the calorie-conscious, using less oil than butter in cooking can help to control normalcy.

Concerning *margarine:* We do not use margarine because even those made totally with vegetable oil—available in natural-food stores—contain color and preservative additives. Further, a new study indicates that margarine may be more instrumental in causing hardening of the arteries than butter or eggs. The study (made in 1976 by Fred A. Kummerow, professor of food chemistry at the University of Illinois) shows that although margarine consists of poly-unsaturated fatty acids, many of these acids change from their natural form to an altered form during the hydrogenation process. This altered form of fatty acids appears to be *more* damaging to arteries than even saturated fatty acids or cholesterol. If "buttered toast" is an individual necessity, we suggest brushing whole-grain bread with safflower oil, sprinkling it with a little herb salt, and toasting it in a 400° oven or under medium heat in the broiler.

An important word about storing oils: Because of their quick tendency to become rancid, oils should be stored in the refrigerator; butter should be stored in the freezer. Because some vitamins contained in the oils are sensitive to light, they should be stored in dark or opaque containers.

A cleaning suggestion: Pans in which foods have been sautéed in hot oil of any type are easier to clean by soaking briefly in baking soda and water.

CORNMEAL: While we know now that a solid diet of cornmeal as the staple grain can invite pellagra, cornmeal is an excellent source of vitamin B_1, B_2, niacin, and iron. It helps diversify menu planning by offering delicious variations in the grain repertoire.

CREAM: See "Milk and Cream," pages 18–19.

DEEP-FRYING: For maximum retention of nutrients, foods to be deep-fried should be small units that will cook quickly. They should be enclosed in a sheath of flour, egg, and bread crumbs, and a light polyunsaturated vegetable oil, such as safflower oil, should be used.

DOUGHS, PASTRY, BATTERS: In this volume we offer short pastry, sponge cake, cream puff dough, crêpes, and soufflés converted to natural ingredients. Changes in ingredients, cooking methods, and results are described in the basic recipes for each type. All convert favorably when prepared naturally. The most notable difference occurs when short pastry is made with vegetable oil instead of solid fat: it becomes a crumbly-type crust.

EGGS: Dione Lucas revered the egg, and her artistry and fame were synonymous with the omelet. For her personal use, she preferred organic eggs, and insisted she could taste the difference between commercial eggs and organic eggs. We can't, but we respect the nutritional superiority of the organic egg and recommend its use exclusively.

What are organic eggs? On the carton of the organic eggs we buy is this legend: "Naturally healthy farm fresh fertile eggs, produced in accordance with established organic farming methods. Chickens are fed a ration rich in essential vitamins and minerals without antibiotics, arsenicals, sulpha drugs, or pesticides." (And the carton is weighed and dated.) Organic eggs are available in many natural-food stores and are priced slightly higher than most commercially available nonorganic eggs. However, on a nutritional cost-comparison basis, organic eggs are a bargain.

Nutritional experts appear to agree that healthy people should eat one egg per day. (The yolk of egg contains cholesterol. This fat is found in all living cells, and eggs are the largest single cells known. But eggs also contain lecithin, a natural emulsifier of cholesterol, which prevents fatty buildup in the arteries. It's probably best not to overdo your egg-eating, as with any other food, but you don't have to worry about cholesterol in eggs that are also rich in lecithin.) They also recommend that egg whites should be solid when eaten; that is, the white should not be translucent and runny as it is in its raw state. In a soft-boiled egg, the white should be just set. The white of raw egg is difficult to digest. Pages 150–153 describe all of the basic methods for cooking eggs best—soft-boiled, hard-boiled, scrambled, *en cocotte* or *en timbale*, fried, poached, and the omelet.

Finally, nutritionists advise us that there is no nutritional difference between a white-shelled egg and a brown-shelled egg. Why pay more?

ENZYMES: Enzymes are substances found in the cells of our bodies, which produce chemical changes in the food we eat, making it easier to digest and assimilate. They are also contained in raw, unprocessed foods, most notably raw fruits and vegetables. Enzymes help keep the body's vital processes going well, but they are very delicate, and can be destroyed by heating, canning, cooking, pasturization, and processing.

FISH AND SHELLFISH: Fish and shellfish are rich in vitamins and minerals and are easier to digest than red meat. It is a fact that classic French cookery contains more recipes for fish and poultry dishes than for red meat. Both fish and poultry recipes translate supremely well when prepared with natural ingredients.

Fish and shellfish are the most easily obtainable natural "meat"; they are not injected with chemicals, and reputable commercial fish retailers can identify their water sources by their government inspection label and will not carry fish from polluted waters. Some natural and specialty-food shops offer frozen fish from declared non-polluted waters (i.e., tested free of DDT and its metabolites) in Canada and Iceland. Certainly it is worth taking heed of announcements by government agencies in newspapers when a certain body of water has been tested and found to contain PCB contamination and querying the fish market or restaurant when ordering fish. Yet it has been said to us by otherwise respected gourmets, "What's one fish?" The problem is that one fish containing toxic chemicals added to the lifelong buildup of other harmful chemicals can be one step closer to disease.

FLAVORINGS AND EXTRACTS: Pure flavorings and extracts are available in natural-food and specialty-food stores and through mail-order sources, in a large variety: vanilla, almond, anise, cinnamon, ginger, lemon, lime, mocha, orange, peppermint, rose, spearmint, wintergreen. They contain only the pure extract and alcohol. They do not contain any imitation flavorings or colorings, synthetics, or preservatives.

FLOUR: Natural foods are whole foods, and in our conversion to natural foods, devitalized white wheat flours are completely avoided, regardless of what claims to "enrichment" or "re-enrichment" there may be. In general we use *stone-ground whole-wheat pastry flour* as an all-purpose flour, *potato flour* when translucency is desired in a thickening, and *arrowroot* when a more delicate thickening agent or binder is desired.

There are now available a variety of brands of organically grown, stone-

KASHA: Kasha is the Russian word for cooked buckwheat. This is one of the most delicious grains to accompany a savory course. Kasha is almost as versatile as rice and can be substituted for rice in most instances. Its nuttiness gives it a rich character, and this makes it an excellent flavor variation as a meat substitute in ~ll-vegetable menus. Kasha is also a time-saver because it can be cooked in a large quantity; what is left over can be refrigerated and reheated successfully with a little water added to the pan.

LEMONS: See "Sour (Acid) Seasoning: Lemon Juice instead of Vinegar," page 22.

MARGARINE: See "Cooking Fats: Butter and Vegetable Oils," pages 12–13.

MARMITE (BREWERS' YEAST EXTRACT) : See "Meat Glaze," page 18.

MAYONNAISE: In our conversion of basic mayonnaise, vinegar, pepper, and Dijon mustard are avoided. Mayonnaise made with organic eggs, herb salt, dry mustard, fresh lemon juice, and cold-pressed safflower oil has a refreshing lightness that is more in keeping with the dishes in which it is used, and is healthier on every count.

MEAT—BEEF, VEAL, LAMB, AND PORK: *Standards for organically grown meat:* "Organically grown meats are products of stock raised on land which is managed organically. Animals are free to run and get adequate exercise for physical fitness. Both feed and environment are free from pesticide and herbicide residues, DES, antibiotics, growth hormones, and irradiation. All young stock must have daylight and well-ventilated housing. All cattle, sheep, and hens shall have free range; permanent housing is prohibited. Routine use of drugs and antibiotics, urea and synthetic proteins is not allowed. If an animal requires drugs or antibiotics due to illness, it is not marketable until chemical analysis proves that all such drugs are no longer in its body. Food supplements include seaweed, bonemeal, and other natural supplements. Animals shall not be sterilized chemically. Grass grazing is encouraged as opposed to heavy grain feeding. Animals shall be periodically examined for vitamin and mineral deficiency. Ninety-five percent of the feed should be grown and harvested on the farm itself. Beef is raised with the view of minimizing, not maximizing the fat content, and this fat content should be 30 percent less than that of commercial beef of the same quality. Meats should be graded carefully, and the highest quality packaging should be used." (*The Organic Directory,* Rodale Press, 1974.)

We recommend eating organic meats instead of commercial meats, and in the overall pattern of the diet, the eating of less meat. Most nutritionists agree that the meat quotient in American diets is too high and should be substantially reduced—to from one to three times per week. (Our own preference, when we are not testing recipes, is to allocate one meal per week to meat or poultry.)

Meat has a high protein content. Unfortunately, the body cannot store any appreciable amount of protein. It uses only what it needs and burns away the rest or retains it as fat. A diet consisting primarily of meat can cause constipation. In addition, 75 percent of all beef sold in America today has been fed rations containing diethylstilbestrol, a synthetic hormone used to fatten livestock. This hormone has been linked to cancer and other serious disorders.

Nutritionists advise that pork should be eaten rarely and always cooked carefully—cooked adequately to destroy the trichinae that infect almost all pork and yet not overcooked so as to destroy the nutritive value. And because pork is a highly concentrated food with high acid excess, nutritionists also advise that it be eaten in small quantities and with plenty of vegetables and fruit. In this first book, with limited space for all the recipes we would like to include, there are no pork recipes. We believe that pork can be avoided or limited to an occasional *pâté* or *cassoulet* without stinting the joy of gourmandise.

More and more natural-food stores are stocking standard cuts of organic beef, veal, and lamb as they become available. (See "Organic," pp. 20–21.) However, organic or natural meats cannot legally be labeled as such, because the government inspector has no directive for accepting an organic certification (which covers the animal from birth to slaughter). At this time, meats, like most natural-food products, force the consumer to rely on the credibility of the retailer and the producer.

MEAT GLAZE (GLACE DE VIANDE) : Our conversion recipes use Marmite (brewers' yeast extract) instead of meat glaze. Meat glaze is avoided for two reasons: first, more and more people wish to avoid animal-based ingredients; second, meat glaze is usually made by searing bones and boiling down meat juices. The glaze on the bottom of the pan left from searing meat or bones is actually burned residue, and burned foods can become toxic. Marmite (brewers' yeast extract) is made by Bovril and has a consistency and flavor concentration similar to meat glaze. It contains brewers' yeast extract flavored with salt, carrots, onions, and spices. It is a good source of vitamin B_1 (thiamine), B_2 (riboflavin), and niacin, and we find it a very acceptable substitute.

MILK AND CREAM: One of the mixed blessings of scientific research in the twentieth century has been "pasteurization" of milk, which not only destroys harmful bacteria but also some of the good bacteria necessary for our life processes. Therefore, where possible, we endorse the use of *raw milk*. Raw milk production is an infant industry, however, and we harbor no illusions that it will be possible to cook with raw milk and raw cream exclusively. But we encourage its use and toward that end specify its preference in the recipes in this book.

What is raw milk? Raw simply means that the milk has not been heated, pasteurized, or cooked, and thereby contains the maximum nutrients of whole milk. Is raw milk safe? "Certified Raw Milk" bearing the seal and trademark of the American Association of Medical Milk Commission is considered to be safe and may even be more safe than pasteurized milk. Gates Homestead Farms of Chittenango, New York, for example, certifies that "both its cows and workers are under vigilant, continuous medical supervision. The cows are washed before each milking, then dried with sterile towels, and the milk is subjected to daily laboratory tests. As another step in the preservation of the delicate nutrients of whole raw milk, some of which are destroyed by exposure to light, Gates markets its milk in black cartons." An extra advantage of raw milk is that the cream settles at the top, and you can skim off your supply of heavy and light cream with a basting bulb. If you can afford it, the best of all milk, for both nutrition and flavor, is *goat's milk*. Nutritionists analyze goat's milk as the closest food parallel to mother's milk.

Nutritionists recommend the use of *dry milk* to supplement skim or whole milk. In some desserts and sauces in this book which call for a large amount of milk and cream, we substitute some of the quantity with extra-strength reconstituted nonfat dry milk. In our use of yogurt, which we offer as an alternative to sweet or sour cream or milk in some recipes, a creamy quality is obtained when nonfat dry milk is added.

There are some very good creamy *sour creams* on the market. Although sour cream is not the *crème fraîche* of Europe, the early works of Dione Lucas frequently use it as a substitute. In this book we have followed this idea, using it often as an option in place of heavy sweet cream when the stiff whipped quality is not required. *Sour goat's cream* defies description in velvety, creamy goodness!

MILLET: Millet is an ancient grain used for centuries in Italy, the Mideast, and Far East. Like all whole grains, it is full of natural nutrients. It is easy and quick to cook, and in addition to being cooked plain, it makes very good Gnocchi alla Romana (p. 176).

MOLASSES: See "Sweetening Agents," page 24.

MUSHROOMS: Organically-grown cultivated mushrooms are available in some natural-food stores. They usually have a brown skin (which should not be peeled away) and are a lovely sturdy product. Edible wild mushrooms—morels, chanterelles, and cepes—in season are organic gourmet delights.

MUSTARD (DRY AND PREPARED): Because mustard is an irritant, we use it sparingly and limit our use to dry mustard. Dry mustard is supposed to be the pure natural powder from the seeds of the mustard plant, although some coloring may be added from the curcuma plant.

We have avoided prepared mustard because it contains vinegar and other undesirable additives. This includes Dijon mustard as well. We avoid vinegar as much as possible. (See "Sour [Acid] Seasoning," p. 22.)

NATURAL: In nutritional parlance, "natural" means a food product that is not synthetic, but rather a food grown and/or produced without artificial elements and containing no chemical additives for growth, development, coloring, flavoring, preservation, or other marketing purposes.

The difference between "natural" and "organic" is a very subtle one. What we attempt to convey through the word "organic" is simply old-fashioned nature, the way in which nature used to be before man attempted, as in recent times, to change and/or alter it. Because of the loose interpretation of "natural," for specific identification of food products which are totally natural in growth and processing, commercial food sellers use the term "organic" (see "Organic," pp. 20–21).

By using the word "natural" in the title of this book we mean to include the use of preferred natural foods, food preparation procedures which maximize the retention of natural nutritive values, and menus that provide for the best possible natural nourishment.

NUTS AND SEEDS: Nuts and seeds have been paired in discussion because they are a primary source of nutrients in natural-food cookery and in many instances can be used in the same ways. They are an excellent source of preferred proteins plus many other nutrients. Quality-grade nuts and seeds no longer need be thought of as an infrequent special treat. Organic, fresh nuts and seeds that have not been artificially treated, such as sunflower seeds, pumpkin seeds, sesame seeds, roasted garbanzos (chick-peas), roasted soybeans, cashews, almonds, black and English walnuts, Brazil nuts, peanuts, pine nuts (pignoli), filberts, pecans, and pistachios are available in most natural-food stores. We suggest using different nuts and seeds for crunch and extra nutrition in various grain pilaffs, vegetables (especially with chopped spinach), and with fresh and dried fruits for a relaxed nibble.

OATS AND OATMEAL: Jethro Kloss in *Back to Eden* contends that "common oatmeal . . . is a most wonderful food; rolled oats is one of the few, if not the only one, cereal food that carries the germs of the grain, and that is important." Oatmeal is an excellent simple dessert with fresh or dried fruit.

OILS: See "Cooking Fats: Butter and Vegetable Oils," pages 12–13.

ORGANIC: "Organic" means produced without the use of chemical fertilizers, pesticides, fungicides, herbicides, hormones, antibiotics, or other chemicals.

Perhaps few people are as qualified as Robert Rodale, son of a pioneer in our return to organic foods, to define "organic food." In his book *Sane Living in a Mad World, A guide to the organic way of life,* he puts it this way: "Organic food is grown in soil that is rich in organic matter, and therefore usually has superior nutritional quality. Organic matter—or humus—is the living part of the soil. In that moist, woodsy part of the soil exists the uncountable billions of bacteria, fungi and other minute organisms which give soil remarkable powers to feed tremendous amounts of minerals and vitamins and other nutrients to plant roots.

"When American land was virgin, before the days of commercial agriculture, our soil contained an average of 3 to 4 percent organic matter. Each growing season a small amount was consumed by plants, then in the fall as leaves fell and annual plants died, the humus was built up again. Insects, earthworms and other small animals burrowed in the soil, sometimes carrying the humus to depths of several feet.

"The past 150 years of large-scale farming have depleted soil organic matter. Now, many soils contain less than 1 percent humus. Manure is spread on fields less often, and the stalks or other waste portions of plants are often removed from the land. Many soils are therefore less alive than they used to be, and the crops they produce are less healthy, and sometimes are lower in nutritional value.

"A constantly growing number of gardeners and farmers are working to restore the organic quality of the soil, and that—basically—is what organically grown food is about. But there is more to the idea. Artificial fertilizers and pesticide poisons are avoided, because they contaminate soil or plant and simply aren't in tune with the idea of producing food that is natural and of high nutritional quality. Organically-grown food is handled differently after it is harvested. It is not refined, chemically treated, or processed beyond the dictates of bare necessity. There is no such thing as organically-grown white bread, for example, since by refining the wheat you would destroy its 'organic' quality. You can see that the word organic has grown beyond its original farm and garden meaning, and has become a matter of interest and concern to all people who want to improve their health.

"Organic food varies in quality according to the area in which it is grown, but almost always it has that good, old-fashioned taste which is sadly lacking in supermarket food. An organic chicken, for example, is fed no drugs to stimulate growth and is allowed to scratch in the ground and eat the worms, bugs and other critters which are delicacies to chickens. As a result, the meat of an organic bird has a hearty flavor that may surprise the taste buds of a child raised on TV dinners or the pale-flavored meat sold in stores. A member of the older generation fed on organic chicken will suddenly remember what white meat used to taste like.

"Blemishes can actually be a mark of quality in organically-grown fruit. An organic apple, for example, will almost always have a few nicks and scars to show that somewhere along the line the bugs got at it. An unmarked apple will most always have been sprayed at least 15 times to keep bugs away.

"Organic vegetables, grains and meats almost always look better as well as taste better. They have a glow of quality and a taste of nature." (See also "Meat," pp. 17–18.)

PASTA: One of the most exciting flavor discoveries in our conversion project has been whole-wheat pasta and whole-wheat gnocchi. Whole-wheat noodles or fettuccini, lasagne, macaroni, and spaghetti of various types are available in natural-food outlets and are far superior in taste and nutritional value to the semolina and white-flour types. There is also some pasta made with buckwheat and American (Jerusalem) artichoke flour which is 100 percent non-starch. The latter is white like traditional pasta, and is supplemented with soy protein.

PEPPER: See "Salt and Pepper," page 22.

POTS AND PANS: The use of aluminum cooking utensils is directly harmful because aluminum is a toxic, porous substance and when food is heated in it, thousands of aluminum particles dislodge and combine with the food. Our preference in cooking utensils is for enamel-coated cast-iron pots and pans, such as the French Creuset ware, tin-lined copper saucepans, porcelain baking dishes, tin-lined copper au gratins, and earthenware or glass bowls.

POULTRY: We urge the use of organic poultry if at all possible (see "Organic," pp. 20–21 and "Meat," pp. 17–18) because of its nutritional quality and because of the inherent dangers in eating commercially raised chickens. More natural-food outlets are stocking organic chickens and chicken parts, as well as turkeys and ducks.

Many respected nutritionists today are urging Americans to reduce their intake of animal meats and poultry. They argue that we would be a healthier nation if we ate more vegetarian meals. We must add, nonetheless, that poultry contains more unsaturated fatty acid than red meat and less saturated fats, and consequently red meats are less advisable to eat than poultry.

The cooking of poultry is discussed on pages 111–112. Nutritionists advise that the lower the cooking temperature, the better the retention of nutrients, and, we add, of flavor, too. Roasting temperatures for poultry preparations have been substantially lowered.

RICE, DOMESTIC AND WILD: Rice is a favorite food in classic cookery, and in our conversion to natural ingredients, only natural brown rice is used, in both savory and dessert dishes. The nutritional value of rice is mainly in the brown coating, the chaff or bran, of the grain, and the process of refining rice into snowy white kernels by removing the vital chaff and relegating it to feed for livestock is robbery. The cooking time for natural brown rice is longer, but the dividends in taste and health are worth waiting for.

Wild rice has no relation to domestic rice. Wild rice is a specialty grain which is found only in the marshes around the lakes of northern Minnesota, Wisconsin, Manitoba, and Ontario. Fortunately wild rice is always "whole grain"; it is not only a gourmet delicacy but also full of food value.

SALT AND PEPPER: For general use of salt we adhere to *sea salt*. Pure sea salt is unrefined salt from the ocean with natural trace minerals including vitally needed natural iodine, of which the ocean is the best source. Packaged sea salt contains no synthetic preservatives, and may be supplemented with iodine, which produces thyroid hormones.

The excessive use of *pepper is avoided*. This includes black and white pepper, peppercorns, as well as cayenne, chili powder, and Tabasco. Nutritionists advise that pepper in large quantities is an irritant which harms the delicate tissues of the digestive organs, and even our gastronomic encyclopedia, the *Larousse,* declares pepper to be "an excitant and a stimulant, and its abuse must therefore be avoided." If pepper must be used, we suggest limiting it to a few freshly cracked grains from the pepper mill as the final touch at the table.

In place of pepper, when a touch of pungency or flavor enhancement is desired, we use an herb salt blend as a "combination salt and pepper" treatment. Specifically we like the *Herbamare* salt which is made in Switzerland and has long been a staple in European cooking. Herbamare is composed of sea salt, organically grown herbs, and marine kelp. In addition to Herbamare there are other good herb and vegetable salts available in natural-food shops. The important considerations are that they contain no preservatives or chemical additives and that they use natural sea salt, if any.

Generally speaking, we add the salt seasoning when the dish is almost finished cooking or when it is completed. Even then the use of salt should be restrained and the seasoning adjusted after a little taste test so as to avoid oversalting.

SEEDS: See "Nuts and Seeds," pages 19–20.

SOUR (ACID) SEASONING: LEMON JUICE INSTEAD OF VINEGAR: Lemon contains the perfect natural acid or piquant agent. A comparison of food values in lemon juice and vinegar (U.S. Department of Agriculture, *Handbook No. 8*) shows lemon juice to be overwhelmingly more nutritious. Vinegar is almost devoid of nutrients; lemon juice is lower in calories and rich in potassium and ascorbic acid with some calcium, phosphorus, and vitamin A value. Therefore, *the use of vinegar is not necessary and is avoided.* We find that cultivation of the taste buds to the use of lemon juice instead of vinegar results in a greater awareness of and pleasure in real flavor sensations. Of course, we mean *fresh* lemon juice exclusively, squeezed and strained. More and more people are preferring vinaigrette and mayonnaise dressings made with lemon juice only. Also hollandaise becomes more delicate, as it is meant to be, with lemon juice instead of vinegar.

SOYBEAN, SOY FLOUR, SOY SAUCE, SOY SPROUTS, SOY STOCK: The nutritious soybean, though used by Eastern peoples for centuries, remains something of an enigma to Western food culture. Thus far in Western cuisines the soybean has been used primarily as a supplement or "food extender," designed to augment the nutritive value of the primary food. The challenge remains, however, for some modern Escoffier to create primary dishes of soy for the gourmet.

The soybean, when sprouted, is rich in iron and vitamin C, and its milk can be used as a substitute for cow's milk for individuals who are allergic to it. The soybean contains twice the protein of beef, and twice the iron as well. It contains 23 times the vitamin B_1 in beef, and 26 times the calcium. It has none of the cholesterol-reducing substances such as lecithin.

The use of soy flour, which is really soy powder, as a supplement is quite simple and is described in the general discussion on Flour (pp. 14–15). Our preferential conversion to "soy stock" made with tamari soy sauce is described in the section on "Stocks" (below). (Tamari is free of chemicals and preservatives and is available in natural- and specialty-food stores and through mail order.) In salads, crisp cool soybean sprouts are a gourmet delight.

SPICES: Our attitude about spices is that if the particular spice has an irritant quality, it should be minimized or eliminated. Therefore, the recipes in this book avoid the use of pepper of all types. For an accent, in lieu of pepper, we frequently use an herb salt (see "Salt and Pepper," p. 22). The use of dry mustard, even though we prefer it to prepared mustard, has also been minimized. Classic cooking requires that spices be used lightly and with finesse, like fine perfume.

STOCKS: Kitchen-made stock has always been hailed as a primary component of gastronomic quality. We find three very good stock options available to the home chef to provide the liquid body for soups and sauces with a subtle measure of marrying flavor. They are: (1) vegetable cooking water, (2) "soy stock," or a combination we term "soy-vegetable stock," and (3) all-purpose chicken stock.

Modern nutritionists implore us not to pour the cooking water from vegetables down the drain. The *Larousse Gastronomique* lists *vegetable stock* (vegetable cooking water) as one of the basic stocks. And you can imagine our surprise and joy when, reviewing Dione Lucas's early files (of the 40's and 50's), we were struck with her frequent note in vegetable preparations to "save the water in which the vegetable was cooked; it is very good for soups and sauces." We have indeed followed this simple, sensible instruction. Nothing is easier than to drain the vegetables through a colander or large wire strainer into another pan or bowl to catch the cooking water, and to transfer the water to a common jar in the refrigerator. The cooking water from different vegetables may be added to the storage jar; the bouquet of multiple flavors improves the vegetable stock. To retain the maximum nutrients, vegetables should be cooked in or with their skins whenever possible.

For soy stock we find that a formula of 1 teaspoon of tamari soy sauce to 1 cup of water and ½ teaspoon of Herbamare salt produces a very acceptable and instant substitute for animal-based stock. It is even better when made with the vegetable stock instead of plain water. As for flavor, the character of the dish is maintained; for nutrition, it is another opportunity to capture the vital treasure of health in the soybean.

In the conversion of classic cookery to natural foods for maximum nutrition, we lean to soy stock, or vegetable stock mixed with soy, rather than chicken stock.

STORAGE: Certain precious vitamins extant in natural foods are sensitive to light and heat. Therefore, it is recommended that whole-grain bread be stored in the freezer and whole-grain flours, grains, wheat-germ oil, cold-pressed vegetable oils, and raw milk and cream be kept in dark or opaque containers in the refrigerator.

SUGAR: See "Sweetening Agents," following entry.

SWEETENING AGENTS: *Raw (unrefined) sugar* and, to a small extent, honey, are used in the recipes we present here. *White refined sugar* from cane and beet is pure sucrose containing neither vitamins nor minerals. Sucrose is a disaccharide, which is hard to digest and must be broken down into simple sugars before it can be absorbed into the bloodstream. Because white sugar lacks vitamins, minerals, or fiber, the human body must deplete its own store of minerals and co-enzymes to metabolize sugar properly. Raw sugar (also called "turbinado") is processed as largish beige crystals from the dried unrefined juice of the sugar cane. It is not the same as commercial brown sugar, which is really refined white sugar colored with a little molasses. Raw sugar still contains its mineral and vitamin content, although it, too, is mostly sucrose.

Honey, while it has no vitamins and few minerals, contains healthier sugars —fructose and glucose—which are easily digested.

In these first steps of conversion to natural foods, we have used raw (dry) sugar where it is more convenient and faster to work with (no sticky granuing utensils to scrape), on a one-for-one quantity basis, instead of white granulated sugar. The only difference in performance is that raw sugar is a little slower to dissolve, particularly in cold mixing, than refined white sugar. We use honey where its nongranular form is a particular asset, as in sweetening whipped cream.

As of this writing we have not found superfine granulated raw sugar and powdered raw sugar available commercially, but they are easy to make in your own kitchen. Using an electric spice grinder, grind regular granulated raw sugar to a superfine degree or completely pulverize it for powdered. It's a good idea to prepare a supply of 1 or 2 cups and store it in an airtight jar.

Molasses is the residue from refined sugar and has a rich mineral content but no vitamins or proteins. We have not used molasses in compound cooking preparations, however, because of its strong, distinctive flavor which might overpower other flavors. We suggest that the characteristic flavor of molasses should be enjoyed as such, in cooked cereal, yogurt, over fruit, or in homemade cookies or cake.

We have experimented with *date sugar* in cooking. Date sugar is simply ground dried dates; therefore, it does not dissolve and its use is limited. It is not quite as sweet as cane or beet sugar, but it has a subtle flavor which is nice sprinkled over cereal or raw fruit.

Saccharin and other artificial sweeteners have been condemned as a health hazard by the Federal Drug Administration. They are *never* used in natural French cooking.

TEA: The tea department in most natural-food stores dazzles the eye. Other countries have long known the health-giving and health-supporting values of a variety of herbal teas, and now a large selection is easily available to Americans. Herbal teas contain no caffeine.

Although tea is not an important part of the classic gastronomic diet, our venerable *Larousse Gastronomique* does introduce its discussion of tea as "the most universally consumed of all beverages." Though coffee, i.e., the demitasse, is usually the finishing touch of a grand dinner, we see no reason why a sturdy cup of tea wouldn't be a welcome option to many people.

TOMATO PASTE: We have not found a *natural* (or organic) tomato paste or concentrate. Walnut Acres (see Appendix, p. 282) offers "natural tomato purée" in 16-ounce cans. You can prepare your own natural tomato paste by cooking and reducing this natural tomato purée to one fourth its original quantity. This paste may be kept in the refrigerator for a long time. If you are using commercial tomato paste, the measurements are the same as given for natural tomato paste.

VANILLA: The scraping and pod of the vanilla bean are preferred. Pure vanilla extract with no artificial flavoring, coloring, or preservative is available in natural-food and specialty-food shops.

VEGETABLES: Nature's original diet for man consisted of fruits and vegetables, and through investigation in the science of nutrition, we are now learning that nature's formula is the best. If we could only return to it! *Organic* vegetables and fruits are the key for maintaining balanced good health. (See "Organic," pp. 20–21.) Also they are the key to gustatory pleasure. Because vegetables are man's primary natural food and offer a limitless palette of menu opportunities, this book contains two categories of vegetable recipes: (1) as main-course vegetable dishes and (2) as garnishes to accompany the main course, be it vegetable, grain, fish, poultry, meat. We urge the use of organic vegetables—which are available in some natural-food stores, farmers' markets, or your own garden—whenever possible.

Vegetable cooking water has always been recognized in classic cookery as providing an excellent stock for soups and sauces (see p. 23).

VEGETABLES, DRIED: Dried vegetables, such as various kinds of beans (pinto, soy, kidney, lima, etc.), chick-peas, lentils, and split peas are extremely nutritious. They are available in abundant variety in natural-food stores. In fine cookery dried vegetables are often used in potages and purées.

VINAIGRETTE (FRENCH SALAD DRESSING): Fresh lemon juice instead of vinegar, sea salt and herb salt instead of commercial salt and pepper, a touch of dry mustard if you like, cold-pressed safflower oil and olive oil, fresh garlic, and eggs or cream to bind, produce an all-purpose vinaigrette that brings any salad into a flavor blend of the finest natural quality. (See "Vinaigrette," p. 38.) Because vinaigrette is synonymous with an acid and oil dressing, we retain the term even though our recipe has no vinegar in it.

VINEGAR: See "Sour (Acid) Seasoning: Lemon Juice instead of Vinegar," page 22.

WATER: All water used for cooking should be *distilled water*. The distillation process boils the raw water, collects the resulting steam, cools and condenses it back into water. Bacteria and germs are immediately killed by heat. Salts, sulfur, arsenic, and mercury do not travel into the cooling, condensing apparatus of the distiller. These impurities are thus left behind in the boiler with only pure water delivered from the distiller's condenser unit.

Bottled water labeled *spring water* is not necessarily pure water since there is no guarantee that the springs from which it comes do not contain undesirable bacteria and harmful minerals.

Rain is pure, natural distilled water. However, it becomes contaminated again due to environmental conditions. Distillation does mechanically what nature does naturally.

WHEAT: See "Flour," pages 14–15, and the introduction to Grains, pages 163–164.

WINE: The recipes in this book use wine as it is traditionally used in classic cookery. We also offer a choice. Depending on the purpose, Grapillon or Lehr's nonsugared wine-grape juice, stock, or water may be substituted.

Concerning wines and nutrition it can be stated that wines contain two types of food elements: those providing energy and those contributing to the maintenance of the body and its nutrition. The energy element is derived chiefly from the carbohydrates, including alcohol; the vital maintenance elements come from minerals (wine contains calcium, phosphorus, magnesium, sodium, potassium, chlorine, sulfur, iron, copper, manganese, zinc, iodine, and cobalt), vitamins (the moderate daily use of wine will provide vitamin B complex to augment the daily intake), and other constituents of wine. In short, not only is wine delicious, it can be nutritionally valuable as well. (Source: *Wine as Food and Medicine,* by Salvatore P. Lucia, New York: The Blakiston Company, Inc., 1954.)

Some wines are subjected to chemicalization, but that is a matter of degree. The grapes for almost all wines have been sprayed; there is little getting away from that at the present time—although it is a subject of concern and study in the wine industry. A few "natural" wines, red and white, that are made from grapes of low sugar content and contain no additives, are now on the market. Most premium wines claim to be "natural," which usually means that they have no special method of preparation and are fined (clarified) with natural agents.

WINE-GRAPE JUICE: We have coined the term "wine-grape juice" to specify pure grape juice made from wine grapes—as opposed to sweeter grape juices made from eating varieties. There are two brands, Grapillon and Lehr's, which offer an option (to those who wish to or must avoid wine) for replacing the wine ingredient in some recipes while still achieving the unique catalytic flavor of wine in cooking. (In savory dishes, the alternative to wine or wine-grape juice is to simply replace the liquid quantity with more water or light stock.) Grapillon and Lehr's come in white and red and are made from selected wine grapes heated to pasteurization temperature before fermentation can begin. No sugar or other additives are used. They are good quality, clear, non-sparkling, and non-alcoholic Swiss 100 percent grape juices. The white is fruity but relatively dry. The red is sweet but not syrupy.

YEAST: Yeast is a very important element in nutrition. In fact more nutrients are more concentrated in yeast than in any other known food, and brewers' yeast is probably the cheapest and best source of B vitamins available. Brewers' yeast and torula yeast are recommended as supplements to regular meals to offset the nutritional deficiencies in modern diets. Uncooked bakers' yeast is not recommended because it grows in the intestine and absorbs the B vitamins supplied by foods or supplements, using them for its own needs.

YOGURT: Yogurt is made from milk thickened by various bacilli (*lactobacillus acidophilus* and *streptococcus thermophilus*). Aside from its rich protein and calcium content, yogurt serves as an agent in improving the intestinal flora which are very important for the absorption and secretion of fluids. Yogurt promotes the growth of desirable intestinal bacteria which in turn produce large amounts of certain necessary B vitamins.

In addition to commercial yogurt, available in whole-milk and low-fat formulas, there are various instructions for making yogurt at home, including the use of an electric yogurt maker. Yogurt eaten plain has a tart acid taste to which many people object. Therefore, it can be mixed with dry milk and/or raw sugar, honey, or molasses, to which are added chunks of any fresh fruit— apple, berries, banana, etc.—to make a delectable, simple, but very healthy dish.

Yogurt has not generally been used in the dishes of French cuisine. In our conversion of classic dishes to more natural-food ingredients and methods, we have taken modest steps toward substituting yogurt for milk, cream, or liquid body in some basic and frequent sauces. These include a yogurt vinaigrette— suitable for all tossed and many composed salads—yogurt mayonnaise, hollandaise, velouté, and a dessert sauce. Yogurt will curdle at high temperatures; this can be retarded by mixing a little potato flour or arrowroot into the yogurt first. To modify the tart flavor of yogurt, mix it with some nonfat dry milk which will also give it a creamier consistency.

Menus for Sensuous
and Organic Enjoyment

A cookbook is only as good as it is practical, and compiling the menus for this chapter was the test of our effort. In these pages we suggest menus which we believe offer gourmets of all creeds the opportunity to enjoy both sensuous and nutritional fulfillment via *cuisine santé*.

Here is a list of basic principles for incorporating maximum nutritional benefits in gourmet menu planning:

1. *Eat foods that are prepared with natural (organic) ingredients as much as possible.*
2. *Eat processed foods and ingredients with no chemical additives whenever possible.*
3. *Eat foods that contain the maximum of their original natural nutrients.*
4. *Eat foods that provide a favorable nutritional balance.*
5. *Eat some raw fruit and/or vegetable each day, ideally at the beginning of each meal.* Eating raw fruits or vegetables at the beginning of the meal helps to increase the flow of the gastric juices and aid good digestion. It also helps to supplement the reduced food values of cooked foods. (As much as fine cooking may delight our senses, there is a loss of nutrients once foods are subjected to heat through cooking.)
6. *Limit the intake of meat, meaning poultry and red meat. One to three meat meals weekly is considered fully adequate for most people.* Nutritionists urge Americans in particular to reduce their intake of meat. Americans eat more meat per capita than any other people, and our high intake of meat and fatty animal foods is related to the increased risk of cancer and heart disease.

Thus, our menu plan:

First course: Raw vegetable salad

Main course: Entrée dish from one of the following categories:

Vegetable	Fish
Egg	Shellfish
Pasta	Poultry
Grain	Red Meat
Savory Pastry	

. . . with appropriate garnishes

Dessert: Most frequently—fresh fruit and cheese.
(Fancy French desserts were always meant for special occasions.)

Soups are a rich nutritional food and may serve as the main course (depending on their substance) or precede it.

A word about wines

For the gourmet who enjoys wine with his meal, there is no rule which says that wine cannot be appreciated with the no-meat meal, and in our sample menus we have suggested wine types for both meat and no-meat menus. Wine guides ad infinitum recommend wine types for fish, poultry, meat, game, and desserts, but what do you drink with the main course of a no-meat meal? Referring to the millions of Europeans who do not eat as many meat meals as Americans but drink much more wine, we remind ourselves that we *can* drink wine with no-meat meals and enjoy it, perhaps with more sensitized palates. One can enjoy wine with a main course of egg, pasta, savory pastry, or vegetable.

Also, eating the salad as the first course—with the white wine section of the meal (if two wines are being served) —seems to make more sense than the tradition of serving it between the main course and the cheese course, during the red or fuller wine serving. (See also "Wine," p. 26.)

In the following menus, recipes for all dishes, including salads, may be located in the index.

NO-MEAT MEALS, LIGHT, SUMMER-ORIENTED

1. Salade Française: Spring Salad (29)
   Spinach Tart
   Cheese Board
   Fresh Fruits of the Season
   Wine suggestion: California Riesling, or Piesporter Goldtröpfchen

2. Consommé à la Madrilène
   Salade Française: Niçoise without Tuna (21)
   Strawberry Mousse
   Wine suggestion: California Pinot Chardonnay

3. French Potato Salad with Green Beans and Tomatoes
   Cold Cheese Soufflé
   Fresh Fruit Tartlets
   Wine suggestion: St. Veran, or California Pinot Chardonnay

4. Poached Eggs on Vegetable Macédoine
   Potage Paysanne
   Flummery Santé, Fresh Fruit Sauce
   Wine suggestion: Niersteiner Domtal

NO-MEAT MEALS, SUBSTANTIAL, SUMMER-ORIENTED

5. Salade Française: Spinach, Cheese, and Croutons (2)
   Rice Ring Provençal, with Eggplant, Peppers, and Tomatoes
   Vanilla French Ice Cream, Fresh Fruit Sauce
   Wine suggestion: Greek St. Helena, or Rodites

6. Salade Française: Fines Herbes (6)
   Vichyssoise
   Eggplant Stuffed with Mushrooms, Celery, and Tomatoes/Kasha
     Pilaff
   Hot Blueberry Soufflé with Blueberry Sauce
   Wine suggestion: Soave, or Orvieto

7. Caesar Salad
   Crème Olga with Raw Mushrooms and Scallions
   Corn Fritters, Thin-sliced Green Beans, Glazed Turnips
   Riz à l'Impératrice Nature
   Wine suggestion: Alsatian Riesling, or Bernkasteler

8. Cold Tomato Soufflé, with Salade Française: Bibb lettuce and
     Watercress (1)
   Crêpes Stuffed with Spinach, Mornay Sauce
   Frozen Rhubarb Soufflé
   Wine suggestion: Loire Valley White—Vouvray or Quincy

NO-MEAT MEALS, LIGHT, WINTER-ORIENTED

9. Artichoke Vinaigrette
   Chick-pea Soup with Mornay Toast
   Hot Orange Marmalade Soufflé, Sour Cream Sauce
   Wine suggestion: Beaujolais Saint-Amour, or California Sau-
     vignon

10. Salade Française: Spinach, Zucchini, Onion, and Parmesan Cheese
    (8)
    Omelet with Eggplant Filling, Tomato Sauce
    Cold Chestnut Soufflé
    Wine suggestion: California Zinfandel, or Côtes du Rhône

11. Endive and Orange Salad
    Onion Tart
    Carob Bavarian Cream (Chocolate flavor)
    Wine suggestion: Rhine white, or Côte Rôtie red

12. Salade Française: Fines Herbes (6)
    Soupe au Pistou
    Hot Carob Soufflé (Chocolate flavor)
    Wine suggestion: California Zinfandel, or Côtes de Provence rosé

NO-MEAT MEALS, SUBSTANTIAL, WINTER-ORIENTED

13. Cucumber Mousse
    Broiled Vegetables on Skewers/Kasha Pilaff
    Dione Lucas's Chocolate Roll with Carob
    Wine suggestion: Alsatian Riesling, or Sauvignon Blanc

14. Salade Française: Bibb Lettuce and Tomato (13)
    Potato Soup with Julienne Vegetables
    Spinach Ring with Mushrooms
    Ile Flottante
    Wine suggestion: Rhinehessen white, or California Sauvignon
       Blanc

15. Salade Française: Romaine, Beets, and Nuts (5)
    Lasagne with Cheese Filling, Tomato and Mushroom Sauce
    Mocha Cream Puffs, Carob Sauce (Chocolate flavor)
    Wine suggestion: Bardolino, or Grignolino

16. Salade Française: Fines Herbes (6)
    Crème Aurore with Potato and Tomato
    Onions Stuffed with Spinach, Mushroom Sauce/Fried Gnocchi
    Cheese Board
    Chestnut Mont-Blanc
    Wine suggestion: California Pinot Chardonnay, or Verdicchio

WITH-MEAT MEALS, LIGHT, SUMMER-ORIENTED

17. Stuffed Eggs on Watercress Cream
    Sautéed Lamb Chops Stuffed with Chicken Mousse/Cucumbers
       with Fresh Herbs

Crème au Caramel
Wine suggestion: Red Burgundy—Volnay, Santenay, Mercurey

18. Cucumber Mousse
Chicken Mallorca with Tomatoes, Green Peppers, Oranges/Rice Pilaff with Almonds
Cold Banana Soufflé
Wine suggestion: Red Portuguese Dão, or red Spanish Rioja

19. Stuffed Tomatoes
Cod Mousse with Sour Cream Sauce
Fresh Fruit Tartlets
Wine suggestion: Alsatian Riesling, or Rüdesheim-Nahe

20. Caesar Salad
Fish Soup in the Manner of the Loire Region
Le Clafouti with Cherries
Wine suggestion: Austrian Sylvaner, or Muscadet

WITH-MEAT MEALS, SUBSTANTIAL, SUMMER-ORIENTED

21. Salade Française: Endive and Watercress (16)
Cold Cream of Asparagus Soup
Chicken Marengo
Cold Carob Soufflé (Chocolate flavor)
Wine suggestion: Red Burgundy—Fixin or Aloxe-Corton

22. Salade Française: Romaine, Chives, Watercress (19)
Gazpacho
Paella Valenciana
Rhubarb French Ice Cream, Strawberry Sauce
Wine suggestion: Red Spanish Rioja, or red Portuguese Dão

23. Salade Française: Spring Salad (29)
Seafood Casserole
Frozen Raspberry Soufflé, Raspberry Sauce
Wine suggestion: Loire Valley white, or Alsatian Riesling

24. Salade Française: Bibb lettuce, Spinach, Onion, Watercress (3)
Ragout of Lamb with Spring Vegetables
Strawberry Mousse
Wine suggestion: Red Médoc, or California Zinfandel

25. Salade Française: Bibb lettuce, Soybean Sprouts (4) /Poached Eggs in Aspic with Tarragon
Roast Shoulder of Lamb with Veal Mousse and Stuffed Eggplant
Cheese Board
Gâteau Favori Nouveau
Wine suggestion: Barbaresco, or California Cabernet Sauvignon

WITH-MEAT MEALS, LIGHT, WINTER-ORIENTED

26. Salade Française: Escarole, Endive, Spinach, Parsley (28)
    Fillets of Sole Véronique
    Cheese Board
    Banana Cream Tart
    Wine suggestion: California Chablis, or Pinot Chardonnay

27. Salade Française: Lettuce, Onion, Avocado (22)
    Scallops and Oysters in Shells
    Cheese Board
    Sweet Omelet with Apricot Sauce
    Wine suggestion: Pinot Chardonnay, or Sancerre

28. Avocado Vinaigrette
    Poached Breasts of Chicken with Mushroom Velouté and Hol-
        landaise/Plain Spinach Ring
    Chestnut Tart
    Wine suggestion: Red Rhône

29. Salade Française: Boston lettuce, Cucumbers, Radishes, Scallions,
        Cherry Tomatoes, Watercress (12)
    Poached Breasts of Chicken with Ricotta-filled Crêpes/Sautéed
        Diced Celery with Almonds
    Hot Lemon Soufflé with Lemon Sauce
    Wine suggestion: Red Givry, or red Nipozzano

30. Salade Française: Boston lettuce, Artichoke hearts, Tomatoes
        (9)
    Veal Scallops with Mushroom Purée/Zucchini Cassolettes with
        Spinach Purée
    Hot Sweet Potato Soufflé, Sabayon Sauce
    Wine suggestion: Soave, or Meursault

WITH-MEAT MEALS, SUBSTANTIAL, WINTER-ORIENTED

31. Avocado Stuffed with Crabmeat
    Chicken with Tarragon, Suprême Sauce/Plain Braised Endive
    Cheese Board
    Grapefruit Crêpes Suzette
    Wine suggestion: Beaujolais Saint-Amour, or light red wine

32. Salade Mimosa
    Sautéed Chicken Demi-deuil style, with Truffles/Gnocchi Parisi-
        enne
    Cheese Board
    Orange Cream Puffs with Carob Sauce (Chocolate flavor)
    Wine suggestion: Fine dry white or red, Californian or French

33. Salade Française: Fines Herbes (6) , with Mornay Toast Fingers
    Fillets of Soles Dugléré with Tomatoes and Mushrooms
    Hot Carob Soufflé (Chocolate flavor) , with Vanilla Sauce
    Wine suggestion: Pouilly-sur-Loire, or Pouilly-Fumé

34. Orange and Escarole Salad
    Nut Soup
    Pike Quennelles, Suprême Sauce
    Cheese Board
    Mocha Cream Puffs, Carob Sauce (Chocolate flavor)
    Wine suggestion: Puligny Montrachet, or Pouilly Vinzelles

35. Salade Française: Endive and Watercress (16)
    Shrimp Bisque
    Roast Rack of Lamb with Mascotte Garnish
    Pears Belle Hélène, with Carob Sauce (Chocolate flavor)
    Wine suggestion: Durfort-Vivens, Château Talbot, or Château
        Duhart-Milon

THANKSGIVING DINNER

36. Salade Française: Mushrooms, Bibb lettuce, Chives, Parsley (24)
    Oysters on the Half Shell with Fresh Lemon
    Roast Stuffed Turkey with Pears/Chestnut-Filled Acorn Squash
    Apple Flan and Lemon Curd Tart
    Dried Fruits and Nuts
    Wine suggestions: with oysters: French Chablis
                    with turkey: Clos de la Roche, Beaune, or Mer-
                    curey

CHRISTMAS DINNER

37. Shrimp Salad in Tomato Aspic Ring
    Boned Stuffed Duck with Orange Sauce and Orange Saffron Rice/
        Broccoli Purée and Chestnut Purée
    Cheese Board
    Dione Lucas's Chocolate Roll with Carob
    Wine suggestions: with salad: Champagne
                    with duck and cheese: fine red Bordeaux, Free-
                    mark Abbey Cabernet, or Inglenook Ca-
                    bernet

PART II
Recipes

The First Course:
Salads

Why "the first course"? For the maximum organic enjoyment of the meal, nutrition experts recommend that the salad not only be served as a separate course but that it be the *first* course. The reason is that raw vegetables and fruits set the gastric juices flowing in a propitious manner, an important consideration in the art of eating.

The best salad is the easiest to make, because it can be made in advance, at your convenience. Imagine making a tossed salad preparation the night before, setting it in the refrigerator, and forgetting about it until the meal when it is to be eaten? True, and not a wilted leaf in the bowl if the dresssing is on the bottom and the salad has not been tossed. When you can afford the time, however, it is preferable to assemble the salad an hour or so before serving to allow for sufficient chilling.

To avoid unnecessary loss of delicate nutrients in washing greens, we suggest plunging them quickly into a large bowl filled with cold water and then giving each leaf a good rinsing under a forceful spray tap (and, of course, drying them well).

If you plan your salad courses a few days to a week ahead, you will avoid salad doldrums. You should install a supply of greens and other salad ingredients, cleaned and dried, in plastic bags, in your refrigerator. They will be nicely chilled and crisped when you wish to assemble your salad bowl or platter. In your menu plan there need not be a repetition of the same tossed salad for weeks—there are so many variations—and it is always a wonderful surprise to present a beautiful composed salad once in a while.

For tossed salads, crystal, silver, or any nonporous bowl is preferred over wood. Wood absorbs the oils, and oils easily become rancid. The old adage "never wash a wooden salad bowl" is nutritional poison. Have ample-sized bowls for thorough, quick tossing and coating.

Composed salads may be served in lovely bowls, platters, or tin-lined copper au gratin dishes. The latter are especially good because when the salad that has been arranged in a tin-lined copper au gratin dish is set in the refrigerator to chill, the copper retains the chill well after it is removed for serving.

BASIC SALAD DRESSINGS

Basic Vinaigrette

¼ teaspoon sea salt
¼ teaspoon herb salt
1 teaspoon raw sugar
1 teaspoon dry mustard
2 tablespoons fresh lemon juice
2 tablespoons cold-pressed virgin olive oil

8 tablespoons cold-pressed safflower oil
1 organic egg, raw, or ⅓ cup light raw cream
1 teaspoon finely chopped fresh garlic

Combine all of the ingredients in a 1-pint screw-top jar and close it tightly. To protect the nutrients in the delicate oils, which are quickly lost when exposed to light, it is best to use a dark glass or opaque jar. Shake the mixture very well, until it emulsifies. Store in the refrigerator.
Approximately 1 cup

Yogurt Vinaigrette

¼ teaspoon sea salt
¼ teaspoon herb salt
1 teaspoon raw sugar
1 teaspoon dry mustard
1 tablespoon fresh lemon juice
5 tablespoons cold-pressed safflower oil

5 tablespoons yogurt (whole-milk or low-fat type)
1 teaspoon finely chopped fresh garlic

Follow the preparation given for Basic Vinaigrette.
Approximately 1 cup

Variations of Vinaigrette (Basic or Yogurt)

When you have a supply of lovely fresh herbs, you can make interesting variations of these dressings. Measure the amount of dressing you require for one salad and add the herbs, finely chopped, to it.
1. *Dill:* Add 2 tablespoons, finely chopped, with 1 teaspoon raw sugar to ½ cup Vinaigrette.

2. *Basil:* Add a generous amount, say 4 tablespoons, of finely chopped basil to ½ cup Vinaigrette.

3. *Tarragon:* Add 1 tablespoon, finely chopped, to ½ cup Vinaigrette.

4. *Hard-boiled egg:* Add 1 hard-boiled organic egg, finely chopped, to ½ cup Vinaigrette.

5. *Blue Cheese:* Add 1 hard-boiled organic egg and ½ cup natural blue cheese, finely chopped, to 1 cup Vinaigrette.

Salad Bowl Vinaigrette

A simplified version of Basic Vinaigrette may be made directly in the bottom of the salad bowl.

⅛ to ¼ teaspoon herb salt	½ teaspoon finely chopped fresh
½ teaspoon dry mustard	garlic
1 tablespoon fresh lemon juice	1 organic egg, raw, or 1 tablespoon
3 to 4 tablespoons cold-pressed	heavy raw cream, or 1 or 2
safflower oil	tablespoons yogurt (optional)

Combine all of the ingredients in the bottom of the salad bowl. Stir the mixture with the tines of a dinner fork until it is well blended. Then place the salad ingredients on top of this dressing.

Basic Mayonnaise

Yolks of 2 organic eggs, raw	1½ cups cold-pressed safflower oil
½ teaspoon herb salt	Raw cream, for thinning, if
1 teaspoon dry mustard	desired
2 tablespoons fresh lemon juice	

Combine the egg yolks, salt, and mustard in the bowl of an electric mixer and beat well. Add the lemon juice and beat again. Continue beating as you very slowly pour in the safflower oil, literally drop by drop until the sauce begins to thicken; then the pouring may go a little faster. If a thinner mayonnaise is desired, add a little light cream. Store in the refrigerator.

1¾ cups

Yogurt Mayonnaise

Prepare the preceding recipe for Basic Mayonnaise with the following changes:

1. Use 1 tablespoon fresh lemon juice instead of 2 tablespoons.

2. Use 1 cup cold-pressed safflower oil instead of 1½ cups.

3. After all of the oil has been incorporated into the mayonnaise, beat in ½ cup yogurt (whole-milk or low-fat type).

(cont.)

4. Do not use the raw cream.

Note: The addition of yogurt will result in a thinner mayonnaise. If you wish a *thicker consistency* for spreading, dissolve 2 teaspoons unflavored gelatin in 2 tablespoons warm water and stir it into the yogurt mayonnaise. Allow it to chill and thicken.

Variations of Mayonnaise (*Basic or Yogurt*)

1. *Coating mayonnaise:* To bring Basic Mayonnaise to a pouring consistency for coating, add light cream. With Yogurt Mayonnaise, add more yogurt.

2. *With gelatin for coating:* If you do not plan to serve a dish that has been coated with mayonnaise right away, you may set the mayonnaise coating by mixing 1 tablespoon unflavored gelatin dissolved in 2 tablespoons hot water (which mixture has been cooled a little) into 1¾ cups thinned Basic Mayonnaise or Yogurt Mayonnaise.

3. *Creamier, fluffier mayonnaise:* Fold whipped or sour cream into *Basic Mayonnaise.* For *creamier Yogurt Mayonnaise,* prepare Yogurt Mayonnaise through the addition of the oil. Mix ½ cup yogurt with ½ cup nonfat dry milk and fold the mixture into the mayonnaise. For a *fluffy Yogurt Mayonnaise,* beat the white of 1 organic egg and fold it into the mayonnaise.

4. *Mustard Mayonnaise:* Add more dry mustard to Basic or Yogurt Mayonnaise and beat thoroughly.

5. *Horseradish Mayonnaise:* For a nippy character in either Mayonnaise, add finely chopped fresh horseradish.

6. *Herb Mayonnaise:* Add finely chopped fresh herbs such as dill or tarragon to either Mayonnaise. For other herb ideas, please see discussions on herbs on pages 16 and 259–261.

7. *Green Mayonnaise:* Add 1 cup very finely chopped parsley or spinach to 1¾ cups Mayonnaise, and purée in the blender.

8. *Pink Mayonnaise:* Add natural tomato paste to either Mayonnaise.

Salade Française

Tossed Salad

A Salade Française is a *salade ordinaire,* a tossed salad, a selection of fresh greens and vegetables, accented with fresh herbs, from hundreds of variations, dressed with one good all-purpose vinaigrette dressing. Here are some choices for the salad bowl from nature's garden:

GREENS	
Arugula (rocket)	*Chinese cabbage*
Beet tops	*Cress*
Carrot tops	*Dandelion leaves*
Chicory (curly endive)	*Endive, Belgian*
	Escarole

Lettuces: Bibb, Boston, romaine, salad bowl, iceberg (least preferred)
Nasturtium leaves
New Zealand spinach
Purslane
Sea kale
Sorrel
Spinach
Watercress

RAW VEGETABLES
Alfalfa sprouts
Avocado
Bean sprouts
Cabbage: green, white, red, Savoy
Carrots
Cauliflower, tiny florets or paper-thin slices
Celery
Cucumber
Fennel
Jicama
Mushrooms
Peppers: green and red sweet bell
Radishes
Tomatoes: cherry, regular, plum, beefsteak
Zucchini

VEGETABLES CRISP-COOKED
AND CHILLED
Asparagus tips
Green beans
Kidney beans
Lima beans
Beets
Cactus (nopal)
Celeriac (celery root)
Garbanzo (chick-pea)

Potato
Water chestnut

HERBS
Basil
Celery leaf
Chervil
Coriander
Dill
Fennel leaf
Garlic
Horseradish, fresh
Mustard leaves
Onion varieties: Bermuda, red, silverskins (white), yellow; also chives, scallions, shallots
Orégano
Parsley varieties: curly, hamburg, Italian
Savory
Sweet Cicely
Tarragon
Thyme

OTHER SALAD CONTRIBUTIONS
Anchovy fillets
Artichoke hearts
Cheese: freshly grated Parmesan or Romano; cubed or julienne-cut tangy cheeses such as Swiss, Monterey Jack, Cheddar
Croutons: cubes of whole-wheat bread sautéed in oil (p. 258)
Hard-boiled eggs
Olives, green and ripe
Herring fillets
Italian sweet peppers, roasted
Nuts: walnuts, pecans
Sardines

Dressing
Basic or Yogurt Vinaigrette, page 38
(Prepare a supply for a week and keep it in the refrigerator.)

PROCEDURE
By assembling a tossed salad in the following manner, the vegetables are never mixed with the dressing until the salad is served. This per-

mits making the salad preparation as much as a day before and allowing the whole composition, including the bowl, to chill thoroughly in
the refrigerator.

Into a large, clean, nonporous bowl, add the following ingredients
in the order given:
1. Pour the dressing into the bottom of the bowl.
2. Break the sturdier green leaves into bite-size pieces on top of the
dressing. (Avoid cutting the greens with a knife, unless you specifically
want a shredded texture.)
3. If you are using a combination of greens, break the more delicate
green leaves on top of the sturdier ones.
4. If you are using a raw or cooked vegetable, or any combination
thereof, arrange it on top of the greens. This includes chunks of onion.
5. If you are using any other contributions, such as cheese or croutons,
cuts of herring or sardines, scatter them on top of the vegetables.
6. Last, sprinkle the herbs, which are usually finely chopped, over all.

Cover the bowl with a piece of plastic wrap and set it in the refrigerator to chill. *Do not toss or mix the salad in any way until you are
ready to eat it.* When you do toss the salad, toss gently, thoroughly,
and quickly so that each leaf is coated with the dressing and has the
finely chopped herbs clinging to it, but is not bruised. Serve immediately.

PRESENTATIONS

Over 25 salad combinations are suggested here. You will think of
many more. Assemble each combination in the order of ingredients as
given. All of them include the use of Basic Vinaigrette dressing—or a
variation if you wish—which contains all of the seasonings necessary
for the entire salad. Quantities of each salad ingredient depend on the
number of servings needed.

The ingredient which represents the bulk quantity of the salad,
usually the greens, is marked with an asterisk. All other ingredients are
considered garnishes and are used in appropriate, smaller quantities.

1. *Vinaigrette*
   *Bibb lettuce
   Shallots, finely chopped
   Watercress, a few clusters

2. *Vinaigrette*
   *Spinach
   Parmesan cheese, freshly grated
   Whole-wheat croutons
   Curly parsley, finely chopped

3. *Vinaigrette*
   *Bibb lettuce
   *Spinach, tender little leaves
   *Baby white onion or shallot,
   finely chopped*
   Watercress, a few clusters

4. *Vinaigrette*
   *Bibb lettuce
   Soybean sprouts
   *Sprinkling of red sweet bell
   pepper, diced*

5. *Vinaigrette*
   *Arugula, or Romaine lettuce
   Beets, cooked and cubed
   Walnuts or pecans, halved or coarsely chopped

6. Classic Fines Herbes Salad
   Vinaigrette
   *Bibb lettuce
   Shallot, finely chopped
   Chives, finely chopped
   Tarragon (only if fresh is available), finely chopped
   Curly parsley, finely chopped

7. *Vinaigrette*
   *Romaine
   *Spinach
   Bermuda onion rings, halves
   Avocado, chunks

8. *Vinaigrette*
   *Spinach
   Zucchini, thinly sliced
   Baby white onion, thinly sliced
   Parmesan cheese, freshly grated
   Parsley, curly or Italian, chopped

9. *Vinaigrette*
   *Boston lettuce
   Artichoke hearts, quartered
   Tomato, wedges

10. *Vinaigrette*
    *Boston lettuce
    Bermuda or red onion, large dice
    Roasted Italian sweet peppers
    Sardines
    Ripe olives

11. *Vinaigrette*
    *Spinach
    *Curly endive
    Zucchini, thinly sliced
    Parsley, chopped

12. *Vinaigrette*
    *Boston or salad bowl lettuce
    Cucumbers, sliced

    Radishes, sliced
    Scallions, 1-inch cuts
    Cherry tomatoes, cut into halves
    Watercress, a few clusters

13. *Vinaigrette*
    *Bibb lettuce
    Tomato, wedges
    Scallions, 1-inch cuts

14. *Vinaigrette*
    *Boston lettuce
    *New Zealand spinach
    Baby white onion, rings
    Cherry tomatoes, cut into halves
    Cheese, julienne strips

15. *Vinaigrette*
    *Romaine lettuce
    Mung-bean sprouts
    Watercress clusters
    Parsley, finely chopped

16. Elegant Salad
    Vinaigrette
    *Belgian endive, 1-inch slices
    *Watercress, clusters

17. Mexican Salad
    Vinaigrette
    *Boston lettuce, cut into ½-inch shreds
    Bermuda onion, large dice
    Tomato, cubes or thin wedges
    Fresh coriander or parsley, chopped
    Parmesan cheese, freshly grated
    Sour cream, one dollop on the top

18. *Vinaigrette*
    *Boston lettuce, cut into ½-inch shreds
    *Beet greens, cut into ½-inch shreds
    Cucumbers, peeled, halved, seeded, cut into ½-inch slices

Red onion rings, cut into
  halves
Parsley, chopped

19. Vinaigrette
    *Romaine, center leaves
    Chives, finely chopped
    Watercress, clusters

20. Vinaigrette
    *Romaine lettuce
    Parmesan cheese, freshly grated
    Whole-wheat croutons
    Hard-boiled egg, wedges
    Parsley, finely chopped

21. Salade Niçoise without Tuna
    (see pp. 54–55 for the classic
    version)
    Vinaigrette
    *Boston or Romaine lettuce
    Potatoes, boiled, skinned, cut
      into large dice, separately
      mixed with Vinaigrette
    Green beans, barely cooked,
      1-inch cuts
    Hard-boiled egg, wedges
    Tomato wedges, or cherry to-
      matoes, halved
    Ripe olives
    Parsley, chopped

22. Vinaigrette
    *Boston or Romaine lettuce
      heart, cut into ½-inch shreds
    Bermuda onion, cut into ¼-
      inch-thick slices and halved
    Avocado, sliced
    Roasted Italian sweet pepper,
      large dice

23. Vinaigrette
    *Dandelion leaves
    Zucchini, thinly sliced
    Red onion, thinly sliced and
      halved
    Italian parsley, coarsely
      chopped

24. Vinaigrette
    *Mushrooms, sliced
    *Bibb lettuce or young spinach
    Chives, finely chopped
    Parsley, finely chopped

25. Vinaigrette
    *Chinese cabbage, cut into ½-
      inch shreds
    *Spinach
    Mung-bean sprouts
    Red bell pepper, small dice

26. Vinaigrette
    *Romaine lettuce
    *Bibb lettuce
    Cauliflower, sliced paper-thin
    Fines herbes: parsley, chives,
      shallots, or other leaf herbs,
      finely chopped

27. Vinaigrette
    *Boston lettuce
    Asparagus, barely cooked,
      chilled, cut into 1-inch
      pieces
    Hard-boiled egg, chopped
    Parsley, chopped

28. Vinaigrette
    *Escarole
    Belgian endive, 1-inch slices
    Few spinach leaves
    Shallot, finely chopped
    Parsley, finely chopped

29. Spring Salad
    Vinaigrette
    *Boston, salad bowl, or Ro-
      maine lettuce, or combina-
      tion
    Cucumbers, cubed
    Radishes, thinly sliced
    Green bell pepper, short shreds
    Tomato, small wedges or cubes
    Scallions, 1-inch cuts
    Parsley, chopped
    Hard-boiled egg, wedges

Artichoke is also very good cold with Blue Cheese Dressing (p. 39), and warm with Sauce Hollandaise (pp. 268–269).

4 globe artichokes	*1 finely chopped hard-boiled*
2 tablespoons fresh lemon juice	*organic egg and 2 teaspoons*
1 tablespoon sea salt	*finely chopped parsley mixed*
1 cup Basic or Yogurt Vinaigrette	*with the vinaigrette (optional)*
(p. 38)	

Cut the tops off the artichokes, about one third of the way down. With a scissors, trim off all the points on the leaves. Bring a large pot of water with the lemon juice and sea salt to a boil. Place the trimmed artichokes in the boiling water and cook for 15 to 25 minutes, depending on their size. The flesh on the bottom of the leaves and the under part of the artichoke should be tender but firm. Remove and drain on paper towels. Chill the artichokes in the refrigerator.

PRESENTATION. When the artichokes are to be served, scoop out the thistle choke in the center of each artichoke with a little spoon. Place the artichokes on individual salad plates. Fill the center cavities with ¼ cup of vinaigrette.

4 servings

2 ripe but firm avocados, peeled	*Watercress sprigs*
2 medium-size tomatoes, skinned	
½ cup Basic or Yogurt Vinaigrette	
(p. 38)	

On 4 individual salad plates, or one large serving platter, arrange alternating slices of avocado and tomato. Drizzle the vinaigrette over all. Garnish with sprigs of crisp watercress.

4 servings

4 beets, 3 to 3½ inches in diameter	*⅓ cup Basic or Yogurt Vinaigrette*
Sea salt	*(p. 38), or ½ cup Basic or Yo-*
½ cup small dice of celery	*gurt Mayonnaise (pp. 39–40)*
¼ cup chopped organic walnuts or	*Small bunch of crisp fresh*
pecans	*watercress*

Cook the beets in boiling water, seasoned with 1 teaspoon sea salt, until they are just tender. Drain and chill them in the refrigerator.

Remove the skins from the beets; these can be slipped off with your fingers. Trim the bottom of each beet so that it has about the same flat surface as the top. Cut the beets horizontally into halves. Cut out a hollow in the cut sides, shaping each beet half like a little saucer.

Chop the beet pulp that was scooped out to pieces about the same size as the celery dice. Bind the chopped beet, celery, and nuts with vinaigrette or mayonnaise. Fill the beet halves with this mixture.

PRESENTATION. Arrange the stuffed beets on an au gratin dish or shallow serving dish. Garnish with the watercress and chill before serving.

4 servings of 2 cassolettes each

Salade de Tomates
Tomato and Onion Salad

2 pounds firm ripe tomatoes (regular, beefsteak, or plum), skinned

2 medium-size onions (Bermuda, 4 to 6 baby white, red, or yellow), thinly sliced

1 tablespoon raw sugar

1 tablespoon chopped fresh parsley

½ cup Basic or Yogurt Vinaigrette (p. 38)

Cut the tomatoes into slices or wedges. Arrange the slices in overlapping fashion (or the wedges in circles) on a serving platter. Or they may be piled into a salad bowl. Sprinkle the tomatoes with the sugar.

Separate the onion slices into rings and scatter them on top of the tomatoes. Pour the vinaigrette over the onions and tomatoes, and sprinkle the chopped parsley over the top.

4 servings

Tomates au Basilic
Tomatoes and Basil

2 pounds firm ripe tomatoes (regular, beefsteak, or plum), skinned

1 tablespoon raw sugar

½ cup Basic or Yogurt Vinaigrette (p. 38)

½ cup chopped fresh basil

Prepare the tomatoes and arrange them in a serving dish as described for Salade de Tomates (above). Pour the vinaigrette over the tomatoes. Scatter the chopped basil over the top.

4 servings

Salade des Endives et des Oranges
Endive and Orange Salad

½ cup Basic or Yogurt Vinaigrette, (p. 38)

Grated rind of 1 orange

4 fairly large Belgian endives, cut into 1-inch pieces

Skinned sections of 4 oranges

2 tablespoons chopped fresh parsley

Few small watercress sprigs

around the edge of the mousse. In the center of each cornucopia set a tiny sprig of the reserved dill.

Peel, seed, and chop very finely the remaining piece of cucumber, and mix it into the mayonnaise. Beat the remaining egg white to soft peaks and fold it into the mayonnaise. Fold in the reserved whipped cream. Serve this sauce separately with the mousse.

4 to 6 servings

POTATO SALAD

4 or 5 large Idaho potatoes
Sea salt
¼ cup finely chopped shallots
¼ cup finely chopped fresh parsley
2 tablespoons finely chopped fresh chives (optional)
½ cup Soy Stock (p. 262)
1 cup or more Basic or Yogurt Vinaigrette (p. 38)

Herb salt

GARNISHES

1 pound green beans
1 head of Boston lettuce
Cold-pressed safflower oil for mold
4 small ripe tomatoes, skinned and quartered
12 ripe olives

Salade des Pommes de Terre

French Potato Salad with Green Beans and Tomatoes

POTATO SALAD. Boil the potatoes in their skins in water seasoned with sea salt, until they are soft. Drain, and while they are still warm, remove the skins. Cut the potatoes lengthwise into quarters and then across into chunks. Combine the potatoes with the shallots, parsley, and chives in a mixing bowl. Warm the soy stock and pour it over the potatoes and toss lightly. Mix enough vinaigrette into the potatoes so that each chunk is nicely moist. Season with a little herb salt, if necessary.

BEANS. Top and tail the green beans. Cover them with water seasoned with sea salt and cook until they are barely tender. Drain the beans, mix them with a little vinaigrette, and chill.

Cut the lettuce into ½-inch shreds and spread them over the surface of a serving platter.

PRESENTATION. Brush a round-bottomed mixing bowl with a little safflower oil and press the potato salad into it, like a mold. Invert the bowl onto the serving platter, and turn out the potato salad, which is now dome-shaped. On the opposite sides of the potato mound set a bundle of green beans. On the other two sides of the potato mound arrange piles of tomato sections. Scatter the olives over the tomato sections.

4 to 6 servings

Oeufs Pochés à la Macédoine

Poached Eggs on Vegetable Macédoine

VEGETABLE MACÉDOINE
1 cup baby lima beans, plain cooked
1 cup diced green beans, plain-cooked
1 cup diced carrots, plain-cooked
1 cup diced turnips, plain-cooked
1 cup green peas, plain-cooked
1 cup diced, peeled, and seeded cucumber
1 cup chopped, skinned, and seeded tomatoes

1 teaspoon fresh lemon juice
Herb salt

6 organic eggs, poached (see p. 152)
1¾ cups Basic or Yogurt Mayonnaise for coating (pp. 39–40)
6 sprigs of watercress

VEGETABLE MACÉDOINE. Combine all of the vegetables in a large bowl, add the lemon juice, and toss all together lightly. Season with herb salt. Arrange the macédoine on the bottom of an au gratin dish and let it chill in the refrigerator.

Drain the poached eggs on paper towels, trim any shaggy edges with a kitchen scissors, and carefully set them on the vegetable macédoine. PRESENTATION. Coat the eggs with some of the mayonnaise. Set a little sprig of watercress on top of each egg. Return the dish to the refrigerator until it is to be served. Serve the extra mayonnaise in a bowl.
6 servings

Oeufs Farcis à la Crème de Cresson

Stuffed Eggs on Watercress Cream

2 bunches of fresh crisp watercress
1 cup raw sour cream
Herb salt
¼ teaspoon freshly grated nutmeg
6 organic eggs, hard-boiled and shelled
1 cup thinned Basic or Yogurt Mayonnaise (pp. 39–40)

1 teaspoon dry mustard
1 tablespoon natural tomato paste
2 teaspoons unflavored gelatin
6 thin slices of black truffle or 6 halves of pitted ripe olive

Reserve about 6 sprigs of watercress for decoration. Trim the stems off the rest of the watercress (save them for a soup pot). Chop the watercress very fine and mix it thoroughly with the sour cream. Season with herb salt and nutmeg. Shape this watercress cream like a bed on a serving plate.

Cut the hard-boiled eggs lengthwise into halves. Remove the yolks without damaging the whites and rub yolks through a fine wire strainer. Beat the strained yolks with 1 tablespoon thinned mayonnaise in a mixer. Add the mustard, season with herb salt, and beat again. Fill the hollows of the egg whites level with this mixture and stick the egg halves back together to resemble whole eggs. Set the eggs on the watercress cream.

Mix remaining mayonnaise with the tomato paste. Dissolve the gelatin in 2 tablespoons hot water, allow it to cool a little, and mix it into the mayonnaise. Coat each egg with some of this mayonnaise.

PRESENTATION. Garnish the top of each egg with a thin slice of truffle or half of a ripe olive. Decorate the serving plate with the reserved watercress sprigs. Chill the preparation.

6 servings

Oeufs à la Parisienne

Stuffed Eggs and Tomatoes with Anchovy Mayonnaise

4 organic eggs, hard-boiled and shelled
1 cup plus 2 tablespoons Basic or Yogurt Mayonnaise (pp. 39–40)
1 tablespoon chopped fresh chives
Herb salt
4 ripe tomatoes, each about 3 inches in diameter, skinned
1 teaspoon raw sugar
½ teaspoon finely chopped fresh garlic
4 anchovy fillets
3 tablespoons raw milk
1 tablespoon unflavored gelatin
1 teaspoon natural tomato paste
⅓ cup light raw cream or yogurt
1 bunch of fresh crisp watercress
8 slices of red radish

Cut the eggs lengthwise into halves. Remove the yolks without damaging the whites and rub yolks through a fine wire strainer. Beat the strained yolks in a mixer with 2 tablespoons mayonnaise. Add the chopped chives and season with herb salt. Refill the egg whites with this mixture, more or less level.

Cut the tomatoes horizontally into halves and season the top of each with herb salt, raw sugar, and chopped garlic. Place a stuffed egg half, cut side down, on top of each tomato half. Set the tomato and egg combinations on a wire rack over a shallow pan and coat them with anchovy mayonnaise.

ANCHOVY MAYONNAISE. Mash the anchovy fillets in a mortar and beat the anchovy paste into 1 cup of mayonnaise. Warm the milk in a little pan and dissolve the gelatin in it. Cool the gelatin mixture a little, then beat it into the mayonnaise. Add the tomato paste and enough light cream or yogurt to the mayonnaise to reach a coating consistency. Quickly coat the tomato and egg units with this mayonnaise. Allow them to set in the refrigerator.

PRESENTATION. Scatter the watercress on the bottom of a serving plate. Arrange the tomato-and-egg preparations on the watercress. Top each egg with a slice of radish.

4 servings

Salade Mimosa

Mimosa Salad

2 cups finely diced carrots
2 cups finely diced beets
2 cups finely diced garden beans
2 cups finely diced turnips
    Sea salt
1 large or 2 small heads of Boston
    lettuce, cleaned and crisped
¼ cup Basic or Yogurt Vinaigrette
    (p. 38)

6 organic eggs, hard-boiled and
    shelled
6 small ripe tomatoes, skinned and
    thinly sliced
    Small bouquet of watercress or
    parsley
2 cups Creamier Basic or Yogurt
    Mayonnaise (pp. 39–40)

Cook the carrots, beets, beans, and turnips separately, as follows: Place the diced vegetable in a small pan with ½ teaspoon sea salt. Cover with water, bring to a boil, drain immediately, and chill.

Cut the lettuce into fine shreds, toss with the vinaigrette, and arrange it on the bottom of a large shallow salad bowl or platter. Remove the yolks from the whites of the eggs and rub the whites through a coarse wire strainer. Then rub the yolks through the strainer.

PRESENTATION. In a cartwheel pattern, arrange sections of egg white, egg yolk, carrot, beet, turnip, and beans on top of the shredded lettuce. Surround the edge of the dish with the thin slices of tomato, overlapping. Set the bouquet of watercress or parsley in the center. Chill thoroughly. Serve the mayonnaise in a separate bowl.

4 to 6 servings

Salade Niçoise

For a vegetarian meal, the tuna and anchovies may be omitted, and it is still a very ample and delicious salad.

2 cups diced cooked potatoes
    Herb salt
¼ cup finely chopped shallots
5 tablespoons finely chopped
    fresh parsley
1½ cups Basic or Yogurt
    Vinaigrette (p. 38)
1 large head of Boston or
    romaine lettuce, cleaned and
    crisped
½ pound green beans, plain-
    cooked, cut into 1-inch
    lengths

2 cups water-packed white tuna,
    separated into bite-size chunks
3 medium-size ripe tomatoes, cut
    into quarters
3 organic eggs, hard-boiled,
    shelled, and cut lengthwise
    into quarters
12 anchovy fillets
12 to 18 pitted ripe olives

Combine potatoes with a little herb salt, the shallots, 1 tablespoon parsley, and ¾ cup vinaigrette in a mixing bowl and toss lightly. Pour remaining vinaigrette into the bottom of a large salad bowl. Line the bowl with the lettuce torn into bite-size pieces. Arrange the potato mixture on top of the lettuce in the center, leaving a border of lettuce around the side of the bowl. Place the green beans on top of the potatoes. Scatter the chunks of tuna on top of the beans. Sprinkle the remaining parsley on top of the fish. Arrange a border, alternating wedges of tomato and hard-boiled egg, around the edge of the bowl. Lay one anchovy fillet across each section of egg. Strew the olives over the top. Cover the bowl with a piece of plastic wrap and chill in the refrigerator until ready to eat. Toss gently but thoroughly at serving time.

4 to 6 servings

Avocat Farci au Crabe

Avocado Stuffed with Crab Meat

6 beets, about 2½ inches in
    diameter
Sea salt
2 cups small matchstick shapes
    of celery
½ cup coarsely chopped organic
    walnuts

1 cup Basic or Yogurt Mayonnaise
    (pp. 39–40)
3 ripe but firm avocados
½ pound lump crab meat
6 thin slices of black truffle
6 organic walnut halves

Cook the beets in water seasoned with sea salt until they are just tender. Remove the skins. Cut 6 nice ⅛-inch-thick slices and set them aside for the garnish. Cut the rest of the beets into small matchstick shapes. Place the celery in a pan with 1 teaspoon sea salt, cover with water, bring it to a boil, and drain immediately. Combine the beets, celery, and chopped walnuts in a mixing bowl and toss gently with ½ cup of mayonnaise. Arrange this mixture on the bottom of a serving platter or shallow bowl.

PRESENTATION. Cut the avocados into halves, peel them, and remove the pits. Set the avocado halves on top of the vegetable mixture, cut sides up. Mix the crab meat with ½ cup of mayonnaise and spoon it into the hollows of the avocados. On top of each mound of filling place a thin slice of truffle. Garnish around the edge of the dish with the reserved slices of beet and the walnut halves.

6 servings

Salade d'Homard Française

French Lobster Salad

2 hearts of Boston lettuce, cut into
    fine shreds
4 medium-size ripe tomatoes,
    skinned, seeded, and cut into
    fine shreds
2 small cucumbers, peeled, seeded,
    and cut into ¼-inch cubes
Juice of 1 lemon

2 small lobsters, or 4 lobster tails,
    plain-boiled
1 tablespoon natural tomato paste
1 cup Basic or Yogurt Mayonnaise
    for coating (pp. 39–40)
Few ripe olives, or 1 black truffle
Few sprigs of fresh crisp
    watercress

Combine the shredded lettuce, tomatoes, and cucumbers in a mixing bowl and lightly toss and mix them. Sprinkle with the lemon juice and arrange the mixture on the bottom of a shallow serving dish or bowl. Cut the lobster meat into bite-size pieces and place them on top of the lettuce mixture, reserving about 8 nice slices for garnish. Blend the tomato paste with the mayonnaise, and cover the lobster and lettuce with this pink mayonnaise.

PRESENTATION. Garnish the top of the dish with the reserved lobster slices, the olives or slices of truffle, and clusters of watercress.

4 to 6 servings

Salade de Saumon
_____
Salmon Salad

2 pounds raw salmon (preferably the tail, which is more tender)
½ pound raw shrimps
1 bay leaf
1 celery stalk, sliced
1 small carrot, sliced
½ onion, sliced
Juice of 1 lemon
Herb salt
½ cup finely diced green beans
Sea salt
½ cup finely diced carrots
2 cups Natural Brown Rice, Plain-Cooked (see p. 165)

2 small ripe tomatoes, skinned, seeded, and shredded
½ cup cold-pressed safflower oil
¾ cup thinned Basic Mayonnaise or Yogurt Mayonnaise (pp. 39–40)
¾ cup Green Mayonnaise (Basic or Yogurt) (p. 40), thinned with light raw cream, or with yogurt mixed with 1 tablespoon nonfat dry milk powder
Few sprigs of fresh crisp watercress

SALMON AND SHRIMPS. Wrap the salmon in cheesecloth and place it in a fish kettle or shallow pan. Also wrap the shrimps in cheesecloth and place them in the same pan. Scatter over the fish and shrimps the bay leaf, celery, carrot, and onion. Add the lemon juice, ½ teaspoon herb salt, and 2 cups of water. Bring the water to a boil, reduce the heat, and cover the pan. Cook the shrimps for 5 minutes, or until they just turn pink, and remove them from the pan. Cook the salmon for 20 minutes. Uncover the pan, remove it from the heat, and allow the salmon to cool in the liquid.

VEGETABLE AND RICE MACÉDOINE. Place the diced beans in a small pan with ½ teaspoon of sea salt, and cover with water. Bring the beans to a boil and drain immediately. Cook the diced carrots in the same manner. Combine the cooked rice, beans, carrots, and tomatoes in a mixing bowl with the safflower oil and a little herb salt. Arrange the vegetable and rice mixture like a bed on the bottom of a shallow serving dish.

PRESENTATION. Carefully remove skin and bones from the salmon and place fish on the vegetable and rice bed. Coat *half* the surface of the salmon with the thinned Basic or Yogurt Mayonnaise. Coat the *other half* of the salmon with the thinned green mayonnaise. Shell and devein the shrimps. Cut them into halves and decorate the top of the dish with them. Surround the dish with the sprigs of watercress.

6 servings

Salade des Crevettes en Madrilène

Shrimp Salad in Tomato Aspic Ring

Cold-pressed safflower oil for
   mold
3 tablespoons natural tomato paste
3 teaspoons soy sauce
3 tablespoons unflavored gelatin
   Herb salt
½ pound raw shrimps
½ cup Basic or Yogurt Mayonnaise
   (*pp. 39–40*)

8 slices of peeled cucumber, ½
   inch thick
2 small ripe tomatoes, skinned and
   cut into 8 wedges
2 organic eggs, hard-boiled, shelled,
   and cut lengthwise into
   quarters
Bunch of crisp fresh watercress

Have ready a lightly oiled 1-quart ring mold. Combine 3 cups water, the tomato paste, soy sauce, gelatin, and herb salt to taste in a pan, and stir over medium heat until the gelatin dissolves. Set the pan in a bowl of ice and stir until the aspic is on the point of setting. Pour it into the mold and place it in the refrigerator (not the freezer) to set.

Cook the shrimps with 1 teaspoon herb salt in 2 cups boiling water until they just turn pink, 4 to 5 minutes. Drain, shell, and devein them, then chill.

PRESENTATION. When the aspic is firm, turn it out onto a serving plate. Mix the shrimps with the mayonnaise and carefully spoon them into the center of the ring. Surround the aspic ring with alternating cucumber slices and tomato wedges. On each cucumber slice, place an egg quarter. Garnish with clusters of watercress.

4 servings

Salade d'Homard et d'Ananas

Lobster and Pineapple Salad

2 cups rice (see Natural Brown
   Rice, Plain-Cooked, p. 165)
2 medium-size ripe tomatoes,
   skinned, seeded, and shredded
¼ cup Basic or Yogurt Vinaigrette
   (p. 38)
4 to 6 slices of fresh pineapple,
   about ½ inch thick
1 tablespoon raw sugar
1 lobster, about 1½ pounds, in its
   shell, plain-boiled

PINK DRESSING
2 organic eggs, separated
1 tablespoon fresh lemon juice
½ tablespoon dry mustard
1 tablespoon sweet paprika
½ teaspoon herb salt
1 tablespoon natural tomato paste
1 cup cold-pressed safflower oil
2 tablespoons raw heavy cream, or
   yogurt mixed with 2 tablespoons nonfat dry milk
¼ cup raw light cream or yogurt

Mix the cooked rice and shredded tomato pulp with the vinaigrette. Arrange the mixture like a bed on the bottom of a shallow serving dish. Arrange the slices of pineapple on top of the rice and sprinkle them with the sugar.

Carefully remove the lobster meat from the shell, keeping the head and tail shells and little claws intact and reserving them. Cut the lobster meat into bite-size pieces and arrange pieces on top of the slices of pineapple.

PINK DRESSING. Combine the separated egg yolks, lemon juice, dry mustard, paprika, herb salt, and tomato paste in an electric mixer bowl and beat well. Continue beating as you very slowly pour in the safflower oil. Beat in the heavy cream or 2 tablespoons yogurt and dry milk. In a separate bowl beat the egg whites to soft peaks and fold them into the dressing. Stir in the light cream or plain yogurt.

PRESENTATION. Spoon the sauce over the lobster and pineapple. Garnish the dish with the lobster shells and the little claws. Keep chilled until ready to serve.

4 to 6 servings

Cold Seafood, Poultry, or Meat Salad

1 cup cooked rice (see Natural Brown Rice, Plain-Cooked p. 165)
1 cup garden peas, plain-cooked
1 cup diced carrots, plain-cooked
2 cups cooked "meat" (chicken, duck, turkey, seafood, fish, veal, or beef)

2 cups Basic or Yogurt Mayonnaise (pp. 39–40)
¼ cup raw light cream (if needed)
Few sprigs of fresh crisp watercress
1 sweet red bell pepper, seeded and finely diced

Combine the cooked rice with the peas and carrots and arrange the mixture in a mound on a shallow serving plate. Remove all fat, skin, and sinew from the "meat" being used. Cut "meat" into bite-size pieces. Arrange it on top of the rice mixture.

Thin the Basic Mayonnaise with light cream to bring it to a coating consistency. If you are using yogurt mayonnaise, it may be thin enough; if not, thin it with additional yogurt. Coat the "meat" with the mayonnaise. Decorate the dish with the watercress and diced red pepper.

4 to 6 servings

Soups

Soups have nutritional preeminence over many cooked dishes because nutrients lost from the vegetables in the cooking process most likely will be retained in the cooking water, or the soup base. Also in soups you can use precious cooking water saved from other vegetable preparations. Dried-vegetable soups, such as lentil and chick-pea, provide nutritious soaking water. The old technique of discarding the soaking water is taboo; valuable nutrients have passed into the water in the soaking process. In cooking naturally, vegetable oil instead of butter is used in hot soups as well as in cold soups, a traditional use.

When you stop to think about it, soup making really can be quick and easy. Vegetables generally should be undercooked; there should be no long cooking times. Instant stocks—Soy and Vegetable—are always on hand in the quantity you require (pp. 261 and 262). Use your blender—cook a few vegetables in stock, then purée the whole mixture in the blender; you can readily have a potage. Finally, most soups freeze very well. You might concentrate your weekly food preparation activities on one day for the marketing, the prepartion of the salad inventory, and the preparation of a soup recipe or two to be frozen for instant or portable meals.

Homemade soups, made the natural way, are so delicious and nutritious that they make excellent main-course dishes in many meals. Soup main courses can account for more light meals and more no-meat meals, which nutritionists recommend. There is nothing more gratifying to the gourmet than a hot or cold, thick or clear, elaborate or basic "meal in a bowl"—homemade.

Potage de Céleri et des Pommes

Celery and Apple Soup

5 tablespoons cold-pressed safflower oil
2 large celery stalks, sliced
1 medium-size yellow onion, sliced
1 medium-size carrot, sliced
6 medium-size unpeeled apples, cored and sliced

2 cups Soy-Vegetable Stock (p. 262)
1 teaspoon Marmite (brewers' yeast extract)
Herb salt
A little stone-ground whole-wheat pastry flour
Mornay Toast triangles (p. 259)

In a deep heavy pan combine 3 tablespoons safflower oil, the celery, onion, and carrot, and cook over moderate heat for 4 or 5 minutes. Set aside 6 nice apple slices for garnish, and add the rest of the apples to the pan. Cook the mixture over high heat until the apples are soft. Add the soy stock and Marmite yeast extract, season with a little herb salt, and bring the mixture to a boil. Reduce the heat and cook until all of the vegetables are soft. Rub the mixture through a fine vegetable strainer, return it to the pan, adjust the seasoning with herb salt, and reheat for serving.

Dust the reserved slices of apple with whole-wheat flour. Heat remaining 2 tablespoons of safflower oil in a sauté pan and brown the apple slices on each side in the hot oil.

PRESENTATION. Garnish each serving of soup with a sautéed apple ring. (If you do not wish to make the apple rings, the soup is very good garnished with a dollop of raw sour cream.) Serve with a plate of Mornay Toast triangles.

4 to 6 servings

Note: This soup freezes well. Pour it into a plastic container with a tight lid and freeze. When the soup is to be served, thaw it a little; then transfer it to a heavy pan, cover, and heat it slowly, stirring occasionally.

Bisque des Crevettes

Shrimp Bisque

1 pound fish bones or head
1 cup dry white wine, or additional water
2 quarts water
Herb salt
1 pound raw shrimps, in the shells, wrapped in cheesecloth
1 medium-size carrot, sliced
1 yellow onion, sliced
½ teaspoon finely chopped fresh garlic
4 tablespoons stone-ground whole-wheat pastry flour

8 tablespoons cold-pressed safflower oil
1 tablespoon natural tomato paste
½ cup raw light cream
1 bay leaf
1 tablespoon chopped fresh parsley
Bowl of fried stone-ground whole-wheat Croutons (p. 258)

Combine the fish bones or head, wine, water, and ½ teaspoon herb salt in a deep heavy pan, and bring it to a boil. Add the shrimps, carrot, onion, and garlic. Simmer until the shrimps are just pink and remove them at once. Continue to boil the liquid in which the shrimps were cooked until it is reduced to about 6 cups. Strain and return it to the pan.

Blend the flour with 2 tablespoons of the safflower oil and stir it into the stock. Add the tomato paste, cream, and bay leaf. Season with herb salt, if necessary, and bring the mixture to a boil. Reduce the heat and simmer for 5 minutes. Remove the bay leaf.

Cut the feet and tails from the shrimps but keep the shells on. Reserve 3 or 4 shrimps for garnish and coarsely chop the rest of the shrimp. Place the chopped shrimps and shells in a blender container with remaining 6 tablespoons safflower oil and blend to a smooth purée. If the mixture becomes too thick to blend, add a little of the soup mixture. Rub the puréed shrimps through a fine vegetable strainer. Over low heat, stir the strained shrimp purée into the soup, bit by bit. Adjust the seasoning with herb salt.

PRESENTATION. Shell and devein the reserved shrimps. Chop them finely, and add to the bisque with the chopped parsley. Serve with a separate bowl of fried whole-wheat croutons.

4 to 6 servings

Note: This bisque will keep well in the refrigerator for about a week.

Potage des Marrons et Gourds

Purée of Chestnut and Squash Soup

2 medium-size acorn squashes
4 tablespoons cold-pressed safflower oil
1 small yellow onion, sliced
1 medium-size carrot, sliced
1 celery stalk, sliced
   Herb salt
3 cups Soy-Vegetable Stock (p. 262), using the water in which the squashes were cooked

1 cup Chestnut Purée (p. 192), or unflavored natural canned chestnut purée
½ cup raw light sweet cream or raw sour cream
2 tablespoons chopped fresh parsley
   Toasted triangles of stone-ground whole-wheat bread (p. 259)

Cut the acorn squashes into quarters, remove the seeds, and cook them in boiling salted water until they are soft. Drain, and reserve the water for the soy stock. Remove the skins from the squashes, and set them aside.

Combine the following ingredients in a deep heavy pan: safflower oil, onion, carrot, and celery; season with herb salt to taste. Cook the vegetables over moderate heat for 5 minutes. Add the soy stock and simmer until vegetables are soft. Stir in chestnut purée and cooked squash; rub the mixture through a fine vegetable strainer or purée it in an electric blender. Return the puréed soup to the pan, stir in the cream and parsley, adjust the seasoning with herb salt, and gently reheat the soup. If the soup is too thick (depending on the size of the squashes), thin it with more stock or cream.

PRESENTATION. Serve the soup with a plate of toasted whole-wheat bread triangles. Garnish with a dollop of sour cream, if you like.

4 to 6 servings

Note: This soup freezes well. After adding the cream and parsley, pour the soup into a plastic container with a tight lid and freeze. When the soup is to be served, thaw it a little; then transfer it to a heavy pan, cover, and heat it slowly, stirring occasionally.

Potage Soissonnaise

Chick-pea or Garbanzo Soup

Soybeans or pinto beans can be substituted for the chick-peas to give a tasty and nutritious variation.

1 pound dried chick-peas
  Juice of 1 lemon
4 tablespoons cold-pressed safflower oil
1 medium-size yellow onion, sliced
1 large carrot, sliced
1 large celery stalk, sliced
  Herb salt
1 cup Soy Stock (p. 262) using the water in which the chick-peas were soaked

2 cups raw milk
  Yolks of 2 organic eggs
½ cup raw heavy sweet cream, or raw sour cream
½ cup fresh parsley or chervil, or scallions, finely chopped
1 cup fried stone-ground whole-wheat Croutons (p. 258)

Soak the chick-peas in water with the lemon juice overnight or for at least 12 hours.

Combine the following ingredients in a deep heavy pan: the safflower oil, soaked chick-peas and soaking water, the onion, carrot, and celery. Season with herb salt to taste. Cover with additional cold water to about 1 inch above the vegetables. Bring the water slowly to a boil, cover the pan, and simmer until the chick-peas are soft. Do not drain, but rub the whole mixture through a fine vegetable strainer, or purée it in an electric blender. Return the soup to the cooking pan. Add the soy stock and milk, and adjust the seasoning with herb salt. Bring it slowly to a boil, stirring constantly.

PRESENTATION. Mix the egg yolks and cream in the bottom of a warm tureen or casserole. Slowly stir in the hot soup. Scatter the chopped herbs on top of the soup. Serve with a bowl of fried whole-wheat croutons.

6 to 8 servings

Note: This soup freezes well. Prepare it through the step of adding the stock and milk. Pour it into a plastic container with a tight lid, and freeze. When the soup is to be served, thaw it a little; then transfer it to a heavy pan, cover, and heat it slowly, stirring occasionally. When the soup is entirely melted, stir it into the egg-yolk mixture.

This soup can become a substantial main course by adding more fish and potato for each serving.

Soupe aux Poissons de la Loire

Fish Soup in the Manner of the Loire Region

2 *pounds fish bones and heads*	2 *shallots, finely chopped*
3 *cups water*	½ *teaspoon finely chopped fresh*
1½ *cups dry white wine, or*	*garlic*
additional water	*Herb salt*
½ *teaspoon dried thyme*	8 *baby or 4 medium-size potatoes,*
1 *bay leaf*	*neatly peeled*
2 *sprigs of fresh parsley*	8 *pieces of fish, two for each*
2 *tablespoons cold-pressed*	*individual serving (haddock,*
safflower oil	*whiting, or red mullet)*
1 *medium-size carrot, finely sliced*	*Toasted triangles of stone-*
2 *large leeks, well washed and*	*ground whole-wheat bread*
finely sliced	*(p. 259)*

Prepare a good fish stock: Place fish bones and heads in a pan. Add the water, wine, thyme, bay leaf, and parsley. Bring the ingredients to a boil, reduce the heat, and allow to simmer gently for 45 minutes.

Heat the safflower oil in a deep heavy pan. Add the carrot, leeks, shallots, and garlic. Season with herb salt. Cook the vegetables for a few minutes without browning. Strain the fish stock into the vegetable mixture. Add the potatoes. Bring the soup to a boil, cover, and cook over low heat until the potatoes are just tender. Add the pieces of fish, and simmer the soup uncovered for about 5 minutes, until the fish flesh just turns white and firm. Adjust the seasoning, if necessary, with herb salt.

PRESENTATION. Serve 2 pieces of fish and 2 baby potatoes with each portion. Accompany the soup with a plate of toasted stone-ground whole-wheat bread.

4 servings

Fruit Soup, Hot or Cold

2½ cups natural red fruit juice (cherry, strawberry, raspberry, etc. Good-quality bottled fruit juices are available in natural-food stores.)

¼ cup fresh lemon juice

2 teaspoons potato flour

1 to 2 teaspoons natural currant jelly

1 tablespoon shredded orange rind

1 tablespoon shredded grapefruit rind

Skinned sections of 1 grapefruit

Skinned sections of 2 oranges

1 cup sliced fresh strawberries, or whole raspberries

½ cup sweet sherry or Marsala wine

Pour the fruit juice and lemon juice into a deep heavy pan. In a small bowl, mix the potato flour with ¼ cup of cold water. Off the heat stir the potato-flour mixture into the fruit juice. Add the currant jelly and the shredded orange and grapefruit rinds. Place the pan over moderate heat and bring the mixture to a boil, stirring all the while. Remove the pan from the heat and add the orange and grapefruit sections, the berries, and the wine.

PRESENTATION. Serve hot, or chill and serve over crushed ice.

4 to 6 servings

Potage des Lentilles

Purée of Lentil Soup

1½ cups dried lentils

1 lemon slice

4 tablespoons cold-pressed safflower oil

2 medium-size yellow onions, finely chopped

1 teaspoon finely chopped fresh garlic

3½ cups Soy Stock (p. 262), using the water in which the lentils were soaked

¼ cup dry white wine, or additional stock

¼ cup Madeira wine, or additional stock

1 small bay leaf

1 small white onion stuck with 2 whole cloves

¼ cup raw light cream

Yolks of 2 organic eggs

2 tablespoons dry sherry

¼ cup raw heavy cream or raw sour cream

1 cup fried stone-ground whole-wheat Croutons (p. 258)

Soak the lentils in water with the lemon slice in it overnight, or for at least 12 hours.

Combine the safflower oil, chopped onions, and garlic in a deep heavy pan and cook slowly for 2 or 3 minutes without browning. Add the lentils, the soy stock, white wine, and Madeira. Bring the soup to a boil. Add the bay leaf and the onion stuck with cloves. Cover the pan, reduce the heat, and allow the soup to simmer gently until the lentils are soft.

Rub the soup through a fine vegetable strainer, or purée it in an electric blender. Return the soup to the pan and stir in the light cream. Reheat the soup gently.

PRESENTATION. In the bottom of a warm tureen or casserole, mix the egg yolks, dry sherry, and heavy or sour cream. Slowly pour the hot soup into the yolk mixture, stirring all the time. Serve with a bowl of whole-wheat croutons.

4 to 6 servings

Note: This soup freezes well. Prepare it through the step of adding the light cream. Pour it into a plastic container with a tight-fitting lid and freeze. When the soup is to be served, thaw it a little; then transfer it to a heavy pan, cover, and heat it slowly, stirring occasionally. When it is entirely melted, stir it into the egg-yolk mixture.

Crème Olga

Raw Mushroom and Scallion Soup

4 tablespoons cold-pressed safflower oil
2 bunches (about 24) of scallions, chopped
½ teaspoon finely chopped fresh garlic
4 tablespoons stone-ground whole-wheat pastry flour
3 cups Light Soy Stock (p. 262)
Herb salt

2 cups chopped fresh mushrooms, not too firmly packed
½ cup raw light cream
1 tablespoon finely chopped fresh tarragon or chives
½ cup raw heavy sweet cream, whipped, or raw sour cream

Combine the safflower oil, scallions, and garlic in a deep heavy pan, and cook slowly until the scallions are soft but not browned. Off the heat blend in the flour and stir in the stock. Set the pan over moderate heat and stir until the soup comes to a boil. Season with herb salt to taste, reduce the heat, and allow to simmer gently for a few minutes. Add the chopped mushrooms. Rub the mixture through a fine vegetable strainer, or purée it in a blender.

Return the soup to the pan and stir in the light cream and tarragon or chives. Adjust the seasoning with herb salt and gently reheat for serving.

PRESENTATION. Serve in individual cream-soup bowls. Garnish each serving with a dollop of whipped or sour cream.

4 to 6 servings

Soupe aux Noix

Nut Soup

3 cups Soy Stock (p. 262)
1 tablespoon cold-pressed safflower oil
2 tablespoons stone-ground whole-wheat pastry flour
Yolks of 2 organic eggs
Herb salt

1 cup shelled organic English or black walnuts, very finely chopped, almost to a meal texture
4 tablespoons raw sour cream
2 teaspoons chopped fresh tarragon, or 2 tablespoons chopped fresh parsley

Pour the stock into a deep heavy pan and bring it to a boil. Remove it from the heat. Blend the safflower oil with the flour and add it, bit by bit, to the hot stock, stirring all the while. In a small bowl mix the egg yolks with 2 or 3 tablespoons of the hot stock. Pour the egg-yolk mixture into the soup in the pan, still off the heat. Season with herb salt to taste. Add the chopped nuts and stir in the sour cream.

Reheat the soup for serving over very low heat; do not allow it to boil or it will separate.

PRESENTATION. Garnish the soup with chopped tarragon or parsley.

4 to 6 servings

Soupe aux Oignons au Gratin
Onion Soup

4 tablespoons cold-pressed safflower oil
6 medium-size yellow onions, finely sliced
Herb salt
½ teaspoon dry mustard
½ teaspoon potato flour
2½ cups Soy-Vegetable Stock (p. 262)

1 cup dry white wine, or additional stock
6 tablespoons freshly grated Gruyère or Swiss-type natural cheese
4 tablespoons freshly grated Parmesan cheese
8 to 12 triangles of Mornay Toast (p. 259)

Heat the safflower oil in a deep heavy pan. Add the onions, herb salt to taste, and dry mustard, and cook slowly, stirring occasionally, until the onions are golden brown. This may require about 30 minutes. Off the heat blend in the flour. Stir in the stock and wine. Return the pan to moderate heat and bring the soup to a boil. Reduce the heat and allow the soup to simmer gently for 25 minutes. Adjust the seasoning, if necessary, with herb salt.

PRESENTATION. Serve the soup in individual earthenware bowls. Sprinkle the top with grated Gruyère or Swiss-type cheese and Parmesan cheese, and brown it quickly under the broiler. Serve with a plate of Mornay Toast.

4 to 6 servings

Potage Paysanne
Peasant Soup

This soup uses up all remnants of lettuces, parsley, celery leaf, watercress, spinach—any leaf greens. They are added after the soup base has been cooked; therefore, except for warming the soup, the greens are never cooked and the maximum nutritive values are preserved. With a salad and a bowl of whole-wheat croutons, this soup can be an excellent meal in itself.

4 *large potatoes*
3 *large yellow onions*
3 *large celery stalks*
4 *cups water*
½ *teaspoon sea salt*
1 *teaspoon herb salt*
4 *tablespoons cold-pressed virgin*
   olive oil
6 *tablespoons cold-pressed*
   safflower oil

1 *pound fresh spinach, well washed,*
   or any mixture of leftover
   spinach, lettuces, parsley, celery
   leaf, watercress, etc.
1 *cup raw light sweet cream or*
   raw sour cream
1 *cup fried stone-ground whole-*
   wheat Croutons (p. 258)

Peel and slice the potatoes and onions. Slice the celery. Place all of these vegetables in a heavy pan with the water, sea salt, herb salt, olive oil, and safflower oil. Cover the pan and slowly cook the vegetables until they are soft. Remove the pan from the heat and stir in the leaf vegetables, allowing them to wilt in the hot soup mixture. Rub the soup through a fine vegetable strainer. Return the strained soup to the pan, add the cream, and adjust the seasoning with herb salt.

PRESENTATION. Serve with a separate bowl of whole-wheat croutons.

6 to 8 servings

Note: This soup freezes well. Pour it into plastic containers with tight-fitting lids, and freeze. When the soup is to be served, thaw it a little; then transfer it to a heavy pan, cover, and heat it slowly, stirring occasionally. Prepare the garnish and serve.

Soupe au Pistou

Provençal
Vegetable Soup
with Basil and
Parmesan Cheese

1 *pound green beans, cut into*
   1-inch chunks
2 *medium-size yellow onions,*
   chopped
2 *large potatoes, peeled and diced*
3 *large ripe tomatoes, peeled,*
   seeded, and chopped
1 *cup dried white beans or chick-*
   peas, plain-cooked
2 *quarts Soy-Vegetable Stock*
   (p. 262), more if necessary

1 *pound small unpeeled zucchini,*
   cut into ½-inch-thick slices
½ *cup whole-wheat vermicelli,*
   broken into small pieces
1 *cup packed fresh basil leaves*
½ *cup freshly grated Parmesan*
   cheese
½ *cup cold-pressed virgin olive oil*
2 *teaspoons finely chopped fresh*
   garlic
Herb salt

In a large deep heavy pan combine the green beans, onions, potatoes, tomatoes, cooked white beans or chick-peas, and the stock. Bring the soup to a boil and allow it to simmer over low heat until the green beans and potatoes are just tender. Add the zucchini and vermicelli and cook for another 10 minutes.

Combine the basil leaves, Parmesan cheese, olive oil, and garlic in a blender and blend to a smooth paste. Stir this paste into the soup, little by little. Adjust the seasoning with herb salt to taste.

PRESENTATION. To serve, warm the soup but do not allow it to cook for any length of time.

8 to 10 servings

Note: Preferably, soak the beans or chick-peas and plain-cook them the day before; the alternative is to use natural canned white beans or chick-peas.

This soup will keep very well in the refrigerator for about 1 week.

Le Pot-au-Feu

Broth with Chicken and Vegetables

1 whole chicken, including giblets
1 pound chicken backs and/or wings
1½ pounds beef flank (optional)
2 or 3 veal bones
2 medium-size yellow onions, sliced
1 very small white or green cabbage, cut into quarters and tied in a cheesecloth
1 large leek, sliced
2 medium-size carrots, sliced
Few mushrooms
1 large celery stalk, sliced

Few tomato skins or slices of tomato
Bouquet of herbs tied in a cheesecloth: 1 bay leaf, few sprigs of parsley, celery leaf, and any other fresh herbs on hand, plus 2 whole cloves and 1 garlic clove
Herb salt

GARNISH
2 large potatoes, peeled
4 large carrots, scraped
Sea salt
½ cup freshly grated horseradish

Truss the chicken and place it in a large heavy pot with the giblets, the chicken backs and/or wings, the beef if used, and the veal bones. Cover with cold water, 5 to 6 quarts, and bring it to a boil slowly. Turn off the heat and skim off the scum from the top of the water. Add to the pot the onions, cabbage, leek, carrots, mushrooms, celery, tomato, bouquet of herbs, and 1 tablespoon herb salt. Bring the stock to a boil again, reduce the heat to a bare simmer, and allow it to cook for 2 to 3 hours. After 30 minutes, remove the whole chicken and set it aside. When the cabbage is tender, remove it from the pan.

After the stock has simmered, adjust the seasoning with more herb salt, if necessary. Line a colander with a damp cloth, set it over a large bowl, and strain the stock through it. Remove the piece of beef. Remove the meat from the chicken wings and backs, if any (it can be used for salads or stuffed crêpes). Pour the strained stock into plastic containers, cover with tight-fitting lids, and let stock chill in the refrigerator or the freezer. When it has set, remove the fat that has solidified on the top. (You now have good all-purpose chicken stock which can be frozen and used when desired.)

GARNISH. Cut the potatoes and carrots into olive-shape chunks. Place them in a pan, cover with water, season with a little sea salt, and boil until the vegetables are just soft.

PRESENTATION. Warm the chicken, beef, cabbage, and potato and carrot chunks in some of the stock in a casserole. Carve the chicken and the meat and arrange it on a warm platter with the vegetables. Spoon over a little warm stock. Serve meat and vegetables with individual cups of warm stock, and with condiment dishes of sea salt and freshly grated horseradish. (The *cornichons* and Dijon mustard, traditionally served with the *pot-au-feu,* are avoided in the natural-food version.)
Approximately 4 quarts stock; 4 to 6 servings

Potage Parmentier à la Julienne

Potato Soup with Julienne Vegetables

6 tablespoons cold-pressed safflower oil
5 large potatoes, peeled and sliced
1 large yellow onion, finely chopped
Herb salt
3 cups Vegetable Stock (p. 261) or plain water
2 medium-size carrots, scraped
2 large leeks
1 small Boston lettuce
Yolks of 2 organic eggs
¼ cup chopped fresh chervil or parsley

Heat 3 tablespoons safflower oil in a deep heavy pan. Add the potatoes and onion, season with a little herb salt, and stir over high heat for 2 or 3 minutes. Add 1½ cups vegetable stock or plain water, cover the pan, and cook very slowly until the potatoes are soft. Rub the mixture through a fine vegetable strainer. If the strained purée is too thick, add more water to bring it to a thick soup consistency.

Prepare the following julienne: Cut the carrots and white part of the leeks into matchstick shape. Cut the lettuce into fine shreds. Heat remaining 3 tablespoons safflower oil in a sauté pan. Add the vegetables with a little herb salt. Cover the pan and cook very slowly until the vegetables are quite soft. Mix these vegetables into the purée. In a small bowl mix the egg yolks with 3 tablespoons water. Pour a little of the soup into the yolks; then pour the yolk mixture into the soup, stirring all the while. Adjust the seasoning with herb salt.

PRESENTATION. To serve, gently reheat the soup, but do not let it boil or it will separate. Sprinkle the chopped chervil or parsley on top of the soup and serve.
6 to 8 servings

Potage Crème de Tomate

Cream of Tomato Soup

6 tablespoons cold-pressed safflower oil
1 medium-size yellow onion, finely chopped
½ teaspoon finely chopped fresh garlic
5 medium-size ripe tomatoes, sliced, with skins on
2 tablespoons natural tomato paste

2 tablespoons stone-ground whole-wheat pastry flour
2 cups Soy-Vegetable Stock (p. 262)
¾ cup raw light cream
Herb salt
2 tablespoons chopped fresh chives or parsley
1 medium-size ripe tomato, skinned, seeded, and shredded

Heat 4 tablespoons safflower oil in a deep heavy pan. Add the onion and garlic and cook over low heat for 1 minute. Add the sliced tomatoes and cook briskly for 5 minutes. Mix the tomato paste and flour with remaining 2 tablespoons safflower oil; off the heat, blend it into the tomatoes. Stir in the stock. Return the pan to moderate heat and stir until the soup comes to a boil.

Rub the soup through a fine vegetable strainer. Return it to the pan and simmer gently for 15 minutes. Stir in the light cream, adjust the seasoning with herb salt, and gently reheat.

PRESENTATION. Stir the chopped chives and shredded tomato into the hot soup and serve.

4 to 6 servings

Note: This soup freezes well. Pour it into a plastic container with a tight-fitting lid and freeze. When the soup is to be served, thaw it a little; then transfer it to a heavy pan, cover, and slowly heat, stirring occasionally. Mix in the chives and shredded tomato garnish and serve.

Crème Aurore

Cream of Tomato and Potato Soup

6 tablespoons cold-pressed safflower oil
4 large potatoes, peeled and sliced
2 medium-size yellow onions, sliced
1 teaspoon finely chopped fresh garlic
1 cup water
1 cup raw milk

Herb salt
1 pound ripe tomatoes, sliced, with skins on
3 tablespoons natural tomato paste
¼ teaspoon dried sage, pulverized
¼ cup raw light cream
2 teaspoons chopped fresh parsley

Heat 2 tablespoons safflower oil in a deep heavy pan. Add the potatoes, half of the sliced onions, the garlic, 1 cup of water, and the milk. Season with herb salt to taste. Cover the pan and cook over low heat until the potatoes are soft. Set the potato mixture aside.

Heat remaining 4 tablespoons safflower oil in a sauté pan. Add the tomatoes, tomato paste, the rest of the onions, the sage, and herb salt to taste. Mix well, and allow to cook slowly for 10 to 12 minutes. Combine the tomato mixture with the potato mixture.

Rub the soup through a fine vegetable strainer. Return the soup to the pan and add enough light cream to reduce the soup to a thick creamy consistency. Adjust the seasoning with herb salt.

PRESENTATION. Reheat the soup gently to serve. Sprinkle the parsley on the top.

4 to 6 servings

Note: This soup freezes well. Pour it into a plastic container with a tight-fitting lid and freeze. When the soup is to be served, thaw it a little; then transfer it to a heavy pan, cover, and slowly heat, stirring occasionally.

Soupe aux Légumes

Vegetable Garden Soup

5 tablespoons cold-pressed safflower oil, or cold-pressed virgin olive oil

2 medium-size yellow onions, finely sliced

2 medium-size carrots, shredded

1 large celery stalk, finely sliced

2 medium-size turnips, shredded (if available)

2 medium-size parsnips, shredded (if available) , or 2 potatoes, peeled and cubed

1 cup diced green beans

6 cups Soy-Vegetable Stock (p. 262) , or Vegetable Stock (p. 261)

½ cup whole-wheat vermicelli, broken into small pieces

Herb salt

½ cup shelled garden peas (optional)

Sea salt

1 cup coarsely chopped spinach leaves

3 medium-size ripe tomatoes, skinned and sliced

½ pound skinny zucchini, cut into ½-inch slices

Heat the oil in a deep heavy pan and add the onions, carrots, celery, turnips, and parsnips or potatoes. Cook these vegetables for a few minutes; then add the green beans. Cook the vegetables for another 5 minutes. Add the stock and vermicelli, and season with herb salt to taste. Reduce the heat and cook slowly until the vegetables are tender but still crisp.

If you are using fresh garden peas, place them in a small pan with ¼ teaspoon sea salt, and cover with water. Bring the water to a boil and cook until the peas are tender. Drain and add them to the soup with the spinach, tomatoes, and zucchini. Continue cooking the soup over very low heat for another 10 to 15 minutes. Adjust the seasoning with herb salt.

6 to 8 servings

Note: This soup will keep very well in the refrigerator for about 1 week.

Potage Cressonnière

Watercress and Potato Soup

2 tablespoons cold-pressed safflower oil
4 large potatoes, peeled and sliced
2 medium-size yellow onions, skinned and sliced
2 cups water

Herb salt
2 bunches of watercress
1 cup raw milk
¾ cup raw light cream
1½ cups fried stone-ground whole-wheat Croutons (p. 258)

Heat the safflower oil in a deep heavy pan and add the potatoes, onions, and water. Season with herb salt to taste. Cover the pan and cook slowly until the potatoes are soft. Carefully remove the leaves from 1 bunch of watercress and set them aside. Add the remaining stems plus the leaves and stems of the second bunch of watercress to the potato mixture. Rub the potato and watercress mixture through a fine vegetable strainer.

Return the soup to the pan and add the milk and the cream. Adjust the seasoning with herb salt. Reheat. Add the reserved watercress leaves. Serve with a separate bowl of stone-ground whole-wheat croutons.

4 to 6 servings

Note: This soup freezes well. Pour it into a plastic container with a tight-fitting lid and freeze. When the soup is to be served, thaw it a little; then transfer it to a heavy pan, cover, and heat it slowly, stirring occasionally.

Crème des Asperges Glacée

Cold Cream of Asparagus Soup

18 stalks of asparagus, ½ inch in diameter
Sea salt
2 cups water
Handful of spinach, well washed
1 bunch of scallions (about 12)
2 tablespoons cold-pressed safflower oil

Herb salt
4 tablespoons rice flour
1 cup raw light cream, or 1 cup yogurt mixed with ¼ cup nonfat dry milk

Cut the small tips from the asparagus. Place the tips in a pan with ¼ teaspoon sea salt and cover them with 2 cups water. Bring the water to a boil slowly. As soon as the water boils, drain it from the asparagus tips over the spinach. Set the asparagus tips aside to cool. Allow the spinach to stay in the hot water for 4 to 5 minutes, until it is wilted. Drain the water from the spinach and reserve it. Chop the spinach roughly. Slice the scallions coarsely.

Heat the safflower oil in a deep heavy pan. Add the scallions, season with a little herb salt, and cook over low heat for 1 or 2 minutes. Cut the asparagus _spears_ into chunks and add them to the scallions with ½ cup of the reserved spinach water. Cover and cook slowly until the asparagus chunks are nearly soft. Remove the pan from the heat and blend in the rice flour. Add the rest of the water from the spinach. Return the pan to moderate heat and stir until the soup comes to a boil. Rub the soup through a fine vegetable strainer. If the soup is too thick, a little more water may be added. Adjust the seasoning with herb salt. Set the soup in the refrigerator to chill thoroughly.

PRESENTATION. At serving time, stir in the light cream, or yogurt and dry-milk mixture. Gently mix in the reserved asparagus *tips,* saving 6. Serve the soup in small bowls surrounded with crushed ice. Place 1 asparagus tip in the center of each bowl.

4 to 6 servings

Soupe d'Avocat
Avocado Soup

2 medium-size ripe avocados
2 small white onions, chopped
½ cup raw heavy cream
1 cup Soy-Vegetable Stock (*p. 262*)
½ cup raw light cream, or ½ cup yogurt mixed with 2 table- spoons nonfat dry milk

Herb salt
2 teaspoons finely chopped fresh chives, or grated lime rind

Combine the avocados, onions, and heavy cream in a blender container and blend to a smooth purée. Add the stock, light cream or yogurt mixture, and a little herb salt, and blend again. Adjust the seasoning with herb salt and add more stock, light cream, or yogurt if the consistency is too thick. Chill the soup thoroughly.

PRESENTATION. Serve soup in small bowls over ice. Sprinkle the chives or grated lime rind over the top of each serving.

4 servings

Gazpacho
Andalusian Salad Soup

6 large ripe tomatoes, skinned
2 medium-size cucumbers, peeled, seeded, and finely chopped
½ cup finely chopped yellow, red, or Bermuda onion
1 teaspoon finely chopped fresh garlic
½ cup finely chopped green or red sweet bell pepper

Additional natural tomato juice, as required to thin the soup
⅓ cup cold-pressed virgin olive oil
3 tablespoons fresh lemon juice
½ teaspoon dry mustard
½ cup chopped fresh parsley
1 teaspoon sea salt
Herb salt
Mornay Toast (*p. 259, optional*)

Seed the tomatoes and chop the pulp finely. Rub the seed sections through a fine vegetable strainer and set aside the juice.

(cont.)

Combine in a large bowl the chopped tomato pulp, cucumbers, onion, garlic, and pepper. Mix the fresh tomato juice with the canned natural tomato juice to make 3 cups and add it to the vegetables. Add the olive oil, lemon juice, dry mustard, parsley, sea salt, and herb salt to taste. Mix well. Allow the soup to marinate and chill thoroughly, ideally at least 24 hours.

PRESENTATION. Serve in chilled bowls surrounded by crushed ice, with a plate of Mornay toast.

6 to 8 servings

Note: Gazpacho will keep in the refrigerator for at least 1 week, possibly longer. It seems to improve day by day.

Consommé à la Madrilène

Jellied Tomato Consommé

Whites of 3 organic eggs
5 cups Soy-Vegetable Stock (p. 262)
4 tablespoons natural tomato paste
4 medium-size ripe tomatoes, sliced but not skinned
¼ cup dry sherry, or additional stock

1 tablespoon raw sugar
4 tablespoons unflavored gelatin
2 medium-size firm ripe tomatoes, skinned, seeded, and finely shredded or diced
1 tablespoon mixed finely chopped tarragon and parsley

Beat the egg whites to soft peaks. Combine the stock, tomato paste, sliced tomatoes, sherry, sugar, stiffly beaten egg whites, and the gelatin in a pan. Set the pan over moderate heat and stir the mixture with a wire whisk until it comes to a boil. Remove the pan from the heat and let it sit without moving for 15 minutes.

Line a colander with a damp cloth and strain the stock through it. Return the clarified stock (consommé) to a clean pan, add the shredded tomatoes, and reheat for 1 or 2 minutes. Pour the consommé into a serving dish and let it chill until it is set.

PRESENTATION. Set the serving dish over crushed ice. Sprinkle fresh tarragon and parsley over the top.

4 servings

Vichyssoise

Cold Leek and Potato Soup

4 large leeks, well cleaned and sliced
4 large potatoes, peeled and sliced
1 large celery stalk, sliced
1 Bermuda onion, sliced
3 cups light soy stock (p. 262)

1 to 2 cups raw light cream, or 1 to 2 cups yogurt mixed with ½ cup nonfat dry milk per cup
Herb salt
2 tablespoons chopped fresh chives

Place the leeks, potatoes, celery, and onion in a deep heavy pan with the soy stock. Cover the pan and cook slowly until the vegetables are soft. Rub the soup through a fine vegetable strainer. Thin it to a thick cream consistency with the light cream or yogurt mixture. Adjust the seasoning with herb salt.

PRESENTATION. Serve the soup in individual bowls surrounded by crushed ice. Sprinkle chopped chives over the top.

4 to 6 servings

Main-Course Dishes

Perhaps the most unorthodox chapter in our cookbook is this one, a master chapter on main-course dishes subdivided by types of foods:

Vegetables
Fish and Shellfish
Poultry and Meat
Eggs
Grain, Pasta, and Savory Pastry

Our purpose is to make menu planning easier, especially in organizing a greater frequency of no-meat meals.

As the sample menus demonstrate, it is possible to create a variety of "gourmet-quality" no-meat menus. The no-meat recipes in the Main-Course chapter are substantial dishes in themselves. In addition, delectable no-meat main courses can be a composition of simpler preparations; for example, a grain with two purées, or plain-cooked green beans with corn fritters, or refilled baked potatoes with broccoli polonaise. Good fresh vegetables, properly cooked and presented, and eaten without the competing taste of a meat, offer a taste experience of natural splendor. Happily, these no-meat dishes also enhance the libation of the juice of the vine.

VEGETABLES

At any season of the year there is a wide selection of beautiful vegetables from which to create a variety of main courses. The first requirement for giving vegetables "main-course" stature is that they must be properly cooked. To enjoy vegetables at their nutritional and palatable best, they should be "under-cooked," that is cooked just to the point of edibility. Remember that the vegetable will continue cooking in its own heat after it has been removed from the stove. Soggy vegetables provide one of the reasons many people dislike vegetables. Also, heat is destructive to some of the natural nutrients.

Other ways of capturing natural nutrients are through adjusting our cooking methods; for example:

1. Whenever possible, cook potatoes in their jackets to preserve the nutrients just under the skin. This includes preparing boiled potatoes for any purpose; skin them *after* they are cooked and save the cooking water for vegetable stock.

2. Boil garden peas with their pods. Our method is to shell the peas, tie the shelled peas in a cheesecloth, and cook peas with the empty pods in a large pot. The pods are then discarded, and the rich cooking water is stored in the vegetable-stock container in the refrigerator.

3. Save the water in which all vegetables are cooked. This is nutritious "vegetable stock" (see p. 261) which can be used in soup and sauce preparations.

Vegetable main-course dishes, like fish and meat main-course dishes, can be given attractive presentations at table. The fine art of French cooking includes a mastery of presentation, and here are just some of the possibilities:

• molded vegetable preparations;
• cut shapes, such as potatoes, carrots, and turnips cut into olive shapes; potato balls made with a melon scoop; julienne—fine shreds; matchstick—larger shreds; large and small dice;
• green beans or asparagus neatly arranged like piles of logs;
• eggplant, beets, zucchini cut into halves and scooped out to serve as cassolettes;
• vegetable soufflé preparations, hot and cold;
• crêpes stuffed with vegetable preparations;
• purées in various ways of serving—piped into rosette shapes, sometimes atop artichoke bottoms, shaped into croquettes—coated and deep-fried, or mounded into prepared vegetable cassolettes;
• tomatoes, peppers, onions, mushrooms, variously stuffed.

Céleri Provençale

Celery with Tomatoes, Olives, and Cheese

6 *hearts of celery, or 3 bunches cut below the leaves and split lengthwise*
Sea salt
4 *teaspoons fresh lemon juice*
Olive oil for pan

4 *large ripe tomatoes, skinned and thickly sliced*
12 *anchovy fillets*
4 *thin slices of natural Swiss-type cheese*
6 *pitted ripe olives*

(cont.)

SAUCE

½ teaspoon sea salt	1 teaspoon finely chopped fresh
½ teaspoon herb salt	garlic
1 tablespoon fresh lemon juice	1 tablespoon anchovy oil (from
½ cup cold-pressed virgin olive oil	anchovy tin)

Preheat the oven to 375°. Wash the celery and place it in a pan with 1 teaspoon sea salt and the lemon juice. Cover with water and bring it to a boil. Reduce to a simmer, cover the pan, and cook until the celery is nearly soft, but still firm. Drain it well between paper towels.

SAUCE. Combine all of the sauce ingredients in a screw-top jar and shake well.

Brush an au gratin dish with a little olive oil and arrange the sliced tomatoes in it. Lay the celery on top of the tomatoes. Lay the anchovies over the celery. Spoon the sauce over all. Cover the dish with slices of cheese. Bake in the preheated oven for 15 to 20 minutes.

PRESENTATION. When the celery is baked, scatter the black olives over the top and serve.

6 servings

Casserole d'Aubergines

Eggplant Casserole

3 small or 2 medium-size eggplants, peeled and cut into ½-inch-thick slices	1 tablespoon stone-ground whole-wheat pastry flour
Sea salt	2 tablespoons natural tomato paste
4 tablespoons cold-pressed safflower oil	½ teaspoon finely chopped fresh garlic
1 ounce dried mushrooms, soaked in a little water	Herb salt
3 medium-size ripe tomatoes, skinned and sliced	4 tablespoons freshly grated Parmesan cheese
	1 tablespoon cold-pressed safflower oil for topping

TOMATO SAUCE

1 tablespoon cold-pressed safflower oil

Place the eggplant slices in a large bowl, sprinkle them liberally with sea salt, and allow them to sit for at least 30 minutes. Rinse the slices in cold water and dry them between paper towels. Heat 4 tablespoons safflower oil in a sauté pan. Quickly brown the eggplant slices on each side, using more oil if necessary, and set them aside. Preheat the oven to 375°. Drain the soaked mushrooms. Chop them and quickly sauté them in the pan in which the eggplant was browned. Add the tomatoes and cook briskly for 4 or 5 minutes.

SAUCE. Heat 1 tablespoon safflower oil in a saucepan. Off the heat blend in the flour, tomato paste, garlic, and 1¼ cups water. Season with herb salt to taste. Bring the sauce to a boil, reduce the heat, and let it simmer for 2 or 3 minutes.

PRESENTATION. In a small casserole arrange a layer of half of the eggplant, half of the tomato sauce, and half of the mushroom and tomato mixture. Repeat the sequence for the second layer. Sprinkle grated cheese over the top and dot with 1 tablespoon safflower oil. Bake in the preheated oven for 20 minutes.

4 to 6 servings

---

2 *small eggplants*
  Sea salt
4 *tablespoons cold-pressed safflower*
  oil
1 *medium-size yellow onion, finely*
  chopped
2 *celery stalks, finely chopped*
2 *teaspoons finely chopped fresh*
  garlic
3 *fresh firm mushrooms, coarsely*
  chopped

  Herb salt
2 *medium-size ripe tomatoes,*
  skinned and coarsely chopped
2 *teaspoons natural tomato paste*
6 *tablespoons dry whole-wheat*
  Bread Crumbs (p. 258)
12 *finger-size pieces of natural*
  Swiss-type cheese
½ *cup freshly grated Parmesan*
  cheese

Aubergines à la Parisienne

Eggplant Stuffed with Mushrooms, Celery, and Tomatoes

Cut the eggplants lengthwise into halves. Slit them around the edge with a sharp knife, and cut them crisscross on top, but do not cut through the skin. Sprinkle the tops well with sea salt and let the eggplants sit for at least 30 minutes. Rinse them well in cold water and dry on paper towels.

Heat the safflower oil in a sauté pan. When it is quite hot, add the eggplants and cook them slowly, about 5 minutes or so on each side, until they are soft. Remove them from the pan and set aside to cool a little. Add to the pan in which the eggplants were cooked the onion, celery, garlic, and mushrooms, also adding a little more safflower oil, if necessary. Cook these vegetables slowly until they begin to brown a little. Season with herb salt to taste.

Carefully scoop the pulp out of the eggplants, without puncturing the skins. Chop the pulp and add it with the chopped tomatoes to the chopped vegetable mixture in the sauté pan. Season with herb salt to taste, and stir in the tomato paste and 2 tablespoons of the bread crumbs.

PRESENTATION. Fill the eggplant skins with the stuffing mixture. Sprinkle the tops with the remaining 4 tablespoons of the bread crumbs. Arrange 3 fingers of cheese on top of each eggplant and sprinkle with the grated cheese. Brown the eggplants under a broiler until the cheese begins to melt.

4 servings

Aubergine et Tomates Hollandaise

Eggplant and Tomatoes Hollandaise

Zucchini may be substituted for the eggplant.

1 large eggplant, or 6 small zucchini (about 1½ pounds)
Sea salt
8 tablespoons cold-pressed virgin olive oil
4 medium-size ripe tomatoes, skinned and sliced
1 medium-size yellow onion, finely chopped
1 teaspoon finely chopped fresh garlic
Herb salt

HOLLANDAISE SAUCE
Yolks of 2 organic eggs
Herb salt
2 tablespoons fresh lemon juice
2 tablespoons raw sour cream, or yogurt
8 tablespoons cold-pressed safflower oil
½ teaspoon natural tomato paste
½ teaspoon Marmite (brewers' yeast extract)

If you are using eggplant: Peel the eggplant, and cut it into strips about 1 inch wide, 3 inches long, and ½ inch thick. *If you are using zucchini:* Cut the zucchini into ½-inch-thick slices. Do not peel them. Place the strips of eggplant or zucchini in a large bowl, sprinkle them liberally with sea salt, and allow them to sit for at least 30 minutes. Rinse slices in cold water and dry between paper towels. Heat 4 tablespoons olive oil in a sauté pan. Quickly brown the eggplant or zucchini pieces on each side and set them aside.

Add 4 tablespoons olive oil to the pan, and stir in the tomatoes, onion, and garlic. Season the mixture with herb salt to taste, and cook briskly for 3 or 4 minutes.

HOLLANDAISE SAUCE. In a small bowl mix the egg yolks, ¼ teaspoon herb salt, the lemon juice, and the sour cream or yogurt. Set the bowl in a small sauté pan half-filled with hot water, over low heat. With a small wire whisk beat the egg-yolk mixture until it is thick. Very slowly add the safflower oil, beating constantly. Beat in the tomato paste and Marmite yeast extract. Remove the sauce from the heat, cover it with plastic wrap, and set it aside until you are ready to use it.

PRESENTATION. Combine the eggplant or zucchini with the tomato mixture and warm it over low heat for a few minutes, arrange the vegetables in a warm au gratin dish, and cover with the hollandaise sauce.

4 to 6 servings

Cold-pressed safflower oil for
    soufflé dish and collar
4 tablespoons cold-pressed safflower
    oil
1 cup thinly sliced firm fresh
    mushrooms
1 teaspoon fresh lemon juice
    Herb salt
3 tablespoons stone-ground whole-
    wheat pastry flour

Sea salt
¾ cup raw milk
    Yolks of 4 organic eggs
2 tablespoons freshly grated
    Parmesan cheese
    Whites of 5 organic eggs
    Canapé Sauce (p. 269, optional)

Soufflé des Champignons

Mushroom Soufflé

Preheat the oven to 350°. Lightly brush a 1-quart (No. 6) soufflé dish with safflower oil. Tear off a length of wax paper 1½ times the outer girth of the soufflé dish, fold it in half lengthwise, and brush it with safflower oil. Wrap the wax paper around the soufflé dish and tie it with kitchen string. Set the soufflé dish in a roasting pan and have a pan of hot water ready.

Heat 2 tablespoons safflower oil in a small sauté pan and briskly cook the sliced mushrooms with the lemon juice for 2 minutes. Season with herb salt to taste.

Heat 2 tablespoons safflower oil in a saucepan. Remove the pan from the heat and stir in the flour and ½ teaspoon sea salt. Add the milk, return the pan to low heat, and continue stirring until the sauce thickens. Remove the pan from the heat and mix in the mushrooms, egg yolks, and grated cheese. Beat the egg whites to soft peaks. Fold them lightly and smoothly into the egg-yolk mixture. Spoon the soufflé mixture into the prepared dish. Place dish in the roasting pan and half-fill pan with hot water. Set the soufflé dish in its water bath in the preheated oven and bake for 1 hour and 15 minutes, or until the top is firm to the touch.

PRESENTATION. When the soufflé is baked, carefully remove it from the oven and the water bath. Gently place the soufflé dish on a serving plate, remove the paper collar, and serve at once. Serve some of the top crust and the creamy center with each portion. Spoon a little canapé sauce on the side.

4 servings

Cold-pressed safflower oil for
    soufflé dish and collar
4 tablespoons cold-pressed
    safflower oil
1 large yellow onion, chopped
½ teaspoon finely chopped fresh
    garlic

    Herb salt
3 tablespoons stone-ground whole-
    wheat pastry flour
    Sea salt
½ teaspoon curry powder
¾ cup raw milk

Soufflé d'Oignon au Cari

Curried Onion Soufflé

(cont.)

2 tablespoons freshly grated Parmesan cheese	Whites of 5 organic eggs
Yolks of 4 organic eggs	Mornay Sauce (p. 268, optional)

Preheat the oven to 350°. Lightly brush a 1-quart (No. 6) soufflé dish with safflower oil. Tear off a length of wax paper 1½ times the outer girth of the soufflé dish, fold it in half lengthwise, and brush it with safflower oil. Wrap the wax paper around the soufflé dish and tie it with kitchen string. Set the soufflé dish in a roasting pan and have a pan of hot water ready.

Heat 2 tablespoons safflower oil in a small sauté pan. Add the onion and garlic, season with herb salt, and cook slowly until the onion is golden brown. Set the mixture aside for a moment.

Heat 2 tablespoons safflower oil in a saucepan. Off the heat blend in the flour, ½ teaspoon sea salt, the curry powder, and milk. Stir over moderate heat until the mixture thickens. Remove the pan from the heat and stir in the grated cheese, onion mixture, and egg yolks, and adjust the seasoning with sea salt. Beat the egg whites to soft peaks and fold them into the egg-yolk mixture. Spoon the soufflé mixture into the prepared dish. Place the dish in the roasting pan and half-fill the pan with hot water. Set the soufflé dish in its water bath in the preheated oven and bake for 1 hour and 15 minutes, or until the top is firm to the touch.

PRESENTATION. When the soufflé is baked, carefully remove it from the oven and the water bath. Gently place the soufflé dish on a serving plate, remove the paper collar, and serve immediately. Serve some of the top crust and creamy center with each portion. Spoon a little Mornay sauce on the side.

4 servings

Oignons Farcis aux Epinards, Sauce aux Champignons ou Hollandaise

---

Onions Stuffed with Spinach, Mushroom Sauce or Hollandaise

Large Bermuda onions prepared for stuffing in this manner may also be stuffed with a pilaff or with the tomato and eggplant mixture in the recipe for Eggplant and Tomatoes Hollandaise (p. 80). Hollandaise Sauce (pp. 268–269) may be substituted for the Mushroom Sauce.

6 Bermuda onions, about 3 inches in diameter	½ cup raw sour cream
Sea salt	¼ cup freshly grated natural Swiss-type cheese
Herb salt	¼ cup freshly grated Parmesan cheese
6 teaspoons plus 4 tablespoons cold-pressed safflower oil	Dry whole-wheat bread crumbs (p. 258)
1½ pounds spinach, well washed	Chopped fresh parsley
4 tablespoons stone-ground whole-wheat pastry flour	

MUSHROOM SAUCE
4 *firm fresh mushrooms, coarsely chopped*
1 *cup raw heavy cream*
2 *tablespoons cold-pressed safflower oil*

Herb salt
Yolk of 1 organic egg
1 *teaspoon potato flour*
1 *tablespoon Madeira wine, or 1 teaspoon natural guava jelly*

Skin the onions and place them in a pan with 1 teaspoon sea salt. Cover with water, and bring to a boil. Drain at once, and set the onions on paper towels to blot. Cut the onions horizontally into halves, and carefully remove the centers, leaving a shell of 3 outside skins. (The removed centers may be refrigerated and used in salads.) Season the inside of each onion shell with herb salt and ½ teaspoon safflower oil.

Place the spinach in a large pan with ½ cup water and 1 teaspoon sea salt. Cover the pan and cook until the spinach is just wilted, turning it once or twice. Drain it thoroughly, set it on a board, and chop finely. Heat 4 tablespoons safflower oil in a saucepan, stir in the flour, and cook slowly for a minute or two. Then mix in the spinach, sour cream, and herb salt to taste, and cook over low heat for 5 minutes. Fill the onion shells with this mixture and arrange them on a shallow heatproof serving dish.

MUSHROOM SAUCE. Purée the mushrooms in a blender with the heavy cream and 2 tablespoons safflower oil. Pour the mixture into a saucepan, season with herb salt to taste, and bring to a boil. Remove the pan from the heat. In a small bowl mix the egg yolk with the potato flour and Madeira wine. Stir in a little of the warm mushroom mixture, then pour the yolk mixture into the rest of the sauce. Stir the sauce over low heat until it thickens a little, but do not let it boil, or it will separate.

PRESENTATION. Pour half of the *mushroom sauce* over the onions, sprinkle the top with the grated Swiss-type cheese, then pour over the rest of the sauce. Sprinkle the tops with Parmesan cheese and bread crumbs, and dot with safflower oil. Brown the stuffed onions lightly under the broiler. Garnish with chopped fresh parsley. Serve with a pilaff (see pp. 168–169 and pp. 171–172) in a separate bowl.

If you are using hollandaise sauce, arrange the stuffed onions on a bed of the pilaff. Eliminate the cheese and crumb topping. Just sprinkle with chopped parsley, spoon hollandaise sauce over all, and pass briefly under a hot broiler to brown a little.

6 servings

Petits Pois Parisienne

Garden Peas with Lettuce and Scallions

2 to 3 pounds fresh garden peas, shelled (reserve the pods)
Sea salt
Bouquet of fresh herbs tied in cheesecloth (parsley, celery leaf, thyme, whatever is available)
1 Boston lettuce, cut into 8 sections

1 bunch of scallions, about 12, cut horizontally into halves
1 tablespoon raw sugar
Herb salt
3 tablespoons cold-pressed safflower oil
2 tablespoons stone-ground whole-wheat pastry flour

Tie the shelled peas in a cheesecloth and put them with the pods in a pan with 1 teaspoon sea salt and 3 or 4 cups water. Bring the water to a boil slowly and drain, reserving the peas and the cooking water and discarding the pods. Place the peas in a deep heavy pan and remove the cheesecloth. Add the bouquet of herbs, lettuce sections, scallions, 1 cup of the reserved cooking water, and the sugar; season with herb salt. Bring to a boil, cover the pan with a tight-fitting lid, and cook very slowly until the peas are tender. Remove the bouquet of herbs.

Blend the safflower oil and flour to a smooth paste and stir it into the peas bit by bit. Adjust the seasoning and serve.
4 servings
Note: The rest of the cooking water may be stored in the refrigerator for future use in soups and sauces.

Soufflé Froid des Petits Pois au Cari

Cold Peas with Curry Soufflé

2 pounds fresh garden peas, shelled, enough to supply 2 cups (reserve the pods)
Sea salt
1/2 cup Chestnut Purée (p. 192), or natural, unflavored canned purée
2 tablespoons cold-pressed safflower oil
2 tablespoons cold-pressed virgin olive oil
1/2 teaspoon finely chopped fresh garlic
1 tablespoon finely chopped yellow or white onion
1 tablespoon finely chopped celery
1 teaspoon Marmite (brewers' yeast extract)

1/2 teaspoon natural tomato paste
1 teaspoon curry powder
1 1/2 tablespoons unflavored gelatin mixed with 3 tablespoons stone-ground whole-wheat pastry flour
1 cup Soy Stock (p. 262), using cooking water from the peas
3 organic eggs, separated
3/4 cup raw sour cream or whole-milk yogurt
Cold-pressed safflower oil for soufflé collar
2 tablespoons chopped fresh chives
1/4 cup freshly grated Parmesan cheese

Tie the shelled peas in a cheesecloth and place them with the pods in a pan with 1 teaspoon sea salt. Cover with cold water and bring it to a boil. Cover the pan and cook until the peas are tender. Drain, reserving the cooking water for use as stock in soups or sauces. Discard the pods. Press the cooked peas through a fine vegetable strainer. Combine the pea purée and the chestnut purée in an electric mixer with 2 tablespoons safflower oil and beat until light and fluffy. Season with sea salt.

Heat the olive oil in a saucepan and add the garlic, onion, and celery. Cook over low heat for 2 or 3 minutes. Off the heat stir in the Marmite yeast extract, tomato paste, 1/2 teaspoon of the curry powder, and the mixed gelatin and flour. When the mixture is blended, stir in the soy stock. Return the pan to moderate heat and stir until the mixture comes to a boil. Pour it into a shallow plate to cool in the freezer. Mix it into the pea and chestnut purée. Beat the egg yolks into the mixture, one at at time. Adjust the seasoning with herb salt. Beat the egg whites to soft peaks and lightly and smoothly fold them into the pea and chestnut mixture. Fold in the sour cream or yogurt.

Tear off a length of wax paper 1 1/2 times the outer girth of a 1-quart No. 6 soufflé dish. Fold it in half lengthwise and brush it with safflower oil. Wrap the wax paper around the soufflé dish and tie it with kitchen string. Fill the dish with the soufflé mixture and put it in the refrigerator to set.

PRESENTATION. When the soufflé is set, carefully remove the paper collar. Stick the chopped chives around the side of the soufflé that rises above the dish. Mix the grated cheese with remaining 1/2 teaspoon curry powder and sprinkle it over the top. Store the soufflé in the refrigerator until serving time.

4 to 6 servings

This spinach ring may also be served without the mushrooms as a vegetable accompaniment.

Bordure d'Epinards aux Champignons

Spinach Ring with Mushrooms

SPINACH RING
- 2 *pounds spinach, well washed*
  Sea salt
- 3 *tablespoons cold-pressed safflower oil*
- 3 *tablespoons stone-ground whole-wheat pastry flour*
- 3/4 *cup raw milk*
  Herb salt
- 2 *whole organic eggs*
  White of 1 organic egg
  Cold-pressed safflower oil for ring mold

- 1 *cup raw sour cream, or 1 cup yogurt mixed with 1/4 cup nonfat dry milk*
- 1 *teaspoon finely chopped fresh garlic*

MUSHROOMS
- 2 *tablespoons cold-pressed safflower oil*
- 1/2 *pound firm fresh mushrooms (if large, cut them into halves or quarters)*
- 1 *teaspoon fresh lemon juice*
  Herb salt

SPINACH RING. Preheat the oven to 350°. Put the spinach in a pan and cook it with ½ cup water and 1 teaspoon sea salt, covered, until it is wilted. Drain it through a colander, pressing out all of the moisture with a small plate. Chop the spinach finely.

CREAM SAUCE. Heat the safflower oil in a saucepan. Off the heat blend in the flour and the milk. Season with herb salt, return the pan to moderate heat, and stir until the sauce comes to a boil. Beat the whole eggs and the extra egg white together and mix with the chopped spinach. Add the cream sauce to the spinach.

Brush a 1-quart ring mold with safflower oil and fill it with the spinach mixture. Set the filled mold in a roasting pan and pour hot water into the pan to about half the height of the mold. Set the mold in its water bath in the preheated oven and bake for 45 minutes, or until the spinach is set.

MUSHROOMS. Heat the safflower oil in a sauté pan and add the mushrooms, lemon juice, and a little herb salt. Cook briskly for 2 or 3 minutes only.

PRESENTATION. When the spinach ring is baked, remove it from the oven and let it stand for 5 minutes. Loosen the edges with a small sharp knife and turn it out onto a warm serving platter. Fill the center of the ring with the mushrooms. Mix the sour cream, or yogurt mixture, with the chopped garlic and season with herb salt. Serve this sauce in a separate bowl. Garnish each serving of spinach and mushrooms with a dollop of sauce.

4 to 6 servings

Crêpes aux Epinards, Sauce Mornay

Crêpes Stuffed with Spinach, Mornay Sauce

8 to 12 crêpes, about 6 inches
    in diameter (p. 232)

SPINACH FILLING
1 pound fresh spinach, well
    washed
4 tablespoons cold-pressed
    safflower oil
    Sea salt
6 ounces firm fresh mushrooms,
    coarsely chopped
1 teaspoon fresh lemon juice
    Herb salt
    Yolks of 4 organic eggs

½ cup natural ricotta cheese
½ teaspoon freshly grated nutmeg
½ teaspoon finely chopped fresh
    garlic
    Mornay Sauce (p. 268)

GARNISH
2 tablespoons dry whole-wheat
    Bread Crumbs (p. 258)
2 tablespoons freshly grated
    Parmesan cheese
1 tablespoon cold-pressed
    safflower oil

Prepare crêpes and pile them on a wire rack. Prepare Mornay sauce and set it aside until you are ready to use it.

SPINACH FILLING. Combine the spinach, 2 tablespoons safflower oil, ½ teaspoon sea salt, and 2 tablespoons water. Cook the spinach over high heat for 4 to 5 minutes, just until it wilts. Stir to turn it. Drain the spinach through a colander, pressing it dry with a small plate, and cool it a little. Chop the spinach coarsely. Heat 2 tablespoons safflower oil in a sauté pan. Add the mushrooms and lemon juice, season with herb salt, and cook briskly for 2 minutes. Beat the egg yolks with the ricotta cheese and add to the spinach. Mix in the mushrooms, nutmeg, and garlic, and season with herb salt.

PRESENTATION. Spread 2 tablespoons of the filling on the "under side" (the second side to be cooked) of each crêpe. Roll up the crêpes and arrange them on an au gratin dish. Spoon over the Mornay sauce, sprinkle the bread crumbs and grated cheese over the sauce, and dot with 1 tablespoon safflower oil. Brown lightly under the broiler and serve.

4 to 6 servings

Cold-pressed safflower oil for soufflé collar	1 cup Soy-Vegetable Stock (p. 262)	**Soufflé Froid de Tomates**
3 tablespoons cold-pressed safflower oil	2 tablespoons natural tomato paste	Cold Tomato Soufflé
2 pounds ripe tomatoes, sliced but not skinned	½ teaspoon Marmite (brewers' yeast extract)	
¼ cup finely chopped yellow or white onion	3 tablespoons unflavored gelatin Whites of 4 organic eggs	
1 teaspoon finely chopped fresh garlic Herb salt	1 medium-size ripe tomato, skinned, seeded, and cut into 8 wedges	

Tear off a length of wax paper 1½ times the outer girth of a 1-quart (No. 6) soufflé dish. Fold it in half lengthwise and brush it with safflower oil. Wrap the wax paper around the soufflé dish and tie it with kitchen string.

Heat 3 tablespoons safflower oil in a pan, about 3-quart size. Add the sliced tomatoes, the onion, garlic, and a little herb salt. Cook the mixture briskly for 4 or 5 minutes, stirring occasionally. Stir in the stock, tomato paste, and Marmite yeast extract. Bring the mixture to a boil. Reduce the heat and let it simmer gently for 3 minutes. Rub the mixture through a fine vegetable strainer.

Dissolve the gelatin in 6 tablespoons water in a little pan over low heat. Stir the gelatin into the strained tomato mixture and adjust the seasoning with herb salt. Set it in the refrigerator and let it chill until it is at the point of setting. Pour the chilled tomato mixture into an electric mixer bowl and beat it until it becomes very light, fluffy, and thick. In a separate bowl, beat the egg whites to soft peaks and fold them into the tomato mixture. Fill the prepared soufflé dish with this mixture and return it to the refrigerator to set.

PRESENTATION. When the soufflé is firm, carefully remove the paper collar. Garnish the top with the skinned sections of tomato, like petals. Store the soufflé in the refrigerator until it is to be served.

4 to 6 servings

Légumes en Brochette

Broiled Vegetables on Skewers

12 firm fresh mushroom caps, about 1 inch in diameter
16 cherry tomatoes
12 sections of green sweet bell pepper, about 1½ inches square
8 baby white onions, skinned

12 unpeeled zucchini chunks, about 1 inch in diameter and ¾ inch thick
Cold-pressed virgin olive oil
Herb salt
Kasha Pilaff (p. 169)
Bunch of fresh crisp watercress

Thread the vegetables on 4 long skewers in the following sequence: Mushroom / tomato / pepper / onion / zucchini / tomato / pepper / mushroom / zucchini / tomato / pepper / onion / zucchini / tomato / mushroom. Place the prepared skewers on a wire rack on a jelly-roll pan. Brush the vegetables with olive oil. Sprinkle with herb salt. About 10 minutes before you wish to serve the vegetables, place the skewers under the broiler and cook for 4 to 5 minutes. Turn them over and broil a few minutes more.

PRESENTATION. Arrange hot kasha pilaff like a bed on a warm serving platter. Lay the skewers of vegetables over the kasha, and garnish with watercress. Serve at once.

4 servings

Bordure de Nouilles aux Légumes

Whole-Wheat Noodle Ring with Spinach and Carrots

The spinach and carrot combination in this recipe is unusual and good. It may be used separately as a vegetable garnish instead of a main course.

NOODLE RING
4 tablespoons cold-pressed safflower oil
Sea salt
¾ pound whole-wheat noodles
1 organic egg, beaten

Herb salt
Cold-pressed safflower oil for ring mold
About ½ cup dry whole-wheat Bread Crumbs (p. 258)

SPINACH AND CARROT MIXTURE
4 *medium-size carrots, pared and*
   thinly sliced
1 *pound spinach, well washed*
1 *teaspoon sea salt*
4 *tablespoons cold-pressed virgin*
   olive oil
1 *Bermuda onion, cut into rings*
1 *teaspoon finely chopped fresh*
   garlic

¼ *cup pine nuts (pignoli)*
½ *cup organic raisins, soaked in a*
   little white wine or water
   Herb salt
¾ *cup raw sour cream, or yogurt*
   mixed with 2 tablespoons
   nonfat dry milk

3 *tablespoons freshly grated*
   Parmesan cheese

Preheat the oven to 375°. Fill a large pan ¾ full of water and bring it to a boil with 2 tablespoons safflower oil and 1 tablespoon sea salt. Add the noodles, reduce the heat to a simmer, and cook for 6 to 7 minutes. Drain the noodles well and transfer them to a mixing bowl. Add to the noodles the beaten egg and 2 tablespoons safflower oil, and season with a little herb salt. Lightly brush a 1½-quart ring mold with safflower oil. Dust it with the bread crumbs. Fill the mold with the noodles and bake in the preheated oven for 30 minutes.

SPINACH AND CARROT MIXTURE. Cover the carrots and ½ teaspoon sea salt with cold water. Bring to a boil and drain immediately. Cook the spinach with ½ cup water and ½ teaspoon sea salt until it is wilted. Drain it well and chop it into coarse shreds.

Heat 4 tablespoons olive oil in a heavy pan. Add the Bermuda onion rings and the garlic, and cook until the onion is soft but not brown. Add the carrots, pine nuts, and raisins, and cook until the carrots are soft. Mix in the spinach, season with herb salt to taste, and cook briskly for 2 minutes. Remove the pan from the heat and stir in the sour cream or yogurt mixture.

PRESENTATION. Turn the noodle ring out onto a warm serving platter. Fill the center with the spinach and carrot mixture. Sprinkle the grated cheese over the top of the vegetables.

4 to 6 servings

FISH AND SHELLFISH

As far as nutrition is concerned, fish is distinctly preferred over poultry and red meat because it is much easier to digest and it delivers lean, good proteins. In addition, fish and shellfish contain a generous array of vital minerals including iodine, which is needed by the thyroid gland but is hard to obtain in sufficient quantity in other food. Also, fish is low in saturated fat content. And above all, fish is delicious.

The first rule of good nutrition in cooking fish is to cook the fish as little as possible and to cook it in a container that will catch the juices, every drop of which should be served with the fish. Good fish cookery always serves the cooking liquid in some way—in the classic fish velouté or white-wine sauce, or spooned up with a little wine for a pan sauce, or in a broth or bisque. This is the reason why fish sauces and soups marry so perfectly with the dishes they accompany. When a stronger flavor is desired, a separate stock of fish heads and bones (usually free from the fish market), cooked in water with a *bouquet garni,* is prepared. This may be cooked down in quantity to become an essence, or *fumet* as it is called in classic cookery (see p. 264).

Traditionally white wine is mixed with water for poaching fish or for stirring up pan juices. In this book we offer the option to use or not to use wine. If you choose not, you may prepare your poaching liquids with water and seasonings only; it's the flavor and nutrients in the fish juices you want to capture. Sometimes a little dry white wine-grape juice, Lehr's or Grapillon, can be used instead of wine. Because of its somewhat sweet character, we do not recommend its substitution for wine in large quantities.

Also, with classic fish sauces, such as the fish velouté, because we use stone-ground whole-wheat pastry flour for thickening, the sauce may take on a brownish hue. We find this subtle tone to be a delightful indication of pure natural quality, as well as of richer flavor and less starchy taste.

This chapter contains a grand seafood casserole (*Casserole de Fruits de Mer,* pp. 105–107) which is marvelous for entertaining a large group; it is a gastronomic and nutritional masterpiece with mussels, shrimps, lobster, scallops, and rich natural brown rice. For convenience, this casserole may be prepared ahead of time and rewarmed. Also we like the different idea of covering *coquilles Saint-Jacques* with thinly sliced tomatoes as a change from the duchess potato garnish. The *Baked Bass with Oyster Stuffing and Eggplant,* the *Filets de Sole Véronique* with white grapes *and tomatoes,* and *Filets de Soles Saint-Tropez—* sautéed with scallops and a delicious sauce, are some dishes which Dione Lucas created just before her death.

Bar Farci aux Huîtres et Aubergine

Baked Bass with Oyster Stuffing and Eggplant

2 medium-size eggplants
  Cold-pressed safflower oil for
    eggplant skins and baking dish
6 tablespoons cold-pressed safflower
  oil
2 whole small sea bass, about 1½
    pounds each, or 1 large bass

2 tablespoons and few drops of
    fresh lemon juice
  Herb salt
8 oysters on the half shell
2 firm fresh mushrooms, finely
    chopped
3 tablespoons dry whole-wheat
    Bread Crumbs (p. 258)

1 teaspoon finely chopped fresh
   garlic
1 tablespoon finely chopped fresh

herbs (parsley, thyme,
   tarragon, etc.)
½ *cup raw sour cream, or yogurt*

Preheat the oven to 350°. Brush the eggplants with a little safflower oil, wrap them in a double thickness of wax paper, and bake them in the preheated oven for about 30 minutes, or until they are soft to the touch.

The bass may be boned, leaving the head and tail on the body, in which case the stuffing will reshape it. Or you may choose not to bone the fish, in which case the stuffing will be cooked in the belly cavity. Wash the fish in water with 1 tablespoon lemon juice. Dry it between paper towels. Rub it with a little herb salt and a few drops of lemon juice.

Chop the oysters as fine as possible and combine them with any liquid from the shells, plus the chopped mushrooms, bread crumbs, ½ teaspoon garlic, and the herbs. Season with herb salt to taste. Stuff the fish with this mixture.

Brush an ovenproof dish with safflower oil and place the stuffed fish on it. Mix 2 tablespoons safflower oil with 1 tablespoon lemon juice and pour it over the fish. Sprinkle with a little herb salt. Bake the fish in the preheated oven, allowing 25 minutes for a 1½- to 2-pound fish.

When the eggplants are cooked, remove them from the oven, carefully scrape the pulp from the skins, and chop it. Mix the pulp with ½ teaspoon garlic and the sour cream or yogurt, and season with herb salt.

PRESENTATION. When the fish is baked, remove it from the oven and let it sit for a moment. Warm the eggplant mixture and spread it like a bed on a warm serving platter. Lay the baked fish on the eggplant. Heat 4 tablespoons safflower oil in a small pan and add the liquid from the dish in which the fish was baked, a few drops of lemon juice, and a dash of herb salt. Warm this mixture a little and spoon it over the fish. Serve.

4 to 6 servings

1 *live 1½-pound lobster*
¾ *cup cold-pressed virgin olive oil*
12 *mussels, well scrubbed*
1 *whole mackerel, dressed*
1 *whole small bluefish, dressed*
2 *small eels, dressed*
½ *pound salmon steak*
½ *pound cod steak*

2 *tablespoons dry sherry*
   (optional)
1 *Bermuda onion, finely chopped*
2 *teaspoons finely chopped fresh*
   garlic
1 *pound ripe tomatoes, skinned*
   and sliced

             (cont.)

Bouillabaisse

Fish Stew,
Marseilles Style

2 tablespoons stone-ground whole-
wheat pastry flour
1 teaspoon Marmite (brewers'
yeast extract)
1 tablespoon natural tomato
paste
½ cup dry white wine, or additional
water

¼ teaspoon ground saffron
Herb salt
½ pound sea scallops
4 slices of stone-ground whole-
wheat bread, cut into
triangular halves

Split the lobster down the back with a sharp knife. Remove the sac behind each eye and the intestinal vein. With a kitchen scissors, cut away the small claws and the large claws; also cut open the shells of the large claws. Cut the tail into 1-inch pieces. Heat ¼ cup olive oil in a large heavy pan and cook the lobster pieces, cut sides down, over low heat for 8 minutes.

Place the mussels in a pan with 1 cup water, cover, and steam for about 5 minutes, or until the shells open. Remove the heads of the mackerel, bluefish, and eels, and cut the fish crosswise into 2-inch pieces. Cut the salmon and cod steaks into 4 serving pieces each.

Heat the dry sherry in a little pan, ignite, and pour it over the lobster. Remove the lobster from the pan. Add another ¼ cup olive oil to the pan with the onion, garlic, and tomatoes. Cook these vegetables over moderate heat until the onion is translucent. Off the heat blend in the flour, Marmite yeast extract, and tomato paste. Stir in 2 cups water, the wine, and saffron, and season with herb salt to taste. Return the pan to moderate heat and bring the mixture to a boil.

Add to the sauce in the pan the mackerel, bluefish, eels, scallops, cod, and salmon. Place the cooked lobster and mussels in their shells on top of the fish. Also add the strained liquid from the mussels. Cover the pan and cook for 5 to 10 minutes—only until the pieces of fish are cooked. They should be a little underdone because they will continue cooking in the hot sauce.

Meanwhile preheat the oven to 400°. Brush the bread triangles with the remaining olive oil, sprinkle with a little herb salt, and set them on a baking sheet. Toast them in the preheated oven for about 10 minutes, until they just begin to brown.

PRESENTATION. Place a piece of toasted bread on the bottom of a deep plate. Carefully, with a large spoon, serve a variety of the fish and shellfish on top of the bread for each serving, including some of the sauce.

4 to 6 servings

1½ *pounds raw salmon, boned*
  Whites of 3 organic eggs
2 *cups raw light cream*
2 *teaspoons sea salt*
3 *tablespoons dry sherry, or dry*
  white wine, or white wine-
  grape juice
  Safflower oil for mold
5 *medium-size firm fresh*
  mushrooms, coarsely chopped
8 *tablespoons cold-pressed*
  safflower oil
2 *tablespoons and few drops of*
  fresh lemon juice

  Herb salt
3 *ounces raw shrimps, shelled,*
  deveined, and coarsely chopped
2 *ounces bay scallops, or sea scallops*
  cut into quarters
2 *teaspoons chopped fresh dill or*
  parsley
4 *tablespoons raw heavy sweet*
  cream or raw sour cream
  Yolks of 2 organic eggs
3 *small cucumbers*
3 *teaspoons finely chopped fresh*
  mint

Mousse de Saumon Farcie, Sauce Hollandaise

Salmon Mousse Filled with Shrimps and Scallops, Hollandaise Sauce, Blanched Cucumbers

Preheat the oven to 350°. Pass the boned salmon through a fine meat grinder twice. In an electric mixer, beat it with the egg whites until it is smooth. Continue beating as you very slowly add the light cream. Add 2 teaspoons sea salt and 2 tablespoons sherry. Brush a decorative mold or charlotte mold with safflower oil and fill it with three quarters of the mousse mixture. Make a well in the center of the mixture, using the back of a large spoon, dipped into water to prevent sticking. Fill the well with the shrimp mixture.

SHRIMP AND SCALLOP FILLING. Sauté the chopped mushrooms with 1 tablespoon safflower oil, a few drops of lemon juice, and a little herb salt. Add the chopped shrimps to the pan and cook until shrimps are pink. Mix in the scallops, dill or parsley, and 2 tablespoons heavy cream or sour cream; season with herb salt to taste.

After the shrimp mixture has been set in the well in the mousse, cover with the remaining mousse. Cover the mold with a piece of oiled wax paper and stand the mold in a roasting pan half-filled with hot water. Place the mousse in its water bath in the preheated oven, and bake for 25 to 30 minutes, until it is set.

HOLLANDAISE SAUCE. In a small bowl combine the egg yolks, 2 table-spoons lemon juice, 1 tablespoon sherry or wine (optional), ¼ tea-spoon herb salt, and 2 tablespoons heavy or sour cream. Half-fill a small sauté pan with hot water. Stand the bowl in the pan, over low heat, and beat the sauce with a small wire whisk until it is thick. Very slowly add 6 tablespoons safflower oil, beating constantly. Remove the bowl from the water and cover it with plastic wrap until you are ready to use it.

BLANCHED CUCUMBERS. Peel the cucumbers, cut them lengthwise into halves, and remove the seeds. Cut them into ½-inch slices. Put the cucumber slices in a pan with 1 teaspoon herb salt, cover with cold water, and bring it to a boil. Drain immediately and return the cucumbers to the pan. Add remaining 1 tablespoon safflower oil, the chopped mint, and a little herb salt. Cover and cook for 1 minute. PRESENTATION. Remove the mousse from the oven and let it stand for about 5 minutes. Slip a thin-bladed knife around the edge to loosen it, and carefully turn it out onto a warm serving dish. Spread the hollandaise sauce over the mousse. Arrange a garnish of cucumbers on either side of the mousse.

4 to 6 servings

Quenelles de Brochet, Sauce Suprême

Pike Dumplings, Suprême Sauce

FISH STOCK
> *Head and bones of 1 pike (see pike under "Quenelles")*
> 2 *cups water*
> 1 *cup dry white wine, or additional water*
> 1 *small celery stalk, sliced*
> 1 *small yellow onion, sliced*
> 1 *bay leaf*

QUENELLES
> 1 *cup water*
> 12 *tablespoons cold-pressed safflower oil*
> 2 *teaspoons sea salt*
> 1 *cup, plus additional for coating, sifted stone-ground whole-wheat pastry flour*
> 2 *organic eggs*
> ⅓ *cup whites of organic eggs*
> ¾ *pound ground pike*
> ½ *teaspoon freshly grated nutmeg*

¼ *cup raw heavy cream*

SUPRÊME SAUCE
> 5 *tablespoons cold-pressed safflower oil*
> 3 *tablespoons sifted stone-ground whole-wheat pastry flour*
> 1½ *cups fish stock (from above)*
> ⅓ *cup raw light cream*
> *Sea salt*
> *Yolks of 2 organic eggs*
> 2 *tablespoons raw heavy sweet cream or raw sour cream*
> 1 *tablespoon dry sherry (optional)*
> 1 *black truffle, shredded*
>
> *Cold-pressed safflower oil for serving platter and topping*
> ¼ *cup freshly grated Parmesan cheese*

FISH STOCK. Place the fish head and bones in a pot with the water and wine and bring the liquid to a boil; reduce the heat to a simmer and skim. Add the celery, onion, and bay leaf. Simmer for about 5 minutes. Strain the stock through a colander lined with a damp cloth and set aside.

QUENELLES. Combine the water, 4 tablespoons safflower oil, and ½ teaspoon sea salt in a saucepan, and slowly bring the mixture to a boil. Add 1 cup flour all at once, and stir over low heat until the mixture forms a mass and comes away from the sides of the pan. Transfer the mixture to an electric mixer and beat in the eggs, one at a time. Then beat in the egg whites. Continue beating as you add, very slowly, 8 tablespoons safflower oil. When the mixture is well blended, beat in the ground pike. Add 1½ teaspoons sea salt, the nutmeg, and heavy cream, and beat again. Press the pike mixture through a fine vegetable strainer, spread it out on a shallow dish, and set it in the freezer for 30 minutes or so to chill.

When the pike mixture is firm, but not frozen, form it into cork shapes on a lightly floured board. Gently pat off excess flour. Try to make the quenelles smooth—no wrinkles. Fill a large pan ¾ full of water seasoned with sea salt. Bring the water to a boil and reduce the heat to a gentle simmer. Drop the quenelles into the hot water. Place a double thickness of paper towels on top of them and poach gently until the quenelles are set, about 20 to 25 minutes. Do *not* allow the water to boil actively. The quenelles can remain in the hot—not boiling—water until they are to be transferred to a serving dish.

SUPRÊME SAUCE. Mix 3 tablespoons safflower oil with the flour in a saucepan and stir over low heat until the mixture bubbles. Off the heat add 1½ cups of the strained fish stock; stir the sauce over moderate heat until it comes to a boil. Add the light cream and adjust the seasoning with sea salt. Reduce the heat to a simmer, stir in 2 tablespoons safflower oil, and allow to cook for 5 minutes. Beat the egg yolks, sweet or sour cream, and sherry in a small bowl. Pour a little of the sauce into the egg-yolk mixture; then pour the egg-yolk mixture into the sauce in the pan. Add the chopped truffle. Gently reheat the sauce but do not allow it to boil, or it will separate.

PRESENTATION. Brush an au gratin dish or ovenproof serving platter with safflower oil. Drain the quenelles with a slotted spoon and arrange them on the platter. Spoon over the sauce. Sprinkle with the grated cheese and dot with a little safflower oil. Brown lightly under the broiler, not too long or sauce will separate and scorch.

4 to 6 servings

This exquisite mousse can be made with salmon instead of cod.

Mousse de Cabillaud, Sauce Smitane

Cod Mousse with Sour Cream Sauce

1 pound fresh cod, boned
  Whites of 2 organic eggs
¼ cup cold-pressed safflower oil
¼ cup raw light cream
1 tablespoon finely chopped fresh
    parsley
  Sea salt
  Cold-pressed safflower oil for
    mold

SOUR CREAM SAUCE
2 tablespoons cold-pressed
    safflower oil
1 tablespoon stone-ground whole-
    wheat pastry flour
1½ cups raw sour cream
2 teaspoons chopped fresh chives
  Herb salt
  Yolk of 1 organic egg

Preheat the oven to 350°. Pass the cod through a fine meat grinder twice. In an electric mixer combine the ground cod with the egg whites and beat until smooth; then rub the mixture through a fine vegetable strainer. Set the bowl with the cod mixture in another bowl filled with ice cubes. Using a small wire whisk, beat in 1/4 cup safflower oil, then the cream. Add the chopped parsley and season with sea salt.

Brush a 1-quart mold with safflower oil and fill it with the cod mousse. Cover the mold with oiled wax paper and stand it in a roasting pan half-filled with hot water. Place the mousse in its water bath in the preheated oven and bake for 20 minutes.

SOUR CREAM SAUCE. Mix the safflower oil with the flour in a saucepan and stir over moderate heat until it bubbles. Off the heat add 1 1/4 cups sour cream; stir the sauce over moderate heat until it comes to a boil. Add the chives and season with herb salt to taste. In a little bowl mix the egg yolk with the remaining sour cream. Pour a little sauce into the egg-yolk mixture; then pour the egg-yolk mixture into the sauce in the pan and mix thoroughly. The sauce may be reheated gently, but do not allow it to boil or it will separate.

PRESENTATION. When the mousse is baked, remove it from the oven and allow it to stand for about 5 minutes. Slip a thin-bladed knife around the edge of the dish to loosen it, and carefully turn the mousse out onto a warm serving dish. Spoon the sauce over the mousse and serve.

4 servings

Filets de Soles Bonne Femme

Poached Fillets of Sole with Mushrooms, Velouté and Hollandaise Sauces

Duchess Potatoes (p. 194)
4 to 6 fillets of gray sole
2 tablespoons and 1 teaspoon fresh lemon juice
Sea salt
Cold-pressed safflower oil for baking dish and mushrooms

2 tablespoons cold-pressed safflower oil
8 large firm fresh mushrooms (slice 4 and leave 4 whole)
1/4 cup water
1/2 cup dry white wine, or additional water, or white wine-grape juice

HOLLANDAISE SAUCE (pp. 268–269), prepared while the fish is cooking.

VELOUTÉ SAUCE
5 tablespoons cold-pressed safflower oil
3 tablespoons stone-ground whole-wheat pastry flour

1 cup strained stock from the fish
1/2 cup raw light cream
Herb salt

Fit a pastry bag with a No. 9 star tube, and fill the bag with the duchess potatoes. Pipe a border of scallop shapes around the edge of an oval au gratin dish. Brown the potato border lightly under the broiler and set the dish aside.

Preheat the oven to 350°. Wash the fillets of sole in water and 2 tablespoons lemon juice and dry them between paper towels. Season the skin side with a little sea salt, fold them lengthwise with the flesh side showing, and arrange them on a large baking dish brushed with safflower oil.

Heat 2 tablespoons safflower oil in a small saucepan. Add the *sliced* mushrooms and 1 teaspoon lemon juice and cook briskly for 2 minutes. Add the water and wine and bring to a boil. Spoon this mixture over the fish. Cover the fish with a piece of oiled wax paper and set it in the preheated oven to poach for 12 minutes.

Prepare Hollandaise sauce, remove it from the heat, cover with plastic wrap, and set it aside for a moment.

When the fish is cooked, remove it from the oven, and immediately, with great care, transfer the fillets to the au gratin dish with the potato border. Strain the stock and reserve it and the mushrooms.

VELOUTÉ SAUCE. Heat 3 tablespoons safflower oil in a saucepan. Off the heat blend in 3 tablespoons flour. Add the strained fish stock. Return the sauce to moderate heat and stir until it thickens. Add the light cream and bring the sauce to a boil. Stir in another 2 tablespoons safflower oil, little by little, and season with herb salt to taste.

Quickly sauté the 4 *whole* mushrooms in a little safflower oil and a few drops of lemon juice.

PRESENTATION. Scatter the reserved *sliced* mushrooms over the fish. Spoon the velouté sauce over the fish, completely coating the fillets but not the potato border. Carefully spoon a wide ribbon of hollandaise down the center of the dish. Brown lightly under the broiler, not too long or the sauce will separate and scorch. Set a row of the whole mushrooms down the center and serve.

4 to 6 servings

Duchess Potatoes (p. 194)
4 to 6 large fillets of gray sole
2 tablespoons and 1 teaspoon fresh lemon juice
Sea salt
Cold-pressed safflower oil for baking dish and topping
2 tablespoons cold-pressed safflower oil
2 firm fresh mushrooms, thinly sliced
½ cup water

½ cup dry white wine, or additional water, or white wine-grape juice

VELOUTÉ SAUCE AND GARNISH
4 medium-size ripe tomatoes, skinned
3 tablespoons cold-pressed safflower oil
3 tablespoons stone-ground whole-wheat pastry flour
Stock from the fish, about 1 cup

(cont.)

Filets de Soles Duglèré

Fillets of Sole with Tomatoes, Mushrooms, Velouté Sauce

½ cup chopped onion
⅓ cup raw light cream
    Herb salt
    Reserved mushrooms, from fish
2 teaspoons chopped fresh parsley

3 tablespoons freshly grated
    Parmesan cheese
2 tablespoons dry whole-wheat
    Bread Crumbs (p. 258)

Fit a pastry bag with a No. 9 star tube, and fill the bag with the duchess potatoes. Pipe a border of scallop shapes around the edge of an oval au gratin dish. Brown the potato border lightly under the broiler.

Preheat the oven to 350°. Wash the fillets of sole in water and 2 tablespoons lemon juice and dry them between paper towels. Season the skin side with a little sea salt, fold them lengthwise with the flesh side showing, and arrange them on a large baking dish brushed with safflower oil. Heat 2 tablespoons safflower oil in a saucepan. Add the sliced mushrooms and 1 teaspoon lemon juice and cook briskly for 2 minutes. Add the water and wine and bring to a boil. Spoon this mixture over the fish. Cover the fish with a piece of oiled wax paper and set it in the preheated oven to poach for 12 minutes.

Remove the fish from the oven and immediately, with great care, transfer the fillets to the au gratin dish with the potato border. Strain the stock and reserve it and the mushrooms.

VELOUTÉ SAUCE. Cut the skinned tomatoes into quarters. Remove the seeds and rub the seed parts through a fine vegetable strainer, reserving the juice. Cut the outer pulp into coarse shreds. Heat 3 tablespoons safflower oil in a saucepan. Off the heat stir in 3 tablespoons flour. Add the reserved stock and stir the sauce over moderate heat until it thickens. Add the strained tomato juice, chopped onion, and light cream, and season with herb salt to taste. Stir over low heat until the sauce comes to a boil. Add the reserved mushrooms, shredded tomatoes, parsley, and 1 tablespoon grated cheese.

PRESENTATION. Spoon the sauce over the fish, completely coating the fillets but not the potatoes. Sprinkle the bread crumbs and 2 tablespoons grated cheese over the top. Dot with a few drops of safflower oil and brown lightly under the broiler.

4 to 6 servings

Filets de Soles Joinville

Poached Turban
of Sole with
Salmon Mousse

6 fillets of gray sole
2 tablespoons fresh lemon juice
    Cold-pressed safflower oil for
    mold
1¼ pounds fresh salmon
    Whites of 2 organic eggs

1 cup raw light cream
2 teaspoons sea salt
⅛ teaspoon ground cardamom
2 tablespoons dry sherry
    (optional)

SUPRÊME SAUCE
> Fish head and bones (from
>> sole, if possible)
> 3 cups water
> ½ cup dry white wine, or
>> additional water, or white
>> wine-grape juice
> 1 large sprig of fresh dill
> 1 bay leaf
> 1½ teaspoons herb salt
> 1 allspice berry
> 1 small white onion, quartered
> 1 small piece of celery, sliced
> 1 small piece of carrot, sliced
> 4 tablespoons cold-pressed
>> safflower oil
> 3 tablespoons stone-ground whole-
>> wheat pastry flour

> ⅓ cup raw light cream
> Yolks of 2 organic eggs
> 2 tablespoons dry sherry
>> (optional)
> 3 tablespoons raw heavy sweet
>> cream or raw sour cream

GARNISH
> Herb salt
> 1 pound raw shrimps
> 2 tablespoons cold-pressed
>> safflower oil
> 12 fresh firm small mushrooms,
>> fluted if desired
> 2 teaspoons fresh lemon juice
> 2 teaspoons chopped fresh parsley

Preheat the oven to 350°. Wash the fillets of sole in water with 2 table-spoons lemon juice and dry them between paper towels. Brush a 1½-quart ring mold with safflower oil, and line it with the fillets of sole, placing the flesh side against the mold. Fill the mold with salmon mousse.

SALMON MOUSSE. Remove the skin and bones from the salmon. Pass the salmon through a fine meat grinder. Transfer it to the bowl of an electric mixer and beat in the egg whites. Continue beating as you very, very slowly add the light cream. Add 2 teaspoons sea salt, the cardamom, and sherry. Pack the mousse into the fish-lined mold and cover it with the ends of the fillets. Cover the mold with a piece of wax paper brushed with safflower oil and stand it in a roasting pan half-filled with hot water. Place the filled mold in its water bath in the preheated oven and bake for 30 minutes.

SUPRÊME SAUCE. Combine the fish head and bones, the water, wine, dill, bay leaf, 1½ teaspoons herb salt, the allspice, onion, celery, and carrot in a pan and bring to a boil. Reduce the heat and simmer gently for 45 minutes. Strain and reserve the liquid. Heat 3 tablespoons safflower oil in a saucepan. Off the heat mix in 3 tablespoons flour. Add 1½ cups of the strained fish stock and stir over moderate heat until the sauce comes to a boil. Add the light cream and bring the sauce to a boil again. Reduce the heat to a simmer, stir in another tablespoon of safflower oil, and adjust the seasoning with herb salt. In a small bowl mix the egg yolks, sherry, and sweet or sour cream. Add a little of the hot sauce to the egg-yolk mixture, then pour the egg-yolk mixture into the sauce in the pan, stirring all the while. Reheat but do not boil.

GARNISH. Heat 2 cups water with 1 teaspoon herb salt to a boil. Add the raw shrimps and cook until they turn pink. Drain the shrimps and shell and devein them. Heat 2 tablespoons safflower oil in a sauté pan. Add the mushrooms and lemon juice, season with a little herb salt, and cook briskly for 2 minutes. Add the shrimps and cook for another 2 minutes. Add the chopped parsley.

PRESENTATION. When the fish is cooked, remove it from the oven. Let it stand in the mold for about 5 minutes. Slip a thin-bladed knife around the edge of the mold to loosen it, and carefully invert it onto a warm serving dish. Coat the fish mold with the sauce. Fill the center of the mold with the mushroom and shrimp mixture.

4 to 6 servings

Filets de Soles Marguery

Poached Fillets of Sole with Mussels and Shrimps, Velouté and Hollandaise Sauces

8 small fillets of gray sole
3 tablespoons and 1 teaspoon fresh lemon juice
Sea salt
Cold-pressed safflower oil for baking dish
1½ pints large mussels
1 teaspoon dry mustard
¼ cup dry white wine, or white wine-grape juice, or water
2½ cups water
4 tablespoons dry sherry (optional)
1 bay leaf
4 medium-size firm fresh mushrooms

10 tablespoons cold-pressed safflower oil
Herb salt
8 to 10 raw shrimps, shelled and deveined
1 tablespoon chopped fresh parsley
3 tablespoons stone-ground whole-wheat pastry flour
¼ cup raw light cream
Yolks of 2 organic eggs
2 tablespoons raw heavy sweet cream or raw sour cream

Preheat the oven to 350°. Wash the fish in water and 2 tablespoons lemon juice and dry them between paper towels. Season the skin side with a little sea salt, fold them lengthwise with the flesh side showing, and arrange them on a large baking dish brushed with safflower oil.

Wash the mussels in water with the dry mustard. (The mustard helps to clean the mussels.) Place the cleaned mussels in a saucepan with the white wine, ½ cup water, the sherry, and bay leaf. Bring to a boil and simmer for 3 or 4 minutes, until the shells open.

Remove the stems from the mushrooms and slice the stems and 1 whole mushroom. Heat 1 tablespoon safflower oil in a small pan and sauté the sliced mushrooms with 1 teaspoon lemon juice for a minute or two. Strain the mussel liquid over the mushrooms and bring the mixture to a boil. Pour this mixture over the fillets of sole. Cover fillets with a piece of oiled wax paper and set them in the preheated oven to poach for 12 minutes.

In a saucepan bring 2 cups water with ½ teaspoon herb salt to a boil. Add the shrimps and cook until they are pink. Drain and cut the shrimps into slices. Slice the 3 remaining mushroom caps. Heat 1 tablespoon safflower oil in a sauté pan; add the shrimps to the mushrooms. Remove the mussels from the shells and add them and the chopped parsley to the mushrooms and shrimps.

When the fish is cooked, remove it from the oven immediately, and, with great care, transfer the fillets to a warm au gratin or shallow serving dish. Strain the liquid from the fish and reserve it.

VELOUTÉ SAUCE. Heat 2 tablespoons safflower oil in a saucepan. Off the heat blend in the flour. Add the reserved fish stock, about 1 cup, return the sauce to moderate heat, and stir until it comes to a boil. Add the light cream and adjust the seasoning with herb salt.

HOLLANDAISE SAUCE. In a small bowl combine the egg yolks, 1 table-spoon lemon juice, sweet or sour cream, and ¼ teaspoon herb salt, and mix well. Set the bowl in a small sauté pan half-filled with hot water over low heat. Beat the yolk mixture with a small wire whisk until it is thick. Very slowly add 6 tablespoons safflower oil, beating constantly. Fold the hollandaise sauce into the velouté sauce.

PRESENTATION. Scatter the mushroom, shrimp, mussel mixture over the fish. Cover with the sauce. Brown lightly under the broiler, not too long or the sauce will separate and scorch.

4 servings

Filets de Soles Meunière

Sautéed Fillets of Sole Garnished with Cucumber, Tomato, and Mushrooms

1 cucumber, peeled, seeded, and cut into ½-inch chunks
Sea salt
4 tablespoons cold-pressed safflower oil
4 large firm fresh mushrooms, quartered
1 teaspoon and 3 tablespoons fresh lemon juice
Herb salt
3 medium-size ripe tomatoes, skinned and quartered
4 fillets of gray sole
Stone-ground whole-wheat pastry flour, for coating the fish
1 teaspoon finely chopped yellow or white onion
¼ teaspoon finely chopped fresh garlic
2 tablespoons chopped fresh herbs (parsley, thyme, tarragon, chives, etc.)
3 tablespoons dry white wine, or white wine-grape juice, or water
4 thin slices of lemon

GARNISHES. Cover the cucumber slices and ½ teaspoon sea salt with cold water, bring to a boil, and drain immediately. Return the cucumbers to the pan with 1 tablespoon safflower oil, cook over low heat for 2 minutes, and set aside. Heat 1 tablespoon safflower oil in a sauté pan, add the mushrooms with 1 teaspoon lemon juice, and cook briskly for 2 minutes. Season them with a little herb salt and remove them from the pan. In the same pan warm the tomato sections and season with herb salt. Keep these garnishes warm while you prepare the fish.

FISH. Wash the fillets in cold water and 2 tablespoons lemon juice, and dry them between paper towels. Sprinkle them with a little sea salt and dust them lightly with flour. Heat 2 tablespoons safflower oil in a sauté pan. When it is very hot, brown the fish quickly on both sides. (This should cook the fish perfectly.) Carefully remove the fish from the pan, arrange the fillets on a warm serving dish, and keep them warm.

Add the onion and garlic to the pan in which the fish was cooked, and cook for 1 minute. Add the herbs, wine, 1 tablespoon lemon juice, and 1/4 teaspoon herb salt. Gently cook the mixture for 2 minutes, stirring with a wooden spoon.

PRESENTATION. Spread the pan mixture over the fillets of sole. Set a thin slice of lemon on each. Garnish the dish with the cucumbers, mushrooms, and tomatoes, in separate mounds.

4 servings

Filets de Soles Saint-Tropez

Sautéed Fillets of Sole with Scallops

Fish head and bones
1 cup dry white wine, or additional water, or white wine-grape juice
1/2 cup mixed sliced onion, carrot, and celery
1 bay leaf
Herb salt
4 large sea scallops
10 tablespoons cold-pressed safflower oil
6 ounces firm fresh mushrooms, finely chopped
1/3 cup finely chopped shallot
1 medium-size yellow onion, finely chopped
1 tablespoon chopped fresh parsley
1 tablespoon chopped fresh tarragon

1 teaspoon chopped fresh chives
1 teaspoon finely chopped fresh garlic
8 small fillets of gray sole
2 tablespoons fresh lemon juice
Sea salt
About 1/4 cup raw milk
Stone-ground whole-wheat pastry flour for dusting fish
3 tablespoons stone-ground whole-wheat pastry flour
1/2 cup freshly grated Parmesan cheese
1 cup raw heavy sweet cream or raw sour cream
Cold-pressed safflower oil for topping

Combine the fish head and bones, 1/2 cup water, the wine, *sliced* onion, carrot, and celery, the bay leaf, and a little herb salt, and bring the mixture to a boil. Simmer for 20 minutes and strain. Boil the strained stock down to 1 cup in quantity.

Cut the scallops into small dice. Heat 2 tablespoons safflower oil in a sauté pan and add the scallops, mushrooms, shallots, *chopped* onion, parsley, tarragon, chives, and garlic. Season with herb salt. Cook this mixture briskly for 4 or 5 minutes; reduce the heat and cook for another 5 minutes, stirring occasionally. Set the mixture aside while you prepare the fish.

Wash the fillets in cold water with 2 tablespoons lemon juice. Dry fillets between paper towels, and fold them lengthwise, with the flesh side out. Rub the fillets with a little sea salt, brush them with a little milk, and pat lightly with flour. Heat 4 tablespoons safflower oil in a large sauté pan. Brown the fillets on each side and carefully transfer them to a warm serving platter or au gratin dish. Keep them warm while you prepare the sauce.

Heat 4 tablespoons safflower oil in a saucepan. Off the heat blend in 3 tablespoons flour and the reduced fish stock. Season with herb salt and add ¼ cup grated cheese. Stir the sauce over moderate heat until it comes to a boil. Stir in the sweet or sour cream.

PRESENTATION. Spread the scallop mixture over the fish. Cover the top of the dish with the sauce. Sprinkle with the rest of the grated cheese and dot with a few drops of safflower oil. Brown lightly under the broiler and serve.

4 servings

Filets de Soles Véronique

Fillets of Sole with White Grapes and Tomatoes, Hollandaise Sauce

4 to 6 large fillets of gray sole
2 tablespoons fresh lemon juice
  Cold-pressed safflower oil for
    baking dish
7 tablespoons cold-pressed
    safflower oil
1 tablespoon finely chopped white
    onion
1 tablespoon chopped fresh dill
  Herb salt
¼ cup dry white wine, or water, or
    white wine-grape juice
1 tablespoon dry sherry
    (optional)
¾ cup fresh white grapes, skinned
    and pitted
3 small ripe tomatoes, skinned,
    seeded, and cut into shreds
1 tablespoon chopped fresh
    parsley
3 small ripe tomatoes, whole, not
    skinned
1 teaspoon raw sugar
½ teaspoon finely chopped fresh
    garlic
6 wafer-thin slices of yellow or
    Bermuda onion
2 tablespoons whole-wheat Bread
    Crumbs (p. 258)
2 tablespoons freshly grated
    Parmesan cheese

HOLLANDAISE SAUCE
  Yolks of 3 organic eggs
1 tablespoon fresh lemon juice
¼ teaspoon herb salt
2 tablespoons raw heavy sweet
    cream or raw sour cream
8 tablespoons cold-pressed
    safflower oil

Preheat the oven to 350°. Wash the fillets in cold water with 2 table-spoons lemon juice and dry them between paper towels. Lay the fillets on a lightly oiled baking dish. Heat 4 tablespoons safflower oil in a small pan. Add the chopped onion, dill, and a little herb salt. Sauté the onion mixture over low heat for 1 minute. Add the white wine, ¼ cup water, and the sherry, and bring to a boil. Pour this mixture over the fish and cover with a piece of oiled wax paper. Set the fish in the preheated oven and poach for 12 minutes. When the fillets are cooked, carefully transfer them to an au gratin or shallow serving dish and keep them warm.

Strain the liquid from the fish into a sauté pan and reheat with 2 tablespoons safflower oil. Add the white grapes, shredded tomatoes, and chopped parsley, and season with herb salt. Warm the mixture over low heat and remove the grapes and tomatoes with a slotted spoon, scattering them over the fish.

HOLLANDAISE SAUCE. In a small bowl combine the egg yolks, 1 table-spoon lemon juice, ¼ teaspoon herb salt, and the sweet or sour cream. Mix well. Set the bowl in a small sauté pan half-filled with hot water over low heat. Beat the yolk mixture with a small wire whisk until it is thick. Very slowly add 8 tablespoons safflower oil, beating constantly. Remove the sauce from the heat, cover it with plastic wrap, and set it aside while you prepare the tomato garnish.

Core the 3 whole unskinned tomatoes and cut into halves. Sprinkle the tops with a little herb salt, the raw sugar, and garlic. Cover each with a slice of onion. Sprinkle with the bread crumbs and grated cheese and dot with 1 tablespoon safflower oil. Brown lightly under the broiler.

PRESENTATION. Spoon a wide ribbon of hollandaise over the fish prep-aration and brown it lightly under the broiler, not too long or the sauce will separate and scorch. Decorate the dish with the broiled tomatoes and serve.

4 servings

Truite Farcie aux Crevettes

Sautéed Trout Stuffed with Shrimps

4 small trout, dressed
2 tablespoons fresh lemon juice
  Herb salt
¼ pound raw shrimps, shelled and deveined
6 firm fresh mushrooms
6 tablespoons cold-pressed safflower oil
1 cup finely chopped onion

½ teaspoon finely chopped fresh garlic
½ cup dry whole-wheat Bread Crumbs, plus more for dusting (p. 258)
2 tablespoons chopped fresh parsley
  A little stone-ground whole-wheat pastry flour

1 organic egg, beaten
1 lemon, cut into 4 wedges
  Few sprigs of crisp fresh
    watercress

HOLLANDAISE SAUCE
½ cup dry red wine (if traditional
    hollandaise is preferred, use

  2 tablespoons fresh lemon
    juice)
  Yolks of 3 organic eggs
¼ teaspoon herb salt
  2 tablespoons raw heavy sweet
    cream or raw sour cream
  8 tablespoons cold-pressed
    safflower oil

Wash the trout in cold water with 2 tablespoons lemon juice and dry them between paper towels. Cut off the heads and carefully remove the backbone. Wash the insides well and season with a little herb salt.

Bring to a boil 1 cup water with ½ teaspoon herb salt, and add the shrimps. Cook until they are pink, and drain immediately. Pass the cooked shrimps through the fine blade of a food grinder; also put the mushrooms through the grinder. Heat 2 tablespoons safflower oil in a pan and sauté the chopped onion until it is soft and translucent. Combine the onion, shrimps, mushrooms, garlic, ½ cup bread crumbs, and the parsley in a bowl and mix well. Season with herb salt. Stuff the trout with this mixture and reshape the fish. Dust them lightly with flour, brush with beaten egg, and dust with bread crumbs.

Heat 4 tablespoons safflower oil in a large sauté pan with a lid. Carefully brown the stuffed trout on both sides. Cover the pan and finish cooking the fish for 5 minutes. Remove the fish to a warm au gratin dish or shallow serving dish.

HOLLANDAISE SAUCE. Boil the red wine down to half the original quantity. In a small bowl combine the reduced wine (or 2 tablespoons lemon juice), the egg yolks, ¼ teaspoon herb salt, and sweet or sour cream. Set the bowl in a small sauté pan half-filled with hot water over low heat, and beat the mixture with a small wire whisk until it is thick. Very slowly add 8 tablespoons safflower oil, beating constantly.

PRESENTATION. Decorate the fish with the lemon wedges and watercress. Serve the hollandaise in a separate bowl.

4 servings

MUSSELS
1½ dozen mussels
  1 teaspoon dry mustard
½ cup mixed sliced carrot, celery,
    and onion
½ cup dry white wine, or
    additional water, or white
    wine-grape juice
  1 bay leaf
    Herb salt

SAFFRON RICE
  4 tablespoons cold-pressed
    safflower oil
  1 medium-size onion, finely
    chopped
  1 teaspoon finely chopped fresh
    garlic
1½ cups natural brown rice
  2 teaspoons sea salt

(cont.)

**Casserole de
Fruits de Mer**

*Seafood Casserole
(Mussels,
Shrimps, Lobster,
and Scallops)
with Saffron Rice*

1 teaspoon whole saffron, crushed
and soaked in 1 tablespoon
cold water
1 pound raw shrimps, shelled and
deveined

LOBSTER

1 live lobster, any size
2 tablespoons cold-pressed
safflower oil
3 tablespoons dry sherry
(optional)

MUSHROOMS

2 tablespoons cold-pressed
safflower oil
4 firm fresh mushrooms, sliced
1 teaspoon fresh lemon juice
Herb salt

SAUCE

4 tablespoons cold-pressed
safflower oil
½ teaspoon finely chopped fresh
garlic
2 teaspoons finely chopped
shallots

½ teaspoon Marmite (brewers'
yeast extract)
½ teaspoon natural tomato paste
2 tablespoons stone-ground whole-
wheat pastry flour
1 cup stock reserved from the
mussels
⅓ cup raw light cream
Yolks of 2 organic eggs
1 tablespoon dry sherry
(optional)
2 tablespoons raw heavy sweet
cream or raw sour cream

SCALLOPS

½ pound sea scallops
2 tablespoons fresh lemon juice
2 tablespoons cold-pressed
safflower oil
Herb salt

FINISH

2 or 3 tablespoons whole-wheat
Bread Crumbs (p. 258)
2 or 3 tablespoons freshly grated
Parmesan cheese
Cold-pressed safflower oil for
topping

MUSSELS. Wash the mussels in water with 1 teaspoon dry mustard (which helps to clean them). Place the mussels in a pan with the carrot, celery, onion, wine, bay leaf, a little herb salt, and 2 cups water. Bring slowly to a boil, cover, and shake over high heat for a minute or two, or until the shells open. Discard any mussels with unopened shells; they are not good. Strain and reserve the liquid. Remove the mussels from the shells and set them aside.

SAFFRON RICE. Preheat the oven to 350°. Heat 4 tablespoons safflower oil in a deep heavy pan with a tight-fitting lid. Add the onion and cook very slowly, until the onion is translucent. Add the garlic and the rice, and stir until the rice is coated with oil. Add 3¾ cups of liquid, using all but 1 cup of the liquid from the mussels plus additional water. Add 2 tablespoons sea salt and the saffron. Bring the rice mixture to a rolling boil and remove it from the heat. Mix the raw shrimps into the rice, cover with the lid, and set the pan in the preheated oven to cook for 45 minutes. Remove the rice from the oven, add the shelled mussels, and fluff the mixture with 2 forks. Set aside and keep warm.

LOBSTER. Kill the lobster by cutting through the cross in the head shell behind the eyes with the point of a long chef's knife. Cut off the tail and split the tail and the head lengthwise. Remove the sac behind each eye and the intestine. Remove the claws. Heat 2 tablespoons safflower oil in a heavy pan and add the lobster pieces. Cover the pan and warm the lobster through for about 3 minutes. If desired, flame the lobster with 3 tablespoons dry sherry. Cover the pan and cook briskly until the lobster blushes, about 7 or 8 minutes. Remove the lobster from the pan and carefully extract the meat from the large claws and tail. Cut the lobster meat into bite-size chunks and mix it into the rice. Reserve the head shell and small claws for decoration.

MUSHROOMS. Heat 2 tablespoons safflower oil in a sauté pan and add the sliced mushrooms, lemon juice, and a little herb salt. Cook briskly for 2 minutes and mix the mushrooms into the rice.

SAUCE. Strain any liquid from the lobster pan, and add it to a saucepan with 4 tablespoons safflower oil. Add the garlic and shallots, and cook for 1 or 2 minutes. Off the heat blend in the Marmite yeast extract, tomato paste, and flour. Add the reserved cup of mussel stock and stir over moderate heat until sauce comes to a boil. Add the light cream and allow the sauce to simmer for 3 minutes. In a small bowl mix the egg yolks with the dry sherry and sweet or sour cream. Pour a little of the hot sauce into the egg-yolk mixture; then pour the egg-yolk mixture into the sauce in the pan and mix well. Reheat the sauce gently, but do not let it boil.

SCALLOPS. Wash the scallops in water and lemon juice, and dry them between paper towels. Heat 2 tablespoons safflower oil in a small sauté pan. When oil is very hot, add the scallops, brown them quickly on each side, and season with herb salt. Remove scallops from the pan and cut each one into halves.

PRESENTATION. Arrange the rice mixture like a mound on a large oval au gratin dish. Spoon over the sauce and sprinkle with the bread crumbs and grated cheese. Dot with a few drops of safflower oil, and brown lightly under the broiler. Decorate with the lobster shells, putting the head shells at one end of the dish and the little claws on the sides. Set the halved scallops, brown side up, in a row down the center of the dish, like buttons on a vest.

6 to 8 servings

2 *large live lobsters (size optional)*	2 *large yellow onions, finely chopped*	**Homard Thermidor**
6 *tablespoons cold-pressed safflower oil*	¼ *cup dry white wine, or additional water, or white wine-grape juice*	Lobster Thermidor
2 *tablespoons dry sherry (optional)*		

(cont.)

Herb salt

3 tablespoons stone-ground whole-
   wheat pastry flour
½ teaspoon dry mustard
1 cup raw milk
¼ cup raw heavy sweet cream or
   raw sour cream
⅓ cup freshly grated Parmesan
   cheese

A little sweet paprika
A few dry whole-wheat Bread
   Crumbs (p. 258)
Cold-pressed safflower oil for
   topping
Small bunch of crisp fresh
   watercress

Cut the lobsters into halves, starting from the cross in the center of the head. Remove the small sac from behind each eye and the intestines. With a kitchen scissors, cut off the large and small claws. Heat 2 tablespoons safflower oil in a large pan with a lid. Put the pieces of lobster, shell side down, in the pan, cover the pan, and cook for 2 minutes. Heat the sherry in a little pan, ignite, and pour it over the lobster. Re-cover the lobster and continue cooking until the shells are bright red. Remove the lobster from the pan and carefully extract the meat from the tail and the large claws. Arrange the 4 large half-shells, empty, on a shallow serving dish and set aside. Cut the lobster meat into even dice, and set it aside for a moment.

Add to the pan in which the lobster was cooked another 4 tablespoons safflower oil, and warm it. Add the chopped onions and cook until onions are soft but not brown. Add the wine, season with a little herb salt, and allow the mixture to boil down a little. Off the heat blend in the flour, dry mustard, and milk. Stir the sauce over moderate heat until it comes to a boil. Add the cream and half of the cheese, sprinkle with a little paprika, adjust the seasoning with herb salt, and mix well.

PRESENTATION. Mix the diced lobster into the sauce. Divide the mixture evenly among the 4 lobster shells. Sprinkle the tops with a few bread crumbs and the rest of the cheese. Dot with a few drops of safflower oil. Brown the lobsters lightly under the broiler. Garnish with watercress, and serve.

4 servings

**Coquilles
Saint-Jacques
Nantua**

*Scallops and
Oysters in Shells*

1 pound bay or sea scallops
2 tablespoons plus 1 teaspoon
   fresh lemon juice
1 cup dry white wine, or water, or
   white wine-grape juice
1 sprig of parsley or celery leaf
1 bay leaf
8 oysters on the half shell

3 tablespoons cold-pressed
   safflower oil
½ cup sliced firm fresh mushrooms
Herb salt
1½ tablespoons stone-ground
   whole-wheat pastry flour
Yolk of 1 organic egg

2 tablespoons raw heavy sweet
cream or raw sour cream
2 small tomatoes, about 2½
inches in diameter, skinned
and thinly sliced

½ cup freshly grated Parmesan
cheese
Cold-pressed safflower oil for
topping

Wash the scallops in water and 2 tablespoons lemon juice. Place them in a pan, and add the wine, parsley or celery leaf, and the bay leaf. Bring to a boil, and simmer for 5 minutes. Drain and reserve the liquid. If you are using sea scallops, slice them into bite-size pieces and set aside.

Remove the oysters from their shells and place them in a small pan. Cover them with the liquid from the scallops and bring to a boil Drain immediately and add the oysters to the scallops. Strain and reserve the liquid.

Heat 1 tablespoon safflower oil in a small sauté pan, add the mushrooms, 1 teaspoon lemon juice, and a little herb salt, and cook briskly for 2 minutes. Add the mushrooms to the scallops and oysters.

Heat 2 tablespoons safflower oil in a saucepan. Off the heat blend in the flour and 1 cup of the liquid from the oysters. Stir the sauce over moderate heat until it comes to a boil. Adjust the seasoning with herb salt. In a small bowl mix the egg yolk with the cream. Pour a little of the hot sauce into the egg-yolk mixture; then stir the egg-yolk mixture into the sauce in the pan. Warm the sauce for a minute but do not let it boil. Combine it with the scallop, oyster, and mushroom mixture and fill 4 scallop shells, about 6 inches across.

PRESENTATION. Cover the filled shells with overlapping slices of tomato. Sprinkle with the grated cheese, dot with a little safflower oil, and brown lightly under the broiler.

4 servings

Crevettes à la Créole

Shrimps Creole

3 tablespoons cold-pressed virgin
olive oil
3 tablespoons cold-pressed
safflower oil
¼ cup finely diced celery
½ cup finely diced fennel root
2 large carrots, finely diced
1 large yellow onion, finely
chopped
2 teaspoons finely chopped fresh
garlic
3 firm fresh mushrooms, finely
diced

Herb salt
1 teaspoon curry powder
2 green sweet bell peppers, finely
diced
3 medium-size ripe tomatoes,
skinned, seeded, and diced
2 teaspoons potato flour
1 tablespoon natural tomato paste
1 cup Soy-Vegetable Stock (p. 262)
4 cups raw shrimps, shelled and
deveined
1 cup raw sour cream
Saffron Rice (pp. 170–171)

Heat the olive oil and safflower oil in a heavy pan with a tight-fitting lid. Add the celery, fennel root, carrots, onion, garlic, and mushrooms. Season with herb salt and the curry powder. Press a piece of wax paper over the vegetables, cover the pan, and cook slowly until the vegetables are soft.

In a separate pan cover the diced green peppers with cold water, bring to a boil, and drain. Add the peppers and the tomatoes to the first vegetable group.

Off the heat, blend the potato flour, tomato paste, and stock with the vegetable mixture. Stir over moderate heat until it comes to a boil. Add the shrimps and cook over low heat until the shrimps turn pink. Then stir in the sour cream, spoonful by spoonful, and adjust the seasoning with herb salt.

PRESENTATION. Serve the shrimp mixture in a warm casserole with a separate bowl of the saffron rice.

4 to 6 servings

Aubergines Farcies aux Crevettes

Eggplant Stuffed with Shrimps

2 medium-size eggplants	Herb salt
Sea salt	¾ cup raw sour cream
9 tablespoons cold-pressed safflower oil	1 tablespoon stone-ground whole-wheat pastry flour
1 cup finely chopped yellow onion	1 tablespoon natural tomato paste
1 teaspoon finely chopped fresh garlic	1 medium-size ripe tomato, skinned, seeded, and cut into shreds
1 pound raw shrimps in their shells	Thin slices of natural Swiss-type cheese, enough to cover the tops of 4 eggplant halves
½ cup freshly grated Parmesan cheese	
1 tablespoon chopped fresh chives	

Cut the eggplants lengthwise into halves. Make a few incisions in the pulp from the cut side with a sharp knife, and sprinkle the surface with sea salt. Let the eggplants sit for at least 30 minutes. Rinse eggplants in cold water and dry between paper towels. Heat 4 tablespoons safflower oil in a large sauté pan. Cook the eggplants in the hot oil slowly, for about 5 minutes on each side. Remove them from the pan and carefully scoop out the pulp, leaving the skins whole. Chop the pulp and set it aside.

Heat 2 tablespoons safflower oil in a sauté pan and add the onion and ¾ teaspoon garlic. Cook over low heat until the onion is soft but not brown. Add the onion to the eggplant pulp. Add 2 tablespoons safflower oil to the sauté pan and cook the shrimps. Shake them over moderate heat until they turn pink. Remove the shells, devein, and slice them finely. Mix the sliced shrimps, grated cheese, and chives with the eggplant mixture. Adjust the seasoning with herb salt and mix in the sour cream.

TOMATO SAUCE. Heat 1 tablespoon safflower oil in a saucepan. Off the heat blend in the flour, tomato paste, ¼ teaspoon garlic, and 1 cup water. Season with herb salt. Stir over moderate heat until the sauce comes to a boil, reduce the heat, and allow to simmer for 5 minutes. Mix in the shredded fresh tomato.

PRESENTATION. Carefully fill the eggplant shells with the shrimp mixture. Cover the tops with the slices of cheese. Arrange the eggplants on an au gratin dish or heatproof serving platter. Brown lightly under the broiler, coat with the tomato sauce, and serve.

4 servings

POULTRY AND MEAT

Poultry, meat, and good health are a matter for knowledge, judgment, and moderation. As the gourmet strives for the ultimate in *cuisine santé,* perhaps the most drastic change in his diet will be to program fewer meals based on meat.

Almost nowhere else in the world do people eat as much meat per capita as in the United States. Most nutritionists advise that a meat meal once or twice a week is adequate; some say that it is not necessary at all. The nutritional problem with a heavily meat-oriented diet is that meat, as a rule, contains a higher percentage of acidity than does poultry or fish. (Of the three, fish contains the least.) Also a substantial meat diet means a high intake of saturated fat. But it is the overchemicalization of meat and the mass-production and synthetic feeding processes of poultry—for instance, the health hazards posed by nitrates, nitrites, and Red Dyes No. 2 and 40—that give impetus to the question: "Do we really need to eat as much meat?"

The following recipes include a broad selection of poultry and meat dishes for sensuous and organic pleasure in eating. We urge you, though, to use discretion in the *amounts* as well as the *quality* of the poultry and meat you consume. (Note: The meat chapter contains recipes for lamb, veal, and beef, but none for pork. Our reasons are given on p. 18.)

Nutritional aspects for cooking poultry and meat: Here are some basic principles which have been followed in the poultry and meat recipes.

1. Cook poultry and meat slowly with low temperatures. The meat will be more tender and flavorful, and the proteins—the chief nutrients in

poultry and meat—and other vitamins will be preserved. Harsh high heat kills vital elements.

In her later experiments, Mrs. Lucas worked with various low cooking temperatures but settled on a 300° temperature for roasting chicken or meat, and a 350° temperature for sautéing or braising in a sauce which would also be eaten. (If you have the time, by all means sauté and braise at the lower temperature, too. The lower the cooking heat, the less chance of harming the vitamins and proteins.) When cooking a whole bird or a large piece of meat, use a meat thermometer in order to cook only until the desired temperature is reached.

2. Chicken and meat should be browned only lightly, if at all. Adelle Davis notes that "although searing has long been used as a means of developing flavor (and a nice color), it may cause carcinogenic substances."

3. Generally, meat and poultry should not be salted until the end of the cooking, if at all. Mrs. Lucas believed—and we agree—that a well-seasoned sauce accompanying the meat or fowl will usually provide the proper balance.

4. Baste minimally. The only purpose is to catch the juices from the meat and prevent their burning away in the bottom of the pan. These vitamin-rich juices will be used later to prepare a tasty and nutritious sauce. The basting liquid does not moisturize the meat.

How the sauces change: Basic ingredients in sauces served with poultry and meat dishes are re-interpreted as follows: (All of these ingredients are discussed in the Encyclopedia.)

1. Cold-pressed safflower oil replaces butter.

2. Stone-ground whole-wheat pastry flour (or potato flour for a clear sauce) is used instead of refined white flour.

3. Marmite (brewers' yeast extract) is substituted for meat glaze (*glace de viande*).

4. Herb salt and fresh herbs are used for seasoning in place of pepper and other spices of an irritant quality.

5. Wine is used, as in traditional methods, but may be replaced by additional stock or water. If a recipe calls for flaming the meat or poultry with sherry or Marsala, this step may be skipped.

6. The stocks we like to use are Soy-Vegetable Stock (p. 262), when we want a good sturdy stock, and Light Soy Stock (p. 262). Dione Lucas generally used an all-purpose chicken stock for sauces and soups; although this stock is excellent and may be used in any of the recipes calling for stock, the Soy-Vegetable Stock also produces a good sauce, is much more convenient, and utilizes nutrition-rich vegetable cooking water which might otherwise be discarded.

In all of the recipes, organic meats and poultry are recommended. They are available in limited supply—usually through natural-food stores or fancy meat suppliers—but you will have to trust your supplier as to their organic purity. If you cannot obtain organic meat and poultry, the cooking methods and sauce ingredients given in these recipes used with commercial meat or poultry will still be a big step toward better nutrition.

This is a basic recipe for roast chicken. The garnish of meatballs is optional.

Poulet Rôti à la Viennoise

Roast Chicken with Meatballs

1 *whole dressed chicken, about*
   3½ pounds
  About 3 tablespoons cold-pressed
   safflower oil
  Herb salt
2 *sprigs of fresh parsley*
1 *baby white onion, cut into*
   quarters
1 *garlic clove*
  About 2 tablespoons fresh lemon
   juice
  Sea salt
1 *cup mixed water and dry white*
   wine, or water and white wine-
   grape juice, or light Soy Stock
   (p. 262), for basting

MEATBALLS
2 *chicken livers*
¼ *pound ground veal or beef*
¼ *teaspoon finely chopped fresh*
   garlic
½ *teaspoon chopped fresh thyme,*
   or ¼ teaspoon dried thyme
  White of 1 organic egg
  Herb salt
  Stone-ground whole-wheat
   pastry flour for coating
  About 2 tablespoons cold-
   pressed safflower oil

GARNISH
  Broiled Tomatoes (p. 211)

Preheat the oven to 300°. Wipe the chicken inside and out with paper towels. Insert in the cavity 2 tablespoons safflower oil, 1 teaspoon herb salt, the parsley, onion, and garlic clove. Truss the chicken with kitchen string. Rub it all over with lemon juice and sea salt and brush it with safflower oil. Set the chicken in a small roasting pan and pour the mixed water and wine into the pan. Insert a meat thermometer into the flesh of the chicken. Roast in the preheated oven until the thermometer registers 170° to 175°, about 2½ hours. During roasting, baste the chicken about every 30 minutes, using the liquid from the bottom of the pan and more mixed water and wine, if necessary.

MEATBALLS. Chop the raw chicken livers finely. In the bowl of an electric mixer combine the chopped livers, ground veal or beef, garlic, thyme, and egg white. Beat the mixture well and season with herb salt. Roll the mixture into little balls, dust them lightly with flour, and sauté them in hot safflower oil until they are golden brown all over.

PRESENTATION. When the chicken is cooked, it may be served whole and carved at the table, or it may be carved in the kitchen and the pieces arranged on a shallow serving dish. Either way, moisten the chicken with the juices from the pan, and garnish it with the broiled tomatoes and piles of meatballs.

4 to 6 servings

Poulet Rôti Lorette

Boned Stuffed Chicken with Lorette Potatoes

1 whole dressed chicken, about 3½ pounds
Herb salt
¾ pound ground veal
Whites of 2 organic eggs, raw
1 cup raw light cream
2 black truffles, chopped
Sea salt
4 chicken livers
2 organic eggs, hard-boiled and shelled
About 4 tablespoons cold-pressed safflower oil
1 cup mixed water and dry white wine, or water and white wine-grape juice, or Light Soy Stock (p. 262), for basting

3 teaspoons potato flour
1 teaspoon Marmite (brewers' yeast extract)
1 teaspoon natural tomato paste
2 cups Soy-Vegetable Stock (p. 262)
¾ pound firm fresh mushrooms
1 teaspoon fresh lemon juice

GARNISHES
Lorette Potatoes (p. 209)
Broiled Tomatoes (p. 211)

Preheat the oven to 300°. Carefully bone the chicken completely. Spread it out on a board, skin side down, and sprinkle the top with herb salt. Spread it with veal mousse.

VEAL MOUSSE. Beat the ground veal and raw egg whites in the electric mixer until well blended. Continue beating as you very slowly add the light cream. Mix in 1 chopped truffle, 1 teaspoon herb salt, and ½ teaspoon sea salt.

On top of the mousse arrange the whole chicken livers and the whole hard-boiled eggs. Roll up the chicken and sew it together with thread. Place it in a roasting pan and brush it all over with safflower oil. Insert a meat thermometer. Pour the water and wine mixture or stock in the pan. Set the chicken in the preheated oven and roast until the thermometer registers 170° to 175°, about 3 hours. During the roasting, baste the chicken about every 30 minutes, using liquid from the bottom of the pan and more water and wine, or stock, if necessary.

When the chicken is roasted, remove it from the pan and keep it warm while you prepare the sauce. Add to the roasting pan the potato flour, Marmite yeast extract, and tomato paste, and blend well. Add the stock and stir the sauce over moderate heat until it comes to a boil. Continue stirring, and add 1 tablespoon safflower oil and the remaining truffle. Simmer the sauce over low heat for 5 minutes.

Flute the mushroom caps, if desired. Sauté them quickly in a little safflower oil with 1 teaspoon lemon juice, and season with herb salt.

PRESENTATION. Cut as many slices of the chicken as needed for one serving. Arrange the slices overlapping at one end of a warm serving dish. Place the uncut chicken at the other end. Spoon the sauce over the chicken. Place a pile of Lorette potatoes at each end of the serving dish. Arrange the broiled tomatoes and mushrooms on the sides of the dish.

4 to 6 servings

Poulet Sauté en Demi-Deuil

Sautéed Chicken in Half-Mourning

1   whole dressed chicken, about
    4 or 5 pounds
3   *large black truffles*
6   *tablespoons cold-pressed*
    safflower oil
    Herb salt
2   *or 3 sprigs of fresh parsley*
1   *yellow onion, quartered*
1   *garlic clove, bruised*
⅓   *cup dry sherry (optional)*
¼   *teaspoon natural tomato paste*
1   *teaspoon Marmite (brewers'*
    yeast extract)

4   *teaspoons potato flour*
3½   *cups Soy-Vegetable Stock*
    (p. 262)
1   *teaspoon natural currant or*
    guava jelly

GARNISH
    Gnocchi alla Romana, whole-
    wheat (p. 176), or Gnocchi
    Parisienne without Mornay
    Sauce (pp. 176–177)
    Bunch of crisp fresh watercress

Preheat the oven to 300°. Wipe the chicken inside and out with paper towels. Thinly slice 2 truffles. Carefully loosen the skin from the legs and breast of the chicken and insert the truffle slices in neat rows down both sides of the breastbone and on the thighs and drumsticks. Insert in the cavity of the chicken 2 tablespoons safflower oil, 1 teaspoon herb salt, the parsley, onion, garlic, and the chicken neck and gizzard. Carefully truss the chicken.

Heat 3 tablespoons safflower oil in a deep heavy pan. When it is hot, carefully and slowly brown the chicken on all sides, taking great care not to break the skin. Do not have the oil so hot as to scorch the skin. You want to achieve a golden, translucent look. Also sauté the chicken liver in the pan and then set aside. Heat the dry sherry in a little pan, ignite, and pour it over the chicken. Remove the chicken from the pan and set it aside while you prepare the sauce.

Add to the pan, off the heat, the tomato paste, Marmite yeast extract, and potato flour. Blend these ingredients to a smooth paste and then stir in the stock. Chop the remaining truffle and add it to the sauce with the jelly. Adjust the seasoning, if necessary, with herb salt.

Stir the sauce over moderate heat until it comes to a boil. Reduce the heat to a simmer and let the sauce cook for 10 minutes. Return the chicken to the pan with the sauce. Insert a meat thermometer in the flesh of the chicken. Set the pan in the preheated oven and cook until the thermometer registers 170° to 175°, about 3 hours.

PRESENTATION. When the chicken is cooked, remove the string and place the whole chicken on a warm serving platter. Garnish with the gnocchi and the watercress. Slice the chicken liver, add it to the sauce, and serve the sauce in a separate bowl. (If you prefer, the chicken may be carved in the kitchen and the pieces arranged on the platter.)
4 to 6 servings

Poulet Mallorca

Chicken with Tomatoes, Green Peppers, Oranges

2 *small whole dressed chickens, 2½ to 3 pounds each*
4 *tablespoons cold-pressed safflower oil*
¼ *cup dry sherry (optional)*
½ *teaspoon finely chopped fresh garlic*
2 *teaspoons natural tomato paste*
½ *teaspoon Marmite (brewers' yeast extract)*
2 *teaspoons potato flour*
1¼ *cups Soy-Vegetable Stock (p. 262)*
¼ *cup Madeira wine, or additional stock*
Herb salt
2 *sprigs of fresh tarragon*

1 *green sweet bell pepper*
1 *red sweet bell pepper, or additional green pepper*
Sea salt
3 *medium-size ripe tomatoes, skinned*
2 *tablespoons cold-pressed safflower oil*
2 *teaspoons finely chopped fresh garlic*
4 *firm fresh mushrooms, cut into thick slices*
1 *teaspoon fresh lemon juice*
Herb salt
Herbed Potatoes (p. 207), or Rice Pilaff (pp. 168–169)

GARNISH
2 *large oranges*

Dry the chickens inside and out with paper towels and truss them. Heat 3 tablespoons safflower oil in a deep heavy pan. Slowly brown the chickens in the hot oil until the skin is golden and translucent, not scorched. Heat the sherry in a little pan, ignite, and pour it over the chickens. Remove the chickens from the pan and set them aside for a moment.

Add another tablespoon of safflower oil to the pan. Off the heat add the garlic, tomato paste, Marmite yeast extract, and potato flour, and blend to a smooth paste. Add the stock and Madeira and stir the sauce over moderate heat until it comes to a boil. Adjust the seasoning with herb salt and add the sprigs of tarragon. Reduce the heat to very low and return the chickens to the pan. Cover the pan with a piece of wax paper and a tight-fitting lid. Cook over low heat until the chicken is tender.

GARNISH. Peel the rind from 1 orange and cut it lengthwise into fine shreds. Peel the other orange, discard the peel, and cut both oranges into neat sections. Remove the seeds from the green and red peppers and cut them into strips $3/8$ inch wide. Put the pepper strips in a pan, cover with cold water and $1/2$ teaspoon sea salt, bring the water to a boil, and drain immediately. Cut the tomatoes into quarters and remove the seeds.

Heat 2 tablespoons safflower oil in a sauté pan and add the shredded orange rind and the chopped garlic. Cook slowly for 2 minutes. Add the sliced mushrooms and lemon juice, season with a little herb salt, and cook for 2 minutes. Add the red and green peppers, season with a little more herb salt, and cook for another 2 or 3 minutes. Add the tomato and orange sections. Gently warm the mixture for a minute or two but not longer; you do not want the tomatoes and oranges to disintegrate.

PRESENTATION. When the chickens are cooked, cut them into quarters, if small, or smaller serving pieces if they are larger. Arrange the chicken in a casserole dish. Spoon the garnish mixture over the chicken. Pour over the sauce. Serve the Herbed Potatoes or Rice Pilaff separately.

8 servings

Poulet Marengo

Chicken Marengo —with Lobster and Eggs

2 small whole dressed chickens, 2 to 2½ pounds each
6 tablespoons cold-pressed safflower oil
3 tablespoons dry sherry (optional)
1 tablespoon natural tomato paste
2 tablespoons stone-ground whole-wheat pastry flour
1½ cups Soy-Vegetable Stock (p. 262)

3 firm fresh mushrooms, finely chopped
4 medium-size ripe tomatoes, skinned and sliced
1 bay leaf
Herb salt
Sea salt
1 small live lobster
4 to 6 organic eggs (1 per serving)
8 triangular Croutons of stone-ground whole-wheat bread, fried (p. 258)

Preheat the oven to 350°. Cut the chickens into quarters. Heat 3 tablespoons safflower oil in a deep heavy pan and lightly brown the pieces of chicken. Heat the sherry in a little pan, ignite, and pour it over the chicken. Remove the chicken from the pan and set it aside for a moment.

Add to the pan the tomato paste and flour and blend to a smooth paste. Add the stock and stir over moderate heat until the sauce comes to a boil. Add the chopped mushrooms, tomatoes, and bay leaf, and season with herb salt. Bring the sauce to a boil again. Return the chicken to the pan, cover it with the lid, and cook in the preheated oven for about 35 minutes, or until the chicken is tender.

Fill a pan large enough for the whole lobster ¼ full of water and add 1 teaspoon sea salt. Bring the water to a boil, add the lobster, and cover the pan. Cook the lobster in the boiling water until it turns red. Remove it from the pan and carefully extract the meat from the shell, saving the head and tail shells and little claws for decoration.

Heat 3 tablespoons safflower oil in a small sauté pan. Break 1 egg into a cup. Tilt the sauté pan so there is a pool of oil in one side. Pour the egg into the pool of oil. When the white begins to set, carefully fold it over the yolk. Carefully turn the egg so that it browns on both sides. Cook all the eggs in this manner and set them in a bowl of warm water.

PRESENTATION. When the chicken is cooked, arrange it on a warm au gratin or shallow serving dish. Slice the lobster meat and scatter it over the chicken. Cover all with the sauce. Drain the eggs on paper towels and carefully set them around the edge of the chicken dish. Stick the fried croutons around the sides also, with the points sticking up.

8 servings

Poulet Smitane aux Cerises

Chicken with Sour Cream Sauce and Cherries

1 whole dressed chicken, about
   3½ pounds
4 tablespoons cold-pressed
   safflower oil
2 tablespoons dry sherry
   (optional)
¼ pound fresh mushrooms,
   finely chopped
¼ teaspoon finely chopped fresh
   garlic
½ teaspoon natural tomato paste

1 teaspoon Marmite (brewers'
   yeast extract)
2 tablespoons stone-ground whole-
   wheat pastry flour
1 cup Soy-Vegetable Stock (p. 262)
1 cup raw sour cream
   Herb salt
1 cup fresh black cherries, or
   unsweetened water-packed
   black cherries

Preheat the oven to 350°. Dry the chicken inside and out with paper towels and tie it with string. Heat 3 tablespoons safflower oil in a deep heavy pan. Slowly brown the chicken on all sides, turning it over and over until the skin is translucent and golden brown. Heat the sherry in a small pan, ignite, and pour it over the chicken. Remove the chicken from the pan while you prepare the sauce.

Add to the pan another tablespoon of safflower oil, the mushrooms, and garlic, and cook for 1 minute. Off the heat add the tomato paste,

Marmite yeast extract, and flour, and blend to a smooth paste. Add the stock, and stir over moderate heat until the sauce comes to a boil. Spoonful by spoonful, stir in the sour cream. Adjust the seasoning with herb salt.

Carve the chicken into serving pieces and return it to the pan. Cover it with the lid and cook in the preheated oven for 45 minutes, or until the chicken is tender.

PRESENTATION. When the chicken is cooked, arrange it on a warm au gratin dish or shallow serving dish. Add the cherries to the sauce and warm them over low heat. Spoon the sauce over the chicken and lightly brown the top of the dish under the broiler.

4 servings

6 *half-breasts of chicken*
  Herb salt
4 *tablespoons dry sherry (optional)*
3 *tablespoons cold-pressed safflower oil*

DUXELLES STUFFING
2 *cups finely chopped fresh mushrooms*
2 *tablespoons cold-pressed safflower oil*
2 *tablespoons chopped yellow onion*
1 *teaspoon finely chopped shallot*
  Herb salt
1 *tablespoon natural tomato paste*

BÉARNAISE SAUCE
  Yolks of 3 organic eggs
2 *teaspoons fresh lemon juice*
2 *tablespoons raw light cream*
¼ *teaspoon herb salt*
8 *tablespoons cold-pressed safflower oil*
¼ *teaspoon natural tomato paste*
¼ *teaspoon Marmite (brewers' yeast extract)*
1 *tablespoon mixed chopped fresh herbs (tarragon, parsley, thyme, etc.)*

Pea Purée (p. 194)

Suprêmes de Volaille Farcis, Sauce Béarnaise

Sautéed Stuffed Breasts of Chicken, Béarnaise Sauce, on Pea Purée

Carefully remove the skin and bones from the chicken breasts. Cut a pocket in the thick side. Season the breasts with herb salt. Brush them with 1 tablespoon sherry and let them marinate while you prepare the stuffing.

DUXELLES STUFFING. Put the chopped mushrooms in a cloth; twist the cloth tightly and squeeze out all of the liquid. Heat 2 tablespoons safflower oil in a sauté pan and add the mushrooms, onion, and shallot. Season with herb salt and cook for 4 or 5 minutes. Mix in the tomato paste and cook over low heat for another 4 or 5 minutes. Carefully fill the pockets in the chicken with the mushroom mixture and reshape them.

Heat 3 tablespoons safflower oil in a large sauté pan. Lightly brown the breasts on each side. Heat 3 tablespoons dry sherry in a little pan, ignite, and pour over the chicken. Reduce the heat to very low and cook until the chicken is tender, about 15 to 20 minutes, turning the breasts once.

BÉARNAISE SAUCE. In a small bowl combine the egg yolks, lemon juice, cream, and herb salt. Set the bowl in a small sauté pan half-filled with hot water, over low heat, and beat with a small wire whisk until the mixture is thick. Very slowly beat in the safflower oil. After all of the oil has been incorporated, beat in the tomato paste, Marmite yeast extract, and herbs.

PRESENTATION. Spread the pea purée on the bottom of a warm au gratin dish or shallow serving dish, like a bed. Place the chicken breasts on top of it. Coat the chicken with the béarnaise sauce. Brown lightly under the broiler, not too long, or the sauce will separate, and serve.

6 servings

Crêpes Niçoise Variées

Savory Filled Crêpes (Poultry, Seafood, or Meat)

To prepare this dish with cooked crab, lobster, shrimps, duck, turkey, or veal, substitute 1 cup of any of the preceding ingredients for the chicken in the recipe given below. Follow the rest of the recipe ingredients and procedure as given. (Instead of finishing the dish with grated cheese, it may be covered with Canapé Sauce [p. 269] and browned under the broiler.)

8 to 12 crêpes, about 6 inches in diameter (p. 232)

FILLING AND GARNISH
5 tablespoons cold-pressed safflower oil
5 or 6 firm fresh mushrooms, sliced
1 teaspoon fresh lemon juice
Herb salt

1 cup cooked chicken, shredded
2 organic eggs, hard-boiled and chopped
1 tablespoon chopped fresh parsley
4 tablespoons raw sour cream
½ cup freshly grated Parmesan cheese

Prepare the crêpes and gently pile them on a wire rack.

FILLING. Heat 2 tablespoons safflower oil in a sauté pan. Add the mushrooms, lemon juice, and a little herb salt, and cook briskly for 1 or 2 minutes. Add the chicken, hard-boiled eggs, parsley, sour cream, and a little more herb salt if necessary. Cook the mixture over low heat for a few minutes.

PRESENTATION. Place a spoonful of the filling in the middle of each crêpe. Roll them up tightly and arrange them in a row on a warm au gratin dish or shallow serving dish. Brush them lightly with about 3 tablespoons safflower oil and sprinkle the grated cheese over the top. Brown lightly under the broiler and serve.

4 servings

8 half-breasts of chicken

3 cups light Soy-Vegetable Stock (p. 262)

½ cup mixed sliced carrot, celery, and onion
Herb salt

8 to 12 crêpes, about 6 inches in diameter (p. 232)

1 pound natural ricotta cheese

VELOUTÉ SAUCE

4 tablespoons cold-pressed safflower oil

3 tablespoons stone-ground whole-wheat pastry flour

1½ cups stock (from the liquid in which chicken was cooked)

1 cup raw light cream

Herb salt

HOLLANDAISE SAUCE

Yolks of 2 organic eggs

¼ teaspoon herb salt

1 tablespoon fresh lemon juice

2 tablespoons raw sour cream

8 tablespoons cold-pressed safflower oil

Suprêmes de Volaille Lucia

Poached Breasts of Chicken with Crêpes Filled with Ricotta Cheese

Place the chicken breasts in a heavy pan, cover them with the stock, and add the carrot, celery, onion, and 1 teaspoon herb salt. Bring to a boil, cover, and simmer gently for 25 minutes. Remove the chicken from the stock; strain the stock, and reserve it. Carefully remove the skin and bones from the chicken. Place the breasts in a row on a warm serving platter, and keep them warm.

Prepare the crêpes and gently pile them on a wire rack. Spread a little ricotta cheese on the second side of each crêpe, roll them up, and arrange around the chicken breasts.

VELOUTÉ SAUCE. Heat 2 tablespoons safflower oil in a saucepan. Off the heat blend in the flour, 1½ cups strained stock, and the light cream. Adjust the seasoning with herb salt and bring the sauce to a boil over moderate heat, stirring constantly. Reduce the heat to a simmer and stir in another 2 tablespoons safflower oil.

HOLLANDAISE SAUCE. In a small bowl combine the egg yolks, herb salt, lemon juice, and sour cream, and mix well. Set the bowl in a small sauté pan half-filled with hot water, over low heat, and beat with a small wire whisk until the sauce is thick. Slowly add 8 tablespoons safflower oil, beating constantly.

PRESENTATION. Coat the chicken breasts and the stuffed crêpes with the velouté sauce. Spoon a ribbon of the hollandaise sauce on top of the velouté sauce down the center of the dish. Brown the top lightly under the broiler, not too long, or it will separate, and serve.

8 servings

Suprêmes de Volaille, à l'Aubergine, Hollandaise

Breasts of Chicken on Eggplant, Hollandaise Sauce

1 large eggplant
  Sea salt
4 tablespoons cold-pressed
  safflower oil plus additional
  oil for topping
1 Bermuda onion, chopped
½ cup sliced firm fresh mushrooms
  Herb salt
¾ cup raw sour cream
½ cup dry whole-wheat Bread
  Crumbs (p. 258)
½ cup freshly grated Parmesan
  cheese
4 to 6 half-breasts of chicken

BROWN SAUCE
1 tablespoon cold-pressed
  safflower oil
2 tablespoons Marsala wine, or red
  wine-grape juice
2 tablespoons stone-ground whole-
  wheat pastry flour

1 teaspoon natural tomato paste
1 teaspoon Marmite (brewers'
  yeast extract)
1½ cups Soy-Vegetable Stock
  (p. 262)
  Herb salt

HOLLANDAISE SAUCE
  Yolks of 2 organic eggs
1 tablespoon fresh lemon juice
¼ teaspoon herb salt
1 tablespoon raw sour cream
6 tablespoons cold-pressed
  safflower oil

GARNISH
4 whole firm fresh mushrooms,
  fluted if desired
1 tablespoon cold-pressed
  safflower oil
  Few drops of fresh lemon juice
  Herb salt

Preheat the oven to 350°. Cut the eggplant lengthwise into quarters. Sprinkle pieces with sea salt and set them on a jelly-roll pan. Bake the eggplant in the preheated oven for about 30 minutes, until the pulp is soft. Scoop out the pulp, leaving the skin sections intact. Heat 2 tablespoons safflower oil in a sauté pan. Add the onion and cook until it is translucent. Add the sliced mushrooms with a little herb salt, and cook for 1 or 2 minutes longer. Chop the eggplant pulp and put it in a mixing bowl with the onion and mushroom mixture and the sour cream, and adjust the seasoning with herb salt if necessary. Place the eggplant skins on a shallow serving dish or au gratin dish. Spread the eggplant mixture on the skins. Sprinkle the tops with the bread crumbs and cheese, dot with a few drops of safflower oil, and brown under the broiler.

Sprinkle the chicken breasts with a little herb salt. Heat 2 tablespoons safflower oil in a sauté pan. When it is quite hot, lightly brown the chicken breasts on both sides and cook over low heat until done. Place 1 chicken breast on top of each eggplant section.

BROWN SAUCE. Add 1 tablespoon safflower oil to the pan in which the chicken was cooked. Off the heat add the Marsala wine, flour, tomato paste, and Marmite yeast extract, and blend. Add the stock and stir over moderate heat until the sauce comes to a boil. Adjust the seasoning with herb salt.

HOLLANDAISE SAUCE. In a small bowl combine the egg yolks, lemon juice, ¼ teaspoon herb salt, and the sour cream. Set the bowl in a small sauté pan half-filled with hot water, over low heat, and beat with a small wire whisk until it is thick. Slowly beat in the safflower oil.

Quickly sauté the whole mushrooms in 1 tablespoon safflower oil with a few drops of lemon juice and herb salt to taste.

PRESENTATION. Pour the brown sauce around the edge of the chicken dish. Put a spoonful of hollandaise sauce on top of each chicken breast, and brown lightly under the broiler, not too long, or the sauce will separate. Set a whole mushroom on top of each chicken breast, and serve.

4 to 6 servings

Suprêmes de Volaille au Limon

Breasts of Chicken with Lime Sauce

4 to 6 half-breasts of chicken, skinned and boned

3 tablespoons stone-ground whole-wheat pastry flour plus additional for coating

6 tablespoons cold-pressed safflower oil

5 tablespoons dry sherry, or white wine-grape juice

Finely grated rind of 2 large or 3 small limes

2 teaspoons finely chopped fresh garlic

1 teaspoon natural tomato paste

1 teaspoon Marmite (brewers' yeast extract)

1½ cups light Soy-Vegetable Stock (p. 262)

Herb salt

1 cup raw sour cream

½ cup raw heavy sweet cream, whipped

Juice of 1 lime

2 teaspoons raw sugar, or organic honey

1 teaspoon natural guava jelly

½ cup freshly grated Parmesan cheese

Dust the chicken breasts lightly with flour. Heat 4 tablespoons safflower oil in a large sauté pan. When it is hot, quickly brown the chicken breasts on both sides. Heat 3 tablespoons dry sherry in a little pan, ignite, and pour it over the chicken. If you are using the grape juice, pour it over the chicken. Remove the chicken from the pan, setting it aside for a moment.

Add 2 tablespoons safflower oil to the pan. Add the lime rind and chopped garlic and cook very slowly for 2 or 3 minutes. Off the heat add the tomato paste, Marmite yeast extract, 3 tablespoons whole-wheat flour, the stock, and 2 tablespoons sherry or grape juice. Stir the sauce over moderate heat until it comes to a boil. Season with herb salt, reduce the heat, and allow the sauce to simmer gently.

Fold the sour cream into the whipped cream. Stir the combined cream into the sauce, spoonful by spoonful. Add the lime juice, sugar or honey, and jelly. Adjust the seasoning with herb salt. Return the chicken breasts to the pan, coat them with the sauce, and cook over low heat for about 20 minutes, until the chicken is tender.

PRESENTATION. Arrange the chicken breasts on a warm au gratin dish or shallow serving dish. Cover them with the sauce, sprinkle the top with the grated cheese, and brown lightly under the broiler.

4 to 6 servings

Suprêmes de Volaille Parisienne

Poached Breasts of Chicken with Mushroom Velouté and Hollandaise

8 half-breasts of chicken, skinned and boned
Herb salt
4 tablespoons stone-ground whole-wheat pastry flour plus additional for dusting
8 tablespoons cold-pressed safflower oil
4 tablespoons dry sherry, or white wine-grape juice
1 ounce dried mushrooms, soaked in ½ cup water
2½ cups light Soy-Vegetable Stock (p. 262)

½ cup chopped fresh mushrooms
8 whole firm fresh mushrooms, fluted if desired
1 teaspoon fresh lemon juice

HOLLANDAISE SAUCE
Yolks of 2 organic eggs
¼ teaspoon herb salt
1 tablespoon fresh lemon juice
2 tablespoons raw heavy sweet cream, or raw sour cream
6 tablespoons cold-pressed safflower oil

Sprinkle the chicken breasts with a little herb salt and dust them lightly with whole-wheat flour. Heat 3 tablespoons safflower oil in a sauté pan. When it is quite hot, add the chicken breasts and brown them quickly on each side. Pour over sherry or grape juice. Drain the water from the dried mushrooms and have it handy to the sauté pan. Cover the chicken, reduce the heat, and cook for 15 to 20 minutes, until tender, gradually adding ¼ cup mushroom water. When the chicken breasts are done, remove them from the pan with a slotted spoon, arrange them on a shallow serving dish, and keep them warm.

MUSHROOM VELOUTÉ SAUCE. Heat 3 tablespoons safflower oil in a saucepan. Off the heat add 4 tablespoons flour, the light stock, chopped fresh mushrooms, and a little herb salt. Stir over moderate heat until the sauce comes to a boil. Chop the drained mushrooms and add them to the sauce; also add the liquid from the sauté pan in which the chicken was cooked. Simmer the sauce for 5 minutes.

HOLLANDAISE SAUCE. In a small bowl combine the egg yolks, ¼ teaspoon herb salt, 1 tablespoon lemon juice, and the cream. Set the bowl in a small sauté pan half-filled with hot water, over low heat, and beat with a small wire whisk until the mixture is thick. Very slowly, beat in the safflower oil.

Heat 2 tablespoons safflower oil in a small sauté pan and briskly sauté the whole mushrooms with 1 teaspoon lemon juice and a little herb salt.

PRESENTATION. Cover the chicken breasts with the mushroom velouté sauce. Spoon a ribbon of the hollandaise sauce down the center of the dish. Brown the top lightly under the broiler. Set a whole mushroom on top of each chicken breast.

8 servings

Poulet à l'Estragon, Blanc

Chicken with Tarragon, Suprême Sauce

6 half-breasts of chicken, or 1 whole dressed chicken, about 3½ pounds
1 yellow onion, sliced
1 medium-size carrot, sliced
1 small celery stalk, sliced
½ cup dry white wine, or white wine-grape juice
  Herb salt
3 tablespoons cold-pressed safflower oil

3 tablespoons stone-ground whole-wheat pastry flour
1½ cups liquid in which chicken was cooked
¼ cup raw heavy sweet cream, or raw sour cream
  Yolk of 1 organic egg
1 tablespoon raw milk
¼ cup fresh tarragon leaves
3 sprigs of fresh tarragon
  Rice Pilaff (pp. 168–169)

If you are using chicken breasts, carefully remove the skin and bones. *If you are using a whole chicken,* wipe it inside and out with paper towels and truss it. Set the breasts or whole chicken in a deep heavy pan with the onion, carrot, celery, and wine. Pour in just enough water to cover the chicken, and add 1½ teaspoons herb salt. Bring the water to a boil and cover the pan. Simmer the breasts for 25 minutes. Simmer the whole chicken for about 45 minutes. When the chicken is cooked, remove it from the stock and strain the stock.

SUPRÊME SAUCE. Heat the safflower oil in a saucepan and blend in the flour. Off the heat add 1½ cups of the strained chicken stock. Stir the sauce over moderate heat until it comes to a boil. Season with herb salt. Reduce the heat and stir in the cream. Gently simmer the sauce for 5 minutes. Mix the egg yolk and milk in a little bowl. Add 2 or 3 tablespoons of the sauce to the egg-yolk mixture, then pour the egg-yolk mixture into the sauce in the pan, stirring all the while. Add the tarragon leaves. The sauce may be reheated, but do not let it boil or it will separate.

PRESENTATION. Arrange the rice pilaff on a warm au gratin dish or shallow serving dish. Place the chicken breasts on the rice. Or carve the whole chicken into serving pieces and set them on the rice. Coat the chicken with the sauce and garnish with the sprigs of fresh tarragon.

4 to 6 servings

**Côtelettes de
Volaille Pojarsky**

Chicken Cutlets,
Pojarsky

4 half-chicken breasts, skinned
 and boned
4 ounces natural sweet butter,
 firm and cold
1 cup raw heavy sweet cream,
 whipped, or good thick raw
 sour cream
 Herb salt
 A little freshly grated nutmeg
 Stone-ground whole-wheat pastry
 flour, sifted, for dusting the
 cutlets
1 organic egg, beaten

 Dry whole-wheat Bread Crumbs
 (p. 258)
4 tablespoons cold-pressed
 safflower oil
1 tablespoon and 1 teaspoon fresh
 lemon juice
 About 12 pieces of wide
 macaroni, raw (for "chicken
 legs")
 About 12 paper cutlet frills
½ pound fresh button mushrooms
 Bunch of crisp fresh watercress

Put the chicken breasts and the cold butter through the fine blade of a
food grinder three or four times, until the mixture is very smooth. Rub
the mixture through a fine vegetable strainer. Fold in the whipped
or sour cream and season with herb salt and nutmeg.

Divide the chicken mixture into 12 portions. On a lightly floured
board, roll each portion into a ball with lightly floured hands. With a
small palette knife, flatten out the balls a little, and form them into
cutlet shapes. Brush them with the beaten egg, then coat with the
bread crumbs. Set the cutlets in the freezer for 1 hour.

Heat the safflower oil in a sauté pan with 1 tablespoon lemon juice
and a little herb salt. Get the oil quite hot and brown the cutlets on
each side. Cover the pan and cook them over low heat for another 3
minutes on each side.

PRESENTATION. Arrange the cutlets on a warm shallow serving dish in
the shape of a crown. Stick a piece of macaroni at the narrow end of
each cutlet like the end bone of a chop. Cover the macaroni with a
paper cutlet frill. In the pan in which the cutlets were cooked, quickly
sauté the mushrooms with 1 teaspoon lemon juice and a little herb
salt. Garnish the dish with the mushrooms and the watercress.

4 to 6 servings

**Timbales de
Poulet, Riz au
Safran**

Chicken
Timbales with
Saffron Rice

6 half-breasts of chicken, skinned
 and boned
 Whites of 4 organic eggs
1¼ cups raw light cream
 Sea salt
 Herb salt
 Cold-pressed safflower oil for
 molds
3 tablespoons cold-pressed
 safflower oil

3 tablespoons stone-ground
 whole-wheat pastry flour
1½ cups light Soy-Vegetable Stock
 (p. 262)
 Yolks of 2 organic eggs
2 tablespoons raw milk
 Saffron Rice (pp. 170–171)

Preheat the oven to 350°. Pass the boned chicken breasts through the fine blade of a food grinder twice. In an electric mixer beat the ground chicken with the egg whites. Rub this mixture through a fine vegetable strainer into a round-bottomed metal bowl. Set the bowl in another bowl filled with ice, and with a small wire whisk beat in 1 cup of the light cream, little by little. Add 1/2 teaspoon sea salt and 1/2 teaspoon herb salt. Taste for seasoning and add more salt if necessary.

Brush 8 dariole or baba molds or custard cups with safflower oil. Fill each with some of the chicken mixture. Wrap the molds in wax paper and stand them in a roasting pan. Pour hot water in the pan up to half the height of the molds. Set the filled molds in their water bath in the preheated oven and bake for 25 minutes.

SAUCE. Heat 3 tablespoons safflower oil in a saucepan and blend in the flour. Off the heat add the stock. Stir the sauce over moderate heat until it comes to a boil. Season with herb salt and stir in remaining 1/4 cup light cream. Mix the egg yolks with the milk in a small bowl. Add 2 or 3 tablespoons of the sauce to the egg yolks; then pour the egg-yolk mixture into the sauce in the pan, stirring all the while. Reheat the sauce over low heat, but do not let it boil or the sauce will separate.

PRESENTATION. When the chicken timbales are baked, carefully turn them out onto a warm au gratin dish or shallow serving dish. Pour the sauce over them. Serve the saffron rice in a separate bowl.

4 servings

Canard Farci à l'Orange

Boned Stuffed Duck with Orange Sauce and Orange Saffron Rice

1 whole dressed duck, 4 to 5 pounds
Herb salt
3 tablespoons dry sherry (optional)
1 pound ground lean veal
2 organic eggs
1/2 cup raw heavy cream
1 medium-size yellow onion, finely chopped
1/2 teaspoon finely chopped fresh garlic
2 tablespoons dried mushrooms, soaked in a little water for 30 minutes
1 teaspoon fresh thyme, or 1/2 teaspoon dried thyme
1/2 teaspoon freshly grated nutmeg
1/2 teaspoon fresh sage, or 1/4 teaspoon dried sage
1 tablespoon chopped fresh parsley or chives
1/2 cup port wine, or red wine-grape juice, or stock
1/2 cup natural orange marmalade

ORANGE SAUCE

3 large oranges
3 tablespoons dry sherry, or white wine-grape juice
2 tablespoons cold-pressed safflower oil
1/2 teaspoon finely chopped fresh garlic
2 teaspoons potato flour

(cont.)

1 teaspoon Marmite (brewers'
    yeast extract)
¼ cup fresh orange juice
1 cup Soy-Vegetable Stock
    (p. 262)

2 teaspoons natural currant jelly
    or rose-hip jelly
½ cup natural orange marmalade
    Herb salt
    Orange Saffron Rice (p. 171)

Preheat the oven to 300°. Carefully bone the duck. Spread the boned duck out on a board, skin side down, and sprinkle it with herb salt and the sherry. Roll the duck and set it aside while you prepare the stuffing.

In the bowl of an electric mixer combine the ground veal, eggs, cream, onion, garlic, mushrooms, drained and finely chopped, the thyme, nutmeg, sage, and parsley or chives. Season with herb salt. Spread this mixture on the duck, wetting your hands with water so that the stuffing doesn't stick. Fold the duck back together and sew it securely with thread.

Set the stuffed duck on a rack in a roasting pan. Mix the port wine with ½ cup water and pour half of this mixture over the duck. Prick the skin in a few places with the tines of a fork to release the fat while the duck is cooking. Stick a meat thermometer into the duck and set it in the preheated oven. Cook the duck, basting occasionally with the wine and water mixture, until the thermometer registers 180°, about 3 hours. Thirty minutes before the duck is finished roasting, spread the top of it with the orange marmalade, and raise the oven heat to 400° for a nice glaze.

ORANGE SAUCE. Pare the rind from 2 oranges and cut the rind lengthwise into very fine shreds. Pour the sherry over the rind and let it marinate for a few minutes. Drain the rind but reserve the sherry. Skin all 3 oranges, cut out the sections neatly, and set them aside. Heat 2 tablespoons safflower oil in a heavy pan. When it is quite hot, brown the liver of the duck in the oil. Remove the liver, reduce the heat a little, and add the drained orange rind and the chopped garlic. Cook over low heat for 2 or 3 minutes. Off the heat add the potato flour and Marmite yeast extract, and stir to a smooth paste. Add the orange juice, the reserved sherry, the stock, jelly, and marmalade. Stir the sauce over moderate heat until it comes to a boil. Adjust the seasoning with herb salt. Reduce the heat and let the sauce simmer gently for 10 minutes. Add the orange sections, but do not cook the sauce any longer; you do not want the orange sections to disintegrate.

PRESENTATION. When the duck is roasted, cut enough slices for one serving per person. Arrange the slices overlapping on one end of a warm serving platter and set the uncut part of the duck at the other end. Pour the sauce over the duck. Serve the orange saffron rice in a separate bowl.

4 to 6 servings

2 small wild ducks, or 1 domestic
  duck, 4 pounds, dressed
7 tablespoons cold-pressed safflower
  oil, approximately
2 tablespoons natural tomato paste
2 teaspoons potato flour
2 cups Soy-Vegetable Stock (p. 262)
4 tablespoons Marsala wine, or red
  wine-grape juice, or additional
  stock
  Herb salt
1 bay leaf
6 firm fresh mushrooms, sliced
1 teaspoon fresh lemon juice

½ red sweet bell pepper, finely
  diced
½ green sweet bell pepper, finely
  diced
  Grated rind of 1 large orange
  Sections of 2 large oranges
3 medium-size ripe tomatoes,
  skinned, seeded, and cut into
  shreds

GARNISH
  Stuffed Baked Potatoes (pp.
  208–209)

Canard Maison

*Sautéed Duck
(wild or
domestic) with
Tomato and
Orange Sauce*

Cut the ducks into serving pieces. Heat a deep heavy pan with a tight-fitting lid. *If you are using wild ducks* with little or no fat under the skin, add 3 tablespoons safflower oil to the pan. *If you are using domestic duck* which has a thick layer of fat under the skin, use no fat in the pan. Slowly brown the pieces of duck on all sides in the hot pan, and set them aside for a moment.

If the pan in which the ducks were browned is dry, add 1 or 2 table-spoons safflower oil to the pan. Add the tomato paste and potato flour and blend to a paste. Add the stock and wine and stir over moderate heat until the sauce comes to a boil. Season with herb salt. Return the duck to the pan with the bay leaf, cover the pan, and simmer on top of the stove until the duck is tender.

In a separate sauté pan, heat 2 tablespoons safflower oil. Add the sliced mushrooms and the lemon juice, season with herb salt, and cook briskly for 2 or 3 minutes. Add the red and green pepper and orange rind and cook for another 3 or 4 minutes. Add the orange sections and the shredded tomatoes to the pan but do not cook. Season with herb salt.

PRESENTATION. When the duck is cooked, arrange the pieces on a warm au gratin dish or shallow serving dish. With a baster, skim the fat off the top of the sauce in the pan in which the duck was cooked. Add the tomato and orange mixture to the pan in which the duck was cooked and gently warm the sauce for 2 or 3 minutes. Spoon this mixture over the duck. Accompany the duck with stuffed baked potatoes.

4 servings

Dindonneau Rôti Farci aux Poires

Roast Stuffed Turkey with Pears

For a grand presentation, serve Chestnut-Filled Acorn Squash (pp. 210–211) for an additional garnish.

1 whole dressed turkey, 7 to 10 pounds
2 large black truffles, thinly sliced (optional)
½ cup chopped yellow onion
6 tablespoons cold-pressed safflower oil
1½ cups whole-wheat Bread Crumbs (p. 258)
2 cups plain Chestnut Purée (p. 192), or natural unflavored canned purée
½ pound ground veal
½ teaspoon finely chopped fresh garlic
½ teaspoon freshly grated nutmeg
½ teaspoon dried thyme
  Herb salt
  A little raw light cream for stuffing
  Cold-pressed safflower oil for brushing on turkey

½ cup dry sherry and 1 cup water, mixed, or ¾ cup white wine-grape juice mixed with ¾ cup water, or 1½ cups Soy Stock (p. 262)
1 teaspoon potato flour
½ teaspoon Marmite (brewers' yeast extract)

PEAR GARNISH
24 Seckel pears
  A little fresh lemon juice
24 whole cloves
1 cup raw sugar, or ¾ cup organic honey
  Grated rind and juice of 2 limes
1½ cups white wine-grape juice, or water

Preheat the oven to 300°. Dry the turkey inside and out with paper towels. For special flavor and elegance, thin slices of black truffle may be inserted under the skin. Carefully loosen the skin from the legs and breast and insert the truffle slices in neat rows.

STUFFING. Sauté the onion in 2 tablespoons safflower oil. Mix the bread crumbs with 4 tablespoons oil until oil is absorbed. Combine in a large bowl the chestnut purée, ground veal, sautéed onion, bread crumbs, garlic, nutmeg, and thyme. With your hands mix ingredients thoroughly. Season with herb salt. If the mixture is too stiff, add a little raw light cream. Fill the cavity of the turkey with this mixture.

Sew both ends of the turkey and truss it tightly. Place it on a rack in a roasting pan and brush it all over with safflower oil. Pour half of the sherry/water mixture, or alternate, into the pan. Insert a meat thermometer into the deepest part of the turkey. Place the turkey in the preheated oven and roast until the thermometer registers 170° to 175°, or approximately 45 minutes per pound. (Turkey and chicken should be served slightly underdone to be moist, tender, and flavorful at its maximum.) Baste the turkey approximately every 30 minutes, using the liquid from the bottom of the pan and more of the sherry/

water mixture, if necessary. Once or twice during the roasting brush the top of the turkey with safflower oil.

PEAR GARNISH. Wash the pears in a little lemon juice and water. Prick them a few times with a wooden food pick. Stick a clove in the bottom of each. In a deep heavy pan cook the sugar, grated lime rind and juice, and the grape juice or water until the mixture forms a light syrup. Stand the pears in the syrup and cook until they are just soft, about 15 minutes.

PRESENTATION. When the turkey has finished roasting, place it on a large warm platter. Stick a paper frill on each leg. Drain the pears and arrange them around the turkey. Make pan sauce.

PAN SAUCE. Add a little water to the juices in the bottom of the roasting pan, enough to make 1½ cups. Stir in 1 teaspoon potato flour and ½ teaspoon Marmite yeast extract. Adjust the seasoning with herb salt. Stir the sauce over low heat until it comes to a boil. Spoon a little pan sauce over the bird, and serve the rest of the sauce in a separate bowl.

10 to 12 servings

Ragoût d'Agneau Printanière

Ragout of Lamb with Spring Vegetables

½ *pound baby potatoes, whole, or 2 large Idaho potatoes, peeled and cut into olive shapes*
½ *pound baby carrots, whole, or 2 large carrots, cut into olive shapes*
12 *baby white onions, skinned*
1 *pound fresh garden peas, shelled and tied in a cheese-cloth (reserve the empty pods)*
½ *pound green beans, tops and tails removed*
Sea salt
3 *cups Soy-Vegetable Stock, using the vegetable cooking water (p. 262)*
3 *pounds boned shoulder of lamb, or 6 lamb shanks*
14 *tablespoons cold-pressed safflower oil*
1 *teaspoon natural tomato paste*
½ *teaspoon Marmite (brewers' yeast extract)*
4 *teaspoons potato flour*
½ *cup dry red wine, or additional stock*
¼ *cup Marsala wine, or dry sherry, or additional stock*
1 *teaspoon natural currant or guava jelly*
Herb salt
1 *small bay leaf*
12 *small firm fresh mushrooms*
1 *teaspoon fresh lemon juice*
2 *tablespoons organic honey*
3 *small ripe tomatoes, skinned and quartered*
2 *tablespoons chopped fresh parsley*

First cook the potatoes, carrots, onions, peas, and green beans individually, in the following manner: Put the vegetable in a pan, cover it with water, and add ½ teaspoon sea salt. Bring water to a boil, and cook until the vegetable is just tender; it should still be crisp. Drain immediately through a colander set over a bowl to catch the liquid. Set the vegetables aside. (Skin the baby potatoes.) Use 3 cups of the cooking liquid for the soy-vegetable stock and store the rest for future use.

Preheat the oven to 350°. Trim the excess fat, sinew, and skin from the lamb and cut the shoulder meat into 1½-inch cubes. If you are using shanks, leave them whole. Heat 3 tablespoons safflower oil in a large deep heavy pan. Lightly brown the pieces of meat quickly on all sides. Put only a few pieces of meat in the pan at a time; if they touch each other, they will not brown. When all the meat is browned, set it aside while you prepare the sauce.

Off the heat, blend 3 tablespoons safflower oil, the tomato paste, Marmite yeast extract, and potato flour in the pan in which the meat was browned. Add the stock, red wine, Marsala or sherry, and jelly. Stir over moderate heat until the sauce comes to a boil. Adjust the seasoning with herb salt and add the bay leaf. Return the lamb to the pan, cover it, and set it in the preheated oven to cook for 1½ hours, or until the meat is tender. After 30 minutes, remove the cover. Once or twice, while the lamb is cooking, spoon some sauce over it.

Finish the vegetables as follows: In a small sauté pan, heat 2 tablespoons safflower oil. Add the mushrooms, lemon juice, and herb salt to taste, and cook briskly for 2 minutes. Transfer the mushrooms to a bowl. Add 2 tablespoons safflower oil to the pan and get it quite hot. Add the potatoes, season them with herb salt, and shake them until they are a nice brown. Transfer the potatoes to the bowl with the mushrooms. Add another 2 tablespoons safflower oil to the pan and get it quite hot. Add the carrots with 1 tablespoon honey and a little herb salt. Shake the carrots until they are glazed to a golden brown. Transfer the carrots to the vegetable bowl. If necessary, add another 2 tablespoons safflower oil to the pan and get it quite hot. Add the onions with 1 tablespoon honey and a little herb salt. Shake the onions until they are glazed a golden brown. Transfer the onions to the vegetable bowl. Also add the previously cooked peas and beans and the uncooked quartered tomatoes to the vegetable bowl.

PRESENTATION. Five minutes before the ragout is finished, add the vegetables to it. When the ragout is cooked, carefully transfer it to a warm serving container, either a casserole or deep serving dish. Sprinkle fresh parsley over the top.

4 to 6 servings

1 large half-breast of chicken,
  skinned and boned
White of 1 organic egg
½ cup raw light sweet cream, or
  raw sour cream
Herb salt
1 tablespoon very finely chopped
  fresh chives
1 tablespoon very finely chopped
  yellow or white onion

1 tablespoon very finely chopped
  celery
¼ teaspoon finely chopped fresh
  garlic
2 tablespoons cold-pressed
  safflower oil
Sauce Périgueux (p. 265), or
  Demi-Glace (p. 265)
8 double-rib lamb chops, trimmed

Côtelettes d'Agneau à la Française

Sautéed Lamb Chops Stuffed with Chicken Mousse

Pass the chicken breast through a fine meat grinder twice and transfer it to an electric mixer bowl. Add the raw egg white and beat thoroughly. Continue beating as you slowly add the cream. Season with herb salt and add the chives, onion, celery, and garlic. Cut a pocket in each chop and fill it with the chicken mixture. Close the pocket and secure it with a food pick.

Heat 2 tablespoons safflower oil in a sauté pan and lightly brown the chops on each side. Set a flat lid and a weight on top of the chops in the pan. Reduce the heat and cook very slowly until the meat is done.

PRESENTATION. Remove the food picks from the stuffed chops and arrange the meat on a warm shallow serving dish. Pour over the périgueux or demi-glace sauce.

4 servings

1 small eggplant, large enough for
  12 cubes of 1½ inches
Sea salt
About ½ cup cold-pressed virgin
  olive oil
1 teaspoon finely chopped fresh
  garlic
Herb salt
4 loin lamb chops
4 lamb kidneys

1 green sweet bell pepper, seeded
  and cut into 8 squares
8 firm fresh white mushrooms
4 small white onions, skinned and
  cut into halves
Pilaff—Rice, Kasha, Cracked
  Whole Wheat, or Wild Rice
  (see pp. 168–169)
Bunch of crisp fresh watercress

Brochettes d'Agneau

Loin of Lamb on Skewers, with Kidneys and Eggplant

Cut the stem from the eggplant but do not peel it. Cut the eggplant into 1½-inch cubes, put them in a bowl, toss with 1 teaspoon sea salt, and let them stand for 30 minutes. Rinse the eggplant cubes in cold water and dry them between paper towels. Heat 2 or 3 tablespoons olive oil in a sauté pan. When the oil is very hot, quickly and lightly brown the cubes; do not let them cook to the soft stage. Drain on paper towels.

(cont.)

Combine ¼ cup olive oil with the chopped garlic and ½ teaspoon herb salt in a little pan and heat it a little. Trim the meat from the lamb chops and cut it into 3 chunks—2 from the loin and 1 from the tail end. Skin the kidneys, cut them into halves, and remove the cores.

Thread 4 long skewers more or less in the following sequence: mushroom/lamb/pepper/kidney/eggplant/lamb/onion/kidney/eggplant/ pepper/lamb/onion/eggplant/mushroom. Lay the skewers on a rack on a jelly-roll pan or a broiler pan. Brush the meat and vegetables with the olive oil and garlic mixture. About 10 minutes before they are to be served, run the skewers under the broiler and cook them for about 5 minutes on one side; turn them and cook for 5 minutes on the other side.

PRESENTATION. Spread the pilaff over the bottom of a warm shallow serving dish, like a bed. Lay the broiled skewers over it. Garnish with a bouquet of watercress.

4 servings

Gigot d'Agneau Rôti aux Flageolets

──────────

Roast Leg of Lamb with Flageolets

The flageolets need to be soaked in water for at least 8 hours.

FLAGEOLETS
1 cup dried flageolets (narrow, light green beans)
  Sea salt
2 tablespoons cold-pressed virgin olive oil
½ teaspoon finely chopped fresh garlic
2 or 3 medium-size ripe tomatoes, skinned and cut into quarters
  Herb salt

LAMB
1 leg of lamb

3 tablespoons cold-pressed safflower oil
1 teaspoon finely chopped fresh garlic
  Herb salt
½ cup dry white wine mixed with ½ cup water, or 1 cup Light Soy Stock (p. 262)
1 cup Soy-Vegetable Stock (p. 262)

FLAGEOLETS. Cover the dried flageolets with 2 cups water and soak them for at least 8 hours. Put the beans in a pan with the soaking water and 1 teaspoon sea salt. Bring to a boil, reduce the heat, cover, and allow the beans to simmer until they are soft. Drain. Heat the olive oil with the chopped garlic in a deep heavy pan and cook over low heat for 2 or 3 minutes. Add the tomatoes and cooked flageolets and season with herb salt. Cook over low heat for 30 minutes.

LAMB. Preheat the oven to 300°. Combine 3 tablespoons safflower oil with the garlic and 1 teaspoon herb salt in a little pan and warm the mixture for 2 or 3 minutes. Trim most of the fat from the lamb and brush the meat all over with the safflower-oil mixture. Set the meat on a rack in a roasting pan. Pour the wine and water mixture, or the light stock, in the bottom of the pan. Insert a meat thermometer into the thickest part of the meat. Set the meat in the preheated oven and let it roast until the thermometer registers 155° (for pink), about 25 to 30 minutes per pound. Turn the meat once or twice during roasting and baste occasionally with the liquid from the bottom of the pan, adding more if necessary.

When the meat is cooked, transfer it to a carving board and let it stand while you prepare the sauce. Pour the soy-vegetable stock into the roasting pan and whisk it around to mix the pan juices. Simmer over low heat for 4 or 5 minutes, and pour the juices into a small bowl.

PRESENTATION. Carve enough slices for 1 serving and arrange them overlapping at one end of a warm serving platter. Place the uncut piece of lamb at the other end of the platter. Spoon the flageolet and tomato mixture along one side of the dish. Serve the sauce separately.
4 servings

Carré d'Agneau à la Mascotte

Roast Rack of Lamb with Artichoke Bottoms, Potatoes, and Truffles

3 tablespoons cold-pressed safflower oil
1 teaspoon finely chopped fresh garlic
    Herb salt
1 rack of lamb, French-trimmed and chined
½ cup dry sherry, or Light Soy Stock (p. 262)
½ cup water
1 cup Soy-Vegetable Stock (p. 262)
1 teaspoon potato flour

½ teaspoon Marmite (brewers' yeast extract)

MASCOTTE GARNISH
2 large Idaho potatoes, peeled and cut into olive shapes
    Sea salt
3 tablespoons cold-pressed safflower oil
    Herb salt
4 to 6 plain-cooked artichoke bottoms
2 black truffles, sliced

LAMB. Preheat the oven to 300°. Combine 3 tablespoons safflower oil with the garlic and 1 teaspoon herb salt in a little pan and warm the mixture for 2 or 3 minutes. Trim the excess fat from the lamb and brush the meat all over with the safflower-oil mixture. Set the meat on a rack in a roasting pan. Pour the sherry, or light stock, and water into the bottom of the pan. Insert a meat thermometer into the thickest part of the meat. Set the meat in the preheated oven and cook it until the thermometer registers 155° (for pink), 25 to 30 minutes per pound. Turn the meat over after 30 minutes, then turn it back after 20 minutes. Baste a few times with the liquid from the bottom of the pan. If you wish to brown the top a little more, increase the oven temperature to 400° during the last 5 to 10 minutes.

When the meat is cooked, transfer it to a carving board. Pour the soy-vegetable stock into the roasting pan, the amount depending on the quantity of liquid already in the pan; you want about 1 cup all together. Blend the potato flour and Marmite yeast extract into the pan juices and stir over low heat for 3 or 4 minutes.

MASCOTTE GARNISH. Put the potatoes in a pan, cover them with water, and add 1 teaspoon sea salt. Bring to a boil, drain immediately, and return the potatoes to the pan to dry over heat for a moment. Heat 3 tablespoons safflower oil in a sauté pan and add the potatoes. Shake them briskly until they are lightly browned, and season with herb salt. Add the quartered artichoke bottoms and sliced truffles and warm the mixture over low heat for a few minutes.

PRESENTATION. Carve the lamb into individual chops and arrange them overlapping on a warm serving platter. Place the garnish at one end of the dish. Serve the sauce in a separate bowl.

2 to 4 servings

Epaule d'Agneau Farcie, Provençale

Roast Shoulder of Lamb with Veal Mousse and Stuffed Eggplant

1 boned shoulder of lamb
2 tablespoons dry sherry (optional)
  Herb salt
½ teaspoon finely chopped fresh garlic
½ pound ground veal
  White of 1 organic egg
½ cup raw light cream
3 anchovy fillets, crushed to a paste

1 tablespoon very finely chopped shallot
1 tablespoon very finely chopped fresh parsley
  About 2 tablespoons cold-pressed safflower oil
1 cup Light Soy Stock (p. 262), or more, if necessary
  Eggplant Stuffed with Mushrooms (pp. 201–202)

Preheat the oven to 300°. Spread the boned shoulder of lamb out on a board and brush it with the sherry. Sprinkle with herb salt and chopped garlic. Spread veal mousse over the surface.

VEAL MOUSSE. Beat the ground veal and egg white together in the electric mixer. After it is thoroughly mixed, continue beating as you slowly add the cream. Season with a little herb salt, add the anchovy paste, shallot, and parsley, and mix well.

Carefully roll up the lamb and tie it with string in several places. Place it on a rack in a roasting pan and brush it all over with safflower oil. Insert a meat thermometer into the thickest part of the meat. Pour the stock into the bottom of the pan and set it in the preheated oven to roast until the thermometer registers 155° (for pink), approximately 2 to 2½ hours. Turn the meat twice and baste occasionally with the liquid from the bottom of the pan, adding more stock if necessary. While the meat is cooking, prepare the stuffed eggplant.

PRESENTATION. Cut enough slices of meat for 1 serving and arrange them overlapping at one end of a warm serving platter. Set the uncut piece of meat at the other end. If necessary, add additional stock to the roasting pan to make 1 cup. Heat the liquid in the pan for a moment and strain it over the meat. Garnish the platter with the stuffed eggplant, or serve it separately.

4 servings

Blanquette de Veau

Poached Veal in Velouté Sauce with Vegetables and Rice

2 pounds boned shoulder of veal
5 tablespoons cold-pressed safflower oil
1 cup mixed sliced onion, carrot, celery, and turnip
Herb salt
1 bay leaf
2 tablespoons stone-ground whole-wheat pastry flour
3 tablespoons raw heavy sweet cream, or raw sour cream
Yolk of 1 organic egg
1 tablespoon dry sherry, or raw milk

CHOICE OF VEGETABLES FOR GARNISH
Baby onions, skinned
Baby carrots, scraped
Garden peas, shelled
Cucumbers, skinned, seeded, and cut into chunks
Celery hearts, halved
Leeks, halved
Fresh firm baby mushrooms, lightly sautéed in oil

Cold-pressed safflower oil for vegetable garnishes
Sea salt
Natural Brown Rice, Plain-Cooked (p. 165)

Cut the veal into neat 1-inch cubes or 2-inch oblong slices. Heat 2 tablespoons safflower oil in a deep heavy pan. Add the sliced onion, carrot, celery, and turnip, and coat with the oil. Set the meat on top of the vegetables and just cover with water. Season with a little herb salt and add the bay leaf. Bring the water to a boil, reduce the heat to low, cover with a tight-fitting lid, and simmer the meat very gently until it is tender. When the meat is cooked, carefully transfer it with a slotted spoon to another dish and keep it warm. Strain the liquid in which the veal was cooked and reserve it.

VELOUTÉ SAUCE. Heat 2 tablespoons safflower oil in a saucepan. Off the heat stir in the flour. Add 1¼ cups of the liquid from the veal and stir over moderate heat until the sauce comes to a boil. Reduce the heat and stir in the cream. Adjust the seasoning with herb salt and stir in another tablespoon of safflower oil. In a small bowl mix the egg yolk with the sherry or milk. Pour a little of the sauce into the egg-yolk mixture, then pour the egg-yolk mixture into the sauce in the pan, stirring all the while.

GARNISHES. Prepare the vegetables you plan to use in the following manner: Put each kind of vegetable in a pan, cover with cold water and add a little sea salt, and bring the water to a boil. Continue cooking until the vegetable is just tender; it should remain a little crisp. Drain and toss each kind of vegetable with a little safflower oil and herb salt to taste.

PRESENTATION. The veal may be arranged on top of the rice on a warm shallow serving dish, or the rice may be served in a separate bowl. Pour the sauce over the veal, and arrange the vegetables around the meat.

4 to 6 servings

Paupiettes de Veau à la Foyot

Veal Birds with Chicken Mousse

8 thin slices of veal, each about 6 by 4 inches
8 tablespoons dry sherry (optional)
Herb salt
2 half-breasts of chicken, skinned and boned
Whites of 2 organic eggs
¾ cup raw light sweet cream, or raw sour cream
Sea salt
2 large black truffles, or 8 green olives stuffed with pimiento

4 tablespoons cold-pressed safflower oil
2 teaspoons potato flour
1 teaspoon Marmite (brewers' yeast extract)
1½ cups Soy-Vegetable Stock (p. 262)
¼ cup dry white wine, or additional Soy-Vegetable Stock
2 teaspoons natural currant or rose-hip jelly
2 cups Pea Purée (p. 194)

Preheat the oven to 350°. Lay the slices of veal on a strip of wax paper and cover them with another piece of wax paper. Slap them with the side of a heavy cleaver to flatten them until they are almost translucent. Remove the top piece of paper. Brush them with 3 tablespoons dry sherry, and sprinkle with a little herb salt.

CHICKEN MOUSSE. Pass the chicken breasts through the fine blade of a food grinder twice. Beat the ground chicken with the egg whites in an electric mixer. Continue to beat as you very slowly add the cream. Season with 1 to 2 teaspoons sea salt. The salt will help to thicken the mousse, but taste it before adding the second teaspoon.

If you are using the truffles, they may be chopped and added to the mousse mixture at this point, or they may be cut into quarters and placed on top of the mousse later. *If you are using the stuffed olives,* they would be placed on top of the mousse later.

Spread the mousse on the slices of veal. Set a quarter of truffle or 1 stuffed olive in the center of each slice, carefully roll it up, and tie it in 2 places with kitchen string. Heat 3 tablespoons safflower oil in a deep heavy pan. Lightly brown the veal birds all over. Heat 2 tablespoons dry sherry in a little pan, ignite, and pour it over the veal. Remove the veal from the pan and set it aside while you prepare the sauce.

Add 1 tablespoon safflower oil to the pan with the potato flour and Marmite yeast extract. Blend to a smooth paste and stir in the stock, white wine, 3 tablespoons dry sherry, and the jelly. Continue stirring over moderate heat until the sauce comes to a boil. Adjust the seasoning with herb salt and return the veal birds to the pan. Cover the pan with a tight-fitting lid and set it in the preheated oven to cook for about 45 minutes.

PRESENTATION. Spread the pea purée like a mound on a warm au gratin dish or shallow serving dish. When the veal birds are cooked, remove them from the pan, carefully remove the strings, and cut them into halves. Arrange the halves, with the cut side facing the outside of the dish, on the pea purée. Strain the sauce over all.

4 servings

¾ cup organic seedless white
    raisins, soaked in ¼ cup dry
    sherry or water for at least
    30 minutes
4 tablespoons cold-pressed
    safflower oil
2 pounds boned veal, from
    shoulder or leg, cut into
    1½-inch cubes
¼ cup finely chopped onion
1 teaspoon finely chopped fresh
    garlic

1 teaspoon Marmite (brewers'
    yeast extract)
1 teaspoon natural tomato paste
3 tablespoons stone-ground
    whole-wheat pastry flour
1 cup Light Soy Stock (p. 262)
1½ cups raw sour cream
    Herb salt
1 tablespoon chopped fresh
    tarragon, or fresh thyme, or
    chives
    Rice Pilaff (pp. 168–169)

Veau en Casserole

Casserole of Veal with Sour Cream and Raisin Sauce

Preheat the oven to 350°. Drain the sherry or water from the raisins and set it aside. Heat 2 tablespoons safflower oil in a deep heavy pan and lightly brown the pieces of veal on all sides. Heat the reserved sherry in a little pan, ignite, and pour it over the veal. If you soaked the raisins in water, just add it to the pan to loosen the glaze. Remove the veal and set it aside while you prepare the sauce.

Add 2 tablespoons safflower oil to the pan with the chopped onion and garlic and cook over low heat for 2 or 3 minutes. Add the soaked raisins and cook slowly for another 2 or 3 minutes. Off the heat stir in the Marmite yeast extract, tomato paste, and flour. Add the stock and stir over moderate heat until the sauce comes to a boil. Reduce the heat to low and, little by little, stir in the sour cream. Adjust the seasoning with herb salt and add the chopped fresh herb. Return the veal to the pan, cover with the sauce, and cover the pan with a tight-fitting lid. Cook in the preheated oven for 1¼ hours, or until the meat is tender.

PRESENTATION. Serve the veal in a warm casserole with a separate bowl of rice pilaff.

4 to 6 servings

Côtes de Veau Soubise

Veal Chops with Onion Purée and Stuffed Mushrooms

8 small veal chops
  About 6 tablespoons cold-
    pressed safflower oil
4 Bermuda onions, skinned and
    sliced
1 cup raw milk
  Herb salt
  White of 1 organic egg
½ cup freshly grated Parmesan
    cheese
6 small firm fresh mushrooms

12 large firm fresh mushrooms
1 teaspoon fresh lemon juice
1 teaspoon natural tomato paste
1 teaspoon Marmite (brewers'
    yeast extract)
2 teaspoons potato flour
1 cup Light Soy Stock (p. 262)
2 tablespoons dry sherry
    (optional)
½ cup dry red wine, or additional
    stock

Preheat the oven to 300°. Arrange the chops on a rack on the broiler pan, brush the tops with safflower oil, and brown them lightly under the broiler on one side only. Place the chops, browned side down, on a flat baking dish.

ONION PURÉE. Combine the onions, milk, and a little herb salt in a heavy pan. Cover and cook over low heat until the onions are soft. Drain the milk and store it for other use (in soups or cream sauce). Rub the onions through a fine vegetable strainer. Beat the onion purée with the egg white in an electric mixer. Adjust the seasoning with herb salt. Using a spoon, shape the onion purée on top of the veal chops like domes. Sprinkle with grated cheese, dot with a few drops of saf-flower oil, and bake in the preheated oven for about 45 minutes.

MUSHROOM GARNISH. Chop the small mushrooms and the stems from the large mushrooms very finely. Heat 1 tablespoon safflower oil in a sauté pan. Add the large mushroom caps with the lemon juice and cook them briskly for 2 minutes. Season with herb salt and remove them from the pan. Add the chopped mushrooms to the pan, season with herb salt, and cook briskly for 2 minutes. Fill the mushroom caps with the chopped mushrooms.

SAUCE. Heat 1 tablespoon safflower oil in a saucepan. Off the heat blend in the tomato paste, Marmite yeast extract, and potato flour. Mix in the stock, dry sherry, and red wine. Stir the sauce over moderate heat until it comes to a boil. Adjust the seasoning with herb salt.

PRESENTATION. When the veal chops are finished cooking, arrange them on a serving dish in a circle, like a crown. Surround them with the stuffed mushrooms. Spoon the sauce over the veal chops and stuffed mushrooms.

4 servings

This dish was one of Mrs. Lucas's personal favorites. If fresh morels are not available, wholesome brown organic cultivated mushrooms are an excellent substitute.

Escalopes de Veau à la Toscana

Veal Scallops with Morels and Looseleaf Potatoes

1½ cups sliced morels, or firm fresh cultivated mushrooms	4 cups Soy-Vegetable Stock (p. 262)
2 teaspoons fresh lemon juice	1 cup dry white wine, or additional stock
12 small, thin slices veal Herb salt	½ cup morel or mushroom soaking water
⅔ cup and 2 tablespoons dry sherry, plus a few drops to sprinkle the veal	2 teaspoons natural guava jelly
7 tablespoons cold-pressed safflower oil	2 tablespoons cold-pressed virgin olive oil
1 teaspoon natural tomato paste	12 thin slices natural mozzarella cheese
1 teaspoon Marmite (brewers' yeast extract)	3 tablespoons freshly grated Parmesan cheese
4 teaspoons potato flour	Looseleaf potatoes (p. 208)

Barely cover the sliced morels or cultivated mushrooms with cold water and lemon juice and allow to soak while you prepare the veal. Lay the slices of veal on a strip of wax paper and cover them with another piece of wax paper. Slap them with the side of a heavy cleaver to flatten them a little. Remove the top piece of wax paper, sprinkle the veal with a little herb salt and a few drops of sherry, and allow it to marinate for a few minutes. Heat 2 tablespoons safflower oil in a heavy shallow sauté pan. When it is hot, put in the pieces of veal, taking care not to let the meat overlap. Set a flat oiled lid on top and set a weight on top of it. Brown the veal quickly on one side; then turn the pieces of veal over and brown quickly on the other. Heat ⅓ cup sherry in a little pan, ignite, and pour it over the veal. Remove the veal and set it aside in a warm place.

Add to the sauté pan, off the heat, 2 tablespoons safflower oil, the tomato paste, Marmite yeast extract, and potato flour, and stir until the mixture is smooth. Add the stock, dry white wine, ⅓ cup sherry, morel or cultivated mushroom soaking water, and guava jelly, and season with herb salt. Stir over moderate heat until the sauce comes to a boil. Reduce the heat and allow to simmer while you prepare the mushrooms.

Heat 1 tablespoon safflower oil and the olive oil in a small sauté pan. Add the morels or cultivated mushrooms, season with herb salt, and cook briskly for 3 or 4 minutes. Heat 2 tablespoons sherry in a small pan, ignite, and pour it over the mushrooms. Add the mushrooms and the veal to the sauce and warm the combined ingredients a little.

PRESENTATION. Arrange the veal slices on a warm serving platter and set a slice of mozzarella on top of each. Spoon over the mushroom sauce, sprinkle with Parmesan cheese, and dot with a few drops safflower oil. Brown under the broiler and garnish around the edge of the platter with looseleaf potatoes.

6 servings

Escalopes de Veau Beau Séjour

Veal Scallops with Mushroom Purée

About 4 tablespoons cold-pressed safflower oil
2 cups finely chopped fresh mushrooms
2 teaspoons fresh lemon juice
Herb salt
2 tablespoons raw sour cream
1/4 teaspoon freshly grated nutmeg
1 tablespoon stone-ground whole-wheat pastry flour
8 small thin slices of veal, about 4 inches in diameter
1/2 cup freshly grated Parmesan cheese

2 tablespoons dry sherry (optional)
1/2 teaspoon Marmite (brewers' yeast extract)
1/2 teaspoon natural tomato paste
1 1/2 teaspoons potato flour
1 cup Light Soy Stock (p. 262)
2 tablespoons dry white wine, or additional stock
1 teaspoon natural rose-hip or guava jelly
Glazed Carrots (pp. 196–197)
Glazed Turnips (pp. 196–197)

Heat 1 tablespoon safflower oil in a pan. Add the chopped mushrooms, lemon juice, and a little herb salt, and cook briskly for about 2 or 3 minutes. Add the sour cream, nutmeg, and flour, and cook for 3 or 4 minutes. Press the mixture through a fine vegetable strainer. Set the mushroom purée aside for a moment.

Lay the slices of veal on a strip of wax paper and cover them with another piece of wax paper. Slap them with the side of a heavy cleaver to flatten them a little. Heat 2 or 3 tablespoons safflower oil in a sauté pan and lightly brown the veal slices on each side. Place the slices on a jelly-roll pan or baking sheet and sprinkle them with a little herb salt. Spread a little mushroom purée on each slice, sprinkle a little grated cheese on top, and add a drop or two of safflower oil.

Add to the pan in which the veal was browned the sherry, Marmite yeast extract, tomato paste, and potato flour, and blend to a smooth paste. Add the stock, white wine, and jelly, and stir over moderate heat until the sauce comes to a boil. Season with herb salt and strain.

PRESENTATION. Lightly brown the prepared veal scallops under the broiler, and arrange them carefully on a warm shallow serving platter. Garnish the dish with the glazed carrots and turnips. Serve the sauce in a separate bowl.

4 servings

2½ to 3 pounds boned shoulder of
    veal
3 tablespoons dry sherry
    (optional)
    Herb salt
½ teaspoon finely chopped fresh
    garlic
2 half-breasts of chicken, skinned
    and boned
    White of 1 organic egg
1 cup raw light cream
1 teaspoon sea salt
1 black truffle, chopped
    (optional)
4 tablespoons cold-pressed
    safflower oil
½ cup dry white wine, or Soy-
    Vegetable Stock (p. 262)

¼ cup water
1 teaspoon Marmite (brewers'
    yeast extract)
1 teaspoon natural tomato paste
2 teaspoons potato flour
1¼ cups Soy-Vegetable Stock
    (p. 262)
1 teaspoon natural currant or
    rose-hip jelly

GARNISHES
2 tablespoons cold-pressed
    safflower oil
6 to 8 artichoke bottoms, cooked
6 to 8 firm fresh mushrooms
1 teaspoon fresh lemon juice
    Herb salt
6 to 8 Broiled Tomatoes (p. 211)

Epaule de Veau
Farcie Rôtie

Roast Stuffed
Shoulder of Veal
with Tomatoes,
Artichoke
Bottoms,
Mushrooms

Preheat the oven to 300°. Spread the veal out on a board; cut it into a thinner slab if necessary. Brush the surface with dry sherry and season with herb salt and the chopped garlic.

CHICKEN MOUSSE. Pass the boned chicken breasts through the fine blade of a food grinder twice. Beat the ground chicken with the egg white in an electric mixer. Continue beating as you slowly add the cream. Add 1 teaspoon sea salt and a little herb salt. The salt will help to thicken the mousse, but do not get it too salty. Mix in the chopped truffle. Spread the mousse over the veal.

Roll up the meat and tie it in several places with string. Place it on a rack in a roasting pan and brush all over with safflower oil. Pour ¼ cup dry white wine or stock and ¼ cup water into the bottom of the pan. Insert a meat thermometer into the thickest part of the meat. Place the meat in the preheated oven and cook until the thermometer registers 180°, or about 3 hours. Carefully turn the meat 2 or 3 times during roasting. Baste occasionally with the juices from the bottom of the pan, adding more wine and water, if necessary.

GARNISHES. Heat 2 tablespoons safflower oil in a sauté pan. Carefully remove the stems from the mushrooms. Add the artichoke bottoms and mushroom caps to the sauté pan with the lemon juice and a little herb salt and warm. Remove them from the pan and set 1 mushroom cap on top of each artichoke bottom. Prepare the broiled tomatoes.

SAUCE. When the meat has finished cooking, remove it from the pan and let it stand for about 10 minutes before slicing it. Meanwhile prepare the sauce in the roasting pan on top of the stove: Blend 2 tablespoons safflower oil with the Marmite yeast extract, tomato paste, and potato flour. Off the heat mix in the stock, 1/4 cup wine, and the jelly. Stir over moderate heat until the sauce comes to a boil. Adjust the seasoning with herb salt, and strain.

PRESENTATION. Carefully remove the string from the veal. Cut as many slices as are needed for 1 serving and arrange them slightly overlapping on one end of a warm serving platter. Place the uncut meat at the other end of the dish. Surround the dish with the broiled tomatoes and artichoke bottoms with mushroom caps. Pour the sauce over the meat. *6 to 8 servings*

Foie de Veau Smitane

Calf's Liver with Sour-Cream and Raisin Sauce

This sauce varies from that for Casserole of Veal. The mustard and curry seasoning makes this especially companionable with liver.

8 slices of calf's liver, 1/2 inch thick (2 per serving)

2 tablespoons stone-ground whole-wheat pastry flour plus additional for dusting the liver

5 tablespoons cold-pressed safflower oil

1/2 teaspoon finely chopped fresh garlic

4 medium-size fresh mushrooms, thinly sliced

1 teaspoon fresh lemon juice

3/4 cup Soy-Vegetable Stock (p. 262)

1/2 cup organic white or dark raisins, soaked in 1/2 cup of the stock

1 teaspoon Marmite (brewers' yeast extract)

1/2 teaspoon natural tomato paste

1/4 teaspoon dry mustard

1/4 teaspoon curry powder

1 cup raw sour cream

Herb salt

Pea Purée (p. 194)

Lightly dust the slices of liver with flour and pat off the excess. Heat 2 or 3 tablespoons safflower oil in a sauté pan and quickly and lightly brown the slices on each side. Remove them from the pan and prepare the sauce.

SOUR-CREAM AND RAISIN SAUCE. Add 2 tablespoons safflower oil to the pan with the chopped garlic, sliced mushrooms, and lemon juice. Shake these ingredients briskly over moderate heat for 2 minutes. Drain the raisins, reserving the stock, and add them to the pan to cook over low heat for 3 minutes. Remove the pan from the heat and mix in the Marmite yeast extract, tomato paste, dry mustard, curry powder, and 2 tablespoons whole-wheat pastry flour. Add ¾ cup stock and stir over moderate heat until the sauce thickens. Stir in the sour cream, spoonful by spoonful. Adjust the seasoning with herb salt and return the liver to the pan with the sauce. Cook the liver over low heat for 10 to 15 minutes.

PRESENTATION. Spread the pea purée on the bottom of a shallow serving dish, like a bed. Lay the slices of liver on top, overlapping. Pour the sauce over the liver.

4 servings

Ris de Veau en Brochette

Sweetbreads on Skewers

2 *pair sweetbreads*
Sea salt
1 *Bermuda onion, skinned*
2 *green sweet bell peppers, seeded and cut into 1½-inch pieces*
8 *firm fresh mushrooms*
About 2 tablespoons cold-pressed safflower oil
Herb salt
Rice or Kasha Pilaff (pp. 168–169)

SAUCE
3 *tablespoons cold-pressed safflower oil*
½ *teaspoon natural tomato paste*
½ *teaspoon Marmite (brewers' yeast extract)*
2 *teaspoons potato flour*
1½ *cups Soy-Vegetable Stock (p. 262)*

Bring the sweetbreads slowly to a boil in water seasoned with ½ teaspoon sea salt. Drain them and remove all membranes and blood vessels. Cut them into large chunks, about 1½ inches in size.

Cut the onion into 1½-inch pieces. Divide the sweetbreads, onions, peppers, and mushrooms into 4 equal groups and thread them onto 4 skewers. Brush them with safflower oil and sprinkle with a little herb salt. About 10 minutes before you wish to serve them, brown the skewers under the broiler, turning them once.

SAUCE. Heat 3 tablespoons safflower oil in a saucepan and blend in the tomato paste, Marmite yeast extract, and potato flour. Off the heat add the stock. Stir the sauce over moderate heat until it comes to a boil. Season with herb salt.

PRESENTATION. Fluff the pilaff like a bed on a warm shallow serving dish. Lay the cooked skewers of sweetbreads on top of the pilaff. Serve

the sauce in a separate bowl and pour a little over the individual servings.
4 servings

Tournedos Béarnaise

Sautéed Tournedos with Mushrooms and Béarnaise

BÉARNAISE SAUCE
   Yolks of 2 organic eggs
  1 tablespoon fresh lemon juice
  1 tablespoon raw heavy sweet cream, or raw sour cream
  ¼ teaspoon herb salt
  8 tablespoons cold-pressed safflower oil
  ¼ teaspoon Marmite (brewers' yeast extract)
  ¼ teaspoon finely chopped shallot
  ⅛ teaspoon finely chopped fresh garlic
  1 teaspoon chopped fresh tarragon, or ½ teaspoon dried tarragon

1 teaspoon chopped fresh parsley

1½ pound piece of beef tenderloin (fillet), about 2½ inches in diameter
About 2 tablespoons cold-pressed safflower oil
8 large firm fresh mushrooms
1 teaspoon fresh lemon juice
Herb salt
Bunch of fresh crisp watercress

BÉARNAISE SAUCE. In a small bowl combine the egg yolks, lemon juice, cream, and herb salt. Stand the bowl in a small sauté pan half-filled with hot water, over low heat, and beat with a small wire whisk until the sauce is as thick as you want it. Very slowly, beat in the safflower oil. Mix in the rest of the sauce ingredients. Cover the bowl with a piece of plastic wrap and set it aside, off the heat, until you are ready to use it.

Trim the excess fat from the beef and cut the meat into 4 equal slices. Tie a string around the girth of each slice to keep it compact. Brush the meat with safflower oil, on both sides. Heat a sauté pan and quickly brown the meat in it on both sides. This is all the cooking tenderloin should require. Remove the meat from the pan and keep it warm.

Carefully remove the stems from the mushrooms. Add the mushroom caps to the sauté pan with the lemon juice. Sprinkle with a little herb salt and cook briskly for 1 minute. Remove the mushroom caps from the pan.

PRESENTATION. Remove the strings from the tournedos and arrange them on a warmed small platter. Set 1 mushroom cap, bottom side up, on top of each tournedos. Fill the mushroom cap with the sauce and cover it with another mushroom cap, top side up. Garnish with a bouquet of watercress.
4 servings

1½ pounds beef tenderloin (fillet)
3 teaspoons fresh lemon juice
5 tablespoons cold-pressed
    safflower oil
1 cup finely sliced yellow onion
    Herb salt
1 cup sliced firm fresh mushrooms

About 3 tablespoons stone-
    ground whole-wheat pastry
    flour
1 cup raw sour cream
12 pitted small ripe olives
12 pitted small green olives
    Rice Pilaff (pp. 168–169)

Filet de Boeuf Stroganoff

Beef Tenderloin in Sour Cream Sauce with Olives

Trim the excess fat and sinew from the beef and cut the meat into finger-size pieces. Sprinkle the meat with 2 teaspoons lemon juice and let it sit for 30 minutes.

Heat 3 tablespoons safflower oil in a sauté pan and add the onion. Season with a little herb salt and cook over moderate heat until the onion begins to brown. Remove the onion with a slotted spoon and set it aside. Add the mushrooms to the pan with 1 teaspoon lemon juice and a little herb salt. Cook them briskly for 1 minute and remove them with a slotted spoon.

Dust the pieces of beef lightly with flour. Add 2 tablespoons safflower oil to the sauté pan, and when it is quite hot, add the beef. Shake the pan over high heat for 3 or 4 minutes. Add the onions and mushrooms to the meat and stir in the sour cream. Cook the mixture for 3 or 4 minutes, and adjust the seasoning with herb salt.

PRESENTATION. Serve the meat in a warm casserole and scatter the ripe and green olives over the top. Serve the rice pilaff in a separate bowl.
4 servings

This is a good ragout with or without the Burgundian touch.

Boeuf Bourguignonne

Ragout of Beef with Red Burgundy Wine

2 pounds top round of beef
4 tablespoons cold-pressed
    safflower oil
2 tablespoons dry sherry (optional)
1 teaspoon finely chopped fresh
    garlic
2 teaspoons natural tomato paste
1 teaspoon Marmite (brewers'
    yeast extract)
3 teaspoons potato flour
1 cup Soy-Vegetable Stock (p. 262)
1 cup dry red wine, or additional
    Soy-Vegetable Stock

    Herb salt
1 bay leaf
1 teaspoon natural guava or rose-
    hip jelly
24 baby white onions, skinned
12 large firm fresh mushrooms,
    quartered
    Sea salt
1 tablespoon raw sugar
1 teaspoon fresh lemon juice
2 tablespoons chopped fresh
    parsley

Preheat the oven to 350°. Trim all excess fat from the beef and cut the meat into large cubes. Heat 2 tablespoons safflower oil in a deep heavy pan with a tight-fitting lid. Lightly brown the pieces of beef on all sides. Return all of the meat to the pan. Heat the sherry in a little pan, ignite, and pour it over the meat. Remove the meat from the pan for a moment.

Add to the pan, off the heat, the chopped garlic, tomato paste, Marmite yeast extract, and potato flour, and blend. Add the stock and wine and stir the mixture over moderate heat until it comes to a boil. Adjust the seasoning with herb salt and add the bay leaf and jelly. Return the meat to the pan and cover it with a piece of wax paper. Cook in the preheated oven for about 2 hours, until the meat is tender but not disintegrating.

While the meat is cooking, prepare the onions and mushrooms. Cover the onions with water and 1 teaspoon sea salt and bring them to a boil. Drain immediately. Heat 2 tablespoons safflower oil in a sauté pan and add the onions with the brown sugar and a little herb salt. Shake the onions over high heat until they are nicely glazed. Remove the onions from the pan and add to the pan the mushrooms with the lemon juice and a little herb salt. Cook the mushrooms over high heat for 2 minutes.

PRESENTATION. When the beef is cooked, transfer it to a warm serving casserole or dish. Add the onions and mushrooms and pour the sauce over all. Sprinkle with chopped parsley.

4 to 6 servings

Boeuf en Gelée

Roast Beef in Aspic, Garnished with Tomatoes and Eggs Stuffed with Cream Cheese

4 pounds top sirloin of beef
   About 3 tablespoons cold-pressed
    safflower oil
1 cup Soy-Vegetable Stock
   (p. 262)
   Herb salt
4 cups Aspic (p. 264)
6 organic eggs, hard-boiled and
   shelled

½ pound natural cream cheese
1 tablespoon thick raw sour cream
2 tablespoons natural tomato paste
2 tablespoons very finely chopped
   chives
   Herb salt
6 small ripe tomatoes
1 black truffle (optional)
   Bunch of fresh crisp watercress

Preheat the oven to 300°. Trim the excess fat from the beef and brush it all over with safflower oil. Heat a deep heavy pan and slowly brown the piece of meat lightly on all sides. Pour over it 1 cup stock. Insert a meat thermometer into the thickest part of the meat and set it in the pan in the preheated oven to roast until the thermometer registers 150°, or about 3 hours. Turn the meat once after it has been in the oven for about 1 hour. When the meat is cooked, sprinkle it all over with herb salt and chill it thoroughly. The meat must be completely cold in order to coat it with aspic.

While the meat is chilling, prepare the aspic and the garnishes.
GARNISHES. Cut the eggs lengthwise into halves. Carefully remove the yolks and rub them through a fine wire strainer. Put the cream cheese in an electric mixer and beat it until it is smooth. Add the sour cream and the strained egg yolks and beat thoroughly. Mix in the tomato paste and chopped chives, and season with herb salt to taste. Fit a pastry bag with a No. 6 or No. 7 star tube, and fill the bag with this mixture. Set aside for a moment.

Neatly core but do not skin the tomatoes. Cut them into halves. Pipe a rosette of the cream-cheese mixture on the cut side of each tomato half. Pipe the rest of the mixture into the egg-white halves.

When the meat is chilled, trim off any remaining bits of fat from the outside. Carve 4 or 5 slices of meat and set them aside. Set the uncut piece of beef on a wire rack on a jelly-roll pan. Set the pan of aspic over a bowl of ice and stir until it is on the point of setting. Spoon aspic over the piece of meat several times. If the aspic becomes too thick, remelt it and stir it over ice until it is at the point of setting again. Slice the truffle, dip the slices into aspic, and set them on the meat in a decorative pattern.

PRESENTATION. Set the aspic-coated meat on one end of a flat oval serving dish. Put the rest of the aspic in a cake pan and chill it in the refrigerator until it is firm. Turn it out onto a piece of wax paper and cut it into dice with a long knife. Place the slices of beef overlapping at the other end of the serving dish. Fit a pastry bag with a No. 6 or No. 7 plain tube and fill the bag with the chopped aspic. Pipe some aspic between each slice of meat. Surround the dish alternately with the stuffed tomatoes and eggs. Set the bouquet of watercress at one end of the dish, behind the uncut piece of meat. Keep the dish chilled until ready to serve.

8 to 12 servings

EGGS

In classic French cuisine there are many tempting and satisfying egg dishes because, to the French, an egg dish is a meal. We hope that by including egg dishes in the chapter devoted to the main course, perhaps egg meals will come to our minds more frequently in menu planning. Eggs are quick and easy to prepare—the cooking time is brief, to begin with—when you have mastered the basic methods of egg preparation. Here you will find the best way to *soft-boil* or *hard-boil* an egg, and to *scramble;* the exquisite and too-rarely-thought-of *egg en cocotte;* perfect *fried eggs—French and American* styles; the classic method of *poaching eggs*—the appearance is so much more inviting than one poached in a mold; *baked or shirred eggs*—there are so many ways to garnish them; and the ultimate egg meal—the *omelet*.

Simple explanations for the 8 methods are given on the following pages, and in the menu chapter you will find menus featuring eggs with a suggested wine.

Remember, too: *The "organic egg" is the natural egg,* rich with the substances of life and good health. If organic eggs are at all available to you, use them! Their superiority over commercial eggs is described in detail in the Encyclopedia (pp. 13–14).

Bon appétit!

BASIC METHODS FOR PREPARING EGGS

Oeufs Mollets

Soft-boiled Eggs

There are several methods for the seemingly simple matter of soft-boiling an egg, but in all of them it is absolutely necessary that the eggs be fresh. The following method is excellent to achieve tender, set soft-boiled eggs.

Set room-temperature organic eggs into boiling water with a pair of tongs (so that they do not crack). Remove the pan from the heat, and leave the eggs in the hot water for 8 to 10 minutes, depending upon the size of the eggs. Plunge the eggs into ice water for 2 minutes, after which the shell may be easily removed without damaging or breaking the egg inside. Put the shelled egg back in warm water or broth until ready to serve or until added to other ingredients in a recipe.

By putting room-temperature eggs into boiling water and then removing them from the heat, the eggs will lower the temperature of the water to about 180°, about 30° lower than the boiling point. The white will then be just set.

Another method of soft-boiling eggs is to set room-temperature eggs in enough water to cover and bring the water to a boil slowly. The eggs are then ready to serve.

Oeufs Durs

Hard-boiled Eggs

In order that eggs should be properly hard-boiled, they should be put into boiling water with 1 teaspoon sea salt and allowed to cook in the boiling water for 10 minutes for medium-size eggs, to 15 minutes for jumbo-size eggs, and then immediately cooled in cold water.

Remember that eggs which are cooked and cooled, and then found to be insufficiently done, will not cook any more if they are put back into boiling water.

Hard-boiled eggs can be kept in a cool place for several days if they remain in their shells. If they are shelled, they should be rinsed with a weak solution of lemon juice and water and used as soon as possible.

For a dish of scrambled eggs to be at its best, it should be served immediately after leaving the hands of the cook; scrambled eggs tend to deteriorate rapidly in taste and quality.

Some cooks use cream or cream sauce to keep scrambled eggs in condition for a reasonable period of time. We do not recommend the use of a sauce unless it is absolutely necessary. Cream or water is much more satisfactory. The most important point is never, on any account, to overcook the eggs. This basic recipe is excellent if the directions are strictly followed.

Put 2 tablespoons cold-pressed safflower oil, or 3 tablespoons natural sweet butter, in the top part of a double boiler. Add 6 well-beaten organic eggs, and season with 1/2 teaspoon sea salt. Stir constantly with a wooden spoon until the eggs become creamlike in consistency. If the eggs can't be served instantly, add approximately 1 tablespoon raw sour or raw heavy sweet cream for every 3 eggs, or 1 teaspoon cold water for each egg, *before* cooking.

Oeufs Brouillés

Scrambled Eggs

For eggs *en cocotte* or *en timbale,* the eggs are put in individual molds, the molds are set in a water bath, and the eggs are cooked in the water bath in the oven.

The term *timbale* in cookery is properly applied to anything having the shape of a small goblet. However, today many molds of different shapes are termed timbales. Eggs molded in timbales are put in oiled molds, such as baba or dariole molds, which are set in a pan with hot water added until it reaches halfway up the side of the mold. The whole preparation is then set in a preheated 350° oven and the eggs are gently cooked until they are just set. The molds are then turned out onto a serving dish.

Eggs *en cocotte* are prepared in much the same way as eggs cooked in timbales with the exception that the eggs are *not* turned out of the molds to serve. The cocottes should be made of fine porcelain or earthenware, preferably with little handles attached. They are set in a water bath for cooking in the oven. Cooking time is about 10 minutes, or according to the specific recipe. If the cocottes are lined with forcemeat, the cooking time will be lengthened accordingly.

Eggs en Cocotte or en Timbale

There are 2 distinct methods of frying eggs, one which may be termed the French way and the other the American or English way.

1. French cooks include under frying anything that is immersed and cooked in *very hot* fat (oil, lard, or butter) .

Oeufs Frits

Fried Eggs

2. The American or English cook applies the term "frying" to anything that is cooked with the aid of a fatty substance, generally at a moderate temperature.

From our point of view the American or English way of frying with a small quantity of oil or butter over moderate heat preserves the lightness and digestibility of the egg better than the French method. To prepare eggs the American way: Melt 2 tablespoons cold-pressed safflower oil or natural butter per egg in a heavy sauté pan and cook over moderate heat for 3 minutes. No seasoning should be added except at the table.

Oeufs Pochés
Poached Eggs

Poached eggs are merely eggs cooked in water without the shells. The most important requisite is that the egg be fresh; a stale egg will not poach well. There are 2 methods of poaching eggs—in a deep pan of water and in a poached-egg mold.

The first method is to fill a deep pan, such as the top part of a double boiler, ¾ full of water; add 1 teaspoon of sea salt and 1 tablespoon of fresh lemon juice for each quart of water. Bring the water to a boil, reduce the heat, and allow the water to simmer gently. Break the egg into a cup. Stir the water with a long-handled spoon to make a whirlpool. Slide the egg from the cup into the whirlpool. Simmer for 3½ minutes and remove the egg at once with a large slotted spoon. Put it in a bowl of warm or cold water with a little lemon juice, depending on whether you plan to use the eggs hot or cold.

The second method is to stand the lightly oiled poaching mold in a pan of shallow hot water. Break the eggs into each mold and simmer gently for 3½ minutes.

The first method is the best because it allows the yolks to be completely surrounded by the whites, and we think the eggs look more elegant.

Oeufs sur le Plat
Baked Eggs or Shirred Eggs

Baked eggs are cooked and served in small shallow china dishes especially made for the purpose. To prepare a baked egg, first preheat the oven to 300°. Brush the egg dish lightly with cold-pressed safflower oil or natural butter and break the egg into it. Pour a little oil or melted butter over the yolk and set the dish in the preheated oven to cook until the yolk looks as though it is covered with a veil. The seasoning of the egg, if no sauce accompanies it, should be left to the eater, as salt and pepper would destroy its beauty.

There are three very important rules to be followed in the preparation of an omelet. *First,* the omelet pan should be kept extremely clean and never used for any other purpose. When not in use, it should always be left coated with a little oil, wrapped in paper towels and a plastic bag, and kept in a cool place. Water or any other liquid should *never* touch the pan. In the rare and unhappy event that it has to be cleaned, heat the pan gently first and then rub it out with plain steel wool. Use a clean cloth and vegetable oil to wipe off any steel wool that may be left there. *Second,* the eggs should be well beaten. *Third,* the pan must always be heated before any oil is put in the pan, and the omelet should be cooked over moderate heat. A fork is the best implement for making an omelet.

To make a basic (or plain) omelet for 1 serving you will require these ingredients:

3 organic eggs	1 tablespoon cold-pressed safflower
1 teaspoon water	oil
¼ teaspoon sea salt	

Beat the eggs, water, and sea salt together with a rotary beater or whisk until they are well mixed. Preheat the omelet pan over low-medium heat for 10 minutes. Add the oil and allow it to heat for 1 minute. Add the egg mixture to the pan. Stir the eggs with a fork in your right hand and shake the pan briskly with your left hand concurrently until the eggs are nearly set. With the back of the fork, spread out the mixture so no holes are left on the bottom of the pan. Slightly tip the pan and with the fork begin to fold the omelet over on itself, starting with the edge nearest the handle of the pan. Flip half of it over on itself and turn it out onto a hot flat serving dish. The best way is to grasp the handle of the pan with the left hand, hold the dish near the end of the pan, and tip the two together.

Once the eggs are in the pan, the whole preparation should not take more than 2 minutes, and great care should be taken not to overcook the omelet. The egg mixture should be stirred so quickly that it never touches the bottom of the pan without being moved. This will insure a perfect omelet.

The basic sweet omelet is described on pages 244–245.

3 tablespoons cold-pressed safflower oil	½ teaspoon dry mustard
3 tablespoons stone-ground whole-wheat pastry flour	¾ cup freshly grated Gruyère or natural Swiss-type Cheese
¾ cup raw milk	½ cup plus 2 tablespoons freshly grated Parmesan cheese

(cont.)

Omelette

Basic or Plain Omelet

Oeufs Mollets en Surprise

Soft-boiled Eggs in Cheese Soufflé

4 organic eggs, separated
    Herb salt
¼ cup dry whole-wheat Bread
    Crumbs (p. 258)
3 ounces firm fresh mushrooms,
    sliced
1 teaspoon fresh lemon juice

6 organic eggs, soft-boiled (p. 150)
2 teaspoons chopped fresh parsley
2 teaspoons chopped fresh dill
6 tablespoons raw sour cream
    Cold-pressed safflower oil for
    soufflé dish and topping

Preheat the oven to 350°. Heat 2 tablespoons safflower oil in a sauce-pan and blend in the flour. Off the heat pour in the milk. Stir the sauce over moderate heat until it comes to a boil. Remove the pan from the heat and mix in the dry mustard, Gruyère cheese, ¼ cup Parmesan cheese, and 4 egg yolks. Season with herb salt. Beat the 4 egg whites to soft peaks and fold the egg-yolk mixture into them.

Lightly brush a shallow baking dish with safflower oil and dust the inside with half of the bread crumbs and ¼ cup Parmesan cheese. Spread half of the soufflé mixture on the bottom of the prepared baking dish. Make 6 indentations in the soufflé with the back of a wet spoon.

Heat 1 tablespoon safflower oil in a sauté pan and add the mushrooms, lemon juice, and a little herb salt. Cook the mushrooms over moderate heat for 2 minutes. With a slotted spoon, gently set equal amounts of mushrooms in each indentation. Carefully set the shelled soft-boiled eggs on top of the mushrooms.

Mix the parsley and dill with the sour cream, season with a little herb salt, and put a spoonful on top of each egg. Cover with the rest of the soufflé mixture. Sprinkle the top with the rest of the bread crumbs and 2 tablespoons Parmesan cheese. Dot with a few drops of safflower oil. Set the preparation in the preheated oven and bake for 30 minutes. Remove and serve at once.

6 servings

Oeufs à la Tripe

Hard-boiled Eggs and Onions in Mornay Sauce

4 tablespoons cold-pressed
    safflower oil
2 Bermuda onions, skinned and
    sliced
3 tablespoons stone-ground
    whole-wheat pastry flour
1½ cups raw milk
½ cup freshly grated Parmesan
    cheese

½ teaspoon dry mustard
    Herb salt
    Yolk of 1 organic egg
¼ cup raw sour cream
6 organic eggs, hard-boiled and
    shelled (p. 150)

Preheat the oven to 300°. Heat 2 tablespoons safflower oil in a sauté pan, add the sliced onions, and cook slowly until they are translucent and slightly golden. Set them aside for a moment.

Heat 2 tablespoons safflower oil in a saucepan and stir in the flour. Off the heat add the milk. Stir the sauce over low heat until it comes to a boil. Add ¼ cup grated cheese and the dry mustard, and season with herb salt. Simmer the sauce for about 5 minutes. In a small bowl mix the egg yolk with the sour cream. Pour a little of the sauce into the egg-yolk mixture, then pour the egg-yolk mixture into the rest of the sauce, stirring all the while.

Slice the hard-boiled eggs thickly. Layer the eggs and the onions alternately in a small au gratin dish or casserole. Cover the eggs and onions with the sauce and sprinkle the rest of the grated cheese over the top. Dot with a little safflower oil and bake in the preheated oven for about 30 to 45 minutes. Set the dish under the broiler to brown lightly. Serve in the baking dish.
4 servings

Oeufs Zéphyr au Champignon

Light Scrambled Eggs with a Mushroom

5 organic eggs
1 tablespoon cold-pressed safflower oil
2 tablespoons raw sour cream
3 tablespoons freshly grated Gruyère or Parmesan cheese

Herb salt
2 mushroom caps, browned slightly in a little cold-pressed safflower oil
1 tablespoon chopped fresh parsley

Beat the eggs lightly and combine them in the top part of a double boiler with the safflower oil, sour cream, grated cheese, and herb salt. Set the top pan over hot water and stir gently as the eggs cook.
PRESENTATION. When the eggs are just beginning to set but are still creamy, they are ready to be eaten. Transfer them immediately to a shallow serving dish, or 2 individual serving plates. Set a mushroom cap on top of each serving and sprinkle with chopped parsley.
2 servings

Oeuf en Cocotte à la Crème

Egg in Cocotte with Cream

2 tablespoons raw sour cream, or whipped raw heavy sweet cream
1 teaspoon cold-pressed safflower oil

Herb salt
1 organic egg

Please note basic recipe on page 151. Preheat the oven to 350°. Put 1 tablespoon cream on the bottom of a cocotte. Add 1 teaspoon safflower oil and a little herb salt. Break the egg into the cocotte. Cover the egg with 1 tablespoon cream and season again with herb salt. Set the cocotte in a pan half-filled with hot water, and set the pan in the preheated oven. Bake until the egg is just set, about 20 minutes, depending on the size of egg. Serve at once in the mold.

Follow this procedure for as many eggs as you wish to serve.

1 serving

Oeufs Pochés Salon

Poached Eggs on Toast with Curried Hollandaise Sauce

SAUCE
 Yolks of 4 organic eggs
1 teaspoon curry powder
 Herb salt
1 teaspoon natural tomato paste
1 teaspoon Marmite (brewers' yeast extract)
4 tablespoons raw sour cream
8 tablespoons cold-pressed safflower oil

4 to 6 rounds of toasted stone- ground whole-wheat bread, about 3½ inches in diameter (p. 259)
4 to 6 organic eggs, poached (p. 152), and set in warm water

SAUCE. In a small bowl combine the egg yolks, curry powder, ¼ teaspoon herb salt, the tomato paste, Marmite yeast extract, and sour cream. Set the bowl in a small sauté pan half-filled with hot water, over low heat, and beat with a small wire whisk until the mixture is thick. Continue beating as you slowly add 8 tablespoons safflower oil. Cover the bowl with a piece of plastic wrap, remove it from the water, and set aside for a moment.

PRESENTATION. Arrange the toast rounds on a warm au gratin dish or shallow heatproof serving dish. Drain the poached eggs on paper towels and place an egg on each toast round. Spoon the sauce over the eggs and brown lightly under the broiler, not too long, or the sauce will separate.

4 to 6 servings

Oeufs en Gelée à l'Estragon

Poached Eggs in Aspic with Tarragon

4 to 5 cups Aspic (p. 264)
¼ cup fresh tarragon leaves

6 organic eggs, poached (p. 152), and set in cold water

Chill a 1½-quart ring mold. Stir the aspic over a bowl of ice until it is on the point of setting. Pour half of the aspic into the mold and allow it to set in the refrigerator. Decorate the top of the set aspic with the tarragon leaves. Dry the eggs on paper towels and arrange them on top of the aspic, evenly spaced. Cover with remaining aspic, and set the mold in the refrigerator until it is firm. Pour the rest of the aspic in a cake pan and chill it also.

PRESENTATION. Remove the mold from the refrigerator and dip it quickly into boiling water. Slip a small sharp knife around the edge of the mold. Turn mold out onto a chilled flat serving dish. Turn the aspic in the cake pan out onto a piece of wax paper on a cutting board and chop it coarsely. Fit a pastry bag with a No. 8 or No. 9 plain tube, and fill the bag with chopped aspic. Pipe a border around the mold. Serve cold.

6 servings

Oeufs sur le Plat Flamenco

Baked Eggs with Potatoes, Peas, and Tomatoes

3 *large potatoes*
  Sea salt
1 *cup shelled fresh garden peas*
3 *tablespoons cold-pressed safflower oil*
  Herb salt
½ *cup coarsely diced sweet red bell pepper*

3 *medium-size ripe tomatoes, skinned and cubed*
2 *tablespoons chopped fresh parsley*
1 *teaspoon Marmite (brewers' yeast extract)*
4 *organic eggs*
2 *tablespoons raw heavy sweet cream, or raw sour cream*

Preheat the oven to 300°. Place the potatoes in a pan, cover them with water, and add 1 teaspoon sea salt. Bring water to a boil and cook potatoes until they are tender. Drain, and remove the skins. Cut potatoes into small cubes. Put the peas in a saucepan, cover with water, and add 1 teaspoon sea salt. Bring to a boil, and continue to cook until peas are just tender. Drain.

Heat the safflower oil in a sauté pan and lightly brown the potato cubes. Season them with a little herb salt. Add the peas, red pepper, tomatoes, parsley, and Marmite yeast extract. Cook only for 1 or 2 minutes. Spread the mixture over the bottom of an au gratin dish or shallow baking dish. Break the eggs on top of the vegetable mixture and sprinkle them with a little herb salt. Set the preparation in the preheated oven and bake until the eggs are set. Spoon the cream over the eggs and return them to the oven for another 2 or 3 minutes. Serve at once in the baking dish.

4 servings

Omelette Bonne Femme

Omelet Filled with Potato and Onion

BONNE FEMME POTATOES
2 *medium-size Idaho potatoes*
4 *tablespoons cold-pressed safflower oil*
1 *medium-size yellow onion, sliced*
  Herb salt

2 *tablespoons finely chopped fresh parsley*

6 *organic eggs*
½ *teaspoon sea salt*

Pare the potatoes, cut them lengthwise into halves, and then cut them into ¼-inch slices. Put 2 tablespoons safflower oil in a small heavy pan with a tight-fitting lid. Add the sliced onion; lay the potatoes on top of the onion. Season with herb salt and cover the pan. Cook over low heat for 15 to 20 minutes, stirring once or twice. When the potatoes are tender, carefully mix in half of the parsley.

Beat the eggs, 2 teaspoons water, and ½ teaspoon sea salt in a bowl with a rotary beater until they are well mixed. Using half of the egg mixture, prepare 1 omelet according to the basic procedure (p. 153). Just before you are ready to fold it in the pan, add half of the filling in the center of the eggs. Fold the omelet and turn it out onto a warm plate. Brush the top with a little safflower oil and sprinkle with parsley. Prepare the second omelet in the same manner and serve at once.
2 servings

Omelette aux Champignons

Omelet with Mushrooms

½ pound firm fresh mushrooms	Herb salt
3 tablespoons cold-pressed safflower oil	4 organic eggs
1 teaspoon fresh lemon juice	½ teaspoon sea salt

Slice all but two of the mushrooms. Heat 2 tablespoons safflower oil in a sauté pan, add the sliced and whole mushrooms and the lemon juice, and season with a little herb salt. Cook briskly for 3 minutes only.

Beat the eggs, 1½ teaspoons water, and ½ teaspoon sea salt in a bowl with a rotary beater. Add the sliced mushrooms to the egg mixture. Set the whole mushrooms aside for garnish. Using half of the egg mixture, prepare 1 omelet according to the basic procedure (p. 153). Turn the omelet out onto a warm serving plate. Prepare the second omelet in the same manner. Set a whole mushroom on top of each, and serve at once.
2 servings

Omelette Fines Herbes

Omelet with Herbs

2 teaspoons finely chopped aromatic herb (e.g., tarragon, chervil, dill, rosemary, basil, marjoram)	¼ teaspoon finely chopped fresh garlic, or ½ teaspoon finely chopped shallot
2 tablespoons very finely chopped fresh parsley	3 organic eggs
1 teaspoon finely chopped baby white onion	¼ teaspoon sea salt
	2 tablespoons cold-pressed safflower oil

Chop the aromatic herb, parsley, onion, and garlic or shallot together. Beat the eggs, 1 teaspoon water, and ¼ teaspoon sea salt in a bowl with a rotary beater. Prepare the omelet according to the basic procedure (p. 153), but put the herb mixture in the pan *before* you add the egg mixture. Stir the herb mixture around a little to warm it, then add the eggs. Mix the herbs with the eggs, and turn the omelet out onto a warm serving plate. Brush the top with a little safflower oil and serve at once.
1 serving

Omelette au Fromage

Cheese Omelet

3 organic eggs
¼ teaspoon sea salt
¼ teaspoon dry mustard
1 tablespoon dry sherry (optional)
3 tablespoons freshly grated Gruyère cheese or natural Swiss-type cheese

1 tablespoon freshly grated Parmesan cheese
2 tablespoons cold-pressed safflower oil

Beat the eggs, 1 teaspoon water, the sea salt, mustard, and sherry in a bowl with a rotary beater until well mixed. Prepare the omelet according to the basic procedure (p. 153). Just before folding it in the pan, put the grated Gruyère or natural Swiss-type cheese in the center; then fold and turn the omelet out onto a warm serving plate. Brush the top of the omelet with safflower oil and sprinkle with Parmesan cheese. Serve at once.
1 serving

Omelette aux Huîtres

Omelet with Oyster and Potato Garnish

2 tablespoons cold-pressed safflower oil
2 tablespoons finely chopped celery
2 tablespoons finely chopped yellow or white onion
1 large Idaho potato, pared and sliced ⅛ inch thick
½ teaspoon finely chopped fresh garlic

Herb salt
6 oysters on the half shells
¼ cup raw sour cream
1 tablespoon finely chopped fresh parsley
6 organic eggs
½ teaspoon sea salt

Heat 1 tablespoon safflower oil in a small sauté pan. Add the celery, onion, potato, and garlic, season with herb salt, and cook slowly until the vegetables are soft but not browned. Remove the oysters from the shells and add them to the potato mixture.

(cont.)

If there is any oyster liquid in the shells, pour it into a small pan and boil it down to about 1 tablespoon in quantity. Add this to the potato and oyster filling with the sour cream. Mix well, adjust the seasoning with herb salt, and reheat gently so that the oysters are not overcooked. Mix in the parsley.

Beat the eggs, 2 teaspoons water, and ½ teaspoon sea salt in a bowl with a rotary beater until well mixed. Using half of the egg mixture, prepare 1 omelet according to the basic procedure (p. 153). Turn omelet out onto a warm serving plate. Prepare the second omelet in the same manner. Cut a slit in the top center of each omelet and fill it with the potato and oyster mixture. Serve at once.

2 servings

Omelette Provençale

Omelet with Eggplant Filling, Tomato Sauce

1 small eggplant
  Sea salt
3 tablespoons cold-pressed virgin olive oil
1 tablespoon cold-pressed safflower oil plus 1 tablespoon for cooking omelet
1 baby white onion, finely chopped

½ teaspoon finely chopped fresh garlic
3 small ripe tomatoes, skinned and cut into ½-inch-thick slices
1 teaspoon finely chopped fresh basil
  Herb salt
6 organic eggs

Remove the stem from the eggplant, but do not peel it. Cut the eggplant into ¾-inch cubes, put them in a bowl, and sprinkle with sea salt. Let the eggplant stand for 30 minutes. Rinse eggplant in cold water, drain, and dry well between paper towels. Heat the olive oil in a sauté pan, add the cubed eggplant, and shake the eggplant over high heat to brown it lightly. Remove it from the pan at once; do not cook it.

Add 1 tablespoon safflower oil to the sauté pan with the onion and garlic. Cook for 2 minutes; add the tomatoes and basil, and season with herb salt. Cook the tomato mixture over moderate heat for 2 or 3 minutes.

Beat the eggs, 2 teaspoons water, and ½ teaspoon sea salt in a bowl with a rotary beater until well mixed. Using half of the egg mixture, prepare 1 omelet according to the basic procedure (p. 153). Just before you are ready to fold the omelet, add half of the eggplant in the center. Fold the omelet and turn it out onto a warm serving plate. Prepare the second omelet in the same manner. Spoon the tomato mixture over the omelets and serve at once.

2 servings

This very delicate creamy omelet, a variation of the plain omelet, is like the fluffy dessert omelet. A mousseline omelet may be plain, as here, or it may have a filling such as mushroom.

3 organic eggs
Herb salt
2 tablespoons raw sour cream, or raw heavy sweet cream

2 tablespoons cold-pressed safflower oil

Separate the eggs and beat the yolks in a mixer until they are thick and pale. Beat 1/4 teaspoon herb salt and the cream into the yolks. In a separate bowl beat the whites to soft peaks. Fold the egg-yolk mixture into the whites.

Prepare the omelet following the basic procedure for a plain omelet (p. 153), using 2 tablespoons safflower oil instead of 1. Do not overcook the omelet; it should be creamy. Fold the omelet and turn it out onto a warm serving plate. Serve at once.

1 or 2 servings

3 tablespoons cold-pressed safflower oil
8 scallions, finely sliced
4 tablespoons finely chopped celery
1 tablespoon tamari soy sauce

1/2 teaspoon raw sugar
1 cup diced cooked lobster
Herb salt
4 organic eggs
4 tablespoons raw sour cream

Heat 1 tablespoon safflower oil in a sauté pan and add the scallions and celery. Cook until the vegetables are just soft but not brown. Add 1/2 cup water, the soy sauce, sugar, and lobster meat, and season with herb salt. Simmer the mixture until it is well heated.

Separate the eggs, and beat the yolks in a mixer until they are thick and pale. Beat in a good 1/2 teaspoon herb salt and the sour cream. In a separate bowl beat the whites to soft peaks. Fold the egg-yolk mixture into the whites. Prepare the omelet following the basic procedure for a plain omelet (p. 153), using 2 tablespoons safflower oil instead of 1. Before folding the omelet, add the lobster mixture. Fold omelet and turn it out onto a warm serving platter. Serve at once.

2 servings

**Omelette Soufflé
en Tomates**

*Tomatoes Stuffed
with Egg Soufflé*

This dish is attractive and delicious served on a bed of rice pilaff. For a simpler preparation, the tomatoes may be filled with plain Scrambled Eggs (p. 151).

4 firm medium-size ripe tomatoes,
   skinned
Herb salt
2 teaspoons raw sugar
4 organic eggs, separated

4 tablespoons freshly grated
   Parmesan cheese
Rice Pilaff (pp. 168–169,
   optional)

Preheat the oven to 375°. Cut the tops off the tomatoes and carefully scoop out the centers. Sprinkle the insides with a little herb salt and ½ teaspoon sugar each.

Beat the egg yolks and mix in 2 tablespoons grated cheese and ½ teaspoon herb salt. Beat the whites to soft peaks and fold them into the egg-yolk mixture. Arrange the tomatoes on an au gratin dish. Fill them with the egg mixture. Sprinkle the rest of the grated cheese on the top. Bake in the preheated oven for 15 minutes. If you are serving the rice pilaff, arrange the tomatoes on a bed of pilaff. If not, serve the tomatoes in the au gratin dish in which they were baked.

4 servings

Frittata

Italian Omelet

This is a good way to use up leftovers, cooked and uncooked. For a frittata, the same egg mixture is used as that for the Basic Omelet (p. 153). The procedure differs in that the filling is mixed with the eggs before the mixture is poured into the omelet pan. Also, the frittata is not folded; it is served like a large pancake.

Fillings for frittatas usually consist of *vegetables* such as sliced onions, carrots, potatoes, zucchini, mushrooms, green and lima beans, or any suitable combination. The vegetables, if raw, are finely sliced or coarsely diced and cooked in a little salted water until just tender but still crisp. The vegetables are usually, but not necessarily, combined with sliced or diced cooked meats or cooked fish. You may use any combination of vegetables, meats, or fish.

A *sweet frittata* can be made by adding *fruits* instead.

To cook the frittata, heat 2 tablespoons cold-pressed safflower oil or cold-pressed virgin olive oil in an omelet pan and pour in the egg and filling mixture. The frittata is usually about ½ inch thick. It is served flat instead of folded. It can be cooked on one side only until the eggs are set and then flipped over, or it may be put under the broiler for a minute to finish the top, or it may be covered for a moment while cooking.

A frittata may also be prepared in an au gratin dish in which the filling may have been cooked in advance. The egg mixture is poured over the filling and cooked until set. It is served in the same dish.

GRAIN, PASTA, AND SAVORY PASTRY

Ever since we discovered the wonderful world of natural grains, we have found it hard to understand how the gourmet palate ever came to favor the bland, refined forms of these grains in which not only flavor but vital nutrients are discarded. Whole grains are nutritionally and gastronomically superior to their devitalized, processed counterparts in every way, and we readily—and enthusiastically—admit to being "hooked." We now include a natural grain—in a classic preparation—in our menus every day.

Entrenched as we are in the "grain experience," we venture to say that, once you've eaten whole-wheat fettuccini, you will never be satisfied with white semolina pasta again. Once you've savored stone-ground whole-wheat bread, even the best French and Italian bread will pale in comparison. If you've always had a so-so attitude about rice, including well-seasoned pilaffs, your palate will take notice, happily, when it experiences the richness of natural brown rice.

Pilaffs and gnocchi, multiplied by variations in whole wheat, millet, cornmeal, bulgur, and kasha, will open up a whole new world of sensuous delights for you. Moreover, the main course will have an excitingly different appeal as natural grains make their appearance in pilaffs or risottos, gnocchi and pasta of all types and forms, macédoines in salads, savory pastries (the shell for Quiche Lorraine or onion tart, for example), rich soufflés, and filled crêpes. Whole-grain preparations served with a vegetable dish are so delicious and satisfying that they offer very acceptable no-meat meals. And vitamins will have never tasted so good!

Cooking with natural grains: The first thing to know about natural grains is that they should be stored in the refrigerator; whole grains contain enzymes and should be kept cool to avoid rancidity. The second thing to know is that whole grains, in general, need to be cooked longer than refined grains. Most of them, however—wheat, barley, buckwheat, for instance—are available in various degrees of milling—cracked or coarse, medium, fine; the terms vary from producer to producer.

Some natural grains have a tendency to become sticky during the longer cooking process, more so than refined grains. We have found the following procedure to be effective in helping prevent stickiness: Put the grain in a deep heavy pan in which it is to be cooked. Add a beaten egg and stir the grain over moderate heat until the kernels are separate and dry. Then add the liquid plus any other ingredients and proceed to cook as directed in the recipe. This is an optional procedure, of course. The natural grain may be cooked as described in the following recipes with the egg step eliminated.

For the purpose of using these grains within the context of French cooking, we offer the following notes on individual grains (also, please note the discussions in the Encyclopedia) .

Whole wheat: Whole-kernel wheat takes several hours to cook. For a cereal texture, in pilaffs and stuffed peppers, for instance, we use "cracked wheat"; for a finer texture as for Gnocchi alla Romana, a crushed wheat is available; as a substitute for "all-purpose white re-fined re-enriched flour" in any recipe, we use organic stone-ground whole-wheat pastry flour. (Semolina, traditionally used for gnocchi, in commercial forms is often refined and degerminated.) *Bulgur wheat* is a Mideastern treatment of wheat much favored by the Persians, and is available in this country.

Natural brown rice: Natural (organic) brown rice is available in long and short grains. We use natural brown rice in both savory and dessert dishes. For cooking natural brown rice, add 2½ cups liquid to 1 cup of rice; cook in a 350° oven for 45 minutes. This compares with 2 cups liquid and 25 minutes of cooking time for polished white rice. With natural brown rice especially we recommend coating the kernels with beaten egg before cooking.

Millet: The grain we feed our feathered friends is also very healthy and good-tasting food for us humans.. This grain has nourished man-kind since prehistoric times—in the Far East (China and Japan) , in the Middle East, and in pre-Columbian America. Whole hulled millet is used in the recipes for plain-cooked millet and Gnocchi alla Romana.

Barley: Although this ancient grain is thought of mainly for soups and spirits, barley grits are good when plain-cooked or in gnocchi served as a garnish, and hulled (pearl) barley is delicious as a pilaff.

Kasha (Buckwheat): Kasha is the name for cooked buckwheat. Buck-wheat groats are the hulled or hulled-and-coarsely-cracked grain. In today's market buckwheat is available in whole, medium, or fine grade. It is an especial favorite of ours for its rich nutty flavor, and it cooks rather quickly—about 20 minutes for any of the textures. We like it with plain-cooked vegetables, with skewered entrées, or with sautéed fruit.

Cornmeal: Cornmeal and corn grits can be wholesome, tasty changes in a variety of traditional recipes and should appear more often as gar-nishes with vegetable, poultry, or meat entrées. Simply cooked cornmeal is *mamaliga* in Rumania, *polenta* in Italy, and johnnycake in America.

Wild Rice: Gourmets have long acclaimed wild rice for its unique delicacy. It is a genuine American native, found only in the lake country of Northern Minnesota and adjoining Canada. Also called Indian rice, or water oats, its seeds were used by the American Indian for food before the white man discovered it. It remains one of our original, unadulterated natural foods, untampered by notions of progress.

All of these grains are available in natural- and specialty-food stores or through mail-order sources (pp. 281–282).

Natural Brown Rice, Plain-Cooked

1 cup natural brown rice, long or short grain
1 organic egg, beaten (optional)
2½ cups water or stock, Soy, Vegetable, or Chicken (pp. 261–262)
1 tablespoon cold-pressed safflower oil
1 teaspoon herb salt

Cook the rice in the oven or on top of the stove over low heat. To cook it in the oven, which avoids the risk of scorching the bottom of the pan, preheat the oven to 350°.

Put the rice in a deep heavy pan with a tight-fitting lid. To prevent stickiness, add the beaten egg and stir the mixture over moderate heat until the kernels are separate and dry. Whether or not you have coated the rice with egg, add the water or stock, safflower oil, and salt, and stir over moderate heat until the mixture comes to a boil. Cover the pan with the lid and cook it in the preheated oven for 45 minutes, without disturbing it. Or cook it, covered, on top of the stove over very low heat for approximately 45 minutes—until it is tender.

PRESENTATION. Fluff the rice with 2 forks and serve it in the hot baking dish, or transfer it to a warm serving dish. Or press it into a lightly oiled mold, and turn out onto a warm flat serving dish.

2 cups

Millet, Plain-Cooked

To plain-cook millet, follow the recipe for Natural Brown Rice (preceding recipe).

Kasha
(Buckwheat),
Plain-Cooked

1 cup medium-ground kasha
  (buckwheat groats)
1 organic egg, beaten (optional)
2 cups water or stock, Soy,
  Vegetable, or Chicken
  (pp. 261–262)

2 tablespoons cold-pressed safflower
  oil
1 teaspoon herb salt

Put the kasha (buckwheat groats) in a deep heavy pan with a tight-fitting lid. To prevent stickiness, add the beaten egg and stir the mixture over moderate heat until the kernels are dry and separate. Whether or not you have coated the rice with egg, add the water or stock, safflower oil, and salt, and stir over moderate heat until it comes to a boil. Cover the pan, reduce the heat to very low, and cook for 20 minutes.
PRESENTATION. Fluff the kasha with 2 forks and serve it in the hot cooking dish, or transfer it to a warm serving dish. Or press it into a lightly oiled mold, and turn out onto a warm flat serving dish.
2 cups

Hulled Barley,
Plain-Cooked

1 cup hulled (pearl) barley
2½ cups water or stock, Soy,
  Vegetable, or Chicken (pp.
  261–262)

½ teaspoon sea salt

Bring the water or stock and the salt to a boil in a deep heavy pan with a tight-fitting lid. Add the barley and bring the liquid to a boil again. Cover the pan, reduce the heat to low, and cook for 45 minutes.
PRESENTATION. Fluff the barley with 2 forks and serve it in the hot cooking dish, or transfer it to a warm serving dish.
2 cups

Bulgur Wheat,
Plain-Cooked

2 tablespoons cold-pressed safflower
  oil
1 cup bulgur wheat
2 cups water or stock, Soy,
  Vegetable, or Chicken
  (pp. 261–262)

½ teaspoon sea salt

Preheat the oven to 350°. Heat the safflower oil in a deep heavy pan with a tight-fitting lid. Add the bulgur and cook it in the oil until it just begins to become golden. Add the water or stock and salt, and bring it to a boil. Cover the pan and cook in the preheated oven for 30 minutes without disturbing it.

PRESENTATION. Fluff the bulgur with 2 forks and serve it in the hot baking dish, or transfer it to a warm serving dish. Or press it into a lightly oiled mold, and turn out onto a warm flat serving dish.

2 cups

Cracked Wheat, Plain-Cooked

Plain-cooked cracked wheat is delicious with vegetables, poultry, or meat instead of rice or potatoes. It is also a delightful dish with fruit (apples, peaches, bananas, for instance) that has been sautéed in a little oil and raw sugar. The *whole* grain wheat (uncracked) takes a very long time to cook, at least 4 hours; therefore, for easier and more frequent serving, we recommend the cracked wheat.

1 cup cracked wheat
1 organic egg, beaten (optional)
2 cups water or stock, Soy, Vegetable, or Chicken (pp. 261–262)

2 tablespoons cold-pressed safflower oil
1 teaspoon herb salt

Put the cracked wheat in a deep heavy pan with a tight-fitting lid. To prevent stickiness, mix in the beaten egg and stir the mixture over moderate heat until the kernels are dry and separate. Whether or not you have coated the wheat with egg, add the water or stock, safflower oil, and salt, and stir over moderate heat until it comes to a boil. Cover the pan, reduce the heat to very low, and cook for 20 minutes; or follow the time recommended on the package of the brand you are using; the time may vary according to the milling.

PRESENTATION. Fluff the cooked cracked wheat with 2 forks and serve it in the hot cooking dish, or transfer it to a warm serving dish. Or press it into a lightly oiled mold, and turn out onto a warm flat serving dish.

2 cups

Wild Rice, Plain-Cooked

1 cup wild rice
3 cups water or stock, Soy, Vegetable, or Chicken (pp. 261–262)

1 teaspoon herb salt
2 tablespoons cold-pressed safflower oil

Put the wild rice in a deep heavy pan with the water or stock, herb salt, and safflower oil, and bring it to a boil. Reduce the heat to very low and continue cooking until the rice has absorbed all the liquid and is

soft. While the rice is cooking, stir it occasionally. If all of the liquid is absorbed before the rice is tender, add more stock and continue cooking. Transfer the rice to a warm serving dish.
2 cups

Creamy Kernels, Plain-Cooked

Creamy Kernels are a white, whole-grain buckwheat product which we found from Birkett Mills of Penn Yan, New York. They are delicious and wholesome and offer another excellent variation within the grain repertoire.

3 cups raw milk or water
1 cup Creamy Kernels
1 teaspoon herb salt

2 tablespoons cold-pressed safflower oil

Pour the milk or water into a deep heavy pan with a tight-fitting lid. Stir in the Creamy Kernels, herb salt, and safflower oil. Cover the pan and cook over very low heat for 20 minutes. Serve in a warm bowl or au gratin dish, or as a bed for an arrangement of vegetables, fish, shellfish, or meat.
2 cups

Riz Pilaf
Rice Pilaff

3 tablespoons cold-pressed safflower oil
1 medium-size yellow onion, finely chopped
½ teaspoon finely chopped fresh garlic
Herb salt
1 cup natural brown rice, long or short grain

1 organic egg, beaten (optional)
2½ cups water or stock, Soy, Vegetable, or Chicken (pp. 261–262)
¼ cup sunflower seeds or pine nuts (optional)

Preheat the oven to 350°. Heat the safflower oil in a small sauté pan. Add the onion and garlic and season with a little herb salt. Cook until the onion is translucent but not brown. Set the onion mixture aside for a moment.

Put the rice in a deep heavy pan with a tight-fitting lid. To avoid stickiness, add the beaten egg and stir the mixture over moderate heat until the kernels are dry and separate. Whether or not you have coated the rice with egg, mix it with the cooked onion and garlic, water or stock, and ½ teaspoon herb salt, and bring the mixture to a boil. If you are using sunflower seeds or pine nuts, add them to the mixture. Cover the pan and cook in the preheated oven for 45 minutes without disturbing it.

PRESENTATION. Fluff the pilaff with 2 forks and serve it in the baking dish, or transfer it to a warm serving dish. Or press it into a lightly oiled mold, and turn out onto a warm flat serving dish.
2 cups

All of these grains make delicious pilaffs. For a pilaff, each grain type is cooked in the same manner as in the recipe for plain-cooking it except that stock is generally preferred over water and sautéed onions are added before the grain is cooked. Sunflower seeds, pine nuts, almond slivers, or lightly sautéed sliced mushrooms may be added, if desired. Use the ingredients for the plain-cooked version of the grain.

Various Grain Pilaffs: Cracked Wheat, Kasha, Bulgur, Wild Rice

Kasha (Buckwheat) (p. 166)
Cracked Wheat (p. 167)
Bulgur Wheat (pp. 166–167)
Wild Rice (pp. 167–168)

ONION MIXTURE
2 tablespoons cold-pressed safflower oil
1 medium-size yellow onion, finely chopped

½ teaspoon finely chopped fresh garlic
Herb salt
¼ cup sunflower seeds, pine nuts, almond slivers, or lightly sautéed sliced mushrooms (optional)

ONION MIXTURE. Heat the safflower oil in a small sauté pan. Add the chopped onion and garlic and season with herb salt. Cook until the onion is translucent but not brown. Add the sunflower seeds or pine nuts and set the mixture aside for a moment.

Prepare the plain-cooked recipe for the grain you are using. At the point when you add the liquid, also add the onion mixture, and then proceed to finish cooking according to the basic recipe.
PRESENTATION. Fluff the pilaff with 2 forks and serve it in the hot baking dish, or transfer it to a warm serving dish. Or press it into a lightly oiled mold and turn out onto a warm flat serving dish.
2 cups

This rice is good with skewered fish or meat or curries.

Riz aux Bananes

Rice with Bananas

4 tablespoons cold-pressed safflower oil
4 bananas, on the green side, skinned and cut into 1-inch slices
2 tablespoons chopped yellow or white onion
1 teaspoon herb salt

1 cup natural brown rice, long or short grain
1 organic egg, beaten (optional)
1 teaspoon sweet paprika
2½ cups water, or Light Soy Stock (p. 262)
4 tablespoons freshly grated Parmesan cheese

Preheat the oven to 350°. Heat the safflower oil in a sauté pan. Add the sliced bananas and onion, and season with the herb salt. Cook over moderate heat for 2 minutes. Set the mixture aside for a moment.

Put the rice in a deep heavy pan with a tight-fitting lid. To prevent stickiness, mix in the beaten egg and stir the mixture over moderate heat until the kernels are dry and separate. Whether or not you have coated the rice with egg, combine the rice with the paprika and water or stock, and bring the mixture to a boil. Add the bananas and onion, cover the pan, and cook in the preheated oven for 45 minutes without disturbing it.

PRESENTATION. Fluff the rice with 2 forks and serve it in the hot baking dish, or transfer it to a warm serving dish. Sprinkle the top with the grated cheese.

About 3 cups

Riz aux Raisins et aux Amandes

Rice with Raisins and Almonds

This rice preparation is good with skewered fish or meat entrées.

1 cup natural brown rice, long or short grain
1 organic egg, beaten (optional)
¼ cup dark or white raisins
¼ cup shredded blanched almonds

2 tablespoons cold-pressed safflower oil
2½ cups water
1 teaspoon sea salt
1 teaspoon sweet paprika

Preheat the oven to 350°. Put the rice in a deep heavy pan with a tight-fitting lid. To prevent stickiness, mix in the beaten egg and stir the mixture over moderate heat until the kernels are dry and separate. Whether or not you have coated the rice with egg, combine the rice with the raisins, almonds, safflower oil, water, salt, and sweet paprika, and stir over moderate heat until the mixture comes to a boil. Cover the pan with the lid and cook in the preheated oven for 45 minutes without disturbing it.

PRESENTATION. Fluff the rice with 2 forks and serve it in the hot baking dish, or transfer it to a warm serving dish.

Approximately 3 cups

Riz au Safran

Saffron Rice

2 tablespoons cold-pressed virgin olive oil
2 tablespoons cold-pressed safflower oil
1 medium-size yellow onion, finely chopped
1 cup natural brown rice, long or short grain

1 organic egg, beaten (optional)
2½ cups water or Light Soy Stock (p. 262)
½ teaspoon herb salt
1 teaspoon whole saffron, crushed

Preheat the oven to 350°. Heat the olive oil and safflower oil in a sauté pan, add the chopped onion, and cook it until it is translucent but not browned. Set the onion aside for a moment.

Put the rice in a deep heavy pan with a tight-fitting lid. To prevent stickiness, mix in the beaten egg and stir the mixture over moderate heat until the kernels are dry and separate. Whether or not you have coated the rice with egg, combine it with the cooked onion, stock or water, and herb salt, and bring the mixture to a boil. Stir in the crushed saffron. Cover the pan and cook in the preheated oven for 45 minutes without disturbing it.

PRESENTATION. Fluff the rice with 2 forks and serve it in the hot baking dish or transfer it to a warm serving dish. Or press it into a lightly oiled mold, and turn out onto a warm flat serving dish.

2 cups

Riz Safran à l'Orange

Orange Saffron Rice

1 cup natural brown rice, long or short grain
1 organic egg, beaten (optional)
1 tablespoon cold-pressed virgin olive oil
2 teaspoons whole saffron, crushed
Grated rind of 2 oranges

2½ cups Light Soy Stock (p. 262)
½ teaspoon sea salt
2 tablespoons orange liqueur, or 2 teaspoons natural orange flavoring with 1 tablespoon cold-pressed safflower oil

Preheat the oven to 350°. Put the rice in a deep heavy pan with a tight-fitting lid. To prevent stickiness, add the beaten egg and stir the mixture over moderate heat until the kernels are dry and separate. Whether or not you have coated the rice with egg, combine it with the olive oil, saffron, and orange rind, and stir over low heat for 2 minutes. Add the stock and sea salt and bring to a boil. Cover the pan and cook in the preheated oven for 45 minutes without disturbing it.

PRESENTATION. Add the orange liqueur or flavoring mixed with oil to the cooked rice and fluff it with 2 forks. Serve it in the hot baking dish, or transfer it to a warm serving dish. Or press it into a lightly oiled mold, and turn out onto a warm flat serving dish.

2 cups

Riz Pilaf Birman

Burmese Pilaff

2 cups natural brown rice, long or short grain
2 organic eggs, beaten (optional)
3 tablespoons cold-pressed safflower oil
1 teaspoon Marmite (brewers' yeast extract)

1 teaspoon natural tomato paste
1 teaspoon whole saffron, crushed
5 cups Light Soy Stock (p. 262)
½ teaspoon herb salt
¼ cup pine nuts
¼ cup whole almonds, blanched

Preheat the oven to 350°. Put the rice in a deep heavy pan with a tight-fitting lid. To prevent stickiness, add the beaten eggs and stir over moderate heat until the kernels are dry and separate. Whether or not you have coated the rice with egg, add to the rice 2 tablespoons saf-flower oil, the Marmite yeast extract, tomato paste, and saffron, and mix well. Add the stock and ½ teaspoon herb salt, and bring the mixture to a boil. Cover the pan and cook in the preheated oven for 1 hour without disturbing it. Lightly sauté the pine nuts and almonds in 1 tablespoon safflower oil and set them aside.

PRESENTATION. When the rice is cooked, add the pine nuts and al-monds and fluff the whole mixture with 2 forks. Serve in the hot baking dish, or transfer the rice to a warm serving dish. Or press it into a lightly oiled mold, and turn out onto a warm flat serving dish.

Approximately 4 cups

Riz Provençale

Rice Ring Provençal, with Eggplant, Peppers, and Tomatoes

For the presentation of this dish, the rice may be molded in a ring and the center filled with the Provençal vegetables, or the rice and vege-tables may be served in separate bowls.

Rice Pilaff (pp. 168–169), double recipe
1 large eggplant
Sea salt
5 tablespoons cold-pressed virgin olive oil
2 yellow onions, each cut into eighths
1 teaspoon finely chopped fresh garlic
1 green sweet bell pepper, seeded and cut into eighths

1 red sweet bell pepper, seeded and cut into eighths (if a red bell pepper is not available, use another green one)
Herb salt
4 firm fresh mushrooms, thickly sliced
1 teaspoon fresh lemon juice
3 medium-size ripe tomatoes, each skinned and cut into eighths
1 tablespoon finely chopped fresh parsley

PROVENÇAL VEGETABLES. Cut the stem end from the eggplant but do not peel it. Cut the eggplant lengthwise into halves, and then into ½-inch-thick slices. Sprinkle the sliced eggplant with sea salt and let it marinate for 30 minutes. Rinse the eggplant in cold water and dry it between paper towels.

Heat 3 tablespoons olive oil in a large sauté pan. When it is quite hot, quickly brown the eggplant slices on each side, using more oil if necessary. Do not keep the eggplant in the pan too long; you do not want the slices to be soft or mushy. Drain the eggplant on paper towels. Add 2 tablespoons olive oil to the pan with the onions and gar-lic. Cook briskly until the onions begin to brown. Add the peppers and cook over moderate heat for 3 minutes. Season the mixture with herb salt. Add the sliced mushrooms and lemon juice and cook for 2 minutes.

Gently mix the eggplant and tomatoes with the pepper mixture, and cook over low heat for 2 minutes. Adjust the seasoning with herb salt. *Note:* The tomatoes and sautéed eggplant should be added just before serving. You do not want to "cook" these vegetables because you do not want them to disintegrate in the hot mixture.

PRESENTATION. Spoon the Provençal vegetables into the center of the rice ring, or serve in a separate bowl. Sprinkle the chopped parsley over the top.

4 servings

Paella Valenciana

Paella with Chicken and Seafood

5 tablespoons cold-pressed safflower oil
1 whole dressed chicken, 3 to 3½ pounds
¾ cup dry sherry (optional)
1 teaspoon Marmite (brewers' yeast extract)
2 teaspoons natural tomato paste
4 teaspoons potato flour
2 cups Light Soy Stock (p. 262)
1½ cups dry white wine, or ½ cup additional stock and 1 cup water
2 teaspoons natural currant or guava jelly
Herb salt
24 mussels, well cleaned
½ cup mixed sliced onion, carrot, and celery
1 bay leaf
2 or 3 sprigs of fresh herb (parsley, dill, tarragon, etc.)
1 live lobster, any size
11 tablespoons cold-pressed virgin olive oil

2 cups natural brown rice, long or short grain
2 organic eggs, beaten
¾ cup finely chopped yellow onion
1½ teaspoons finely chopped fresh garlic
2 teaspoons whole saffron, crushed
1 pound raw shrimps, shelled and deveined
3 yellow onions, each cut into eighths
½ pound firm fresh mushrooms
2 teaspoons fresh lemon juice
1 green sweet bell pepper, seeded and cut into eighths
1 red sweet bell pepper, seeded and cut into eighths (if red bell pepper is not available, use another green one)
4 medium-size ripe tomatoes, each skinned and cut into eighths
1 teaspoon raw sugar

Heat 2 tablespoons safflower oil in a deep heavy pan with a tight-fitting lid, large enough for the chicken. Truss the chicken and brown it lightly on all sides in the hot oil. Also brown the chicken liver. Heat ¼ cup dry sherry in a little pan, ignite, and pour it over the chicken. Remove the chicken from the pan and set it aside.

(cont.)

In the same pan, off the heat, combine 3 tablespoons safflower oil, the Marmite yeast extract, tomato paste, and potato flour, and blend to a smooth paste. Add the stock, ½ cup dry white wine, ¼ cup dry sherry or additional stock, and the jelly. Adjust the seasoning with herb salt. Stir the sauce over moderate heat until it comes to a boil. Carve the chicken into small serving pieces and put it back in the pan with the sauce. Cover the pan and set it over low heat on top of the stove to cook until the chicken is tender. Meanwhile, preheat the oven to 350°.

Put the mussels in a pan with 4 cups of water and 1 cup white wine or additional water, the sliced onion, carrot, and celery, bay leaf, and fresh herb. Cover, bring slowly to a boil, and cook for 3 or 4 minutes, until the shells open. Strain the liquid and reserve it. Discard any mussel shells that have not opened; they are not good. Remove the top shells of the opened mussels, and set the mussels on the half shells aside.

Set the live lobster on a cutting board. With a large chef's knife, slit the lobster into halves, starting at the center of the back of the head and cutting down through the tail. Remove the sac behind each eye and the large vein. Cut off the large and small claws. Heat 4 tablespoons olive oil in a large heavy pan, about 8-quart size, with a tight-fitting lid. Place the lobster in thé pan, shell side down, and the claws. Cover the pan and cook for 3 minutes. Heat ¼ cup dry sherry in a little pan, ignite, and pour it over the lobster. Re-cover the pan and allow the lobster to cook over moderate heat until the shells are red. Remove the lobster and set it aside.

Put the rice in a separate dry pan, mix it with the beaten eggs, and stir it over heat until the kernels are dry and separate. Set the rice aside.

In the pan in which the lobster was cooked, heat another 4 tablespoons olive oil. Add the chopped onion and 1 teaspoon garlic, and cook over moderate heat until the onion is translucent but not brown. Add the rice and mix it with the onion. Add the reserved liquid from the mussels and additional water to make 5 cups. Also add the saffron and 2 teaspoons herb salt. Stir the mixture over moderate heat until the liquid comes to a boil. Cut the raw shrimps into halves and add them to the rice mixture. Cover the pan and cook in the preheated oven for 1 hour.

While the rice is cooking prepare the vegetables. Heat 3 tablespoons olive oil in a large sauté pan and add the cut-up onions and ½ teaspoon chopped garlic. Cook over moderate heat until the onions just begin to brown. Add the sliced mushrooms, the lemon juice, and peppers, and season with herb salt. Cook the vegetables over low heat for 4 or 5 minutes. Add the tomatoes and raw sugar, and adjust the seasoning with herb salt.

PRESENTATION. It is nice to serve the paella in the traditional paella pan, which is a large round shallow metal pan with handles at either end. However, a large casserole will serve as well. As soon as the rice is cooked, remove it from the oven and fluff it with 2 forks. Arrange half of the rice on the bottom of the serving dish. Place the pieces of chicken and mussels on the half shells on top of it. Spoon the vegetables over. Cover with the rest of the rice. Cut the lobster into bite-size pieces, leaving it attached to the shells. Scatter these over the top of the rice. The prepared dish may be warmed in a low oven prior to serving.

6 to 8 servings

This creative mixture is delicious accompanied with plain-cooked vegetables, poultry, or meat.

Riz Sauvage Dione

Wild Rice Dione

1 cup wild rice
3. cups Light Soy Stock (p. 262), more if necessary
1 teaspoon herb salt
Bouquet garni (parsley, celery leaf, orégano, thyme, or any other fresh leaf herbs on hand), wrapped and tied in cheesecloth
¼ cup cold-pressed virgin olive oil
2 tablespoons dried currants

4 tablespoons cold-pressed safflower oil
1 cup finely chopped yellow onion
½ cup finely chopped green sweet bell pepper
1 cup finely chopped fresh mushrooms
2 tablespoons chopped fresh basil, or 2 teaspoons dried basil
½ cup pine nuts (pignoli)

Put the rice in a deep heavy pan with the stock, herb salt, and *bouquet garni,* and bring to a boil over moderate heat, stirring occasionally. Add the olive oil and currants, cover with a tight-fitting lid, and allow to cook over very low heat until the rice has absorbed all the stock and is soft. While the rice is cooking, stir it occasionally. If all of the liquid has been absorbed before the rice is cooked, add more stock.

Heat the safflower oil in a sauté pan and add the onion and green pepper. Cook over low heat until the onion is translucent. Add the mushrooms, basil, and pine nuts, and season with a little herb salt. Stir the mixture over low heat for about 4 minutes. When the rice is tender, remove the *bouquet garni* and mix in the ingredients from the sauté pan. Serve in a warm casserole.

Approximately 3 cups

Gnocchi alla Romana

Variations: Whole Wheat, Millet, Kasha, Creamy Kernels, or Barley

Gnocchi alla Romana prepared with natural grains are far tastier and more nutritious than when they are made with the traditional white or yellow semolina or cream of farina. For this recipe you will want the following milling:

Whole wheat—crushed, cereal texture (not flour)
Millet meal—medium fine
Kasha (Buckwheat) —grits, fine, hulled

Creamy Kernels (special millled buckwheat)
Barley—grits

Or you may experiment with other organic whole-grain cereals of similar milling.

2 cups plain-cooked cereal-texture grain prepared according to package directions for a thick mixture
¾ cup freshly grated Parmesan cheese

½ teaspoon dry mustard
2 tablespoons cold-pressed safflower oil
Herb salt

Plain-cook the cereal but reduce the liquid by about one quarter so that you get a thick consistency. Add to the cooked cereal ½ cup grated cheese, the dry mustard, and 1 tablespoon safflower oil. Adjust the seasoning with herb salt. Stir over low heat for 3 or 4 minutes until mixture is well blended.

Rinse a shallow pan, like a cake pan, with cold water and spread the mixture over the bottom, about ½ inch thick. Set it in the freezer or refrigerator to set.

PRESENTATION. Cut the chilled cereal with a cookie cutter into rounds 1½ inches in diameter, and arrange them overlapping on a lightly oiled au gratin dish or shallow baking dish. Sprinkle the rest of the grated cheese over the top and dot with a few drops of safflower oil. Brown lightly under the broiler and serve.

4 servings

Gnocchi Parisienne

Whole-Wheat Chou-Paste Gnocchi, Mornay Sauce

WHOLE-WHEAT CHOU-PASTE GNOCCHI
1 cup water
4 tablespoons cold-pressed safflower oil
Sea salt
1 cup stone-ground whole-wheat pastry flour
3 organic eggs

½ teaspoon dry mustard
¾ cup freshly grated Parmesan cheese
¼ teaspoon freshly grated nutmeg

MORNAY SAUCE
2 tablespoons cold-pressed safflower oil

2 tablespoons stone-ground whole-
    wheat pastry flour
1 cup raw milk
    Herb salt
¼ cup freshly grated Parmesan
    cheese

½ teaspoon dry mustard
    Yolk of 1 organic egg
3 tablespoons raw sour cream, or
    raw heavy sweet cream

GNOCCHI. Combine the water, 2 tablespoons safflower oil, and ½ teaspoon sea salt in a saucepan, and bring the mixture to a boil. While the
liquid is boiling, add the flour. Stir until smooth with a small whisk.
Transfer the mixture to the bowl of an electric mixer and beat in the
eggs, one at a time. Beat in the dry mustard, ¼ cup grated cheese, and
the nutmeg.

Fill a large pan three-quarters with water and 1 teaspoon sea salt
and bring it to a boil. Reduce the heat to a bare simmer. Fit a pastry
bag with a No. 8 or No. 9 plain tube, and fill the bag with the gnocchi
mixture. Pipe out 1-inch-long pieces of dough into the pan of simmer-
ing water, cutting the pieces off with a small knife. Place a double
thickness of paper towel over the top of the gnocchi and allow them to
simmer, *but not boil,* for 20 minutes, or longer, if you wish. Carefully
remove them from the water with a slotted spoon onto paper towels to
drain. Pile them into a lightly oiled au gratin dish or shallow baking
dish.

PRESENTATION. *If the gnocchi are to be served without sauce,* sprinkle
½ cup grated cheese over the top and dot with 2 tablespoons safflower
oil. Brown the dish lightly under the broiler and serve.

If the gnocchi are to be served with sauce, prepare Mornay sauce and
spoon it over the gnocchi.

MORNAY SAUCE. Heat 2 tablespoons safflower oil in a saucepan. Off the
heat blend in the flour. Add the milk and stir over moderate heat until
the sauce comes to a boil. Reduce the heat, season with herb salt, and
add ¼ cup grated cheese and the dry mustard. Simmer the sauce for
5 minutes. Mix the egg yolk with the cream in a small bowl. Add 2 or 3
tablespoons of sauce to the egg-yolk mixture, then pour the egg-yolk
mixture into the sauce in the pan, stirring all the while.

Sprinkle ½ cup grated cheese over the sauce and dot with 2 tablespoons safflower oil. Brown the dish lightly under the broiler and
serve.

4 servings

Gnocchi Sauté

Fried Gnocchi

Whole-wheat Chou-Paste Gnocchi
    (see preceding recipe)
Stone-ground whole-wheat pastry
    flour, for dusting
1 organic egg, beaten

Dry whole-wheat Bread Crumbs,
    for coating (p. 258)
4 tablespoons cold-pressed safflower
    oil, or more if needed for
    frying

Prepare the gnocchi through the step of cooking them in the water. Drain them well on paper towels. Lightly dust the gnocchi with flour, brush them with beaten egg, and roll them in bread crumbs.

Heat the safflower oil in a large sauté pan and fry the gnocchi in it until they are golden brown, turning them gently. Drain them on paper towels and carefully transfer them to the serving dish.

4 servings

Nouilles Bis aux Fines Herbes

Whole-Wheat Noodles with Mixed Herbs

Cooked whole-wheat spaghetti, shells, or bows are also good tossed with this herb mixture. The herb mixture will keep in the freezer.

HERB MIXTURE
- 6 tablespoons cold-pressed safflower oil
- 2 teaspoons very finely chopped white onion
- 1 tablespoon finely chopped fresh tarragon
- 1 teaspoon finely chopped fresh thyme, or ½ teaspoon dried thyme
- 2 tablespoons finely chopped fresh parsley

- ¼ teaspoon ground sage
- ¼ teaspoon ground rosemary
- ½ teaspoon herb salt
- ¼ teaspoon dry mustard

- 1 pound whole-wheat noodles
- 3 tablespoons cold-pressed safflower oil
- 2 teaspoons sea salt
- 4 tablespoons raw sour cream

HERB MIXTURE. Put all of the ingredients in the blender and purée.
NOODLES. Fill a large pan three-quarters with water and add the safflower oil and sea salt. Bring it to a rolling boil and put in the noodles. Cook whole-wheat noodles no more than 10 minutes, or according to the time given on the package. Drain immediately through a colander or wire strainer and transfer them to a hot serving dish.
PRESENTATION. Put the sour cream on top of the noodles with about half of the herb mixture and toss lightly but well with 2 forks. Add only enough additional herb mixture to coat the noodles lightly.
4 servings

Fettuccini alla Italiana

Whole-Wheat Fettuccini with Oil, Cream, and Cheese

This dish may also be prepared with whole-wheat spaghetti, shells, or bows.

- 9 tablespoons cold-pressed safflower oil, or 3 tablespoons safflower oil and 8 tablespoons natural sweet butter

- 1 teaspoon finely chopped fresh garlic
- 1 teaspoon herb salt
- 1 pound whole-wheat noodles

2 *teaspoons sea salt*
1 *to 1½ cups freshly grated*
  Parmesan cheese

3 *tablespoons raw sour cream, or*
  raw heavy sweet cream

If you are using safflower oil only, put 6 tablespoons safflower oil, the garlic, and herb salt in a blender and blend well. *If you are using butter,* cream the butter in the mixer until it is very light and fluffy. Then beat in the chopped garlic and herb salt.

NOODLES. Fill a large pan three-quarters with water and add 3 tablespoons safflower oil and the sea salt. Bring to a rolling boil and put in the noodles. Cook whole-wheat noodles no more than 10 minutes, or according to the time given on the package. Drain them immediately through a colander or wire strainer and transfer them to a hot serving dish.

PRESENTATION. Put a little of the butter or safflower-oil mixture on top of the noodles and toss lightly with 2 forks. Next, toss in a little of the grated cheese. Continue adding oil or butter mixture and cheese alternately, using about ¾ cup of cheese and only enough oil or butter to coat the pasta. Last, toss with the cream. Serve immediately with the rest of the grated cheese in a separate bowl.

4 servings

This dish may also be made with whole-wheat spaghetti, shells, and bows. When fresh basil is in season, the pesto can be made in extra quantity and frozen for future use.

Fettuccini al Pesto

Whole-Wheat Fettuccini with Fresh Basil and Parmesan Cheese

PESTO
½ *cup firmly packed fresh basil*
  leaves
⅓ *cup cold-pressed virgin olive oil*
½ *teaspoon chopped fresh garlic*
⅓ *cup freshly grated Parmesan*
  cheese

1 *pound whole-wheat noodles*
3 *tablespoons cold-pressed*
  safflower oil
2 *teaspoons sea salt*
¾ *cup freshly grated Parmesan*
  cheese

PESTO. Combine the fresh basil leaves, olive oil, garlic, and grated cheese in the blender and blend well.

NOODLES. Fill a large pan three-quarters with water and add 3 tablespoons safflower oil and the sea salt. Bring it to a rolling boil and put in the noodles. Cook whole-wheat noodles for 10 minutes only, or according to the time given on the package. Drain immediately through a colander or wire strainer and transfer them to a hot serving dish.

PRESENTATION. Spoon a little of the pesto on top of the noodles and toss lightly with 2 forks. Continue to add the sauce and toss until all of the noodles are lightly coated. Serve immediately with the rest of the grated cheese in a separate bowl.

4 servings

Whole-Wheat Lasagne with Cheese Filling, Tomato and Mushroom Sauce

12 to 14 strips of whole-wheat
    lasagne
3 tablespoons cold-pressed
    safflower oil
2 teaspoons sea salt
    Cold-pressed safflower oil for
    baking dish
1 pound natural mozzarella
    cheese
1 cup freshly grated Parmesan
    cheese
¼ cup finely chopped fresh chives

FILLING
1½ cups natural cottage cheese
1½ cups natural ricotta cheese
8 ounces natural cream cheese
1 tablespoon finely chopped
    white onion
½ teaspoon finely chopped fresh
    garlic
1 tablespoon finely chopped fresh
    dill

Herb salt
2 tablespoons cold-pressed virgin
    olive oil

TOMATO AND MUSHROOM SAUCE
1 pound firm fresh mushrooms,
    coarsely chopped
3 tablespoons cold-pressed virgin
    olive oil
2 medium-size yellow onions,
    finely chopped
1 teaspoon finely chopped fresh
    garlic
2 medium-size ripe tomatoes,
    skinned and sliced
2 tablespoons natural tomato
    paste
½ cup Light Soy Stock (p. 262), or
    water
1 teaspoon Marmite (brewers'
    yeast extract)
Herb salt

LASAGNE. Three-quarters fill a large pan with water, add 3 tablespoons safflower oil and the sea salt, and bring to a rolling boil. Carefully put the strips of lasagne in the boiling water and cook for 10 minutes, or according to the time given on the package. Drain immediately through a colander or wire strainer, rinse the strips with cold water, and spread them on paper towels to dry.

FILLING. Rub the cottage cheese through a fine vegetable strainer. In the electric mixer, combine the strained cottage cheese, ricotta cheese, cream cheese, onion, garlic, and dill. Beat until the mixture is light and fluffy, and season with herb salt. Add 2 tablespoons olive oil and beat again. Spread a thick layer of the cheese mixture on top of each strip of lasagne. Roll them up like small jelly rolls. Brush a shallow baking dish with safflower oil and place the rolled lasagne in it. Preheat the oven to 300°.

SAUCE. Put the chopped mushrooms in a towel and squeeze out all of the juice, catching as much of it as possible in a small container. Heat the olive oil in a large sauté pan. Add the chopped onions and garlic and cook over moderate heat for 2 or 3 minutes, until the onions become soft but not brown. Add the sliced tomatoes and tomato paste and cook the mixture briskly for 3 minutes. Mix in the chopped mushrooms, any reserved mushroom juice, the soy stock, and Marmite yeast extract; season with herb salt. Reduce the heat and simmer for 20 minutes.

Spoon the sauce over the lasagne. Cut 1 slice of mozzarella cheese for each rolled lasagna and lay the slices on top of the sauce. Liberally sprinkle grated Parmesan cheese over the top. Bake the lasagne in the preheated oven for 20 minutes.

PRESENTATION. Serve the lasagne in the baking dish. Sprinkle the rest of the Parmesan cheese and the chopped chives on the top before serving.

6 to 7 servings

12 strips of whole-wheat lasagne
5 tablespoons cold-pressed safflower oil
2 teaspoons sea salt
1 pound natural mozzarella cheese
1 cup freshly grated Parmesan cheese
2 tablespoons finely chopped Italian parsley

FILLING
1 pound fresh spinach, well washed
Herb salt
Yolks of 4 organic eggs
½ cup natural ricotta cheese
½ teaspoon freshly grated nutmeg
½ teaspoon finely chopped fresh garlic

TOMATO SAUCE
3 tablespoons cold-pressed virgin olive oil
2 medium-size yellow onions, finely chopped
1 teaspoon finely chopped fresh garlic
6 medium-size ripe tomatoes, skinned and sliced
2 tablespoons natural tomato paste
2 teaspoons potato flour mixed with 4 tablespoons water
1 teaspoon Marmite (brewers' yeast extract)
2 tablespoons finely chopped Italian parsley
Herb salt

Whole-Wheat Lasagne with Spinach Filling, Fresh Tomato Sauce

LASAGNE. Three-quarters fill a large pan with water, add 3 tablespoons safflower oil and the sea salt, and bring to a rolling boil. Carefully put the lasagne in the boiling water and cook for 10 minutes, or according to the time given on the package. Drain immediately through a wire strainer or colander, rinse the strips with cold water, and spread them on paper towels to dry.

FILLING. Put the spinach in a pan with ¼ cup water and sprinkle with a little herb salt. Cook over high heat until it just wilts, stirring occasionally to turn it. Drain the spinach well through a colander, pressing it down with a saucer. Pass the spinach through the fine blade of a food grinder. Beat the egg yolks and ricotta cheese in an electric mixer. Add the ground spinach, nutmeg, and garlic, and season with herb salt. Spread a layer of this filling on top of each strip of lasagne. Roll them up like small jelly rolls. Brush a shallow baking dish with safflower oil and place the rolled lasagne in it. Preheat the oven to 300°.

SAUCE. Heat the olive oil in a large sauté pan. Add the chopped onions and garlic, and cook over moderate heat for 2 or 3 minutes, until the onions begin to get soft but not brown. Add the sliced tomatoes and tomato paste and cook briskly for 3 minutes. Add the potato-flour-and-water mixture, the Marmite yeast extract, and chopped parsley, mix well, and season with herb salt. Reduce the heat and let the sauce simmer for about 20 minutes.

Spoon the sauce over the lasagne. Cut 1 slice of mozzarella cheese for each rolled lasagna and lay the slices on top of the sauce. Liberally sprinkle about half of the grated cheese over the top. Set the lasagne in the preheated oven to cook for 20 minutes.

PRESENTATION. Serve the lasagne in the baking dish. Sprinkle the rest of the cheese and the chopped parsley on top before serving.

6 servings

Spaghetti Napoletana

Whole-Wheat Spaghetti with Tomato Sauce

Whole-wheat and buckwheat pasta in any shape gives a rich, nutty taste treat. There is also an excellent quality and highly nutritious pasta made of artichoke flour, which is white (see p. 21). Prepare in the lusty Neapolitan manner, topped with fresh tomato sauce, or with tomato and mushroom sauce, and with a generous sprinkling of freshly grated Parmesan cheese.

1 pound whole-wheat, buckwheat, or artichoke-flour pasta
3 tablespoons cold-pressed safflower oil
2 teaspoons sea salt

Fresh Tomato Sauce (p. 181), or Fresh Tomato and Mushroom Sauce (p. 180)
1½ cups freshly grated Parmesan cheese

Prepare the selected sauce and set it aside.

SPAGHETTI OR OTHER PASTA. Fill a large pan three-quarters with water, add the safflower oil and the sea salt, and bring to a rolling boil. Put the pasta in the boiling water and cook for no more than 10 minutes, or according to the time given on the package. Drain immediately through a colander or wire strainer and transfer the hot pasta to a warm serving dish.

PRESENTATION. Cover the pasta with the sauce. Sprinkle some grated cheese over the sauce and serve the rest of the cheese in a separate bowl.

4 servings

SOME COMMENTS ABOUT SAVORY TARTS

The recipes for savory tarts in this section suggest a whole-wheat short pastry made with grated cheese, which happens to go very well with savory fillings. If you prefer, the plain whole-wheat short pastry given on page 220 may be used.

The use of stone-ground whole-wheat pastry flour and cold-pressed safflower oil in making pastry produces a somewhat crumbly shell, more so than a short pastry made with refined white flour and butter. Therefore, instead of using a flan ring in which to shape the pastry shell, which is removed for serving, we recommend that savory tarts made with stone-ground whole-wheat flour and safflower oil be baked in a neat pie pan or in one of the attractive French porcelain round baking dishes that are 1 inch deep, and that the tart be served in its baking dish. The baking dish may be set on a napkin or doily on a serving plate or tray for presentation at the table. We think you will find the eating reward worth the adjustment.

Cheese Short Pastry for Savory Tarts

2 *cups stone-ground whole-wheat*
    pastry flour
3 *tablespoons freshly grated*
    Parmesan cheese
¼ *teaspoon sea salt*
4 *tablespoons cold-pressed*
    safflower oil
⅓ *cup water*

Put the flour, cheese, and salt in a bowl. Add the safflower oil and mix it into the flour mixture thoroughly with your fingers. Add only enough water to work the mix to a firm ball. Wrap the dough in plastic wrap or wax paper and leave it in the refrigerator for 1 hour, or longer if you wish.

When you are ready to bake the pastry shell, have a 10-inch baking pan or dish ready and preheat the oven to 375°. Set the dough on a lightly floured surface and flatten it with a rolling pin to about the size of the baking container. Carefully transfer it to the baking container. Working from the center to the edge, press the dough evenly to cover the pan and sides. Trim off the excess neatly with a small knife and flute the edge with pastry pincers.

Press a piece of wax paper on top of the pastry and fill it with rock salt or dried beans to weight it. Set the container in the preheated oven and bake for 30 minutes. Remove the weight and the paper. At this point the pastry shell may be filled and the baking finished; or it may be frozen, unfilled, for future use.

1 pastry shell, 10-inch size

Tarte aux Champignons
_____
Mushroom Tart

1 baked 10-inch whole-wheat
    pastry shell (p. 183 or p. 220)
2 tablespoons cold-pressed
    safflower oil
6 nice firm fresh mushrooms caps,
    medium size, whole
2 teaspoons fresh lemon juice
½ cup chopped yellow onion
8 ounces firm fresh mushrooms,
    sliced
1 tablespoon finely chopped fresh
    herb (parsley, tarragon, dill—
    any choice)

Herb salt
¾ cup freshly grated Gruyère or
    natural Swiss-type cheese
3 whole organic eggs
    Yolks of 2 organic eggs
2 cups raw light cream, scalded
¼ cup freshly grated Parmesan
    cheese

If you have just baked the pastry shell in a 375° oven, remove the wax paper and weight and bake the shell for another 10 minutes. Remove it from the oven but leave the oven heated, reducing the temperature to 300°. If the pastry shell was frozen, finish baking it, if necessary.

Heat the safflower oil in a sauté pan and add the whole mushroom caps with 1 teaspoon lemon juice. Quickly brown the tops lightly and remove them from the pan. Set them aside to use for garnish. Add the chopped onion to the pan and cook it over moderate heat until it is soft but not brown. Add the sliced mushrooms, 1 teaspoon lemon juice, the fresh herb, and a little herb salt. Cook the mixture briskly for 2 minutes. Stir in the grated Gruyère cheese. Remove the pan from the heat and set the mixture aside for a moment.

Mix the whole eggs and extra egg yolks in a bowl and add the scalded cream. Add the sliced-mushroom mixture to the eggs and season with herb salt. Spoon this filling into the pastry shell and set it in the pre-heated oven. Bake the filled tart until it is firm to the touch, about 45 minutes.

PRESENTATION. Sprinkle the top of the baked tart with grated Parmesan cheese, and set a whole mushroom cap at even intervals around the tart. Serve hot.

6 servings

Tarte aux Oignons
_____
Onion Tart

1 baked 10-inch whole-wheat
    pastry shell (p. 183 or p. 220)
4 tablespoons cold-pressed virgin
    olive oil or cold-pressed
    safflower oil
2 large Bermuda onions, skinned,
    halved, and sliced

½ teaspoon finely chopped fresh
    garlic
    Herb salt
2 whole organic eggs
    Yolk of 1 organic egg
½ cup freshly grated Parmesan
    cheese

1 *teaspoon dry mustard*
¾ *cup raw light cream*
2 *tablespoons dry whole-wheat*

Bread Crumbs (p. 258)
A little sweet paprika

If you have just baked the pastry shell in a 375° oven, remove the wax paper and weight and bake the shell for another 10 minutes. Remove it from the oven but leave the oven heated, reducing the temperature to 350°. If the shell was frozen, finish baking it, if necessary.

Heat the oil in a sauté pan and add the sliced onions and garlic. Cook until the onions are soft but not brown. Season with a little herb salt and set the mixture aside for a moment.

Mix the whole eggs and extra egg yolk in a bowl with a wire whisk. Add ¼ cup grated cheese and the dry mustard, and season with herb salt. Scald the cream and pour it into the egg mixture, stirring all the time. Mix the sautéed onions into the egg mixture. Spoon this filling into the baked pastry shell. Set it in the preheated oven to bake for 15 to 20 minutes, or until it is firm to the touch.

PRESENTATION. When the tart is baked, sprinkle the top with the bread crumbs, the rest of the cheese, and a few dashes of paprika. Return it to the oven for a moment to brown a little.

6 servings

Tarte d'Epinards
Spinach Tart

1 *baked 10-inch whole-wheat*
   pastry shell (p. 183 or p. 220)
2 *tablespoons dry whole-wheat*
   Bread Crumbs (p. 258)
2 *tablespoons freshly grated*
   Parmesan cheese

FILLING

1 *pound fresh spinach, well*
   washed
7 *tablespoons cold-pressed*
   safflower oil
1 *cup finely chopped yellow onion*
½ *cup finely chopped celery*
½ *teaspoon finely chopped fresh*
   garlic
   Herb salt
1 *tablespoon dried juniper berries,*
   finely crushed

3 *whole organic eggs*
   Yolks of 2 organic eggs
½ *teaspoon dry mustard*
2¼ *cups raw milk, scalded*
⅓ *cup freshly grated Parmesan*
   cheese

GARNISH (optional)

   About 24 onion rings, ½ inch
   thick
   Stone-ground whole-wheat
   pastry flour, for coating
1 *organic egg, beaten*
   Dry whole-wheat Bread Crumbs
   for coating (p. 258)
   Cold-pressed safflower oil for
   deep-fryer

If you have just baked the pastry shell in a 375° oven, remove the wax paper and weight and bake the shell for another 10 minutes. Remove it from the oven but leave the oven heated, reducing the temperature to 350°. If the pastry shell was frozen, finish baking it, if necessary. Mix 2 tablespoons bread crumbs and 2 tablespoons grated cheese, and sprinkle this mixture on the bottom of the pastry shell.

FILLING. Wilt the spinach in a large pan with 2 tablespoons water over high heat. Drain it thoroughly, using a small saucer to press out as much moisture as possible. Put the spinach on a cutting board and chop it fine. Heat 2 tablespoons safflower oil in a sauté pan, add the chopped onion, celery, and garlic, and cook these vegetables over medium heat for 3 or 4 minutes. Season with herb salt and add the crushed juniper berries and chopped spinach. Mix the whole eggs, extra egg yolks, and dry mustard in a bowl with a whisk and season with herb salt. Mix in 5 tablespoons safflower oil, then the scalded milk, then the spinach mixture. Spoon the filling into the baked tart shell and sprinkle half of the grated cheese on the top. Bake the filled tart in the preheated oven for 30 minutes, or until it is firm to the touch.

GARNISH. Dust the onion rings with whole-wheat flour, brush them with the beaten egg, and coat them with the dry bread crumbs. Heat some safflower oil in a deep-fryer to 375°. Lightly fry the onion rings in it and drain them on paper towels.

PRESENTATION. When the tart is baked, arrange the onion rings on the top in an overlapping circle. Sprinkle the rest of the grated cheese over the top. Serve hot.

6 servings

Soufflé au Fromage, Sauce Hollandaise à la Moutarde

Cheese Soufflé with Mustard Hollandaise Sauce

Cold-pressed safflower oil for soufflé dish and collar
¾ cup freshly grated Parmesan cheese
3 tablespoons cold-pressed safflower oil
3 tablespoons stone-ground whole-wheat pastry flour
¾ cup raw milk
½ teaspoon dry mustard
Herb salt
Yolks of 4 organic eggs

Whites of 6 organic eggs
Sweet paprika

MUSTARD HOLLANDAISE SAUCE (optional)
Yolks of 2 organic eggs
1 teaspoon dry mustard
2 teaspoons fresh lemon juice
2 tablespoons raw sour cream
¼ teaspoon herb salt
8 tablespoons cold-pressed safflower oil

Preheat the oven to 325°. Brush a 1-quart (No. 6) soufflé dish with safflower oil. Tear off a piece of wax paper 1½ times the outer girth of the soufflé dish, fold it in half lengthwise, and brush it with safflower oil. Wrap it around the soufflé dish and tie it with kitchen string. Dust the inside with ¼ cup grated Parmesan cheese. Set the soufflé dish in a roasting pan and have a pan of hot water ready.

In a saucepan heat 3 tablespoons safflower oil and blend in the flour. Off the heat stir in the milk. Return the pan to moderate heat and stir until the sauce comes to a boil. Stir in the remaining ½ cup of grated cheese and the dry mustard, and season with herb salt. Remove the pan from the heat and stir in the egg yolks, one by one. Beat the egg whites to soft peaks and gently and smoothly fold the yolk mixture into the whites. Spoon the soufflé mixture into the prepared soufflé dish. Pour hot water into the roasting pan until it reaches halfway up the side of the soufflé dish. Set the soufflé in its water bath in the pre-heated oven, and bake for 1 hour or until the top tests firm.

MUSTARD HOLLANDAISE SAUCE. In a small bowl combine the egg yolks, dry mustard, lemon juice, sour cream, and ¼ teaspoon herb salt. Set the bowl in a small sauté pan half-filled with hot water over low heat. Beat with a small wire whisk until the sauce is thick. Add the safflower oil, little by little, beating all the time. Cover the bowl with a piece of plastic wrap, remove it from the heat, and set it aside until the soufflé is baked.

PRESENTATION. When the soufflé is baked, carefully remove it from the oven and the water bath. Set it on a serving plate, remove the paper collar, and sprinkle a few dashes of sweet paprika over the top. Serve immediately. For each portion, serve some of the top crust and some of the creamy inside with a dollop of the sauce.

4 servings

Soufflé Froid au Fromage

Cold Cheese Soufflé

Cold-pressed safflower oil for
   soufflé dish and collar
3 tablespoons cold-pressed
   unrefined safflower oil
2 tablespoons unflavored gelatin
4 tablespoons stone-ground
   whole-wheat pastry flour
1¼ cups raw milk
1 teaspoon dry mustard
4 tablespoons freshly grated
   Gruyère or natural Swiss-type
   cheese

6 tablespoons freshly grated
   Parmesan cheese
Sea salt
Yolks of 4 organic eggs
2 tablespoons raw sour cream
Whites of 6 organic eggs
Sweet paprika

Prepare a 1-quart (No. 6) soufflé dish as follows: Tear off a piece of wax paper 1½ times the outer girth of the soufflé dish, fold it in half lengthwise, and brush it with safflower oil. Wrap it around the soufflé dish and tie it with kitchen string.

In a saucepan warm 3 tablespoons safflower oil. Mix the gelatin with the flour and blend this mixture into the oil in the pan. Remove the pan from the heat and stir in the milk. Mix in the dry mustard, grated Gruyère, and 2 tablespoons of the grated Parmesan, and season with sea salt. Cook over low heat for 3 minutes to blend the mixture; transfer it to the bowl of an electric mixer. Beat in the egg yolks, one by one; then add the sour cream. Adjust the seasoning with sea salt. Beat the egg whites to soft peaks and fold them into the egg-yolk mixture. Fill the soufflé dish with the mixture and set it in the refrigerator or freezer to set.

PRESENTATION. Carefully remove the wax-paper collar and coat the sides and top with the rest of the grated Parmesan cheese. Sprinkle a few dashes of paprika on the top. Store in the refrigerator until the soufflé is to be served.

6 servings

Crêpes au Fromage
———————
Crêpes with Cheese Fondue Filling

8 to 12 whole-wheat crêpes, about 6 inches in diameter (see p. 232)
1 cup beer, or Light Soy Stock (p. 262)
2 cups grated natural Cheddar cheese
¾ cup freshly grated Parmesan cheese

¼ cup freshly grated Gruyère or natural Swiss-type cheese
½ teaspoon dry mustard
Herb salt
Yolks of 3 organic eggs
¾ cup raw light cream
2 tablespoons cold-pressed safflower oil

Heat the beer or stock in the top part of a double boiler. Slowly stir in the Cheddar, ½ cup of the Parmesan, and the Gruyère. Season with the dry mustard and a little herb salt. When all of the cheese has been added and the mixture is smooth, remove it from the heat. Beat the egg yolks and cream together in a separate bowl. Add the egg-yolk mixture to the cheese mixture. Return the cheese fondue to the heat and cook until it is thick.

PRESENTATION. Spread each crêpe with some of the cheese fondue and roll it up. Arrange the filled crêpes on an au gratin dish or heatproof serving dish. Brush the top with the safflower oil and sprinkle with remaining ¼ cup grated Parmesan cheese. Set the dish under the broiler to brown lightly and serve immediately.

4 servings

Vegetable Garnishes and
Accompaniments

Vegetables are an integral part of the diet for good health, and nature has made this life source available to us in plenty. Some 280 different vegetables appear in the markets of America—indeed, a vegetable for everyone, if it is presented, raw or cooked, to its best natural advantage.

The art of French cooking has invented many beautiful, nutritious ways to add vegetables to main courses of fish, shellfish, poultry, meat, eggs, grains, etc. In this chapter we try to provide a fair sampling of vegetable garnishes in the classic manner, cooked in the spirit of *cuisine santé*.

How to get the most health out of your vegetables: Like most other foods, vegetables can lose much of their vitamin and mineral content during handling and cooking. Here are some general pointers which are reflected in the recipes of this book:

1. The nutritional superiority of the organic vegetable in the nutrients it contains and its freedom from chemical processes, is uncontested, so use organic vegetables if you can get them. Apart from growing your own, some natural-food stores and farmer markets specialize in organic produce.

2. To reduce vitamin and mineral loss at the outset, always clean vegetables quickly; do not soak them. Also, keep them chilled in the refrigerator until they are ready to be used.

3. Whenever possible cook vegetables in their skins.

4. If you are boiling the vegetable, cook it for the minimum amount of time. Use a timer, and test the tenderness with an ice pick, to avoid breaking it apart with the tines of a fork. Cease boiling when the vegetable is slightly *underdone;* it will continue cooking in its own heat. A

perfectly cooked vegetable *holds its shape;* it is not limp, it is still *crisp in the eating,* and it does not need MSG to zap up its flavor.

5. Boil vegetables in a minimum amount of water, seasoned with a little salt. Always reserve the cooking water, as it contains much of the vitamin and mineral content from the vegetable. You can use this rich water as stock in sauces or soups.

6. Avoid if possible using aluminum or nickel- or chromium-plated cooking utensils, as flecks of the metal containers pass into the cooking water and the food and are toxic. Enameled cast-iron cooking utensils are excellent, and good ones last a lifetime. Pressure cookers are to be avoided, not only because they are usually aluminum but because they can be dangerous, and often cook the vegetable to a too-soft state within seconds.

7. Thumb through this chapter and other cookbooks to pick up different vegetable suggestions. Interpret them according to your own ideas. You will develop a gastronomic galaxy of garnishes and accompaniments worthy of sensuous and organic acclaim.

Vegetable Purées

With the emphasis on natural cookery, the classic vegetable purée shines with new glory. In addition to using a purée in the usual manner, as a garnish with fish, meat, poultry, or egg dishes, often as the bed on which the main dish is presented, a vegetable purée offers a delectable entrée when paired with rich natural-grain pilaffs. You can have a satisfying and different main-course presentation consisting of natural brown rice pilaff pressed into a simple mold (perhaps an oiled soufflé dish), turned out, and surrounded with artichoke bottoms filled alternately with two different purées—for example, pea and carrot, chick-pea and broccoli, turnip and spinach, or cauliflower and sweet potato. Or just serve the various purées in little bowls or au gratin dishes.

Preparation of purées: Purées are easy to prepare. In many cases the vegetable can be puréed in a blender, although we recommend that certain vegetables—to insure that the purée will be absolutely smooth—be rubbed through a fine vegetable strainer.

There are various ways in which to prepare vegetable purées. A béchamel sauce is often used to thicken the purée, as in the manner of the onion purée (classically known as Sauce Soubise), given in the Sauce section of this book. For most vegetable purées to be used as garnishes, however, Dione Lucas generally simplified the procedure by plain-cooking the vegetable until it was soft, then puréeing it through a strainer or in the blender, thickening it with a little flour and butter or oil, and finishing it with a dash of cream. Purées may be made ahead of time and reheated in a heavy pan over low heat.

Presentation of purées as separate dishes:
1. Put the purée(s) in a separate bowl or small au gratin dish. If desired, spoon a little raw sour cream or raw heavy sweet cream on top of the purée and brown it lightly under the broiler. Place triangular croutons of toasted whole-wheat bread around the dish and serve.
2. Warm some cooked artichoke bottoms in a little cold-pressed safflower oil. Put the purée in a pastry bag fitted with a large star tube (No. 8 or No. 9), and pipe a rosette into the artichoke bottom; or fill the artichoke bottom by using a small spoon, shaping the purée like a mound, and covering it with a sautéed mushroom cap.

Purée de Brocoli ou Chou-Fleur

Broccoli or Cauliflower Purée

1 bunch of broccoli or 1 cauliflower, about 2 pounds
Juice of ½ lemon
1 teaspoon sea salt
3 tablespoons cold-pressed safflower oil
2 tablespoons stone-ground whole-wheat pastry flour
2 tablespoons raw sour cream
Herb salt
¼ teaspoon freshly grated nutmeg (for cauliflower)

Trim the tough ends of the stems and excess leaves from the broccoli. Or remove the outer leaves and some of the core from the cauliflower.

Put the broccoli or cauliflower with 1 or 2 cups of water in a pan with a tight-fitting lid; the water should be about ½ inch deep. Add the lemon juice and sea salt. Bring the water to a boil, cover the pan, and cook over low heat until the vegetable is tender. Drain immediately and rub through a fine vegetable strainer.

Heat the safflower oil in a heavy pan. Blend in the flour and stir over low heat for a minute or two. Mix in the vegetable purée and sour cream. Adjust the seasoning with herb salt and add the nutmeg to the cauliflower. Stir the purée over low heat for 2 or 3 minutes.
Approximately 1 cup

Purée des Carottes, Panais, ou Navets

Carrot, Parsnip, or Turnip Purée

3 cups sliced carrots or parsnips, about 1-inch chunks, well-washed but not pared; or 3 cups turnips, pared and cut into about 1-inch chunks
Juice of ½ lemon
1 teaspoon sea salt
1 teaspoon raw sugar
2 tablespoons cold-pressed safflower oil
2 tablespoons stone-ground whole-wheat pastry flour
2 tablespoons raw sour cream
Herb salt

Put the prepared carrots, parsnips, or turnips in a pan, cover them with water, and add the lemon juice, sea salt, and sugar. Bring to a boil, reduce the heat, and simmer until the vegetable is tender. Drain and reserve the cooking water for future use as vegetable stock. In a blender reduce the vegetable to a smooth purée. If the outer skin of the parsnips seems a little fibrous, rub them through a vegetable strainer instead of blending.

Heat the safflower oil in a heavy pan. Blend in the flour and stir over low heat for a minute or two. Mix in the vegetable purée and the sour cream. Adjust the seasoning with herb salt. Stir over low heat for 2 or 3 minutes.

Approximately 2 cups

Purée de Marrons

Chestnut Purée

PLAIN CHESTNUT PURÉE. If you are preparing a dish that calls for plain chestnut purée, use the strained chestnuts in this recipe, without the safflower oil, cream, and seasoning.

Instead of raw chestnuts, you may use 1 cup natural-packed un-flavored chestnut purée.

1½ *pounds raw chestnuts*	2 *tablespoons raw sour cream*
2 *cups Soy-Vegetable Stock* (*p. 262*)	*Herb salt*
3 *tablespoons cold-pressed safflower oil*	

If you are using raw chestnuts: Put the chestnuts in a pan, cover them with water, and bring the water to a boil. Continue boiling for 4 or 5 minutes to soften the shells. Let the chestnuts stand in the water as you take them out one by one to remove the outer and inner skins. Discard the water and return the shelled chestnuts to the pan. Cover them with the stock and simmer until they are soft. Rub the cooked chestnuts through a fine vegetable strainer.

Heat the safflower oil in a heavy pan. Blend in the chestnut purée and the sour cream. Season with herb salt. Stir over low heat for 2 or 3 minutes.

Approximately 1 cup

Purée Soissonnaise

Chick-Pea Purée

½ *pound dried chick-peas*	1 *teaspoon sea salt*
Juice of ½ lemon	2 *tablespoons cold-pressed safflower oil*
1 *cup mixed sliced onion, carrot, and celery*	

2 tablespoons stone-ground whole-
    wheat pastry flour

3 tablespoons raw sour cream
Herb salt

Put the chick-peas in a pan and cover them with water and the lemon juice. Let them soak overnight or for at least 12 hours. Cook the chick-peas in the water in which they were soaked with the sliced onion, carrot, and celery. If necessary, add more water to the pan, to bring it to about 1 inch above the chick-peas. Add 1 teaspoon sea salt and bring the water to a boil. Reduce the heat to a simmer, cover the pan, and cook until the chick-peas are soft. Drain them, reserving the water for soups or other uses. Purée the chick-peas in a blender, using a little of the cooking water if necessary, or rub them through a fine vegetable strainer.

Heat the safflower oil in a heavy pan. Blend in the flour and stir over low heat for a minute or two. Mix in the chick-pea purée and the sour cream. Adjust the seasoning with herb salt. Stir over low heat for 2 or 3 minutes.

Approximately 1 cup

¾ cup dried lentils
    Juice of ½ lemon
2 teaspoons soy sauce
¼ cup Madeira wine (optional)
1 bay leaf
1 small white onion stuck with
    3 or 4 whole cloves

1 teaspoon sea salt
2 tablespoons cold-pressed safflower
    oil
2 tablespoons stone-ground whole-
    wheat pastry flour
3 tablespoons raw sour cream
Herb salt

Purée
de Lentilles

Lentil Purée

Put the lentils in a pan and cover them with cold water and the lemon juice. Let them soak overnight or for at least 12 hours. Cook the lentils in the water in which they were soaked. If necessary, add more water to the pan to bring it to about ½ inch above the lentils. Add the soy sauce and wine and bring the liquid to a boil. Add the bay leaf, onion with cloves, and 1 teaspoon sea salt. Reduce the heat to a simmer, cover the pan, and cook until the lentils are soft. Drain and reserve the water for soups and other uses. Rub the lentils through a fine vegetable strainer.

Heat the safflower oil in a heavy pan. Blend in the flour and stir for a minute or two over low heat. Mix in the lentil purée and the sour cream. Adjust the seasoning with herb salt. Stir over low heat for 2 or 3 minutes.

Approximately 1 cup

Onion Purée

Onion purée is Sauce Soubise, the recipe for which is given on page 268 in the chapter on Staples, Stocks, and Sauces.

Purée de Pois Frais

Pea Purée

2 cups shelled fresh garden peas
    and their pods
Juice of ½ lemon
1 teaspoon sea salt
2 tablespoons cold-pressed safflower
    oil

2 tablespoons stone-ground whole-
    wheat pastry flour
2 tablespoons raw sour cream
Herb salt

Tie the shelled peas in a cheesecloth and put them in a pan with the pods. Add about 3 cups water, the lemon juice, and sea salt, and bring to a boil. Reduce the heat and cook until the peas are tender. Drain and reserve the cooking water for future use in soups and sauces. Rub the peas through a fine vegetable strainer.

Heat the safflower oil in a heavy pan. Blend in the flour and stir for a minute or two over low heat. Mix in the pea purée and the sour cream. Adjust the seasoning with herb salt. Stir over low heat for 2 or 3 minutes.

Approximately 1 cup

Pommes de Terre Duchesse

Duchess Potatoes (Firm Potato Purée for Rosettes or Other Shapes)

4 large Idaho potatoes, scrubbed
1 teaspoon sea salt
2 organic eggs
3 tablespoons cold-pressed safflower
    oil

Herb salt
For rosettes, 1 organic egg, beaten

Cut the potatoes into halves, put them in a pan, cover with cold water, add 1 teaspoon sea salt, and bring them to a boil. Continue cooking until the potatoes are soft through the center. Drain, reserving the water for vegetable stock. Remove the skins from potatoes and put the potatoes in an electric mixer. Beat the potatoes until they are completely smooth. Beat in the 2 eggs, then the safflower oil, and season with herb salt.

To pipe into shapes: Put the puréed potato mixture into a pastry bag fitted with a No. 8 or No. 9 star tube. Pipe *scallop shapes as a border* around an au gratin dish for a sole preparation, or as a ribbon around scallop shells for *coquilles Saint-Jacques.* As a separate garnish for other dishes, pipe *rosettes* onto a lightly oiled baking sheet, gently brush the tops with beaten egg, and brown lightly under the broiler.

2 to 3 cups

3 large Idaho potatoes, scrubbed
1 teaspoon sea salt
   Yolks of 2 organic eggs
2 tablespoons cold-pressed safflower
   oil

   Herb salt
½ cup raw milk

Pommes de Terre Mousseline

Soft Potato Purée

Cut the potatoes into halves, put them in a pan, cover with cold water, add 1 teaspoon sea salt, and bring to a boil. Continue cooking until the potatoes are soft through the center. Drain the potatoes and reserve the cooking water for vegetable stock. Remove the skins from potatoes and put the potatoes in a mixer. Beat the cooked potatoes until they are completely smooth. Or you may rub them through a fine vegetable strainer.

Beat in the egg yolks, safflower oil, and ½ teaspoon herb salt. Heat the milk and add it to the potatoes. Beat thoroughly.
Approximately 2 cups

1½ pounds sorrel or spinach,
   well washed
   Juice of ½ lemon
1 teaspoon sea salt
4 tablespoons cold-pressed
   safflower oil

1 tablespoon stone-ground whole-
   wheat pastry flour
2 tablespoons raw sour cream
   Herb salt

Purée d'Oseille ou d'Epinards

Sorrel or Spinach Purée

Put the sorrel or spinach in the pan with the lemon juice, sea salt, and 2 tablespoons safflower oil. Cover the pan and cook until the leaves are just wilted; turn the leaves once or twice. Drain in a colander and press down with a saucer to remove as much moisture as possible. Rub the vegetable through a fine strainer, or put it through the fine blade of a food grinder.

Heat 2 tablespoons safflower oil in a heavy pan. Blend in the flour and stir for a minute or two over low heat. Mix in the purée and the sour cream. Adjust the seasoning with herb salt. Stir over low heat for 2 or 3 minutes.
Approximately 1 cup

2 or 3 acorn squashes, about 5
   inches in diameter, or 2 to 3
   pounds Hubbard squash
2 teaspoons sea salt
2 tablespoons cold-pressed safflower
   oil

2 tablespoons stone-ground whole-
   wheat pastry flour
2 tablespoons raw sour cream
   Herb salt

Purée de Courge

Squash Purée

Cut the acorn squashes into quarters or the larger squash into chunks, and remove the seeds. Put them in a pan, cover with water, and add 2 teaspoons sea salt. Bring the water to a boil, reduce the heat, and cover the pan. Cook until the squashes are soft. Drain and reserve the cooking water for future use as vegetable stock. Remove the pulp from the skins and put it in a blender with a little of the water in which it was cooked. Blend to a smooth purée, or rub through a fine strainer.

Heat the safflower oil in a heavy pan. Blend in the flour and stir for a minute or two over low heat. Mix in the squash purée and sour cream. Adjust the seasoning with herb salt. Stir over low heat for 2 or 3 minutes.

Approximately 2 cups

Purée de Patates

Sweet-Potato
Purée

2 pounds sweet potatoes	2 tablespoons raw sour cream
Sea salt	1/4 teaspoon freshly grated nutmeg
2 tablespoons cold-pressed safflower oil	Herb salt
2 tablespoons stone-ground whole-wheat pastry flour	

Potatoes may be baked or boiled. *To bake them,* put them (in their skins) in a 400° oven and bake until they are soft, about 1 hour. *To boil them,* put them in a pan, cover with water and 1 teaspoon sea salt, and boil until they are soft. When the potatoes are cooked, remove the potato pulp from the skins and rub it through a fine vegetable strainer.

Heat the safflower oil in a heavy pan. Blend in the flour and stir for a minute or two over low heat. Mix in the sweet-potato purée and sour cream. Season with the grated nutmeg and herb salt. Stir over low heat for 2 or 3 minutes.

Approximately 2 cups

Carottes Glacées, ou Oignons Glacés, ou Navets Glacés

Glazed Carrots,
Onions, or
Turnips

1 pound baby carrots, or	3 tablespoons cold-pressed safflower oil
1 pound baby white onions, about 1 inch in diameter, or	Herb salt
1 pound baby turnips	1 tablespoon raw sugar
Juice of 1/2 lemon	2 tablespoons organic honey
1 teaspoon sea salt	

Scrape carrots. If they are large, cut them into olive shapes. Skin the onions. Pare the turnips. If turnips are large, cut them in olive shapes. Put the carrots, onions, or turnips in a pan and just cover the vegetable with water. Add the lemon juice and sea salt and slowly bring to a boil. Reduce the heat and cook until the vegetable is tender but still crisp. Drain well.

Heat the safflower oil in a sauté pan, add the carrots, or onions, or turnips, and season with herb salt. Sprinkle the carrots, or onions, or turnips with the raw sugar and shake them briskly. Add the honey and shake over moderate heat until they have a golden glaze. Serve as a garnish or in a small vegetable dish.

4 servings

*4 whole globe artichokes, about
    3½ inches in diameter*
1 tablespoon fresh lemon juice

*1 tablespoon sea salt
    Hollandaise Sauce (pp. 268–269)*

Artichauts à la Hollandaise

Artichokes with Hollandaise Sauce

Cut the stalk even with the bottom of the artichoke. Cut off about one third of the top of the artichoke. With a kitchen scissors, cut off the tips of the rest of the uncut leaves. Fill a large pan three-quarters with water, add the lemon juice and 1 tablespoon sea salt, and bring to a boil. Put the artichokes in the boiling water and cook for about 30 minutes, until the heart in the bottom is just tender. Remove them with tongs and drain on paper towels. Carefully cut out the small leaves and thistle choke in the center and discard.

PRESENTATION. Set the artichokes on warm individual serving plates. Fill the center cavity with hollandaise sauce and serve the artichokes warm.

4 servings

*24 to 32 medium-size fresh
    asparagus*
*4 slices stone-ground whole-wheat
    bread*

Hollandaise Sauce (pp. 268–269)

Asperges à la Hollandaise

Asparagus with Hollandaise Sauce

Cut the tough ends off the asparagus and rinse them under cold water. Have ready a vegetable steamer. Tie the asparagus in a bundle, and set it aside for a moment.

Trim the crusts off the bread slices and reserve crusts for making bread crumbs for future use. Toast the bread squares on each side in the oven or under the broiler.

Prepare the hollandaise sauce, remove it from the heat, cover it with plastic wrap, and set it aside.

Bring 1 cup water to a boil in the vegetable steamer, put in the bundle of asparagus, and steam for 4 minutes. Remove immediately. The asparagus should be crisp.

PRESENTATION. Arrange the slices of toast in a row on a serving plate, or one on each of 4 individual serving plates. Carefully put equal piles of asparagus on each. Spoon the hollandaise sauce over the asparagus and serve at once.

4 servings

Note: If you do not have a vegetable steamer, use a double boiler. Put the water and the asparagus in the *bottom* of the double boiler, tips uppermost, and cover with the inverted top of the double boiler.

Betteraves à la Crème

Baby Beets in Sour Cream

1½ pounds beets, baby beets preferred
1 teaspoon sea salt
2 tablespoons cold-pressed safflower oil

⅓ cup raw sour cream
Herb salt
1 tablespoon chopped fresh green herb (tarragon, chives, parsley, etc.)

Put the beets in a pan, cover with cold water, add the sea salt, and bring to a boil. Reduce the heat and simmer until the beets are tender but still firm. Drain them and remove the skins. If they are baby beets, of 1-inch diameter or less, leave them whole. If they are large, cut them into large dice, about ½-inch size.

Heat the safflower oil in a pan and add the cooked beets. Add the sour cream and mix carefully, just to coat the beets, and warm them a little. If necessary, season with herb salt. Put them in a warm serving dish and sprinkle the chopped herb over the top.

4 servings

Brocoli à la Polonaise

Broccoli with Hard-boiled Egg and Bread-Crumb Sauce

1 bunch of broccoli, 1½ pounds
Juice of 1 lemon
1 teaspoon sea salt

POLONAISE SAUCE
6 tablespoons cold-pressed safflower oil
3 tablespoons dry whole-wheat Bread Crumbs (p. 258)

2 teaspoons finely chopped white onion
2 organic eggs, hard-boiled and finely chopped
Herb salt

Trim the tough ends of the stems and excess leaves from the broccoli. Put the broccoli and about 2 cups of water in a pan with a tight-fitting lid. Add the lemon juice and sea salt. Bring the water to a boil, cover the pan, and cook over low heat until the broccoli is just tender. Drain it immediately and arrange it on a warm serving dish. Spread polonaise sauce thickly over the broccoli clusters.

POLONAISE SAUCE. Combine the safflower oil, bread crumbs, and chopped onion in a pan, and cook over moderate heat for about 2 minutes, being careful not to let the bread crumbs get too brown or burned. Add the chopped hard-boiled egg and a little herb salt. Stir over moderate heat for 1 minute. Serve as a garnish or in a separate vegetable dish.

4 servings

Céleri Amandine

Sautéed Diced Celery with Almonds

5 tablespoons cold-pressed safflower oil

4 cups coarsely diced young celery stalks

Herb salt

2 tablespoons finely chopped fresh chives

2 tablespoons finely chopped yellow or white onion

1 cup shredded blanched organic almonds

½ teaspoon finely chopped fresh garlic

2 tablespoons dry white wine (optional)

Heat 3 tablespoons safflower oil in a deep heavy pan with a tight-fitting lid. Add the celery and season with a little herb salt. Stir the celery in the oil, cover the pan, and cook over very low heat until the celery is tender. Occasionally stir the celery to prevent scorching. While the celery is cooking, sprinkle it with the chives and onion. Adjust the seasoning with herb salt.

When the celery is cooked, arrange it on a warm au gratin dish. Add 2 tablespoons safflower oil to the pan in which the celery was cooked. Add the almonds and shake them over medium heat until they are lightly browned. Add the chopped garlic and white wine, and season with herb salt. Cook for 1 minute, and spoon the almond mixture over the celery. Serve as a separate vegetable dish or as a garnish.

4 to 6 servings

Beignets de Maïs

Corn Fritters

This recipe also includes the best procedure for cooking corn on the cob—with the leaves and silk.

6 full ears of very fresh corn

Herb salt

8 tablespoons stone-ground whole-wheat pastry flour

1 teaspoon freshly grated nutmeg

¼ teaspoon dry mustard

Sea salt

1 whole organic egg

1 organic egg, separated

½ cup raw sour cream

2 tablespoons cold-pressed safflower oil

White of 1 organic egg

Safflower oil for frying

COOKING CORN ON THE COB. Remove and reserve all the green leaves and silk from the ears of corn. Barely cover the bottom of a deep pan with water, about ½ inch. Place reserved corn leaves and silk in the pan. Slowly heat the water so that the leaves are warm. Set the corn ears on top of the leaves, cover the pan, and steam the corn very quickly, about 5 to 6 minutes. Remove the ears; with a very sharp small knife, cut off the kernels. Season them with a little herb salt and set them aside.

FRITTERS. Combine the flour, nutmeg, dry mustard, and ½ teaspoon sea salt in a small bowl with 1 whole egg and 1 egg yolk, ¼ cup sour cream, and 2 tablespoons safflower oil. Beat with a wire whisk until the batter is quite smooth; it will be thick. Chill it in the refrigerator for at least 30 minutes.

When you are ready to cook the fritters, stir the rest of the sour cream and the corn kernels into the batter. Beat the 2 egg whites to soft peaks and fold them into the batter. Heat a sauté pan. When it is very hot, rub the bottom with a wad of wax paper dipped into safflower oil. Drop teaspoons of the mixture, about the size of a silver dollar, onto the bottom of the pan. Brown them lightly on one side; they brown quickly. Turn them over and brown the other side. Remove them with a spatula and drain on paper towels on a wire rack. Set the rack in a warm-oven with the door open, until you have finished making all of the fritters. Arrange them on a warm shallow dish and serve.
6 servings

Concombres aux Herbes

Cucumbers with Fresh Herbs

4 medium-size cucumbers
3 tablespoons cold-pressed safflower oil
2 tablespoons any fresh green herb, finely chopped (dill, tarragon, thyme, mint, parsley mixed with 1 teaspoon chopped shallot)
Herb salt

Cut the tops and bottoms from the cucumbers and peel them with a potato parer. Cut them lengthwise into quarters and cut out the seed sections. Cut the pulp into 1- or 1½-inch chunks.

Put the cucumber chunks in a heavy pan. Cover them with water, bring it to a boil, and drain immediately. Return the cucumbers to the pan and add the safflower oil and chopped herb, and season with herb salt. Press a piece of wax paper on top of the cucumbers and cover with the pot lid. Cook over very low heat until the cucumbers are just tender, only 2 or 3 minutes, as they will continue to cook after they are removed from the heat. Serve in a warm dish.
4 servings

Prepare Concombres aux Herbes (preceding recipe). After adding the herbs, stir in ½ to ¾ cup raw sour cream, enough to coat and sauce the cucumbers. Adjust the seasoning with herb salt and warm the cucumbers in the cream for 1 or 2 minutes. Serve in a warm vegetable dish.

Concombres à la Crème

Cucumbers in Cream

---

1 medium- to large-size eggplant
   Sea salt
   Stone-ground whole-wheat pastry
     flour for dusting eggplant slices
2 tablespoons cold-pressed virgin
   olive oil
5 tablespoons cold-pressed safflower
   oil
1 tablespoon finely chopped yellow
   or white onion

½ teaspoon finely chopped fresh
   garlic
3 or 4 tablespoons dry white wine,
   or Light Soy Stock (p. 262)
2 or 3 tablespoons chopped fresh
   parsley
   Herb salt

Aubergine Meunière

Sautéed Eggplant

Cut the stem off the eggplant and cut the eggplant into round slices a good ½ inch thick. Sprinkle the slices with sea salt and allow them to stand for at least 30 minutes. Rinse slices in cold water and dry well between paper towels. Lightly dust the eggplant slices with whole-wheat pastry flour and pat off the excess.

Heat 2 tablespoons olive oil and 2 tablespoons safflower oil in a large sauté pan. When the oil is quite hot, quickly brown the eggplant slices on each side. Do not cook them too long; they continue to cook even after they are removed from the pan, and become soft very quickly. Use more oil, if necessary. Set them on paper towels to drain. Arrange them on a warm au gratin dish and keep them warm while you finish the pan seasoning.

Add 2 tablespoons safflower oil to the pan with the chopped onion and garlic. Stir over low heat for 2 minutes. Add the white wine or stock, another tablespoon of safflower oil, and the chopped parsley. Season with a little herb salt. Stir the mixture over low heat for 2 minutes. Spoon the sauce over the eggplant and serve.

4 servings

---

2 small eggplants, each 4 to 5
   inches long
   Sea salt
4 tablespoons cold-pressed
   safflower oil
6 ounces firm fresh mushrooms,
   sliced

1 teaspoon fresh lemon juice
   Herb salt
2 tablespoons stone-ground whole-
   wheat pastry flour
½ teaspoon dry mustard
1 cup raw milk

              (cont.)

Aubergine Farcie aux Champignons

Eggplant Stuffed with Mushrooms

½ cup freshly grated Parmesan cheese	½ cup dry whole-wheat Bread Crumbs (p. 258)
¼ cup raw heavy sweet cream, or raw sour cream	Cold-pressed safflower oil for topping
3 or 4 tablespoons cold-pressed virgin olive oil	

Cut the eggplants lengthwise into halves. Sprinkle the cut sides with sea salt and let them stand for 30 minutes.

MUSHROOMS. Heat 2 tablespoons safflower oil in a sauté pan. Add the mushrooms and lemon juice and season with a little herb salt. Cook briskly for 2 minutes and set aside.

SAUCE. Heat 2 tablespoons safflower oil in a saucepan. Stir in the flour and dry mustard. Off the heat add the milk and season with herb salt. Return the pan to moderate heat and stir until the sauce comes to a boil. Add the Parmesan cheese and the sweet or sour cream. Reduce the heat and simmer gently for about 5 minutes.

Rinse the eggplants in cold water and dry them between paper towels. With a small knife, score the cut side of the eggplant in a criss-cross pattern, but do not cut through. Heat the oilve oil in a sauté pan and cook the eggplant halves in it, cut side down, until they are slightly browned and getting a little soft. Turn them over, skin side down, and cook for a little longer. Remove the eggplant halves from the pan and carefully scoop out the meat, leaving the skins intact. Chop the eggplant pulp and mix it with the mushrooms. Add 2 or 3 tablespoons of the sauce to bind the mixture. Fill the eggplant skins with the mushroom and eggplant-pulp mixture.

PRESENTATION. Arrange the stuffed eggplants on an au gratin dish. Coat the tops with the rest of the sauce, sprinkle with the bread crumbs, and dot with a little safflower oil. Brown lightly under the broiler, and serve.

4 servings

Endives Braisées, Sauce Mornay

Braised Endives with Cheese Sauce

8 fat fresh Belgian endives	1 bay leaf
1 tablespoon and 1 teaspoon fresh lemon juice	Herb salt
½ teaspoon sea salt	**TO SERVE WITHOUT MORNAY SAUCE**
2 tablespoons cold-pressed safflower oil	1 teaspoon potato flour
1 cup mixed finely sliced onion, carrot, and celery	**MORNAY SAUCE**
1 teaspoon Marmite (brewers' yeast extract)	3 tablespoons cold-pressed safflower oil
½ teaspoon natural tomato paste	4 tablespoons stone-ground whole-wheat pastry flour
2 cups Light Soy Stock (p. 262)	1¼ cups raw milk

⅔ cup freshly grated Gruyère
    cheese or natural Swiss-type
    cheese
¼ *cup raw heavy sweet cream,*
    whipped, or ½ *cup raw sour*
    cream

Herb salt
Yolks of 2 organic eggs
¼ *cup raw light cream*

Preheat the oven to 350°. Put the endives in a pan, cover them with water, 1 tablespoon lemon juice, and ½ teaspoon sea salt, and bring to a boil. Drain immediately and dry the endives between paper towels.

Heat 2 tablespoons safflower oil in a deep heavy pan with a lid and add the sliced onion, carrot, and celery. Cook over moderate heat for 2 or 3 minutes. Stir in the Marmite yeast extract, tomato paste, and stock, and bring to a boil. Add the bay leaf, season with herb salt, and arrange the endives on top of the vegetables. Spoon a little of the liquid over the endives, and cover the pan with the lid. Cook in the preheated oven for 45 minutes, occasionally spooning some of the liquid over the vegetable.

Carefully remove the endives with a slotted spoon. Arrange them on a warm au gratin dish or shallow serving dish, and sprinkle with 1 teaspoon of lemon juice.

If you are not using the mornay sauce, strain the liquid and return it to the pan. Mix 2 or 3 tablespoons of the pan stock with the potato flour and stir it into the stock in the pan. Adjust the seasoning with herb salt. Spoon this sauce over the endives and serve hot.

MORNAY SAUCE. Heat the safflower oil in a saucepan and blend in the flour. Off the heat add the milk. Return the pan to moderate heat and stir until the sauce comes to a boil. Add the grated cheese and heavy cream and season with herb salt. In a separate bowl, mix the egg yolks with the light cream. Add 2 or 3 tablespoons of the sauce to the egg-yolk mixture; then stir the egg-yolk mixture into the rest of the sauce. Spoon the sauce over the endives, lightly brown under the broiler, and serve.

4 servings

1 *pound young fresh green beans*
1 *teaspoon sea salt*
3 *tablespoons cold-pressed safflower*
    oil

1 *teaspoon fresh lemon juice*
Herb salt

**Haricots Verts
Parisienne**

*Thin-Sliced
Green Beans*

Cut the tops and tails from the beans and cut them diagonally into very thin slices. Put them in a pan, cover with water and 1 teaspoon sea salt, and bring them to a boil. Drain immediately.

Heat the safflower oil in a deep heavy pan with a tight-fitting lid.

Add the beans, lemon juice, and 4 tablespoons water. Season with herb salt and gently toss the beans. Cover with a piece of wax paper and the lid, and cook over very low heat until the beans are just tender but still crisp. This will require only a few minutes, the time depending on the beans. Transfer the beans with a slotted spoon from the pan to a warm serving dish.

4 servings

Haricots Verts Amandine

Green Beans with Almonds

Prepare Haricots Verts Parisienne (preceding recipe) and add the following almond garnish:

3 tablespoons cold-pressed safflower oil
½ cup shredded blanched organic almonds

1 teaspoon finely chopped fresh garlic

Heat the safflower oil in a sauté pan and add the almonds. Over low heat slowly brown the almonds. Mix in the chopped garlic and cook for another 1 or 2 minutes.

Champignons Sautés à la Crème

Sautéed Mushrooms in Cream

1 pound firm fresh mushrooms of uniform size
3 teaspoons fresh lemon juice
4 tablespoons cold-pressed safflower oil
¼ cup any combination of finely chopped fresh herbs (parsley, chives, basil, tarragon, dill, with a speck of finely chopped fresh garlic and white onion)

4 tablespoons raw sour cream
1 teaspoon Marmite (brewers' yeast extract)
Herb salt

Wash the mushrooms in 2 tablespoons lemon juice and water and drain them well. Cut the stems off even with the caps; reserve the stems for soups or sauces. If the caps are about 1 inch in diameter or smaller, leave them whole. If they are larger, cut them into halves or quarters, according to size.

Heat the safflower oil in a large sauté pan and add the mushrooms with 1 teaspoon lemon juice. Toss the mushrooms in the oil over moderate heat for 1 minute. Add the chopped herbs, sour cream, and Marmite yeast extract, and cook for another minute or two. Adjust the seasoning with herb salt. Serve in a warm au gratin dish or vegetable dish.

4 servings

8 to 12 firm fresh mushroom caps,
    about 2 to 2½ inches in
    diameter
2 cups finely chopped fresh
    mushrooms, including the stems
    from the caps
4 teaspoons fresh lemon juice
2 tablespoons cold-pressed safflower
    oil
    Herb salt

2 tablespoons finely chopped
    shallots
1 tablespoon natural tomato paste
¼ cup freshly grated Parmesan
    cheese
2 tablespoons finely chopped fresh
    parsley
    Cold-pressed safflower oil for
    topping

Champignons Farcis

Stuffed Mushrooms

Wash the mushrooms in 2 teaspoons lemon juice and cold water and dry them between paper towels. Carefully remove the stems from the choice mushrooms and set the caps aside. Chop the remaining mushrooms and stems to produce 2 cups. Put the chopped mushrooms in a cloth and squeeze out the juice.

Heat the safflower oil in a sauté pan. Add the mushroom caps with 2 teaspoons lemon juice, and sprinkle with a little herb salt. Cook over fairly high heat for 1 minute, then remove them from the pan. Put the chopped mushrooms in the pan with the chopped shallots, season with herb salt, and cook over moderate heat for 2 minutes. Mix in the tomato paste and cook for another 2 minutes. Fill the mushroom caps with the chopped mushroom mixture.

PRESENTATION. Arrange the stuffed mushrooms on an au gratin dish and sprinkle them with the grated cheese. Dot with a few drops of safflower oil and lightly brown them under the broiler. Sprinkle fresh parsley over the tops and serve. Or, the stuffed mushrooms may be used to garnish a main dish.

4 servings

1 pound fresh okra
1 teaspoon sea salt
6 or 7 chicken livers (optional)
3 tablespoons cold-pressed safflower
    oil
    Herb salt
1 teaspoon finely chopped fresh
    garlic

3 medium-size ripe tomatoes,
    skinned and thickly sliced
1 tablespoon chopped fresh chives
¼ cup freshly grated Parmesan
    cheese

Gombos à la Tomate

Okra with Tomato Sauce

Put the okra in a pan and cover it with water. Add the sea salt, bring to a boil, and cook until just tender. Drain and cut the okra into 1-inch chunks. If you are using the chicken livers, sauté them in 1 tablespoon safflower oil, season with herb salt, and set them aside.

Heat 2 tablespoons safflower oil in a pan, add the garlic, and cook over moderate heat for 1 minute. Add the okra and tomatoes and season with herb salt. Bring the mixture to a boil over moderate heat and cook for 4 or 5 minutes. Cut the chicken livers into halves and add them to the okra with the chives.

PRESENTATION. Serve the okra in an au gratin dish or heatproof shallow serving dish. Sprinkle grated cheese over the top and brown lightly under the broiler.

4 servings

Croquettes de Panais

Parsnip Croquettes with Fried Parsley

These croquettes may be prepared in advance up to the step of frying and stored in the freezer.

6 *medium-size parsnips*
1 *teaspoon sea salt*
1 *teaspoon raw sugar*
  About ¼ cup raw milk
  Yolks of 2 organic eggs
1 *tablespoon cold-pressed safflower oil*
  Herb salt
  Stone-ground whole-wheat pastry flour, for coating

1 *organic egg, beaten*
  Dry whole-wheat Bread Crumbs (p. 258), for coating
  Cold-pressed safflower oil for deep-frying
1 *bunch of fresh parsley, well washed and dried between paper towels*

Wash the parsnips but do not pare them. Cut them into chunks and put them in a pan. Cover them with water, add the sea salt and raw sugar, and bring to a boil. Reduce the heat and cook until the parsnips are tender but still crunchy. You do not want them too soft or the croquettes will fall apart. Drain; reserve the cooking water for vegetable stock in soups and sauces.

Rub the parsnips through a coarse vegetable strainer and transfer the purée to the bowl of an electric mixer. Heat the milk and beat in only enough hot milk to make a thick mixture that holds its shape fairly well. Beat in the egg yolks and 1 tablespoon safflower oil and adjust the seasoning with herb salt. Spread the mixture on a shallow dish and chill it in the freezer or refrigerator.

With floured hands, shape the parsnip mixture into small croquettes of cork shape and roll them lightly in flour. Gently brush them with beaten egg and roll them in bread crumbs. (At this point the croquettes may be frozen for later use.) Heat the safflower oil in a deep-fryer with a thermometer. When it registers 350°, fry the parsnip croquettes until they are golden brown. Drain on paper towels.

FRIED PARSLEY. Plunge clusters of dry fresh parsley into the hot deep fat. As soon as each cluster is crisp, remove it instantly and drain on paper towels.

PRESENTATION. Arrange the parsnip croquettes like piles of logs on a warm serving platter. Garnish with fried parsley.

4 servings

---

2 cups shelled fresh garden peas (reserve the pods)
1 cup baby white onions, ideally ½ to ¾ inch in diameter
1 teaspoon sea salt
3 tablespoons cold-pressed virgin olive oil

½ pound small firm fresh mushrooms, thickly sliced
2 teaspoons fresh lemon juice
Herb salt

Petits Pois à la John Scoville

Garden Peas with Mushrooms and Onions

Tie the shelled peas and the onions in a cheesecloth and put them in a pan with the pods. Add 3 cups water and the sea salt and bring to a boil. Drain; save the water for use as vegetable stock. Discard the pods, and set the peas and onions aside.

Heat the olive oil in a deep heavy pan with a tight-fitting lid, and add the mushrooms and lemon juice. Season with a little herb salt and cook the mushrooms briskly for 2 minutes. Add the peas and onions to the pan with the mushrooms. Cover with the lid and cook over low heat for 10 to 15 minutes, or until the peas are tender. Shake the pan occasionally while cooking. Serve in a warm casserole.

4 to 6 servings

---

3 large Idaho potatoes
1 teaspoon sea salt
3 tablespoons cold-pressed safflower oil

1 or 2 tablespoons chopped fresh herbs (parsley, chives, rosemary, tarragon, thyme, etc.)
Herb salt

Pommes de Terre aux Herbes

Herbed Sautéed Potatoes

Pare the potatoes, cut them lengthwise into halves, and then into slices ¼ inch thick. Put them in a pan with 1 teaspoon sea salt and cover with water. Bring the water to a boil and drain the potatoes immediately. Blot them between paper towels.

Heat 3 tablespoons safflower oil in a sauté pan. Add the potatoes and sauté them until they are a golden brown. When they are almost cooked, add the herbs and season with herb salt. Serve in a warm vegetable dish or as a garnish.

4 to 6 servings

Looseleaf Potatoes

A Dione Lucas "Invention"

6 medium-size Idaho potatoes
Herb salt
4 tablespoons cold-pressed safflower oil

6 tablespoons freshly grated Parmesan cheese
Cold-pressed safflower oil to oil baking dish

Preheat the oven to 400°. Pare the potatoes and cut them into leaves like a notebook. (The easiest way to cut them "almost but not completely through" is by placing them against the edge of a thin [about ¼-inch-thick] chopping board and cutting to the level of the board.) Place the potatoes cut-side up on an oiled shallow baking dish. Brush thoroughly with safflower oil and season with herb salt. Roast the potatoes in the preheated oven, basting them several times with the oil that is in the pan (or additional, if necessary). When the potatoes are cooked, sprinkle them with a little more herb salt and the Parmesan cheese, and raise the oven temperature to 450°, allowing them to brown lightly. Serve as a garnish or on a warm vegetable dish.
6 servings

Pommes de Terre Delmonico

Potatoes Sautéed in Cream

2 pounds potatoes
4 tablespoons cold-pressed safflower oil

¾ cup raw light cream
Herb salt

Peel the potatoes and cut them into small cubes. Heat the safflower oil in a heavy sauté pan, and add the potatoes with a little of the cream. Season with herb salt. Cover the pan and cook over moderate heat, shaking the pan occasionally. Add the rest of the cream slowly until the potatoes are just soft. Serve hot in a warm au gratin dish.
4 servings

Pommes de Terre Farcies

Stuffed Baked Potatoes

4 large Idaho potatoes
About 4 tablespoons cold-pressed safflower oil
½ teaspoon finely chopped fresh garlic
Herb salt
2 tablespoons finely chopped celery

2 tablespoons finely chopped yellow or white onion
1 large organic egg, or 2 small eggs
2 tablespoons raw sour cream
4 tablespoons freshly grated Parmesan cheese

Preheat the oven to 375°. Wash and dry the potatoes. Set them in the preheated oven and bake until they are soft; the time will depend on the size of the potatoes. Allow 1 hour or more. When the potatoes are baked, cut the tops off lengthwise and carefully scoop out most of the potato meal. In a little pan heat 2 tablespoons safflower oil with the chopped garlic for 2 or 3 minutes. Sprinkle a little of this oil in the bottom of each potato shell and also sprinkle with herb salt.

Rub the potato meal through a fine vegetable strainer and put it in an electric mixer bowl. Cook the celery and onion in a little safflower oil until they are soft, and add them to the potato meal. Also add the egg, 1 tablespoon safflower oil, the sour cream, and grated cheese. Beat very well and season with herb salt. Put the potato mixture into a pastry bag fitted with a No. 8 or No. 9 star tube, and pipe it into the potato shells. Dot the tops with a few drops of safflower oil, and brown them lightly under the broiler. Serve as a garnish or on a separate warm platter.

4 servings

2 pounds potatoes	Herb salt
1½ teaspoons sea salt	Dry whole-wheat Bread Crumbs
4 tablespoons cold-pressed	(p. 258) for coating
safflower oil	Stone-ground whole-wheat pastry
1 cup stone-ground whole-wheat	flour for coating
pastry flour	Cold-pressed safflower oil for
5 organic eggs	deep-frying

Pommes de Terre Lorette

Lorette Potatoes (croquettes)

Place the potatoes in a pan, cover them with water and 1 teaspoon sea salt, and boil until the potatoes are soft. Drain; return the potatoes to the pan over heat for a moment to dry. Remove the skins and cut potatoes into quarters. Put the potatoes in the bowl of an electric mixer and beat until they are smooth. Allow them to cool a little while you prepare the dough.

Heat 1 cup water, 4 tablespoons safflower oil, and ½ teaspoon sea salt in a saucepan. When it comes to a boil, add 1 cup flour. Stir over low heat until the mixure is smooth and comes away from the sides of the pan. Transfer the dough to the electric mixer and beat in 4 eggs, one at a time. Allow the dough to cool a little; then beat in the potatoes. Adjust the seasoning with herb salt.

Roll the mixture into a sausage about 1½ inches in diameter. Cut off 1½-inch lengths. Beat the remaining egg. Roll the potato sections in flour, brush with beaten egg, and roll in the bread crumbs. Deep-fry the potatoes in oil heated to 375° until they are golden brown. Remove with a slotted spoon and drain on paper towels. Arrange the Lorette potatoes in piles on a warm serving dish, or serve as a garnish with the main dish.

4 to 6 servings

Pommes de Terre Provençale

Casserole of Potatoes and Tomatoes

4 large Idaho potatoes
1 teaspoon sea salt
1 large organic egg, or 2 small eggs
3 tablespoons cold-pressed safflower oil
Herb salt
Cold-pressed safflower oil for baking dish and topping
2 tablespoons cold-pressed virgin olive oil
½ teaspoon finely chopped fresh garlic
3 large ripe tomatoes, skinned and cut into thick slices
2 tablespoons dry whole-wheat Bread Crumbs (p. 258)
¼ cup freshly grated Parmesan cheese

Preheat the oven to 350°. Cut the potatoes into halves, put them in a pan, and cover with water. Add the sea salt and boil until the potatoes are soft. Drain the potatoes and return to the pan over heat for a moment to dry. Remove the skins, cut the potatoes into quarters, and put them in an electric mixer bowl. Beat the potatoes until they are smooth. Beat in the egg and 3 tablespoons safflower oil, and season with herb salt.

Lightly brush a baking dish with safflower oil and spread half of the potatoes on the bottom. Heat the olive oil in a pan with the chopped garlic. Add the sliced tomatoes and cook for 3 or 4 minutes. Season with herb salt. Spoon the tomatoes on top of the layer of potatoes. Cover the tomatoes with the rest of the potato mixture. Sprinkle the top with the bread crumbs and grated cheese and dot with a few drops of safflower oil. Cook the casserole in the preheated oven for 45 minutes.
4 to 6 servings

Chestnut-Filled Acorn Squash

3 or 4 small acorn squashes
Cold-pressed safflower oil for brushing on squashes
2 cups Chestnut Purée (p. 192)
½ cup freshly grated Parmesan cheese
¼ cup dry whole-wheat Bread Crumbs (p. 258)
4 tablespoons cold-pressed safflower oil
½ cup organic honey
Herb salt

Preheat the oven to 350°. Cut the squashes into halves and scoop out the seeds. Boil the halves in salted water for 5 minutes and drain them. Brush the inside hollows with safflower oil, set them on a jelly-roll pan, and bake in the preheated oven until they are soft.

Carefully remove the pulp of the squash, leaving the skins intact. Set the skins aside to be refilled later. Rub the pulp through a fine vegetable strainer. Combine the puréed squash with the chestnut purée in the bowl of an electric mixer and beat until the mixture is smooth. Add half of the grated cheese, half of the bread crumbs, 2 tablespoons safflower oil, and the honey. Season with herb salt, and beat again.

Refill the squash skins with this mixture. Sprinkle the tops with remaining bread crumbs and grated cheese, and dot with 2 tablespoons safflower oil. Brown lightly under the broiler. Serve as a garnish with the main dish or on a separate warm platter.

6 to 8 servings

2 medium-size ripe tomatoes, or smaller if they are to be a garnish Herb salt 2 teaspoons raw sugar ½ teaspoon finely chopped fresh garlic 4 very thin slices of yellow or Bermuda onion, about the same diameter as the tomatoes, or 4 tablespoons finely chopped yellow or white onion	4 teaspoons dry whole-wheat Bread Crumbs (p. 258) 4 teaspoons freshly grated Parmesan cheese About 1 tablespoon cold-pressed safflower oil or virgin olive oil	**Tomates Gratinées** ——— *Broiled Tomatoes*

Core the tomatoes and cut them horizontally into halves. Set them, cut sides up, on a broiler pan or shallow baking dish. Season each half well with herb salt. Sprinkle with ½ teaspoon brown sugar and ⅛ teaspoon chopped garlic. Cover with the onion slice, or 1 tablespoon chopped onion, and sprinkle with 1 teaspoon bread crumbs and 1 teaspoon grated cheese. Dot with safflower oil and brown lightly under the broiler. Serve as a garnish with the main dish or on a separate warm platter.

4 servings

This is a good way to serve leftover pilaff, using as many tomatoes as you have rice to fill.

Tomates Farcies au Pilaf

Tomatoes Stuffed with Rice Pilaff

Rice Pilaff (pp. 168–169), cooked with pine nuts (pignoli) or sunflower seeds 3 tablespoons finely chopped fresh parsley 6 medium-size firm ripe tomatoes, skinned	Herb salt About 4 teaspoons cold-pressed safflower oil 3 tablespoons dry whole-wheat Bread Crumbs (p. 258) 3 tablespoons freshly grated Parmesan cheese

(cont.)

FRESH TOMATO SAUCE (*optional*)
  2 *tablespoons cold-pressed safflower oil*
  ½ *teaspoon finely chopped fresh garlic*
  ½ *teaspoon Marmite (brewers' yeast extract)*

  2 *teaspoons potato flour*
  2 *tablespoons natural tomato paste*
    Juice from scooped-out tomatoes
  1 *cup Light Soy Stock (p. 262)*
    Herb salt

Prepare the rice pilaff. When it is cooked, fluff it with 1 tablespoon chopped parsley. Cut a thin slice off the tops of the skinned tomatoes and carefully scoop out the seeds and pulp. Rub the seeds and pulp through a fine vegetable strainer and set the juice aside to use later. Preheat the oven to 350°.

Carefully dry the tomatoes with a soft cloth or soft paper towel, and arrange them on an au gratin dish or heatproof serving dish. Season the inside of each tomato with a little herb salt and pour in ½ teaspoon safflower oil. Stuff the tomatoes with the rice. Sprinkle the tops with the bread crumbs and grated cheese. Dot with a few drops of safflower oil. Warm the tomatoes in the preheated oven for about 5 minutes; then pass them under the broiler to brown the tops lightly.

TOMATO SAUCE. Heat 2 tablespoons safflower oil in a saucepan. Add the garlic, Marmite yeast extract, potato flour, and tomato paste; and blend well. Off the heat add the reserved tomato juice and the stock. Stir over moderate heat until the sauce comes to a boil. Season with herb salt. Reduce the heat and simmer for 10 minutes. Spoon the sauce around the tomatoes in the serving dish. Sprinkle the rest of the parsley over the top of the tomatoes and serve.

6 servings

Courgettes Florentine
────────────
Zucchini Cassolettes with Spinach Purée, Sauce Hollandaise

  2 *or 3 zucchini, about 6 inches long and 2 to 2½ inches in diameter*
    Juice of ½ lemon
  ½ *teaspoon sea salt*

  Spinach Purée (p. 195)
  Hollandaise Sauce (pp. 268–269), or 8 to 12 tablespoons whipped raw heavy sweet cream, or raw sour cream

Peel the zucchini with a potato parer. If the zucchini are of the size suggested, cut them lengthwise into halves and again horizontally into halves, making 4 pieces per vegetable. Trim the corners on each piece so they are oval shaped. Carefully scoop out a shallow hollow in the center of each piece, like a saucer. This will give you 8 to 12 zucchini cassolettes about 3 inches long and 2 inches wide. If you cannot get the zucchini in the size suggested, this description of its use as a container for the spinach purée will guide you in adapting larger or smaller zucchini accordingly.

Put the zucchini cassolettes in a pan, cover them with water, and add the lemon juice and ½ teaspoon sea salt. Slowly bring them to a boil and drain immediately. Dry the zucchini between paper towels.

Fill the zucchini with the spinach purée and arrange them on an au gratin dish or shallow baking dish. Spoon some hollandaise sauce over each zucchini cassolette and brown it lightly under the broiler. If you are using the cream topping instead of the hollandaise, spoon a dollop of cream on top of each and brown it lightly under the broiler. Serve in the baking dish or as a garnish with the main dish.

4 to 6 servings

Desserts

Cooking Naturalized Desserts

French cooking made desserts an art, but *refined foods* have weakened their nutritional impact. In this chapter, we have attempted to maintain the character, flavor, and presentation of a selection of classic French desserts while converting their ingredients and cooking methods for improved nutritional values. The following are the major conversion factors which apply in dessert-making:

1. *Stone-ground whole-wheat pastry flour instead of refined white flour*—in cakes, short pastry, cream-puff dough, pastry cream, crêpes, and soufflés. Also on the subject of grains, the delicious rice custard desserts, such as *Riz à l'Impératrice,* are made with natural brown rice, to the advantage of gourmandise.

2. *Cold-pressed safflower oil instead of butter*—except when a buttercream consistency is required (as in the filling for the Chestnut Tart).

3. *Raw sugar (which is beige in color) and honey instead of refined white sugar.* It's easy to make your own superfine and powdered raw sugar (you are not likely to find them in markets). Use an electric spice grinder to produce superfine and powdered raw sugar from regular granulated raw sugar, removing it when it has reached either the superfine or powdered stage. You might wish to make a small supply of superfine and powdered raw sugar to keep on hand. To sweeten whipped cream, honey is used. It blends with the cream immediately.

4. *Carob instead of chocolate.* The nutritional comparison of these ingredients is discussed in detail in the Encyclopedia. Carob is a one-for-one conversion from chocolate, in powder, nuggets, and solid bar. The flavor is like chocolate. It is possible, however, to distinguish the

difference between chocolate and carob, and you may like the taste of carob better.

5. *Natural (organic) fruit preserves should be used exclusively.*

6. When possible, *organic eggs, organic fruits and nuts, raw milk and cream.* When the cream ingredient is substantial, we offer the option of using double-strength nonfat dry milk, reconstituted. The result is not quite par with cream, but you will achieve a more than acceptable ice cream or custard.

The eating difference: Dione Lucas was famous for her desserts, especially the chocolate roll Leontine, chocolate mousse, lemon-curd tart, *gâteau favori* (with carob, now called *gâteau favori nouveau*), *tart aux fraises, charlotte aux pommes* with that incredible sour cream sauce, chocolate Bavarian cream, and rediscovered in old files—frozen rhubarb soufflé, blueberry soufflé with blueberry sauce, and *mousse aux fraises.* They are still as delicious, but now they are healthier.

Natural or organic fruit preserves are usually of superior quality. They are available in wide variety and offer wonderful variations for the delicate, easy-to-bake, health-oriented sponge roll. Carob filling offers an excellent chocolate-flavor roll without the sins of chocolate, and the lemon-curd filling without butter is as fresh and zesty as its forebear. To compound the blessing, this sponge roll freezes very well, filled or unfilled. A good standby dessert idea is to make 2 sponge rolls, each with a different filling, and freeze them. The filled roll can be served by itself or accompanied by fresh berries, peaches, ice cream, or custard.

Biscuit Roulé

Sponge Cake Roll with Various Fillings

Cold-pressed safflower oil for
  baking pan
4 large, or 5 small, organic eggs
¼ teaspoon sea salt
1 cup granulated raw sugar
¾ cup sifted *stone-ground whole-
  wheat pastry flour*

1 teaspoon natural flavoring
  (extract of vanilla, almond,
  orange, lemon, rose, etc.)
¼ cup powdered raw sugar
  (p. 214)
1 cup filling (see suggestions
  following)

Preheat the oven to 350°. Oil a 17-inch jelly-roll pan and line it with a strip of wax paper, with an overhang at each end to serve as handles. Thoroughly brush the wax paper and the sides of the pan with oil.

Beat the eggs with the salt and ¾ cup granulated raw sugar in an electric mixer until eggs are stiff. Sprinkle the flour over the egg mixture; with a rubber scraper, gently and smoothly fold it into the mixture. Fold in the flavoring. Spread the mixture on the prepared jelly-roll pan and set it on the top shelf of the preheated oven to bake for 17 minutes, or until it rebounds to the touch.

Spread a kitchen towel or clean cloth on a work surface. Mix ¼ cup granulated raw sugar with the powdered raw sugar and sprinkle the mixed sugar over the cloth. When the cake has finished baking, remove it from the oven and loosen the sides of the cake from the pan with a little knife. Turn the cake out onto the sugared cloth and carefully peel off the paper now on top. With a large knife, trim off the crisp ends, to facilitate rolling the cake. Carefully roll the cake like a jelly roll, and put it in the refrigerator or freezer to cool. It can stay there any length of time until you are ready to fill it, providing it is well wrapped.

To fill the cake roll: Unroll the chilled cake and spread it with the filling. Roll up the cake again, quite tightly. Serve on a jelly-roll board, or arrange cut slices on a cake plate.

To store: Wrap the cake in a double thickness of wax paper and then in a sheet of foil. Fasten the foil ends securely.
One 17-inch cake roll

Fillings for Sponge Cake Roll

AUX CONFITURES
(with Natural Fruit Preserves)
*1 cup natural fruit preserves,
apricot, black raspberry, rose
hips, currant*

2 teaspoons fresh lemon juice

Dissolve the preserve or jelly with the lemon juice over moderate heat. Press the mixture through a fine wire strainer and allow it to cool a little before spreading it over the sponge cake roll. Reroll the cake.
1 cup

AU CITRON (with Fresh Lemon)

1 cup lemon curd (pp. 225–226)

Spread the prepared lemon curd over the cake roll and reroll the cake.
1 cup

A LA CAROUBE (chocolate flavor)
*6 ounces carob nuggets or solid bar
1 tablespoon instant decaffeinated
coffee dissolved in ¼ cup hot
water
2 tablespoons cold-pressed safflower
oil*

*½ cup coarsely grated carob, from
nuggets or solid bar
¼ cup powdered raw sugar
(p. 214)*

If you are using bar carob, cut it into small pieces. Put the carob in a small pan with the coffee essence and stir it over low heat until it is completely dissolved. Stir in the safflower oil, then stir the mixture over ice until it begins to cool and thicken a little.

Set aside 2 or 3 tablespoons of the carob sauce for the top of the cake roll. Unroll the cake and spread it with the rest of the carob sauce. Reroll the cake, quite tightly. Spread the reserved sauce on top of the cake. Sprinkle the coarsely grated carob all over the cake roll. Dust with the powdered raw sugar. Chill to set the filling and coating a little.

One 17-inch cake roll

Dione's "Chocolate Roll" with Carob

(The original Chocolate Roll Leontine)

This famous dessert roll freezes very well.

Cold-pressed safflower oil for
   baking pan
8 ounces carob nuggets or solid bar
2 teaspoons instant decaffeinated
   coffee dissolved in ⅓ cup hot
   water, and cooled
8 organic eggs, separated
1 cup superfine granulated raw
   sugar (p. 214)

Sea salt
½ cup carob powder
1½ cups raw heavy cream
2 tablespoons organic honey
   Scraping of 2-inch piece of
   vanilla bean, or 1 teaspoon
   natural vanilla extract

Preheat the oven to 350°. Oil a jelly-roll pan and line it with a strip of wax paper, leaving an overhang at each end to serve as handles.

If you are using bar carob, cut it into small pieces. Combine the carob with the dissolved coffee in a small pan and stir over low heat until carob is completely dissolved. Set the mixture aside and let it cool a little.

Beat the separated egg yolks with the superfine granulated raw sugar and a pinch of sea salt in the electric mixer until the mixture is very stiff. Beat in the dissolved carob. In a separate bowl, beat the egg whites to soft peaks. With a rubber scraper, carefully and smoothly fold them into the egg-yolk mixture. Pour the mixture onto the prepared jelly-roll pan and spread it evenly over the surface. Set the pan on the top shelf of the preheated oven and bake for 17 minutes, or until it rebounds to the touch.

Have ready a length of 4 paper towels, folded in half and wrung out with cold water. As soon as you remove the dessert roll from the oven, gently cover it with the damp paper towels. Lay a strip of dry paper towels on top of the damp ones. Allow the dessert roll to cool for a moment, then loosen the sides with a knife. Remove the paper towels. Sprinkle the top with the carob powder. Lay 2 strips of wax paper over the top of the dessert roll; holding the sides firmly, quickly turn the pan bottom side up. Carefully lift the pan away from the roll, and carefully peel off the wax paper that is now on the top.

Beat the heavy cream in a metal bowl set in another bowl of ice. Add the honey and vanilla and continue beating until the cream is stiff. With a rubber scraper, put dollops of whipped cream around the top of the roll. Gently spread them out to cover the surface. Place a jelly-roll serving board alongside the dessert roll. Using the wax paper that is under the dessert roll, carefully roll it into a jelly-roll shape and transfer it on to the board.

PRESENTATION. Serve the dessert roll on the board. If you plan to serve it the same day, store it in the refrigerator, covered with wax paper, until serving time. If you wish to keep it for a longer period, the roll on the board may be wrapped in foil and stored in the freezer. It will thaw in a few minutes when it is removed.

One 17-inch cake roll

Pâte à Foncer

Pastry for Lining Sweet and Savory Tarts

Preparing a pastry shell with stone-ground whole-wheat pastry flour (a fine-milled whole-grain flour now generally available in natural-food and specialty-food stores and by mail order), and substituting vegetable oil for butter, produces a rich-flavored crisp and crunchy shell. It lacks cohesion, however, and it will break or crumble easily. Therefore, for baking and serving whole-wheat pastry shells, we recommend using a neat pie pan or one of the attractive round French porcelain baking dishes with a 1-inch high rim, instead of the usual flan ring on a baking sheet. The reasons are twofold: First, the dough must be patted into the pan with the fingers. It will break if you attempt to roll it out to the size of the flan ring and transfer it from board to ring. Second, after the tart is baked, if it is hot and filled (as in the case of a savory tart), it will be impossible to transfer it from the baking sheet to a serving plate without breaking it. Even a chilled sweet tart might break. Placed on a doily on a serving platter, the tart in its baking pan makes a regal presentation, and its genuine home-made credentials are underscored.

There is an option: the basic pastry shell recipe may be made with *sifted* stone-ground whole-wheat flour but with *natural butter* instead of oil. With these substitutions the dough is less crumbly. The Pâte à Foncer II recipe can be rolled to line a flan ring and lifted from the ring after it is baked. The recipe for Pâte Sucrée II with butter is less crumbly than the safflower-oil version, but because of the sugar it is delicate to handle.

Tart and tartlet shells can be prepared weeks in advance and stored, either completely baked or unbaked, in the freezer. If they have been prebaked, crisp them in the oven before using them. If they are unbaked, complete the baking according to the pastry recipe when you plan to use them. It is a nice convenience to have a couple of prepared tart shells on hand ready for a quick savory or sweet tart.

Pâte à Foncer I

Short Pastry with Oil

This recipe produces a crumbly pastry shell. Please note the general comments about pastry shells on pages 218–219.

2 cups stone-ground whole-wheat
    pastry flour
¼ teaspoon sea salt
4 tablespoons cold-pressed
    safflower oil

⅓ cup ice water
    Cold-pressed safflower oil for
    brushing pastry

Preheat the oven to 375°. Have ready a 10-inch pie pan or round porcelain or heatproof glass baking dish with 1-inch-high rim. Put the flour and salt in a bowl and blend in 4 tablespoons safflower oil with your fingers. Add only enough water to gather up the mixture into a ball. Wrap the dough in a piece of wax paper and chill it in the refrigerator or freezer for about 1 hour.

On a lightly floured board flatten the dough to a round 9 or 10 inches in diameter. Using the rolling pin or a spatula, transfer the dough to the baking container. Working from the center toward the edge, pat the dough to cover the pan neatly. Using a small knife, trim the excess dough off the rim, and flute the edge with pastry pincers.

Brush the surface of the pastry shell with very little safflower oil, and cover with a piece of wax paper. Weight the paper with a cup of dried beans or rice. Bake in the preheated oven for 25 to 30 minutes, or until the edge begins to brown. Remove the beans or rice and wax paper and return the pastry shell to the oven for another 10 minutes. *One 10-inch pastry shell*

Pâte à Foncer II

Short Pastry with Butter

This recipe produces a less crumbly, more flaky shell. Please note the general comments about short pastry on pages 218–219.

2 cups sifted stone-ground whole-
    wheat pastry flour
½ teaspoon sea salt
8 tablespoons natural sweet butter

¼ cup ice water
    Cold-pressed safflower oil to
    brush pastry

Preheat the oven to 375°. Have ready a 10-inch flan ring and baking sheet, or pie pan. Put the flour and salt in a bowl. Cut the butter into small pieces and rub it into the flour with your fingertips until the mixture is like coarse meal. Add enough water to gather up the mixture into a ball. Wrap it in a piece of wax paper and chill in the refrigerator or freezer for about 1 hour.

On a lightly floured board roll out the dough to a round about 12 inches in diameter. Lay it over the rolling pin and transfer it to the inside of the flan ring on a baking sheet, or over the pie pan. Depending on the granular texture of the flour, the sheet of dough may break. If it does, simply set it in the pan and pat it into place. Shape the dough firmly into the ring or pan. Roll the rolling pin over the rim to trim off the excess. Flute the edge with pastry pincers.

Brush the surface of the pastry shell with very little safflower oil and cover with a piece of wax paper. Weight the paper with a cup of dried beans or rice. Bake in the preheated oven for 25 to 30 minutes, until the edge begins to brown. Remove the beans or rice and wax paper and return the pastry shell to the oven for another 10 minutes. *One 10-inch pastry shell*

Pâte Sucrée I
"Sugar and Egg" Short Pastry with Oil

This recipe produces a crumbly pastry shell. Please note the general comments about the pastry shell on pages 218–219.

2 cups stone-ground whole-wheat pastry flour
Yolks of 4 organic eggs, beaten
5 tablespoons granulated raw sugar
4 tablespoons cold-pressed safflower oil
Sea salt

Preheat the oven to 350°. Have ready a 10-inch pie pan or round porcelain or heatproof glass baking dish with 1-inch-high rim. Put the flour on a pastry board or marble slab. Make a well in the center and add the beaten egg yolks, raw sugar, safflower oil, and a pinch of sea salt. Blend the *center ingredients* and then quickly work in the flour. Roll out, not too thin. Using a rolling pin or a spatula, transfer the dough to the baking container. Working from the center toward the edge, pat the dough to cover the pan neatly. Using a small knife, trim the excess dough off the rim, and flute all around the edge with pastry pincers.

Cover the top of the pastry with a piece of wax paper. Weight the paper with a cup of dried beans or rice. Bake in the preheated oven for 25 to 30 minutes, or until the edge begins to brown. Remove the beans or rice and wax paper and return the pastry shell to the oven for another 10 minutes. *One 10-inch pastry shell*

This recipe produces a more cohesive pastry. Please note the general comments about short pastry on pages 218–219.

2 cups sifted stone-ground whole-
    wheat pastry flour
  Yolks of 4 organic eggs, beaten
5 tablespoons granulated raw sugar

4 tablespoons natural sweet butter,
    at room temperature
Sea salt

Preheat the oven to 350°. Have ready a 10-inch flan ring and baking sheet, or pie pan. Put the flour on a pastry board or marble slab. Make a well in the center and add the egg yolks, sugar, butter, and a pinch of sea salt. Mix the *center ingredients* to a smooth paste and quickly work in the flour. Roll out, not too thin. Using a rolling pin, lay it over the flan ring on the baking sheet, or the pie pan. Pat the dough firmly in the ring. Roll the rolling pin over the rim to trim off the excess. Flute the edge with pastry pincers.

    Cover the top of the pastry with a piece of wax paper. Weight the paper with a cup of dried beans or rice. Bake in the preheated oven for 25 to 30 minutes, or until the edge begins to brown. Remove the beans or rice and wax paper and return the pastry shell to the oven for another 10 minutes.
One 10-inch pastry shell

TARTLET SHELLS. Any of the short pastry doughs, Pâte à Foncer I or II (pp. 219–220) or Pâte Sucrée I or II (pp. 220–221), may be used to line little tartlet molds. Just pat the pastry dough over the inside of the mold with your fingertips. The quantity of one recipe should line 12 molds 3¼ inches in diameter.

Tartlets

    To bake tartlet shells: Preheat the oven to 375°. Cut squares of wax paper large enough to cover the inside of each mold. Brush the pastry with a little cold-pressed safflower oil and press a square of wax paper against it. Put some dried beans or rice on top of the wax paper to weight it. Set the molds on a baking sheet and bake for about 25 minutes, or until the edges of the pastry begin to brown. Remove the pastry from the oven and remove the weight and wax paper. Either fill the shells immediately or store them in the freezer for future use.

Fill the tartlet shells with pastry cream, arrange the fruit on the cream, and glaze with fruit jelly. Or prepare the tartlets without using pastry cream; simply fill the baked tartlet shells with fresh fruit and

Fresh Fruit
Tartlets

glaze the top with jelly. If you have a supply of tartlet shells in the freezer, you can make a quick instant dessert by filling them with any fresh fruit on hand. It's nice to serve a selection of different fruit fillings.

12 baked tartlet shells	*2 tablespoons granulated raw sugar*
CRUMB MIXTURE (with Pâte à Foncer only)	*½ teaspoon ground cardamom*
2 tablespoons dry whole-wheat Bread Crumbs (p. 258)	*Vanilla Pastry Cream (p. 228)*

FILLING AND GLAZE SUGGESTIONS
1. 2 cups fresh *strawberries* with 1 cup natural currant jelly
2. 2 cups fresh *blueberries* with 1 cup natural currant jelly
3. 2 cups fresh *raspberries* with 1 cup natural currant jelly
4. 2 cups thinly sliced *bananas* with 1 cup natural apricot preserve
5. 2 cups seedless *white grapes,* skinned, with 1 cup natural apricot preserve
6. 2 cups thinly sliced pared *apples,* sprinkled with a little fresh lemon juice, with 1 cup natural apricot preserve
7. 2 cups sliced fresh *apricots* with 1 cup natural apricot preserve
With each of these: 2 teaspoons fresh lemon juice

CRUMB MIXTURE. Mix the bread crumbs, sugar, and cardamom together and sprinkle this mixture on the bottom of the *pâte à foncer* shells only. (This is not used with *pâte sucrée*.)

To fill the fruit tartlets: If you are using pastry cream, spread a layer of it on the surface of each tartlet shell. With or without the pastry cream, fill the tartlet shells with one of the suggested fruits. If you are using the sliced bananas or apples, arrange the slices on top like a pinwheel.

GLAZE. To glaze the top of the fruit, dissolve the currant jelly or apricot preserve with the fresh lemon juice in a little pan. Rub mixture through a fine wire strainer and let it cool a little. When it is still liquid, gently brush the top of the fruit in each tartlet shell with the glaze.

To finish the apple tartlets, set them in a preheated 375° oven to bake for 15 minutes. Remove and brush with a little more apricot glaze.

DECORATION (optional). Sprinkle glazed tartlets with chopped nuts just before serving, or pipe a ribbon of plain whipped cream around the edge.

Chopped nuts, about ½ cup	*Whipped cream, 1 cup*

PRESENTATION. Chill the tartlets in their molds until they are to be served. Then carefully remove them from the molds and arrange them on a paper doily on a serving tray.
12 tartlets

12 tartlet baked shells (*Pâte à Foncer I or II, pp. 219–220, or Pâte Sucrée I or II, pp. 220–221*)

CRUMB MIXTURE (with *pâte à foncer* only)
2 tablespoons dry whole-wheat Bread Crumbs (*p. 258*)

2 tablespoons granulated raw sugar
½ teaspoon ground cardamom

Lemon Curd (*pp. 225–226*), well chilled (*without meringue*)

Tartelettes au Citron

Lemon-Curd Tartlets

CRUMB MIXTURE. Mix the bread crumbs, sugar, and cardamom together, and sprinkle this mixture on the bottom of the *pâte à foncer* shells only.

To fill the lemon-curd tartlets: Put spoonfuls of the lemon curd on top of the crumb mixture. This does not need to be smooth; it can look "spooned." The tartlets may be served just this way, with no topping, or a ribbon of whipped cream may be piped around the rim of each tartlet. Keep the tartlets in their molds and chilled until ready to serve.

PRESENTATION. At serving time carefully remove the tartlets from the molds and arrange on a paper doily on a serving tray.
12 tartlets

Pâte Sucré (*pp. 220–221*) for 10-inch short pastry shell
5 large green apples, skinned, cored, and thinly sliced
¾ cup granulated raw sugar

1 cup natural apricot preserve
2 teaspoons fresh lemon juice
¼ cup powdered raw sugar (*p. 214*)

Tarte aux Pommes Ménagère

Apple Flan

Preheat the oven to 350°, and prepare the pastry shell ready for baking. Bake it in the preheated oven for 25 to 30 minutes, or until the edge begins to brown. Remove the beans or rice and the wax paper.

Reserve about one third of the nicest apple slices for the top. Put the rest of the apple slices in the pastry shell. Sprinkle them with about two-thirds of the granulated raw sugar. Arrange the reserved apple slices in a pattern on the top, neatly overlapping them in 3 concentric circles. Sprinkle with remaining granulated sugar. Return the tart to the 350° oven and bake it for about 20 minutes, or until the apples become a little tinged with brown. Remove the flan from the oven and let it cool.

Dissolve the apricot preserve and lemon juice in a little pan over low heat. Rub mixture through a fine wire strainer and let it cool a little. When it is still liquid, gently brush it all over the top of the apples, but do not touch the rim of the pastry. Sprinkle powdered raw sugar all around the edge of the flan. Chill thoroughly before serving.

6 to 8 servings

Tarte aux Bananes

Banana Cream Tart

Pâte Sucrée (pp. 220–221) for 10-inch short pastry shell, baked
5 organic eggs
6 tablespoons granulated raw sugar
1 tablespoon unflavored gelatin
1½ cups raw milk

2½ cups raw heavy sweet cream, whipped
1 teaspoon pure vanilla extract
1 cup banana purée (ripe bananas rubbed through a fine vegetable strainer)

BANANA CREAM FILLING. Separate the eggs. Beat the egg yolks with the granulated raw sugar in an electric mixer until the mixture is light and creamy. Mix in the gelatin. Bring the milk to a boil and pour it into the egg-yolk mixture, beating all the time. Pour the combined mixture into the saucepan and stir over low heat until the custard coats the back of a metal spoon. Set the saucepan in a bowl of ice and stir with a wire whisk until the custard is cool and on the point of setting.

Beat the egg whites to soft peaks and fold them into the custard mixture, over ice. Fold in half of the whipped cream, spoonful by spoonful, blending it smoothly into the custard. Finally mix in the vanilla extract and the banana purée. Spread this mixture on the baked pastry shell and chill it in the refrigerator until the cream is set.

To decorate the tart, spread about half of the remaining whipped cream over the top of the tart. Put the rest of the whipped cream into a pastry bag fitted with a No. 6 or No. 7 star tube, and pipe rosettes or scallops around the edge of the tart. Leave the tart in the refrigerator until it is to be served.

6 to 8 servings

1 baked 10-inch short pastry shell
    (*Pâte Sucrée*, pp. 220–221, or
    Pâte à Foncer, pp. 219–220)
Yolks of 3 organic eggs
1 cup granulated raw sugar
1 cup plain Chestnut Pureé
    (p. 192) , or natural-packed
    canned purée

1 cup natural sweet butter
1 cup natural apricot preserve
¼ cup powdered raw sugar
    (p. 214)
1 cup raw heavy sweet cream,
    whipped

Tarte aux Marrons

Chestnut Tart

Beat the egg yolks in an electric mixer until they are light and thick. Combine 1 cup granulated sugar and ¼ cup water in an unlined copper pan. Stir over high heat until the mixture comes to a boil and the sugar is dissolved. Let the syrup cook until it forms a light syrup (225° on a candy thermometer) . Pour the syrup in a very thin stream into the yolks, beating all the time. Continue beating until the mixture is thick and cool.

Beat the chestnut purée into the yolk mixture. When it is well blended, beat in the butter, a little at a time. Continue beating until the mixture is thick and has a spreading consistency. Fill the baked tart shell with the chestnut mixture. Set it in the refrigerator or freezer to chill while you prepare the topping.

Dissolve the apricot preserve in a small pan over moderate heat. Rub it through a wire strainer and let it cool a little. Sprinkle the chestnut tart with ¼ cup powdered raw sugar. While the strained apricot preserve is still liquid, gently brush it all over the top of the tart. Fill a pastry bag fitted with a No. 4 or No. 5 star tube with the whipped cream and pipe a border all around the edge. Keep the tart chilled until it is to be served.

6 to 8 servings

1 baked 10-inch short pastry shell
    (*Pâte à Foncer*, pp. 219–220,
    or *Pâte Sucrée*, pp. 220–221)

CRUMB MIXTURE
(for *Pâte à Foncer* only)
2 tablespoons dry whole-wheat
    Bread Crumbs (p. 258)
2 tablespoons granulated raw
    sugar
½ teaspoon ground cardamom

LEMON CURD
10 tablespoons cold-pressed
    safflower oil

3 organic eggs, well beaten
1 cup granulated raw sugar
    Grated rind and juice of 2 large
    lemons

MERINGUE TOPPING
    Whites of 5 organic eggs
12 tablespoons superfine granulated
    raw sugar (p. 214)

Tarte au Citron

Lemon-Curd Tart

LEMON CURD. In the top part of a douse boiler combine the safflower oil, beaten eggs, granulated raw sugar, grated lemon rind, and the lemon juice. Stir the mixture over low heat until it coats the back of a metal spoon. Pour the mixture into a shallow pan and chill it in the freezer until it becomes very thick and set.

CRUMB MIXTURE. Mix the bread crumbs, granulated raw sugar, and the cardamom, and sprinkle this mixture over the bottom of the *pâte à foncer* shell.

Fill the pastry shell with the chilled, thick lemon curd. It can be almost frozen.

MERINGUE. Preheat the oven to 375°. Beat the egg whites to soft peaks in an electric mixer. Continue beating as you slowly add the superfine raw sugar. Continue beating until the meringue is stiff and holds its shape. Fill a pastry bag fitted with a No. 8 or No. 9 star tube with the meringue, and pipe circles of scallop shapes to cover the top of the tart. Set the tart in the preheated oven to brown the top of the meringue lightly.

Transfer the tart to the freezer for at least 1 hour before serving. You may leave the tart in the freezer; take it out about 30 minutes before serving.

6 to 8 servings

Tarte aux Fraises

Strawberry Tart

1 baked 10-inch short pastry shell
   (*Pâte à Foncer, pp. 219–220,*
   or Pâte Sucrée, pp. 220–221)

CRUMB MIXTURE
(for *Pâte à Foncer* only)
2 tablespoons dry whole-wheat
   Bread Crumbs (*p. 258*)
2 tablespoons granulated raw sugar
½ teaspoon ground cardamom

Mocha Pastry Cream (*pp. 228–229*)
3 cups cleaned, hulled fresh strawberries
1½ cups natural currant jelly
1 tablespoon Port or Madeira wine, or fresh lemon juice
About ¼ cup powdered raw sugar (*p. 214*)

CRUMB MIXTURE. Mix together the bread crumbs, granulated raw sugar, and cardamom, and sprinkle the mixture over the bottom of the baked *pâte à foncer* pastry shell.

Spread the mocha pastry cream over the bottom of the tart shell. Stand the whole strawberries on top of the pastry cream, hulled end down. Dissolve the currant jelly with the wine over low heat. Rub it through a fine wire strainer and let it cool a little. When the jelly is still liquid, gently brush it all over the strawberries, leaving about a 1-inch margin around the edge of the tart not covered. Sprinkle the

powdered sugar all around the edge of the tart. Chill thoroughly before serving.
6 to 8 servings

Pâte à Chou

Dessert and Savory Cream Puff Pastry

Cream puffs can be made in any size, from ½ inch in diameter, used as garnish in consommé, to the big round *Gâteau Favori Nouveau,* a circle of 8-inch diameter. The 1-inch size is perfect for hors d'oeuvre fillings. The 2-inch size is nice for dessert fillings; present 2 or 3 puffs on an individual serving plate. Cream-puff shells can be made in advance and frozen. Just allow them to thaw at room temperature and recrisp in a moderate oven for a moment; then fill.

1 cup water
8 tablespoons cold-pressed safflower oil
Sea salt
1 cup sifted *stone-ground whole-wheat pastry flour*

4 organic eggs
½ cup shredded blanched organic almonds (optional)

Preheat the oven to 350°. Combine the water, safflower oil, and a pinch of sea salt in a saucepan and slowly bring it to a boil. Throw the flour all at once into the boiling liquid. Stir with a small whisk until the mixture is smooth and comes away from the sides of the pan. Transfer the dough to an electric mixer and beat in 3 eggs, one at a time. Beat the fourth egg in a cup and add half of it to the dough. Continue beating until the dough is shiny. Let it sit in the refrigerator for at least 30 minutes.

Put the dough into a pastry bag fitted with a plain tube with about a ½-inch opening (No. 6 or No. 7). Pipe small balls of dough on an unoiled baking sheet. For cream puffs of 2-inch diameter when baked, pipe mounds about 1½ inches in diameter and ½ inch high. Brush the top of each mound with beaten egg reserved from the fourth egg. Take care not to use too much egg; it should not drip down the side onto the pan or the cream puff will not puff. Sprinkle the shredded almonds over the top. Bake the cream puffs in the preheated oven for 30 minutes. Reduce the heat to 325° and bake for another 30 minutes, or until puffs are firm to the touch. Turn off the heat; if you have the time, let the cream puffs cool in the oven, with the door ajar.

To fill the cream puffs, make a round hole in the bottom of each, using a small pointed knife. Put the filling into a pastry bag and pipe it through the opening in the bottom of the cream puff.
18 to 24 cream puffs, 2 inches in diameter

**Crème Pâtissière
à la Vanille**

Vanilla Pastry
Cream

1 whole organic egg
  Yolk of 1 organic egg
3 tablespoons stone-ground whole-
  wheat pastry flour
3 tablespoons granulated raw sugar
1 tablespoon unflavored gelatin

¾ cup raw milk
¼ vanilla bean, scraped
  Whites of 2 organic eggs
1 cup raw heavy sweet cream,
  whipped

Combine 1 whole egg and 1 extra egg yolk, the flour, and sugar in a bowl and beat well with a wire whisk. Mix in the gelatin. Bring the milk to a boil with the vanilla bean scraping; pour the hot milk into the egg mixture, stirring all the time. Pour the egg and milk mixture into a saucepan and stir over low heat until mixture comes to a boil. Remove the pan from the heat and set it over a bowl of ice. Continue to stir the mixture, using a wire whisk, until it cools and thickens. Beat the egg whites to soft peaks and fold them into the custard. Fold in the whipped cream, spoonful by spoonful.

Store the pastry cream in the refrigerator until you are ready to use it.

Approximately 2 cups

**Crème Pâtissière
au Moka**

Mocha Pastry
Cream

1 whole organic egg
  Yolk of 1 organic egg
3 tablespoons stone-ground whole-
  wheat pastry flour
3 tablespoons granulated raw sugar
1 tablespoon unflavored gelatin
2 tablespoons instant decaffeinated
  coffee dissolved in 3 tablespoons hot water, and cooled

¾ cup raw milk
  Whites of 2 organic eggs
1 cup raw heavy sweet cream,
  whipped

Combine 1 whole egg and 1 extra egg yolk, the flour, and sugar in a bowl, and beat well with a wire whisk. Stir in the gelatin and the dissolved coffee. Bring the milk to a boil and pour it into the egg mixture, stirring all the time. Pour the egg and milk mixture into a saucepan and stir over low heat until mixture comes to a boil. Remove the pan from the heat, set it over a bowl of ice, and stir until the mixture cools and thickens. Beat the egg whites to soft peaks and fold them into the sauce. Fold in the whipped cream, spoonful by spoonful.

Store the pastry cream in the refrigerator until you are ready to use it.

Approximately 2 cups

3 ounces carob nuggets or solid bar
2 tablespoons instant decaffeinated
    coffee dissolved in 3 table-
    spoons hot water, and cooled
1 whole organic egg
    Yolk of 1 organic egg
3 tablespoons stone-ground whole-
    wheat pastry flour

3 tablespoons granulated raw sugar
1 tablespoon unflavored gelatin
¾ cup raw milk
    Whites of 2 organic eggs
½ cup raw heavy sweet cream,
    whipped

Crème Pâtissière à la Caroube (le goût du chocolat)

Carob Pastry Cream (chocolate flavor)

If you are using bar carob, cut it into small pieces. Over low heat, melt the carob with the dissolved coffee and stir until it is smooth. Let the carob cool until you are ready to add it to the pastry cream.

Combine 1 whole egg and 1 extra egg yolk, the flour, and sugar in a bowl and beat well with a wire whisk. Mix in the gelatin. Bring the milk to a boil slowly and pour it into the egg mixture, stirring all the time. Pour the egg and milk mixture into a saucepan and stir over low heat until mixture comes to a boil. Remove the pan from the heat and set it over a bowl of ice. Continue to stir the mixture with a wire whisk until it cools and thickens. Add the cooled melted carob. Beat the egg whites to soft peaks and fold them into the pastry cream. Fold in the whipped cream, spoonful by spoonful.

Store the pastry cream in the refrigerator until you are ready to use it.

Approximately 2 cups

2 organic eggs
3 tablespoons stone-ground whole-
    wheat pastry flour
3 tablespoons granulated raw sugar
1 tablespoon unflavored gelatin

¼ cup tart fresh orange juice
½ cup raw milk
    Grated rind of 1 orange
½ cup raw heavy sweet cream,
    whipped

Crème Pâtissière à l'Orange

Orange Pastry Cream

Combine 1 whole egg and 1 egg yolk, the flour, and sugar in a bowl, and beat well with a wire whisk. Mix in the gelatin. Add the orange juice and milk. Pour the mixture into a saucepan and stir over low heat until it comes to a boil. Remove the pan from the heat and set it in a bowl of ice. Continue to stir the mixture until it cools and thickens. Beat the remaining egg white to soft peaks and fold it into the custard. Sprinkle the orange rind over the custard, and mix it in as you fold in the whipped cream, spoonful by spoonful.

Store the pastry cream in the refrigerator until you are ready to use it.

Approximately 2 cups

Crème Pâtissière Pralinée

Praline Pastry Cream

PRALINE POWDER

1 cup granulated raw sugar
1 cup filberts or blanched organic
     almonds

Vanilla Pastry Cream (p. 228)

PRALINE POWDER. Praline powder keeps well indefinitely in the refrigerator; it is a good idea to prepare a supply and have it on hand to garnish other desserts or to sprinkle over ice cream. Put the sugar in an unlined copper pan with the nuts. Stir this dry mixture slowly over moderate heat until the sugar dissolves. When the color is a rich medium caramel, pour the mixture on an oiled baking sheet and let it set. It will become brittle very quickly. Cool it in the refrigerator. When praline is very hard, break it into chunks and put them in a blender. Crush chunks in the blender to any texture you wish. For use in the pastry cream you will want a powder.

Mix 5 tablespoons praline powder into the prepared vanilla pastry cream. Store the pastry cream in the refrigerator until you are ready to use it.

Approximately 1½ cups praline powder
Approximately 2 cups pastry cream

Profiteroles à la Praline, Sauce à la Caroube (le goût du chocolat)

Praline Cream Puffs, Carob Sauce (chocolate flavor)

Baked cream puffs (p. 227), in the
   size desired

Praline Pastry Cream (above)
Carob Sauce (p. 271), hot

The cream puffs, pastry cream, and sauce may be made several days in advance and assembled on the day you wish to serve the dessert.

To fill the cream puffs, put the praline pastry cream into a pastry bag fitted with a plain tube and pipe it into the holes in the bottoms of the cream puffs. Keep the filled cream puffs chilled in the refrigerator until they are to be served.

PRESENTATION. Arrange the chilled cream puffs on a paper doily on a serving tray. Serve with the hot carob sauce in a separate bowl.

6 to 8 servings

Profiteroles à l'Orange, Sauce à la Caroube (le goût du chocolat)

Orange Cream Puffs, Carob Sauce (chocolate flavor)

Prepare these cream puffs following the procedure described for Profiteroles à la Praline, substituting Orange Pastry Cream (p. 229) for the Praline Pastry Cream.

Prepare these cream puffs following the procedure described for Profiteroles à la Praline (p. 230), substituting Mocha Pastry Cream (p. 228) for the Praline Pastry Cream.

Profiteroles au Moka, Sauce à la Caroube (le goût du chocolat)

Mocha Cream Puffs, Carob Sauce (chocolate flavor)

Prepare these cream puffs following the procedure described for Profiteroles à la Praline (p. 230), substituting Carob Pastry Cream (p. 229) for the Praline Pastry Cream.

Instead of serving the carob-filled cream puffs with carob sauce, a rosette of whipped cream may be piped on top of each. Beat 1 cup raw heavy sweet cream with 1 tablespoon organic honey and 1 teaspoon pure vanilla extract. Fill a pastry bag fitted with a No. 6 or No. 7 star tube with the whipped cream and decorate the filled cream puffs when ready to serve.

Profiteroles à la Caroube (le goût du chocolat)

Chocolate-flavored (Carob) Cream Puffs, Carob Sauce

Cream-Puff Pastry (p. 227), chilled	1 tablespoon organic honey
1 cup shredded blanched organic almonds	1 teaspoon pure vanilla extract
	Carob Pastry Cream (p. 229)
1 cup raw heavy sweet cream	¼ cup powdered raw sugar (p. 214)

Gâteau Favori Nouveau

Cream-Puff Ring with Carob Pastry Cream (chocolate flavor)

Preheat the oven to 375°. Using a plate of 7- or 8-inch diameter as a stencil, mark a circle on a dry baking sheet with the point of an ice pick or other sharp pointed tool. Put the cream-puff dough in a pastry bag fitted with a No. 8 or No. 9 plain tube, and pipe out a ring of dough on the circle. Carefully pipe another ring of dough on top of the first one. Gently brush the top of the dough with the remaining beaten egg (see pastry recipe), and sprinkle the top generously with shredded almonds. Allow the dough to stand at room temperature for 30 minutes.

Bake the ring in the preheated oven for 45 minutes. Reduce the oven temperature to 350° and bake for another 15 minutes. Remove the ring from the oven and let it cool.

Beat the heavy cream over ice. When it is almost stiff, add the honey and vanilla. Continue to beat until cream holds its shape.

PRESENTATION. Split the cream-puff ring horizontally into halves and

set the bottom on a paper doily on a serving plate. Fill one pastry bag fitted with a No. 8 or No. 9 plain round tube with the carob pastry cream. Fill another pastry bag fitted with a No. 6 or No. 7 star tube with the whipped cream. On the bottom half of the ring pipe mounds of pastry cream all around the circle. Between the mounds of pastry cream pipe rosettes of whipped cream. Carefully set the top half of the ring on top of the filling. Dust the top lavishly with powdered raw sugar. Store the Gâteau in the refrigerator until time to serve.
6 to 8 servings

Crêpes, Dessert and Savory

For crêpes, the conversion to stone-ground whole-wheat flour and cold-pressed safflower oil is simple and the result is a distinctly richer and just as delicate crêpe. The following recipe makes 10 to 12 crêpes of 6-inch diameter which may be used with savory or sweet fillings. The unfilled crêpes can be frozen. Put a piece of plastic wrap or wax paper between each and seal them in a plastic bag.

8 tablespoons stone-ground whole-wheat pastry flour
Sea salt
1 whole organic egg
Yolk of 1 organic egg

3 tablespoons cold-pressed safflower oil
About ¾ cup raw milk
Cold-pressed safflower oil for crêpe pan

Put the flour, a pinch of sea salt, the whole egg, the extra egg yolk, 3 tablespoons safflower oil, and 4 tablespoons of milk in a small bowl. Beat the mixture with a small whisk until it is smooth. Add additional milk to give the batter the consistency of light cream; it should just coat the back of a metal spoon. Cover the bowl with plastic wrap and let it set in the refrigerator for at least 30 minutes, or a day if you wish.

When you are ready to make the crêpes, heat a sauté pan until it is smoking hot. Arrange near the pan the batter, some safflower oil, a wad of wax paper, a ladle, and a spatula. If the batter has thickened, add a little more milk. Dip the wax paper into safflower oil and wipe out the pan. Ladle a little of the batter into the pan. Tilt the pan to cover the bottom with a thin coating of the batter. Brown the crêpe on one side; very carefully turn it over with the spatula and brown it on the other side (or "underside"). Pile the crêpes on a wire rack.
10 to 12 crêpes

8 to 10 Crêpes (*p. 232*)

GRAPEFRUIT BUTTER
3 tablespoons natural sweet butter
2 tablespoons granulated raw sugar
  Grated rind of ½ grapefruit

GRAPEFRUIT SAUCE
3 tablespoons cold-pressed safflower
  oil, or natural sweet butter

Juice of 1 grapefruit
Finely shredded rind of ½
  grapefruit
½ cup granulated raw sugar
3 tablespoons dry sherry
  (*optional*)
Skinned sections of 1 grapefruit

Crêpes Suzette
Pamplemousse

Grapefruit
Crêpes Suzette

GRAPEFRUIT BUTTER. Beat the butter and sugar in the bowl of an electric mixer until the mixture is light and fluffy; add the grapefruit rind and beat a little longer. Spread this butter over the underside of each crêpe. Fold the crêpes in half, then fold them in half again.

GRAPEFRUIT SAUCE. Combine the safflower oil or butter, grapefruit juice, shredded rind, and the sugar in a sauté pan, and stir the ingredients over low heat until the grapefruit rind becomes translucent. Let the sauce simmer gently for 5 minutes. Heat the sherry in a little pan, ignite, and pour it onto the sauce. Add the skinned sections of grapefruit and warm them in the sauce for just a moment.

PRESENTATION. Arrange the folded crêpes, overlapping, on a serving dish. Pour over the sauce. Serve warm.

4 to 5 servings

SOUFFLÉ
2½ cups fresh blueberries
  1 tablespoon fresh lime juice or
    fresh lemon juice
1½ cups granulated raw sugar
  2 teaspoons potato flour
  2 tablespoons dry sherry
    (*optional*)
  1 teaspoon grated lemon rind
    Cold-pressed safflower oil for
    soufflé dish and collar

Whites of 8 organic eggs
  Granulated raw sugar for soufflé
    dish
½ cup blanched shredded organic
  almonds

BLUEBERRY SAUCE
12 ounces natural blueberry
  preserve
  2 teaspoons fresh lemon juice
  1 cup fresh blueberries

Hot Blueberry
Soufflé with
Blueberry Sauce

Have ready a 1½-quart (No. 7) soufflé dish. Purée the blueberries in a blender. Sprinkle the blueberry purée with the lime or lemon juice, and let it sit in a cool place for about 1 hour. Combine ¾ cup water and the sugar in an unlined copper pan and stir until it comes to a boil. Let the syrup boil without stirring until it spins a thread (225° on a candy thermometer). Slowly stir this syrup into the puréed blueberries. In a separate small bowl mix 2 or 3 tablespoons of the blueberry mixture with the potato flour, then add it to the rest of the blueberry mixture. Pour the blueberry mixture into a saucepan and stir over low heat until it thickens. Add the dry sherry and lemon rind. Remove mixture from the heat and set it aside to cool.

Preheat the oven to 375°. Lightly brush the soufflé dish with safflower oil. Tear off a length of wax paper 1½ times the outer girth of the soufflé dish, fold it in half lengthwise, and brush it with safflower oil. Wrap the wax paper around the outside of the soufflé dish and tie it with kitchen string. Dust the inside of the prepared soufflé dish with granulated raw sugar. Set the soufflé dish in a roasting pan and have a pan of hot water ready.

Beat the egg whites to soft peaks and gently fold them into the cooled blueberry mixture. Spoon the soufflé mixture into the dish. Half-fill the roasting pan with hot water. Set the soufflé preparation in its water bath in the preheated oven and bake for 50 minutes to 1 hour. About 10 minutes before the soufflé is finished baking, have the shredded almonds at hand; quickly open the oven door and sprinkle them on top of the soufflé.

BLUEBERRY SAUCE. Strain the blueberry preserve and put it in a pan with the lemon juice. Bring it to a boil, stir in the fresh blueberries, and remove the sauce from the heat immediately. This sauce may be served hot or cold.

PRESENTATION. When the soufflé has finished baking, carefully remove it from the oven and from the water bath. Gently place it on a serving tray and carefully peel off the wax-paper collar. Dust the top with powdered raw sugar, if desired. Serve at once with the blueberry sauce.
6 servings

Soufflé à la Caroube (le goût du chocolat)

Hot Chocolate-flavor Soufflé (with Carob), Carob (chocolate flavor) or Vanilla Custard Sauce

Cold-pressed safflower oil for soufflé dish and collar
Granulated raw sugar for soufflé dish
3 tablespoons cold-pressed safflower oil
3 tablespoons sifted stone-ground whole-wheat pastry flour
3 ounces carob, nuggets or solid bar
1½ cups raw light cream
Scraping of 1-inch piece of vanilla bean
Yolks of 4 organic eggs
4 tablespoons granulated raw sugar
Whites of 6 organic eggs
Sea salt
A little powdered raw sugar (p. 214, optional)
Carob Sauce (p. 271), or Vanilla Custard Sauce (p. 273)

Preheat the oven to 350°. Lightly brush a 1-quart (No. 6) soufflé dish with safflower oil. Tear off a length of wax paper 1½ times the outer girth of the soufflé dish, fold it in half lengthwise, and brush it with saf-flower oil. Wrap the wax paper around the soufflé dish and tie it with kitchen string. Dust the inside of the soufflé dish with a little granu-lated raw sugar. Set the soufflé dish in a roasting pan and have a pan of hot water ready.

Heat 3 tablespoons safflower oil in a saucepan. Off the heat stir in the flour. If you have solid carob, cut it into small pieces. Melt the carob with the light cream in a small pan over low heat, stirring until it is smooth. Pour the carob mixture slowly into the oil and flour mixture. When it is blended, return the mixture to low heat and stir until it just comes to a boil. Remove the pan from the heat, add the scraping of the piece of vanilla bean, cover, and set aside for a moment.

Put the egg yolks and 4 tablespoons granulated raw sugar in the bowl of an electric mixer, and beat until they are light and fluffy. Add the egg yolks to the carob mixture. Beat the egg whites with a pinch of sea salt to soft peaks and gently and smoothly fold them into the carob mixture. Carefully spoon the soufflé mixture into the prepared dish. Half-fill the roasting pan with hot water. Set the soufflé dish in its water bath in the preheated oven and bake for 30 minutes. Increase the heat to 375° and bake for another 30 minutes, or until the soufflé is firm to the touch.

PRESENTATION. When the soufflé has finished baking, carefully remove it from the oven and from the water bath. Gently place it on a serving tray and carefully peel off the wax-paper collar. Dust the top with the powdered raw sugar, if desired. Serve at once with Vanilla Custard or Carob Sauce.

4 to 6 servings

Soufflé au Citron Chaud, Sauce Citron

Hot Lemon Soufflé, Lemon Sauce

Cold-pressed safflower oil for soufflé dish and collar
Granulated raw sugar for soufflé dish
4 teaspoons cornstarch or potato flour
Grated rind and juice of 1 large lemon or 2 small lemons
Sea salt
¾ cup creamy raw milk
3 teaspoons cold-pressed safflower oil
Yolks of 4 organic eggs
6 tablespoons superfine granulated raw sugar (p. 214)
Whites of 6 organic eggs
Powdered raw sugar (p. 214, optional)
Lemon Sauce (p. 271)

Preheat the oven to 375°. Lightly brush a 1-quart (No. 6) soufflé dish with safflower oil. Tear off a length of wax paper 1½ times the outer girth of the soufflé dish, fold it in half lengthwise, and brush it with safflower oil. Wrap the wax paper around the soufflé dish and tie it with kitchen string. Dust the inside of the soufflé dish with a little granulated raw sugar. Set the soufflé dish in a roasting pan and have a pan of hot water ready.

Blend the cornstarch with the lemon juice and a pinch of sea salt in a little bowl. Bring the milk to a boil and pour it slowly into the lemon juice and cornstarch mixture. Return the mixture to the pan and stir over low heat until it comes to a boil. Cook over low heat for 2 or 3 minutes, stirring all the time. Stir in 3 teaspoons safflower oil, spoonful by spoonful. Add the grated lemon rind.

Beat the egg yolks and the superfine sugar in the bowl of an electric mixer until they are very light and fluffy. Add the egg-yolk mixture to the lemon sauce. Beat the egg whites with a pinch of salt to soft peaks, and gently and smoothly fold them into the lemon and egg-yolk mixture. Carefully fill the prepared soufflé dish with this mixture. Half-fill the roasting pan with hot water. Set the soufflé dish in its water bath in the preheated oven and bake for 50 minutes to 1 hour, or until the soufflé is firm to the touch.

PRESENTATION. When the soufflé has finished baking, carefully remove it from the oven and from the water bath. Gently place it on a serving tray and carefully peel off the paper collar. Dust the top with the powdered raw sugar, if desired. Serve at once with lemon sauce.

4 to 6 servings

Soufflé à la Marmelade d'Oranges, Sauce Smitane

Hot Orange Marmalade Soufflé, Sour Cream Sauce

Cold-pressed safflower oil for soufflé dish and collar
1 cup grated organic pecans
Granulated raw sugar for soufflé dish
2 tablespoons cold-pressed safflower oil
3 tablespoons stone-ground whole-wheat pastry flour
¾ cup raw milk
Grated rind of 1 lemon
Grated rind of 1 orange
4 tablespoons natural bitter orange marmalade

Sea salt
1 tablespoon granulated raw sugar
Yolks of 3 organic eggs
Whites of 5 organic eggs
A little powdered raw sugar (p. 214, optional)

SOUR CREAM SAUCE
¾ cup thick raw sour cream
1 tablespoon granulated raw sugar
Grated rind of 1 lemon
1 teaspoon freshly grated nutmeg

Preheat the oven to 375°. Lightly brush a 1-quart (No. 6) soufflé dish with safflower oil. Tear off a length of wax paper 1½ times the outer girth of the soufflé dish, fold it in half lengthwise, and brush it with safflower oil. Wrap the wax paper around the soufflé dish and tie it with kitchen string. Dust the inside of the soufflé dish with grated pecans and a little granulated raw sugar. Set the soufflé dish in a roasting pan and have a pan of hot water ready.

Heat 2 tablespoons safflower oil in a saucepan. Off the heat stir in the flour. Add the milk and stir over moderate heat until the mixture thickens. Add the grated lemon and orange rinds, the marmalade, a pinch of sea salt, and 1 tablespoon granulated raw sugar. Stir in the egg yolks.

Beat the egg whites to soft peaks and gently and smoothly fold them into the egg-yolk mixture. Carefully fill the prepared soufflé dish with this mixture. Half-fill the roasting pan with hot water. Set the soufflé dish in its water bath in the preheated oven and bake for 45 to 55 minutes.

SOUR CREAM SAUCE. Combine the sour cream with the granulated raw sugar, lemon rind, and nutmeg, and chill the sauce well.

PRESENTATION. When the soufflé has finished baking, carefully remove it from the oven and from the water bath. Gently place it on a serving tray and carefully peel off the paper collar. Dust the top with a little powdered raw sugar, if desired. Serve at once with the cold sour cream sauce.

4 to 6 servings

The sweet-potato soufflé can be served either as a savory vegetable course without the fruit or Sabayon sauce, or as a delicious dessert course.

Soufflé aux Patates, Sauce aux Fruits Secs ou Sabayon

Hot Sweet-Potato Soufflé, Dried Fruit or Sabayon Sauce

2 pounds sweet potatoes or yams (to produce 2 cups cooked and puréed)
Sea salt
Cold-pressed safflower oil for soufflé dish and collar
1 cup raw sour cream
2 tablespoons Marsala wine, or 1 tablespoon natural honey mixed with 1 tablespoon warm water

4 tablespoons cold-pressed safflower oil
1/4 teaspoon freshly grated nutmeg
Grated rind of 1/2 lemon
Yolks of 4 organic eggs
Whites of 5 organic eggs
Dried Fruit Sauce (p. 272), or Sabayon Sauce (p. 272)

Boil the sweet potatoes in their skins with 1 teaspoon sea salt until they are soft. When the potatoes are cooked, drain them, remove the skins, and rub them through a fine vegetable strainer. Measure out 2 cups of the purée.

Preheat the oven to 375°. Lightly brush a 1-quart (No. 6) soufflé dish with safflower oil. Tear off a length of wax paper 1½ times the outer girth of the soufflé dish, fold it in half lengthwise, and brush it with safflower oil. Wrap the wax paper around the soufflé dish and tie it with kitchen string. Set the soufflé dish in a roasting pan and have a pan of hot water ready.

Beat the puréed potatoes in the bowl of a mixer and gradually add the sour cream and Marsala wine. Mix in 4 tablespoons safflower oil, the nutmeg, ½ teaspoon sea salt, and the lemon rind. Add the egg yolks and beat thoroughly.

Beat the egg whites to soft peaks and fold them into the egg-yolk mixture gently and smoothly. Spoon the soufflé mixture into the prepared dish. Half-fill the roasting pan with hot water. Set the soufflé dish in its water bath in the preheated oven and bake for 50 minutes to 1 hour, or until it is firm to the touch.

PRESENTATION. Gently remove the soufflé from the water bath and set it on a serving plate. Carefully peel off the paper collar. Serve at once with the sauce, or plain if you prefer.

Soufflé Froid aux Bananes

Cold Banana Soufflé

Cold-pressed safflower oil for soufflé dish and collar
4 organic eggs
  Yolks of 3 organic eggs
6 tablespoons granulated raw sugar
2 tablespoons unflavored gelatin
1 tablespoon fresh lemon juice

6 ripe bananas
  Sea salt
1½ cups raw heavy sweet cream
¼ cup chopped blanched organic pistachio nuts, or other chopped organic nuts

Tear off a length of wax paper 1½ times the outer girth of the soufflé dish. Fold it in half lengthwise and brush it with safflower oil. Wrap the wax paper around a 3-cup (No. 5) soufflé dish and tie it with kitchen string.

Beat the whole eggs, egg yolks, and the granulated raw sugar in the electric mixer until the mixture is very thick and holds its shape. Dissolve the gelatin with the lemon juice and 4 tablespoons water in a small pan over low heat. Then cool the solution a little.

Beat the heavy cream in a metal bowl over another bowl of ice until it is stiff. Rub 5 of the bananas through a fine vegetable strainer and add a pinch of salt. Carefully and smoothly fold the dissolved gelatin into the egg mixture. Fold in the banana purée. Then fold 1 cup of the whipped cream into the mixture. Store the rest of the whipped cream in the refrigerator until the soufflé is ready to be decorated.

Fill the soufflé dish with the mixture. It should come to about 2 to 3 inches above the top of the dish. Set it in the refrigerator or freezer to chill and set.

PRESENTATION. When the soufflé is set, carefully remove the paper collar. Stick the chopped almonds around the side of the soufflé. Put the rest of the whipped cream in a pastry bag fitted with a No. 4 or No. 5 star tube, and pipe rosettes all over the top. Dip the whole chestnuts into honey and set them on top of the whipped cream. Chill again before serving.
4 to 6 servings

FRENCH ICE CREAM AND FROZEN SOUFFLÉS

The following group of recipes can be served as ice cream or they can be fancied up and served in a soufflé dish to look like a soufflé.

For service like ice cream: Prepare each recipe as directed. When the mixture in the freezer thickens and the churn stops, remove the paddle, pack the mixture in the drum, and allow it to freeze to a firm state in the freezer container. After that it may be served or packed into plastic containers and stored in the freezer.

For service like a frozen soufflé: When the mixture in the freezer thickens and the churn stops, spoon the mixture into a soufflé dish with a paper collar around it (as described in the recipe) and put in the freezer until it is firm. Decorate it as you would a cold soufflé. When served this way, it is an especial gastronomic delight especially if served with a delicious complementary sauce such as a simple fresh Fruit Sauce (pp. 273–274) or chocolate-flavor Carob Sauce (p. 271).

The sight of all that cream in ice cream can cause the most svelte to hesitate. Here is where we suggest that some of the fat content may be offset with the use of reconstituted nonfat dry milk, double-strength, in place of the liquid cream in the egg mixture, but bowing to the retention of the whipped cream ingredient.

If you have a spacious freezer, you can prepare a frozen soufflé or a supply of ice cream days ahead of when you wish to serve it.

½ cup granulated raw sugar	Sea salt
Yolks of 4 organic eggs	1 cup raw heavy cream, whipped
2 cups reconstituted nonfat dry	
milk, double-strength, or raw	
light cream, or raw heavy	FOR SOUFFLÉ DECORATION
cream	1 cup raw heavy cream
2-inch piece of vanilla bean,	
scraped, or 1 teaspoon pure	
vanilla extract	

Glace à la Vanille et Soufflé Glacé à la Vanille

Vanilla French Ice Cream and Frozen Vanilla Soufflé

Combine the sugar with ¼ cup water in an unlined copper pan and stir over high heat until sugar dissolves. Stop stirring and continue to boil the syrup until it forms a light thread (225° on a candy thermometer). Beat the egg yolks in the bowl of a mixer until they are light and fluffy. Slowly pour the syrup into the yolks, beating all the time, and continue beating until the mixture is thick and cold.

Heat the reconstituted milk or the cream with the vanilla bean (scraping and pod) or extract, but do not let it boil. Pour the milk or cream slowly into the egg mixture, stirring all the time. Add a pinch of salt. Pour the mixture through a wire strainer into the top part of a double boiler, and stir it over hot water until the custard thickens. Cool the custard in the refrigerator. When it is chilled, fold in the whipped cream.

Directions for freezing: Pour the chilled custard into the drum of an ice-cream freezer. Insert the paddle and cover it. Pack the freezer with ice and freezing salt, and churn until the mixture is thick. At this point the paddle will usually stop churning.

For ice cream: Remove the paddle, pack the ice cream down in the drum, cover it again, and allow the ice cream to freeze to a firm state, either in the ice cream freezer or by placing the drum in the freezer.

For a frozen soufflé: Have ready a 3-cup (No. 5) soufflé dish. Tear off a length of wax paper 1½ times the outer girth of the soufflé dish. Fold it in half lengthwise. Wrap the wax paper around the soufflé dish and tie it with kitchen string. Spoon the thick-frozen custard into the prepared soufflé dish; it should fill above the dish. Put it in the freezer to become firm.

To decorate the soufflé: When the mixture is frozen, remove the paper collar. Beat the heavy cream until it is stiff. Put it into a pastry bag fitted with a No. 4 or No. 5 star tube. Pipe rosettes all over the top of the frozen soufflé. At this point the dish can be returned to the freezer and stored until it is to be served.

1½ quarts, 6 servings

Glace à la Caroube et Soufflé Glacé à la Caroube (le goût du chocolat)

Chocolate-flavor French Ice Cream and Chocolate-flavor Frozen Soufflé (with carob)

Ingredients for Vanilla French Ice Cream (preceding recipe)
8 ounces carob nuggets or solid bar
3 teaspoons instant decaffeinated coffee mixed with 3 tablespoons hot water

FOR SOUFFLÉ DECORATION
1 cup raw heavy sweet cream
½ cup coarsely grated carob bar or nuggets

If you are using bar carob, cut it into small pieces. Melt the carob with the coffee essence in a small pan over low heat, stirring until it is smooth. Prepare the mixture for Vanilla French Ice Cream. *After the mixture has been cooked in the double boiler, mix it with the dissolved carob.* Cool the mixture in the refrigerator. When it is chilled, fold in the whipped cream. Follow the same procedure for freezing as for Vanilla French Ice Cream or frozen vanilla soufflé.

To decorate soufflé: When the soufflé is frozen, remove the paper collar. Beat the heavy cream until it is stiff. Put it in a pastry bag fitted with a No. 4 or No. 5 star tube. Pipe rosettes all over the top. Scatter the coarsely grated carob over the whipped-cream topping. At this point the dish may be returned to the freezer and stored until it is to be served.

1½ quarts, 6 servings

Natural-food stores offer many varieties of interesting honeys. For this simple, no-egg, all-cream ice cream or frozen soufflé, use the honey of your choice.

Glace au Miel et Soufflé Glacé au Miel

Honey Ice Cream and Frozen Honey Soufflé

2 cups raw heavy sweet cream
½ cup natural honey
    Grated rind of 1 lemon, 1
      orange, and 1 lime
    Sea salt

½ teaspoon pure almond flavoring

FOR SOUFFLÉ DECORATION
½ cup chopped organic almonds

Beat the heavy cream in a metal bowl over another bowl of ice until it is slightly thick. Gradually fold in the honey with a rubber scraper, blending the mixture well. Fold in the grated rinds of lemon, orange, and lime, a pinch of sea salt, and the almond flavoring. Follow the same directions for freezing as for Vanilla French Ice Cream or Frozen Vanilla Soufflé (pp. 241–242).

To decorate soufflé: When the soufflé is frozen, remove the paper collar and sprinkle the top with the chopped almonds. At this point the dish may be stored in the freezer until it is to be served.

1 quart, 4 servings

Rhubarb ice cream is a delicious discovery even if you've never been a rhubarb fancier.

Glace aux Fraises, Framboises, Mûres, ou à la Rhubarbe et Soufflé Glacé

Fresh Strawberry, Raspberry, Blackberry, or Rhubarb French Ice Cream and Frozen Soufflé

Ingredients for French Vanilla
   Ice Cream (p. 241)

FRUIT PURÉE
2 cups puréed fresh strawberries,
   raspberries, or blackberries
2 teaspoons fresh lemon juice
2 tablespoons granulated raw sugar

Or 2 cups cooked Rhubarb
   Purée (recipe follows)

FOR SOUFFLÉ DECORATION
1 cup raw heavy sweet cream
¾ cup whole fresh berries
   (strawberries for rhubarb)

Mix the fresh fruit purée with the lemon juice and raw sugar. If you are using rhubarb, prepare it according to the special recipe.

Prepare the mixture for Vanilla French Ice Cream. *After the mixture has been cooked in the double boiler, mix it with the puréed fruit.* Cool the mixture in the refrigerator. When it is chilled, fold in the whipped cream. Follow the same procedure for freezing as for Vanilla French Ice Cream or Frozen Vanilla Soufflé.

To decorate soufflé: When the soufflé is frozen firm, remove the paper collar. Beat the heavy cream until it is stiff. Put it in a pastry bag fitted with a No. 4 or No. 5 star tube, and pipe rosettes all over the top. At this point the dish can be returned to the freezer until it is to be served. Just before serving, arrange the whole fresh fruit on top of the whipped cream.

1½ quarts, 6 servings

Rhubarb Purée

2 pounds rhubarb
1 cup raw sugar

Grated rind of 1 lemon

Cut the rhubarb into 1-inch chunks and put them in a deep heavy pan with the sugar and lemon rind. Cover and cook over low heat until the rhubarb is soft. Stir occasionally to avoid scorching. Purée the rhubarb in a blender and chill it.

2 cups

Omelette Soufflé, Sauce Abricot

Basic Sweet Omelet, with Apricot Sauce

The sweet dessert omelet is a fluffy concoction, the egg yolks being folded into stiffly beaten whites. It can be filled with fruit or preserves, or served plain with a fruit or other sweet sauce or garnish.

2 organic eggs
2 teaspoons superfine or regular
    granulated raw sugar (see
    p. 214 concerning superfine)
Sea salt
1 tablespoon cold-pressed safflower
    oil
3 tablespoons powdered raw sugar
    (p. 214)

APRICOT SAUCE (optional)
½ cup natural apricot preserve
2 tablespoons granulated raw
    sugar
Grated rind and juice of
    1 lemon
2 tablespoons dry sherry or
    Madeira wine, optional

Set the omelet pan or a heavy sauté pan, 8 to 10 inches in diameter, over low heat and let it gradually heat through.

APRICOT SAUCE. Mix all of the sauce ingredients together and stir in a pan over moderate heat until the mixture is dissolved. Allow to cool while you prepare the omelet.

Separate the eggs. Beat the yolks and 2 teaspoons superfine or regular granulated raw sugar with a wire whisk until the mixture is light and fluffy. Add 1 teaspoon water and a pinch of sea salt to the egg whites and beat them with a whisk or an electric mixer until they hold their shape. Fold the egg-yolk mixture into the whites.

Turn the heat to moderate and get the omelet pan fairly hot. Add the safflower oil and spread it over the bottom of the pan with a wad of wax paper. Put the egg mixture into the pan and spread it over the surface with the back of a fork. Let it cook without stirring until the edges are a light brown. Fold the omelet in half with the side of the fork and turn it out onto a hot flat dish. Sift the powdered sugar on top of the omelet and brown it lightly under the broiler. Spoon the sauce over the top and serve immediately.

2 servings

CARAMEL
1½ *cups granulated raw sugar*

CUSTARD
   3 *whole organic eggs*
   Yolks of 2 organic eggs
½ *cup superfine raw organic
      sugar (p. 214)*

½ *vanilla bean, scraped*
   1 *cup raw milk, or 1 cup double-
      strength reconstituted nonfat
      dry milk*
   1 *cup raw heavy sweet cream*

***Crème au
Caramel***

*Custard with
Caramel*

Preheat the oven to 300°. CARAMEL. Put the granulated sugar and ¾ cup water in an unlined copper pan. Stir over high heat until the sugar dissolves. Allow the mixture to cook until the syrup becomes amber in color. Immediately remove syrup from the heat and set the pan in another pan of cold water to halt any further cooking and browning. Pour the caramel into a 1-quart (No. 6) soufflé dish. Tilt the dish in all directions so that the syrup completely coats the inside of the dish. Pour the excess caramel back into the saucepan. Add ¼ cup water to the caramel in the pan and stir over moderate heat until it dissolves. Pour it into a container and store in the refrigerator until it is to be served as a sauce.

CUSTARD. Combine the whole eggs and the extra egg yolks with the superfine sugar in a bowl and stir with a whisk until the mixture is blended but not frothy. Add the scraping from the vanilla bean. Bring the milk and cream with the vanilla pod to a boil. Pour the hot milk and cream into the egg mixture, stirring all the time. Strain the custard mixture into the caramel-lined soufflé dish. Set the soufflé dish in a roasting pan half-filled with hot water. Set the custard in its water bath in the preheated oven and bake for 2 hours, or until a cake tester inserted into the custard comes out clean. Remove the custard from the water bath and set it in the refrigerator to cool and set, at least 8 hours.

PRESENTATION. Slide a small sharp knife around the edge of the custard to loosen it. Set a serving plate face down on top of the custard and invert the custard onto it. Pour the reserved caramel over the custard.

4 servings

Ile Flottante
Floating Island

This classic dish is also known as *Oeufs à la Neige* or "Snow Eggs."

Yolks of 6 organic eggs
9 tablespoons granulated raw sugar
    (a superfine texture is
    preferred; see p. 214)
3-inch piece of vanilla bean,
    scraping and pod
2 cups raw light cream (or 1 cup
    raw light cream with 1 cup
    reconstituted nonfat dry milk,
    double-strength)

¼ cup raw heavy sweet cream,
    whipped
1 tablespoon Marsala or
    Madeira wine (optional)
1½ tablespoons unflavored gelatin
1 teaspoon fresh lemon juice
    Whites of 2 organic eggs

CARAMEL GARNISH (optional)
¼ cup granulated raw sugar

Beat the egg yolks, 6 tablespoons granulated sugar, and the scraping of the vanilla bean in an electric mixer until the mixture is light and fluffy. Bring the light cream with the vanilla pod to a boil and slowly pour it into the egg-yolk mixture, beating all the time. Transfer the egg-yolk and cream mixture to a saucepan and stir over low heat until the custard coats the back of a metal spoon. Set the pan in a bowl of ice and continue stirring until the custard cools. Fold in the whipped cream and the wine. Pour the custard into a shallow serving bowl and chill it in the refrigerator.

Dissolve the gelatin in the lemon juice and 3 tablespoons water over low heat and let it cool a little. Beat the egg whites until they are stiff, almost dry. Beat in 3 tablespoons granulated sugar and mix in the dissolved gelatin. Form the meringue into egg shapes with 2 large spoons and float them on top of the custard.

CARAMEL GARNISH. Combine ¼ cup raw sugar with 4 tablespoons water in an unlined copper pan. Stir the mixture over high heat until it boils. Continue to cook the syrup without stirring until it becomes light brown in color. Dip a fork into the caramel syrup and drizzle strands of it all over the floating islands. Serve well chilled.

4 servings

2 cups raw milk or more
  (reconstituted nonfat dry
  milk may be used)
¼ cup natural brown rice (short
  grain preferred)
1 tablespoon unflavored gelatin
  Yolks of 2 organic eggs
4 tablespoons granulated raw
  sugar
  Whites of 4 organic eggs

1½ cups raw heavy sweet cream,
  whipped with 1 tablespoon
  organic honey
  Skinned sections of 2
  grapefruits
2 cups strawberries (if they are
  small, cut them into halves;
  if large, cut into quarters)
12 select whole fresh strawberries,
  for garnish

Riz à
l'Impératrice
Nature

Natural Rice
Custard with
Strawberries and
Grapefruit

Combine the milk with the rice in a heavy pan and bring it to a boil over low heat. Reduce the heat as much as possible, and continue to cook until the rice is very soft and has absorbed the milk. Stir occasionally to avoid scorching. If the rice absorbs all of the milk before it is tender, add more milk. When the rice is soft, stir in the gelatin and remove the rice from the heat.

Beat the egg yolks and sugar in the bowl of an electric mixer until the mixture is light and fluffy. Set the cooked rice over a bowl of ice and stir in the egg-yolk mixture. Continue to stir gently until the mixture is cool and at the point of setting.

Beat the egg whites to soft peaks and fold them into the rice and egg-yolk mixture. Fold in half of the whipped cream. Drain the grapefruit sections and dry between paper towels. Gently mix grapefruit and cut strawberries into the rice mixture.

PRESENTATION. Spoon the rice custard and fruit mixture into a crystal serving bowl and set it in the refrigerator. When it is set, put the rest of the whipped cream in a pastry bag fitted with a No. 6 or No. 7 star tube and pipe 12 rosettes around the edge. Set a whole strawberry in each rosette. Store the dish in the refrigerator until it is to be served.

4 to 6 servings

  Cold-pressed safflower oil (to
  oil baking dish)
5 tablespoons granulated raw
  sugar
⅛ teaspoon cardamom
1 to 1½ pounds ripe black
  cherries (not pitted), or
  prune plums (pitted)
3 organic eggs

5 tablespoons sifted stone-ground
  whole-wheat pastry flour
2 cups raw milk, raw light cream,
  or reconstituted nonfat dry
  milk
  Pinch of sea salt
½ cup powdered raw sugar
  (p. 214)

Le Clafouti

Large Baked
Pancake with
Fresh Fruit

Preheat the oven to 375°. Brush a 10-inch diameter pie pan or a shallow round baking dish with safflower oil. Dust it with 2 tablespoons granulated sugar mixed with the cardamom. Scatter the fruit over the bottom of the prepared dish.

Beat the eggs in the electric mixer. Add the flour and mix well. Pour in the milk and add the salt. Beat for at least 5 minutes. During this time slowly add 3 tablespoons of granulated sugar. Pour this mixture into the baking dish with the fruit. Bake in the preheated oven for 40 to 45 minutes, until the top is lightly browned and puffy. Chill the clafouti. Sprinkle the top lavishly with powdered sugar. Cut it into wedges and serve.

6 servings

Crème Bavaroise à la Caroube

Chocolate-flavor Bavarian Cream (with carob)

8 *ounces carob nuggets or solid bar*
1 *cup raw milk*
1 *cup raw light cream*
5 *organic eggs*
8 *tablespoons superfine granulated raw sugar (p. 214)*
2 *tablespoons unflavored gelatin*
1 *tablespoon natural orange flavoring*

2 *cups raw heavy sweet cream*
1 *tablespoon organic honey*
1 *teaspoon pure vanilla extract*
   Cold-pressed safflower oil for oiling the mold

CAROB DISCS (optional)
4 *ounces carob nuggets or solid bar*

If you are using bar carob, break it into little pieces. Put the carob in a saucepan and set it aside for a moment. In another pan bring the milk and light cream to a boil. Pour the combined milk and cream over the carob. Stir the carob and milk/cream over low heat until the carob is completely dissolved.

Separate the eggs and beat the yolks with the superfine sugar in the bowl of an electric mixer until they are light and fluffy. Remove the bowl from the machine and, with a rubber scraper, fold in the gelatin. Mix in the dissolved carob and milk/cream mixture. Pour the mixture into a pan and stir it over low heat until the custard coats the back of a metal spoon. Set the pan in a bowl of ice and stir until the mixture is cool. Mix in the orange flavoring.

Beat the egg whites to soft peaks and fold them into the carob mixture. Beat the heavy cream in a metal bowl set in another bowl of ice. When cream is almost stiff, add the honey and vanilla extract. Continue beating until cream holds its shape. Fold one third of the whipped cream into the carob mixture. Reserve the remaining whipped cream for garnish.

Brush the inside of a 9-inch springform cake pan with safflower oil. Invert the pan on top of paper towels, and let the excess oil drain. Fill the cake pan with the Bavarian cream mixture and set it in the refrigerator for at least 2 hours.

CAROB DISCS. While the Bavarian cream is setting, prepare the carob discs. Prepare 24 to 30 rounds of wax paper about 1½ inches in diameter. If you are using bar carob, cut it into small pieces. Put the carob on a plate or in a shallow pan over a pan of hot water and let the carob dissolve. Remove the carob from the heat and stir it with a spatula until it cools a little. Spread the rounds of wax paper with a thin coating of carob, being sure that the surface is covered and there are no holes. Set the carob-coated papers on a jelly-roll pan and put them in the freezer to harden.

PRESENTATION. When the Bavarian cream is set, slide a thin-bladed knife around the edge to loosen it, and turn it out onto a flat serving dish. Spread the reserved whipped cream over the top and sides. Remove the papers from the hardened carob discs and stick the discs on the whipped cream around the sides of the Bavarian cream. Or coat the sides with grated carob. Return the dessert to the refrigerator and keep it chilled until it is to be served.

4 to 6 servings

This is Dione Lucas's famous Chocolate Mousse converted to carob. It retains the rich chocolate flavor but is much less acid and has only 180 calories per portion (100 grams) compared to 507 for chocolate.

Mousse à la Caroube

Chocolate-flavor Mousse (with carob)

8 ounces carob nuggets or solid bar	GARNISH (optional)
3 teaspoons instant decaffeinated coffee dissolved in ½ cup hot water	*1 cup raw heavy sweet cream, whipped with 1 tablespoon natural honey and 1 teaspoon pure vanilla extract*
Yolks of 5 organic eggs	
Whites of 5 organic eggs	*¼ cup coarsely grated carob*

You may serve this mousse in individual custard cups or small ramekins, or in a serving bowl of about 1-quart size.

If you are using bar carob, cut it into small pieces. Melt the carob with the dissolved coffee in a small pan over low heat and stir until it is smooth. Remove the pan from the heat and beat the egg yolks into the carob, one at a time, using a small wire whisk.

Beat the egg whites to soft peaks. Add the carob and egg-yolk mixture to the whites and beat with a wire whisk until it is absolutely smooth, frothy, and shiny. Pour the mousse from the mixing bowl into a pitcher and then pour it into the serving cups or bowl. Put the mousse in the refrigerator or freezer to set.

PRESENTATION. When the mousse is set, garnish it. Put the whipped cream in a pastry bag fitted with a large star tube, No. 8 or No. 9. Pipe a large rosette on top of each cup of mousse, or all over the top of the bowl. Sprinkle the grated carob over the top of the whipped cream. Store the mousse in the refrigerator until it is to be served. This mousse may be frozen.

6 servings

Mousse aux Fraises

Fresh Strawberry Mousse

6 whole organic eggs
  Yolks of 4 organic eggs
8 tablespoons superfine granulated
    raw sugar (p. 214)
  Grated rind of 1 orange
  Grated rind of 1 lemon
2 tablespoons unflavored gelatin
  Juice of 1 orange
1 teaspoon fresh lemon juice

¾ cup raw heavy sweet cream,
    whipped
1½ cups crushed fresh strawberries
1½ cups natural currant jelly
2 teaspoons pure orange or
    lemon flavoring
30 or more perfect strawberries,
    cleaned and hulled

Combine the whole eggs, extra egg yolks, and superfine sugar in the bowl of an electric mixer and beat until the mixture is very light and stiff, at least 10 minutes. Remove the bowl from the mixer and fold in the orange and lemon rinds. Combine the gelatin, orange juice, lemon juice, and 3 tablespoons water in a small pan, and stir over low heat until the gelatin is dissolved. Carefully and smoothly blend the gelatin mixture into the egg mixture. Fold in the whipped cream. Finally fold in the crushed strawberries.

PRESENTATION. Spoon the mousse into a crystal serving bowl and put it in the refrigerator to set. When it is firm, decorate it. Combine the currant jelly and the orange or lemon flavoring in a pan and stir over low heat until the jelly is dissolved. Strain the mixture through a fine wire strainer and let it cool a little. Cover the top of the mousse with the whole strawberries, hulled end down. Carefully brush the strawberries with the currant jelly to give them a nice glaze. Return the mousse to the refrigerator for at least 30 minutes for the glaze to set, or until it is to be served.

6 to 8 servings

Charlotte aux Pommes

Apple Charlotte

Cold-pressed safflower oil for
    charlotte mold and for
    sautéing bread strips
Granulated raw sugar for
    charlotte mold
1 loaf of stone-ground whole-wheat
    bread
4 pounds green apples, skinned,
    cored, and cut into thick slices

Grated rind of 2 lemons
1½ cups natural apricot preserve
4 tablespoons cold-pressed
    safflower oil
½ teaspoon freshly grated nutmeg
½ teaspoon ground ginger
¾ cup granulated raw sugar
  Sour Cream Sauce (p. 273), or
  Mousseline Sauce (p. 272)

Brush the inside of a 6-cup charlotte mold or a 7-inch springform cake pan with safflower oil, and dust it with granulated sugar. Preheat the oven to 375°. Trim the crusts off the bread (save crusts to make bread crumbs). Cut each slice into 3 equal strips. Heat some safflower oil in a sauté pan and sauté the strips on one side only. Drain the sautéed side of the bread on paper towels. Completely line the mold or cake pan with the bread, placing the sautéed side against the pan. You should have about one quarter of the bread strips left, which will be used to cover the top after the pan is filled with the apple mixture.

Put the apples in a heavy pan, sprinkle them with a little water, cover, and steam them until they are soft but not mushy. Add to the apples the grated lemon rind, apricot preserve, 4 tablespoons safflower oil, the nutmeg, ginger, and ¾ cup raw sugar. Mix well and continue cooking over low heat until the apples are quite soft, but they should not be puréed; you want to keep the apple mixture a little chunky. Spoon the apple mixture into the lined mold. Cover the top with the reserved strips of bread. Set the mold on a baking sheet and bake it in the preheated oven for 40 minutes.

PRESENTATION. To serve the charlotte, warm or at room temperature, let it stand for a while after removing it from the oven. Slide a thin-bladed knife around the edge to loosen it and turn the mold out onto a warm flat serving plate. The sides will bulge when the charlotte is turned out of the mold. Or you may store the charlotte in the refrigerator and remove it 30 minutes or so before you plan to serve it; then turn it out of the mold as described above. Serve the sour cream sauce or mousseline sauce, well chilled, in a separate bowl.

6 to 8 servings

---

4 tablespoons cold-pressed
    safflower oil
2 large green apples, skinned,
    cored, and cut into thick
    slices
  Granulated raw sugar for
    sprinkling on apples, and for
    baking dish
3 tablespoons stone-ground
    whole-wheat pastry flour
¾ cup raw light cream
4 tablespoons granulated raw
    sugar
  Grated rind of 1 lemon
  Yolks of 3 organic eggs
  Whites of 3 organic eggs

  Cold-pressed safflower oil for
    baking dish
  About ¼ cup dry whole-wheat
    Bread Crumbs (p. 258)

APRICOT CREAM SAUCE
  2-inch piece of vanilla bean,
    scraped
1 cup raw light cream
1 teaspoon cornstarch or potato
    flour
2 tablespoons raw milk
¼ cup chopped dried organic
    apricots
2 tablespoons Madeira wine
    (optional)

Cocotte aux Pommes Provençale

Baked Apple Pudding with Apricot Cream Sauce

Preheat the oven to 300°. Heat 2 tablespoons safflower oil in a sauté pan and brown the sliced apples on each side. Sprinkle the apples with a little granulated sugar and cook for a minute longer to give them a nice glaze. Set the apples aside.

Heat 2 tablespoons safflower oil in a saucepan and stir in the flour. Cook for a minute or two, stirring all the time, and remove the pan from the heat. Mix in the light cream, return the pan to low heat, and stir until the mixture is thick and smooth. Add 4 tablespoons raw sugar and the grated lemon rind. Remove the pan from the heat and stir in the egg yolks, one at a time, and beat well. Remove the apples from the sauté pan with a slotted spoon and gently mix them into the sauce. Beat the egg whites to soft peaks and fold them into the mixture.

Brush a soufflé dish or other deep baking dish with safflower oil and dust it with the bread crumbs and a little sugar. Spoon the apple mixture into the prepared dish. Cover the dish with a piece of oiled wax paper and set it in a roasting pan. Half-fill the pan with hot water. Set the pudding in its water bath in the preheated oven and bake it until it is firm to the touch, about 45 minutes to 1 hour.

APRICOT CREAM SAUCE. Add the scraping and pod of the vanilla bean to the cream in a pan and bring it to a boil. Mix the potato flour or cornstarch with 2 tablespoons milk in a bowl. Stir in the hot cream. Return the cream to the saucepan and stir over low heat until it thickens. Add chopped dried appricots and Madeira wine. Reduce the heat to very low and simmer the sauce gently for 3 or 4 minutes. Purée the sauce in a blender until it is smooth.

PRESENTATION. When the pudding is baked, remove it from the oven and water bath and let it stand for about 3 minutes. Slide a thin-bladed knife around the edge to loosen it. Set a shallow serving dish face side down on top of the pudding and invert the pudding onto it. Serve the sauce in a separate bowl.

4 to 6 servings

Mont Blanc aux Marrons

Mont Blanc with Chestnuts

1½ pounds raw chestnuts
  A little raw milk and water to cook chestnuts
2-inch piece of vanilla bean, scraped, or 1 teaspoon pure vanilla extract
¾ cup granulated raw sugar
  Cold-pressed safflower oil for mold and baking sheet

Whites of 3 organic eggs
¾ cup superfine granulated raw sugar (p. 214)
  Granulated raw sugar to sprinkle on meringues
1 cup raw heavy sweet cream, whipped
¼ cup carob nuggets or solid bar, coarsely grated

CHESTNUT MIXTURE. Put the chestnuts in a pan, cover them with water, and boil for 5 minutes. Leave them soaking in the warm water as you remove them one by one to cut away the outer and inner skins with a small sharp knife. Return the skinned chestnuts to the pan and barely cover them with a weak solution of milk and water. Add the scraping and pod of the vanilla bean or the vanilla extract. Let the chestnuts simmer gently in this stock until they are soft, adding a little more of the same liquid if it runs dry. When the chestnuts are thoroughly soft, drain them and rub through a fine vegetable strainer. Mix the puréed chestnuts with ¾ cup granulated raw sugar. Lightly brush a deep round-bottomed bowl with safflower oil and press the chestnut purée into it. Let it chill until you are ready to decorate it with the meringues.

MERINGUES. Preheat the oven to 300°. Beat the egg whites to soft peaks and continue beating as you gradually add the superfine sugar. Fill a pastry bag fitted with a plain round tube (No. 7, No. 8, or No. 9) with the meringue mixture. Brush a baking sheet with safflower oil and cover it with a strip of wax paper. Pipe little mounds of meringue, like mushroom caps, on the wax paper. Sprinkle the tops with granulated sugar. Bake the meringues in the preheated oven until they are firm, 45 minutes to 1 hour.

PRESENTATION. Unmold the chestnut mound onto a serving plate. Fill a pastry bag fitted with a No. 6 or No. 7 star tube with the whipped cream, and pipe rosettes all over the surface of the chestnut mound. Stick the meringues all over the mound on top of the whipped-cream rosettes. Sprinkle the coarsely grated carob on the top. Chill in the refrigerator until serving.

4 servings

Poires Belle Hélène à la Caroube

Poached Pears with Carob Sauce (chocolate flavor)

6 large ripe pears (Comice or Bartlett)
¾ cup granulated raw sugar, or ½ cup organic honey
½ vanilla bean, scraping and pod
¼ teaspoon ground cardamom
¼ cup chopped organic nuts
¼ cup finely chopped dried organic apricots
¼ cup finely chopped seedless organic raisins
2 tablespoons dry whole-wheat Bread Crumbs (p. 258)
Carob Sauce (chocolate flavor) (p. 271)
¼ cup blanched shredded organic almonds

Peel the pears with a potato parer, leaving the stem attached. With the potato parer, carefully remove the core from the bottom without disturbing the stem at the top.

Preheat the oven to 325°. Pour the sugar, 1½ cups water, the vanilla bean scraping and pod, and the cardamom into a heavy pan large enough to set all of the pears on the bottom. Cook until the mixture has a syrupy consistency. Set the pears in the syrup, spoon some syrup over them, and set the pan in the preheated oven. Cook the pears in the oven until they are just soft. Mix the chopped nuts, chopped apricots and raisins, and bread crumbs together. When the pears are cooked, remove them from the syrup and chill them a little. Fill the pear centers with the fruit/nut mixture and return them to the refrigerator.

PRESENTATION. When the pears are to be served, heat the carob sauce a little, thinning it, if necessary, with milk or water. Pour hot carob sauce over the bottom of a shallow serving dish. Stand the pears in the sauce. Sprinkle the shredded almonds over the pears. Serve at once, while the sauce is hot and the pears are cold.

6 servings

Flummery Santé

Health Flummery with Fresh Fruit Sauce

We embellished the name of this English classic because, made with whole wheat instead of semolina, the natural beauty of the flummery is exposed. We think it is one of the most elegant and delightful ways to eat whole wheat.

1 cup dry white wine, or white wine-grape juice	1 tablespoon fresh lemon juice
Sea salt	Whites of 4 organic eggs
8 tablespoons whole-wheat cereal (fine, not cracked, texture)	¾ cup raw heavy sweet cream, whipped
¾ cup granulated raw sugar	Cold-pressed safflower oil for oiling mold
2 teaspoons pure vanilla extract	Fresh Fruit Sauce, any choice (pp. 273–274)
1½ tablespoons unflavored gelatin	

Combine the wine or wine-grape juice and 1 cup water in a heavy pan and bring it to a boil. Add a pinch of sea salt and stir in the whole-wheat cereal. Continue to cook over low heat, stirring frequently, until the mixture becomes very thick and comes away from the sides of the pan. Remove the pan from the heat and stir in the sugar and vanilla extract. Dissolve the gelatin in the lemon juice and 2 tablespoons water in a little pan over low heat. Mix the dissolved gelatin into the whole-wheat mixture.

Beat the egg whites to soft peaks. Set the whole-wheat mixture over ice and stir until it begins to cool. Fold in the egg whites. Finally, carefully and smoothly fold in the whipped cream.

Brush the inside of a 6-cup mold or 7-inch springform pan with safflower oil. Fill the mold with the whole-wheat mixture and put it in

the refrigerator to set. Prepare fresh fruit sauce and chill thoroughly.
PRESENTATION. When the flummery is thoroughly chilled and set, turn it out onto a serving plate. Spoon the fresh fruit sauce over the molded flummery and serve.

6 servings

Staples, Stocks, and Sauces

A natural inventory for your staple shelf

REFRIGERATOR STORAGE
Stone-ground whole-wheat pastry
*   flour*
Natural brown rice, long and short
*   grain*
Buckwheat groats, medium
Cracked wheat
Hulled barley
Cold-pressed safflower oil
Cold-pressed virgin olive oil
Fresh lemons
Organic eggs
Raw milk
Raw light and heavy sweet cream
Raw sour cream
Basic Vinaigrette dressing (p. 38)
Basic Mayonnaise (p. 39), 1 pint
Reserved vegetable cooking water,
*   2-quart jar*
Freshly grated Parmesan cheese
*   (p. 259)*
Yellow onions
Baby white onions
Fresh garlic

PANTRY
Granulated raw sugar

Superfine raw sugar (homemade,
*   p. 214)*
Powdered raw sugar (homemade,
*   p. 214)*
Potato flour
Sea salt
Herb or vegetable salt
Lentils
Chick-peas
Soybeans
Blanched organic almonds, whole
*   and shredded*
Dry bread crumbs (homemade,
*   p. 258)*
Fried croutons (homemade, p. 258)
Natural tomato paste (homemade,
*   pp. 24–25)*
Marmite (brewers' yeast extract)
Dry mustard
Tamari soy sauce
Cardamom
Cinnamon
Ginger
Nutmeg
Bay leaves
Sweet paprika
Saffron

Vanilla beans
Black and white organic raisins
Dried organic apricots
Instant decaffeinated coffee
Teas
Unflavored gelatin
Natural flavorings: vanilla, orange,
lemon, almond
Organic honey
Natural preserves: apricot, currant,
guava, rose hip
Whole-wheat and/or artichoke-
flour noodles, spaghetti, and
macaroni

Sunflower seeds
Pine nuts (pignoli)
Green and ripe olives
Instant nonfat dry milk
16 ounces carob in bars
Carob powder
Potatoes (Idaho preferred)
Dry sherry
Marsala
Madeira
Dry white wine (or white wine-
grape juice)
Dry red wine (or red wine-grape
juice)

The natural attitude toward stocks and sauces: Natural cooking stock options are discussed in the Encyclopedia (Stocks, p. 23) and in this chapter on pages 261–264. Whether you wish to use a meat-base stock (the all-purpose chicken stock, which must be made in advance) or an instant, and nutritious, nonmeat stock is a matter of personal preference. Nonmeat stock refers to vegetable stock (the water reserved from cooking vegetables, which catches the nutrients and flavor lost from the vegetables), soy stock, and soy-vegetable stock.

The use of wine in stock and sauce recipes is also a matter of choice, as it is throughout this book, and an alternative is offered. One cannot expect to duplicate the effect of wine in a sauce; there is a difference. However, the nonwine sauce is a delicious sauce in its own right because its basic concept is expressed in its naturalness.

The basic sauce recipes here are selected from dozens of variations in Dione Lucas's files; they represent versatile sauces that can be used independently with different dishes. In the naturalized method of French cooking, the fine egg sauces, hollandaise and béarnaise, are even better when made with lemon juice instead of vinegar and safflower oil instead of butter. They have a lighter, fresher quality, and are less inclined to separate. And mayonnaise made with lemon juice, instead of vinegar, is lighter too.

A group of natural dessert sauces is also included in this chapter. They can expand our repertoire of simple desserts, providing a delectable extra touch to a compote of fresh fruit, ice cream, or perhaps a serving of sponge roll.

**Bread Crumbs,
Croutons, and
Toasts**

Stone-ground whole-wheat bread is suggested as an all-purpose bread for making bread crumbs, croutons, and toasts. The use of the whole-grain bread for these garnishes offers a rich, natural flavor and high nutritional assets.

DRY BREAD CRUMBS. Accumulate all crusts when trimming slices of bread for croutons, toasts, or canapés, and any odd slices of bread that may have hardened too much for use on the table, and allow them to dry thoroughly. If more bread is needed for a supply of crumbs, dry some slices by setting them out overnight or on a baking sheet in a 250° to 300° oven. When the bread is absolutely dry, break it into pieces small enough to put in the blender. Pulverize it in the blender until it is as fine as you want it. A supply of dry bread crumbs may be stored in an airtight screw-top jar for handy, everyday use.

FRIED BREAD CRUMBS. Prepare fried bread crumbs as needed. To produce ½ cup of fried bread crumbs, heat 2 tablespoons cold-pressed safflower oil in a sauté pan. When it is quite hot, add ½ cup dry bread crumbs. Turn them continually with a wooden spoon as they brown. As soon as they are golden, turn them out onto paper towels to drain.

CROUTONS, TOASTED AND FRIED. Croutons may be made from whole-wheat bread, as well as from a marvelous variety of whole-grain breads from different grains. Because whole-grain breads can become rancid and chemical preservatives are usually avoided, it is recommended they be kept in the freezer. Frozen bread has another advantage—its firmness facilitates sharp, neat cutting of croutons and toasts. Also, if the bread is frozen, it is possible to cut a stack of 3 or 4 slices at a time neatly. Use a sharp chef's knife and hone it just before using. The coarse texture of whole-grain breads is not conducive to making tiny croutons because the bread must be sliced for half-thickness.

For all cube croutons: Trim the crusts from slices of bread and cut slices into even cubes.

For toasted croutons: Preheat the oven to 400°. Spread the bread cubes on a baking sheet and leave them in the oven until they are golden brown.

For fried croutons: For 1 cup bread cubes, heat 4 tablespoons cold-pressed safflower oil in a sauté pan. When the oil is quite hot, add the bread cubes. If desired, they may be sprinkled with a little herb salt. Brown them in the hot oil, gently turning them with a wooden spoon to color them on all sides. Turn the croutons out of the pan onto paper towels to drain. Set them in a 400° oven for a few minutes to crisp.

A supply of toasted or fried croutons may be stored in an airtight screw-top jar.

TOASTS. A plate of toast fingers of various shapes, plain-toasted, fried, or Mornay, made with whole-grain breads, is especially good served with soups and salads.

Trim the crusts from the bread. For *large triangles,* cut the bread squares diagonally. For *small triangles,* cut the large triangles into halves. Or cut the trimmed bread slices into 4 *squares,* or into 3 equal *vertical strips.* For toast *rounds,* use a cookie cutter (save the trimmings for bread crumbs) .

For plain toast, cut any of the shapes. Preheat the oven to 400°. Spread the pieces of bread on a baking sheet and toast them in the oven until they are golden brown.

For fried toast: Using oil instead of butter, the effect of toast fried crisp in fat is better achieved in the oven than in a sauté pan. Preheat the oven to 400°. Arrange the cuts of bread on a baking sheet and brush each with cold-pressed safflower oil or olive oil. If desired, sprinkle them with a dash of herb salt. Toast the bread in the preheated oven until the edges become tinged with brown. Use to garnish an entrée, or serve in a warm napkin.

CROÛTES DE MORNAY OR MORNAY TOAST (WITH CHEESE) . Follow the procedure for preparing fried toast (preceding recipe) . Instead of sprinkling the bread with herb salt, sprinkle it liberally with freshly grated Parmesan cheese. This toast also may be used to garnish a soup or entrée, or can be served separately in a warm napkin on a bread plate.

Fried toast and Mornay Toast can be prepared in advance and stored in an airtight container, to be recrisped in a warm oven at serving time.

Freshly Grated Cheese

Prepare your own supply of grated cheese. A little grated Parmesan cheese is often used as a garnish, and it is good sprinkled over tossed salads.

Freshly grated Parmesan cheese is unquestionably more fragrant and economical than commercially prepared grated Parmesan. Grate ½ to 1 pound of good Parmesan cheese. Store it in a plastic bag or airtight jar in the refrigerator and use as needed.

Other grated cheeses, such as Swiss-type or Cheddar, should be grated in the quantity required as needed.

Herbs

Gastronomically and nutritionally, herbs are the best seasoning agents, and natural-food stores have been a strong force in making a variety of fresh and dried herbs more easily available. For a clear understanding of herbs used in cooking, it is necessary to divide the culinary herbs into two distinct groups: the fine herbs and the robust herbs. Herbs are considered so basic in classic French cookery that they have long been codified into groups and uses led by the classic *fines herbes* which include sweet basil, chervil, sweet marjoram, French or garden thyme, rosemary, tarragon, and chives.

The following notes on *fines herbes* were penned by Dione Lucas:

"*Sweet basil:* There are two kinds of basil: One is the *royal basil* which is a home decorative plant and is often used most effectively as a finishing touch to a green salad. But it is the curly leaves of *sweet basil* with the rich herb quality that can enliven the most insipid-tasting dishes such as vegetables and meats; also some fish. It is also one of the salad herbs; individually it is used in a butter for rolled sandwiches; and it is delicious in egg dishes and with tomatoes and onions.

"*Chervil:* Chervil is a relative of parsley but, of course, of a much finer quality. The flavor of chervil is so tender that it should be used much more generously than any other herb, and sometimes it is the support of other herbs. Chervil is very good in combination with basil and/or chive. It is highly recommended for use in soups, egg dishes, green sauce or mayonnaise for fish, sprinkled finely chopped over potato or celery-root salad, or in a dressing for heart of artichoke.

"*Sweet marjoram:* Marjoram resembles thyme and can be used interchangeably or together, although I personally prefer it to thyme. It is very good with coleslaw, parsnips, green peas. Also, it is the most popular herb for modifying heavy meats such as pork, duck, mutton, also turkey; and you will find it a very good fresh substitute for sage in stuffing.

"*Rosemary:* Rosemary is an herb of Biblical legend. It is a very beautiful herb—a slender, dignified, soft green herb; it reminds me very much of incense. Rosemary is good in a marinade for spring or baby lamb. In the Easter offerings in Florence, braised fennel, or finnochio, will have rosemary in its juices, and sometimes you will find it in bouillabaisse.

"*Tarragon:* Tarragon is, of course, the delight of gourmets. It came originally from the south of Russia and was called *estragon* (as it is known all over the world except in the United States). Tarragon has beautiful spearlike leaves, a velvety sheen, and an exquisite fragrance. It can be used in almost any savory dish to create a most unusual taste experience.

"*French or garden thyme:* Thyme is the all-around herb of the kitchen, either individually or in a *bouquet garni*. It certainly has the quality of a good mixer; it is a great medium in the workings of perfumes and it has valuable medicinal qualities. (In Switzerland thyme is always used medicinally. Thyme as a tisane brings happy dreams. In the Alps one is served a goat cheese permeated with wild thyme, and for me, fortunately, it is the thyme that overpowers the goat.)

"*Chives:* Although chive is of the onion family, it really functions as an herb, and as such, it is indispensable. When chive, with the slight and very delicate flavor of onion, is added to the other herbs it will improve, tone down, or heighten—according to how one uses it. Chive can be the cook's best friend: when soup is really insipid or the sauce colorless, a dash of chive will enliven and make it more hopeful looking. There should never be a kitchen sill that does not contain one or two pots of chives.

"*Fines herbes* mixtures can be used in omelets, sauces, ragouts, soups, eggs, sandwiches, salads."

The robust herbs are all those not codified as *fines herbes,* for example—dill, bay leaves, mint, garlic, shallot, etc.

Vegetable Stock

Vegetable cooking water that has been seasoned with a little salt is simple vegetable stock. It has long been recognized as an excellent flavoring agent for soups and sauces, for cooking rice and other grains, and for many other cooking uses in place of poultry or meat stocks. It is very easy to have a supply of vegetable stock on hand at all times by following these few suggestions.

1. Tend to use a little less salt when you blanch and boil vegetables. As the water reduces in cooking, it becomes saltier and it might become too salty for future use as stock.

2. Drain vegetables through a colander or wire strainer into a bowl or pan to catch the cooking water. Pour the liquid into a 2-quart jar reserved for the purpose, and store it in the refrigerator.

3. Be certain that the vegetables are properly cleaned before you cook them. If they are not thoroughly cleaned, it may be necessary to strain the cooking water through a damp cloth lining the colander or strainer.

4. Collect the cooking water from different vegetables in the same storage jar. The mixture improves the bouquet. The only vegetable whose cooking water we do not save is the beet—because of its strong color.

5. Use vegetable stock cup-for-cup as an alternative for chicken, meat, or soy stock. It may be supplemented with soy sauce to add a meatlike flavor and more nutrients, if desired. Use $1/2$ to 1 teaspoon soy sauce per cup of vegetable stock, depending on the strength you wish. (See Soy-Vegetable Stock, following recipe.)

Soy Stock and Soy-Vegetable Stock

"Soy stock" is soy sauce and herb salt mixed with plain water. We find this simple formula a satisfactory alternative for chicken or veal stock in most uses. Besides being easy and convenient to prepare, soy stock is an excellent way of obtaining the nutrients of the miracle soybean. (See soybean discussion in Encyclopedia, pp. 22–23.)

"Soy-vegetable stock" is soy stock made with vegetable cooking water, and generally it is our preference since it combines the nutrients of two vital food sources. If you have vegetable cooking water on hand, use it plus additional plain water, if necessary, to prepare the quantity of soy-vegetable stock you require.

1 cup plain water, or water reserved from cooking vegetables, or combination
1 teaspoon tamari soy sauce

½ teaspoon herb salt (amount depending on saltiness of soy sauce and vegetable stock)

Mix all of the ingredients in a measuring cup and use as directed in the recipe.
1 cup

Light Soy Stock

1 cup plain water, or water reserved from cooking vegetables, or combination
½ teaspoon tamari soy sauce

½ teaspoon herb salt (amount depending on saltiness of soy sauce and vegetable stock)

Mix all ingredients in a measuring cup and use as directed in the recipe.
1 cup

Chicken Stock

Stocks should not contain any fat. Therefore, in preparing an animal-based stock, such as chicken stock, remove all skin and fat from the bones before cooking the stock. After the stock is made, chill it or freeze it and then remove the rest of the fat which has solidified on the top.

2 pounds raw chicken bones, or wings and backs with skin and fat removed
1 veal knuckle, cracked (an excellent source of connective tissue and gelatin, optional)
2 cups sliced onion, carrot, and celery; also leeks if available

Bouquet garni: 2 whole cloves, 1 bay leaf, 2 large sprigs of parsley, 2 sprigs of celery leaves, 2 sprigs of other fresh herb such as thyme, tarragon, or orégano (if available, 2 whole allspice) —all tied in a cheesecloth bag

4 quarts plain water, vegetable
    cooking water, or combination
1 teaspoon sea salt

1 teaspoon herb salt (amount of
    either salt depending on
    saltiness of vegetable stock)

Put the raw chicken bones or pieces and the veal knuckle in a large pot, at least 8-quart size, and add the water and/or vegetable cooking water. Bring it slowly to a boil, turn off the heat, and skim. Add all of the other ingredients and cook at a gentle simmer for 2½ to 3 hours.

Line a large wire strainer or colander with a damp cloth, set it over a large bowl or pot, and pour the cooked stock through it. Ladle the strained stock into plastic containers with tight-fitting lids. Chill the stock and remove any fat that may have formed on the top. Freeze the stock and use as needed.

If you used chicken wings and backs with any meat on them, remove the meat and use it in a salad or as a crêpe filling.

3 to 4 quarts

Court Bouillon

Seasoned liquid for poaching fish and shellfish, which after poaching becomes the stock for the sauce.

The use of a substantial amount of white wine in court bouillon and fish stock is traditional and marries well with the fish juices. In the natural conversion it is a matter of choice. If you prefer, the wine ingredient may be substituted with additional water, or with white wine-grape juice, which will add a fruitiness.

2 tablespoons cold-pressed
    safflower oil
A few mushroom pieces or stems
    (optional)
1 cup mixed sliced onion, carrot,
    and celery
4 cups water
1 cup dry white wine, or
    additional water, or white
    wine-grape juice

¼ cup dry sherry (optional)
Bouquet garni: 1 small bay leaf,
    2 large sprigs of parsley, 1 or
    2 sprigs of fresh celery leaves,
    and 1 or 2 sprigs of other
    fresh green herb, if available
    —all tied in a cheesecloth bag
1 teaspoon sea salt

Heat the safflower oil in a pan and add the mushrooms pieces. Sauté the mushrooms for 1 or 2 minutes; then add the onion, carrot, and celery, and cook for another 2 or 3 minutes. Pour over the water, dry white wine, and sherry, and add the *bouquet garni*. Bring the liquid to a boil. The court bouillon is now ready to pour over the fish in a fish cooker, to plunge shrimps or other seafood into for brief cooking, or to use as specified in the recipe.

4 cups

Fish Stock

Prepare the Court Bouillon (preceding recipe), adding 1 to 2 pounds fish bones and/or heads and 2 teaspoons fresh lemon juice to the pot. After bringing the stock to a boil, allow it to simmer gently for 30 minutes. Strain and use as directed in the recipe.

Fumet de Poisson

Fish Stock Concentrate

Boil down ½ cup fish stock, either from fish that has been poached, or prepared from the recipe above, to 1 tablespoon in quantity.
1 tablespoon

Aspic

6 cups Soy Stock, Soy-Vegetable
    Stock (p. 262), or Chicken
    Stock (pp. 262–263)
6 tablespoons natural tomato
    paste, or 4 ripe medium-size
    tomatoes, sliced but not
    skinned

⅓ cup dry sherry (optional)
1 tablespoon raw sugar
4 tablespoons unflavored gelatin
    Whites of 4 organic eggs,
    beaten stiff

Combine all of the ingredients, including the beaten egg whites, in a pan and bring the mixture slowly to a boil, stirring all the time with a wire whisk. When the mixture comes to a rolling boil, stop stirring, remove the pan from the heat, and let it stand without disturbing it for 15 minutes.

Line a large wire strainer or colander with a damp cloth and set it over a large bowl or pan. Pour the mixture through it. You now have aspic, or clarified stock with gelatin. It may be stored in the refrigerator but *not* in the freezer, where it would become cloudy. Use the aspic as directed in the recipe for the dish you plan to prepare.
4 to 5 cups

Sauce Brune

Brown Sauce

3 tablespoons cold-pressed
    safflower oil
¾ cup mixed sliced onion, carrot,
    and celery
½ teaspoon finely chopped fresh
    garlic
    A few pieces of fresh
    mushroom, if on hand
3 tablespoons stone-ground
    whole-wheat pastry flour
2 teaspoons natural tomato paste

1 teaspoon Marmite (brewers'
    yeast extract)
1½ cups stock (Soy, Vegetable, or
    Chicken, pp. 261–263)
¼ cup dry sherry, or additional
    stock
1 teaspoon natural guava,
    currant, or rose-hip jelly
1 bay leaf
    Herb salt

Heat the safflower oil in a pan and sauté the onion, carrot, celery, and garlic in it for 2 or 3 minutes. Add the mushroom pieces and cook for another 2 minutes. Blend in the flour, tomato paste, and Marmite yeast extract, and cook for another 1 or 2 minutes. Off the heat add the stock and wine. Stir the sauce over moderate heat until it comes to a boil. Add the jelly and bay leaf, adjust the seasoning with herb salt, and simmer gently for 30 to 45 minutes. Pour the sauce through a fine wire strainer or purée it in the blender.
1½ cups

**Sauce
Demi-Glace**

Prepare the recipe for Brown Sauce (preceding recipe), substituting 3 teaspoons potato flour for the whole-wheat pastry flour in order to make the sauce translucent. When the sauce is cooked, strain it through a fine wire strainer instead of puréeing it in the blender.

Sauce Madère

Madeira Sauce

Prepare the recipe for Brown Sauce (pp. 264–265), with the following substitutions:
1. *Use 3 teaspoons potato flour* instead of 3 tablespoons stone-ground whole-wheat pastry flour.
2. *Use 1¼ cups stock and ½ cup Madeira wine* instead of 1½ cups stock and ¼ cup sherry.
3. When the sauce is cooked, strain it through a fine wire strainer instead of puréeing it in the blender.

Sauce Périgueux

*Madeira Sauce
with Truffles*

Prepare the recipe for Brown Sauce (pp. 264–265), with the following substitutions:
1. *Use 3 teaspoons potato flour* instead of 3 tablespoons whole-wheat pastry flour.
2. *Use 1¼ cups stock and ½ cup Madeira wine* instead of 1½ cups stock and ¼ cup sherry.
3. When the sauce is cooked, strain it through a fine wire strainer instead of puréeing it in the blender.
4. Add 1 large black truffle, finely chopped, about ¼ cup, to the strained sauce.

Sauce Velouté

White Sauce made with Stock

This is a conversion of the basic chicken stock velouté, which is usually finished with cream and egg yolk to become Sauce Suprême (following recipe), or which is used as the basis for a compound sauce to be mixed with other ingredients from the dish being prepared. In its natural robe, the rich wheat color of the whole grain is apparent in this traditionally white sauce.

3 tablespoons cold-pressed
    safflower oil
3. tablespoons stone-ground whole-
    wheat pastry flour (sifted, if
    you object to any minuscule
    particles of whole wheat)

1½ cups stock (Soy, Vegetable, or
     Chicken, pp. 261–263)
¼ cup raw light cream, or raw
    milk, or reconstituted
    nonfat dry milk
    Herb salt

Heat the safflower oil in a saucepan, blend in the flour, and cook for 1 or 2 minutes. Off the heat add the stock. Return the pan to moderate heat and stir until the sauce comes to a boil. Add the cream or milk and adjust the seasoning, if necessary, with herb salt. Reduce the heat to very low and simmer the sauce gently for 5 minutes, stirring occasionally to be sure that it does not burn on the bottom of the pan.
1½ cups

Sauce Suprême

Velouté Sauce Finished with Cream and Egg

1 to 1½ cups Velouté Sauce
    (preceding recipe), or for fish
    or shellfish, use Velouté de
    Poisson (following recipe)
    Yolk of 1 organic egg

3 tablespoons raw heavy sweet
    cream, or raw sour cream, or
    raw milk
1 tablespoon dry sherry (optional)

Prepare the velouté sauce as directed in the recipe. In a small bowl mix the egg yolk with the cream or milk and dry sherry. When the velouté has finished cooking, mix 2 or 3 tablespoons of it into the yolk mixture. Then pour the yolk mixture into the sauce in the pan, stirring all the time. At this point the sauce may be reheated gently, but do not allow it to boil or it will separate.
1¾ cups

Velouté de Poisson

White Sauce made with Fish Stock

If the fish stock used in this recipe contains the dry white wine as given in the recipe on page 264, this sauce would also be called White-Wine Sauce (*Sauce Vin Blanc*). This sauce may be finished with cream and egg yolk, according to the recipe for Sauce Suprême (preceding recipe).

3 tablespoons cold-pressed
    safflower oil
3 tablespoons stone-ground
    whole-wheat pastry flour
    (sifted, if you object to any
    minuscule particles of whole
    wheat)
1½ cups fish stock (strained from
    the fish preparation if a
    court bouillon was used, or
    the plain Fish Stock on
    p. 264)

¼ cup raw light cream or raw
    milk, or reconstituted nonfat
    dry milk
Herb salt

Heat the safflower oil in a saucepan, blend in the flour, and cook for 1 or 2 minutes. Off the heat add the stock. Return the pan to moderate heat and stir until the sauce comes to a boil. Add the cream or milk and adjust the seasoning, if necessary, with herb salt. Reduce the heat to very low and simmer the sauce gently for 5 minutes, stirring occasionally to be sure that it does not burn on the bottom of the pan.
1½ cups

Sauce Béchamel

Savory Cream Sauce

The thickening ingredient in this recipe gives the sauce a coating consistency. If the sauce is to be used as a binder (as for fillings) or mixed with cooked vegetables which have a high moisture content, a thicker sauce is required and the flour should be increased.

2 cups raw milk
1 sprig of fresh celery leaf
1 bay leaf
1 baby white onion, halved
½ teaspoon herb salt
3 tablespoons cold-pressed
    safflower oil

3 tablespoons stone-ground
    whole-wheat pastry flour
½ cup raw sour cream or raw
    heavy sweet cream

Combine the milk, celery leaf, bay leaf, onion, and herb salt in a saucepan and bring it to a boil. Lower the heat and let the milk simmer very gently for 5 to 10 minutes.

In another pan heat the safflower oil, blend in the flour, and cook for 1 or 2 minutes. Off the heat strain the hot milk into the flour mixture. Stir the sauce over moderate heat until the sauce comes to a boil. Reduce the heat, adjust the seasoning, and stir in the cream. Allow the sauce to cook over very low heat for 3 or 4 minutes.
2½ cups

Sauce Mornay

Cheese Sauce

3 tablespoons cold-pressed
    safflower oil
3 tablespoons stone-ground whole-
    wheat pastry flour
1 teaspoon dry mustard
2 cups raw milk
1 sprig of fresh celery leaf
1 bay leaf

½ teaspoon herb salt
⅓ cup freshly grated Parmesan
    cheese
⅓ cup freshly grated Gruyère or
    natural Swiss-type cheese
⅓ cup raw light sweet cream or
    raw sour cream

Heat the safflower oil in a saucepan, blend in the flour and dry mustard, and cook for 1 or 2 minutes. Off the heat stir in the milk. Return the pan to moderate heat and continue stirring until the sauce comes to a boil. Add the celery leaf, bay leaf, and herb salt. Lower the heat and let the sauce simmer gently for 5 minutes, stirring occasionally. Remove the celery sprig and bay leaf and stir in the cheeses and cream. Cook over low heat for another 2 or 3 minutes.
3 cups

Sauce Soubise

*Onion Cream
Sauce or Onion
Purée*

4 Bermuda onions, skinned and
    sliced
1 cup raw milk
    Herb salt
2 tablespoons cold-pressed
    safflower oil

2 tablespoons stone-ground
    whole-wheat pastry flour
2 tablespoons raw sour cream
⅛ teaspoon freshly grated nutmeg

Combine the sliced onions with the milk and a little herb salt in a pan, cover, and cook over low heat until the onions are very soft. Drain the onions and reserve the milk. Purée the onions in a blender until they are smooth.

Heat the safflower oil in a saucepan, blend in the flour, and cook over moderate heat for 1 or 2 minutes. Off the heat add the onion purée. Stir over low heat until the mixture thickens. Stir in the sour cream and grated nutmeg, and adjust the seasoning with herb salt. Cook over low heat a little longer, stirring all the time. This is now a thick purée to be used for a spread or filling.

If you wish a thinner consistency for sauce, add the reserved milk, using as much as is required for the desired liquidity. After the milk has been added, warm the sauce over low heat.
2 cups

**Sauce
Hollandaise**

Yolks of 2 organic eggs
2 tablespoons fresh lemon juice
2 tablespoons raw sour cream, or
    yogurt

¼ teaspoon sea salt
8 tablespoons cold-pressed
    safflower oil

In a small bowl combine the egg yolks, lemon juice, sour cream, and sea salt, and mix well with a small wire whisk. Stand the bowl in a small sauté pan half-filled with hot water. Over low heat, stir the sauce until it is as thick as you want it. Continue beating as you very slowly add all of the safflower oil. Cover the bowl with a piece of plastic wrap, remove it from the heat, and let it stand until you are ready to use it.

1 cup

Sauce Béarnaise

Herbed Hollandaise Sauce

Yolks of 3 organic eggs
4 teaspoons fresh lemon juice
3 tablespoons raw light sweet cream or raw sour cream, or yogurt
8 tablespoons cold-pressed safflower oil
¼ teaspoon sea salt
1 teaspoon very finely chopped white onion
⅛ teaspoon very finely chopped fresh garlic

1 tablespoon chopped fresh parsley
1 teaspoon chopped fresh tarragon, or ½ teaspoon dried tarragon
1 teaspoon chopped fresh chervil, or ½ teaspoon dried chervil
¼ teaspoon natural tomato paste
¼ teaspoon Marmite (brewers' yeast extract)

In a small bowl combine the egg yolks, lemon juice, and cream, and mix well with a small wire whisk. Stand the bowl in a small sauté pan half-filled with hot water. Over low heat, stir the sauce until it is as thick as you want it. Continue beating as you very slowly add all of the safflower oil. Stir in the rest of the ingredients. Cover the bowl with a piece of plastic wrap, remove it from the heat, and let it stand until you are ready to use it.

1½ cups

Canapé Sauce

Egg Sauce for Savory Crêpes and Soufflés

Yolks of 3 organic eggs
2 tablespoons cold-pressed safflower oil
1 tablespoon dry sherry (optional)
2 tablespoons freshly grated Parmesan cheese

¼ teaspoon dry mustard
½ teaspoon sweet paprika
Herb salt
¾ to 1 cup raw light cream, depending on the thickness of sauce desired

In the top part of a double boiler combine the egg yolks, safflower oil, dry sherry, grated cheese, dry mustard, paprika, and a little herb salt. Add the cream and stir the sauce over hot water until it thickens. Adjust the seasoning with herb salt, and add more cream if a thinner sauce is desired.

Approximately 1½ cups

Sauce Tomate

Fresh Tomato Sauce

4 large firm ripe tomatoes
3 tablespoons cold-pressed virgin olive oil or cold-pressed safflower oil
1 teaspoon finely chopped fresh garlic
2 tablespoons natural tomato paste
Herb salt

2 tablespoons stone-ground whole-wheat pastry flour
2 tablespoons dry whole-wheat Bread Crumbs (p. 258)
1 teaspoon granulated raw sugar
2 cups stock (Soy, Vegetable, or Chicken, pp. 261–263), or water

Slice 3 tomatoes with the skins on and set them aside. Skin the fourth tomato, seed it, and cut the pulp into fine shreds; rub the seed parts through a fine vegetable strainer and reserve the juice.

Heat the oil in a large saucepan or heavy pan, add the chopped garlic, and cook over low heat for a minute or two. Add the sliced tomatoes and the tomato paste, and season with a little herb salt. Raise the heat, cover the pan, and cook briskly for about 2 minutes.

Mix the flour with the bread crumbs. Remove the tomato mixture from the heat, sprinkle the flour and bread-crumb mixture over the tomatoes, and blend it into the sauce. Add the sugar and stock or water. Return the sauce to moderate heat and bring it to a boil. Rub the sauce through a fine vegetable strainer.

Return the sauce to the pan and simmer it gently for 5 minutes. Add the strained fresh tomato juice (from the strained seeds) and the reserved shredded tomato, and adjust the seasoning with herb salt. Cook over low heat for another 3 minutes.

About 4 cups

Crème Chantilly

Flavored Whipped Cream

1 cup raw heavy sweet cream
1 tablespoon organic honey
Scraping from 4-inch piece of vanilla bean, or 1 teaspoon pure vanilla extract

Set a round-bottomed metal bowl in a bowl of ice and pour in the heavy cream. Using a large piano-wire whisk, beat the cream until it thickens. Add the honey and vanilla-bean scraping and continue beating until the cream holds its shape. Do not beat beyond that point, or it will separate.

Whipped cream may be held in the refrigerator for 2 or 3 hours. After that it may begin to "set" and be less workable for decorating. Cover it with a piece of plastic wrap when it is in the refrigerator.

2 cups

Please note comments concerning carob and chocolate in the Encyclopedia, pages 11 and 12.

pages 11 and 12

Sauce à la Caroube (*le goût de chocolat*)

Carob Sauce (chocolate flavor)

8 ounces carob nuggets or solid bar
3 teaspoons instant decaffeinated
    coffee mixed with 3 tablespoons
    hot water, or 3 tablespoons
    plain water without the coffee
1 cup raw light cream

1-inch piece of vanilla bean,
    scraping and pod
½ cup granulated raw sugar
Yolks of 2 organic eggs
⅓ cup raw heavy sweet cream,
    whipped

If you are using bar carob, cut it into small pieces. Combine the carob with the coffee essence or plain water in a saucepan and dissolve it over low heat, stirring all the time.

In another pan combine the light cream with the scraping and pod of the vanilla bean and the raw sugar. Bring it to a boil and remove it from the heat immediately.

Beat the egg yolks in a small bowl. Strain the scalded cream onto the egg yolks, stirring all the time. Stir the egg-yolk mixture into the dissolved carob. Set the pan over low heat and stir the sauce until it coats the back of a metal spoon.

For a *hot sauce,* stir the whipped cream into the heated sauce. For a *cold sauce,* chill the sauce first, then fold in the whipped cream.
Approximately 2 cups

This sauce may be served hot or cold.

Sauce au Citron

Fresh Lemon Sauce

¾ cup granulated raw sugar
3 teaspoons potato flour
    Yolks of 3 organic eggs, well
        beaten
¾ cup cold water
2 tablespoons cold-pressed
    safflower oil

½ cup fresh lemon juice
    Grated rind of 2 lemons
1 teaspoon grated orange rind
1 teaspoon grated lime rind

Combine the sugar and potato flour in the top part of a double boiler and stir in the beaten egg yolks. Add the cold water and stir the sauce over boiling water for about 10 minutes. Stir in the safflower oil, a few drops at a time. Stir in the lemon juice and the lemon, orange, and lime rinds. Serve hot or cold.
Approximately 2 cups

Sauce aux Fruits Secs

Dried Fruit Sauce

A Nesselrode-type of sauce using natural dried organic fruits instead of candied fruits. Serve hot or at room temperature.

2 *tablespoons cold-pressed safflower oil*
2 *tablespoons sifted stone-ground whole-wheat pastry flour*
1½ *cups raw light cream*
¾ *cup finely chopped mixed dried organic fruits (dates, raisins, prunes, apricots, currants, etc.), soaked in ½ cup Madeira wine or white wine-grape juice*

5 *tablespoons granulated raw sugar*
½ *cup raw heavy sweet cream, whipped*

Heat the safflower oil in a saucepan, blend in the flour, and cook for 1 or 2 minutes. Off the heat add the light cream and the soaked dried fruits with the soaking wine or wine-grape juice. Stir the sauce over moderate heat until it comes to a boil. Add the sugar and simmer the sauce gently for 2 or 3 minutes, stirring it occasionally. Just before serving, fold in the whipped cream.
Approximately 2½ cups

Sauce Sabayon and Sauce Mousseline (for desserts)

These sauces may be flavored with the addition of a variety of excellent natural flavorings to complement the dessert.

SABAYON SAUCE
1 *whole organic egg*
   Yolks of 3 organic eggs
5 *tablespoons granulated raw sugar*
¼ *cup sherry, Madeira, or Marsala wine, or 1 teaspoon natural flavoring extract (orange, lemon, almond, cinnamon, anise, rose, etc., optional)*

MOUSSELINE SAUCE
⅓ *cup raw heavy sweet cream, whipped*

SABAYON SAUCE. Combine all of the sabayon ingredients in the top part of a double boiler over hot water and beat with a rotary beater until the sauce holds its shape. Serve at once.
MOUSSELINE SAUCE. Prepare the sabayon sauce. Fold the whipped cream into the finished sabayon sauce and serve at once.
Sabayon Sauce, 1 cup
Mousseline Sauce, 1½ cups

PART III
Appendixes

Measurements and Metric Conversions

MEASUREMENTS: All recipes contain specific liquid and dry measurements where specifics are considered necessary. All dry measurements are level.

METRIC MEASURES CONVERSION CHART (approximate)

TO METRIC MEASURES

Symbol	When you know	Multiply by	To find	Symbol
		LENGTH		
in	inches	2.5	centimeters	cm
ft	feet	30	centimeters	cm
		MASS (weight)		
oz	ounces	28	grams	g
lb	pounds	0.45	kilograms	kg
		VOLUME		
fl oz	fluid ounces	30	milliliters	ml
c	cups	0.24	liters	l
pt	pints	0.47	liters	l
qt	quarts	0.95	liters	l
gal	gallons	3.8	liters	l
		TEMPERATURE (exact)		
°F	Fahrenheit temperature	5/9 after subtracting 32	Celsius temperature	°C

FROM METRIC MEASURES

LENGTH

mm	millimeters	0.04	inches	in
cm	centimeters	0.4	inches	in
m	meters	3.3	feet	ft

MASS (weight)

g	grams	0.035	ounces	oz
kg	kilograms	2.2	pounds	lb

VOLUME

ml	milliliter	0.03	fluid ounces	fl oz
l	liters	2.1	pints	pt
l	liters	1.06	quarts	qt
l	liters	0.26	gallons	gal

TEMPERATURE (exact)

°C	Celsius temperature	9/5 then add 32	Fahrenheit temperature	°F

Shopping Sources
by Mail

The following suppliers have mail-order service and may be able to help you if you are unable to obtain any of the natural or organic ingredients, as noted, in your area. The addresses of these companies are given after the table.

Product Category	Shiloh Farms	Walnut Acres	Erewhon	East Ridge Store
Books	X	X	X	X
Breads and bread mixes	X	X		X
Carob		X	X	
Cheeses	X	X	X	X
Eggs				X
Fish and seafood, frozen	X			X
Flavoring extracts		X		
Flours	X	X	X	X
Fruit, dried	X	X	X	X
Fruit juices	X	X	X	X
Fruit preserves		X	X	X
Fruits, natural-canned	X	X		
Gelatin		X		
Grains and beans	X	X	X	X
Grapillon		X		
Herbs and spices		X	X	X
Honeys	X	X	X	X
Meat, frozen	X			
Milk products		X	X	X
Nuts and seeds	X	X	X	X
Oils	X	X	X	X
Pasta (whole wheat)		X	X	X
Poultry	X			

Salts		X	X	X
Soups, frozen	X			
Sugar, raw				X
Tamari soy sauce		X	X	X
Teas	X			
Tomato purée		X		X
Vegetables, natural-canned	X	X		

Shiloh Farms, Inc.
Route 59
Sulphur Springs, Arkansas
72768

Erewhon Natural and Organic
  Foods
33 Farnsworth Street
Boston, Massachusetts 02210

North of Wash., D.C. and east of
  Ohio:
Shiloh Farms Eastern Branch
  Whse.
White Oak Road
Martindale, Pennsylvania
17549

New York area:
Erewhon Natural and Organic
  Foods
303 Howe Avenue
Passaic, New Jersey 07055

East Ridge Store
Callicoon, New York 12723

Walnut Acres
Penns Creek, Pennsylvania 17862

Specialties
Inquiries concerning the following ingredients may be addressed as
follows:
Breads (Seven Grain, Sprouted Wheat, Sprouted Rye, Sprouted Wheat
Raisin, Whole-Wheat with Gluten Soya Carob, Soy Sunflower, Home-
style White, Date-Nut Bread, Wheat Free—100% Sprouted Rye, Low
Sodium) :

Breads For Life
P. O. Box 3484
Springfield, Missouri 65804

Certified Raw Milk:
The Gates Homestead Farms
Chittenango, New York 13037

*Carob Powder, Nuggets and
  Solid Bar:*
El Molino Mills
Division of ACG Co.
City of Industry, California
  91746

*Marmite (brewers' yeast
  extract) :*
Bovril (Canada) Limited
Montreal, Canada

Raw Sugar:
Balanced Foods, Inc.
North Bergen, New Jersey 07047

Kasha and Creamy Kernels:
Wolff's
Birkett Mills
Penn Yan, New York 14527

A Basic Nutritional
Bibliography

Abrahamson, E. M., and A. W. Pezet. *Body Mind and Sugar*. New York: Henry Holt & Co., 1951.

Adams, Ruth, and Frank Murray. *All You Should Know About: Health Foods*. New York: Larchmont Books, 1975.

Airola, Paavo. *Are You Confused?* Phoenix, Ariz.: Health Plus, 1971.

———. *Health Secrets from Europe*. New York: Arco Publishing Co., Inc., 1975.

Ashley, Richard, and Heidi Duggal. *Dictionary of Nutrition*. New York: St. Martin's Press, 1975.

Bailey, Herbert. *The Vitamin Pioneers*. Emmaus, Pa.: Rodale Press, Inc., 1968.

Carson, Rachel. *Silent Spring*. Boston: Houghton Mifflin Company, 1962.

Chen, Philip S., with Helen D. Chung. *Soybeans for Health and a Longer Life*. New Canaan, Conn.: Keats Pub., Inc., 1956.

Davis, Adelle. *Let's Cook It Right*. New York: Harcourt Brace & Co., 1947.

———. *Let's Eat Right To Keep Fit*. New York: Harcourt Brace & Co., 1954.

Douris, Larry, and Mark Timon. *Dictionary of Health and Nutrition*. New York: Pyramid Communications, Inc., 1975.

Fredericks, Carlton. *Psycho-Nutrition*. New York: Grosset & Dunlap, 1976.

Fredericks, Carlton, and Herbert Bailey. *Food Facts & Fallacies*. New York: Arco Publishing Co., Inc., 1965.

Hauser, B. Gayelord, and Ragnar Berg. *Dictionary of Foods*. New York: Benedict Lust Publications, 1970.

Hunter, Beatrice Trum. *Consumer Beware!* New York: Simon & Schuster, 1971.

———. *Food Additives and Federal Policy: The Mirage of Safety*. New York: Charles Scribner's Sons, 1975.

———. *Food and Your Health*. New Canaan, Conn.: Consumers' Research, Inc., Keats Pub., Inc., 1974.

Kirschmann, John D., Nutrition Search, Inc. *Nutrition Almanac*. New York: McGraw-Hill Book Company, 1973.

Kloss, Jethro. *Back to Eden*. New York: Benedict Lust Publications, 1951.

Nittler, Alan H. *A New Breed of Doctor*. New York: Pyramid Communications, Inc., 1972.

Organic Gardening and Farming Staff. *The Organic Directory*. Completely revised. Emmaus, Pa.: Rodale Press, Inc., 1974.

Rodale, Robert. *Sane Living in a Mad World, A Guide to the Organic Way of Life*. Emmaus, Pa.: Rodale Press, Inc., 1972.

United States Department of Agriculture. *Composition of Foods*. Washington, D.C.: Agriculture Handbook No. 8, 1975.

Watson, George. *Nutrition and Your Mind*. New York: Harper & Row, 1972.

Williams, Roger J. *Nutrition Against Disease*. New York: Pitman Pub. Co., 1971.

———. *Nutrition in a Nutshell*. New York: Doubleday & Company, 1962.

———. *You Are Extraordinary*. New York: Random House, 1967.

Index